Syntax of Hungarian
Postpositions and Postpositional Phrases

Comprehensive Grammar Resources

Syntax of Hungarian

General editor:
István Kenesei

Syntax of Hungarian
Postpositions and Postpositional Phrases

Editors:
Katalin É. Kiss
Veronika Hegedűs

Routledge
Taylor & Francis Group
LONDON AND NEW YORK

The research leading toward the publication of this volume and all other volumes of the *Syntax of Hungarian* in the Comprehensive Grammar Resources series was supported by Grant No. 100804 from OTKA, the Hungarian National Research Fund. The publication of this volume was sponsored by Grant No. 120073 *Open access book series on the syntax of Hungarian* from the National Research, Development and Innovation Office.

This book is published in print and online through the online OAPEN library (www.oapen.org).

OAPEN (Open Access Publishing in European Networks) is a collaborative initiative to develop and implement a sustainable Open Access publication model for academic books in the Humanities and Social Sciences. The OAPEN Library aims to improve the visibility and usability of high quality academic research by aggregating peer reviewed Open Access publications from across Europe.

First published in 2021 by Amsterdam University Press Ltd.

Published 2025 by Routledge
4 Park Square, Milton Park, Abingdon, Oxon OX14 4RN
605 Third Avenue, New York, NY 10158

Routledge is an imprint of the Taylor & Francis Group, an informa business

ISBN: 9789463725910 (hbk)
ISBN: 9781041186977 (pbk)
ISBN: 9781003704829 (ebk)
NUR 616 | 624

Cover design: Studio Jan de Boer, Amsterdam

DOI: 10.5117/9789463725910

For Product Safety Concerns and Information please contact our EU representative:
GPSR@taylorandfrancis.com
Taylor & Francis Verlag GmbH, Kaufingerstraße 24, 80331 München, Germany

Contents

Abbreviations and symbols

This appendix contains a list of abbreviations and symbols that are used in this volume. When referring to a chapter or section of the other volumes in this series, the following notational convention is used; otherwise the volumes are referred to with their titles.

A+section#	A3.2 refers to Section 3.2. in Huba Bartos ed. (to appear). *Adjectival Phrases.*
C+section#	C3.2 refers to Section 3.2. in Zoltán Bánréti ed. (to appear). *Coordination and Ellipsis.*
E+section#	E3.2 refers to Section 3.2. in Zsuzsanna Gécseg ed. (to appear). *Finite Embedding.*
F+section#	F3.2 refers to Section 3.2. in Tibor Laczkó & Gábor Alberti eds. (to appear). *Non-Finite and Semi-Finite Verb Phrases.*
M+section#	M3.2 refers to Section 3.2. in Balázs Surányi ed. (to appear). *Sentence Structure.*
N+section#	N3.2 refers to Section 3.2 in Gábor Alberti and Tibor Laczkó eds. (2018) *Nouns and Noun Phrases*
V+section#	V3.2 refers to Section 3.2. in Károly Bibok ed. (to appear). *Verb Phrases in General and Finite Verb Phrases.*

Abbreviations used in both the main text and the examples

AP	Adjectival Phrase	NumP	Numeral Phrase
CP	Complementizer Phrase	PP	Postpositional Phrase
CTopic	Contrastive Topic	PredP	Predicative Phrase
DP	Determiner Phrase	VM	Verb Modifier
NP	Noun Phrase	VP	Verb Phrase

Symbols, abbreviations and conventions (primarily) used in the examples

'	stressed word
"	focus-stressed word
°	unstressed word
□	intonational break
XXX	Small caps indicates that XXX constituent is in focus

Abbreviations used in the glosses of examples

1/2/3	1st, 2nd, 3rd person	Iter	Iterative suffix
Abl	Ablative	Loc	Obsolete locative case
Acc	Accusative	Min	Minimizing particle
Ade	Adessive	Mod	Modality suffix
Adj	Adjectivalizer	Mult	Multiplicative suffix
Adv	Adverbial suffix	Nmn	Nominalizer
All	Allative	Nom	Nominative
Attr	Attributivizer	Part	Participle
Car	Caritive suffix	Past	Past Tense (-*t*)
Cau	Causal(-final)	Perf	Perfectivizing verbal particle
Caus	Causative derivational suffix	Pl	Plural
Cl	Classifier	Poss	Possessed
Comp	Comparative	Posr	Possessor (-*é*)
Cond	Conditional	Pred	Predicate
Dat	Dative	Prox	Proximal
DefObj	Definite object	Quant	Quantifier
Del	Delative	QPart	Question particle (-*e*)
Dim	Diminutive	Rec	Reciprocal suffix
Dist	Distributive suffix	Sg	Singular
Dst	Distal	Sprl	Superlative prefix
Ela	Elative	Soc	Sociative suffix
Emph	Emphatic particle	Sub	Sublative
FoE	Essive-Formal	Subj	Subjunctive
For	Formal suffix	Sup	Superessive
Fut	Future	Ter	Terminative
Ill	Illative	Tmp	Temporal suffix
Ine	Inessive	TrE	Translative(-essive)
Inf	Infinitive	Vrb	Verbalizer
Ins	Instrumental		

Diacritics used for indicating acceptability judgments

*	Unacceptable
*?	Relatively acceptable compared to *
??	Intermediate or unclear status
?	Marked: not completely acceptable or disfavored form
(?)	Slightly marked, but probably acceptable
no marking	Fully acceptable
✓	Fully acceptable (after unacceptable or marked variants)
%	Not (fully) acceptable due to non-syntactic factors *or* varying judgments among speakers
#	Unacceptable under intended reading
$	Special status: old-fashioned, archaic, very formal, incoherent, etc.
†	Extinct

Other conventions

xx/yy	Acceptable both with xx and with yy
*xx/yy	Unacceptable with xx, but acceptable with yy
xx/*yy	Acceptable with xx, but unacceptable with yy
[y ... z]	A unit (but not necessarily a constituent) consisting of more than one word
xx / [y ... z]	Acceptable both with xx, which is a word, and with [y ... z], which is a unit (but not necessarily a constituent) consisting of more than one word
(xx)	Acceptable both with and without xx
*(xx)	Acceptable with, but unacceptable without xx
(*xx)	Acceptable without, but unacceptable with xx
(xx) ... (xx)	Alternative placement of xx in an example
XX_i ... YY_i	Coindexing indicates coreference
XX_i ... YY_j	Counter-indexing indicates disjoint reference
$XX_{*i/j}$	Unacceptable with index *i*, acceptable with index *j*
$XX_{i/*j}$	Unacceptable with index *j*, acceptable with index *i*
$[_{XP}$ ...]	Constituent brackets of a constituent XP

The Syntax of Hungarian

General introduction

István Kenesei
General Editor

1. The series

This is the third volume of the second series of books in what we hope will become a monumental international project, which began sometime in 1992 as a modest attempt at launching *The Syntax of Dutch* at Tilburg University under the sponsorship of Henk van Riemsdijk. Originally, the plan was only meant to include Dutch, but as that project, after a long period of gestation, finally lifted off the ground, Henk van Riemsdijk approached István Kenesei early 2008 with a proposal that was to include a number of other languages. The enterprise was named *Comprehensive Grammar Resources* and a detailed plan was submitted by the two co-editors to Mouton de Gruyter, where Ursula Kleinheinz adopted and supported the series.

Its objectives were outlined in our conspectus in 2009 as follows. "With the rapid development of linguistic theory, the art of grammar writing has changed. Modern research on grammatical structures has tended to uncover many constructions, many in depth properties, many insights that are generally not found in the type of grammar books that are used in schools and in fields related to linguistics. The new factual and analytical body of knowledge that is being built up for many languages is, unfortunately, often buried in articles and books that concentrate on theoretical issues and are, therefore, not available in a systematized way. The *CGR* series intends to make up for this lacuna by publishing extensive grammars that are solidly based on recent theoretical and empirical advances. They intend to present the facts as completely as possible and in a way that will 'speak' to modern linguists but will also, and increasingly, become a new type of grammatical resource for the semi- and non-specialist."

The fate of the series hung by a thread when Ursula Kleinheinz unexpectedly fell ill and to our great sorrow subsequently passed away. After intensive negotiations with Mouton de Gruyter the editors approached Amsterdam University Press, which not only welcomed the plan but offered an advantageous online publication scheme, deemed necessary from its inception for such gigantic work. The final agreement was signed in 2011, just in time for the first installments of *The Syntax of Dutch* to come out with AUP in 2012.

The Dutch project was concluded in 2019 after having produced eight volumes, between c. 400 and 800 pages each, all available also online, and as the Dutch project was nearing its last stage, the first two volumes of *The Syntax of Hungarian* were published, thus inaugurating the second series of books under the general heading *Comprehensive Grammar Resources*. We note here with sorrow that the founding editor of the series, Henk van Riemsdijk has decided to resign, but we will cherish the memory of his initiative and continue to appreciate his indispensable judgment and wisdom in setting up this project and advising us throughout. Hans Broekhuis joined the board at the final phase of the Dutch project, and following Henk van Riemsdijk's resignation Norbert Corver was willing to accept our invitation.

2. Previous research into the grammar of Hungarian

Research into Hungarian in a generative framework started in the 1960's after a number of linguists had returned to Hungary from study trips in the USA. Modern linguistics began to be taught first in Budapest then at other universities in the country, early results got published soon (Telegdi 1969), and by the mid-1970's there arose a community whose systematic work has been continuous ever since. By the end of the next decade the tangled issues of Hungarian word order were given a fresh start (É. Kiss 1978) and concurrently a research team was set up at the Research Institute for Linguistics (RIL) of the Hungarian Academy of Sciences with the aim of producing extensive studies of the grammar within a generative framework. In the 1980's Hungarian had become the topic of international publications (É. Kiss 1981, 1987, Horvath 1986), the only international linguistics journal in Hungary, *Acta Linguistica Hungarica,* started to publish more and more articles in modern frameworks, a new series of collections of papers in English on Hungarian, *Approaches to Hungarian*, was started at the University of Szeged (subsequently moved to Akadémiai Kiadó, Budapest, and currently published by John Benjamins, Amsterdam), individual conferences were organized with particular attention to Hungarian in the Netherlands, Germany, and Austria (cf., e.g., Abraham and de Meij 1986), and a biennial conference series on "The Structure of Hungarian" was conceived, following the first of its kind at Indiana University, Bloomington, in 1992, now regularly held at alternate venues in Hungary and abroad.

The first concerted effort of the 'middle generation' of generative linguists resulted in a voluminous book on the syntax of Hungarian (Kiefer 1992), soon to be published in a modified and somewhat abridged English version (Kiefer and É. Kiss 1994). By the 1990's, issues, analyses and properties of the Hungarian language in general had become household items in linguistics journals, and the language had appeared as one of the best described and analyzed non-Indo-European languages, often making a substantial presence in arguments and illustrations even in textbooks in syntax or linguistics at large (e.g., Haegeman and Guéron 1999). In the meantime a number of students graduated in Hungary and abroad, due to grants primarily in the Netherlands and the USA, and have either come back or remained in close contact with the linguistic scene in Hungary.

The 'hot' topics in Hungarian that have long attracted the attention of linguists at large include some of the basic features of this language. Early on, as was mentioned above, problems of the word order were of paramount significance, since it was extremely difficult to render in a rigid NP – Aux – VP framework. É. Kiss's work from the late 1970's on threw new light on the configurationality issue, and while she offered a 'flat' VP, a controversial issue ever since, her assumptions relating to the left periphery have radically changed our thinking of the constituency, order, and functions of the syntactic material below and above the Complementizer, inducing work opening new perspectives, such as Brody (1990) or Rizzi (1997).

Another highly popular and frequently cited chapter of the grammar has been the DP, and in particular possessive constructions. Since Szabolcsi (1981, 1987) laid down the foundations of the analysis on the pattern of the clause and drew the analogy that, among other things, contributed to introducing the Spec-Head division in the X-bar system and adding more structure to the Comp layer, it has challenged many an acute mind offering various solutions to problems like the 'nominative–dative alternation' on the possessor DP, the movement of the possessor out of the possessive DP, and discovered new traits in the constructions, such as antiagreement phenomena, or the problem of genitive case (Den Dikken 1999, É. Kiss 2002, Dékány 2015).

The order and relative scopes of quantifiers and operators in the left periphery as well as postverbally have also been of central importance. Ever since Anna Szabolcsi, and following her, Ed Williams, quipped that "Hungarian wore its Logical Form on its sleeve", it has been in the foreground. Hungarian is a language exhibiting well-defined properties of contrastive topics (Szabolcsi 1983, Molnár 1998, Gyuris 2009), interesting ambiguous properties of *only* (É. Kiss 1998), the interaction of focus, quantifiers, and negation (Puskás 2006), or in general, the properties of the left periphery (Kenesei and Lipták 2009).The study of adverbs and adverbial adjuncts in Hungarian has also produced a collection of papers (É. Kiss 2009).

Another result of the concerted efforts of generative grammarians has been the research into the historical syntax of Hungarian, owing to projects devised and managed, roughly concurrently and with a partially overlapping personnel with this project, by Katalin É. Kiss (2014a, 2014b). The large number of conference presentations, articles in journals, and the two collections of research papers serve as evidence that this non-Indo-European language has quite a few surprises in store in tracking down syntactic changes.

Let us conclude at this point that the linguistic community studying the properties of Hungarian in and outside Hungary is particularly well motivated to embark on a project producing a generative-based, but in effect theory-neutral, descriptive survey of the language.

Incidentally, although traditional descriptive grammars have been in currency in Hungary, the latest of which is a 583-page (text)book, their approaches have been unprincipled, nonexhaustive, and on the whole unsystematic (cf. Tompa 1961, Bencédy *et al.* 1968, Keszler 2000). Of the two English-language grammars in print, Rounds (2001) is intended for the language-learner, while Kenesei *et al.* (1998) was written on the pattern of the so-called "Lingua questionnaire", which had a pre-defined structure so that all languages would be described in an identical fashion. As a result of this, and because of scope limitations, they could not address a number of issues at all or in sufficient depth. On the other hand, the promise of generative grammars to provide exhaustive surveys, descriptions, and analyses has never been fulfilled, primarily because the discovery of problems and exploring the principles have always taken precedence over exhaustive descriptions. This promise can now be realized, that is, at least in the field of syntax, or in other words, in 'grammar proper', an extensive treatise of the results available can be summed up. It was with this objective in mind that the team behind this project set to work.

3. The project

When the grant proposal was ultimately approved in 2011 and the project was ready to start early 2012, it had 38 participants with senior and junior staff members roughly in equal numbers. They formed eight teams in view of the main themes of the volumes to be compiled.

Although we were aware of the structure of our Dutch forerunner, based on the distinction between the internal and external syntax of the four major lexical categories (nouns, verbs, adjectives, and adpositions, i.e., N, V, A, P) and their phrases (NP, VP, AP, PP), we followed a somewhat different pattern owing mainly to the nature of the problems discussed in the literature on Hungarian. The Dutch project included the complementation and modification of each lexical category in the respective chapters, then proceeded to discuss the functional categories associated with the lexical category under review, and concluded with the broader syntactic environment of the phrase in question.

The Hungarian project also covers the four major lexical categories noun, verb, adjective and adposition in separate volumes, discussing their characteristics, complementation, and modification much like the *Syntax of Dutch*, but retains a more traditional division of labor by devoting individual volumes to clausal phenomena. The structure of the project, that is, the eight areas in which the teams were organized, and titles (as well as the currently foreseeable order) of publications are as follows: Nouns and Noun Phrases (Vols. 1 and 2), Postpositions and Postpositional Phrases, The Structure of the Main Clause, Verb Phrases in General and Finite Verb Phrases, Adjectival Phrases, Non-Finite and Semi-Finite Verb Phrases, Finite Embedding, Coordination and Ellipsis.

The four volumes that deal with lexical categories and their phrases (NP, VP, PP, AP) need no special justification. Let us, however, argue now for the four remaining topics. It is well-known that perhaps the most distinctive feature of the syntax of Hungarian is the order of the constituents arranged not with respect to grammatical functions but according to their logical or communicative properties. Rather than extending the number of volumes discussing the VP, we have decided to devote a separate volume to the constituent order and related problems, such as negation, questions, or modality. It is also in this volume that the characteristics of the intonational patterns are presented. Since finite embedded clauses, whether *that*-clauses complementing nouns, verbs, or adjectives, or relative clauses adjoined to APs, NPs, or PPs, show a remarkable similarity, it was also reasonable to compile a volume specifically for them. There are several subtypes of nonfinite clauses in this language, and although some of them could have easily been treated as complements to or modifiers of major lexical categories, due to properties overarching several of them it was again more economical to put them in a single volume. Finally, the description of and the problems relating to ellipsis and coordination are again difficult to envision as belonging to any one of the lexical categories, so they again are assembled in a separate volume. While all of these four sets of topics could have been divided and thus added to the volumes on the NP, the AP, the PP, and the VP, this solution would have resulted in more repetitions, as well as a more imbalanced structure regarding the sizes and contents of the individual volumes. Let us hope that the trial of our pudding is in the eating and our prospective readership will not turn away from the dish served to them.

Again, in distinction to the Dutch project, we had decided on a different structure of the team producing the grammar. First of all, since we were intent on funding the project with grant money and grants, as a rule, last for four years, with a possible one-year extension (but without extra funding), it was clear that the 'small team' approach was not viable: no panel of three to five people could have put aside the time on top of their usual chores to write the grammar or work on the project full time by giving up their main occupations as professors or researchers. Moreover, in the unlikely case of their being financed full time by the grant, it would still have been dubious whether the project could come to conclusion in four (or five) years.

The alternative was to set up a relatively large group comprised of eight teams led by senior researchers, each having considerable expertise in the subjects of the volumes to be written. This option has had several advantages. First of all, it called on all syntacticians who were capable and ready to contribute, thus forming a nationwide enterprise unparalleled before. Moreover, it offered salaried positions to unemployed young linguists so they could write up chapters that had not been covered by independent research before. And the teams could work according to their own schedules. Among the difficulties of this type of organization are the inevitable differences in approaching similar issues. Although we had planned regular meetings of, and consultations with, the team leaders as well as two all-project conferences each year, the end result will show some divergence in particular analyses, mostly due to the convictions of team leaders regarding lesser issues, which we hope will not hinder the general intelligibility or decrease the value of the work.

The research personnel encompassed three generations of researchers, from internationally acknowledged professors to the middle generation to post-docs or promising graduate (PhD/MA) students. The team leaders, who have all 'grown' into becoming volume editors, were of course from the first two age groups and their responsibilities are listed as follows.

Nouns and Noun Phrases – Gábor Alberti and Tibor Laczkó
Postpositions and Postpositional Phrases – Katalin É. Kiss
The Structure of the Main Clause – Balázs Surányi
Verb Phrases in General and Finite Verb Phrases – Károly Bibok
Adjectival Phrases – Huba Bartos
Non-Finite and Semi-Finite Verb Phrases – Tibor Laczkó and Gábor Alberti
Finite Embedding – Zsuzsa Gécseg
Coordination and Ellipsis – Zoltán Bánréti

Collaborators came from the Universities of Debrecen, Pécs, and Szeged, Eötvös Loránd University (Budapest), Pázmány Péter Catholic University (Piliscsaba/Budapest), that is, from all major universities in Hungary with linguistics curricula, as well as from the Research Institute for Linguistics (of the Academy of sciences until 2019, and since then in the newly formed Eötvös Loránd Research Network). Altogether exactly 50 researchers worked for some time for the project, with almost exclusively junior team members entering and leaving midterm, due to their changing job situations, maternity leaves, or, exceptionally, for reasons of quality of the work they submitted. All told, 17 of them were employed by the project for at least a period of six months. Apart from these junior researchers, all senior and junior staff worked unpaid, compensated for their contribution only by receiving occasional international travel grants to conferences as part of the project.

The project had an international aspect as well, and not only because the principal collaborator of the Dutch project, Dr. Hans Broekhuis, provided help in the first year by coming to our all-project conference to give an overview of their work and offering, as it were, advice online throughout, for which we express our thanks to him, but, more significantly, by inviting Hungarian syntacticians working outside Hungary, notably in France, Germany, The Netherlands, Norway, Romania (Transylvania), and the USA, which underscores the lively contacts between the local and the 'expat' communities and their active collaboration.

4. The language

The choice of Hungarian as the subject of the second series of books in the project *Comprehensive Grammar Resources* followed not only from the fact that the junior series editor is a Hungarian, but also from this language having been elevated in the past 40-odd years to the rank of one of the most thoroughly investigated non-Indo-European languages in the generative framework (together with perhaps Basque, Chinese, and Japanese, to list a few others), as was mentioned above. So the time was ripe to embark on an enterprise that would bring all the knowledge previously published in various monographs, dissertations, articles, etc., into a single set of books accessible to the linguistic community at large.

Hungarian belongs to the Ugric branch of Finno-Ugric languages within the Uralic family. Its closest relatives are Mansi and Khanti, with c. 30,000 and 10,000 speakers respectively, while Hungarian has c. 13-14 million speakers, of which somewhat less than 10 million are in Hungary; most of the rest are in the neighboring countries of Romania, Slovakia, Serbia, and Ukraine (in decreasing numbers from 1.5 million to 140,000) and a few tens of thousands in Croatia, Slovenia, and Austria, living mostly in the areas along their borders with Hungary, except for the Székelys and Csángós in Transylvania and beyond. In addition, several hundred thousand Hungarian speakers are themselves recent immigrants or descendants of earlier waves in (Western) Europe, the Americas, Israel, Australia and New Zealand.

The first charters written in part in Hungarian came down from the mid-11th century, while the first text, the *Funeral Sermon and Prayer* dates from c. 1195. Grammars were written as early as the 17th century, and following the foundation of the Academy of Sciences in 1828 historical and later descriptive studies of the language were published in large numbers. It was the Hungarian astronomer Johannis Sajnovics who discovered the relationship between Finno-Ugric languages in 1770, well before Sir William Jones' famous lecture on Sanskrit in 1786. Antal Reguly, Bernát Munkácsi, and Joseph Budenz carried out research into the historical origins of the language, while Sámuel Brassai, János Fogarasi, József Szinnyei and Zsigmond Simonyi published extensive grammars and studies of the nature of the grammatical system of Hungarian during the second half of the 19th century.

Hungarian is a remarkably uniform language as far as its dialects are concerned: with the exception of the Eastern dialect of the Csángós, there are practically no dialects that are not mutually intelligible to any of the others, although there are differences mostly in phonology, morphology and vocabulary. The standard language exists in regional varieties, and since this project has a membership drawn from various regions, these varieties are not excluded from the sources. The main dialects are shown in the map below.

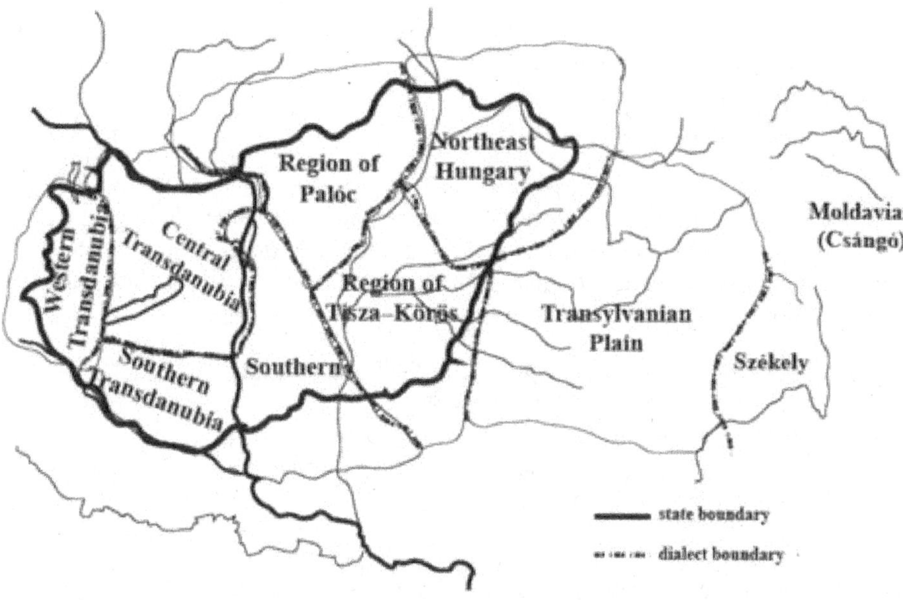

Figure 1: Main Hungarian dialects

The most conspicuous differences are in pronunciation and vocabulary. For example, speakers in the Palóc region have an unrounded short /a/ instead of the majority dialects' round /ɔ/, as in *alma* 'apple'. Common Hungarian *egres* 'gooseberry' has regional varieties like *piszke, büszke, köszméte*. Morphological distinctions between dialects are also frequent; one set has come to signal and/or serve social differentiation between educated or standard *versus* non-standard or 'low' varieties as corroborated by 'purists' and due to indoctrination at schools. One characteristic example is that of the use of subjunctive for indicative conjugation in some verb-forms like dialectal *ért-sük* [e:rʧyk] 'understand-Ind/Subj.1Pl' as against *ért-jük* [e:rcyk] 'understand-Ind.1Pl', both meaning 'we understand (it)' in the case in question, but only the latter is acceptable as the indicative form in educated speech, whereas the former is strongly stigmatized. Since in case of other verbs the subjunctive and indicative verb-forms coincide on the one hand, and on the other the [c] → [ʧ] change in inflections is a natural phenomenon in the phonology of Hungarian, the distinction is, from a descriptive point of view, quite unfounded.

Syntactic differences are harder to put one's finger on except if they are used to indicate social distinctions. The position of the question clitic *-e* illustrates the point. In educated Hungarian it attaches to the finite verb, as in (1a,c). In dialectal varieties it can land on any other head as well, including any preverb, e.g., *le* 'down' (1b) or the negative word *nem* 'not' (1d).

(1) a. Anna le szaladt-e? [Standard]
Anna down ran QPart
'Did Anna run down?'

b. Anna le-e szaladt? [Dialectal]
'idem.'

c. Anna nem szaladt-e le? [Standard]
Anna not ran QPart down
'Didn't Anna run down?

d. Anna nem-e szaladt le? [Dialectal]
'idem.'

Other syntactic variations are not accompanied by value judgments, i.e. stigmatization, like the occurrence of the complementizer *hogy* 'that' adjacent to a number of initial sentence adverbials, cf. (2a-b) as contrasted with standard versions without the complementizer in parentheses.

(2) a. Valószínű-leg (hogy) Anna le- szaladt
probable-Adv that Anna down ran
'Probably Anna ran down.'

b. Természetes-en (hogy) Anna le-szaladt
natural-Adv that Anna down-ran
'Naturally Anna ran down.'

While this phenomenon was first noticed by purists, and then analyzed both by sociolinguists and generative/descriptive grammarians as was reviewed by Nemesi (2000), curiously it has not been adopted as a 'shibboleth' for social stigmatization, unlike the examples above. Moreover, it has never been studied as to its geographical distribution either.

Colloquial Hungarian, much like some South German dialects, tolerates the use of definite articles with proper names when referring to people, except in the North-Eastern dialect as was discussed by Szabolcsi (1994: 200f). She demonstrated that in that dialect the definite article can only occur if it is part of the possessive construction, cf. (3a-b).

(3) a. az Anna kalap-ja
the Anna hat-Poss
'Anna's hat'

b. (*Az) Anna isz-ik.
the Anna drink-3Sg
'Anna drinks.'

In the clause in (3b) the proper name can only be used without the definite article in this dialect, while in the colloquial idiom in other dialects the use of the article is quite frequent. However, in these dialects the possessive construction is acceptable also without the definite article.

There are also distinctions that have passed below the radar range of purists or sociolinguists, as for example the use of multiple negation with negative quantifiers, cf. (4), in which the negation word can be omitted in some dialects while it is obligatory in others, cf. Surányi (2007), Kenesei (2009, 2012).

(4) Nem a déli vonattal (nem) érkezett senki.
not the noon train.Ins not arrived nobody
'It is not the noon train that nobody arrived by.'

Unlike the phonological, morphological or lexical differences illustrated, these or similar syntactic properties have not been charted onto territorial dialects or sociolects as yet, but the *Syntax of Hungarian* makes an effort to register them as far as possible.

Since there has not been any systematic survey of syntactic variation in the dialects and/or sociolects of Hungarian, notwithstanding the reliable statistics of predominantly morphological variation in Kontra (2003), we do not venture to identify the variations presented in these volumes in terms of geographical or social coordinates. We will apply a fairly loose definition of Standard Hungarian, which includes all major regional varieties, especially since several of our authors come from or are located in dialectal areas. These observations are represented also in the grammaticality judgments, a moot issue in all works of generative intent. Members of the project have decided to rely on the individual team's decision as to marking the forms by means of the intricate system of notation.

Since the grammars in this series steer clear of technicalities, there are no principles, conditions, filters, barriers, phases, etc., listed or discussed, let alone introduced, no tree diagrams, no movement operations and/or constraints on them illustrated, although their consequences are demonstrated in simple language.

As was argued in the Preface to the *Syntax of Dutch*, we are concerned with how words are put together to form larger units, and how clauses and ultimately sentences are constructed out of these larger units. We do not discuss the structure of words, i.e., (derivational) morphology, except when it is relevant to the discussion of argument structure, nor do we pay attention to phonological processes, such as vowel harmony or assimilation. However, for our purposes inflectional morphology is part and parcel of syntax, especially since Hungarian is an agglutinative language.

We are intent on representing the native Hungarian speaker's knowledge of the grammar of the language as understood in this more restricted sense, but with a 'descriptive twist' as it were, that is concentrating on the results of several decades of generative research that can be summarized by giving systematic overviews of the phenomena to any practitioner of the field notwithstanding their allegiances to grammatical theories (or the lack thereof).

5. Acknowledgments

As was mentioned in the description of the project, except for a few junior members, all collaborators worked *gratis*. As general editor of *Comprehensive Grammar Resources: Hungarian* I am particularly grateful to the volume editors, Katalin É. Kiss, Research Professor at RIL and Professor Emerita and former Chair of the Doctoral School in Linguistics at Pázmány Péter Catholic University, and Veronika Hegedűs, Senior Research Fellow (RIL), whose expertise and motivation were essential in producing this volume. In addition to them, the contributions were authored by Éva Dékány, Senior Research Fellow (RIL), Barbara Egedi, Senior Research Fellow (RIL), and György Rákosi, Associate Professor and Chair, Department of English Linguistics, University of Debrecen.

The management of the project as well as issues concerning the template were in the hands of Veronika Hegedűs (RIL), who was available almost day and night if problems arose.

Since practically almost the entire community of Hungarian syntacticians has been involved in the project, it was particularly difficult to find internal reviewers who would read and comment on the inevitable inconsistencies, deficiencies, and of course typos. We are very fortunate that there are a few dedicated linguists, both in and outside Hungary, who have volunteered to devote their time and expertise to this mission. We continue to express our gratitude to Prof. Péter Siptár, a phonologist of high esteem, whose interests encompass almost all aspects of language and is an exceptionally experienced and meticulous reader as well. Without his contribution this volume on the Postpositional Phrase would surely have been more error-ridden than as we hope it is.

No book in linguistics written in English by nonnative speakers can be perfect without an expert copy-editor who understands the subject but does not tolerate nonidiomatic English. In our case this important, though not quite rewarding, job was performed by Dr. Mark Newson.

Finally, we are grateful to OTKA, the Hungarian National Research Fund, for awarding the original grant, and to its successor, the National Research, Development and Innovation Office, for managing it since 2015, and having given us a complementary grant to finance the Open Access publication of the following volumes of *CGR Hungarian.*

References

Abraham, Werner and Sjaak de Meij (eds.) 1986. *Topic, Focus, and Configurationality*. Amsterdam: John Benjamins.

Bencédy, József, Pál Fábián, Endre Rácz and Mártonné Velcsov. 1968. *A mai magyar nyelv*. Budapest: Nemzeti Tankönyvkiadó.

Brody, Michael. 1990. Remarks on the order of elements in the Hungarian focus field. In *Approaches to Hungarian Volume* 3, ed. István Kenesei, 95–122. Szeged: JATE.

Dékány, Éva. 2015. The syntax of anaphoric possessives in Hungarian. *Natural Language and Linguistic Theory* 33: 1121–1168.

Dikken, Marcel den. 1999. On the structural representation of possession and agreement: the case of (anti-)agreement in Hungarian possessed nominal phrases. In *Crossing Boundaries*, ed. István Kenesei, 137–178. Amsterdam: John Benjamins.

É. Kiss, Katalin. 1978. A magyar mondatok egy szintaktikai modellje. *Nyelvtudományi Közlemények* 80: 261–286.

É. Kiss, Katalin. 1981. Syntactic relations in Hungarian, a 'free' word order language. *Linguistic Inquiry* 12: 185–215.

É. Kiss, Katalin. 1987. *Configurationality in Hungarian*. Dordrecht: Reidel.

É. Kiss, Katalin. 1998. Identificational focus versus information focus. *Language* 74: 245–273.

É. Kiss, Katalin. 2002. *The Syntax of Hungarian.* Cambridge: Cambridge University Press.

É. Kiss, Katalin (ed.) 2009. *Adverbs and Adverbial Adjuncts at the Interfaces*. Berlin: Mouton de Gruyter.

É. Kiss, Katalin (ed.) 2014a. *Magyar generatív történeti mondattan.* Budapest: Akadémiai Kiadó.

É. Kiss, Katalin (ed.) 2014b. *The Evolution of Functional Left Peripheries in Hungarian Syntax.* Oxford: Oxford University Press.

Gyuris, Beáta. 2009. *The Semantics and Pragmatics of the Contrastive Topic in Hungarian.* Budapest: The Library of the Hungarian Academy of Sciences and Lexica Ltd.

Haegeman, Liliane and Jacqueline Guéron. 1999. *English Grammar: A Generative Perspective*. Oxford: Blackwell.

Horvath, Julia. 1986. *Focus in the Theory of Grammar and the Syntax of Hungarian*. Dordrecht: Foris.

Kenesei, István. 2009. Quantifiers, negation, and focus on the left periphery in Hungarian. *Lingua* 119: 564–591.

Kenesei, István. 2012. Negation in syntactic dialects in Hungarian. In *Discourse & Grammar. A Festschrift in Honor of Valéria Molnár*, eds. Johan Brandtler, David Håkansson, Stefan Huber and Eva Klingvall, 373–386. Lund: Centre for Languages and Literature, Lund University.

Kenesei, István and Anikó Lipták (eds.) 2009. Special Issue: New Perspectives on the Hungarian Left Periphery. *Lingua* 119.

Kenesei, István, Robert M. Vago and Anna Fenyvesi. 1998. *Hungarian: Descriptive Grammar Series*. London: Routledge.

Kenesei, István (series ed.) 1985-2015. *Approaches to Hungarian 1-14*. Editors: Gábor Alberti, Johan Brandtler, Éva Dékány, Marcel den Dikken, Casper de Groot, István Kenesei, Katalin É. Kiss, Tibor Laczkó, Valéria Molnár, Christopher Piñón, Christer Platzack, Csaba Pléh, Catherine O. Ringen, Péter Siptár, Balázs Surányi, Szilárd Szentgyörgyi, Robert M. Vago. Volumes 1-7: JATE, Szeged, Volumes 8-10: Budapest: Akadémiai Kiadó, Volume 11-15: Amsterdam: John Benjamins.

Keszler, Borbála (ed.) 2000. *Magyar grammatika*. Budapest: Nemzeti Tankönyvkiadó.

Kiefer, Ferenc (ed.) 1992. *Strukturális magyar nyelvtan 1. Mondattan*. Budapest: Akadémiai Kiadó.

Kiefer, Ferenc and Katalin É. Kiss (eds.) 1994. *The Syntactic Structure of Hungarian (Syntax and Semantics 27)*. San Diego / New York: Academic Press.

Kontra, Miklós (ed.) 2003. *Nyelv és társadalom a rendszerváltáskori Magyarországon*. Budapest: Osiris.

Molnár, Valéria. 1998. Topic in focus: the syntax, phonology, semantics, and pragmatics of the so-called "contrastive topic" in Hungarian and German. *Acta Linguistica Hungarica* 45: 89–166.

Nemesi, Attila László. 2000. A *természetesen hogy* ... típusú nyelvtani szerkezetről. *Magyar Nyelvőr* 124: 430–442.

Puskás, Genoveva (ed.) 2006. Special Issue: Negation in Finno-Ugric Languages. *Lingua* 116/3.

Rizzi, Luigi. 1997. The fine structure of the left periphery, In *Elements of Grammar*, ed. Liliane Haegeman, 289–330. Dordrecht: Kluwer.

Rounds, Carol H. 2001. *Hungarian: An essential grammar*. Routledge, London.

Surányi, Balázs. 2006. Quantification and focus in negative concord. *Lingua* 116: 272–313.

Szabolcsi, Anna. 1981. The possessive construction in Hungarian: a configurational category in a non-configurational language. *Acta Linguistica Academiae Scientiarum Hungaricae* 31: 261–289.

Szabolcsi, Anna. 1983. Focussing properties, or the trap of first order. *Theoretical Linguistics* 10: 125–146.

Szabolcsi, Anna. 1987. Functional categories in the noun phrase, In *Approaches to Hungarian Volume* 2, ed. István Kenesei, 167–190. Szeged: JATE.

Szabolcsi, Anna. 1994. The Noun Phrase. In Kiefer and É. Kiss (1994), 179–274.

Telegdi, Zsigmond (ed.) 1969. *Általános Nyelvészeti Tanulmányok* VI. Budapest: Akadémiai Kiadó.

Tompa, József (ed.) 1961-1962. A *mai magyar nyelv rendszere* 1-2. Budapest: Akadémiai Kiadó.

Chapter 1
General characteristics and overview

Veronika Hegedűs

1.1. Introduction

This chapter provides a description of the main characteristics of Hungarian postpositions, Postpositional Phrases and related categories. Section 1.2 will describe their basic types and properties, those characteristics that distinguish them from other word classes and those that may be used as characteristics of the whole class. Section 1.3 introduces their syntactic uses, which will be looked at in detail in later chapters.

The categories postposition (P) and Postpositional Phrase (PP) are used in a broad sense in this book; they include not only postpositions proper and their projections, but also postpositions bound to their (most frequently Noun Phrase) complements, i.e., adverbial case suffixes; as well as adverbs, most of which are historically PPs containing an obsolete P; and verbal particles, which are mostly cognate with intransitive Ps or with adverbs. The name adposition (and adpositional phrase) is also used to refer to the broad class in this volume as it is often used when one wants to remain neutral with respect to the internal structure of the PP, espeically when it comes to the order of the P element and its complement.

This broad class of postpositions is different from the other main word classes, i.e., from nouns, verbs and adjectives, in important ways. This chapter outlines the most important distinguishing properties of the class and then will introduce the various types of elements that are included under the umbrella of postpositions. The elements categorized as postpositions and the phrases projected by them all share the basic formal and distributional criteria discussed here and in Chapter 2, where the formal properties of the class will be given a detailed description.

1.2. Basic types and properties of postpositions

1.2.1. Types of postpositions

As Chapter 2 will discuss in detail, Hungarian postpositions come in various types. We can distinguish between case suffixes, case-like postpositions, case-assigning postpositions, verbal particles, and a class of productive derivational suffixes deriving adverbs. These derivational suffixes, called adverbial suffixes, are considered to be Ps since the phrases they head are identical in their distribution to PPs headed by the other, less controversially postpositional elements.

We provide one example for each of these types here (1), and an exhaustive list will be given with the formal characteristics and semantic typology in the next chapter.

(1) a. A gyerekek a kert-ben ugrálnak. [case suffix]
the children the garden-Ine jump.3Pl
'The children are jumping in the garden.'

b. A gyerekek a ház mögött ugrálnak. [case-like P]
the children the house behind jump.3Pl
'The children are jumping around behind the house.'

c. A gyerekek a ház-zal szemben ugrálnak. [case-assigning P]
the children the house-Ins opposite jump.3Pl
'The children are jumping around opposite the house.'

d. A gyerekek fel-ugrálnak. [verbal particle]
the children up-jump.3Pl
'The children keep jumping up.'

e. A gyerekek hangos-an ugrálnak. [adverbial suffix]
the children loud-ly jump.3Pl
'The children are jumping around loudly.'

1.2.2. Properties of the class

The class of postpositions is a relatively closed class, although it is not impossible to add new members to it. New postpositions grammaticalize from members of other classes (mainly from relational nouns marked as heads of possessive constructions and bearing a case suffix, and from adverbial participles) from time to time, and there are some borderline cases in present-day Hungarian, which will be dealt with in Section 2.4. We can provide a more or less exhaustive list of case suffixes (slightly dependent on definitions and defining criteria), of postpositions and verbal particles, and of derivational suffixes as well.

Adverbs are often taken to be a separate word class, either lexical or functional. Here we follow considerations in the literature that have come to the conclusion that what are often classified as adverbs are postpositional in their category (Asbury *et al.* 2007, Kádár 2009, but cf. also É. Kiss 1999, 2002 Chapter 8). Some of these elements include a semantically often opaque but morphologically transparent case suffix (2a) or postposition (2b), thus satisfying the formal criterion of being a PP. Some of them have a more obscure postpositional head which might not be transparent synchronically but which we will still consider postpositional in nature and take it to determine the lexical category of the often very simple (even head-like) phrase. In (3a) we find the productive *-n/-an/-en* suffix (the so-called modal-essive suffix) and in (3b) the *-ul/-ül* suffix (the so-called essive(-modal) suffix), which are equivalents of English *-ly* (and that is how we generally gloss them in the volume). Section 2.2.4 will discuss the productive and semi-productive ways to derive adverbs, including these two productive processes.

(2) a. szerencsé-re
luck-Sub
'luckily'

b. kétség-kívül
doubt-outside_of
'beyond doubt'

(3) a. látható-an
visible-ly
'visibly'

b. kegyetlen-ül
merciless-ly
'mercilessly'

Adverbs are thus taken to be PPs and this decision is not only made simple by the morphosyntactic make-up of these elements, which is a crucial factor in itself, but also by the fact that they are very similar to PPs proper in their phrase internal syntactic properties (e.g. modification) — as shown in Chapter 3 —, and in their external distribution as well, which will become obvious in Chapter 4 to Chapter 7.

As for their general properties, postpositions have a relatively invariant form, the only exception being the group of case-like or inflecting postpositions, which can bear agreement markers. In general, postpositions are not marked for number, which makes them different from nouns and adjectives and are not marked for tense, which makes them different from verbs as well. The so-called case-like postpositions agree with their pronominal complement in person and number but do not agree with regular DP complements (Kenesei *et al.* 1998: 866ff; see also Marácz 1986, who calls them 'dressed' Ps due to their ability to bear agreement marking; although the syntactic analyses differ in details, here we focus on the distinction between the groups). This property will be discussed and illustrated in Chapter 2.

Postpositions often express a relation between two elements in the clause, the so-called Figure and the Ground (Talmy 1972). The relation they express can be spatial or temporal in nature; these two are the most frequent postpositional meanings, although the non-spatial/non-temporal uses of PPs will be covered in later chapters as well.

1.3. Syntactic uses of postpositions

This section introduces the syntactic uses of postpositional phrases, which will be discussed in more detail in the following chapters: predicative PPs in Chapter 4, argument PPs in Chapter 5, obligatory adjunct PPs in Chapter 6, and adjunct PPs in Chapter 7.

1.3.1. Predicative use

Postpositional Phrases are often used predicatively in the clause, in which case they are not simply a selected argument of the verb but are predicated of a Noun Phrase in the clause; that is why the term often used to refer to them in this use is secondary predicates.

Although predicative PPs require the presence of a verb, sometimes it is the PP that is the main syntactic and semantic predicate; the verb just acts as a linking element, one that can express the tense or mood properties of the clause. PPs functioning as main predicates appear with the verb *van* 'be' (4), or with such lexically light verbs as *marad* 'stay, remain'. These are so-called copular verbs, since their function is mostly to provide a verbal link between the nominal that is the subject and the PP that refers to the spatial or temporal location of the subject.

(4) a. Pál a kert-ben van.
Pál the garden-Ine be.3Sg
'Pál is in the garden.'

b. Az előadás dél-után lesz.
the performance noon-after be.Fut.3Sg
'The performance will be in the afternoon.'

Most predicative PPs function as secondary predicates predicated of the internal argument of the verb. Their role is in most cases to telicize the action denoted by the verb. If the verb describes a change of state of the internal argument, the predicative PP (a lexical PP (5a) or a lexically bleached verbal particle (5b)) predicates its result state.

(5) a. A hús puhá-ra főtt.
the meat tender-Sub cook.Past.3Sg
'The meat cooked tender.'

b. Mari be-festette a kerítést.
Mari in-paint.Past.DefObj.3Sg the fence.Acc
'Mari painted the fence [completely].'

Verbs expressing motion or manner of motion are telicized by directional PP complements. The directional PP (a lexical noun phrase with a postposition or case suffix, or a terminative verbal particle, or both a verbal particle and a lexical PP) predicates the end location of the subject in the case of intransitive verbs (6a), and the end location of the object in the case of transitive verbs (6b).

(6) a. Anna a város mellé költözött.
Anna the city next_to move.Past.3Sg
'Anna moved next to the city.'

b. Péter vissza-dobta a halat a tó-ba.
Peter back-throw.Past.DefObj.3Sg the fish.Acc the lake-Ill
'Peter threw the fish back into the lake.'

Predicative PPs can also be selected by lexical verbs expressing existence or spatial configuration. In such cases, the PP predicates the location of the subject (the Figure) of an intransitive predicate (7a), or the location of the object of a transitive predicate (7b) with respect to the Ground, which is the complement of the P.

(7) a. Mari a fotel-ben ül.
Mari the armchair-Ine sit.3Sg
'Mari is sitting in the armchair.'

b. Péter az irodá-ban hagyta a kalapját.
Peter the office-Ine leave.Past.DefObj.3Sg the hat.Poss.3Sg.Acc
'Péter left his hat in the office.'

A further type of predicative PPs predicates the state of a nominal argument of the verbal predicate. For example, in (8), the main predication states that Mary did a lot of good things for the city, and the secondary predication states that she was the director of the company when she did those things. In this example, the PP predicates a property of the subject. The postposition used in this construction is the essive-formal suffix.

(8)

Mari	a	vállalat	igazgatója-ként	sok	jót	tett	a	város-ért.
Mari	the	company	director.Poss-FoE	much	good.Acc	do.Past.3Sg	the	city-Cau

'As the director of the company, Mari did a lot of good for the city.'

In other cases, the PP in the sentence predicates a property of the object of the clause. Thus, the sentence in (9) contains the predications that it is true of everyone that they drink coffee and that the coffee is black when they drink it. The postposition heading the secondary predicate *feketé-n* 'black' is the adverbial suffix *-n/-an/-en*.

(9)

Mindenki	feketé-n	issza	a	kávét.
everybody	black-ly	drink.DefObj.3Sg	the	coffee.Acc

'Everybody drinks coffee black.'

Sometimes sentences that include such a secondary predicate – a so-called depictive secondary predicate – are ambiguous. In (10), for example, the PP *részeg-en* 'drunk' can be understood to be a property of the taxi driver or of the cyclist as well.

(10)

A	taxis	részeg-en	ütötte	el	a	biciklistát.
the	taxi_driver	drunk-ly	hit.Past.DefObj.3Sg	away	the	cyclist.Acc

'The taxi driver hit the cyclist drunk.'

The predicative use of PPs will be discussed in much more detail in Chapter 4.

1.3.2. PPs as arguments

Postpositional phrases may be used as arguments selected by a verb, a noun or an adjective. The PPs selected by verbs are typically headed by a certain case-marker, e.g., by the sublative case selected by the verb *vár* 'wait', or the inessive case selected by the verb *hisz* 'believe'.

(11)

Mari	a	vonat-ra	vár.
Mari	the	train-Sub	wait.3Sg

'Mari is waiting for the train.'

(12)

Pál	hisz	a	csodák-ban.
Pál	believe.3Sg	the	miracle.Pl-Ine

'Pál believes in miracles'

We can thus say that the lexical entry of these verbs contains the information that they require a PP in their argument structure, with the P head being the sublative and the inessive case suffix, respectively.

(13) a. vár [$_{PP}$ DP + Sub]
b. hisz [$_{PP}$ DP + Ine]

It is not always a case-marker that we find as the head of the PP selected by a verb. The verb *küzd* 'fight' can take a PP headed by the postposition *ellen* 'against' (14a). Similarly, we find PPs headed by a postposition proper with the particle verbs (in fact, PP+V complexes) in (14b) and (14c).

(14) a. küzd valami ellen
fight something against
'fight against something'

b. el-törpül valami mellett
away-be.dwarfed something next_to
'be dwarfed by something'

c. ki-áll valami mellett
out-stand something next_to
'make a stand for something'

The PP complement often accompanies an object complement:

(15) figyelmeztet valaki-t valami-re
warn somebody-Acc something-Sub
'warn somebody of something'

The projection of a P head can represent a core (16a) or a non-core argument (16b) of the verb. The different properties of core and non-core arguments will be discussed in detail in Chapter 5.

(16) a. Péter Juli-val csókolózott.
Peter Juli-Ins kiss.Rec.Past.3Sg
'Peter was kissing with Juli.'

b. Péter Juli-val dolgozott.
Peter Juli-Ins work.Past.3Sg
'Peter worked with Juli.'

Adjectives can also take PPs as their complement (selected argument), and this is illustrated with the following examples:

(17) a. büszke valami-re
proud something-Sub
'proud of something'

b. elégedett valami-vel
satisfied something-Ins
'satisfied with something'

A few nouns also take arguments and select for a PP. The noun in (18a) takes a complement with instrumental case, that in (18b) takes a complement with delative case, and the noun in (18c) selects for a PP headed by the postposition *ellen* 'against'.

(18) a. interjú valaki-vel
interview somebody-Ins
'interview with somebody'

b. hír valami-ről
news something-Del
'news about something'

c. tiltakozás valami ellen
protest something against
'protest against something'

Noun phrases with a postnominal PP complement are hard to insert into a sentence; they generally occur as titles, or as subjects of sentences, and become degraded and more difficult to process when the NP bears an oblique case suffix. The productive way of spelling out the argument of a nominal head is to attributivize it by means of the suffix *-i* (19a), by means of the particle *való*, grammaticalized from the participial form of the copula (19b), or by means of a transparent participle (19c). The attributivized argument precedes the nominal head. (The modification and complementation of the NP is discussed in great detail in the volume on Nouns and Noun Phrases; see also 2.2.1.5 and 5.5. in this volume.)

(19) a. a háború ellen-i küzdelem
the war against-Attr struggle
'struggle against the war'

b. a Péter-rel való vita
the Peter-Ins being debate
'the debate with Peter'

c. egy szintaxis-ról szóló könyv
a syntax-Del tell.Part book
'a book about syntax'

It is not always obvious whether something is an obligatory, selected argument or a free adjunct, but when the case or postposition is strictly determined in the lexical requirements of the lexical category, we can often assume that it is an argument. The complementation properties (i.e., argument structures) of verbs, nouns, and adjectives are discussed at length in the relevant chapters in the volumes of this series.

1.3.3. PPs as obligatory and non-obligatory adjuncts

Postpositional phrases, including adverbs, are also used as adjuncts, in which case they are neither selected as arguments, nor used predicatively. Morphologically, adverbial adjuncts can be prototypical PPs headed by case suffixes or postpositions, adverbs that are productively derived from adjectives, and lexicalized elements without a transparent PP structure.

Chapter 6 describes the use of PPs as obligatory adjuncts in sentences where they are not thematically selected, i.e., they are not arguments, but they are obligatory in the sense that the sentence is ungrammatical if the PP is not included.

This use of PPs is typical of verbs of creation and verbs of (coming into) existence, which exhibit the so-called Definiteness Effect. The sentences involving a definite obligatory (internal) argument are ungrammatical (see (20a) and (21a)) but adding a PP will render the sentence grammatical, as (20b) and (21b) illustrate here. The details of these constructions are discussed in Chapter 6.

(20) a. *Van a pénz.
be.3Sg the money
Intended meaning: 'There is the money.'

b. A pénz a fiók-ban van.
the money the drawer-Ine be.3Sg
'The money is in the drawer.'

(21) a. *A baba 'született.
the baby be_born.Past.3Sg
Intended meaning: 'The baby was born.'

b. A baba január-ban született.
the baby January-Ine be_born.Past.3Sg
'The baby was born in January.'

Non-obligatory adjuncts are the topic of Chapter 7, which provides a detailed taxonomy of spatial, temporal and other semantic types of adjuncts. Spatial and temporal adjuncts have to be distinguished from the other adjunct categories as they can freely appear in practically any sentence position, contrary to they other types; moreover, they can be topicalized or focused, which is related to their referential properties.

The position of non-spatial/non-temporal adverbials seems to be more restricted. VP-adverbials (or predicate adverbials) can be distinguished from clausal adverbials (or sentence adverbials), as the former adjuncts modify the predicative part of the sentence (22), while the latter modify larger constituents (23), taking scope over events, propositions, or speech acts. The unmarked position for both types in Hungarian is to appear after the topic constituent, preceding the (extended) predicate. However, even if the two types often appear in the same position within the sentence, as can be observed in the linear order of the elements in these examples, their stress properties reveal the difference between the scopes they take, as will be discussed in Chapter 7 (and also in the volume on Sentence Structure).

(22) A felügyelő könnyen döntésre jutott.
the inspector easily decision.Sub reach.Past.3Sg
'The inspector arrived at a decision easily.'

(23) A felügyelő szerencsére döntésre jutott.
the inspector luckily decision.Sub reach.Past.3Sg
'Luckily, the inspector arrived at a decision.'

When these two basic adjunct types co-occur in the same clause, clausal adverbials precede VP-adverbials:

(24) A felügyelő szerencsére könnyen döntésre jutott.
the inspector luckily easily decision.Sub reach.Past.3Sg
'Luckily, the inspector arrived at a decision easily.'

(25) *A felügyelő könnyen szerencsére döntésre jutott.
the inspector easily luckily decision.Sub reach.Past.3Sg
Intended meaning: 'Luckily, the inspector arrived at a decision easily.'

The relative order of the various adverbial subtypes (evaluative, modal, manner, etc.) is fixed in the preverbal field. At the same time, the postverbal word order of these adjuncts is not so restricted. Moreover, a postverbal adjunct may also have scope over a preverbal one, as in (26).

(26) A felügyelő valószínűleg elkapta szerencsére a gyilkost.
the inspector probably caught luckily the murderer.Acc
'Luckily, the inspector has probably caught the murderer.'

Chapter 7 will also give a general overview on how the various low and high adverbs can be ordered in accordance with their lexical semantics (see Ernst 2002). Special attention will be paid to the so-called exclusive adverbials (also referred to as obligatory focused negative scalar adverbials, following É. Kiss 2009b), such as *alig* 'hardly, scarcely', *ritkán* 'rarely', as well as to adverbial adjuncts with an ambiguous scope, and to clausal adverbials that are obligatorily stressed (e.g. *biztosan* 'certainly').

1.4. Bibliographical notes

A comprehensive traditional description of Hungarian postpositional phrases in the broad sense is given in the monographs of Simonyi (1888, 1892, 1895). The most detailed traditional study of Hungarian PPs in the narrow sense is Sebestyén (1965). The first generative analysis of Hungarian postpositional phrases is by Marácz (1986). *Strukturális magyar nyelvtan III. Morfológia* (ed. by Kiefer 2000c) discusses case endings, adverbial derivational suffixes, and verbal particles at length. The idea of assimilating semantic case morphemes to postpositions, and assimilating adverbs and verbal particles to postpositional phrases was put forth by Asbury *et al.* (2007) and Kádár (2009). The studies of the volume *Adverbs and Adverbial Phrases at the Interfaces* (ed. by É. Kiss, 2009d) discuss the external syntax of postpositional phrases in the broad sense, and the interaction of their syntactic distribution with interpretation and prosody. PPs play a distinguished role in the monograph by Dékány (2011) on the Hungarian DP, and in the monograph by Hegedűs (2013) on non-verbal predicates, as well. Recent analyses of the grammar of the verbal particle include Ackerman (1987), Kiefer and Ladányi (2000b), É. Kiss (2006a), and Surányi (2009a,b). The different syntactic and semantic behavior of PP arguments and PP adjuncts is discussed by Rákosi (2006; 2009a; 2009b), among others. The history of the Hungarian PPs has been investigated by Hegedűs (2014, 2015).

Chapter 2
Postpositions: formal and semantic classification

Éva Dékány and Veronika Hegedűs

2.1. Introduction

This chapter will provide a formal and semantic classification of postpositions and PPs. We will start with the formal classification in Section 2.2. We will turn to their semantic classification in Section 2.3. In Section 2.4 we will address the problem of where to draw the line between the category P and other categories and then discuss some borderline cases.

2.2. Formal characterization

In this section we shall first discuss case suffixes (Section 2.2.1) and then turn to postpositions (Section 2.2.2). Verbal particles will be discussed in Section 2.2.3 and adverbs in Section 2.2.4.

2.2.1. Case suffixes

2.2.1.1. The inventory and form of case suffixes

I. Inventory

A. A bird's-eye view of the case forms

There is some disagreement in the literature on how many case suffixes Hungarian has (see Remark 2.). In this book we consider the 17 suffixes in Table 1 to be true case suffixes because these conform to the formal characteristics discussed in sections 2.2.1.1 through 2.2.1.8. The case allomorphs on lexical nouns will be exemplified in points B through D; the allomorphs on pronouns will be discussed in Section 2.2.1.2 point *V*.

Table 1: The inventory of case suffixes

CLASS	NAME OF CASE	ALLOMORPHS ON LEXICAL Ns	ALLOMORPHS ON PERSONAL PRONOUNS	MEANING
STRUCTURAL	*Nominative*	-∅	-∅	—
	Accusative	*-t, -at, -et, -ot, -öt, -∅*	*-t, -et, -∅*	—
	Dative	*-nak, -nek*	*nek-*	possessor, recipient, beneficiary, goal
OBLIQUE; SPATIAL	*Inessive*	*-ban, -ben*	*benn-*	in(side)
	Illative	*-ba, -be*	*bele-*	into
	Elative	*-ból, -ből*	*belől-*	from inside, from interior
	Superessive	*-n, -on, -en, -ön*	*rajt-*	on, at exterior/ surface
	Sublative	*-ra, -re*	*rá-*	onto, to exterior/ surface

	Delative	*-ról, -ről*	*ról-*	from exterior/ surface
	Adessive	*-nál, -nél*	*nál-*	near, at proximity
	Allative	*-hoz, -hez, -höz*	*hozzá-*	to near, to proximity
	Ablative	*-tól, -től*	*től-*	from near, from proximity
	Terminative	*-ig*	N/A	until, up to, as far as, as long as
OBLIQUE; OTHER	*Instrumental*	*-val, -vel, -Cal, -Cel*	*vel-*	with something or somebody
	Translative(-essive)	*-vá, -vé, -Cá, -Cé*	N/A	into (expressing change of state)
	Causal(-final)	*-ért*	*ért-*	for (reason, aim)
	Essive-formal	*-ként*	N/A	as (role), in the capacity of

B. Structural cases

Nominative case is morphologically unmarked. Subjects bear this case (1), but possessors can also be morphologically unmarked (3). Accusative case appears on direct objects (1).

(1) Ili adott egy könyv-et Imi-nek. [nominative, accusative, dative]
Ili give.Past.3Sg a book-Acc Imi-Dat
'Ili gave a book to Imi.'

Note that Hungarian exhibits Differential Object Marking to some degree: some objects can, others must appear without the accusative suffix. These will be discussed in point *II* and in Section 2.2.1.2 point *V/E*. (On accusative marked pronouns, see also Section 2.2.1.8.) While the nominative and accusative case markers are not exponents of P-heads, thus nominals bearing them are extended NPs, not PPs, these are also cases, so we discuss them in this section.

Dative is the case of recipients, beneficiaries and goals. (1) shows this for a subcategorized noun phrase and (2) for a non-subcategorized NP.

(2) Ezt Ili-nek vettem. [dative]
this.Acc Ili-Dat buy.Past.1Sg
'I bought this for Ili.'

Possessors can also bear dative case (3), but possessors may also be morphologically unmarked (see N2.2.1.2).

(3) János / [János-nak a] kalapja [nominative, dative]
János / János-Dat the hat.Poss
'János' hat'

Dative case is also borne by nominal and adjectival predicates in two environments. Firstly, dative appears on adjectival or nominal predicates of small clauses selected by certain matrix predicates such as *tart* 'consider (sb to be Adj)' and *néz* 'take (sb to be Adj)', as in (4) (see the volume on Adjectival Phrases).

(4) a. Ili okos-nak tartja Imit. [dative]
Ili clever-Dat consider.DefObj.3Sg Imi.Acc
'Ili considers Imi smart.'

b. Ili orvos-nak / hülyé-nek nézte Imit.
Ili doctor-Dat / stupid-Dat take.Past.DefObj.3Sg Imi.Acc
'Ili took Imi to be [a doctor] / stupid.'

Predicates of the small clause complements of the raising verbs *tűnik* 'appear' and *látszik* 'seem' are likewise marked with dative (5).

(5) a. Ili okos-nak tűnik. [dative]
Ili clever-Dat appear.3Sg
'Ili appears to be clever.'

b. Ili okos-nak látszik.
Ili clever-Dat seem.3Sg
'Ili seems to be clever.'

Secondly, fronted nominal and adjectival predicates in the predicate cleft construction also bear dative case (6). On dative-marked adjectival and nominal predicates, see Ürögdi (2006).

(6) a. Szép-nek szép, de túl drága. [dative]
pretty-Dat pretty but too expensive
'As for [being] pretty, it is pretty, but it is too expensive.'

b. Orvos-nak orvos, de nem elég tapasztalt.
doctor-Dat doctor but not enough experienced
'As for being a doctor, he is a doctor, but he is not experienced enough.'

Nominal and adjectival predicates of finite clauses, however, cannot bear dative case; they must be morphologically unmarked (7).

(7) János orvos-(*nak) / okos-(*nak). [dative]
János doctor-Dat / clever-Dat
'János is [a doctor] / clever.'

In a limited number of cases, the dative also has a spatial goal use. This is discussed and illustrated in Section 2.3.1.3.1.

C. Spatial (locative and directional) cases

Hungarian has ten spatial case suffixes; nine of them are arranged in three semantically related triplets. The first triplet relates the Figure to the surface of the Ground object. The superessive case expresses static location on the surface of the Ground (8).

(8) A ház-on sok galamb van. [superessive]
the house-Sup many pigeon be.3Sg
'There are many pigeons on the house.'

The superessive is also the default suffix on names of settlements and geographical areas within the area of the historical Kingdom of Hungary (9). (There are, however, many exceptions where the inessive case is used instead; see below).

(9) Szeged-en / [a Dunántúl-on] sok galamb van. [superessive]
Szeged-Sup / the Dunántúl-Sup many pigeon be.3Sg
'There are many pigeons in [(the city of) Szeged] / [the Dunántúl (region)].'

Names of islands, lowlands / plains and highlands always take the superessive case, regardless of their geographical location (10).

(10) a. a Margitsziget-en, a Zöldfoki Sziget-ek-en [superessive]
the Margaret.island-Sup the green.cape.Attr island-Pl-Sup
'on Margaret Island, on the Cape Verde islands'

b. a Nagyalföld-ön, a Skót Felföld-ön
the big.lowland-Sup the Scottish Highland-Sup
'on the Great (Hungarian) Plain, in the Scottish Highlands'

Days of the month (which take the ordinal form, just like in English) and several temporal adverbs such as 'on Monday', 'in the summer', or 'next week' are also marked with the superessive (11).

(11) a. július 18-á-n [superessive]
July 18-Poss-Sup
'on the 18th of July'

b. hétfő-n, nyár-on, jövő hét-en
Monday-Sup summer-Sup next week-Sup
'on Monday, in the summer, next week'

The superessive is also used to mark the patient in the conative alternation. (12a) encodes a process of hair-drying without commitment that the hair has gotten drier by the end of the event. (12b) expresses a telic event: the hair has gotten dry by the end of the event. Finally, in (12c) the hair has gotten drier, but it has not been dried completely.

(12) a. Ili szárította a haját. [accusative]
Ili dry.Past.DefObj.3Sg the hair.Poss.3Sg.Acc
'Ili was drying her hair.'

b. Ili meg szárította a haját.
Ili Perf dry.Past.DefObj.3Sg the hair.Poss.3Sg.Acc
'Ili has dried her hair.'

c. Ili szárított a hajá-n. [superessive]
Ili dry.Past.3Sg the hair.Poss.3Sg-Sup
'Ili dried her hair a bit.'

The sublative and delative cases express motion to and motion away from the surface of the Ground object (13); they are the directional counterparts of the superessive. As such, they also mark motion into and out of a geographical area or settlement whose locative form involves the superessive case.

(13) a. Sok galamb száll-t [a ház-ra] / Szeged-re. [sublative]
many pigeon fly-Past.3Sg the house-Sub / Szeged-Sub
'Many pigeons flew [onto the house] / [to (the city of) Szeged].'

b. Sok galamb fel-száll-t [a ház-ról] / Szeged-ről. [delative]
many pigeon up-fly-Past.3Sg the house-Del / Szeged-Del
'Many pigeons flew off of [the house] / [(the city of) Szeged].'

The sublative case also obligatorily marks adjectives in resultative constructions (14). See Chapter 4.

(14) Ili lapos-ra kalapálja a vasat. [sublative]
Ili flat-Sub hammer.DefObj.3Sg the iron.Acc
'Ili hammers the iron flat.'

Some measure phrases are also marked with this case (15).

(15) egy méter-re a ház-tól [sublative]
one meter-Sub the house-Abl
'one meter from the house'

The second triplet relates the Figure to the inside of the Ground object. The inessive case expresses static location inside the Ground (16).

(16) A ház-ban sok macska van. [inessive]
the house-Ine many cat be.3Sg
'There are many cats in the house.'

It is also the case to express location in a continent or a country (17a), and the default case to mark location in a county, geographical area or a settlement that is found outside of the area of the historical Kingdom of Hungary (17b) (Tompa 1980, Bartha 1997).

(17) a. Európá-ban / Angliá-ban sok macska van. [inessive]
Europe-Ine / England-Ine many cat be.3Sg
'There are many cats in Europe / England .'

b. Baranyá-ban / London-ban sok macska van. [inessive]
Baranya-Ine / London-Ine many cat be.3Sg
'There are many cats in Baranya [county] / London.

There are numerous exceptions, however. The continent name *Antarktisz* 'Antarctica' and the country name *Magyarország* 'Hungary' take the superessive case rather than the inessive (18).

(18) a. Magyarország-on sok macska van. [inessive]
Hungary-Sup many cat be.3Sg
'There are many cats in Hungary.'

b. Az Antarktisz-on nincsenek macskák. [inessive]
the Antarctica-Sup not_be.3Pl cat.Pl
'There are no cats in Antarctica.'

Remark 1. *Antarktisz* 'Antarctica' behaves more like the name of an island than the name of a continent: as shown in (18), it also requires the definite article (while this is not the case with other continent names).

In addition, in some cases the superessive case is employed on a city name outside of Hungary (19a) and the inessive case is used on a geographical or city name within Hungary (19b).

(19) a. Szentpétervár-on sok macska van. [superessive]
Saint.Petersburg-Sup many cat be.3Sg
'There are many cats in Saint Petersburg.'

b. Győr-ben sok macska van. [inessive]
Győr-Ine many cat be.3Sg
'There are many cats in (the city of) Győr.'

The use of the inessive versus the superessive with certain geographical and settlement names may show variation across speakers and even within the speech of an individual. (It is also attested that a local community in Hungary uses the inessive with the name of its own settlement while the standard language uses the superessive, see Bartha 1997). The inessive also appears on years and the names of months in (static) temporal PPs (20a,b).

(20) a. 2000-ben [inessive]
2000-Ine
'in the year 2000'

b. március-ban
March-Ine
'in March'

The illative and elative cases are the directional counterparts of the inessive; they express motion to and motion away from the inside of the Ground object (21). Geographical names and names of settlements that take the inessive case to express location take the illative and elative cases to express motion into and out of the settlement, respectively.

(21) a. Ili meg-érkez-ett [a ház-ba] / Győr-be. [illative]
Ili Perf-arrive-Past.3Sg the house-Ill / Győr-Ill
'Ili arrived [in the house] / [in (the city of) Győr].

b. Ili távoz-ott [a ház-ból] / Győr-ből. [elative]
Ili leave-Past.3Sg the house-Ela / Győr-Ela
'Ili left [the house] / [(the city of) Győr].'

The last triplet relates the Figure to the vicinity of the Ground object. The adessive case expresses static location near (i.e. in the vicinity of) or at the Ground (22a). The allative and ablative cases are its directional counterparts: these express motion to and motion away from near the Ground, respectively (22b,c).

(22) a. A ház-nál három katona áll. [adessive]
the house-Ade three soldier stand.3Sg
'There are three soldiers standing at the house.'

b. Sok vendég érkez-ett [a ház-hoz]. [allative]
many guest arrive-Past.3Sg the house-All
'Many guests arrived to / at the house.'

c. Az elkövetők el-menekül-t-ek [a ház-tól]. [ablative]
the perpetrator.Pl away-flee-Past-3Pl the house-Abl
'The perpetrators fled from the house.'

The adessive can appear on the object of comparison (23b), though in some dialects the ablative case is used instead (23c). On comparatives and superlatives, see the volume on Adjectival Phrases.

(23) a. Ili magasabb, mint Imi.
Ili taller than Imi
'Ili is taller than Imi.'

b. Ili magasabb Imi-nél. [adessive]
Ili taller Imi-Ade
'Ili is taller than Imi.'

c. %Ili magasabb Imi-től. [ablative]
Ili taller Imi-Abl
'Ili is taller than Imi.'

Finally, the terminative case is used to mark an endpoint in space or time (24a,b). In temporal PPs it can also appear on noun phrases expressing the duration of an event (24c).

(24) a. Hat órá-ig visszajövök. [terminative]
six o'clock-Ter back.come.1Sg
'I will be back by six.'

b. A híd-ig futottam, utána gyalogoltam.
the bridge-Ter run.Past.1Sg after walk.Past.1Sg
'I ran until I reached the bridge, then I walked.'

c. Ili két nap-ig beteg volt.
Ili two day-Ter sick be.Past.3Sg
'Ili was sick for two days.'

D. Other cases

The instrumental case expresses accompaniment (25a) and it is also used to mark instruments (25b).

(25) a. Ili Pál-lal / kutyá-val / hátizsák-kal ment sétálni. [instrumental]
Ili Pál-Ins / dog-Ins / backpack-Ins go.Past.3Sg walk.Inf
'Ili went for a walk [with Pál] / [with a dog] / [with a backpack].'

b. Ili kés-sel nyitotta ki a konzerv-et.
Ili knife-Ins open.Past.DefObj.3Sg out the can-Acc
'Ili opened the can with a knife.'

Some measure phrases also bear this case (26).

(26) egy méter-rel a ház mögött [instrumental]
one meter-Ins the house behind
'one meter behind the house'

The translative(-essive) case marks non-verbal predicates accompanying verbs of change. It expresses the result state of a transformation (27).

(27) a. A hős kutyá-vá változott. [translative(-essive)]
the hero dog-TrE transform.Past.3Sg
'The hero transformed into a dog.'

b. A vér nem válik víz-zé.
the blood not turn.3Sg wanter-TrE
'Blood is thicker than water.' (Lit: Blood will not turn into water.)

Note that the translative(-essive) is not used productively with *lesz* 'will be, become', the future copula (de Groot 2017). It appears only in a few set expressions; these sound archaic or represent a highly elevated style (28).

(28) a. Semmi-vé lett a vagyon. [translative(-essive)]
nothing-TrE become.Past.3Sg the wealth
'The wealth is gone.' (Lit: The wealth has become nothing.)

b. Por-ból lettünk, por-rá leszünk.
dust-Ela become.Past.1Pl dust-TrE become.1Pl
'Ashes to ashes, dust to dust.' (Lit: We are made of dust, we shall become dust.)

In the unmarked, fully productive case, the secondary predicate next to *lesz* 'will be, become' bears the unmarked nominative case (29).

(29) Ili tanár / *tanár-rá lesz. [nominative, translative(-essive)]
Ili teacher / teacher-TrE become.3Sg
'Ili will be / become a teacher.'

The causal(-final) case expresses purpose (30a) or reason / cause (30b).

(30) a. A cicá-ért jöttem. [causal(-final)]
the cat-Cau come.Past.1Sg
'I came for (i.e. in order to fetch) the cat.'

b. Ez-ért nem jó tűz-re olaj-at önteni.
this-Cau not good fire-Sub oil-Acc pour.Inf
'This is why it is not a good idea to pour oil on fire.'

Finally, the essive-formal case is used to express a role held by somebody (31).

(31) a. Ili igazgató-ként sokat tett a vállalat-ért. [essive-formal]
Ili director-FoE lot.Acc do.Past.3Sg the company-Cau
'[As director, Ili did a lot for the company.] / [In her capacity as director, Ili did a lot for the company.]'

b. Ili tanár-ként dolgozik.
the teacher-FoE work.3Sg
'Ili works as a teacher.'

c. A régióban első-ként itt vezették be az új rendszert.
the region.Ine first-FoE here introduce.Past.DefObj.3Pl in the new system
'It was here that the new system was first introduced within the region.'

Remark 2. Drawing the boundaries of the Hungarian case system and thus delineating case suffixes from other nominal suffixes is notoriously difficult. There are altogether 15 suffixes that are accepted as case markers by everybody. These are listed below.

(i) accusative, dative, inessive, illative, elative, superessive, sublative, delative, adessive, allative, ablative, instrumental, translative(-essive), causal(-final), terminative

At the same time, everybody accepts that the inventory of cases is larger than these 15 suffixes; the debate concerns how many and exactly which suffixes should be added to the list. There are two types of suffixes that are problematic in setting up a definitive list of cases. The first type is the nominative case, which has a phonologically zero exponent. Is nominative a case in Hungarian or not? The answer to this question is 'yes' in most works (the most notable exceptions are Olsson 1992 and Payne and Chisarik 2000). The second problematic suffix-type is suffixes with limited productivity, such as the sociative or the essive(-modal). Should all, some, or no suffixes with limited productivity be counted as case markers? Most of the disagreement in the literature stems from the dilemma of where to draw the line between fully productive and less productive suffixes. We will discuss suffixes with a more limited productivity in Section 2.2.4.1.2.

The shortest case inventory with 16 cases can be found in Abondolo (1998: 440) and Payne and Chisarik (2000: 183). The two case-lists are not identical, however. Abondolo adds nominative to the cases in (i), while Payne and Chisarik add the temporal suffix *-kor* and exclude nominative from their list. Antal (1961: 44) and Kornai (1989) add the phonologically zero nominative as well as the essive-formal *-ként* suffix to the 15 strong list above, bringing the total number of cases to 17. Kiefer (2000a: 580, 2003: 202) identifies 18 cases: in addition to the suffixes listed in (i), he also accepts the essive-formal and the modal-essive *-n/-an/-en* suffixes as well as the zero nominative as cases (on the modal-essive, see Section 2.2.4.1.1 point *II*). 22 cases are recognized by Moravcsik (2003: 116-117), 23 by Olsson (1992: 101), and 24 by Lotz (1939: 66) and Rácz (1968: 197-199). There are 25 cases listed by Vago (1980: 100), and 26 by Tompa (1968: 206-29). The longest case-list is found in S. Hámori and Tompa (1961: 557) and Kenesei, Vago and Fenyvesi (1998: 191), with 27 case markers in total.

This diversity in the number of suffixes recognized as cases stems from the fact that many authors do not use explicit formal criteria to delineate cases from other suffixes. The works that do propose formal definitions, on the other hand, use different criteria to identify cases. Compare the definitions of Kiefer (2000a) and Payne and Chisarik (2000); the former picks out 18 suffixes as cases, while the latter picks out 16. (We do not endorse either definition here; we merely show how diverse the definitions in previous research have been.)

(ii) Definitions of case suffixes in Kiefer (2000a) ((iia) and (iib) are equivalent)

a. A suffix is a case marker if and only if a nominal bearing this suffix functions as a selected argument of some verb, and the verb requires its argument to bear precisely this suffix. (our translation)

b. If a noun bearing an inflectional suffix (but not a plural suffix or a possessive suffix) can be modified, then the inflectional suffix in question is a case suffix. If the noun bearing the inflectional suffix cannot be modified, then that suffix is not a case suffix. (our translation)

Based on these definitions, the sociative suffix, for instance, is not a case suffix because no predicate subcategorizes for a sociative marked argument, and nouns bearing the sociative case cannot be modified (Section 2.2.4.1.2).

(iii) Definition of case suffixes in Payne and Chisarik (2000)
Those overt forms which (i) are able to mark maximal noun phrases with a full range of determiners and premodifiers, and (ii) have the [...] property of attaching to noun-phrase premodifiers in case of ellipsis (Payne and Chisarik 2000: 182)

In order for the reader to be able to fully appreciate the Payne-Chisarik definition, let us illustrate the property mentioned in clause (ii) of the definition. Syntactically, case suffixes belong to the whole Noun Phrase, but in the linear string they appear on the nominal head.

(iv) a sok piros almá-t, amit Ili hozott
the many red apple-Acc that Ili bring.Past.3Sg
'the many red apples that Ili brought'

In case the nominal head or an NP sub-constituent containing the nominal head is elided, the case suffix remains overt and receives phonological support from the rightmost overt noun-modifier (this is what Payne and Chisarik call 'noun-phrase premodifier').

(v) a. a ma leszedett három szem piros almá-t
the today down.pick.Part three eye red apple-Acc
'the three red apples picked today'

b. a ma leszedett három szem piros-at [attaching to adjective]
the today down.pick.Part three eye red-Acc
'the three red ones picked today'

c. a ma leszedett három szem-et [attaching to classifier]
the today down.pick.Part three eye-Acc
'the three ones picked today'

d. a ma leszedett hárm-at [attaching to numeral]
the today down.pick.Part three-Acc
'the three picked today'

e. a ma leszedett-et [attaching to participial relative]
the today down.pick.Part-Acc
'the one picked today'

This leaning is possible onto adjectives, classifiers, numerals, quantifiers and prenominal participles, as in (v), but a stranded case suffix cannot lean onto the definite article or demonstratives (see also Lipták and Saab 2014), even though the demonstrative itself can be case-marked, as in (via), and can also stand on its own, as in (vib). As discussed in N2.5.2, adnominal demonstratives can appear both in the pre-D and the post-D zone. *Ez* 'this' and *az* 'that', the demonstratives of the pre-D zone, bear the same case-marking as the head noun (via). The stranded case marking of the nominal head cannot cliticize onto these demonstratives, however, possibly because that would yield a demonstrative with double case-marking (vid).

(vi) • Case suffix leaning onto the definite article and demonstratives in pre-D position

a. ez-en a ház-on
this-Sup the house-Sup
'on this house'

b. ez-en
this-Sup
'on this one'

c. *ez-en a(z)-on [attaching to definite article]
this-Sup the-Sup
Intended meaning: 'on this one'

d. *ez-en-en [attaching to pre-D demonstrative]
this-Sup-Sup
Intended meaning: 'on this one'

Demonstratives in the post-D zone, for instance *eme* 'this' and *ama* 'that', do not show the kind of case-concord that pre-D demonstratives do (viia); they are morphologically invariant. A case suffix stranded under ellipsis cannot lean onto these demonstratives either (viib).

(vii) • Case suffix leaning onto demonstratives in post-D position
a. eme(*-n) ház-on
this-Sup house-Acc
'on this house'
b. *eme-n
this-Sup
Intended meaning: 'on this one'

Note that case-like Ps and the plural marker have the same distribution in elliptical noun phrases as case suffixes: when stranded under N(P) ellipsis, they can lean onto an adjective, classifier, numeral or participial relative clause in the NP, but not on the definite article or a demonstrative (see the volume on Coordination and Ellipsis).

E. The absence of the genitive

Conspicuous by its absence on this list is the genitive case. As shown in (3), possessors are either morphologically unmarked or they bear dative case. Dative marking on possessors can be interpreted in one of two ways: i) Hungarian genuinely has no genitive case (a stance taken in most of the generative literature), or ii) there is a separate genitive case in the grammar, but its exponent is syncretic with that of the dative (cf. Tompa 1961, 1968 and Rácz 1986, among others).

Bartos (2000) and Dékány (2011, 2015) argue that that the possessor suffix *-é* is actually an exponent of the genitive case with a limited distribution. This suffix appears on the possessor if it is not followed by an overt possessum, i.e. if the possessum is elided (32a) and if the possessor is in predicative position (32b).

(32) a. Kinek a pályázata nyert? János-é / *János / *János-nak.
who.Dat the application win.Past.3Sg János-Posr / János / János-Dat
'Whose application won? János'.'
b. Ez a könyv János-é / *János / *János-nak.
this the book János-Posr / János / János-Dat
'This book is János's.'

In adnominal position, possessors cannot bear the *-é* suffix (33).

(33) János / [János-nak a] / *János-é könyv-e
János / János-Dat the / János-Posr book-Poss
'János' book'

There are three main arguments for *-é* being the genitive case. First, *-é* appears only on possessors. Second, demonstratives in the pre-D zone show concord for genuine cases (and the plural marker) of the noun they modify. This is illustrated for the accusative case suffix in (34a). The demonstratives in question also show concord for the *-é* suffix (34b).

(34) • Demonstrative concord for the accusative case suffix and *-é*

a. Kedvelem ez*(-t) a fiú-t.
like.1Sg this-Acc the boy-Acc
'I like this boy.'

b. A könyv ez*(-é) a fiú-é.
the book this-Posr the boy-Posr
'The book is this boy's.'

Note that demonstratives do not show concord for other possession-related suffixes of the head noun such as the possessive suffix (35a) and possessive agreement (35b) (cf. N1.1.1.4.3 and N2.5.2.2); these suffixes definitely do not have the status of case suffixes (see also N2.2.1.2.1.2).

(35) a. a fiú-nak ez(*-e) a cikk-e
the boy-Dat this-Poss the article-Poss
'this article of the boy'

b. nekem ez(*-em) a cikk-em
Dat.1Sg this-Poss.1Sg the article-Poss.1Sg
'this article of mine'

Thirdly, if the head noun is ellipted, then genuine case suffixes (and the plural suffix) are left stranded; they lean onto the linearly last adjectival or numeral modifier of the ellipted noun. (36a') shows this for the accusative case suffix. As shown in (36b'), the *-é* suffix is likewise stranded under noun ellipsis, and is supported by the linearly last adjective (or numeral, not shown here).

(36) • The accusative case suffix and *-é* leaning onto an adjective after N-ellipsis

a. a magas fiú-t
the tall boy-Acc
'the tall boy'

a'. a magas-at
the tall-Acc
'the tall one'

b. a magas fiú-é
the tall boy-Posr
'that of the tall boy'

b' a magas-é
the tall-Posr
'that of the tall one'

For further details on *-é*, see N1.1.1.1 and N1.1.1.4.3, Bartos (2000) and Dékány (2015).

As already mentioned above, possessors can also be morphologically unmarked. This fact has been interpreted in three different ways in the literature: i) they bear nominative case (Szabolcsi 1983) ii) they are caseless (É. Kiss 2002) and iii) the definite article that precedes these possessors has been reanalyzed as a genitive case marker, hence they bear genitive case (Chisarik and Payne 2001).

II. Form

As shown in Table 1, all case suffixes are monosyllabic, and with the exception of the causal(-final), the terminative and the essive-formal suffixes, the quality of their vowel is determined by the word that they attach to (in non-elliptical NPs, by the inflected nominal head, and in elliptical NPs, by the premodifier that gives them phonological support) (37). Most case suffixes show only a front-back vowel harmony, but the vowel of the allative suffix and the linking vowel of the accusative and the superessive also show harmony for roundedness.

(37) • Case suffixes and vowel harmony

a. annak az okos ember-nek
that.Dat the clever man-Dat
'to that clever man'

a'. annak az okos-nak
that.Dat the clever-Dat
'to that clever one'

b. a kedves lány-nak
the kind girl-Dat
'to the kind girl'

b'. a kedves-nek
the kind-Dat
'to the kind one'

The accusative suffix has two allomorphs; an overt one, *-t* (which may be preceded by one of four epenthetic vowels: *a, e, o,* or *ö*) and one that is phonologically zero. The latter is formally identical to the nominative case. The zero allomorph may only appear following a first or second person (singular or plural) possessive agreement suffix (38). The overt allomorph may also appear in this context. (For some speakers, the overt allomorph is, in fact, obligatory after the first or second person plural possessive agreement.)

(38) • Accusative allomorphs in possessed noun phrases

a. Láttad a gyűrű-m(-et)?
see.Past.DefObj.2Sg the ring-Poss.1Sg-Acc
'Have you seen my ring?'

b. Láttad a gyűrű-d(-et)?
see.Past.DefObj.2Sg the ring-Poss.2Sg-Acc
'Have you seen your ring?'

c. Láttad a gyűrű-jé-t / *gyűrű-je?
see.Past.DefObj.2Sg the ring-Poss.3Sg-Acc / ring-Poss.3Sg
'Have you seen her ring?'

d. Láttad a gyűrű-nk(-et)
see.Past.DefObj.2Sg the ring-Poss.1Pl-Acc
'Have you seen our ring?'

e. Láttad a gyűrű-tök(-et)?
see.Past.DefObj.2Sg the ring-Poss.2Pl-Acc
'Have you seen your ring?'

f. Láttad a gyűrű-jük*(-et)?
see.Past.DefObj.2Sg the ring-Poss.3Pl-Acc
'Have you seen their ring?'

On all other object noun phrases, the overt allomorph must be used (39).

(39) • Accusative allomorphs in non-possessed noun phrases

a. Láttad a gyűrű*(-t)?
see.Past.DefObj.2Sg the ring-Acc
'Have you seen the ring?'

b. Láttad a gyűrű-k*(-et)?
see.Past.DefObj.2Sg the ring-Pl-Acc
'Have you seen the rings?'

The inessive, illative, elative, superessive, sublative and allative cases have different allomorphs on lexical nouns and elsewhere (i.e. on pronouns and when used as verbal particles). These will be discussed in Section 2.2.1.2 point *V/B*. Here we illustrate with the superessive. Its *-n* allomorph (potentially preceded by an *o, e* or *ö* linking vowel) is the default form, used everywhere except on personal pronouns (40).

(40) a ház-on, Péter-en, az-on
the house-Sup Peter-Sup that-Sup
'on the house, on Peter, on that'

The second allomorph, *rajt-*, is used when the superessive attaches to an overt or covert personal pronoun (41a), or when it functions as a verbal particle (41b). In other words, the two allomorphs are in complementary distribution. On the use of case markers as particles, see Chapter 4 and Chapter 5.

(41) a. (én-)rajt-am
I-Sup-1Sg
'on me'

b. A könyv rajt-a van az asztal-on.
the book Sup-Poss.3Sg be.3Sg the table-Sup
'The book is on the table.'

Remark 3. Of the two allomorphs of the superessive case, it is *rajt-* that is morphologically related to the sublative *-ra/re* (onto) and the delative *-ről/ről* (from surface). Originally, *rajt-* bore the locative *-(Vt)t* suffix (*rajatt)*; this form then shortened to *rajt-* (Simonyi 1888: 107-108).

The accusative and the superessive have another property, too, which sets them apart from other case markers: these are the only cases that are expressed by non-analytical (synthetic) suffixes. This will be detailed in Section 2.2.1.1 point *III*.

The case suffixes that begin with the consonant *v*, that is, the instrumental and translative(-essive) case suffixes, feature assimilation of their *v* to the last consonant of a consonant-final stem. This is illustrated in (42).

(42) a. autó-val, autó-k-kal, az autó-d-dal az autó-m-mal [instrumental]
car-Ins car-Pl-Ins the car-Poss.2Sg-Ins the car-Poss.1Sg-Ins
'with (a) car, with cars, with your car, with my car'

b. cicá-vá, cicá-k-ká, a cicá-d-dá, a cicá-m-má [translative(-essive)]
cat-TrE cat-Pl-TrE the cat-Poss.2Sg-TrE the cat-Poss.1Sg-TrE
[transform] 'into (a) cat, into cats, into your cat, into my cat'

The expected, regular forms of instrumental and translative(-essive)-marked demonstrative pronouns are shown in (43a). Dialectally or in the spoken register, it is also possible to assimilate the final *z* of the demonstrative to the initial *v* of the case instrumental suffix (43b).

(43) a. az-zal, ez-zel, az-zá, ez-zé
that-Ins this-Ins that-TrE this-TrE
'with that, with this, [transform] into that, [transform] into this'

b. av-val, ev-vel
that-Ins this-Ins
'with that, with this'

As shown in Table 1, Hungarian has ten case markers encoding spatial relations. Nine of these express distinctions along two dimensions. The first dimension is whether the Figure is located with respect to the inside, the surface, or the proximity of the Ground (i.e. cases distinguish between 'in', 'on', and 'at' the Ground). The second dimension is whether the Figure is stationary (place semantics), is in motion towards the Ground (goal semantics) or is in motion away from the Ground (source semantics). The tenth spatial case marker, the terminative -*ig* denotes an endpoint at the goal. This is summarized in Table 2. While case suffixes express distinctions along two dimensions (the part of the Ground in question, i.e. 'in', 'on', and 'at' on the one hand and location versus motion on the other hand), they are indivisible morphemes for contemporary speakers.

Table 2: Case suffixes expressing spatial relations

	INSIDE / IN	SURFACE / ON	PROXIMITY / AT	ENDPOINT
PLACE	*inessive* *-ban, -ben*	*superessive* *-n, -on, -en, -ön*	*adessive* *-nál, -nél*	
GOAL	*illative* *-ba, -be*	*sublative* *-ra, -re*	*allative* *-hoz, -hez, -höz*	*terminative* *-ig*
SOURCE	*elative* *-ból, -ből*	*delative* *-ról, -ről*	*ablative* *-tól, -től*	

For examples with nouns bearing these case suffixes, see (13) through (23). Note that in spoken colloquial Hungarian, the illative and the inessive are often syncretic:

the *-ba/-be* suffix is used in both functions (44). The distinction is strictly maintained in writing, however.

(44) a ház-ba
the house-BA
'[into the house] / %[in the house]'

III. Synthetic vs. analytic cases

Bartos (2000: 712) and Rebrus (2000: 845) distinguish between two types of suffixation in Hungarian: analytical and non-analytical (aka synthetic). Non-analytical suffixes are phonologically tightly integrated into their host: first they are concatenated with the stem, and only then do phonological processes apply, to the stem+suffix unit as whole. Analytical suffixes are less tightly integrated into their host. Phonological rules apply first to the stem alone; this is followed by concatenation with the suffix and another round of phonological rule application, now to the stem+suffix unit.

Case suffixes are analytic suffixes. There are two exceptions, however: the accusative is expressed by a synthetic suffix, and the superessive has both an analytic and a synthetic allomorph (Bartos 2000: 712, Rebrus 2000: 805, 831-832, 845). That these two case suffixes are phonologically more integrated to their host than the others can be observed in two environments: i) when cases combine with a pronoun and ii) when cases combine with nouns showing stem allomorphy.

Consider first case-marked pronouns. A pronoun that bears an analytical case suffix can be dropped without further ado, stranding the case suffix (and the agreement marker following it) (45).

(45) • Dropping a pronominal Ground with analytical cases
a. ő-től-e, ő-nek-i
he-Abl-3Sg he-Dat-3Sg
'from him, to him'
b. től-e, nek-i
Abl-3Sg Dat-3Sg
'from him, to him'

A pronoun bearing accusative case, however, cannot be dropped. In other words, the accusative case suffix requires an overt host and does not combine with *pro*. This is because the exponent of the accusative is a non-analytical suffix, which does not have the (morpho)-phonological independence to stand on its own. Consider (46a) and (46b). Based on (45), we may expect that the pronoun can also be dropped from (46a), leading to (46b). The result, however, is ungrammatical.

(46) a. ő-t
he-Acc
'him'
b. *-t
Acc
Intended meaning: 'him'

The accusative form of first and second person plural pronouns comprises the pronominal base, a person-number suffix reflecting the features of the pronoun, and the accusative case suffix (see point *F* below), as shown in (47a). The pronoun cannot be dropped in these cases either (47b), even though the stranded accusative suffix would receive some phonological support from the person-number affix.

(47) a. mi-nk-et, ti-tek-et
we-1Pl-Acc you.Pl-2Pl-Acc
'us, you(Pl.Acc)'

b. *nk-et *tek-et
1Pl-Acc 2Pl-Acc
Intended meaning: 'us, you(Pl.Acc)'

Note that object *pro*-drop is possible, but it deletes the entire pronoun, together with the case suffix (48).

(48) a. Láttad ő-t / ő-k-et?
see.Past.DefObj.2Sg he-Acc / he-Pl-Acc
'Did you see him / them?'

b. Nem láttam (ő-t / ő-k-et).
not see.Past.1Sg he-Acc / he-Pl-Acc
'No, I didn't.'

c. *Nem láttam -t / -k-et.
not see.Past.1Sg Acc / Pl-Acc

Turning to the superessive, we have already mentioned above that is has two allomorphs: *-(V)n* and *rajt-*. The *-(V)n* allomorph is, in fact, a non-analytical suffix, while the other allomorph, *rajt-*, is a phonologically much heavier, analytical one. The fact that only the latter appears with *pro* (and pronouns in general) is no doubt related to its status as an analytical suffix.

To summarize, analytical case suffixes have enough (morpho)-phonological independence to license *pro*-drop of their associated pronoun. Non-analytical (synthetic) case suffixes are phonologically integrated with their stem to a much larger extent, therefore they do not allow *pro*-drop of their associated pronoun.

Let us now turn to case suffixes on nouns exhibiting stem allomorphy. Some Hungarian nouns have both a free and a bound stem variant (see N1.1.1.2). A few examples are given in Table 3.

Table 3: Some nouns showing stem allomorphy

	HAND	CRANE (THE BIRD)	SNOW	HORSE
FREE	*kéz*	*daru*	*hó*	*ló*
BOUND	*kez-*	*darv-*	*hav-*	*lov-*

Analytical cases always appear with the free stem (49a,b). The synthetic superessive allomorph *-(V)n* often (but not always) takes the free stem: in (49c) it combines with free stems, while in (49d) it combines with the bound stems of the relevant nouns. Finally, the synthetic accusative case appears with bound stems (49e). This shows that the suffix of the accusative case is even more phonologically integrated with its stem than the superessive (Moravcsik 2003).

(49) • Cases on nouns showing stem allomorphy

a. kéz-nek, daru-nak, hó-nak, ló-nak [dative (analytic)]
hand-Dat crane-Dat snow-Dat horse-Dat
'to (a) hand, to (a) crane, to snow, to (a) horse'

b. kéz-ben, daru-ban, hó-ban, ló-ban [inessive (analytic)]
hand-Ine crane-Ine snow-Ine horse-Ine
'in (a) hand, in (a) crane, in snow, in (a) horse'

c. kéz-en, daru-n [superessive + free stem]
hand-Sup crane-Sup
'on (a) hand, on (a) crane'

d. hav-on, lov-on [superessive + bound stem]
snow-Sup horse-Sup
'on snow, on (a) horse'

e. kez-et, hav-at, lov-at [accusative + bound stem]
hand-Acc snow-Acc horse-Acc
'hand(Acc), snow(Acc), horse(Acc)'

Remark 4. The stem class of *daru* 'crane (the bird)' contains three nouns: *daru* 'crane (the bird)', *tetű* 'louse' and *falu* 'village'. In this stem class the free stem ends in a high vowel *u* or *ű* and in the bound stem this vowel is replaced by the consonant *v*. Exceptionally, in this stem class the accusative can attach either to the free or the bound stem (i). In all other stem classes, the accusative combines with the bound stem, as indicated in the main text.

(i) a. daru-t, tetű-t, falu-t [accusative + free stem]
crane-Acc louse-Acc village-Acc
'crane, louse, village'

b. darv-at, tetv-et, falv-at [accusative + bound stem]
crane-Acc louse-Acc village-Acc
'crane, louse, village'

IV. Interaction with stem-final vowels

Before most suffixes, the Low Vowel Lengthening rule causes the stem-final short low vowels [ɔ] and [ɛ] to be replaced by their long counterparts, [a:] and [e:] (see Nádasdy and Siptár 1994, Rebrus 2000, Siptár and Törkenczy 2000 and Szabó 2016, among others). Among other cases, Low Vowel Lengthening applies when the stem is suffixed by a case suffix. Some examples are given in (50).

(50) a. alma, körte
apple pear

b. almá-t, körté-t
apple-Acc pear-Acc
'apple, pear'

c. almá-ra körté-re
apple-Sub pear-Sub
'onto apple, onto pear'

The only exception is the essive-formal case, which does not trigger Low Vowel Lengthening (51).

(51) alma-ként, körte-ként
apple-FoE pear-FoE
'as (an) apple, as (a) pear'

2.2.1.2. Complementation

I. The form of the complement

Case suffixes generally do not stack on each other, thus they take a morphologically unmarked complement (52).

(52) a ház-at, a ház-nak, a ház-on, a ház-ig
the house-Acc the house-Dat the house-Sup the house-Ter
'the house, of/to the house, on the house, up to the house'

See Section 2.2.1.8 on some exceptions to the 'no stacking' generalization.

II. PP-internal position with respect to the complement

Case markers are suffixed to the nominal head of their NP complement (53). Thus similarly to case-like postpositions (Section 2.2.2.2) and unlike case-assigning postpositions (Section 2.2.2.3), they do not allow a prefixal use and do not allow modifiers to intervene between them and their complement.

(53) a. a kert-et, a kert-től
the garden-Acc the garden-Abl
'the garden(Acc), from the garden'

b. *a kert [három méter-re]-től
the garden three meter-Sub-Abl
Intended meaning: 'three meters from the garden'

b'. a kert-től három méter-re
the garden-Abl three meter-Sub
'three meters from the garden'

III. Dropping the complement

Case suffixes cannot occur without a complement. The stars in (54) mean that the intransitive use of the case is ill-formed.

(54) *-t, *-nak, *-ig
-Acc -Dat -Ter

IV. The complement's demonstrative modifier

If the complement of the case is a noun phrase that contains the demonstrative pronoun *ez* 'this' or *az* 'that', then the case must appear twice: once on the nominal head and once on the demonstrative (55) (see also N2.5.2.2).

(55) a. az*(-t) a ház-at
that-Acc the house-Acc
'that house(Acc)'

b. ez*(-ért) a könyv-ért
this-Cau the book-Cau
'for this book'

V. Personal pronoun complements

In this section we discuss case-marked pronouns. It is important to clarify that here and throughout the chapter, the term 'personal pronoun' is meant as a cover for the pronouns *én* 'I', *te* 'you(Sg)', *ő* 'he, she', *mi* 'we ', *ti* 'you(Pl)' and *ők* 'they'. The polite forms of second person pronouns, *Ön* 'you(Sg)', *Önök* 'you(Pl)', as well as *Maga* 'you(Sg)'and *Maguk* 'you(Pl)' are not subsumed by the term 'personal pronoun'. These polite forms are importantly different from the other personal pronouns. (For instance, when combining with a case suffix or a case-like postposition, they are not accompanied by an agreement morpheme.) On pronouns in general, see the volume on Noun Phrases.

A. The availability of a pronominal complement

Most case suffixes can combine with common nouns, proper names as well as personal pronouns. There are three exceptions, however: the translative(-essive), the terminative and the essive-formal case, which combine with common nouns and proper names but not with personal pronouns. Even these three cases can combine with demonstrative pronouns, however. The restrictions on the translative(-essive) case are shown in (56).

(56) • Translative(-essive)

a. A hős cicá-vá változott.
the hero cat-TrE transform.Past.3Sg
'The hero transformed into a cat.'

b. A hős az-zá változott.
the hero that-TrE transform.Past.3Sg
'The hero transformed into that.'

c. *A hős én-vé-m / én-né-m változott.
the hero I-TrE-1Sg / I-TrE-1Sg transform.Past.3Sg
Intended meaning: 'The hero transformed into me.'

In (56c) two potential forms of a translative(-essive) marked personal pronoun are shown. The basic allomorphs of this case are *-va* and *-ve*, but the initial consonant undergoes assimilation to the last consonant of C-final stems. Based on this rule, the **én-né-m* form would be expected. On the other hand, the initial consonant of the instrumental case suffix *-val/vel* also assimilates to the consonant of C-final stems, but this assimilation is suspended with personal pronouns (*én-vel-em* rather than **én-nel-em*, cf. example (77)). Based on analogy with the instrumental case, we might expect the **én-vé-m* form for the translative(-essive). As shown in (56c), neither form is grammatical.

Examples with the essive-formal case are provided in (57).

(57) • Essive-formal

a. János főnök-ként viselkedik.
János boss-FoE behave.3Sg
'János [behaves as] / [acts like] a boss.'

b. János akként viselkedik.
János that.FoE behave.3Sg
'János [behaves as] / [acts like] that.'

c. *János én-ként-em viselkedik.
János I-FoE-1Sg behave.3Sg
Intended meaning: 'János [behaves as] / [acts like] me.'

The intended meaning of (57c) can be approximated with a comparative (58):

(58) János úgy viselkedik, mint én.
János so behave.3Sg as I
'János behaves like me.'

The use of the terminative case is illustrated in (59).

(59) • Terminative

a. János a sarok-ig fut.
János the corner-Ter run.3Sg
'János runs up to (i.e. until he reaches) the corner.'

b. János addig fut.
János that.Ter run.3Sg
'János runs [up to] / until that (point).'

c. *János én-ig-em fut.
János I-Ter-1Sg run.3Sg
Intended meaning: 'János runs up to (i.e. until he reaches) me.'

d. *A kábel el-ér én-ig-em.
the cable away-reach.3Sg I-Ter-1Sg
Intended meaning: 'The cable reaches up to me.'

The intended meaning of (59c) and (59d) can be expressed with the allative case (but while (60b) means exactly what (59d) is meant to express, (60a) and (59c) have a meaning difference, as shown by their English translations).

(60) a. János (én-)hozzá-m fut.
János I-All-1Sg run.3Sg
'János runs to me.'

b. A kábel el-ér (én-)hozzá-m.
the cable away-reach.3Sg I-All-1Sg
'The cable reaches up to me.'

Interestingly, some speakers can add the terminative case suffix to an allative-marked personal pronoun (61) (see also Simonyi 1888: 339).

(61) %A kábel el-ér (én-)hozzá-m-ig.
the cable away-reach.3Sg I-All-1Sg-Ter
'The cable reaches up to me.'

B. The form of the case marker on a personal pronoun complement

Most case markers have the same form on common nouns, proper names and on personal pronouns (62)-(69). Note that oblique case markers on personal pronouns must be followed by an agreement suffix that cross-references the person and number of the pronoun. This property also characterizes case-like postpositions, to be discussed in Section 2.2.2.2.2 point *V*. (The lengthening of the *a* vowel of the sublative case to *á* is a case of Low Vowel Lengthening, a regular morpho-phonological process in the language.) Note that except in the accusative case, the pronoun itself can be dropped. (See Creissels 2006 and Spencer and Stump 2013 for discussion of the oblique forms of personal pronouns.)

(62) • Accusative
a. az őr-t
the guard-Acc
'the guard'
b. ő-t
he-Acc
'him'

(63) • Dative
a. az őr-nek
the guard-Dat
'to the guard'
b. (én-)nek-em
I-Dat-1Sg
'to me'

(64) • Sublative
a. az asztal-ra
the table-Sub
'onto the table'
b. (én-)rá-m
I-Sub-1Sg
'onto me'

(65) • Delative
a. az asztal-ról
the table-Del
'from / about the table'
b. (én-)ról-am
I-Del-1Sg
'from / about me'

(66) • Adessive

a. az asztal-nál
the table-Ade
'at the table'

b. (én-)nál-am
I-Ade-1Sg
'at me'

(67) • Ablative

a. az őr-től
the guard-Abl
'from the guard'

b. (én-)től-em
I-Abl-1Sg
'from me'

(68) • Instrumental

a. a név-vel
the name-Ins
'with the name'

b. (én-)vel-em
I-Ins-1Sg
'with me'

(69) • Causal(-final)

a. az őr-ért
the guard-Cau
'for the guard'

b. (ő-)ért-e
he-Cau-3Sg
'for him'

Five case suffixes, however, exhibit some phonological readjustment or other type of allomorphy when their complement is a pronoun. The inessive *-ban/-ben* is affected by readjustment of its final consonant: the last C undergoes gemination when the complement is an overt pronoun or a silent *pro* (70).

(70) a. az őr-ben
the guard-Ine
'in the guard'

b. (én-)benn-em
I-Ine-1Sg
'in me'

Remark 5. In the spoken register and dialectally, this gemination also affects the last consonant of the adessive, the ablative and the delative case.

(i) (én-)náll-am, (én-)től1-em, (én-)róll-am
I-Ade-1Sg I-Abl-1Sg I-Del-1Sg
'at me, from me, from / about me'

The final consonant of the allative *-hoz/-hez* likewise undergoes gemination. In addition, an *á* vowel is also added, yielding *hozzá-* as the form when the complement is an overt pronoun or a silent *pro* (71).

(71) a. a bor-hoz
the wine-All
'to the wine'

b. (én-)hozzá-m
I-All-1Sg
'to me'

Note that the *á* that appears after the geminated consonant cannot be analyzed as a linking vowel that belongs to the agreement suffix (that is, **hozz-ám*), as a linking vowel is always *a*, *e*, *o* or *ö*, and never a long vowel.

The illative case suffix *-ba/-be* acquires an additional *le* string when it appears with overt pronouns or a *pro*.

(72) a. az őr-be
the guard-Ill
'into the guard'

b. (én-)belé-m
I-Ill-1Sg
'into me'

Remark 6. The illative case suffix *-ba/-be* has grammaticalized from *belé*, the lative (*-á/-é*) marked form of the noun *bel* 'inside' (for a recent discussion see Hegedűs 2014). In contemporary Hungarian *bel* is used as a prefix meaning 'endo-' or 'internal' (i). The related common noun *bél* 'intestine, inside' is exemplified in (ii).

(i) bel-gyógyászat, bel-magasság
inside-medicine inside-height
'endocrinology / [internal medicine], ceiling height'

(ii) kenyér-bél, a kenyér bel-e, a malac bel-e
bread-inside the bread inside-Poss the pig intestine-Poss
'crumb, the inside of the bread, the pig's intestines'

The elative case marker has the *-ból/-ből* allomorph on common nouns and proper names and the longer form *belől-* on pronouns (72).

(73) a. az őr-ből
the guard-Ela
'from (inside) the guard'

b. (én-)belől-em
I-Ela-1Sg
'from (inside) me'

Remark 7. The elative case suffix *-ból/-ből* grammaticalized from the form *belől* (a recent discussion can be found in Hegedűs 2014). The original longer form is still obligatorily used when the elative takes a pronominal complement (73b). *Belől* comprised two morphemes: the *bel* discussed in the previous remark and the source suffix *-Vl* that also appears on case-like Ps with a source semantics (see 2.2.2.2).

Finally, as already mentioned above, the superessive case requires the special *rajt-* allomorph with both overt and covert pronominal complements (74).

(74) a. a híd-on
the bridge-Sup
'on the bridge'

b. (én-)rajt-am
I-Sup-1Sg
'on me'

We can conclude that if a case marker has a different form on common nouns and proper names on the one hand and on pronouns on the other hand, then the form on pronouns is always phonologically heavier.

C. Regular phonological processes suspended

As already pointed out above, most Hungarian case suffixes exhibit vowel harmony: the quality of their vowel is determined by the vowel(s) of the (inflected) stem they attach to. This vowel harmony is suspended when case markers attach to a pronoun; in these cases the vowel has a set value and shows no harmony (75).

(75) a. Case markers with a front vowel: dative (*-nek*), inessive (*-ben*), ablative (*-től*), instrumental (*-vel*)

b. Case markers with a back vowel: sublative (*-ra*), delative (*-ról*), adessive (*-nál*), allative (*-hoz*)

Personal pronouns all have front vowels, so the suspension of vowel harmony can be seen directly only with case suffixes whose vowel quality is set as back in this environment (76).

(76) a. én-rá-m [sublative]
I-Sub-1Sg
'onto me'

b. én-ról-am [delative]
I-Del-1Sg
'from me'

c. én-nál-am [adessive]
I-Ade-1Sg
'at me'

d. én-hozzá-m [allative]
I-All-1Sg
'to (near) me'

Three cases that allow a pronominal complement and exhibit vowel harmony were left out from (75). The superessive was not included because as already discussed above, it has a special allomorph on pronouns (*rajt-*). The illative case was left out because as shown in (72), it has a longer form on pronouns: *bele-*. Finally, the elative was not included in the list because its form on pronouns, *belől-* contains the same stem *bel-* as the illative, and so it gives rise to the same problem as the illative.

As discussed above, the initial *v* segment of the instrumental and the translative(-essive) case assimilates to the final consonant of a C-final stem. This effect, too, is suspended when the complement is a pronoun. In (77) we illustrate this with the instrumental case, as the translative(-essive) case cannot combine with pronouns.

(77) • No *v* assimilation to pronouns

a. én-vel-em
I-Ins-1Sg
'with me'

b. *én-nel-em
I-Ins-1Sg

The facts discussed in this subsection have led Bartos (1999: 68), Moravcsik (2003: 149) and Dékány (2011: 113, fn. 7) to conclude that overt pronouns are always in an appositive-like relation to a phonologically zero complement of oblique cases (as opposed to being the genuine syntactic complement of the oblique case). É. Kiss (2002: 194-195), on the other hand, concludes that oblique cases systematically have postpositional counterparts. While they are morphologically related, the case suffix combines only with lexical nouns and the postposition combines only with pronouns. In this approach, the pronominal examples in (63) through (77) thus feature postpositions rather than oblique cases. Oblique cases show vowel harmony with the lexical nouns they combine with, while their postpositional counterparts do not exhibit vowel harmony with the pronoun they combine with. We refer the reader to the cited works for further details of these analyses.

D. The availability of pro-drop

As discussed above, case suffixes (with the exception of the accusative) allow their pronominal complement to undergo *pro*-drop. Overt pronouns are generally focused or bear contrastive stress.

E. Agreement with a pronominal complement

When case suffixes other than the morphologically zero nominative combine with (overt or covert) personal pronouns, the PP features agreement with the pronoun's person and number features. In the case of accusative-marked personal pronouns, only first and second person pronouns are accompanied by agreement; no agreement is necessary or allowed with a third person (singular or plural) pronoun. In the case of first and second person pronouns the agreement immediately follows the pronoun and precedes the accusative suffix: pronoun-agreement-accusative (78).

(78) a. eng-em-%et, tég-ed-%et, ő-t
I-1Sg-Acc you-2Sg-Acc he-Acc
'me, you(Sg), him'

b. mi-nk-et, ti-tek-et, ő-k-et
we-1Pl-Acc you-2Pl-Acc he-Pl-Acc
'us, you(Pl), them'

With first and second person singular pronouns the accusative suffix itself must be absent in standard Hungarian (*engem, téged*), but it can appear overtly in some substandard varieties (78).

With oblique cases the agreement suffix follows the case marker. The full paradigm of adessive marked personal pronouns is shown in (79).

(79) a. (én-)nál-am, (te-)nál-ad, (ő-)nál-a
I-Ade-1Sg you-Ade-2Sg he-Ade-3Sg
'at me, at you(Sg), at him'

b. (mi-)nál-unk, (ti-)nál-atok, (ő-)nál-uk
we-Ade-1Pl you-Ade-2Pl he-Ade-3Pl
'at us, at you(Pl), at them'

With case suffixes ending in a consonant, the third person singular agreement suffix is either *-a* or *-e* (80a,b). Exceptionally, the agreement is *-i* with the dative case (80c).

(80) • 3Sg agreement with personal pronouns; case ends in C

a. (ő-)benn-e, (ő-)belől-e, (ő)-től-e, (ő)-vel-e, (ő-)ért-e
he-Ine-3Sg he-Ela-3Sg he-Abl-3Sg he-Ins-3Sg he-Cau-3Sg
'in him, from inside him, from him, with him, for him'

b. (ő-)rajt-a, (ő-)ról-a, (ő-)nál-a
he-Sup-3Sg he-Del-3Sg he-Ade-3Sg
'on him, from him, at him'

c. (ő-)nek-i
he-Dat-3Sg
'to him'

With case suffixes whose pronominal allomorph ends in a vowel (the sublative *rá-*, the allative *hozzá-* and the illative *bele-*) there is no overt marking of third person singular agreement. However, we can assume that in this case, too, the agreement is present but a phonologically zero allomorph is employed. The full paradigm of the sublative is shown in (81).

(81) a. (én-)rá-m, (te-)rá-d (ő-)rá-∅
I-Sub-1Sg you-Sub-2Sg he-Sub-3Sg
'onto me, onto you(Sg), onto him'

b. (mi-)rá-nk, (ti-)rá-tok, (ő-)rá-juk
we-Sub-1Pl you-Sub-2Pl he-Sub-3Pl
'onto us, onto you(Pl), onto him'

The 3Sg pronominal forms of all three cases ending in a vowel are shown in (82).

(82) • 3Sg agreement with personal pronouns; case ends in V

(ő-)rá-∅, (ő-)hozzá-∅, (ő-)bele-∅
he-Sub-3Sg he-All-3Sg he-Ill-3Sg
'onto him, to him, into him'

The agreement in PPs is remarkably similar to that in possessive constructions (see N1.1.1.4.1). The possessed noun bears an invariable possessive marker whose allomorphs are *-ja, -je, -a* and *-e*. In addition, the possessed noun also agrees for the person and number features of pronominal possessors (83).

(83) • Possessive agreement

a. az (én) kar-ja-i-m, a (te) kar-ja-i-d, a(z ő) kar-ja-i-∅
the I arm-Poss-Pl-1Sg the you arm-Poss-Pl-2Sg the he arm-Poss-Pl-3Sg
'my arms, your(Sg) arms, his arms'

b. a (mi) kar-ja-i-nk, a (ti) kar-ja-i-tok, a(z ő) kar-ja-i-k
the we arm-Poss-Pl-1Pl the you arm-Poss-Pl-2Pl the he arm-Poss-Pl-3Pl
'our arms, your(Pl) arms, their arms'

c. a(z ő) kar-juk
the he arm-Poss.3Pl
'their arm'

As shown by the examples in (79) through (83), the form of possessive agreement is identical to the form of PP-agreement in first and second person, and the forms in third person show considerable similarity. With the three case suffixes that end in a vowel, some speakers even allow the possessive marker's *-ja* or *-je* allomorph to appear in the third person singular instead of (or in addition to) the standard zero agreement shown in (82) (see É. Kiss 1998, Rákosi 2012b).

(84) • 3Sg pronoun + case marker dialectally

a. (ő-)rá-%ja
he-Sub-Poss
'onto him'

b. (ő-)hozzá-%ja
he-All.3Sg-Poss
'to him'

c. (ő-)belé-%je
he-Ill.3Sg-Poss
'to him'

Pronouns can undergo *pro*-drop in both PPs headed by case markers or postpositions and in possessive noun phrases. Furthermore, the third person plural *ők* is replaced by its singular counterpart *ő* both in the complement position of PPs and in the possessive position; in these cases the plurality of the pronoun is only shown by the agreement (compare (79b) and (81b) with (83c)). The similarities and differences between PPs and possessive noun phrases are discussed in detail in Rákosi (2010) and Dékány (2011, 2018).

VI. Demonstrative pronoun complements

The *z* segment of the demonstratives *az* 'that' and *ez* 'this' undergoes assimilation to the first consonant of C-initial cases (85), except if i) the case suffix is a non-analytical suffix (i.e. the case is accusative or superessive), as in (86) or ii) the case suffix is *v*-initial (i.e. the case is the translative(-essive) or the instrumental).

(85) • *z* assimilation to C-initial analytic cases

a. abban, *azban
that.Ine that.Ine
both: 'in that'

b. ettől, *eztől
this.Abl this.Abl
both: 'from this'

(86) • No *z* assimilation to C-initial synthetic cases

a. azt, *att
that.Acc that.Acc
both: 'that(Acc)'

b. ez-en, *enn
this-Sup this.Sup
both: 'on this'

Forms in which assimilation to *v*-initial case suffixes takes place are attested but they are dialectal or represent the spoken register (87).

(87) • No *z* assimilation to *v*-initial cases (dialectal or depends on register)

a. azzal, avval
that.Ins that.Ins
both: 'with that'

b. ezzé, *evvé
this.TrE this.TrE
both: '[transform] into this'

2.2.1.3. Separability of the suffix and its complement in the clause

Case suffixes cannot be separated from their complement in the clause either by P-stranding under *wh*-movement or by any other means.

Case suffixes can function as verbal particles. Particles must be immediately pre-verbal in neutral sentences. At the same time, there is also the requirement that the case suffix be on its complement. To satisfy both constraints, a doubling pattern emerges: the case suffix (together with 3Sg agreement) appears before the verb and (without the agreement) on the NP/DP in the post-verbal field, too.

(88) a. Pál rá-ugrott a szék-re.
Pál Sub.3Sg-jump.Past.3Sg the chair-Sub
'Pál jumped onto the chair.'

a'. *Pál rá-ugrott a szék.
Pál Sub.3Sg-jump.Past.3Sg the chair
Intended meaning: 'Pál jumped onto the chair.'

b. Pál neki-ment a szék-nek.
Pál Dat.3Sg-go.Past.3Sg the chair-Dat
'Pál bumped into the chair.'

b'. *Pál neki-ment a szék
Pál Dat.3Sg-go.Past.3Sg the chair
Intended meaning: 'Pál bumped into the chair.'

The genuine separated pattern in (88a',b') is ungrammatical. This doubling pattern will be discussed in detail in Chapter 5 Section 5.2.3.5.

2.2.1.4. Combination with the Delative and Sublative case

As will be shown in subsections 2.2.2.2 and 2.2.2.3, locative case-assigning Ps regularly combine with the delative and the sublative case to form directional (goal and source) PPs (89a), and locative case-like Ps marginally do so (89b).

(89) a. a vonal-on alul / alul-ra / alul-ról [case-assigning P]
the line-Sup under / under-Sub / under-Del
'under / [to under] / [from under] the line'

b. a fal mögött / mögött-re / mögött-ről [case-like P]
the wall behind / behind-Sub / behind-Del
'behind / [to behind] / [from behind] the wall'

While case suffixes share many syntactic and morphological properties with postpositions, locative case suffixes cannot combine with the delative or the sublative case; the relevant goal and source PPs feature the appropriate goal and source cases. (90) illustrates this with the superessive case.

(90) a. a ház-on
the house-Sup
'on the house'

b. a ház-ról
the house-Del
'from (on) the house'

c. *a ház-on-ról
the house-Sup-Del
Intended meaning: 'from (on) the house'

d. a ház-ra
   the house-Sub
   'onto the house'

e. *a ház-on-ra
   the house-Sup-Sub
   Intended meaning: 'onto the house'

2.2.1.5. N + case suffix modifying a noun

PPs must appear postnominally in the noun phrase; in the prenominal position they lead to ungrammaticality (91).

(91) a. a ház a kert-nél
   the house the garden-Ade
   'the house at the garden'

b. *a kert-nél ház
   the garden-Ade house
   Intended meaning: 'the house at the garden'

In order to serve as prenominal N-modifiers, locative PPs must be embedded under a present participial head. In the case of non-deverbal nouns, locative PPs combine with the participle *levő* 'being' (92).

(92) a kert-nél levő ház
   the garden-Ade be.Part house
   'the house at the garden'

Directional PPs, on the other hand, are embedded under the present participial form of a contextually appropriate, semantically contentful verb, as in (93).

(93) a. a kert-től indul-ó út
   the garden-Abl start-Part road
   'the road starting from the garden'

b. a kert-hez érkez-ő út
   the garden-All arrive-Part road
   'the road ending at the garden'

In the case of deverbal nouns, locative PPs combine with the participle *való* 'being' in order to be able to appear in the pre-N position (94a). (*Való* and *levő* are both copulas.) Directional PPs combine either with *való* 'being' or the (also participial) *történő* 'happening' (94b).

(94) a. a terem-ben való várakozás
   the room-Ine being waiting
   'the waiting in the room'

b. a kert-hez / kert-től történő / való elsétálás
   the garden-All / garden-Abl happening / being away.walking
   'the walking to / from the garden'

PPs embedded under participles are excluded from the postnominal N-modifier position (95).

(95) a. *a várakozás a terem-ben való
the waiting the room-Ine being
Intended meaning: 'the waiting in the room'

b. *az elsétálás a kert-hez / kert-től történő
the away.walking the garden-All / garden-Abl happening
Intended meaning: 'the walking to / from the garden'

While PPs headed by postpositions can be attributivized by the *-i* suffix in the prenominal modifier position (see Sections 2.2.2.2.5, 2.2.2.3.5 and Kenesei 2014), this is not possible for PPs headed by case suffixes (96).

(96) a. a kert mellett-i ház
the garden next_to-Attr house
'the house next to the garden'

b. *a kert-nél-i ház
the garden-Ade-Attr house
Intended meaning: 'the house at the garden'

2.2.1.6. Modification

PPs headed by an oblique case can be modified by degree modifiers and measure phrases. Degree modifiers must precede the case-marked Noun Phrase (97). The availability of a measure phrase depends on the specific case (98). In the neutral word order measure phrases follow the case marked noun.

(97) a. pontosan a magas ház-ra (*pontosan)
right the tall house-Sub right
'right onto the tall house'

b. pontosan a régi ház-ig (*pontosan)
right the old house-Ter right
'right to the old house'

(98) a. (?két méterre) a ház-tól két méterre
two meter-Sub the house-Abl two meter-Sub
'two meters from the house'

b. *két méterre a ház-nál
two meter.Sub the house-Ade
Intended meaning: 'at the house, two meters from it'

2.2.1.7. Conjunction reduction

PPs headed by case markers allow neither forward or nor backward conjunction reduction (Kenesei 2000: 85), as shown in (99) and (100).

(99) • Forward conjunction reduction

a. a ház-on és a ház-nál
the house-Sup and the house-Ade
'on the house and at the house

b. *a ház-on és -nál
the house-Sup and Ade
Intended meaning: 'on and at the house'

(100) • Backward conjunction reduction

a. a ház-on és a fészer-en
the house-Sup and the shed-Sup
'on the house and on the shed'

b. *a ház- és (a) fészer-en
the house and the shed-Sup
Intended meaning: 'on the house and shed'

The essive-formal case is exceptional in that it can be dropped on the first conjunct of a conjunction (101).

(101) • Conjunction reduction with the essive-formal case

feleség- és anya-ként
mother and mother-FoE
'as a wife and mother'

2.2.1.8. Double case-marking

As a rule, no Hungarian noun bears double case-marking. There are three types of exceptions, however, all of which involve pronouns.

A. Double case-marking by different cases: inessive plus accusative

We saw in Section 2.2.1.2 point *V/E* that accusative marked pronouns have the form in (102).

(102) a. eng-em-%et, tég-ed-%et, ő-t
I-1Sg-Acc you-2Sg-Acc he-Acc
'me, you(Sg), him'

b. mi-nk-et, ti-tek-et, ő-k-et
we-1Pl-Acc you-2Pl-Acc he-Pl-Acc
'us, you(Pl), them'

To recapitulate, first and second person accusative marked pronouns bear agreement that reflects the pronoun's person and number features (agreement is missing on third person pronouns). In the standard dialect the accusative suffix itself is obligatorily dropped on first and second person singular pronouns, but some dialectal varieties retain the accusative marker here as well. When marked with accusative case, pronouns cannot undergo *pro*-drop (see Section 2.2.1.1 point *III*).

First and second person plural pronouns, however, have an alternative accusative form, too. Specifically, an inessive-marked second person pronoun can be adorned with the accusative suffix, and the resulting form can be used as a second person object pronoun. Let us first have a look at the ordinary inessive marked form of first and second person plural pronouns in (103). As characteristic of oblique marked personal pronouns (Section Section 2.2.1.2 point *V/B*), the pronoun is followed by the inessive case suffix, which in turn, is followed by the agreement morpheme cross-referencing the person and number features of the pronoun. The pronoun itself (*mi, ti*) can be dropped.

(103)	(mi-)benn-ünk,	(ti-)benn-etek
	we-Ine-1Pl	you-Ine-2Pl
	'in us, in you(Pl)'	

The forms in (103) can only be used as oblique pronouns in environments where the inessive case is required. However, these forms can be suffixed by the accusative case (104), leading to both an inessive and an accusative case on the same pronoun.

(104)	(mi-)benn-ünk-et,	(ti-)benn-etek-et
	we-Ine-1Pl-Acc	you-Ine-2Pl-Acc
	'us, you(Pl.Acc)'	

The pronouns in (104) serve as alternative accusative forms to the ones seen in (102), in standard Hungarian as well. Similarly to (103) (and unlike in (102)), the pronouns themselves may be dropped in (104); this, in fact, is the highly preferred option. (105) illustrates the use of these doubly case-marked forms in object position.

(105) a.	Ti	láttok	mi-nk-et / benn-ünk-et.
	you(Pl)	see.DefObj.2Pl	we-1Pl-Acc / Ine-1Pl-Acc
	'You(Pl) see us.'		
b.	Mi	látunk	ti-tek-et / benn-etek-et.
	we	see.1Pl	you-2Pl-Acc / Ine-2Pl-Acc
	'We see you(Pl.Acc).'		

The accusative suffix on *bennünk-et* and *bennetek-et* is obligatory (similarly to the case of *mink-et* 'us' and *titek-et* 'you(Pl.Acc)', and unlike *engem-%et* 'me' and *téged-%et* 'you(Sg.Acc').

Personal pronouns other than the first and second person plural do not have similar doubly case-marked forms (106).

(106)	*(én-)benn-em-et,	*(te-)benn-ed-et,	*ő-benn-e-t,	*ő-benn-ük-et
	I-Ine-1Pl-Acc	you(Sg)-Ine-2Pl-Acc	he-Ine-3Sg-Acc	he-Ine-3Pl-Acc
	Intended meaning: 'me, you(Sg.Acc), him, them'			

B. Double case-marking by different cases: allative plus terminative

As already mentioned in connection with (61), repeated here as (107), some speakers can add the terminative case suffix to an allative-marked personal pronoun. This type of double case-marking is substandard.

(107) %A kábel el-ér (én-)hozzá-m-ig.
the cable away-reach.3Sg I-All-1Sg-Ter
'The cable reaches up to me.'

C. Double case-marking by the same case

In dialectal / substandard Hungarian there are also instances of double case-marking by the same case. Firstly, the third person singular pronoun *ő* and the demonstrative pronouns *ez* 'this' and *az* 'that' can dialectally bear double accusative case.

(108) %ő-t-et, %az-t-at, %ez-t-et
he-Acc-Acc that-Acc-Acc this-Acc-Acc
'him, that(Acc), this(Acc)'

Secondly, dialectally, a personal pronoun can also bear double case-marking when it serves as the object of comparison. As already mentioned in Section 2.2.1.1, when the comparative construction has no overt *mint* 'than', then the object of comparison bears overt case: adessive in standard Hungarian and ablative in some dialects. (23) is repeated below as (109) for the reader's convenience.

(109) a. Ili magasabb, mint Imi.
Ili taller than Imi
'Ili is taller than Imi.'

b. Ili magasabb Imi-nél. [adessive]
Ili taller Imi-Ade
'Ili is taller than Imi.'

c. %Ili magasabb Imi-től. [ablative]
Ili taller Imi-Abl
'Ili is taller than Imi.'

Garden variety examples with a personal pronoun as the object of comparison (and no *mint* 'than') are shown in (110).

(110) a. Ili magasabb (én-)nál-am. [adessive]
Ili taller I-Ade-1Sg
'Ili is taller than me.'

b. %Ili magasabb (én-)től-em. [ablative]
Ili taller I-Abl-1Sg
'Ili is taller than me.'

Dialectally and in archaic texts, the adessive case is repeated once more after the agreement suffix, leading to double case-marking by the same case (H. Varga 2008), as in (111).

(111) %Ili magasabb nál-am-nál. [adessive]
Ili taller Ade-1Sg-Ade
'Ili is taller than me.'

Double case-marking of personal pronouns by the adessive case happens only in the comparative construction; it is not possible with the literal locative reading.

2.2.2. *Postpositions*

2.2.2.1. *Introduction: Two classes of postpositions*

Hungarian postpositions fall into two natural classes: case-like postpositions and case-assigning postpositions. Case-like postpositions take a morphologically unmarked Noun Phrase complement. Case-assigning postpositions, on the other hand, require a specific oblique case (e.g. superessive or instrumental) on their Noun Phrase complement. The two types of postpositions are illustrated below: in (112) the case-like P *alatt* 'under' appears with the morphologically unmarked form of *híd* 'bridge', while in (113) the case-assigning P *szemben* 'opposite to' appears with the instrumental-marked form of *híd* 'bridge'.

(112) a híd alatt
the bridge under
'under the bridge'

(113) a híd-dal szemben
the bridge-Ins opposite_to
'opposite to the bridge'

Case-like Ps are sometimes called inflecting or dressed Ps, while case-assigning Ps are also known as non-inflecting or naked Ps. These names reflect the fact that the linear position of the PP-internal agreement suffix depends on which type of P heads the PP. When P's complement is a personal pronoun, then an agreement marker cross-referencing the pronoun's person and number features appears in the PP. In the case of case-like (aka inflecting or dressed) Ps, the agreement appears on the postposition itself – the postposition becomes inflected or 'dressed' (114).

(114) én-alatt-am
I-under-1Sg
'under me'

In the case of case-assigning (aka case-governing, non-inflecting or naked) Ps, on the other hand, the agreement appears on the oblique case marker rather than on the postposition itself (115) – the postposition remains uninflected or 'naked'.

(115) én-vel-em szemben
I-Ins-1Sg opposite_to
'opposite to me'

The two types of postpositions, including their similarities and differences, have been discussed in detail in Marácz (1984, 1986, 1989 Chapter 8), Kenesei (1992: 581ff), Kenesei *et al.* (1998: 86ff), É. Kiss (1999), Hegedűs (2006), Asbury (2008) and Dékány (2011), among others. In Section 2.2.2.2 we turn to the distribution of case-like Ps in detail. The distribution of case-assigning Ps will be taken up in Section 2.2.2.3.

2.2.2.2. Case-like postpositions

2.2.2.2.1. The inventory and form of case-like Ps

The list of case-like Ps is given in Table 4. All of them are at least bisyllabic, and in contrast to case suffixes, they do not exhibit vowel harmony with the noun. Some of them cannot take a personal pronoun complement; these are marked with × in the last column of the table. We shall return to this property below. Note that some Ps listed in the spatial group may also have a temporal reading. Those which are listed in the temporal and the 'other' group do not have a spatial reading. The semantic classes of postpositions will be discussed in Section 2.3.

Table 4: Case-like postpositions

	CASE-LIKE P	MEANING	PRONOMINAL COMPLEMENT POSSIBLE
SPATIAL	*alatt*	under	✓
	alá	to under	✓
	alól	from under	✓
	előtt	(at) in front of, before	✓
	elé	to in front of	✓
	elől	from in front of	✓
	felett/fölött	(at) above	✓
	fölé	to above	✓
	fölül	from above	✓
	körül(ött) / †*körött*	around	✓
	köré	to around	✓
	között, közt	between	✓
	közé	to between	✓
	közül	from between	✓
	mellett	next to, beside	✓
	mellé	to next to	✓
	mellől	from next to	✓
	mögött	behind	✓
	mögé	to behind	✓
	mögül	from behind	✓
	felé	towards	✓
	felől	from the direction of	✓
	iránt	towards	✓
	után	behind, after	✓
TEMPORAL	*múlva* / $*múltán*	in (X time), after (X time)	×
	óta	since	×
	tájban / %*tájt*	around (a point in time)	×

OTHER	*által*	by	✓
	ellen	against	✓
	gyanánt	as, by way of, in lieu of	×
	helyett	instead of	✓
	miatt	because of	✓
	nélkül	without	✓
	szerint	according to	✓
	végett	in order to, due to	% or † (archaic, yet productive in some dialects)

I. Spatial Ps

A. The morphologically related spatial triplets

As shown in Table 4, most case-like postpositions with a spatial meaning come in morphologically related triplets. In each triplet, there is a P expressing location at, a P expressing motion to, and a P expressing motion away from the complement. The triplets share the same bound stem: *al-* in the 'under' series, *el-* in the 'in front of' series, *fel/föl-* in the 'above' series, *köz-* in the 'between' series, and *mell-* in the 'next to' series. These bound stems have grammaticalized from common nouns; *fel/föl-*, *köz-* and *mell-* are homophonous with 'the top of the milk', 'gap, space between', and 'breast' respectively in contemporary Hungarian, too.

Remark 8. The bound stems *fel-* and *föl-* (both: 'up') are in free variation in some Ps, but there are also cases in which the choice between them leads to a difference in meaning. They are interchangeable in the case-like P *felett/fölött* 'above sth', in the case-assiging P *felül/fölül* 'above, in addition' (this P takes a superessive-marked NP/DP complement) and in the verbal particle *fel/föl* 'up (directional)'. However, the case-like Ps *felé* and *fölé* are not interchangeable: while *felé* means 'towards', the meaning of *fölé* is 'to above'. There is also a meaning difference between the case-like Ps *felől* and *fölül*: the former means 'from the direction of', while the latter means 'from above sth'.

Within each triplet, Ps expressing static location bear the locative *-(Vt)t* suffix, Ps expressing motion towards the complement have the obsolete lative case suffix *-á/-é*, and Ps expressing motion away from the complement are adorned with the source suffix *-(V)l*. These suffixes are obsolete case markers and are not productive in contemporary Hungarian; they only combine with the bound P-stems shown in the table and some other adverbial stems (see Section 2.2.4.1.2). They cannot appear on common nouns or proper names.

B. Other uses of the locative -(Vt)t *suffix*

The only exception to the generalization mentioned at the end of the previous paragraph is the locative *-(Vt)t* suffix, which may appear on a handful of Hungarian city names that are i) monosyllabic or ii) end in either *hely* 'place' or *vár* 'castle'. The forms listed in (116) are the most common city names that end in the locative suffix.

(116) a. Győr-ött, Pécs-ett, Vác-ott
Győr-Loc Pécs-Loc Vác-Loc
'in Győr / Pécs / Vác'

b. Hódmezővásárhely-t, Kézdivásárhely-t, Székelyudvarhely-t
Hódmezővásárhely-Loc Kézdivásárhely-Loc Székelyudvarhely-Loc
'in Hódmezővásárhely / Kézdivásárhely / Székelyudvarhely'

c. Kaposvár-t, Kolozsvár-t, Szentpétervár-ott, Székesfehérvár-ott
Kaposvár-Loc Kolozsvár-Loc Saint.Petersburg-Loc Székesfehérvár-Loc
'in Kaposvár / Kolozsvár / Saint Petersburg / Székesfehérvár'

City names with *-(Vt)t* represent an archaic or elevated style and can always be substituted for by forms in which the proper name in question bears a productive locative case suffix (117).

(117) a. Győr-ben, Pécs-en, Vác-on
Győr-Ine Pécs-Sup Vác-Sup
'in Győr / Pécs / Vác'

b. Hódmezővásárhely-en, Kézdivásárhely-en, Székelyudvarhely-en
Hódmezővásárhely-Sup Kézdivásárhely-Sup Székelyudvarhely-Sup
'in Hódmezővásárhely / Kézdivásárhely / Székelyudvarhely'

c. Kaposvár-on, Kolozsvár-on, Szentpétervár-on, Székesfehérvár-on
Kaposvár-Sup Kolozsvár-Sup Saint.Petersburg-Sup Székesfehérvár-Sup
'in Kaposvár / Kolozsvár / Saint Petersburg / Székesfehérvár'

The *-(Vt)t* suffix must combine with the bare form of the proper name, i.e. the name of the city must not bear a plural or a possessive agreement suffix (see also S. Hámori and Tompa 1970: 573), as shown in (119).

(118) a. *Pécs-em-ett, Vác-uk-ott
Pécs-1Sg-Loc Vác-1Pl-Loc
Intended meaning: 'in my Pécs, in our Vác'

b. *Pécs-ek-ett, *Vác-ok-ott
Pécs-Pl-Loc Vác-Pl-Loc
Intended meaning: 'in cities named Pécs, in cities named Vác'

It is, however, possible for the proper name to bear these suffixes when its locative form involves a productive case suffix (119). (Names of settlements rarely occur in the plural form, but this is possible in certain contexts. For instance, different settlements with compound proper names ending in the same morpheme, such as *Kis-Vác* 'small-Vác' and *Nagy-Vác* 'big-Vác', may be referred to together with the shared part of their names, e.g. *a Vác-ok-on*, lit. the Vác-Pl-Sup, 'in the settlements called Vác').

(119) a. Pécs-em-en, Vác-unk-on
Pécs-1Sg-Sup Vác-1Pl-Sup
'in my Pécs, in our Vác'

b. Pécs-ek-en, Vác-ok-on
Pécs-Pl-Sup Vác-Pl-Sup
'in cities named Pécs, in cities named Vác'

The same suffix appears in the case-like Ps *iránt* 'towards', *helyett* 'instead of', *szerint* 'according to' and *végett* 'in order to, due to' (see Table 4 and the discussion below). There are also some locative adverbs that feature this suffix, see (120).

(120) itt, ott, oldalt, lent fent, kint, bent,
here there sideways down up outside inside
más-utt, minden-ütt, †alant
other-Loc every-Loc down.there
'here, there, sideways, down, up, outside, inside, at some other place, everywhere, down there'

C. The morphologically related spatial doublets

In addition to the triplets, there are also two doublets. The first doublet, *körül(ött)* 'around' and *köré* 'to around', involves the bound stem *körül-* 'around', which is related to the common noun *kör* 'circle'. As for the locative *körül(ött)* 'around', the shorter form *körül* is used with a common noun or proper name complement, and the longer form *körülött* is used with a pronominal complement (121).

(121) a. a ház körül(*ött), János körül(*ött)
the house around János around
'around the house, around János'

b. ő-körülött-*(e), †ő-körül-e
he-around-Poss.3Sg he-around-Poss.3Sg
'around him'

Another short form of *körül(ött)* 'around' is *körött* 'around', which is now considered to be archaic.

Körül(ött) 'around' and *köré* 'to around' have no counterpart that expresses direction away from the complement with the directional *-(V)l* suffix. The stem *körül-* may combine with the delative case suffix to express the meaning 'from around' (*körülről*). This form is most frequently used with a temporal reading (122a), but a quasi-directional reading is also possible (122b). The bound stem *körül-* may also take the sublative suffix to express a quasi-directional reading, as in (122b). The combination of postpositions with the delative and the sublative suffix will be taken up in more detail in Sections 2.2.2.3.4 and 2.2.2.2.4.

(122) a. egy 1900 körül-ről származó festmény
a 1900 around-Del originating painting
'a painting from around 1900'

b. A részvények ára 230 Ft körül-ről 250 Ft körül-re
the share.Pl price.Poss 230 HUF around-Del 250 HUF around-Sub
emelkedett.
raise.Past.3Sg
'The price of shares rose from around HUF 230 to around HUF 250.'

The second doublet, *felé* 'towards' and *felől* 'from the direction of', involves the bound stem *fel-* 'towards'. These Ps have no locative counterpart with the locative suffix *-(Vt)t* because the stem itself expresses directionality. Note that the form *felett* 'above' exists, but it is the locative form of the *fel/föl-* 'above' stem.

D. Other spatial Ps

The case-like Ps *iránt* 'towards' and *után* 'behind, after' are not part of morphologically related triplets or doublets. Originally both were case-marked nouns. *Iránt* 'towards' comes from a by now obsolete stem bearing the locative *-(Vt)t* suffix (Benkő 1970: 230).

(123) iránt
toward

Után 'behind, after' grammaticalized from the possessed, superessive (*-n*) marked form of *út* 'road, way' (Benkő 1976: 1039). The morphemic composition has become completely opaque.

(124) Mari a kislány után áll a sorban.
Mari the little.girl behind stand.3Sg the line.Ine
'Mari is standing in line behind the little girl.'

The spatial meaning of *után* 'behind, after' is thus diachronically primary, but in modern Hungarian the temporal use is also wide-spread (125).

(125) karácsony után
Christmas behind
'after Christmas'

In contemporary Hungarian the possessed and superessive marked noun *út* 'road, way' is distinct from the postposition: the former contains a *j* in the possessive suffix (126). As shown in (124), this *j* is missing in the postposition.

(126) a. a falu út-já-n [possessive phrase]
the village road-Poss-Sup
'on the road of the village'

b. a falu után [postposition]
the village behind
'behind / after the village'

Remark 9. There is a curious morpheme, *szerte* '(locative) across, throughout', which resembles case-like Ps in some respects, but not others (therefore it is not included in Table 4). Similarly to case-like Ps, *szerte* combines with a morphologically unmarked noun.

(i) ország-szerte, város-szerte
country-across city-across
'across the country, across the city'

It has a number of properties, however, which set it apart from other case-like Ps. Firstly, the noun must be a bare noun, while the complement of case-like Ps can be modified by N-modifiers such as adjectives, numerals, demonstratives, or the indefinite or definite article.

(ii) a. *régi város-szerte, *szép város-szerte
old city-across nice city-across
Intended meaning: 'across an old city, across a nice city'

b. *két város-szerte, *minden város-szerte, *egész város-szerte
two city-across every city-across whole city-across
Intended meaning: 'across two cities, across every city, across the whole city'

c. *a város-szerte, *eme város-szerte
the city-across this city-across
Intended meaning: 'across the city, across this city'

Secondly, the range of nouns it can combine with is highly restricted. The admissible nouns are names of continents and countries as well as nouns naming canonical geographical regions or other locations. Some examples are given below.

(iii) világ-szerte, Európa-szerte, Anglia-szerte, Dunántúl-szerte,
world-across Europe-across England-across Dunántúl-across
város-szerte
city-across
'across the world / Europe / England / the Dunántúl [region] / the city'

Thirdly, the N+*szerte* sequence has the stress pattern characteristic of compounds rather than other N+P structures (*szerte* does not receive word stress in the examples above). Fourthly, the complement of *szerte* is always understood to be definite. This is trivial in the case of *világ* 'world' and names of continents, countries and canonical geographical regions. However, *ország* 'country' and *város* 'city' are also understood to be definite when they are followed by *szerte* (ivb), even though when not followed by *szerte*, they need a definite article for a definite interpretation (iva). (When followed by *szerte*, it must be inferred from the context which country or city is being referred to.)

(iv) a. város, a város, ország, az ország
city the city country the country
'city, the city, country, the country'

b. (*a) világ-szerte, (*az) ország-szerte, (*a) város-szerte
the world-across the country-across the city-across
'across the world / country / city'

Fifthly, unlike case-like Ps, *szerte* can precede the noun (phrase), and when it does so, it behaves differently than in the post-NP position. With prenominal *szerte*, a noun that is not inherently definite must be accompanied by the definite article. Compare:

(v) szerte *(a) világ-on, szerte *(az) ország-ban, szerte *(a) város-ban
across the world-Sup across the country-Ine across the city-Ine
'across the world / country / city'

N-modifiers other than the definite article or the quantifier *egész* 'whole' are still disallowed, however.

(vi) szerte az (egész) (*három) (*szép) város-ban
across the whole three nice city-Ine
Intended meaning: 'across the whole three nice cities'

Note that prenominal *szerte* requires the noun to be case-marked with the superessive or inessive case (v and vi), depending on which case would normally combine with the noun in ordinary locative expressions (see Section 2.2.1.1).

As pointed out in Fejes (2013), *szerte* also doubles as a verbal particle (on particles, see Section 2.2.3). In this use, its meaning is similar to *szét*; both are best approximated as 'apart, in many directions'. Some examples are given below.

(v) szerte-szór, szerte-ágazik, szerte-foszlik
apart-throw apart-branch apart-ravel
'disperse, branch out, dissipate'

That is, *szerte* has a locative meaning postnominally or prenominally, and a directional meaning in its verbal particle use.

II. Temporal Ps

Of the temporal case-like Ps *múlva* 'in (X time) / after (X time)', *tájban* / *tájt* 'around (a point in time)' and *óta* 'since', the first three appear to be morphologically complex. *Tájt* 'around (a point in time)' is indeed complex, comprising the common noun *táj* 'area, region' and the locative *-t* suffix that appears on spatial case-like Ps, too (see point *I* above) (127).

(127) 6 óra táj-t, éjfél táj-t
6 hour area-Loc midnight area-Loc
'around 6 o'clock, around midnight'

Tájban, which has exactly the same meaning as *tájt*, transparently comprises the common noun *táj* 'area, region' and the productive inessive case suffix *-ban/-ben* (128).

(128) 6 óra táj-ban, éjfél táj-ban
6 hour area-Ine midnight area-Ine
'around 6 o'clock, around midnight'

Given its morphological make-up, *tájban* could be considered to be a case-marked noun rather than a true postposition. However, while inessive marked *táj* 'area, region' may take N-modifiers such as a demonstrative, an article, numerals or adjectives (129a), this is not possible for *tájban* in its temporal P use (129b). To distinguish the inessive marked nominal *táj* 'area, region' from the P *tájban*, we shall henceforth gloss the latter as 'around'.

(129) a. Pál gyönyörködik ebben a három szép táj-ban. [case-marked N]
Pál admire.3Sg this.Ine the three beautiful area-Ine
'Pál admires these three beautiful areas / landscapes.'

b. karácsony (*ebben) (*az) (*egy) (*ünnepi) tájban [postposition]
Christmas this.Ine the one festive around
'around (this one festive time of) Christmas'

Furthermore, analyzing the temporal *tájban* 'around (a point in time)' as a case-marked common noun cannot account for the syntactic relationship between *tájban* and the morphologically unmarked nominal preceding it either. There are only two types of structural relations that may hold between a morphologically unmarked nominal and another nominal following it. Firstly, the unmarked nominal may form a compound with the following nominal (130).

(130) ékszer-doboz, hát-úszás
jewelry-box back-swimming
'jewelry box, backstroke'

Compounds have a single word stress falling on the first member of the compound. This is true of *dél tájban* (lit. noon area.Ine) 'around noon' and *éjfél tájban* (lit. midnight area.Ine) 'around midnight'. However, when *tájban* follows an expression with a numeral, e.g. *6 óra tájban* in (131), then both *tájban* and the nominal preceding it receive word stress. *Tájban* expressions thus cannot be considered to be compounds across the board.

Secondly, an unmarked nominal may serve as the possessive modifier of the noun following it (132).

(132) a diák toll-a, János toll-a
the student pen-Poss János pen-Poss
'the student's pen, János' pen'

In possessive structures the possessum is always marked with the possessive suffix *-a/-e/-ja/-je* (see N2.2.1.2). *Tájban*, however, does not bear this suffix, even though the common noun *táj* 'area, region' always does so when it is a possessum (133a), and possessed *táj* can bear the inessive case (133b).

(133) a. Az ország legcsapadékosabb táj-a az Alpokalja. [case-marked N]
the country most.rainy area-Poss the Alpokalja
'The country's most rainy area is the Alpokalja.'

b. Ili sokáig gyönyörködött az ország legcsapadékosabb táj-á-ban.
Ili for.long admire.Past.3Sg the country most.rainy area-Poss-Ine
'Ili admired the most rainy area of the country for a long time.'

Given the lack of possessive marking, it is not possible to analyze temporal *tájban* expressions as possessive structures.

It would not be possible to analyze *tájban* as a(n inessive marked) nominal and the preceding unmarked NP as its modifier either: apart from possessors, all N-modifying nominals must undergo *-i* attributivization (134a), but this is impossible for the NP preceding *tájban* (134b).

(134) a. éjfél-*(i) mise, tavasz-*(i) szél [case-marked N]
midnight-Attr mass spring-Attr wind
'midnight mass, the wind(s) in / of spring'

b. éjfél-(*i) tájban [postposition]
midnight-Attr around
'around midnight'

The facts laid out above lead to the conclusion that in '*NP tájban*' expressions *tájban* is not a (case-marked) nominal. We take *tájban* to be a genuine case-like postposition, one which grammaticalized from the inessive case-marked common noun *táj* 'area, region'. It is a bi-morphemic P similarly to the members of the spatial triplets discussed in point *I.* above: *mell-ett* 'next_to-Loc, *mell-é* 'next_to-Lative', *mell-ől* 'next_to-from'. Concomitant with the grammaticalization process, this P has acquired a specialized meaning: while the inessive form of the noun *táj* 'area, region' is a spatial expression (135a), the P *tájban* is restricted to temporal PPs (135b,c). (This is an additional fact that the simple nominal analysis of *tájban* would have difficulty capturing.)

(135) a. Pál gyönyörködött a táj-ban.
Pál admire.Past.3Sg the area-Ine
'Pál was admiring the land(scape).'

b. húsvét tájban
Easter around
'around Easter'

c. *a ház tájban
the house around
Intended meaning: 'around the house'

As far as *múlva* 'in (X time), after (X time)' is concerned, this P comprises the verb *múlik* 'elapse, go by' and the adverbial participial suffix *-va/-ve* (136) (see the volume on Non-finite Verb Phrases).

(136) három nap múl-va
three day elapse-Part
'after three days'

However, in '*NP múlva*' phrases *múlva* cannot be taken to be a garden variety adverbial participle (and therefore in the remainder of this section we shall gloss it as 'after'). Firstly, an adverbial participle headed by the participial verb *múl-va* can be modified by adverbs such as 'slowly', as shown by the Googled example in (137a). This is not the case for '*NP múlva*' phrases, however (137b).

(137) a. Életünk lass-an múl-va tovaszáll. [participle]
life.Poss.1Pl slow-ly elapse-Part away.fly.3Sg
'Slowly, our life goes by [and ends].'

b. három nap (*lass-an) múl-va [postposition]
three day slow-ly elapse-Part
Intended meaning: 'after three slowly passing days'

Secondly, if temporal *múlva* 'after' were a genuine adverbial participle, then the morphologically unmarked nominal preceding it would have to be its overt (nominative) subject: in (136), for instance, 'three days' would be the subject of 'elapse'. However, *-va/-ve* adverbial participles cannot have an overt subject (138b): their subject must be covert and must have the same reference as the subject (137a) or object (138b) of the matrix clause.

(138) a. Jánost megkötöz-ve találtuk. [participle]
János.Acc Perf.tie-Part find.Past.DefObj.1Pl
'We have found János tied up.'

b. *Az éjjel el-múl-va, útnak indultunk.
the night away-elapse-Part road.Dat set_out.Past.1Pl
Intended meaning: 'The night having gone by, we set out [on our journey].'

Given these considerations, we take *múlva* in '*NP múlva*' expressions to be a real case-like P which grammaticalized from the adverbial participle *múl-va* 'elapse-Part'.

Múltán 'after (X time)' is a synonym of *múlva*. It is a bit archaic and is used in a higher register. It comprises the verb *múlik* 'pass, go by', the *-t* deverbal nominalizer (see N1.3.1.4), the possessive suffix *-a* and the (superessive) *-n* suffix. The morphemic composition has become opaque, however.

(139) Az edény évek múltán is újnak néz ki.
the pot year.Pl after too new.Dat look out
'The pot looks new even after several years.'

III. Other Ps

Among non-spatial and non-temporal case-like Ps, several bear the *-(Vt)t* locative ending seen in point *I* above. *Helyett* 'instead of' (140) grammaticalized from the noun *hely* 'place' bearing the possessive suffix *-e* and the locative *-(Vt)t* suffix (Zsilinszky 1992: 700). Its original locative meaning 'in its place' has, over time, become the more abstract 'instead of', and the original morphemic composition is not transparent for speakers any more.

(140) János helyett, sírás helyett
János instead_of crying instead_of
'instead of János, instead of crying'

Gyanánt 'as, by way of, in lieu of' (141) likewise has a possessive origin: it is based on *gyanú* 'suspicion' bearing a possessive suffix, an *-n* suffix and the locative *-(Vt)t* suffix (Benkő 1967: 1119).

(141) egy szűrő gyanánt szolgáló ruha
a strainer as serving cloth
'a piece of cloth serving as / [in lieu of] a strainer'

Szerint 'according to' (142) is built on the noun *szer* 'row, order, method' (Benkő 1976: 739) and ends in the locative suffix *-(Vt)t* (Zsilinszky 1992: 700). Whether the bit between the stem and *-(Vt)t* goes back to a possessive structure is debated (see Benkő 1976: 739 pro and Benkő 1994: 1426 contra). In any case, the multi-morphemic origin has become completely opaque.

(142) János szerint, a könyv szerint
János according_to the book according_to
'according to János, according to the book'

While *helyett* 'instead of' and *gyanánt* 'as, by way of, in lieu of' (and perhaps *szerint* 'according to') have their origin in possessive structures, synchronically they are garden variety case-like Ps: their distribution is identical to that of the spatial and temporal Ps discussed above in points *I* and *II*, and they do not show any of the syntactic or morphological trappings of possessive structures. In Section 2.4.2 these Ps will be contrasted with some borderline Ps which are on their way to becoming case-like Ps from possessed Ns, but retain some similarities with possessive structures to date.

Two other case-like Ps in this group also bear the *-(Vt)t* locative ending without having a possessive origin: *végett* 'in order to, due to' is the locative form of the noun *vég* 'end' (Benkő 1976: 1105), while *miatt* 'because of' comes from the interrogative pronoun *mi* 'what' bearing the lative *-á* and a locative *-(Vt)t* suffix (Benkő 1980: 285). To contemporary speakers this is no longer transparent.

(143) a. a félreértések elkerülése végett
the misunderstanding.Pl avoiding.Poss so_as_to
'so as to avoid [any] misunderstandings'

b. Az eső miatt itthon maradtam.
the rain because_of home_at stay.Past.1Sg
'I stayed at home because of the rain.'

Finally, the case-like P *nélkül* 'without' is also originally a bi-morphemic element. This P grammaticalized from a string in which the adessive (*-nál/-nél*) case was followed by the postposition *kül* / *kívül* 'outside of'. The original structure is schematized in (144).

(144) N-nál kül / kívül
N-Ade apart_from / apart_from
'apart from N'

The adessive case suffix was later re-analyzed as the stem of the P *kül* / *kívül* 'apart from, outside of', yielding the contemporary *nélkül* 'without' (145). The original morphemic composition is no longer transparent to speakers.

(145) Esőkabát nélkül indultam el.
raincoat without set_out.Past.1Sg away
'I set out without a raincoat.'

Note that *kívül* 'outside of, apart from' is still used in contemporary Hungarian as a case-assigning P (see Section 2.2.2.3.1), but it assigns the superessive rather than the adessive case (146).

(146) a. Kutyát sétáltatni csak a játszótér-en kívül szabad.
dog.Acc walk.Caus.Inf only the playground-Sup outside_of allowed
'Walking dogs is allowed only outside of the playground.'

b. Víz-en kívül másra nincs szükségem.
water-Sup outside_of other.Sub not_be.3Sg necessity.Poss.1Sg
'Apart from water, I do not need anything else.'

2.2.2.2.2. Complementation

I. The form of the complement

As already mentioned above, case-like postpositions take a morphologically unmarked complement, and if their complement is a personal pronoun, then the PP-internal agreement is borne by the postposition (147).

(147) a. a híd alatt
the bridge under
'under the bridge'

b. én-alatt-am
I-under-1Sg
'under me'

II. PP-internal position with respect to the complement

Within the PP, case-like Ps must immediately follow their complement: no modifier can intervene between them and their complement (148b) and they cannot be used as prepositions (148c). In this respect their distribution is very much like that of case suffixes (Section 2.2.1).

(148) a. a fa mellett
the tree next_to
'next to the tree'

b. *a fa majdnem mellett
the tree almost next_to
Intended meaning: 'almost next to the tree'

c. *mellett a fa
next_to the tree
Intended meaning: 'next to the tree'

III. Dropping the complement

Case-like postpositions must have a syntactic complement. If the complement is a pronoun, then the postposition bears an agreement marker that cross-references person and number features of the pronoun. The full paradigm is illustrated in (149). A pronominal complement can also undergo *pro*-drop. In this case the features of the covert pronoun can be recovered from the agreement on the postposition.

(149) a. A könyv (én-)mellett-em van.
the book I-next_to-1Sg be.3Sg
'The book is next to me.'

b. A könyv (te-)mellett-ed van.
the book you(Sg)-next_to-2Sg be.3Sg
'The book is next to you(sg).'

c. A könyv (ő-)mellett-e van.
the book he-next_to-3Sg be.3Sg
'The book is next to him.'

d. A könyv (mi-)mellett-ünk van.
the book we-next_to-1Pl be.3Sg
'The book is next to me.'

e. A könyv (ti-)mellett-etek van.
the book you(Pl)-next_to-2Pl be.3Sg
'The book is next to you(Pl).'

f. A könyv (ő-)mellett-ük van.
the book he-next_to-3Pl be.3Sg
'The book is next to them.'

These Ps do not agree with lexical N complements, and such complements cannot be dropped either (150).

(150) a. A ház a fa mellett(*-e) van.
the house the tree next_to-3Sg be.3Sg
'The house is next to the tree.'

b. A ház *(a fa) mellett van.
the house the tree next_to be.3Sg
'The house is next to (the tree).'

IV. The complement's demonstrative modifier

If the complement of the case-like P is a Noun Phrase that contains the demonstrative pronoun *ez* 'this' or *az* 'that', then the postposition must appear twice: once after the demonstrative and once after the nominal head (151).

(151) ez / az alatt a fa alatt
this / that under the tree under
'under this / that tree'

V. Personal pronoun complements

As already mentioned above, if there is a personal pronoun in the complement position, then the PP-internal agreement is borne by the postposition (152). Furthermore, personal pronoun complements can undergo *pro*-drop.

(152) (én-)alatt-am
I-under-1Sg
'under me'

Some case-like Ps cannot take a pronominal complement, as shown in Table 4. The postposition *óta* 'since' is a case in point (153b), though its combination with the third person singular pronoun is not ungrammatical (153c). *Óta* has a default temporal interpretation; when it combines with the third person singular pronoun, the resulting expression means 'since his/her time' or 'since his/her work'. The same type of metonymical meaning extension of the complement can also be observed when *óta* 'since' combines with proper names (153d).

(153) a. nyolc óra óta
eight o'clock since
'since eight o'clock'

b. *én óta-m
I since-1Sg
Intended meaning: 'since me'

c. ??ő óta
he since
'since him'

d. Napóleon óta, Einstein óta
Napoleon since Einstein since
'since Napoleon('s time) / since Einstein('s work)'

The ungrammaticality of (153b) may show that apart from the third person singular pronouns, a metonymical meaning extension of the complement is not available to pronouns.

Finally, we note that the postposition *végett* 'in order to, due to' can take a pronominal complement only in non-standard Hungarian (154). In the varieties that allow this, *végett* has a causal meaning ('because of'), and it behaves like other case-like Ps: it bears the agreement itself. (In standard Hungarian, it has a purposive meaning, which may explain why it does not combine with personal pronouns.)

(154) %én-végett-em
I-because_of-1Sg
'because of me'

VI. Demonstrative pronoun complements

If the case-like P begins with a consonant, then the *z* of the demonstrative is dropped (but the demonstrative and the P are still written as two separate words), as in (155).

(155) [e fölé] / [a fölé] a fa fölé
this above / that above the tree above
'above this / that tree'

Keeping the *z* of the demonstrative is possible only dialectally, if the demonstrative refers to an object that is present in the discourse situation and is being pointed at by the speaker, and strong contrast or emphasis is placed on the demonstrative (e.g. 'this, not that') (156).

(156) %EZ fölé
this above
'above THIS'

Other demonstratives such as *ezen*, *e* and *eme* (all: 'this'), as well as *azon* and *ama* (both: 'that') do not combine with case-like Ps; if the noun is modified by one of these demonstratives, then the case-like P appears only after the nominal head (157).

(157) ezen / ama (*alatt) fa alatt
this / that under tree under
'under this / that tree'

The two types of demonstratives differ in a number of other important respects, too; these are detailed in N2.5.2.2.1.

2.2.2.2.3. Separability of the P and its complement in the clause

If the complement of the case-like P is a *wh*-element that needs to undergo *wh*-movement, then the P cannot be stranded (158b). This is due to the above-mentioned restriction that case-like Ps must immediately follow their complement.

(158) a. Ki mögött sétálsz?
who behind walk.2Sg
'Who are you walking behind?'

b. *Ki sétálsz mögött?
who walk.2Sg behind
Intended meaning: 'Who are you walking behind?'

The P-stranding construction becomes possible if and only if i) the *wh*-pronoun bears dative case instead of appearing in the usual unmarked form, and in addition ii) the postposition bears (possessive) agreement (this normally does not happen if its complement is a *wh*- pronoun, see 158a). Compare (159), with dative case on the *wh*-pronoun and agreement on the P, and (158), with a morphologically unmarked *wh*-pronoun and no agreement on the P. (159) is formally similar to an external possessor construction (see N3.2.2.1. point *A*).

(159) Ki-nek sétálsz mögött-e?
who-Dat walk.2Sg behind-3Sg
'Who are you walking behind?'

If both the Ground and the case-like postposition are internal to the PP, then the Ground cannot have dative case (160a,b) and the P cannot bear agreement (160a,c). That is, dative case, P-agreement and P-stranding must go together.

(160) a. *Ki-nek mögött-e sétálsz?
who-Dat behind-3Sg walk.2Sg
Intended meaning: 'Who are you walking behind?'

b. *Ki-nek mögött sétálsz?
who-Dat behind walk.2Sg
Intended meaning: 'Who are you walking behind?'

c. *Ki mögött-e sétálsz?
who behind-3Sg walk.2Sg
Intended meaning: 'Who are you walking behind?'

P-stranding as in (159) does not work with all case-like Ps (161); the possibility depends on the context and is also subject to speaker-variation. Generally, Ps with a directional semantics and argument-like Ps produce better results in this construction.

(161) a. Ki helyett dolgozol?
who instead_of work.3Sg
'Who are you working instead of?'

b. *Ki-nek dolgozol helyett-e?
who-Dat work.3Sg instead_of-3Sg
Intended meaning: 'Who are you working instead of?'

PPs headed by case-like Ps may occupy the so-called verb modifier position, which is the immediately preverbal position (Chapter 4, and also the volume on Sentence Structure), as in (162).

(162) A labda a híd mellett maradt.
the ball the bridge next_to stay.Past.3Sg
'The ball stayed next to the bridge.'

It is also possible for case-like postpositions to occupy the verb modifier position on their own; in this case their complement is in postverbal position (163). (Chapter 4 will feature a detailed discussion of this construction; see also Marácz 1984, 1986, É. Kiss 2002 Chapter 8, Surányi 2009a,b.) As in the case of P-stranding, such separation in the clause is possible if and only if the case-like P bears agreement and the noun phrase complement bears dative case.

(163) A labda mellett-e maradt a híd-nak.
the ball next_to-3Sg stay.Past.3Sg the bridge-Dat
'The ball stayed next to the bridge.'

To summarize, if both the case-like P and the Noun Phrase are within the PP, then the Noun Phrase is morphologically unmarked and the P bears agreement only if the Ground is a personal pronoun. Extraction from a PP with a case-like P is not possible. The case-like P and its complement can be separated in the clause only if a special construction is used, in which both the P and its complement have out-of-the-ordinary (in fact, possessive) morphological marking: the Ground bears dative case, and the P bears agreement (regardless of whether Ground is pronominal or not).

2.2.2.2.4. Combination with the Delative and Sublative case

Case-like Ps with the locative ending *-(Vt)t* may combine with the delative or the sublative case to yield source and goal expressions (164b) (Marácz 1986). This is often a marked option, however, which speakers either disprefer or reject. Compare (164a), the default form of source and goal PPs containing case-like Ps, with (164b), involving the combination of a locative case-like P and a case suffix.

(164) a. a fal mögül, a fal mögé
the wall behind_from the wall behind_to
'from behind the wall, to behind the wall'

b. ?a fal mögött-ről, ?a fal mögött-re
the wall behind-Del the wall behind-Sub
'from behind the wall, to behind the wall'

In some cases, however, this is the only form that can express the intended meaning. Compare (165a) and (165b), where the former example is perfectly grammatical, while the monomorphemic source P yields ungrammaticality. See also Chapter 3 Section 3.2.5 point *III/A*.

(165) a. A váza a római kor előtt-ről származik.
the vase the Roman times before -Del be_from.3Sg
'The vase is from before the Roman times.'

b. *A váza a római kor elől származik.
the vase the Roman times before_from be_from.3Sg
Intended meaning: 'The vase is from before the Roman times.'

2.2.2.2.5. N + case-like posposition modifying a noun

PPs with a case-like postposition (and PPs in general) cannot serve as prenominal modifiers. In order to appear in the prenominal position, PPs must combine with the attributivizer suffix *-i* (166a), or the present participle *levő* 'being' (166b).

(166) a. a ház mellett-*(i) pad, a ház mellett *(levő) pad
the house next_to-Attr bench the house next_to be.Part bench
both: 'the bench next to the house'

b. a palánk mellől-*(i) passz, a palánk mellől *(jövő) passz
the backboard from_next_to-Attr pass the backboard from_next_to come.Part pass
'the pass from next to the backboard, the pass coming from next to the backboard'

Attributivizing with *-i* is possible with locative and source Ps (166) and the Ps classified as 'other' in Table 4 (167).

(167) a vár ellen-i támadás, a vár ellen indított támadás
the castle against-Attr attack the castle against launch.Part attack
'the attack against the castle, the attack launched against the castle'

Attributivizing with *-i* is not grammatical with goal Ps (168a') and temporal Ps (168b'), however: with these Ps only the participial strategy is possible.

(168) a. a ház mellé lőtt lövések
the house next_to fire.Part shot.Pl
'the shots fired to next to the house'

a'. *a ház mellé-i lövések
the house next_to-Attr shot.Pl
Intended meaning: 'the shots [fired] to next to the house'

b. a karácsony óta tartó várakozás
the Christmas since continue.Part waiting
'the waiting since Christmas'

b'. *a karácsony óta-i várakozás
the Christmas since-Attr waiting
Intended meaning: 'the waiting since Christmas'

A PP with a case-like P can serve as a postnominal modifier. In this case combination with the attributivizer suffix *-i*, or the present participle *levő* 'being' is ungrammatical (169).

(169) a. a pad a ház mellett-(*i)
the bench the house next_to-Attr
'the bench next to the house'

b. a pad a ház mellett (*levő)
the bench the house next_to be.Part
'the bench next to the house'

For the modifier use of PPs see also Chapter 5 Section 5.5.

2.2.2.2.6. Modification

PPs with a case-like postposition may be modified by degree modifiers such as *majdnem* 'almost', *szinte* 'almost', *közvetlen* 'right', *teljesen* 'completely', *egészen* 'completely', etc., and measure phrases such as 'two meters'. Degree modifiers must precede the complement of the P (170).

(170) a. majdnem a fa alatt
almost the tree under
'almost under the tree'

b. *a fa majdnem alatt
the tree almost under
Intended meaning: 'almost under the tree'

c. ??a fa alatt majdnem
the tree under almost
'almost under the tree'

Measure phrases may either precede the complement or follow the case-like P (171a,b), but they cannot intervene between the P and its complement (171c).

(171) a. két méterrel a fa mellett
two meter.Ins the tree next_to
'two meters next to the tree'

b. a fa mellett két méterrel
the tree next_to two meter.Ins
'two meters next to the tree'

c. *a fa két méterrel mellett
the tree two meter.Ins next_to
Intended meaning: 'two meters next to the tree'

2.2.2.2.7. Conjunction reduction

PPs containing a case-like P allow forward conjunction deletion (172).

(172) • Forward conjunction reduction

a. a könyv előtt és a könyv mögött
the book in_front_of and the book behind
'in front of the book and behind the book'

b. a könyv előtt és mögött
the book in_front_of and behind
'in front of and behind the book'

PPs containing a case-like P also allow backward conjunction deletion. (173a) and (173b) have different meanings, however: in (173a) the space behind the notebook and the space behind the book are non-identical, while (173b) is ambiguous: here we may have a single space that is behind both the notebook and the book, but a meaning identical to that of (173a) is also available (and can be forced with distributive elements as in (173c)).

(173) • Backward conjunction reduction

a. a füzet mögé és a könyv mögé
the notebook behind and the book behind_to
'to behind the notebook and to behind the book'

b. a füzet és a könyv mögé
the notebook and the book behind_to
'to behind the notebook and the book'

c. A füzet és a könyv mögé is tettem egy tollat
the notebook and the book behind_to too put.Past.1Sg a pen.Acc
'I have put a pen both behind the notebook and the book.'

The reading of (173b) in which we have a single space that is behind both the notebook and the table possibly involves Noun Phrase conjunction rather than PP conjunction plus P-deletion.

2.2.2.2.8. PP-internal coding of reflexivity

As discussed in detail in Rákosi (2010), there is a split between first and second person on the one hand and third persons on the other hand in the coding of PP-internal reflexivity. PP-internal reflexives are, by default, encoded with a reflexive pronoun. In third person, this is the only option (174).

(174) a. János lát maga mellett egy macskát.
János see.3Sg self.3Sg next_to a cat.Acc
'János sees a cat next to himself.'

b. *János$_i$ lát (ő-)mellett-e$_i$ egy macskát.
János see.3Sg he-next_to-3Sg a cat.Acc
Intended meaning: 'János sees a cat next to himself.'

In first and second person, however, many speakers also accept pronominal coding of reflexivity. This is shown for first person singular in (175) and for second person singular in (176); the first and second person plural work similarly.

(175) a. Én látok magam mellett egy macskát.
I see.1Sg self.1Sg next_to a cat.Acc
'I see a cat next to myself.'

b. %Én látok (én-)mellett-em egy macskát.
I see.1Sg I-next_to-1Sg a cat.Acc
'I see a cat next to myself.'

(176) a. Te látsz magad mellett egy macskát.
you(Sg) see.2Sg self.2Sg next_to a cat.Acc
'You see a cat next to yourself.'

b. %Te látsz (te-)mellett-ed egy macskát.
you(Sg) see.2Sg you-next_to-2Sg a cat.Acc
'You see a cat next to yourself.'

2.2.2.3. Case-assigning postpositions

In this section we turn to the characterization of case-assigning postpositions. As already mentioned, these Ps require that their complement bear an oblique case suffix. In the previous literature case-assigning Ps were not unanimously considered to be members of the category P. Antal (1961), É. Kiss (1999, 2002 Chapter 8), Spencer (2008) and Trommer (2008), for instance, consider only case-like Ps to be true Ps. Here we follow Marácz (1984, 1986, 1989); Kenesei *et al.* (1998), Payne and Chisarik (2000); Kádár (2009), Dékány (2011) and Hegedűs (2006, 2013), among others, in treating case-assigning Ps as genuine postpositions.

2.2.2.3.1. The inventory and form of case-assigning postpositions

The list of case-assigning postpositions is given in Table 5. In contrast to case-like Ps, some case-assigning Ps are monosyllabic. These all contain a long vowel. Unlike case suffixes, but similarly to case-like Ps, case-assigning postpositions do not exhibit vowel harmony with the noun that they modify. Note that some Ps listed in the spatial group may also have a temporal reading. There are no case-assigning Ps with only a temporal reading. Case-assigning Ps listed in the 'other' group do not have a spatial reading. See Section 2.3 for the semantic classification of postpositions.

Table 5: Case-assigning postpositions

	CASE-ASSIGNING P	MEANING	SUBCATEGORIZED CASE SUFFIX
SPATIAL	*alul*	below, under	superessive
	át	through, via, across, over	superessive
	belül	inside of	superessive
	felül/fölül	over, above	superessive
	innen	on this side of	superessive

	keresztül	through, via, across	superessive
	kívül	outside of, apart from	superessive
	túl	beyond, over	superessive
	végig	along to the end of	superessive
	szembe	to opposite to	instrumental
	szemben	opposite to	instrumental
	szemből	from opposite to	instrumental
	szemközt	opposite to	instrumental
	közel	close to	allative
OTHER	*együtt*	together	instrumental
	képest	compared to, for	allative

Among case-assigning postpositions, there is a morphologically related quartet: *szemközt* 'opposite to', *szemben* 'opposite to', *szemből* 'from opposite to', and *szembe* 'to opposite to' These involve the bound stem *szem-* 'opposite', which is homonymous with the common noun *szem* 'eye'. However, in order to form a full-fledged postposition, this stem combines with the garden variety inessive (*-ban/-ben*), illative (*-ba/-be*), and elative (*-ból/-ből*) case suffixes rather than with the non-productive suffixes that case-like Ps do (*-(Vt)t* in the case of locative Ps, *-á/-é* in the case of lative Ps, and *-(V)l* in the case of source Ps). In addition, the stem *szem-* 'opposite' may also combine with the case-like P *közt* 'between' to yield the complex locative case-assigning postposition *szemközt* 'opposite to'. (*Közt* is the short form of the case-like P *között* 'between'.)

(177) a. a postá-val szemben / szemközt
the post.office -Ins opposite / opposite
both: 'opposite to the post office'

b. a postá-val szembe / szemből
the post.office-Ins opposite_to / opposite_from
'to opposite to the post office, from opposite to the post office'

Other case-assigning Ps do not come in morphologically related triplets (or doublets or quartets). In addition, no case-assigning P bears the locative suffix *-(Vt)t*, the lative suffix *-á/-é*, or the source suffix *-(V)l*. The case-assigning postpositions *alul* 'below/under', *belül* 'inside of', *felül* 'over/above', *keresztül* 'through/via/across', *kívül* 'outside of', *túl* 'beyond/over', and *közel* 'close to' end in a *-Vl* sequence. These, however, all have a locative rather than a source reading, hence they do not involve the source suffix *-(V)l* that case-like Ps do. The case-assigning postpositions *együtt* 'together' and *képest* 'for/compared to' end in a *-(t)t* sequence, but these do not have a locative reading.

Remark 10. Diachronically, the postposition *együtt* 'together' comprises the numeral *egy* 'one' and the locative suffix *-(Vt)t* (Simonyi 1895: 681). The contemporary meaning thus grammaticalized from the expression 'at one place'. This bimorphemic origin is completely opaque for contemporary speakers, however; in Modern Hungarian *együtt* 'together' is a monomorphemic postposition.

Most case-assigning Ps contain an obsolete or opaque bound stem. The P *alul* 'below, under', for instance, contains the bound stem *al-*. This is the same stem that appears in the case-like Ps *alatt* 'under', *alá* 'to under' and *alól* 'from under' (178).

(178) a. a vonal-on alul
the line-Sup under
'under the line'

b. a vonal alatt / alá / alól
the line under / under_to / under_from
'under / [to under] / [from under] the line'

The bound stem *al-* appears in the words in (179a), too, and it can also be used in compounds with the meaning 'sub-, vice-' (179b). Kenesei (2007) refers to the *al-* of (179b) as a semiword.

(179) a. al-ja, alj, alsó
bottom-Poss skirt underpants
'the bottom of sth, skirt, underpants'

b. al-király, al-elnök, al-ezredes, Al-Duna
AL-king AL-president AL-colonel AL-Danube
'viceroy, vice president, lieutenant-colonel, Lower Danube'

The P *belül* 'inside of sth' contains the bound stem *bel-* 'inner, inside, endo-', which also appears in the expressions in (180a) and in the compounds in (180b).

(180) a. a barlang belse-je, a belső sáv, belső ellenőr, belső szervek
the cave inside-Poss the inner lane inner auditor inner organs
'the inside of the cave, the inner lane, internal auditor, internal organs'

b. bel-gyógyászat, bel-ügy-minisztérium, bel-város, bel-politika
BEL-healing BEL-affair-ministry BEL-city BEL-politics
'internal medicine, ministry of internal affairs, downtown, internal affairs'

The P *közel* 'close to' shares the *köz-* stem with the case-like Ps *között* 'between', *közé* 'to between' and *közül* 'from between' (181b). As mentioned in Section 2.2.2.2.1, this stem is related to the common noun *köz* 'gap, space between'. It also appears in the expressions in (181c).

(181) a. a vonalak-hoz közel
the line.Pl-All close_to
'close to the lines'

b. a vonalak között / közé / közül
the line.Pl between / between_to / between_from
'[in between] / [to between] / [from between] the lines'

c. köz-ös, köz-terület, köz-ügy, köz-társaság
KÖZ-Adj KÖZ-premise KÖZ-case KÖZ-society
'common / shared, public premises, a matter of general concernment, republic'

The stem of the P *felül/fölül* 'above' is similarly shared with case-like Ps: that of *felett/fölött* 'above', *fölé* 'to above', *fölül* 'from above', as well as *felé* 'towards' and *felől* 'from the direction of'.

(182) a. a felhők fölött / fölé / fölül
the cloud.Pl above / above_to / above_from
'above / [to above] / [from above] the clouds'

b. a hegyek felé / felől
the mountain towards / from_the_direction_of
'towards / [from the direction of] the mountains'

The P *végig* 'along to the end of' comprises the common noun *vég* 'end' and the terminative *-ig* case suffix, while the P *kívül* 'outside of' is morphologically related to the verbal particle *ki* 'out' and the locative adverbs *kinn* and *kint*, both meaning 'outside' (see Section 2.2.4.1.2 point *III*). Finally, the P *keresztül* 'through, via, across' is based on the noun *kereszt* 'cross', while the P *képest* 'compared to, for' is related to the noun *kép* 'picture'.

(183) a. az utcá-n végig
the street-Sup end_to
'along to the end of the street'

b. a ház-on kívül
the house-Sup outside_of
'outside the house'

c. az utcá-n keresztül
the street-Sup across
'across the street'

d. a vizsgá-hoz képest
the exam-All compared_to
'compared to the exam'

2.2.2.3.2. Complementation

I. The form of the complement

Case-assigning Ps subcategorize for a Noun Phrase complement with a specific oblique case. Most case-assigning Ps require a superessive-marked complement, but there are also Ps that take an instrumental- or allative-marked complement. The selected case marker is not related to whether the postposition has a locative, directional or 'other' reading (184).

(184) a rét-en keresztül, a rét-hez közel, Mari-val együtt
the meadow-Sup through the meadow-All close_to Mari-Ins together
'through the meadow, close to the meadow, together with Mari'

The superessive and the allative case suffixes do not contribute the locative or directional meaning that they do in PPs headed by case suffixes (185); they are required only for formal (c-selectional) reasons (similarly to *on* in the idiomatic 'choose' reading of *decide on the boat*).

(185) a. a rét-en, a rét-en keresztül
the meadow-Sup the meadow-Sup through
'on the meadow, through the meadow'

b. a rét-hez, a rét-hez közel
the meadow-All the meadow-All close_to
'to the meadow, close to the meadow'

II. PP-internal position with respect to the complement

By default, case-assigning Ps are postpositional, hence they follow their complement. Marácz (1986) claims that these Ps can also freely precede the complement, however, with the two word orders being in free variation. The availability of both orders is shown for *át* 'through, via, across, over' in (186).

(186) a. a híd-on át
the bridge-Sup via
'via the bridge'

b. át a híd-on
via the bridge-Sup
'via the bridge'

Dékány and Hegedűs (2015) have shown that the prepositional order is restricted; it is available only to a subset of case-assigning Ps, specifically *át* 'through, via, across, over', *közel* 'close to', *szemben* 'opposite to', *túl* 'beyond', *végig* '(along) to the end of', *keresztül* 'through, across, via' and *szemközt* 'opposite to' (see also Dér 2012, 2013). Furthermore, the prepositional use of the latter two Ps is somewhat degraded. This is illustrated for *szemközt* 'opposite to' in (187).

(187) a. a fal-lal szemközt
the wall-Ins opposite_to
'opposite to the wall'

b. ?szemközt a fal-lal
opposite_to the wall-Ins
'opposite to the wall'

Other case-assigning Ps such as *felül* 'above sth' cannot precede their complement (188).

(188) a. a vonal-on felül
the line-Sup above
'above the line'

b. *?felül a vonal-on
above the line-Sup
Intended meaning: 'above the line'

The case-assigning Ps that allow the prepositional use are a proper subset of case-assigning Ps that allow the 'NP modifier P' order (see Section 2.2.2.3.8 below). The prepositional order is not discourse-neutral: it is mostly used in enumerations (189a) and when the PP is a contrastive topic (189b).

(189) a. át a híd-on, keresztül a mező-n, majd be az erdőbe
via the bridge-Sup through the meadow-Sup then in the forest.Ill
'through the bridge, through the meadow, then into the forest'

b. [Át a híd-on]$_{\text{CTopic}}$ csak óvatosan szabad menni.
via the bridge-Sup only carefully allowed go.Inf
'As for going through the bridge, one should only do it carefully.'

III. Dropping the complement

The case-assigning Ps *alul* 'below, under', *belül* 'inside of', *felül* 'over, above', *kívül* 'outside of', *közel* 'close to', *szembe* 'to opposite to', *szemben* 'opposite to', *szemből* 'from opposite to', and *szemközt* 'opposite to' can be used without an overt complement. In this case they express a (spatial or temporal) relation between the Figure and an implicit Ground (i.e. a reference point that is recoverable from the context): (190 b,c).

(190) a. A labda a vonal-on alul van.
the ball the line-Sup under be.3Sg
'The ball is under the line.'

b. A labda alul van.
the ball under be.3Sg
'The ball is down / [down there] (with respect to a reference point).'

c. Pál az utca végén állt. A lövések szemből jöttek.
Pál the street end.Poss.Sup stand.Past.3Sg the shot.Pl from_opposite_to come.Past.3Pl
'Pál was standing at the end of the street. The shots came from [the opposite side] / [opposite to him].'

Implicit Grounds are not possible with case suffixes and case-like Ps. In this respect these case-assigning Ps are different. However, they are also different from the group that we categorize as locative adverbs here, which cannot have a syntactically explicit reference point. That is to say, the difference between *alul* 'down (there)' and *kinn/kint* 'outside' (which we list among locative adverbs with the locative suffix *-nn/-nt* in Section 2.2.4.1.2 point *III*) is that the latter must have an implicit reference point, while case-assigning Ps can have a syntactically expressed Ground.

Due to its semantics, *együtt* 'together' can be used without a complement if the subject is semantically plural (191c,d).

(191) a. János Mari-val együtt megy moziba.
János Mari-Ins together go.3Sg cinema.Ill
'János goes to the cinema with Mari.'

b. *János együtt megy moziba.
János together go.3Sg cinema.Ill

c. János és Mari együtt mennek moziba. / Együtt mennek moziba.
János and Mari together go.3Pl cinema.Ill / together go.3Pl cinema.Ill
'János and Mari go to the cinema together.' / 'They go to the cinema together.'

d. A három lány együtt megy moziba.
the three girl together go.3Sg cinema.Ill
'The three girls go to the cinema together.'

IV. The complement's demonstrative modifier

If the complement of the case-assigning P is a noun phrase that contains the demonstrative pronoun *ez* 'this' or *az* 'that', then the case selected by the P appears both on the demonstrative and the nominal head of the complement. In (192) we illustrate this with the case-assigning P *közel* 'close to', which takes an allative-marked complement.

(192) ehhez a ház-hoz közel
this.All the house-All close_to
'close to this house'

Unlike case-like Ps, case-assigning Ps do not appear on the demonstrative themselves (193).

(193) *ehhez közel a ház-hoz közel
this.All close_to the house-All close_to
Intended meaning: 'close to this house'

The case assigning P *kívül* 'outside of' is occasionally claimed to be able to appear on the demonstrative. In our judgment, this is a highly marked option, which allows only the 'apart from' meaning of *kívül*, but not the literal spatial meaning 'outside of'(194b).

(194) %ez-en kívül a ház-on kívül
this-Sup outside_of the house-Sup outside_of
'apart from this house' (Not:'outside of this house')

The case-assigning Ps *át* 'through, via, across, over' and *túl* 'beyond, over' can also exceptionally appear after the demonstrative (195) (though the result is somewhat degraded). In this regard, these two case-assigning Ps behave like case suffixes and case-like Ps (Sections 2.2.1 and 2.2.2.2).

(195) a. ?ezen át a ház-on át
this.Sup through the house-Sup through
'through this house'

b. ??ez-en túl a ház-on túl
this-Sup beyond the house-Sup beyond
'beyond this house'

V. Personal pronoun complements

As already mentioned above, if the case-assigning P combines with a personal pronoun, then the case marker selected by the P must bear an agreement suffix (196). This is because oblique case suffixes with a personal pronoun complement must always be followed by an agreement suffix (see Section 2.2.1.2 point *V/B*).

(196) (én-)rajt-am keresztül, (ti-)hozzá-tok közel, (mi-)vel-ünk együtt
I-Sup-1Sg through you-All-2Pl close_to we-Ins-1Pl together
'through me, close to you, together with us'

2.2.2.3.3. Separability of the P and its complement in the clause

The case-assigning Ps *át* 'through, via, across, over', *közel* 'close to', *végig* 'along to the end of', *keresztül* 'through, via, across, over', *együtt* 'together', *szembe* 'to opposite to', and to a limited extent, also *belül* 'inside of', *szemben* 'opposite to', *szemközt* 'opposite to' and *túl* 'beyond' allow P-stranding under *wh*-movement of their complement (197a,b). The rest of case-assigning Ps do not allow P-stranding (197c). Note that the possibility of P-stranding shows no correlation with either the semantics (locative/static vs. directional) of the P or the oblique case that the P subcategorizes for.

(197) a. Mi-n sétáltál át?
what-Sup walk.Past.2Sg through
'What did you walk through?'

b. ?Mi-vel van szemközt a posta?
what-Ins be.3Sg opposite_to the post.office
'What is the post office opposite to?'

c. *Mi-vel jött szemből a labda?
what-Sup come.Past.3Sg from_opposite_to the ball
Intended meaning: 'What is such that the ball came from opposite to it?'

D-linked interrogative phrases are separable from the case-assigning Ps more easily, however: compare (197c) and (198).

(198) Melyik kereszt-utcá-n van innen a bolt?
which side-street-Sup be.3Sg on_this_side_of the shop
'Which side street is such that the shop is before that street?'

The same case-assigning Ps that can be stranded by with non-D-linked *wh*-phrases can also be used as verbal particles. In neutral sentences, verbal particles appear in the immediately preverbal position (see the volume on Sentence Structure). In this case the P's complement appears in the postverbal field (199a).

(199) a. János át-sétált a mező-n.
János across-walk.Past.3Sg the meadow-Sup
'János walked across the meadow.'

b. *János szemből jött a postá-val.
János from_opposite_to come.Past.3Sg the post_office-Ins
Intended meaning: 'János came from (the place) opposite to the post office.'

2.2.2.3.4. Combination with the Delative and Sublative case

As discussed in Section 2.2.2.2, case-like Ps can be decomposed into a bound stem expressing 'above', 'under', 'next to', etc., and a non-productive suffix that expresses location at (*-(Vt)t*), movement to (*-á/-é*), or movement from (*-(V)l*) the location expressed by the stem. Case-like Ps thus come in morphologically related triplets (200).

(200) a. alatt, alá, alól
under to_under from_under

b. mellett, mellé, mellől
next_to to_next_to from_next_to

Apart from the *szemközt* 'opposite to', *szemben* 'opposite to', *szemből* 'from opposite to', and *szembe* 'to opposite to' series, case-assigning Ps do not come in morphologically related triplets or quartets (see Table 5 and the discussion in Section 2.2.2.3.1). These Ps do not contain the locative *-(Vt)t* suffix, the lative *-á/-é* suffix, or the *-(V)l* source suffix. The case-assigning Ps that express static location combine with the sublative and the delative case suffix in order to form goal and source PPs respectively. Two examples are given in (201).

(201) a. közel, közel-re, közel-ről
close_to close_to-Sub close_to-Del
'close to, to close to , from close to'

b. alul, alul-ra, alul-ról
below below-Sub below-Del
'below, to below, from below'

The combination of the case-assigning P *innen* 'on this side of' and the sublative or delative case suffix is marked, however (202).

(202) a. ??A labda a vonal-on innen-re gurult.
the ball the line-Sup this_side_of-Sub roll.Past.3Sg
'The ball rolled to (the area on) this side of the line.'

b. ??A lövések a vonal-on innen-ről jöttek.
the shot.Pl the line-Sup this_side_of-Del come.Past.3Pl
'The shots came from (the area on) this side of the line.'

Note that *innen* is an ambiguous lexical item: it is used both as a place-denoting P, as in (202), and as a source-denoting adverbial 'from here' (203).

(203) a. itt, ide, innen
here to_here from_here

b. A dokumentum innen letölthető.
the document from_here downloadable
'The document is downloadable from here.'

2.2.2.3.5. N + case-assigning postposition modifying a noun

PPs headed by case-assigning Ps, similarly to PPs headed by case-like Ps, cannot be used as prenominal N-modifiers directly (204a). In the prenominal position they must either bear the attributivizer suffix *-i* (204b), or they must be embedded into a participial clause headed by *levő* 'being' (204c), the present participial form of the future copula.

(204) a. *a vonal-on felül írás
the line-Sup above writing
Intended meaning: 'the writing above the line'

b. a vonal-on felül-i írás
the line-Sup above-Attr writing
'the writing above the line'

c. a vonal-on felül levő írás
the line-Sup above be.Part writing
'the writing above the line'

Attributive *-i* modification works with most case-assigning Ps; it is, however, ungrammatical with **át-i* 'through/via/across-Attr', **végig-i* 'along-Attr', **szembe-i* 'to opposite-Attr', and very limited with *?*szemből-i* 'from opposite to-Attr'. PPs with a case-assigning postposition can serve as postnominal N-modifiers, however, and in this case they cannot combine with either the *-i* attributivizing suffix or *levő* 'being' (205).

(205) a. az írás a vonal-on felül
the writing the line-Sup above
'the writing above the line'

b. *az írás a vonal-on felül-i / [felül levő]
the writing the line-Sup above-Attr / above be.Part

See also Chapter 5 Section 5.5 on PPs as modifiers.

2.2.2.3.6. Modification

PPs containing case-assigning Ps can be modified by degree and measure phrases. Degree modifiers can precede the NP that serves as the P's complement and they can also appear between the NP and the P. They cannot follow the case-assigning postposition, however (206).

(206) a. teljesen a kerítés-en belül
completely the fence-Sup inside.of
'completely inside the fence'

b. a kerítés-en teljesen belül
the fence-Sup completely inside.of
'completely inside the fence'

c. *a kerítés-en belül teljesen
the fence-Sup inside.of completely
Intended meaning: 'completely inside the fence'

Measure phrases may precede the NP complement of the P and may also follow the case-assigning P (207).

(207) a. két méterrel a kerítés-en belül
two meter.Ins the fence-Sup inside.of
'two meters inside the fence'

b. a kerítés-en belül két méterrel
the fence-Sup inside.of two meter.Ins
'two meters inside the fence'

Whether measure phrases can appear between the complement and the case-assigning P varies across individual Ps. This order is the most acceptable with *túl* 'beyond' (208a). With other Ps this order is highly degraded or fully ungrammatical (208b,c).

(208) a. a vonal-on két méterrel túl
the line-Sup two meter.Ins beyond
'two meters beyond the line'

b. ?(?)a vonal-on két méterrel belül
the fence-Sup two meter.Ins inside.of
'two meters inside the line'

c. *a vonal-on két méterrel alul
the fence-Sup two meter.Ins under
Intended meaning: 'two meters under the line'

See also Chapter 3 Section 3.3 on PP-modification.

2.2.2.3.7. Conjunction reduction

PPs headed by case-assigning Ps allow both forward and backward conjunction reduction. This is shown in (209) and (210).

(209) • Forward conjunction reduction

a. a ház-on kívül és a ház-on belül
the house-Sup outside.of and the house-Sup inside.of
'outside of the house and inside of the house'

b. a ház-on kívül és belül
the house-Sup outside.of and inside.of
'outside and inside of the house'

(210) • Backward conjunction reduction

a. a ház-hoz közel és a tó-hoz közel
the house-All close_to and the lake-All close_to
'close to the lake and close to the house'

b. a ház-hoz és a tó-hoz közel
the house-All and the lake-All close_to
'close to the lake and the house'

As with PPs containing case-like Ps, backward conjunction reduction is possibly better analyzed as coordination under the P: while in (210a) the area that is close to the house is not necessarily identical to the area that is close to the lake, in (210b) there is one area that is close to both the house and the lake.

2.2.2.3.8. Case-assigning Ps: summary of the variation

It emerges from the above discussion that not all case-assigning Ps behave alike with respect to certain distributional tests. Some, but not all case-assigning Ps allow P-stranding, use as a particle, the 'NP - degree modifier - P' order and the prepositional order. Of these, the 'NP - degree modifier - P' order is felicitous with most Ps; in fact, only three Ps are not fully acceptable in this order. Case-assigning Ps that allow a particle use and P-stranding form a proper subset of the Ps that are grammatical in the 'NP - degree modifier - P' order. In other words, all Ps that have a particle use and are felicitous with P-stranding also allow the 'NP - degree modifier - P' order, but not vice versa. In addition, the particle use and P-stranding correlate: individual Ps either allow both of these options or neither.

Case-assigning Ps usable as prepositions are, in turn, a proper subset of case-assigning Ps that can serve as verbal particles or can be P-stranded. That is, all case-assigning Ps that allow the prepositional use also allow P-stranding and have a particle use, but not vice versa. The pattern is summarized in Table 6.

Table 6: Case-assigning Ps: prepositional use, particle use and P-stranding

CASE-ASSIGNING P	MEANING	NP-MODIFIER-P SECTION 2.2.2.3.6	PARTICLE USE SECTION 2.2.2.3.3	P-STRANDING SECTION 2.2.2.3.3	PREPOSITIONAL USE SECTION 2.2.2.3.2 POINT *II*
át	through, via, across, over	✓	✓	✓	✓
közel	close to	✓	✓	✓	✓
végig	along to the end of	✓	✓	✓	✓
keresztül	through, via, across	✓	✓	✓	?
szemben	opposite to	✓	restricted	restricted	✓
túl	beyond, over	✓	restricted	restricted	✓
belül	inside of	✓	restricted	restricted	×
együtt	together	✓	✓	✓	×
szembe	to opposite to	✓	✓	✓	×

szemközt	opposite to	✓	??	??	?(?)
alul	below, under	?	×	×	×
felül	over, above	??	×	×	×
innen	on this side of	?	×	×	×
kívül	outside of	✓	×	×	×
kívül-re	to outside of	✓	×	×	×
kívül-ről	from outside of	✓	×	×	×
szemből	from opposite to	✓	×	×	×
túl-ra	to beyond	✓	×	×	×
túl-ról	from beyond	✓	×	×	×
képest	compared to, for	N/A	×	×	×

2.2.2.4. Taking stock: the relation between case suffixes and postpositions

The properties of case suffixes, case-like postpositions and case-assigning postpositions discussed in the preceding sections are summarized in Table 7. Of the three types of P-elements, it is case suffixes that have the tightest connection with their complement, and case-assigning Ps have the greatest degree of morphological/phonological freedom. Case-like Ps share properties both with case suffixes and case-assigning Ps and so they constitute a type of intermediate category between the two.

Table 7: Case-like Ps, case-assigning Ps and suffixes

PROPERTY	CASE SUFFIX	CASE-LIKE P	CASE-ASSIGNING P
visible case on the complement	N/A	×	✓
may precede its complement	×	×	✓ (some)
'NP - degree modifier - P' order	×	×	✓ (some)
P-stranding in wh-questions	×	×	✓ (some)
dropping non-pronominal complement	×	×	✓ (some)
appearing on demonstrative	✓	✓	×
bears agreement	✓	✓	×
vowel harmony with complement	✓	×	×
deletion under conjunction	×	✓	✓
sublative or delative suffixation	×	✓ (limited)	✓
modification by -i	×	✓ (most)	✓ (most)
modification by levő or való	✓	✓	✓

Neither morphological nor phonological criteria can be used to draw a definitive line between case suffixes and postpositions. Suffixhood is not a good diagnostic (Sebestyén 1965, Antal 1961, Asbury *et al.* 2007, Asbury 2005, 2008): case suffixes show postposition-like behavior in that they do not require the pronoun to be overt

(Section 2.2.1.2 points *V/B* and *V/D*). The number of syllables does not distinguish case suffixes from postpositions either. While all case suffixes are monosyllabic, there exist some monosyllabic postpositions, too (cf. case-like *tájt* 'around a point in time' and *közt* 'between' – both of which have longer forms as well – in Table 4 as well as case-assigning *át* 'through, via, across, over' and *túl* 'beyond' in Table 5). The availability of vowel harmony does not completely separate case suffixes from postpositions either. Although postpositions never harmonize, and the majority of case suffixes do, case suffixes containing a neutral vowel (the causal(-final) *-ért*, the terminative *-ig* and the essive-formal *-ként*) do not harmonize. We can conclude that case suffixes, case-like Ps and case-assigning Ps are realizations of the same category: that of adpositions. Their differences can be traced back to the fact that they have different degrees of morpho-phonological freedom from their NP complement.

2.2.3. *Verbal particles*

Verbal particles are a subgroup of the so-called verb modifiers. The name verb modifier is an umbrella term for predicative elements in the VP such as bare objects, resultatives, certain infinitival complements and verbal particles (see Chapter 4, Chapter 5, as well as the volume on Sentence Structure). These constituents have the same syntactic distribution in the clause. In neutral sentences they occupy the immediately preverbal position (the so-called straight order). In clauses with contrastive focus, negation, progressive aspect or imperatives, however, they appear in the post-verbal field (the so-called inverse order).

2.2.3.1. *The inventory of verbal particles*

As was the case with case-suffixes in Section 2.2.1, the boundaries of the class of verbal particles are difficult to draw, and authors disagree about which elements to include in the list of these items (see Komlósy 1992, Kiefer and Ladányi 2000b). A representative but non-exhaustive list of verbal particles is given in (211).

(211) a. meg, el, ki, be, fel, le
Perf away out in up down

b. át, túl, végig, keresztül
through beyond/over to_completion through

c. össze, szét, széjjel, tovább, vissza
together apart apart further back

d. hát-ra, fél-re, tönk-re, új-ra, agy-on, egy-be
back-Sub side-Sub stump-Sub new-Sub brain-Sup one-Ill
'back, aside, (V sth) to ruins, anew, over- / [to death], co- / together'

(211a) contains the oldest Hungarian verbal particles, which were already used in the first written texts (J. Soltész 1959). All of them are monosyllabic. *Ki* 'out' versus *be* 'in' and *fel* 'up' versus *le* 'down' form obvious semantic opposition pairs. In the beginning, *meg* and *el* 'away' were also semantic opposites, as the original meaning of *meg* was 'back' (as in e.g. *meg-jön*, lit. *meg*-come, which meant 'come back, return', cf. D. Mátai 1991: 433 and Hegedűs 2014). However, *meg* has undergone semantic bleaching and completely lost its directional reading over time. In contemporary Hungarian it has no lexical meaning any more; it is a grammatical word that telicizes the event. Today, *meg-jön*, lit. *meg*-come generally means 'arrive', and it does not entail that the agent has returned. (See also Section 2.3.1.3.4.) (211b) shows the case-assigning Ps that are most frequently used as verbal particles, too. They all have a directional meaning. (211c) lists some further verbal particles with a directional meaning. Finally, (211d) lists some verbal particles that originate from case-marked nouns. The internal morphological structure of these particles is still transparent for speakers, but they clearly have the distribution of verbal particles and in many cases the meaning is not compositional any more.

The reason why it is not straightforward to provide a definitive list of verbal particles is that it is not always clear how to draw the line between particles and other verb modifiers (particularly resultatives) or postpositions. Intransitively used case-assigning Ps (Section 2.2.2.3.2 point *III*) share the external distribution of verbal particles, and so do case-like postpositions that are non-adjacent to their NP complement (Section 2.2.2.2.3). Case-suffixes can also show a doubling-like pattern in the clause (Section 2.2.1.3 and Chapter 5 Section 5.2.3.5), appearing both on their NP complement and next to the verb, like ordinary verbal particles. Verb modifiers that qualify as verbal particles should meet the criterion of productivity, that is, they should be able to appear with a large number of verbs with a compositional meaning for the partice+verb unit. If a verb modifier has a semantically bleached, purely telicizing function (perhaps in addition to a semantically more contentful, directional meaning), then it is a good indication that it is a verbal particle. The verbal particle *ki* 'out', for instance, has both a goal-denoting (212a) and a more grammaticalized, purely telicizing use (212b).

(212) a. Ili ki-ment a kertbe. [directional]
Ili out-go.Past.3Sg the garden.Ill
'Ili went out into the garden.'

b. Ili ki-olvasta a könyvet. [telicizing]
Ili out-read.Past.DefObj.3Sg the book.Acc
'Ili has read the book from cover to cover.'

2.2.3.2. Verbal particles are (parts of) PPs

The so-called PP-with-DP construction is a clause type used to identify directional PPs (Hegedűs 2006).

(213) [PP A kuká-ba] a régi újságok-kal!
the bin-Ill the old newspaper.Pl-Ins
'Into the bin with the old newspapers!'

Verbal particles can be used as the sole (214a) or the first element (214b) in the PP-with-DP construction, showing that they are (parts of) PPs (see also Horvath 1978).

(214) a. [PP Ki] a régi újságok-kal!
out the old newspaper.Pl-Ins
'Out with the old newspapers!'

b. [PP Ki a kuká-ba] a régi újságok-kal!
out the bin-Ill the old newspaper.Pl-Ins
'Out into the bin with the old newspapers!'

As this test singles out directional PPs, particles with a non-directional reading are ungrammatical in this construction. (214) features the particle *ki* 'out' in its basic, directional reading, and the PP-with-DP construction is grammatical. When the same particle is used with a purely telicizing reading, as in (215a), then it cannot appear in the PP-with-DP construction. (215b) is grammatical, but only under a directional reading; the telicizing reading seen in (215a) is unavailable.

(215) a. Ili ki-olvasta a könyvet.
Ili out-read.Past.DefObj.3Sg the book.Acc
'Ili has read the book from cover to cover.'

b. [PP Ki] a könyv-vel!
out the book-Ins
'Out with the book!' (Not: 'Read the book from cover to cover.')

Verbal particles that have no directional use never appear in the PP-with-DP construction. (216) illustrates this for the particle *agyon* 'over, to death'.

(216) a. Ili agyon-dicsérte Imit.
Ili over-praise.Past.DefObj.3Sg Imi.Acc
'Ili praised Imi very much.'

b. *[PP Agyon] Imi-vel!
over Imi-Ins

Another particle that has no directional use is *meg*. As already mentioned above, *meg* used to have a directional meaning, 'back', but it has completely lost this reading and is now a purely telicizing particle. While the original directional reading remains in a few particle-verb combinations such as (217a), *meg* is incompatible with the PP-with-DP construction even in these collocations (217b), showing that the directional reading has become completely opaque.

(217) a. Kati meg-ad-ja a tartozást.
Kati Perf-give-DefObj.3Sg the loan.Acc
'Kati pays back the loan.'

b. *[PP Meg] a tartozás-sal!
Perf the loan-Ins

2.2.3.3. Separability from the verb

I. Separation from the verb: the inverse and the interrupted order

Let us take (218) as our baseline sentence. This example features the verbal particle *ki* 'out'. In this so-called straight order the particle is immediately preverbal.

(218) Ili ki-ment a kertbe. [neutral sentence]
Ili out-go.Past.3Sg the garden.Ill
'Ili went out into the garden.'

In non-neutral sentences (declaratives containing contrastive focus, negation, progressive aspect, as well as *wh*-interrogatives and imperatives) verbal particles occur in the post-verbal field (the so-called inverse order). This is shown in (219) with narrow focus and negation.

(219) a. Ili A KERTBE [ment ki]. [narrow focus]
Ili the garden.Ill go.Past.3Sg out
'It was the garden that Ili went out to.'

b. Ili nem [ment ki a kertbe]. [negation]
Ili not go.Past.3Sg out the garden.Ill
'Ili did not go out into the garden.'

Certain elements may intervene between the particle and the verb when the particle is preverbal. These are i) the emphatic particle *is* 'also, too' and its negative counterpart *sem* (220a,a') and ii) the negative particles *nem* 'not' and *ne* 'do not' (220b,c). (*Ne* is used in negative imperatives.) This is the so-called interrupted order.

(220) a. Ili ki is ment a kertbe.
Ili out Emph go.Past.3Sg the garden.Ill
'Ili did go out into the garden.'

a'. Ili ki sem ment a kertbe.
Ili out not.too go.Past.3Sg the garden.Ill
'Ili did not even go out into the garden.'

b. Ili ki nem menne a kertbe.
Ili out not go.Cond.3Sg the garden.Ill
'Ili would not go out into the garden.'

c. Ili ki ne menjen a kertbe!
Ili out not go.Subj.3Sg the garden.Ill
'Ili must not go out into the garden.'

Remark 11. (220c) is a marked version of the negative imperative; it is felicitous only if the action taken by the subject has been under consideration in the previous discourse (Varga 2013). Its more neutral word order involves the inverse order, as shown below.

(i) Ili ne menjen ki a kertbe!
Ili not go.Subj.3Sg out the garden.Ill
'Ili must not go out into the garden.'

All Hungarian verbal particles can appear in the interrupted and the inverse order, that is, they are all separable from the verb and there are no 'non-parting particles'. On their positions in the clause, see also Chapter 4.

II. Non-separability in the scope of nominalization

If a particle-verb combination is nominalized and then verbalized again, then the resulting complex is outwardly verbal, but the particle is no longer separable (Hegedűs and Dékány 2017). Examples are given in (221).

(221)	kifogásol,	befolyásol,	kivonatol,	feltételez,	kivitelez,	kivételez,
	'take objection to,	influence,	précis,	assume,	carry out,	show favor toward
	bevételez,	szemrevételez,	utánvételez,	felvételizik		
	enter as income,	inspect,	collect (value) upon delivery,	take an admission exam'		

The particle-verbs that form the core of the expressions in (221) are nominalized with the productive deverbal nominalizer suffix *-ás/-és* (see N1.3.1.2) or the semi-productive deverbal nominalizer *-t*. After potential attachment of a further nominalizing suffix (or suffixes), the noun is then verbalized again with the *-l* or *-z* verbalizer suffix. A detailed morphemic decomposition of the forms in (221) is given below. (The verbal forms are indicated by the *to* infinitival marker in the translations. This serves the reader's convenience only, the Hungarian forms themselves are not infinitival.) (222) shows the decomposition of those examples that involve one nominalizer suffix between the particle-verb and the outer verbalizing suffix.

(222) a. ki-fog, ki-fog-ás, ki-fog-ás-ol,
out-hold out-hold-Nmn out-hold-Nmn-Vrb
'to catch (by taking sth out of somewhere, e.g. fish), objection, to take objection to'

b. be-foly-(ik), be-foly-ás, be-foly-ás-ol
in-flow-3Sg in-flow-Nmn in-flow-Nmn-Vrb
'to flow in, influence, to influence'

c. ki-von, ki-von-at, ki-von-at-ol
out-pull out-pull-Nmn out-pull-Nmn-Vrb
'to pull out, précis, to précis'

(223) decomposes examples involving two nominalizer suffixes between the particle-verb and the outer verbalizing suffix.

(223) a. fel-tesz, fel-té-t, fel-té-t-el, fel-té-t-el-ez,
up-take up-take-Nmn up-take-Nmn-Nmn up-take-Nmn-Nmn-Vrb
'to [put up] / assume, topping, condition, to assume'

b. (után-vesz), után-vé-t, után-vé-t-el, után-vé-t-el-ez
after-take after-take-Nmn after-take-Nmn-Nmn after-take-Nmn-Nmn-Vrb
'take later, collection on delivery, collecting on delivery, to collect (value) upon delivery'

c. ki-vesz, ki-vé-t ki-vé-t-el ki-vé-t-el-ez
out-take out-take-Nmn out-take-Nmn-Nmn-Vrb out-take-Nmn-Nmn-Vrb
'to take out, business income, exception, to show a favor toward'

d. be-vesz, be-vé-t-el, be-vé-t-el-ez
in-take in-take-Nmn-Nmn in-take-Nmn-Nmn-Vrb
'to take in, proceeds / return, proceeds / return, to enter as income'

e. ki-visz, ki-vi-t-el, ki-vi-t-el-ez
out-take out-take-Nmn-Nmn out-take-Nmn-Nmn-Vrb
'to take out, export / [taking out], to carry out (an action)'

f. szemügyre-vesz szemre-vé-t-el szemre-vé-t-el-ez
sight.into-take on_eye-take-Nmn-Nmn on_eye-take-Nmn-Nmn-Vrb
'to inspect, inspection, to inspect'

(223b) features a particle-verb base that is not used on its own, therefore the base appears in parentheses. In the examples in (223d-f) the two nominalizers always appear together, hence the form with just one nominalizer is not shown separately. In (223f) the particle-verb features a longer form of the particle than the nominalized examples. Finally, (224) shows the morphemic composition of the most complex example.

(224) fel-vesz, fel-vé-t, fel-vé-t-el, fel-vé-t-el-i,
up-take up-take-Nmn up-take-Nmn-Nmn up-take-Nmn-Nmn-Attr
fel-vé-t-el-i-z
up-take-Nmn-Nmn-Attr-Vrb
'to take up, taking up, admission / recording, admission exam, to take an admission exam'

The particle-verb base has two nominalizers and an *-i* attributivizer (on *-i*, see Kenesei 2014). The resulting *felvételi* 'admission exam' is originally an N-modifier of the noun *vizsga* 'exam' (*felvételi vizsga*). With frequent ellipsis of the head noun *vizsga* 'exam', the original attributive form *felvételi* assumed a nominal distribution and came to mean 'admission exam' by itself. As a noun, it now combines with the productive denominal verbalizer *-z*.

The minimal pairs in (225) and (227), both involving the verbal particle *ki* 'out' and the verb *von* 'pull', show the effect that nominalization followed by further verbalization has on a particle-verb combination. (225) involves the partice-verb *ki-von* lit. 'out-take' 'take out, pull out, extract'. As expected, the particle is separable and can appear both in the interrupted and the inverse order.

(225) • Particle plus verb complex predicate

a. A só ki-von-ja a vizet a húsból. [neutral sentence]
the salt out-pull-3Sg the water.Acc the meat.Ela
'Salt extracts water out of meat.'

b. A só ki is von-ja a vizet a húsból. [interrupted order]
the salt out too pull-3Sg the water.Acc the meat.Ela
'Salt does extract water out of meat.'

c. A só nem von-ja ki a vizet a húsból. [inverse order, negation]
the salt not pull-3Sg out the water.Acc the meat.Ela
'Salt does not extract water out of meat.'

d. A SÓ von-ja ki a vizet a húsból. [inverse order, narrow focus]
the salt pull-3Sg out the water.Acc the meat.Ela
'It is salt that extracts water out meat.'

In (226b) we see that when the particle-verb *ki-von* undergoes nominalization by the semi-productive *-t* nominalizing suffix, its meaning changes to 'extract, epitome, abridgement'. After attaching the productive verbalizing suffix *-l* to this noun we get the verb 'to abridge / précis' (226c).

(226) a. ki-von
out-pull
'take out, pull out, extract'

b. ki-von-at
out-pull-Nmn
'extract, epitome, précis'

c. ki-von-at-ol
out-pull-Nmn-Vrb
'to abridge, to précis'

(227) shows that the particle cannot be separated from the derived verb in (226c); it cannot appear either in the inverse or the interrupted order.

(227) • Particle + verb complex predicate after nominalization and further verbalization

a. Ili ki-vonatol-ja a könyvet. [neutral sentence]
Ili out.abridge-3Sg the book.Acc
'Ili abridges the book.'

b. *Ili ki is vonatol-ja a könyvet. [interrupted order]
Ili out Emph abridge-3Sg the book.Acc
Intended meaning: 'Ili does abridge the book.'

b'. Ili ki-vonatol-ja is a könyvet.
Ili out-abridge-3Sg Emph the book.Acc
'Ili does abridge the book.'

c. *Ili nem vonatol-ja ki a könyvet. [inverse order, negation]
Ili not abridge-3Sg out the book.Acc
Intended meaning: 'Ili does not abridge the book.'

c'. Ili nem ki-vonatol-ja a könyvet.
Ili not out-abridge-3Sg the book.Acc
'Ili does not abridge the book.'

d. *ILI vonatol-ja ki a könyvet. [inverse order, narrow focus]
Ili abridge-3Sg out the book.Acc
Intended meaning: 'It is Ili that abridges the book.'

d'. ILI ki-vonatol-ja a könyvet.
Ili out-abridge-3Sg the book.Acc
'It is Ili that abridges the book.'

This shows that in the nominalized and re-verbalized particle verbs in (221) the particle is not visible for syntax. This conclusion is further supported by the fact that while verbal particles normally cannot be stacked on verbs, the nominalized and re-verbalized expressions in question do combine with durative or exhaustive verbal particles. In these cases the two different verbal particles (the inner one in the scope of nominalization and the outer durative or exhaustive one) end up adjacent on the surface (228, 229, data from Hegedűs and Dékány 2017).

(228) • Verbal particle with a durative reading

a. El-fel-vételiz-t-em az időt. [durative *el* 'away']
away-out-entrance.exam.take-Past-1Sg the time.Acc
'I spent all the available time with taking entrance exams.'

b. Át-fel-vételiz-t-em a napot. [durative *át* 'through']
through-up-exam.take.Past.1Sg the day.Acc
'I spent all day with taking entrance exams.'

(229) • Verbal particle with an exhaustive reading

a. [after 5 exams]
mára ki-fel-vételiztem magamat. [exhaustive *ki* 'out']
for.today out-up-exam.take.Past.1Sg myself.Acc
'I got exhausted with entrance exams for the day.'

b. Szét-fel-vételiztem az agyamat. [exhaustive *szét* 'apart']
apart-up-exam.take.Past.1Sg the brain.Poss.1Sg.Acc
'I got exhausted with taking entrance exams.'

When such examples appear in an environment that requires the interrupted or the inverse order, then the durative or exhaustive particle is separated from the complex verb, as expected, while the particle that is in the scope of nominalization remains immediately preverbal (230).

(230) a. [I've been here for hours.]
Mára ki is fel-vételiztem magamat. [interrupted order]
today.Sub out Emph up-exam.take.Past.1Sg myself.Acc
'I did get exhausted with entrance exams for today indeed.'

b. Nem fel-vételiztem át az egész napot. [inverse order, negation]
not up-exam.take.Past.1Sg through the whole day.Acc
'I did not spend all day with taking entrance exams.'

In short answers to questions, the durative or exhaustive particle is used on its own, without the particle in the scope of the nominalization.

(231) a. Szét-fel-vételizted az agyadat?
apart-up-exam.take.Past.2Sg the brain.Poss.2Sg.Acc
'Did you get exhausted with taking entrance exams?'

b. Szét.
apart
'Yes, I did.'

However, of the nominalized and re-verbalized particle verbs in (221) there is one that may undergo re-analysis and as a result its particle may become separable. *Feltételez* 'assume', whose composition is shown in (223a), is frequently re-analyzed (especially in scientific texts) in such a way that its particle *fel-* 'up' is understood to attach to re-verbalized form rather than to the verb in the scope of nominalization (232b).

(232) a. [$_{VP}$ [$_{NP}$ [$_{NP}$ [$_{VP}$ fel-té]-t]-el]-ez] [without reanalysis]
up-take-Nmn-Nmn-Vrb
'assume'

b. fel-[$_{VP}$ [$_{NP}$ [$_{NP}$ [$_{VP}$ té]-t]-el]-ez] [after reanalysis]
up- take-Nmn-Nmn-Vrb
'assume'

When this happens, the particle *fel-* 'up' separates from the morphologically complex verb like ordinary verbal particles do (233).

(233) a. %Ha fel is tételezzük, hogy így van, … [interrupted order]
if up Emph assume.1Pl that so be.3Sg
'Even if we assume that this is so, …'

b. %Tételezzük fel, hogy igazad van. [inverse order, imperative]
assume.Subj.1Pl up that right.Poss.2Sg be.3Sg
'Let us assume that you are right.'

c. %Nem tételeztem fel, hogy hibázol. [inverse order, negation]
not assume.Past.1Sg up that mistake_make.2Sg
'I did not assume that you would make a mistake.'

2.2.3.4. The formal properties of verbal particles

I. Complementation

Generally, verbal particles do not take complements. However, verbal particles that also double as case-assigning Ps, i.e. those in (211b), can take the same complement that they do as postpositions. (234a) shows that in its use as a case-assigning P, *át* 'through, via, across, over' takes a superessive-marked complement. When *át* is used as a verbal particle, the superessive-marked NP can appear in postverbal position (234b).

(234) a. a mező-n át
the meadow-Sup through
'through the meadow'

b. Ili át-gyalogol-t a mező-n.
Ili through-walk-Past.3Sg the meadow-Sup
'Ili walked through the meadow.'

When the Ground element that is being traversed is expressed in the clause ('through, via, across, over X'), then the use of the superessive-marked NP is obligatory in (234b). In this case the superessive case does not contribute any meaning to the structure; it is merely formally required on the NP by this specific P. In these cases we can say that there is a selection / complementation relationship between *át* as a verbal particle and the postverbal case-marked NP. At the same time, the superessive-marked NP complement can be dropped (235a) or replaced by an NP bearing a different case (235b). In the latter case, the Ground that is being traversed remains unexpressed; the case-marked NP denotes the starting or endpoint of the path.

(235) a. Ili át-sétált.
Ili through-walk.Past.3Sg
'Ili walked over.'

b. Ili át-sétált a kert-be / kert-ből.
Ili through-walk.Past.3Sg the garden-Ill / garden-Ela
'Ili walked over to / from the garden.'

In cases like (235b), there is no selection / complementation between *át* and the case-marked NP. In these cases the case suffix on the NP contributes to the meaning of the structure: as clear from (235b), it makes a difference whether the case is illative or elative, for instance.

II. Modification

It is not entirely clear whether verbal particles can be modified or not. A PP containing a verbal particle plus some other material can be modified by a modifier expressing degree or orientation (236).

(236) közvetlenül / majdnem / egyenesen be az ágy alá
directly / almost / straight in the bed under_to
'directly / almost / straight in (to) under the bed'

In these cases, however, it is not clear whether the scope of the modifier is the particle only, or a larger PP structure containing the particle and the other PP-internal material (here: *az ágy alá*).

A degree modifier can also appear when the PP is in the verbal modifier position and contains only the particle (237).

(237) Ili teljesen be-verte a szöget.
Ili completely in-hammer.Past.DefObj.3Sg the nail.Acc
'Ili hammered in the nail completely.'

In these cases it is unclear whether the scope of modification is the PP (i.e., the particle) only, or the whole verb phrase containing the particle and the verb. In some cases a modifier can disambiguate between two different readings of a particle+verb unit. *Be-fut* lit. 'in-run', for instance, has a directional reading, 'run in', and an idiomatic reading, 'make it, become successful'. The modifier *egyenesen* 'straight' is grammatical only with the former reading.

(238) a. A zenész be-futott.
the musician in-run.Past.3Sg
'[The musician ran in.] / [The musician became successful.]'

b. A zenész egyenesen be-futott.
the musician straight in-run.Past.3Sg
'The musician ran straight in.' (Not: 'The musician became successful straight away.')

*III. The particle+*felé *construction*

Directional verbal particles can co-occur with the case-like P *felé* 'towards'. (This P is used by some speakers in the form *fele*). *Felé* expresses an unbounded path and like other case-like Ps, normally takes an NP complement (239).

(239) Ili a folyó felé sétált.
Ili the river towards walk.Past.3Sg
'Ili was walking towards the river.'

Its combination with verbal particles is illustrated in (240).

(240) Ili ki-felé / be-felé / fel-felé / le-felé sétált.
Ili out-towards / in-towards / up-towards / down-towards walk.Past.3Sg
'Ili was walking outwards / inwards / upwards / downwards.'

A verbal particle combined with *felé / fele* 'towards' indicates that the subject is moving along a path towards an endpoint, but this endpoint is not yet reached. Compare (240) with (241):

(241) Ili ki / be / fel / le sétált.
Ili out / in / up / down walk.Past.3Sg
'Ili walked out / in / up / down.'

The combination of *felé / fele* with the particle *el* away is somewhat restricted: it is more felicitous with 'come' than with 'go', for instance (242).

(242) a. Épp mentünk el-(?*fele) a kórházba, amikor ...
just go.Past.1Pl away-towards the hospital.Ill when
'We were going to the hospital when…'

b. Épp jöttünk el-(?fele) a kórházból, amikor ...
just come.Past.1Pl away-towards the hospital.Ela when
'We were coming away from the hospital when…'

In spoken Hungarian, it is not uncommon for a verbal particle with a purely telicizing meaning to combine with *felé / fele* 'towards' either. These combinations express that the event is in progress and has not culminated yet. This construction appears to be best with the *fele* allomorph used in imperative sentences (243), and is especially common in the northeastern dialects (J. Soltész 1959: 180).

(243) a. Írd meg-(%fele) a leckét!
write.Subj.2Sg Perf-towards the homework.Acc
'Write your homework!'

b. Egyed meg-(%fele) a levest!
eat.Subj.2Sg Perf-towards the soup.Acc
'Eat your soup!'

IV. Two particles with one verb

It is normally not possible for one verb to combine with more than one verbal particle. There are, however, some systematic exceptions to this.

A. Reduplication

Verbal particles can be reduplicated (J. Soltész 1959, Piñón 1991, Kiefer 1995, Halm 2015); this expresses irregular iteration of the event (244). Observe that this is a case of full reduplication: with bisyllabic particles both syllables take part in the process.

(244) ki-ki-nyit, meg-meg-áll vissza-vissza-néz
out-out-open Perf-Perf-stop back-back-look
'open (wide) occasionally, stop from time to time, look back from time to time'

As pointed out in Halm (2015), reduplicated particles are compatible with adverbials such as 'daily' or 'regularly' (245). In these cases we still have irregular event iteration, however: there are regular intervals at which the event is irregularly repeated.

(245) Ili rendszeresen / naponta ki-ki-nyitja az ablakot.
Ili regularly / daily out-out-open.DefObj.3Sg the window.Acc
'Ili occasionally opens the window, and this happens regularly / every day.'

In indicative sentences, reduplicated verbal particles must be immediately preverbal. They cannot appear in the interrupted or the inverse order, therefore they are incompatible with the emphatic clitic *is* 'also, too' (246a), or phenomena that require particles to be postverbal (focus, negation, etc.), as in (246b,c). (On the emphatic particle *is*, see the volume on Sentence Structure.)

(246) a. *Ili ki-ki is nyitja az ablakot.
Ili out-out Emph open.DefObj.3Sg the window.Acc
Intended meaning: 'Ili does occasionally open the window.'

b. ??ILI nyitja ki-ki az ablakot.
Ili open.DefObj.3Sg out-out the window.Acc
'It is Ili that occasionally opens the window.'

c. *Ili nem nyitja ki-ki az ablakot.
Ili not open.DefObj.3Sg out-out the window.Acc
Intended meaning: 'Ili does not open the window occasionally.'

In conditional sentences, however, the acceptability of the interrupted order significantly improves (247).

(247) Ha Ili ki-ki is nyitja az ablakot, …
if Ili out-out Emph open.DefObj.3Sg the window.Acc
'Even if Ili occasionally opens the window...'

In conditionals the emphatic particle can also appear postverbally (248a), which is independent of particle reduplication (248b).

(248)a. Ha Ili ki-ki nyitja is az ablakot, ...
if Ili out-out open.DefObj.3Sg Emph the window.Acc
'Even if Ili occasionally opens the window...'

b. Ha Ili ki nyitja is az ablakot, ...
if Ili out open.DefObj.3Sg Emph the window.Acc
'Even if Ili opens the window...'

In contrast to non-reduplicated verbal particles, reduplicated ones cannot serve as short answers to questions. Compare (249) and (250):

(249) a. Ki-nyitotta Ili az ablakot?
out-open.DefObj.3Sg Ili the window.Acc
'Did Ili open the window?'

b. Ki.
out
'Yes, she did.'

(250) a. Ki-ki-nyitotta Ili az ablakot?
out-out-open.Past.DefObj.3Sg Ili the window.Acc
'Did Ili open the window occasionally?'

b. *Ki-ki.
out-out
Intended meaning: 'Yes, she did.'

A further difference between non-reduplicated and reduplicated particles is that the latter cannot undergo contrastive topicalization (251).

(251) a. [Ki]$_{\text{CTopic}}$ ILI nyitotta az ablakot.
out Ili open.Past.DefObj.3Sg the window.Acc
'As for opening the window, it was Ili who did it.'

b. *[Ki-ki]$_{\text{CTopic}}$ ILI nyitotta az ablakot.
out-out Ili open.Past.DefObj.3Sg the window.Acc
Intended meaning: 'As for opening the window occasionally, it was Ili who did it.'

B. Semantic opposites

A single verb can occur with two particles if these have a directional reading and are semantic opposites of each other (J. Soltész 1959, Piñón 1991, Kiefer 1995), as in (252). This is the so-called oppositional construction, which expresses that the event has two (or more) opposite directions.

(252) ki-be ugrál, fel-le jár, oda-vissza szaladgál
out-in jump up-down walk there-back run_around
'jump in and out, pace up and down, run back and forth'

The two particles in the oppositional construction usually have a highly preferred order. While in addition to the default *fel-le* 'up-down' the reverse order *le-fel* 'down-up' is equally possible, *ki-be* 'out-in' is preferred over $^{?}$*be-ki* 'in-out', and the order in *oda-vissza* 'back and forth' is strictly fixed: **vissza-oda*.

In the oppositional construction the two particles can also appear in the interrupted and the inverse order, as in (253) (but they cannot be separated from each other).

(253) a. Ili ki-be is ugrált.
Ili out-in Emph jump.Past.3Sg
'Ili did jump in and out.'

b. ILI ugrált ki-be.
Ili jump.Past.3Sg out-in
'It is Ili that jumped in and out.'

c. Ili nem ugrált ki-be.
Ili not jump.Past.3Sg out-in
'Ili did not jump in and out.'

This indicates that the two particles occupy one syntactic slot and they are probably in an asyndetic coordination structure. In some cases it is even possible for an overt coordinator to appear between the two particles. (In previous stages of Hungarian, this was more widesperead, cf. J. Soltész 1959.)

(254) Ili fel s alá sétál.
Ili up and under walk.3Sg
'Ili is walking up and down.'

Note that the order of the two particles in (254) is fixed: **alá s fel sétál* 'down and up walk'.

The particles in the oppositional construction can undergo contrastive topicalization (but they can only do so together), as shown in (255).

(255) [Ki-be]$_{\text{CTopic}}$ ILI ugrált az ablakon.
in-out Ili jump.Past.3Sg the window.Sup
'As for jumping in and out though the window, it was Ili who did it.'

As short answers to questions such particle combinations are severely degraded (256).

(256) a. Ki-be ugrált Ili az ablakon?
in-out jump.Past.3Sg Ili the window.Sup
'Did Ili jump in and out through the window?'

b. *?Ki-be.
in-out
'Yes, she did.'

2.2.4. Adverbs

As explained in detail in Chapter 1, this book does not assume a lexical category 'adverb'; lexical items that have traditionally been categorized as adverbs are viewed as PPs headed by an opaque P head with little conceptual-semantic content. However, for the sake of convenience, we will retain the term "adverb" to refer to these elements, bearing in mind that they are, in fact, PPs.

In this section we will zoom in on the formal properties of adverbs. We will start the discussion in Section 2.2.4.1 with those adverbs that are formed with the help of a suffix. In Section 2.2.4.2 we turn to adverbs that are form-identical to adjectives. Finally in Section 2.2.4.3 we discuss adverbs that are not derived by an overt affix and are, at the same time, not form-identical to adjectives either.

2.2.4.1. Adverbs derived by suffixation

2.2.4.1.1. Adverbs derived by productive suffixes

I. The -va/-ve *suffix*

The *-va/-ve* suffix productively attaches to verbs to yield adverbial participles (also called converbs). These are used in the clause as adverbials of manner or state (257).

(257) a. Ili áll-va / megkötöz-ve / üvölt-ve várta Petit.
Ili stand-Part / tied_up-Part / shout-Part wait.Past.DefObj.3Sg Peti.Acc
'Ili was waiting for Peti standing / [tied up] / shouting.'

b. Ili megkötöz-ve találta Petit.
Ili tied_up-Part find.Past.DefObj.3Sg Peti.Acc
'Ili found Peti tied up.'

The forms in *-va/-ve* are, in fact, non-finite adverbial clauses. Their clausal status is shown by the fact that a transitive verb with *-va/-ve* takes an accusative-marked direct object and di-transitive verbs also take a dative-marked recipient / beneficiary (258).

(258) a. Ili [a kerítés-t át-ugor-va] jött Petihez.
Ili the fence-Acc across-jump-Part come.Past.3Sg Peti.All
'Ili came to Peti by jumping across the fence.'

b. [A level-et mindenkinek elküld-ve] Ili elkerüli a büntetést.
the letter-Acc everyone.Dat away.send-Part Ili avoid.DefObj.3Sg the punishment.Acc
'By sending the letter to everyone, Ili avoids punishment.'

Given their clausal status, *-va/-ve* forms are discussed in detail in the volume on Non-Finite and Semi-Finite Verb Phrases. The reason why they are also relevant here is that some adverbial participial forms have grammaticalized (or are on their way to grammaticalizing) into adverbs. An example is given in (259): *készakarva* 'on purpose' comprises *kész* 'ready' and the participial form of *akar* 'want', but the full form has a non-compositional lexical meaning and unlike in the case of genuine participial clauses, no adverbial or PP-modifiers are admitted.

(259) készakarva
on.purpose
'on purpose'

Further examples are discussed in Chapter 7.

II. The -n/-an/-en *suffix*

Adverbs can be productively derived from adjectives with the so-called modal-essive suffix *-n/-an/-en*, one of the equivalents of the English *-ly* suffix (260).

(260) szép-en, forró-n, gyors-an, szerencsés-en, piros-an, drágá-n
nice-ly hot-ly quick-ly lucky-ly red-ly expensive-ly
'nicely, hotly, quickly, luckily, red[ly], expensively'

In a few cases, the suffix appears in the *-on* form (261). This, however, is the exception rather than the rule, thus below we will refer to the suffix as *-n/-an/-en.*

(261) nagy-on, szabad-on, vak-on, gazdag-on
big-ly free-ly blind-ly rich-ly
'very, freely, blindly, richly'

Adjectives in the comparative and superlative form (262a) and derived adjectives (262b) are also inputs to *-n/-an/-en* suffixation.

(262) a. gyors-abb-an, a leg-gyors-abb-an
fast-Comp-ly the Sprl-fast-Comp-ly
'more fast, [in] the fastest [way]'

b. erő-s-en, lát-ható-an
power-Adj-ly see-Part-ly
'strongly, visibly'

In a few cases the *-n/-an/-en* adverb is not built directly on the adjective, instead, the adjective and the corresponding adverb are both built on the same bound root (263).

(263) gyakor-, gyakor-i, gyakr-an
frequent frequent-Attr frequent-ly
'frequent (bound stem), frequent, frequently'

Adjectives ending in the *-i* (attributivizing) suffix, the *-beli* (attributivizing) suffix and in the *-nyi* suffix (corresponding to English *-ful*) do not productively serve as inputs to *-n/-an/-en* suffixation (Kiefer and Ladányi 2000a: 208). Relational and abstract adjectives with the *-i* suffix can, however, take the adverbial suffix (Kenesei, Vágó and Fenyvesi 1998: 371-372). Adjectives with the caritive suffix *-tlan/-tlen* cannot be suffixed by *-n/-an/-en;* they take the *-ul/-ül* suffix instead (see below). The *-n/-an/-en* suffix is a closing morpheme: no other suffix can be added after it (Kiefer and Ladányi 2000a, Rebrus 2000).

The adjectives *nagy* 'big' and *kis / kicsi* 'small' form an interesting minimal pair when it comes to *-n/-an/-en* suffixation. *Nagy* 'big' undergoes *-n/-an/-en* suffixation, yielding the degree adverb 'very' (264a). The degree adverb from *kis* and *kicsi* 'small' is formed differently, however: *kis* is suffixed by the translative case (Simonyi 1888: 338, 1895: 644), while *kicsi* takes the special form *kicsit* (264).

(264) a. nagy-on
big-ly
'very'

b. kissé, kicsit
small.TrE a_bit
both: 'a bit, a little'

Adverbs formed with *-n/-an/-en* generally serve as manner and depictive adverbs in the clause.

(265)	Ili	gyors-an / zöld-en	szedte	le	az	almát.
	Ili	quick-ly / green-ly	pick.Past.DefObj.3Sg	down	the	apple.Acc

'Ili picked the apples quickly / [while still] green.'

The modal-essive suffix is cognate with but not identical to the superessive case suffix (see Simonyi 1888: 201, Simonyi 1895: 657, Klemm 1928: 191, Tompa 1968: 205, S. Hámori and Tompa 1970: 575-577, Kádár 2009). While on common nouns and proper names the superessive case has four allomorphs, *-n/-on/-en/-ön* (266a), the modal-essive suffix has the allomorphs: *-n/-an/-en* (266b) and the rare *-on* mentioned in connection with (261).

(266) a.	az almá-n,	az asztal-on,	a szék-en,	a tölgy-ön
	the apple-Sup	the table-Sup	the chair-Sup	the oak-Sup

'on the apple, on the table, on the chair, on the oak'

b.	csúnyá-n,	magas-an,	féltékeny-en,	tömör-en
	ugly-ly	high-ly	jealous-ly	succinct-ly

'in an ugly way, highly, jealously, succinctly'

If the adjective from which the *-n/-an/-en* adverb is built has a complement, then this complement is retained after *-n/-an/-en* suffixation as well (267b).

(267) a.	büszke	valami-re,	féltékeny	valaki-re,	elégedett	valami-vel
	proud	something-Sub	jealous	somebody-Sub	satisfied	something-Ins

'proud of something, jealous of somebody, satisfied with something'

b.	büszké-n	valami-re,	féltékeny-en	valaki-re,	elégedett-en	valami-vel
	proud-ly	something-Sub	jealous-ly	somebody-Sub	satisfied-ly	something-Ins

'proudly of something, jealously of somebody, satisfied with something.'

The adverbs formed by *-n/-an/-en* can be modified by degree modifiers. Some examples of possible modifiers are given in (268).

(268)	nagyon,	túl,	kissé,	valamelyest,	elég
	very	overly	slightly	somewhat	enough

The modification of both adjectives and adverbs formed by *-n/-an/-en* is illustrated in (269).

(269) a. nagyon / túl / kissé / valamelyest / elég drága
very / overly / slightly / somewhat / enough expensive
'very / overly / slightly / somewhat / rather expensive'

b. nagyon / túl / kissé / valamelyest / elég drágá-n
very / overly / slightly / somewhat / enough expensive-ly
'very / overly / slightly / somewhat / rather expensively'

III. The -ul/-ül *suffix*

The so-called essive(-modal) *-ul/-ül* suffix also combines with adjectives to yield adverbs. It is in complementary distribution with the modal-essive suffix *-n/-an/-en*; (Kenesei *et al.* 1998: 371, Kiefer and Ladányi 2000a). Some examples are given in (270): the adjectives listed here only combine with *-ul/-ül* and not with *-n/-an/-en.*

(270) rossz-ul, jó-l, józan-ul
bad-ly good-ly sober-ly
'badly / wrongly, well, soberly'

There are two types of adjectives that always take *-ul/-ül* instead of *-n/-an/-en.* The first type is adjectives of nationality: the adverbs derived by *-ul/-ül* express that somebody is speaking (learning, reading, etc.) a particular language (271). In this use, the vowel of the suffix is always retained, even if the stem ends in a vowel.

(271) magyar-ul, angol-ul, német-ül, igbó-ul, zulu-ul
Hungarian-ly English-ly German-ly Igbo-ly Zulu-ly
'in Hungarian, in English, in German in Igbo in Zulu'

Remark 12. *Magyar-ul* in (271) is ambiguous between the compositional meaning 'speaking or learning Hungarian' and an idiomatic meaning 'bluntly, that is'. The exceptional form *magyarán* only has the idiomatic meaning.

The second type is adjectives ending in the caritive (also known as abessive or privative) suffix *-tlan/-tlen;* these also must take *-ul/-ül* instead of *-n/-an/-en* (272).

(272) erő-tlen-ül, határ-talan-ul, bátor-talan-ul, feltét-len-ül
power-Car-ly boundary-Car-ly brave-Car-ly condition-Car-ly
'feebly, boundlessly, timidly, by all means'

As pointed out in Simonyi (1888: 330), the adjectivalizing suffix *-os/-es/-ös* is the semantic opposite of the caritive suffix (the former expresses the property of having something, while the latter expresses lack of something). Adjectives with *-os/-es/-ös* are adverbialized with the *-n/-an/-en* suffix, e.g. *pont-os-an* point-Adj-ly 'exactly'.

In some cases the base form of the adjective takes the *-ul/-ül* suffix, while the comparative form of the same adjective must (273a) or may (273b) take the *-n/-an/-en* suffix (Simonyi 1888: 330).

(273) a. jó-l, jo-bb-an
good-ly good-Comp-ly
'well, better'

b. vad-ul, vad-abb-an / vad-abb-ul
wild-ly wild-Comp-ly / wild-Comp-ly
'wildly, more wildly'

Note that in addition to adjectives, the *-ul/-ül* suffix can also combine with certain nouns (274).

(274) a. ember-ül / vitéz-ül / paraszt-ul viselkedik
man-ly / hero-ly / peasant-ly behave
'behave bravely / valiantly / boorishly'

b. zálog-ul ad, bizonyíték-ul szolgál, zsákmány-ul ejt, vendég-ül lát,
collateral-ly give proof-ly serve prey-ly take guest-ly see
segítség-ül hív, feleség-ül vesz
help-ly call wife-ly take
'give as a collateral, serve as proof, catch sth as prey, entertain [at home or for a meal], call to help, marry a woman (lit. take as wife)'

c. vég-ül, példá-ul
end-ly, example-ly
'finally, for example'

In this use, its meaning is similar to that of the essive-formal case (*-ként*) discussed in Section 2.2.1.1, and can often be substituted by this suffix as well as the particle *mint* 'as', the case-like postposition *gyanánt* 'as, in the guise of', or the adverbial suffix *-képp(en)* 'as' discussed in Section 2.2.4.1.2. Compare (274) and (275):

(275) a. Ili zálog-ként adta az ékszert.
Ili collateral-FoE give.Past.DefObj.3Sg the jewel.Acc.
'Ili gave the jewel as collateral.'

b. Ili mint zálog-ot adta az ékszert.
Ili as collateral-Acc give.Past.DefObj.3Sg the jewel.Acc
'Ili gave the jewel as collateral.'

c. Ili zálog-képp(en) / [zálog gyanánt] adta az ékszert.
Ili collateral-For / collateral as give.Past.DefObj.3Sg the jewel.Acc
'Ili gave the jewel as collateral.'

The *-ul/-ül* suffix is a closing morpheme, that is, no other suffix can be added after it (Rebrus 2000). Some works regard the *-ul/-ül* on adjectives and the *-ul/-ül* on nouns as two different, homonymous suffixes (see e.g. Kiefer and Ladányi 2000a, de Groot 2017).

2.2.4.1.2. Adverbs formed by semi-productive and miscellaneous suffixes

Adverbs can also be derived by semi-productive or miscellaneous suffixes (which we will take to be spellouts of P heads in syntax). When this is compatible with their meaning, these adverbs, too, can be modified by the degree adverbs in (268).

I. The -lag/-leg *suffix*

Adverbs can be derived from adjectives and present participles with the so-called modal suffix *-lag/-leg*. The meaning of this suffix is basically the same as that of *-n/-an/-en* (S. Hámori and Tompa 1970: 577-578, Kenesei *et al.* 1998: 372); that is, it is comparable to English *-ly*. Stems taking *-lag/-leg* normally end in I) *-ó/-ő* or *-ú/-ű* (276a) or II) the attributivizer *-i* suffix (276b). There are also lexicalized cases in which *-lag/-leg* is added to an uninflected noun (276c).

(276) a. valószínű-leg, utó-lag, futó-lag, állít-ó-lag, fő-leg
likely-ly after-ly passing-ly claim-Part-ly main-ly
'presumably, subsequently, briefly, allegedly, mainly'

b. test-i-leg, elv-i-leg, kép-i-leg, eredet-i-leg, egyén-i-leg
body-Attr-ly principle-Attr-ly picture-Attr-ly original-Attr-ly individual-Attr-ly
'physically, theoretically, pictorially / visually, originally, individually'

c. jelen-leg, név-leg, tett-leg, arány-lag, tény-leg
present-ly name-ly action-ly ratio-ly fact-ly
'right now, nominally, physically, relatively, genuinely'

It is not the case that all stems ending in *-ó/-ő, or -ú/-ű* combine with *-lag/-leg;* some take the modal-essive *-n/-an/-en* suffix instead.

(277) egyszerű-en, feltehető-en, egyértelmű-en, forró-n
simple-ly assumable-ly unambiguous-ly hot-ly
'simply, likely, straightforwardly, hot'

Kiefer and Ladányi (2000a) claim that this suffix is in complementary distribution with both the *-n/-an/-en* suffix and the *-ul/-ül* suffix, though there are some cases in which an adjective can take either *-n/-an/-en* or *-lag/-leg* (278).

(278) feltehető-en, feltehető-leg
assumable-ly assumable-ly
both: 'likely'

Note also that unlike *-n/-an/-en* and *-ul/-ül, -lag/-leg* is not a closing morpheme: other suffixes can be added after it (Rebrus 2000).

(279) eset-leg-es-en, eset-leg-es-ség
case-ly-Adj-ly case-ly-Adj-ness
'perhaps, eventuality'

The use of this suffix is gradually spreading to more adjectives, especially in spoken Hungarian (Kiefer and Ladányi 2000a).

II. The sociative suffix -(V)stul/-(V)stül

The sociative suffix *(-stul/-stül/-ostul/-estül/-östül)* expresses that "the action is carried out in unity with another person or object" (Fekete 2013: 2). Representative examples are given in (280).

(280) a. Az emberek család-ostul mennek a parkokba.
the people.Pl family-Soc go.3Pl the park.Pl.Ill
'People go to the parks with their family.'

b. Ili cipő-stül / ruhá-stul ugrott a medencébe
Ili shoe-Soc / clothing-Soc jump.Past.3Sg the pool.Ill
'Ili jumped into the pool with her shoes / clothes on.'

For some speakers the *u/ü* vowel of the suffix is replaced by *ó/ő* (281):

(281) Az emberek család-ostól mennek a parkokba.
the people.Pl family-Soc go.3Pl the park.Pl.Ill
'People go to the parks with their family.'

The meaning of the sociative suffix is comparable to the comitative function of the instrumental case suffix. In some cases either of them can be used without a change in meaning (282); this mostly happens when the instrumental case suffix follows the possessive suffix.

(282) a. Ili család-ostul jött a rendezvényre.
Ili family-Soc come.Past.3Sg the program.Sub
'Ili came to the program with her family.'

b. Ili a család-já-val jött a rendezvényre.
Ili the family-Poss-Ins come.Past.3Sg the program.Sub
'Ili came to the program with her family.'

In many cases both suffixes can be followed by the postposition *együtt* 'together' (283). (This is not possible with the instrumental use of the instrumental suffix and in set expressions involving the sociative suffix, however.)

(283) a. Ili család-ostul együtt jött a rendezvényre.
Ili family-Soc together come.Past.3Sg the program.Sub
'Ili came to the program with her family.'

b. Ili a család-já-val együtt jött a rendezvényre.
Ili the family-Poss-Ins together come.Past.3Sg the program.Sub
'Ili came to the program with her family.'

In other contexts either the sociative or the instrumental can be used, but with a difference in meaning. In (284a), for instance, Ili had to have her shoes on when she jumped into the pool. In (284b) this is a possible reading, but here it may be the case that Ili had a shoe in her hand when she jumped.

(284) a. Ili cipő-stül ugrott a medencébe.
Ili shoe-Soc jump.Past.3Sg the pool.Ill
'Ili jumped into the pool with her shoes on.'

b. Ili cipő-vel ugrott a medencébe.
Ili shoe-Ins jump.Past.3Sg the pool.Ill
'Ili jumped into the pool with [a shoe] / shoes.'

In some expressions the sociative suffix is the unmarked choice; then it can only be replaced with the combination of the instrumental suffix and the postposition *együtt* 'together' (285).

(285) a.	Ili	kamat-ostul	vissza-fizeti	a	kölcsönt.	
	Ili	interest-Soc	back-pay.3Sg	the	loan.Acc	
	'Ili repays the loan with interest.'					
b.	Ili	kamat-tal	*(együtt)	vissza-fizeti	a	kölcsönt.
	Ili	interest-Ins	together	back-pay.3Sg	the	loan.Acc
	'Ili repays the loan with interest.'					

In a few set expressions, such as the examples in (286), the sociative suffix is completely frozen and irrespective of the presence or absence of *együtt* 'together', it cannot be replaced by the instrumental case suffix.

(286) a.	Ili	fenek-estül	felforgatta	a	házat.		
	Ili	bottom-Soc	up.turn.Past.3Sg	the	house.Acc		
	'Ili turned the house upside down.'						
a'.	*Ili	fenék-kel	(együtt)	felforgatta	a	házat.	
	Ili	bottom-Ins	together	up.turn.Past.3Sg	the	house.Acc	
	Intended meaning: 'Ili turned the house upside down.'						
b.	A	farkas	szőr-östül-bőr-östül	megette	a	nyulat.	
	the	wolf	hair-Soc-skin-Soc	Perf.eat.Past.DefObj.3Sg	the	rabbit.Acc	
	'The wolf ate the rabbit fur and all.'						
b'.	*A	farkas	szőr-rel-bőr-rel	(együtt)	megette	a	nyulat.
	the	wolf	hair-Ins-skin-Ins	together	Perf.eat.Past.DefObj.3Sg	the	rabbit.Acc
	Intended meaning: 'The wolf ate the rabbit fur and all.'						

The use of the sociative suffix is more restricted than that of the instrumental case suffix both in terms of semantics and syntax. As for semantics, the instrumental case has both a comitative and an instrumental use (287).

(287) a.	Ili	Tas-sal	érkezett	a	fogadásra.	
	Ili	Tas-Soc	arrive.Past.3Sg	the	reception.Sub	
	'Ili come to the reception with Tas.'					
b.	Ili	kés-sel	vágta	fel	a	kenyeret.
	Ili	knife-Ins	cut.Past.DefObj.3Sg	up	the	bread.Acc
	'Ili has cut up the bread with a knife.'					

The sociative, on the other hand, has no instrumental use; it can only express a (regular, frequent) comitative relationship. (288) has the pragmatically odd meaning that Ili has cut up both the bread and the knife; the knife cannot be understood as the instrument of cutting.

(288)	#Ili	kés-estül	vágta	fel	a	kenyeret.
	Ili	knife-Soc	cut.Past.DefObj.3Sg	up	the	bread.Acc
	'Ili has cut up the bread together with the knife.'					

As far as syntax is concerned, the nominal complement of the instrumental case can bear nominal inflections (such as the possessive suffix and the plural suffix), and it can also have modifiers such as the demonstrative, the definite article, numerals or adjectives (289).

(289) a. Ili ezzel a három szép rózsá-val lepte meg Editet.
Ili this.Ins the three petty rose-Ins surprise Perf Edit.Acc
'Ili has surprised Edit with these three pretty roses.'

b. a mi könyv-e-i-nk-kel
the we book-Poss-Pl-Poss.1Pl-Ins
'with our books'

The sociative, however, only attaches to an unmodified and uninflected common noun (see also Kiefer 2003: 201). The impossibility of modification is shown in (290).

(290) a. *Ili a cipő-stül ugrott a medencébe. [definite article]
Ili the shoe-Soc jump.Past.3Sg the pool.Ill
Intended meaning: 'Ili jumped into the pool with the shoe on.'

b. *Ili ama cipő-stül ugrott a medencébe. [demonstrative]
Ili that shoe-Soc jump.Past.3Sg the pool.Ill
Intended meaning: 'Ili jumped into the pool with that shoe on.'

c. *Ili egy cipő-stül ugrott a medencébe. [indefinite article]
Ili a shoe-Soc jump.Past.3Sg the pool.Ill
Intended meaning: 'Ili jumped into the pool with a shoe on.'

d. *Ili két cipő-stül ugrott a medencébe. [numeral]
Ili two shoe-Soc jump.Past.3Sg the pool.Ill
Intended meaning: 'Ili jumped into the pool with two shoes on.'

e. *Ili piros cipő-stül ugrott a medencébe. [adjective]
Ili red shoe-Soc jump.Past.3Sg the pool.Ill
Intended meaning: 'Ili jumped into the pool with red shoes on.'

The fact that the complement of the sociative suffix must be uninflected in illustrated in (291).

(291) a. *Ili cipő-jé-stül ugrott a medencébe. [possessive suffix]
Ili shoe-Poss-Soc jump.Past.3Sg the pool.Ill
Intended meaning: 'Ili jumped into the pool with her shoe(s) on.'

b. *Ili cipő-k-östül ugrott a medencébe. [plural suffix]
Ili shoe-Pl-Soc jump.Past.3Sg the pool.Ill
Intended meaning: 'Ili jumped into the pool with shoes on.'

Certain nouns, including kinship terms, are typically possessed. When these nouns combine with the sociative suffix, they do so without the noun taking any possessive suffix. Compare (292a) and (292b): while the former features the sociative suffix combining with a bare noun, the latter features the instrumental suffix, and in this case the noun must be possessed.

(292) a. Imi feleség-estül jött a rendezvényre.
Imi wife-Soc come.Past.3Sg the program.Sub
'Imi came to the program with his wife.'

b. Imi a feleség-é-vel jött a rendezvényre.
Imi the wife-Poss-Ins come.Past.3Sg the program.Sub
'Imi came to the program with his wife.'

That the complement of the sociative must be a common noun in shown in (293).

(293) a. Ili Péter-rel / *Péter-estül megy a parkba. [proper name]
Ili Péter-Ins / Péter-Soc go.3Sg the park.Ill
'Ili goes to the park with Péter.'

b. Ili én-vel-em / *én-estül-em megy a parkba. [personal pronoun]
Ili I-Ins-1Sg / I-Soc -1Sg go.3Sg the park.Ill
'Ili goes to the park with me.'

c. Ili az-zal / *az-ostul megy a parkba. [demonstrative pronoun]
Ili that-Ins / that-Soc go.3Sg the park.Ill
'Ili goes to the park with that [e.g. her dog].'

Taken together, (289) through (293) show that the complement of the sociative suffix must be structurally very small, specifically it must be a bare NP. As all inflectional suffixes and N-modifiers are introduced above this layer, their co-occurrence with the sociative is excluded. Proper names and pronouns also involve more structure than an NP: they are DPs, and so they do not combine with the sociative either.

III. The locative -nn *and* -nt *suffix*

Directional verbal particles (with the exception of *el* 'away') can combine with the *-nn* or *-nt* locative P suffix (294). The resulting forms have a spatial, non-directional (locative) meaning.

(294) a. le, lenn, lent
down(dir) down(loc) down(loc)

b. fel, fenn, fent
up(dir) up(loc) up(loc)

c. ki, kinn, kint
out(dir) outside outside

d. be, benn, bent
in(dir) inside inside

e. el, *el-nn, *el-nt
away away(loc) away(loc)

In the adverbs listed in (294) the choice between *-nn* or *-nt* is a matter of idiolect or dialect. (Note that the final consonant of *fel* 'up' is dropped before these suffixes.) However, in compounds either one or the other form is normally lexicalized, as in the examples in (295).

(295) a. benn-szülött, benn-fent-es
inside-born inside-up-Adj
'aboriginal, insider'

a'. bent-lakás-os iskola
inside-living-Adj school
'boarding school'

b. fenn-sík, fenn-tartó
above-plane above-keeper
'highland, maintainer'

b'. fent-nevezett
above-mentioned
'above mentioned'

The adverbs in (294) have a comparative and a superlative form. Comparatives and superlatives based on the *-nt* versions (297a',b',c',d') are highly preferred over those based on the *-nn* versions (297a'',b'',c'',d''). In the comparative and the superlative *-nt* or *-nn* may be replaced by *-jj* (in the case of *lent* 'down' and *kint* 'outside') or *-lj* (in the case of *fent* 'up' and *bent* 'inside'), as in (297a,b,c,d). For some speakers, these are the most neutral forms.

(296) • Comparative and superlative form of adjectives
magas, magas-abb, leg-magas-abb
tall tall-Comp Sprl-tall-Comp
'tall, taller, tallest'

(297) • Comparative and superlative forms of *-nn* and *-nt* PPs
a. lejj-ebb, leg-lejj-ebb
down-Comp Sprl-down-Comp
'lower down, most down'

a'. lent-ebb, leg-lent-ebb
down-Comp Sprl-down-Comp
'lower down, most down'

a''. %lenn-ebb, %leg-lenn-ebb
down-Comp Sprl-down-Comp
'lower down, most down'

b. felj-ebb, leg-felj-ebb
up-Comp Sprl-up-Comp
'higher up, highest up'

b'. fent-ebb, leg-fent-ebb
up-Comp Sprl-up-Comp
'higher up, highest up'

b''. %fenn-ebb, %leg-fenn-ebb
up-Comp Sprl-up-Comp
'higher up, highest up'

c. kijj-ebb, leg-kijj-ebb
out-Comp Sprl-out-Comp
'further out, furthest out'

c'. kint-ebb, leg-kint-ebb
out-Comp Sprl-out-Comp
'further out, furthest out'

c''. %kinn-ebb, %leg-kinn-ebb
out-Comp Sprl-out-Comp
'further out, furthest out'

d. belj-ebb, leg-belj-ebb
in-Comp Sprl-in-Comp
'further in, furthest in'

d'. bent-ebb, leg-bent-ebb
in-Comp Sprl-in-Comp
'further in, furthest in'

d''. %benn-ebb, %leg-benn-ebb
in-Comp Sprl-in-Comp
'further in, furthest in'

IV.The locative -(Vt)t *suffix*

Some adverbs are formed by the same *-(Vt)t* locative suffix (an obsolete case suffix) that also appears on locative case-like Ps (Section 2.2.2.2.1). Some examples are given in (298a); case-like Ps with *-(Vt)t* are shown in (298b) for comparison.

(298) a. i-tt, o-tt, oldal-t, más-utt, minden-ütt, hany-att
Prox-Loc Dst-Loc side-Loc other-Loc every-Loc on_back-Loc
'here, there, at the side, elsewhere, everywhere, [on one's back] / over'

b. mell-ett, al-att, föl-ött, elő-tt
next_to-Loc under -Loc above -Loc in_front_of-Loc

Remark 13. In some dialects the forms for 'here' and 'there' are adorned with an additional *-an/-en* suffix whose nature and function requires further research. (It is certain that it is not the superessive case, however, as the allomorphs of the superessive are *-on/-en/-ön*; this case has no *-an* allomorph.)

(i) i-tt-en, o-tt-an
Prox-Loc-EN Dst-Loc-AN
'here, there'

Other dialectal forms for 'here' are shown below.

(ii) e-hol, e-hun e-hely-(üt)t
Prox-where Prox-where Prox-place-Loc
all: 'here'

(iii) i-hol
Prox-where
'here'

V. The multiplicative suffix -szor/-szer/-ször

The multiplicative suffix (*-szor/-szer/-ször*) combines with numerals and some quantifiers, including *pár* 'a few', *több* 'more', *kevés* 'few' and *sok* 'many, a lot'. The resulting complex form expresses that the action has taken place X times. An example is given in (299). (See also N2.6.1.1.5.5 and N2.6.2.4.4. point *III*).

(299) Ili három-szor / sok-szor járt Brazíliában.
Ili three-Mult / many-Mult go.Past.3Sg Brazil.Ine
'Ili has been to Brazil three / many times.'

Numerals also combine with the accusative case marker to yield adverbs that quantify over events. The accusative and the multiplicative suffix give rise to different meanings, however. Compare (300a) with (300b):

(300) a. Imi négy-szer kopogott.
Imi four-Mult knock.Past.3Sg
'Imi knocked four times.' (four events of knocking)

b. Imi négy-et kopogott.
Imi four-Acc knock.Past.3Sg
'Imi made four knocks [on the door].' (one event of knocking involving four knocks)

Accusative-marked numerals are used only in combination with transitive verbs. (301) shows that *kopogni* 'to knock', seen in (300b), can take NP/DP objects.

(301) Pál morzejelek-et kopogott az asztalon.
Pál morse.sign.Pl-Acc knock.Past.3Sg the table.Sup
'Pál knocked Morse code on the table.'

(302) demonstrates that *biciklizni* 'to bike' does not take NP/DP objects, and it does not combine with accusative-marked numerals either.

(302) a. Pál (*kirándulások-at / *zarándoklatok-at) biciklizik.
Pál excursion.Pl-Acc / pilgrimage.Pl-Acc bike.3Sg
'Pál goes (on excursions / pilgrimages) biking.'

b. Pál (*négy-et) biciklizik.
Pál four-Acc bike.3Sg
'Pál bikes (four times).'

This can be accounted for if accusative-marked numerals are actually modifiers of an ellipted object. As described in Remark 2., nominal ellipsis affects the head noun (and potentially some of its modifiers), but it strands the noun's number and case-marker. These stranded suffixes then attach to the last overt N-modifier in the nominal phrase. Thus in accusative marked NumPs that consist of a numeral and a noun, nominal ellipsis causes the accusative case suffix to attach to the numeral.

(303) a. [$_{\text{NUMP}}$ numeral [$_{\text{NP}}$ ~~noun~~]]-accusative [syntactic input]
b. numeral-accusative [morphological output]

There is one exception to the generalization that accusative marked numerals combine only with transitive verbs. *Egyet*, the accusative form of *egy* 'one' can also appear with intransitive predicates (304).

(304) Pál biciklizik egy-et.
Pál bike.3Sg one-Acc
'Pál goes biking.'

In this use *egyet* 'one-Acc' is referred to as a pseudo-object. The contrast between (302) and (304) shows that in contrast to accusative marked higher numerals, *egyet* does not have an underlying elliptical syntax. (On pseudo-object *egyet*, see Piñón 2001, Csirmaz 2006c, Farkas 2017, Farkas and Kardos 2018.)

Degree quantifiers may also combine with the accusative case marker to yield adverbs that quantify over events. Here, too, the accusative and the multiplicative suffix give rise to different meanings (305).

(305) a. Imi sok-szor biciklizik.
Imi many-Mult bike.3Sg
'Imi bikes frequently.'

b. Imi sok-at biciklizik.
Imi many-Acc bike.3Sg
'Imi bikes a lot.'

As shown in (305), accusative marked degree quantifiers are not restricted to apprearing with transitive verbs. In this respect they pattern with *egyet* 'one-Acc' rather than with accusative marked numerals.

VI. The distributive suffix -(V)nként

The distributive suffix *-(V)nként* (allomorphs: *-nként/-anként/-enként/-onként/ -önként*) has the meaning 'per N, after every N', as in (306). The *é* vowel of the suffix is not subject to vowel harmony; only the linking vowel is.

(306) Kutyá-nként / Ház-anként 5000 Ft adót kell fizetni
dog-Dist / house-Dist 5000 HUF tax.Acc must pay.Inf
'One must pay 5000 HUF tax per dog / house.'

Names of days productively combine with this suffix, yielding the meaning 'on every name-of-day', as in (307).

(307) Péntek-enként úszni járok.
Friday-Dist swim.Inf go.1Sg
'[On Fridays] / [Every Friday] I go swimming.'

The distributive suffix productively combines with nouns denoting temporal units, too (308).

(308) Het-enként / hav-onként / hónap-onként / év-enként járok úszni.
week-Dist / month-Dist / month-Dist / year-Dist go.1Sg swim.Inf
'I go swimming weekly / monthly / yearly.'

While the noun *nap* 'day' may bear the distributive suffix, *nap-onként* 'day-Dist' is best when a numeral precedes it (309b).

(309) a. $^{?(?)}$János nap-onként úszni jár.
János day-Dist swim.Inf go.3Sg
'János goes swimming daily / [every day].'

b. János két-nap-onként / más-nap-onként úszni jár.
János two-day-Dist / other-day-Dist swim.Inf go.3Sg
'János goes swimming every second / other day.'

The intended meaning of (309a) is best expressed with the iterative suffix discussed in point *VII* below (see (317)).

Hónap 'month' has two stems: the free stem *hónap* and the bound stem *hav-*. The distributive suffix can combine with either, but in both cases a numeral modifier is preferred, just like with *nap-onként* 'day-Dist': (310) and (311).

(310) a. $^{?}$János hav-onként úszni jár. [bound stem]
János month-Dist swim.Inf go.3Sg
'János goes swimming monthly / [every month].'

b. János három-hav-onként úszni jár.
János three-month-Dist swim.Inf go.3Sg
'János goes swimming every three months.'

(311) a. $^{?(?)}$János hónap-onként úszni jár. [free stem]
János month-Dist swim.Inf go.3Sg
'János goes swimming monthly / [every month].'

b. János három-hónap-onként úszni jár.
János three-month-Dist swim.Inf go.3Sg
'János goes swimming every three months.'

The most neutral way of rendering 'monthly' involves the iterative suffix discussed in point *VII* below (see (318e)).

The distributive suffix may also combine with sortal classifiers (e.g. *szál* lit. 'thread', classifying long and thin objects), including the general classifier *darab* 'piece', container classifiers (e.g. *doboz* 'box'), measure classifiers (e.g. *liter* 'liter' or *csepp* 'drop') and group classifiers (e.g. *csapat* 'group'). Examples are given in (312). On classifiers, see N2.4 and N2.6.3.

(312) a. Ez a termék szál-anként / darab-onként / doboz-onként / liter-enként / csepp-enként 100 Ft.
this the product thread-Dist / item-Dist / box-Dist / liter-Dist / drop-Dist 100 HUF
'This product costs 100 HUF per piece / item / box / liter / drop.'

b. A gyerekek csapat-onként két feladatot kapnak.
the child.Pl group-Dist two exercise.Acc get.3Pl
'The children get two [academic] exercises per group.'

Among the names of the times of the day, some but not all combine with the distributive suffix (313).

(313) a. reggel-enként, esté-nként, éjjel-enként
morning-Dist evening-Dist night-Dist
'every morning, every evening, every night'

b. *éjfél-enként, *napnyugtá-nként
midnight-Dist sunset-Dist
Intended meaning: 'every midnight, at every sunset'

Not all names of seasons combine with the distributive suffix either (314). (See also point *VII*).

(314) a. tavasz-onként, nyar-anként, ?tel-enként
spring-Dist summer-Dist winter-Dist
'every spring, every summer, every winter'

b. *ősz-önként
autumn-Dist
Intended meaning: 'every autumn'

The names of the months do not take the distributive suffix (315).

(315) *január-onként, *március-onként, *december-enként
January-Dist March-Dist December-Dist
Intended meaning: 'every January, every March, every December'

There are some set expressions involving the distributive suffix such that the base is an adjective, an adverb or a numeral (316). (Based on Simonyi 1888: 409, it appears to be the case that this suffix was, at some point, used with a wider range of numerals, perhaps productively.)

(316) apránként, lass-anként, egy-enként
tiny.Dist slow-Dist one-Dist
'little by little, bit by bit, one by one'

Another set expression worth mentioning is *hely-enként* lit. place-Dist, which has the meaning 'at a few/some places' rather than the expected 'everywhere'.

VII. The iterative suffix -(V)nta/-(V)nte

A noun denoting a temporal unit such as 'day', 'week' or 'year' may bear the iterative (sometimes also called distributive-temporal) suffix *-(V)nta/-(V)nte* (allomorphs: *-nta/-nte/-onta/-ente/-önte*). The resulting phrase means that the action is repeated regularly, once during every temporal unit denoted by N (317).

(317) Ili nap-onta / het-ente / hav-onta / év-ente eszik egy almát.
Ili day-Iter / week-Iter / month-Iter / year-Iter eat.3Sg an apple.Acc
'Ili eats an apple [once] every day / week / month / year.'

With some nouns naming units of time, either the iterative or the distributive suffix can be used without a change in meaning (318a-d).

(318) a. nap-onta, nap-onként
day-Iter day-Dist
both: 'daily'

b. het-ente, het-enként
week-Iter week-Dist
both: 'weekly'

c. hav-onta, hav-onként
month-Iter month-Dist
both: 'monthly'

d. év-ente, év-enként
year-Iter year-Dist
both: 'yearly'

e. *perc-ente, perc-enként
minute-Iter minute-Dist
both: 'per minute, every minute'

f. *órá-nta, órá-nként
hour-Iter hour-Dist
both: 'hourly'

The distribution of the iterative suffix is much more limited than that of the distributive suffix discussed in the previous point. The iterative suffix only occurs on nouns denoting units of time. However, it does not combine with the names of the months (319).

(319) *január-onta, *március-onta, *december-ente
January-Iter March-Iter December-Iter
Intended meaning: 'every January, every March, every December'

Furthermore, there are lexeme-based idiosyncrasies in the distribution of this suffix. Among the names of the days, only 'Sunday' combines with it (320a,b). All names of days can combine with the distributive suffix, however (320c).

(320) a. Ili vasárnap-onta eszik egy almát.
Ili Sunday-Iter eat.3Sg an apple.Acc
'Ili eats an apple [once] every Sunday.'

b. *hétfő-nte, *kedd-ente, *szombat-onta
Monday-Iter Tuesday-Iter Saturday-Iter
Intended meaning: 'every Monday, every Tuesday, every Saturday'

c. hétfő-nként, kedd-enként, szombat-onként, vasárnap-onként
Monday-Dist Tuesday-Dist Saturday-Dist Sunday-Dist
'every Monday, every Tuesday, every Saturday, every Sunday'

Among nouns denoting the times of the day, *hajnal* 'dawn', *reggel* 'morning' and *éjjel* 'night' take the iterative suffix. *Este* 'evening' is used with this suffix mostly in the literary language (with an *l* consonant appearing between the noun and the suffix). *Éjfél* 'midnight' does not combine with the iterative suffix, and the acceptability of *dél* 'noon' with this suffix is subject to variation (321).

(321) a. Ili hajnal-onta / reggel-ente / éjjel-ente / $este-lente eszik egy almát.
Ili dawn-Iter / morning-Iter / night-Iter / evening-Iter eat.3Sg an apple.Acc
'Ili eats an apple every dawn / morning / night / evening.'

b. *éjfél-ente
midnight-Iter
Intended meaning: 'every midnight'

c. %del-ente
noon-Iter
'every noon'

Este 'evening' combines with the distributive suffix instead (322).

(322) esté-nként
evening-Dist
'every evening'

Dél 'noon' does not take the distributive suffix, however (323).

(323) *del-enként
noon-Dist
Intended meaning: 'every noon'

The intended meaning of (321**c**) and (323) can be rendered with the help of the quantifier *minden* 'every' and the inessive case suffix for all speakers; and the quantifier strategy (in combination with the temporal suffix, which will be discussed in the next point) also works for *éjfél* 'midnight' (324).

(324) minden dél-ben, minden éjfél-kor
every noon-Ine every midnight-Tmp
'every noon, every midnight'

The names of the seasons also combine with the iterative suffix in an idiosyncratic way (325).

(325) a. nyar-anta, tel-ente
summer-Iter winter-Iter
'every summer, every winter'

b. *tavasz-onta, *ősz-önte
spring-Iter autumn-Iter
Intended meaning: 'every spring, every autumn'

b'. minden tavasszal, minden ősszel
every spring.Ins every autumn.Ins
'every spring, every autumn'

VIII. The temporal suffix -kor

The temporal suffix combines with bare numerals (326a) or nouns expressing time units such as hour, minute, etc. (326b) to yield adverbs of time. (Note that the vowel of the suffix does not undergo vowel harmony.)

(326) a. Hat-kor találkozunk.
six-Tmp meet.1Pl
'We shall meet at six.'

b. [Hat óra-kor] / [Hat óra harminc perc-kor] találkozunk.
six-Tmp / six hour thirty minute-Tmp meet.1Pl
'We shall meet at [six o'clock] / [six thirty].'

The Low Vowel Lengthening rule (replacing a stem-final [ɔ] and [ɛ] by [aː] and [eː] before suffixes) does not apply with *-kor* suffixation. Compare (327a) and (327b), the latter with the sublative suffix.

(327) a. napnyugta-kor, vecsernye-kor
sunset-Tmp evening.mass-Tmp
'at sunset, at evening mass'

b. napnyugtá-ra, vecsernyé-re
sunset-Sub evening.mass-Sub
'by sunset, by evening mass'

Remark 14. This suffix has grammaticalized from (case-marked forms of) the noun *kor* 'era, time' (Simonyi 1888: 445, 1895: 703, S. Hámori and Tompa 1970: 575).

The temporal suffix regularly appears on nouns naming holidays (328a), on some other nouns such as *ünnep* 'holiday' (328b), and with event nominals (328c).

(328) a. karácsony-kor, húsvét-kor, pünkösd-kor, újév-kor
Christmas-Tmp Easter-Tmp, Pentecost-Temp New.Year-Tmp
'at Christmas, at Easter, at Pentecost, on New Year's day'

b. ünnep-kor, múlt-kor
holiday-Tmp past-Tmp
'on (a) holiday, the other day'

c. mos-ás-kor, érkez-és-kor, távozás-kor,
wash-Nmn-Tmp arrive-Nmn-Tmp depart-Nmn-Tmp
a zebrá-n való át-kel-és-kor
the zebra.crossing-Sup being through-walk-Nmn-Tmp
'during washing [the clothes], on arrival, at departure, during / when crossing the zebra crossing'

It can also combine with demonstratives. In this case the *z* of the demonstrative undergoes assimilation to the *k* of the suffix (329). This assimilation also takes place when the demonstrative bears a case suffix (see Section 2.2.1.2 point *VI*) and when it bears the formal suffix *-képp(en)* (as discussed in the next point).

(329) ekkor, akkor
this.Tmp that.Tmp
'at this time, at that time'

Not all nouns denoting time units or points in time combine with the temporal suffix however; the names of the days and the months do not, as shown in (330).

(330) a. *január-kor, *március-kor, *december-kor
January-Tmp March-Tmp December-Tmp
Intended meaning: 'in January, in March, in December'

b. *hétfő-kor, *kedd-kor, *vasárnap-kor
Monday-Tmp Tuesday-Tmp Sunday-Tmp
Intended meaning: 'on Monday, on Tuesday, on Sunday'

The names of the months take the inessive case suffix, the names of the days 'Monday' through 'Saturday' take the superessive case, while as a temporal adverb, 'Sunday' remains bare (331).

(331) a. január-ban, március-ban, december-ben
January-Ine March-Ine December-Ine
'in January, in March, in December'

b. hétfő-n, kedd-en, szerdá-n, csütörtök-ön, péntek-en, szombat-on
Monday-Sup Tuesday-Sup Wednesday-Sup Thursday-Sup Friday-Sup Saturday-Sup
'on Monday, on Tuesday, on Wednesday, on Thursday, on Friday, on Saturday'

c. vasárnap
Sunday
'Sunday / on Sunday'

Not all times of the day take the temporal suffix either (332), but see (327a) for further grammatical examples.

(332) a. éjfél-kor
midnight-Tmp
'at midnight'

b. *reggel-kor, *dél-kor, *este-kor
morning-Tmp noon-Tmp evening-Tmp
Intended meaning: 'in the morning, at noon, in the evening'

Dél 'noon' and years combine with the inessive case suffix instead (333), while 'morning' and 'evening' remain uninflected (333). (The former is diachronically an instrumental marked noun, but this morphemic composition has become completely opaque.)

(333) a. dél-ben, 2018-ban
noon-Ine 2018-Ine
'at noon, in 2018'

b. reggel, este
morning evening
'in the morning, in the evening'

Days of the month are in the ordinal form and are marked with the possessive suffix and the superessive case suffix rather than the temporal suffix. The noun *nap* 'day' is likewise marked with the superessive (334).

(334) a. január harmadik-á-n
January third-Poss-Sup
'on the third of January'

b. az-on a nap-on
that-Sup the day-Sup
'on that day'

The names of the seasons do not combine with the temporal suffix; 'summer' and 'winter' take the superessive case, while the relevant forms of 'spring' and 'autumn' diachronically contain the instrumental case (but this fact is not transparent to contemporary speakers) (335).

(335) a. *tavasz-kor, *nyár-kor, *ősz-kor, *tél-kor
spring-Tmp summer-Tmp autumn-Tmp winter-Tmp
Intended meaning: 'in the spring, in the summer, in autumn, in winter'

b. nyár-on, tél-en
summer-Sup winter-Sup
'in summer, in winter'

c. tavasszal, ősszel
spring.Ins autumn.Ins
'in the spring, in autumn'

There are a few exceptional, lexicalized cases in which the temporal suffix combines with an adjective, a numeral or a quantifier (336).

(336) a. jó-kor, jobb-kor, a legjobb-kor
good-Tmp better-Tmp the best-Tmp
'at a good time, at a better time, at the best time'

b. rossz-kor, rosszabb-kor, a legrosszabb-kor
bad-Tmp worse-Tmp the worst-TmP
'at a bad time, at a worse time, at the worst time'

c. más-kor, oly-kor, egy-kor, †minden-kor
other-Tmp such-Tmp one-Tmp every-Tmp
'at another time, sometimes, in the past, always'

Table 8 below summarizes the possible combinations of nouns with the distributive, the iterative and the temporal suffix.

Table 8: The distribution of the distributive, the iterative and the temporal suffix

TYPE OF NOUN	DISTRIBUTIVE SUFFIX -(V)NKÉNT	ITERATIVE SUFFIX -(V)NTA/-(V)NTE	TEMPORAL SUFFIX -KOR
NON-TEMPORAL DENOTING	✓	×	×
NAMES OF DAYS	*some*	*very limited*	×
NAMES OF TIMES OF THE DAY	*some*	*some*	*limited*
NAMES OF MONTHS	×	×	×
NAMES OF SEASONS	×	*some*	×
OTHER TEMPORAL UNITS (*'hour', 'day', 'month', 'year' etc.*)	✓	*most*	*some*
CLASSIFIERS	✓	×	×

IX. The formal suffix -képp, -képpen

The formal suffix attaches to nouns and yields adverbs with the meaning 'as N, in the role of N' (337).

(337) A bankkártya a készpénzfizetés alternatívája-képp(en) szolgál.
the bank.card the cash.payment alternative.Poss-For serve.3Sg
'A bank card serves as an alternative of cash payment.'

It also productively appears after numeral or quantifier *+féle* 'type' combinations (338).

(338) a. egy-féle-képp(en), sok-féle-képp(en), minden-féle-képp(en)
one-type-For many-type-For every-type-For
'in one way, in many ways, by all means'

b. A feladatot két-féle-képp(en) lehet értelmezni.
the task.Acc two-type-For possible understand.Inf
'One can understand the task in two (different) ways.'

In lexicalized cases *-képp(en)* can also be found on adjectives, quantifiers or participles (339).

(339) más-képp(en), minden-képp(en), semmi-képp(en), kivál-t-képp(en)
other-For every-For nothing-For come.out-Part-For
'in another way, by all means, in no way, especially'

The vowel of the suffix does not undergo vowel harmony. When it attaches to a demonstrative, the *z* of the demonstrative undergoes assimilation to the *k* of the suffix. (A similar assimilation also takes place when i) the demonstrative bears the *-kor* temporal suffix, as discussed in the previous point, and ii) when the demonstrative is followed by a case suffix or a case-like postposition. On assimilation to case suffixes and case-like postpositions, see Section 2.2.1.2 point *VI* and Section 2.2.2.2.2 point *VI*).

(340) ekképp(en), akképp(en)
this.For that.For
'in this way, in that way'

The Low Vowel Lengthening rule does not apply with *-képp(en)* suffixation: when attaching to stems ending in [ɔ] or [ɛ], this suffix does not trigger lengthening of the stem-final vowel to [aː] or [eː]. Compare (341a) with (341b), the latter featuring the dative case suffix.

(341) a. ruha-képp(en) használ
clothing-For use.3Sg
'use as clothing'

b. ruhá-nak használ
clothing-Dat use.3Sg
'use as clothing'

As shown in the previous examples, the suffix has a shorter and a longer form: *-képp* and *-képpen*. Rebrus (2000) argues that synchronically, the latter is not a combination of the short form and the modal-essive *-n/-an/-en* suffix discussed above. The *-n/-an/-en* suffix is a closing morpheme, but the *-képpen* suffix is not: it can be further suffixed by the attributivizer *-i* (342). (The shorter form *-képp* is, however, a closing morph; cf. (342) with the ungrammatical **tulajdon-képp-i*.)

(342) tulajdon-képpen-i, valami-képpen-i, más-képpen-i
property-For-Attr somewhat-For-Attr other-For-Attr
'proper / [properly so called], somehow / [in some way], different'

In some cases the formal suffix can be substituted by the essive-formal case suffix (Section 2.2.1.1) without a change in meaning (343).

(343) A bankkártya a készpénzfizetés alternatívája-ként szolgál.
the bank.card the cash.payment alternative.Poss-FoE serve.3Sg
'A bank card serves as an alternative of cash payment.'

In general, however, the distribution of the *-képp(en)* suffix is much more restricted than that of the essive-formal case marker (de Groot 2017).

Remark 15. This suffix originates from (a case-marked form of) the noun *kép* 'picture' (Klemm 1928: 217, S. Hámori and Tompa 1970: 578). The shorter version, *-képp*, is the newer form; before the 18th century only the longer form was in use (Simonyi 1888: 411, 1895: 690, Klemm 1928: 217).

X. Adverbs with transparent case suffixes

Some adverbs comprise a noun or an adjective and a case suffix with bleached semantics (see Section 2.2.1.1). Examples are given in (344).

(344) a. szerencsé-re, rend-re, új-ra, örök-re, jövő-re [sublative]
luck-Sub order-Sub new-Sub eternal-Sub next-Sub
'luckily, regularly, again, forever, next year'

b. elv-ben, titok-ban, első-sor-ban, való-ban [inessive]
theory-Ine secret-Ine first-row-Ine real-Ine
'in principle, in secret, primarily, in reality'

c. valóság-gal [instrumental]
reality-Ins
'practically'

Speakers consider some of these (e.g. *szerencsére, újra*) to be monomorphemic units. Even when the morpheme boundaries are transparent, however, their meaning is often non-compositional (e.g. *valósággal*). This is one reason to consider them to be adverbs rather than ordinary case-marked nouns (or resultative adjectives). The other reason is that as we will see in Chapter 3, bare N complements appear with spatial case suffixes under limited circumstances only (under a generic or type interpretation, in contrastive focus and in the subcategorization frame of certain verbs), but the examples in (344) do not satisfy these criteria.

2.2.4.2. Adverbs which are homophonous with adjectives

There are a handful of adverbs that are homophonous with adjectives (cf. English *fast*: *a fast runner* vs. *to run fast*). Given the view that adverbs are, in fact, opaque PPs (Chapter 1), these can be thought of as being derived from adjectives with a phonologically zero P-head. The examples mostly involve degree modifiers such as *szörnyű* 'horrible', *borzasztó* 'awful', *rettentő* 'terrible', *jó* 'good' (345).

(345) a. egy szörnyű / borzasztó / rettentő / jó nap
a horrible / awful / terrible / good day
'a horrible / awful / terrible / good day'

b. szörnyű / borzasztó / rettentő / jó nagy
horrible / awful / terrible / good big
'horribly / awfully / terribly / very big'

In their adverbial use, *szörnyű* 'horrible', *borzasztó* 'awful' and *rettentő* 'terrible' can optionally be suffixed by the productive modal-essive *-n/-an/-en* suffix (the Hungarian equivalent of English *-ly*, discussed in Section 2.2.4.1.1), as shown in (346).

(346) szörny-en / borzasztó-an / rettentő-en nagy
horrible-ly / awful-ly / terrible-ly big
'horribly / awfully / terribly big'

This is not the case for *jó* 'good', however. Firstly, the adverbial form of *jó* 'good' is formed with the essive(-modal) *-ul/-ül* suffix (with the vowel of the suffix deleted), and secondly, the suffixed form cannot be used as a degree modifier any longer; it is only grammatical as a verb (phrase) modifier (347).

(347) a. *jó-l nagy
good-ly big
Intended meaning: 'very big'

b. Ili jó-l táncol.
Ili good-ly dance.3Sg
'Ili dances well.'

Not all adverbs that are homophonous with adjectives involve degree modifiers, though. *Feltétlen* 'unconditional(ly), by all means, under all circumstances', *hirtelen* 'sudden(ly)' and *külön* 'separate(ly)' are cases in point. The form *feltét-len* comprises the noun *feltétel* 'condition' and the caritive suffix (*-tlen*); the nominal base is shortened before the caritive suffix to *feltét-*. The use of *feltétlen* as an adjective is shown in (348a); its use as an adverb is illustrated in (348b).

(348) a. a feltét-len szeretet
the condition-Car love
'the unconditional love'

b. Feltét-len el akarok jönni.
condition-Car away want.1Sg come.Inf
'I want to come under any circumstance.'

Diachronically, *hirtelen* 'sudden(ly)' is also bi-morphemic, comprising the noun *hír* 'news' and the caritive suffix (*-telen*), but this is no longer transparent for contemporary speakers. Its uses are shown in (349).

(349) a. egy hirtelen mozdulat
a sudden move
'a sudden move'

b. Ili hirtelen befordult az utcába.
Ili sudden in.turn.Past.3Sg the street.Ill
'Ili suddenly turned into the street.'

The adverbial use of both *feltétlen* 'unconditional(ly)' and *hirtelen* 'sudden(ly)' freely alternate with the longer form in (350a,b) that bears the essive(-modal) *-ul/-ül* suffix.

(350) a. Feltét-len-ül el akarok jönni.
condition-Car-ly away want.1Sg come.Inf
'I want to come under any circumstance.'

b. Amilyen váratlan-ul jött, olyan hirtelen-ül tűnt el.
as unexpected-ly come.Past.3Sg so sudden-ly disappear.Past.3Sg away
'He disappeared as suddenly as he came unexpectedly.'

Külön 'separate(ly)' cannot be suffixed either by the modal-essive *-n/-an/-en* suffix or the essive(-modal) *-ul/-ül* suffix in its adverbial use (351).

(351) a. egy különkérdés
a separate question
'a separate question'

b. Ili külön ment haza.
Ili separate go.Past.3Sg home_to
'Ili went home separately / [on her own].'

2.2.4.3. Other adverbs

Other adverbs cannot be given a unified formal characterization. Some examples are given in (352). These adverbs are neither headed by a suffixal P head, nor are they homophonous with adjectives. They can only be defined by their distribution in the clause; see Chapter 7.

(352) tegnap, tavaly, már, még, majdnem, hamar, talán, épp(en), csak
yesterday last_year already yet almost soon perhaps just only
'yesterday, last year, already, yet, almost, soon, perhaps, just, only'

2.3. Semantic classification

This section provides a semantic classification of Hungarian postpositions. We distinguish three main groups and will discuss them one by one. The three semantic groups are: spatial Ps, temporal Ps, and non-spatial/non-temporal Ps.

2.3.1. Spatial Ps

Spatial postpositions (in the broad sense) may be divided into semantic subclasses based on whether they refer to a location in space or to a path (direction). There is another distinction, which is based on whether they refer to a spatial configuration that is dependent on an anchoring point or not. These properties will be discussed in turn, after Section 2.3.1.1 introduces the distinctive properties in a bit more detail.

A note on terminology is in order here: We will use the term spatial as a cover term for all interpretations involving spatial configurations, while locative will be used to refer to Ps denoting a location (point or region in space, stative) and directional will be used to cover meanings related to change of location (e.g. goal, path, source).

2.3.1.1. Basic semantic distinctions

I. Location and direction

The basic semantic classification in terms of spatial relations is whether a P-element refers to a location or to a change of location. The difference between location and change of location or direction can be tested if one tries to use the PP as a complement of stative (semi-)copular predicates such as *be* or *stay* or positional predicates such as *stand* or *lie* as opposed to dynamic locational/transactional predicates such as *put* or *lay* in English. We use this test in the examples below with (353) showing the grammatical locative examples with the Hungarian verb *marad* 'stay', (354) showing ungrammatical sentences where directional PPs are used with the same verb, and (355) and (356) illustrating the reverse of this, when the verb is dynamic and only directional PPs are grammatical, locative ones are not. Furthermore, a verb such as *tesz* 'put' always requires a goal-denoting PP, source-denoting ones are ungrammatical in this context as well, putting a serious limitation on the use of this test with directional Ps.

(353) a. A kutya a szomszéd-nál maradt.
the dog the neighbor-Ade stay.Past.3Sg
'The dog stayed at the neighbor's.'

b. A kutya az ajtó előtt maradt.
the dog the door in_front_of stay.Past.3Sg
'The dog stayed in front of the door.'

(354) a. *A kutya a szomszéd-hoz maradt.
the dog the neighbor-All stay.Past.3Sg
Intended meaning: 'The dog stayed to the neighbor's.'

b. *A kutya a szomszéd-tól maradt.
the dog the neighbor-Abl stay.Past.3Sg
Intended meaning: 'The dog stayed from the neighbor's.'

c. *A kutya az ajtó elé maradt.
the dog the door in_front_of_to stay.Past.3Sg
Intended meaning: 'The dog stayed (to) in front of the door.'

d. *A kutya az ajtó elől maradt.
the dog the door in_front_of _from stay.Past.3Sg
Intended meaning: 'The dog stayed from in front of the door.'

(355) a. Kati az asztal-ra tette a táskát.
Kati the table-Sub put.Past.DefObj.3Sg the bag.Acc
'Kati put the bag on the table.'

b. Kati az asztal alá tette a táskát.
Kati the table under_to put.Past.DefObj.3Sg the bag.Acc
'Kati put the bag under the table.'

(356) a. *Kati az asztal-on tette a táskát.
Kati the table-Sup put.Past.DefObj.Sg the bag.Acc
Intended meaning: 'Kati put the bag (at) on the table.'

b. *Kati az asztal-ról tette a táskát.
Kati the table-Del put.Past.DefObj.3Sg the bag.Acc
Intended meaning: 'Kati put the bag from the table.'

c. *Kati az asztal alatt tette a táskát.
Kati the table under_at put.Past.DefObj.3Sg the bag.Acc
Intended meaning: 'Kati put the bag at a place under the table.'

d. *Kati az asztal alól tette a táskát.
Kati the table under_from put.Past.DefObj.3Sg the bag.Acc
Intended meaning: 'Kati put the bag from under the table.'

Remark 16. For the Hungarian examples, the use of *áll* 'stand' is not always conducive since it is a verb of spatial configuration that is not only used in the simple position sense (which is nonagentive) but can also be used in the 'assume position' sense of Levin & Rappaport Hovav (1995) in the right context, so it can also be used with directional Ps. The use of inanimate, immobile subjects can help us in avoiding this issue. So, examples (i) and (ii) are both correct, with the difference that (i) is a stative event, while (ii) describes a dynamic event, where the car is stopping, 'assuming position' in front of the house. The sentence in (iii) is semantically odd and would only be appropriate in a fairy-tale context where trees can move on their own and thus can stop in front of a house, i.e., with an agentive subject.

(i) Az autó a ház előtt állt.
the car the house in_front_of stand.Past.3Sg
'The car stood in front of the house.'

(ii) Az autó a ház elé állt.
the car the house before_to stand.Past.3Sg
'The car came to stand in front of the house.'

(iii) #A fenyőfa a ház elé állt.
the pine.tree the house before_to stand.Past.3Sg
'The pine tree came to stand in front of the house.'

Hungarian Ps are not ambiguous between locative and directional meanings, their morphological forms correspond very clearly to this semantic distinction as was already mentioned in Section 2.2. Most case-markers and case-like postpositions show a systematic morphological distinction for three semantic types: a stative locative form-meaning pair, a goal-denoting directional one, and a source-denoting directional form-meaning pair.

II. Deictic, inherent and absolute use of Ps

Ps can refer to points (or regions) in space in a way that is deictic. This means that the spatial configuration of the Figure (the entity that is being located) and the Ground (the landmark that is the basis of locating the Figure) depends on the speaker or another anchoring point in space. For example, in (357) the location of Pál with respect to the tree is determined by the vantage point of the speaker who utters the sentence.

(357) Pál a fa előtt áll.
Pál the tree in_front_of stand.3Sg
'Pál is standing in front of the tree.'

The external anchoring point does not necessarily have to be the speaker; it can be independently established as well, as in (358).

(358) Az ablak-ból nézve, Pál pont a fa előtt áll.
the window-Ela looking Pál right the tree in_front_of stand.3Sg
'If one looks out of the window, Pál is standing right in front of the tree.'

Sometimes the anchoring point is in the Ground, in which case we can speak about the inherent use of the postposition. This is generally the case when the Ground has a natural orientation, e.g. a natural front or back (cf. Kiefer 2000b on *előtt* 'in front of' and *mögött* 'behind'). Cars or buildings have an inherent front, so the meaning of (359) or (360) does not necessarily depend on the speaker, although the position of the speaker may overwrite the natural interpretation of 'front' when speaking about an object like a car.

(359) Pál az autó előtt áll.
Pál the car in_front_of stand.3Sg
'Pál is standing in front of the car.'

(360) Pál a templom előtt áll.
Pál the church in_front_of stand.3Sg
'Pál is standing in front of the church.'

These sentences have two distinct readings: one where the spatial configuration between the located object and the Ground is inherently given by the properties of the Ground, e.g. when Pál is in front of the entrance of the church or when he is standing in front of the hood of the car, and another one where an external anchoring point (often the speaker's) determines the interpretation. For example, if Pál's position is between us and the car, we can still utter (359) felicitously even if Pál is standing at the side of the car and not at its hood, which is its natural front.

A third possibility is the absolute interpretation of the P. When the orientation of the Ground does not matter in the interpretation of the spatial configuration, we are dealing with an absolute interpretation. For instance, in (361) the table has a natural top surface, so if we say that the lamp hangs above the table, we understand their location in a way that the top of the table is closest to the lamp but not touching. However, even if we were to turn the table upside down so that technically its legs and the 'underside' part of the table were closest to the lamp, their relation would remain the same, we would still say that the lamp is above the table. This is an absolute interpretation.

(361) A lámpa az asztal felett lóg.
the lamp the table above_at hang.3Sg
'The lamp hangs above the table.'

In this case the orientation of the Ground object (the table) does not change the interpretation of the sentence. This, as well, depends on the context and the objects involved, and it is generally not lexically determined.

III. Non-spatiotemporal use of spatial Ps

Both locative and directional Ps can be used to refer to temporal relations based on their spatial meaning, which will be discussed in Section 2.3.2. However, they can also have non-spatiotemporal uses, when they are lexically selected or are adjuncts, as well as in their use as secondary predicates.

There are spatial case suffixes with non-spatial meaning when they are used as complements (362), and we find adjuncts of this kind as well (363).

(362) a. Ezek a gyerekek hisznek a Mikulás-ban.
these the children believe.3Pl the Santa.Claus-Ine
'These children believe in Santa Claus.'

b. Peti fél a kutyák-tól.
Peti fear.3Sg the dog.Pl-Abl
'Peti is afraid of dogs.'

(363) A diákok pusztán lelkesedés-ből ki-dekorálták a termet.
the student.Pl barely enthusiasm-Ela out-decorate.Past.DefObj.3Pl the room.Acc
'The students decorated the room out of sheer enthusiasm.'

These uses are not spatial even in the extended metaphorical sense, and the morphological form used in such a context depends on the selecting verb in the case of complement PPs and seems to be idiosyncratic in the case of adjuncts, such as (363). As we can see, the English translation also uses a preposition that denotes direction away from the Ground, so it might not be completely arbitrary what semantic class of P appears on which adjuncts.

The sublative suffix is attached to resultative secondary predicates as a marker of the syntactic and semantic relation, a marker of resultativity, which is another use of a spatial element as a formal marking of a configuration (364).

(364) Juli zöld-re festette az ajtó-t.
Juli green-Sub paint.Past.DefObj.3Sg the door-Acc
'Juli painted the door green.'

This use of PPs as secondary predicates will be discussed in Chapter 4.

2.3.1.2. Locative Ps

2.3.1.2.1. Locative case suffixes

Table 9 provides the case suffixes with locative readings (repeating from Table 2):

Table 9: Locative case suffixes

	INSIDE / IN	SURFACE / ON	PROXIMITY / AT
PLACE	*Inessive* *-ban, -ben*	*Superessive* *-n, -on, -en, -ön*	*Adessive* *-nál, -nél*

All of these case suffixes may be used with verbs such as *marad* 'stay' (365) or *áll* 'stand' (366) but are ungrammatical with change-of-state verbs, such as *tesz* 'put' (367), which lets us conclude that they only have locative interpretations.

(365) A könyv [a fiók-ban] / [a polc-on] / [az asztal-nál] maradt.
the book the drawer-Ine / the shelf-Sup / the desk-Ade remain.Past.3Sg
'The book was left [in the drawer] / [on the shelf] / [at the desk].'

(366) A szék [a sarok-ban] / [az erkély-en] / [az ágy-nál] áll.
the chair the corner-Ine / the balcony-Sup / the bed-Ade stand.3Sg
'The chair is standing [in the corner] / [on the balcony] / [at the bed].'

(367) *Mari [a fiók-ban] / [a polc-on] / [az asztal-nál] tette a könyvet.
Mari the drawer-Ine / the shelf-Sup / the desk-Ade put.DefObj.3Sg the book.Acc
Intended meaning: 'Mari put the book [in the drawer] / [on the shelf] / [at the desk].'

The semantics of the inessive case is that the Figure is inside the Ground, while the superessive case means that it is on the surface of the Ground. The interpretation of the adessive marker allows for the Figure to be anywhere in the region close enough to the Ground that it can be considered to be 'at' it, there does not have to be a point where the Figure and the Ground are in contact. For instance in (366), the chair has to be in the vicinity of the bed but they do not have to touch each other. The physical closeness that this requirement of being in the vicinity involves depends both on the Figure and on the Ground and is not strictly grammatically determined.

2.3.1.2.2. Locative case-like postpositions

There are several case-like postpositions with only locative meanings, and they all have directional — goal- and source-denoting — counterparts that we will turn to in Section 2.3.1.3.2. The locative ones end in the old locative suffix *-(Vt)t*, but they are perceived as monomorphemic and otherwise this suffix is very limited in its productivity today, as was discussed in Section 2.2.2.2.1 point *I*. The inventory of locative case-like Ps is given in Table 10.

Table 10: Locative case-like Ps

CASE-LIKE P	MEANING
alatt	(at) under
előtt	(at) in front of
felett/fölött	(at) above
körül(ött)	around
között, közt	between
mellett	beside
mögött	(at) behind

Similarly to the purely locative case suffixes, these Ps can be used with verbs like *stand* or *stay* (368), but not with verbs such as *put* (369).

(368) a. A szék [az asztal előtt] / [az ágy mellett] maradt / állt.
the chair the table in_front_of / the bed next_to stay.Past.3Sg / stand.Past.3Sg
'The chair stayed / stood [in front of the table] / [beside the bed].'

b. A székek az asztalok körül / között maradtak.
the chairs the table.Pl around / between stay.Past.3Pl
'The chairs stayed around / between the tables.'

(369) a. *Mari [az asztal előtt] / [az ágy mellett] tette a széket.
Mari the table in_front_of / the bed next_to put.Past.DefObj.3Sg the chair.Acc
Intended meaning: 'Mari put the chair [at in front of the table] / [at beside the bed].'

b. *Mari az asztalok körül / között tette a székeket.
Mari the table.Pl around / between put.Past.DefObj.3Sg the chair.Pl.Acc
Intended meaning: 'Mari put the chairs at around / between the tables.'

2.3.1.2.3. *Locative case-assigning postpositions*

Many of the case-assigning postpositions have a locative spatial interpretation. A list of these is given in Table 11.

Table 11: Locative case-assigning Ps

	CASE-ASSIGNING P	MEANING
LOCATIVE	*alul*	below
	belül	inside of
	felül	above
	innen	on this side of
	kívül	outside of
	közel	close to
	szemben	opposite
	szemközt	opposite
	túl	beyond

Most of them, like *alul*, *belül*, *felül*, *kívül*, *közel*, are completely opaque in their morphology and the fact that they probably have the old ablative ending *-(V)l* does not play any part in their present interpretation. Contrary to most of the case-like Ps ending in *-(V)l*, which have a directional, source meaning, these case-assigning Ps specify the location of the Figure with respect to the Ground in stative contexts. Some of them are morphologically more transparent, e.g. *szemben* 'opposite' is composed of the noun *szem* 'eye' and the inessive suffix *-ben*, or *szemközt* is made up of the same noun and the locative postposition *közt* 'between'. These are also only locative in meaning.

Most of these Ps take complements with a superessive case ending (370a), the others take instrumental or allative-marked complements, as shown in (370b)-(370c), respectively. As already mentioned in Section 2.2.2.3.2 point *I*, the semantics of the case suffix on the complement of the case-assigning P does not play a real role compositionally, it is a selected case, but the semantics of the whole is determined by the case-assigning P. For instance, the allative case on (370c) has directional semantics on its own, however, here the full phrase is locative.

(370) a. Az autó a folyó-n túl maradt.
the car the river-Sup beyond stay.Past.3Sg
'The car stayed beyond the river.'

b. Az autó az étterem-mel szemben maradt.
the car the restaurant-Ins opposite_to stay.Past.3Sg
'The car stayed opposite the restaurant.'

c. Az autó az út-hoz közel maradt.
the car the road-All close stay.Past.3Sg
'The car stayed close to the road.'

These PPs can be adjuncts with verbs of motion but they are still not directional in those cases. In a sentence like (371a), the verb contributes the motion component to the interpretation and the PP denotes the space where the motion of the Figure (the car) takes place with respect to the Ground (the bicycle). However, the spatial meaning is not directional, i.e., this sentence does not mean that the car was approaching the bicycle; it means that the car was moving along a path which was in the proximity of the bicycle. Similarly in (371b) the PP denotes the area where the car's movement should take place (it should be moving on the far side of the river) rather than the goal of the movement (i.e. the sentence does not mean that the car should cross the river and end up on the far side).

(371) a. Az autó a bicikli-hez közel ment.
the car the bicylce-All close went.3Sg
'The car was moving close to the bike.'

b. A ti autótok a folyó-n túl menjen!
the you(Pl) car.Poss.2Pl the river-Sup beyond go.Subj.3Sg
'Your car should be going beyond the river.'

However, the case-assigning postpositions *túl* 'beyond' and *közel* 'close to' can also be used as verbal particles, as (372) illustrates. In this use the verbal particle equivalent of the case-assigning P is directional in as much as it provides an endpoint, a goal to the movement expressed by the verb. That is, it provides the boundedness of the path, where the path is given by the fact that a motion verb is involved. The sentence in (372b) does mean that the car approached the bicycle: the change of location is contributed by the verb, while the endpoint of the movement is encoded in the particle. The same applies to the simple intransitive particle used in (373).

(372) a Az autó túl-ment a folyón.
the car beyond-went.3Sg the river-Sup
'The car went to a place over the river.'

b. Az autó közel-ment a biciklihez.
the car close_to-went.3Sg the bike-Ade
'The car went close to the bicycle.'

(373) Az autó közel-jött.
the car close_to-come.Past.3Sg
'The car came up close.'

These particles most of the time appear with motion verbs, even in their more idiomatic, metaphorical meanings (374).

(374) Ez túl-megy minden határ-on.
this beyond-go.3Sg every boundary-Sup
'[This crosses every boundary.] / [This is too much.]'

2.3.1.2.4. Locative particles

Particles are typically directional as was shown in Section 2.2.3.1 and thus will be discussed in Section 2.3.1.3.4. However, there is one particle that is formally locative. It contains the locative superessive suffix, which is to some extent still transparent morphologically although it is opaque semantically. This particle is *agyon*, which originally meant 'on the brain/skull' in a locative sense, but now means 'to death, to an extreme degree' as a verbal particle (375).

(375) a. A férfit agyon-ütötte a zuhanó fa.
the man.Acc to_death-hit.Past.DefObj.3Sg the fall.Part tree
'The falling tree killed the man.'

b. Marit agyon-dicsérte a főnöke.
Mari.Acc to_death-praise.Past.DefObj.3Sg the boss.Poss.3Sg
'Her boss praised Mari excessively (lit. to death).'

This is a rare case where the form is locative (superessive, i.e. referring to the Figure being on the surface of the Ground) but it has developed into a particle. That the morphemic composition is semantically opaque and is also on the way to becoming morphologically opaque for (at least some) speakers can be seen from cases when another case ending can be added to it. Interestingly, we can find sentences with the form *agyon-ra*, where the sublative suffix ('onto') is added to the particle (376), i.e., the original case ending is completely opaque for those speakers who accept it.

(376) %Ezt már agyon-ra ismételték.
this.Acc already to_death-Sub repeat.Past.DefObj.3Pl
'This has been repeated ad nauseam (lit. to death).'

This sublative suffix is the one we find on resultative secondary predicates, and in this case, it seems to contribute to the result state meaning that the locative *agyon* formally lacks. Encoding the endpoint morphologically is generally necessary to achieve a resultative interpretation, and the sublative suffix is one of the canonical markers of that meaning component.

2.3.1.2.5. Locative adverbs

Those adverbs that have a spatial meaning are mostly locative, contrary to particles, which are mostly directional. Adverbs ending in the *-nn* and *-nt* suffix, as well as adverbs with the locative *-(Vt)t* suffix belong here.

We find locative adverbs in various semantic opposition pairs: *itt* 'here' – *ott* 'there', *lenn/lent* 'down' – *fenn/fent* 'up', *kinn/kint* 'outside' – *benn/bent* 'inside'. They also have directional counterparts that are classified as verbal particles, i.e., the locative and the directional parts of the semantic pairs are in some descriptions taken to belong to different lexical categories (e.g. Marácz's 1989 detailed discussion of PPs). The locative elements, however, have the same syntactic distribution as the directional ones: they can fill the role of the only locative complement of a stative verb but can also appear together with another locative element, in which case they specify an additional semantic dimension in addition to the one expressed by the other locative expression (see Section 2.3.1.3.4, and cf. Kiefer 2000b on particles). In (377), the adverbs are the only locative elements, they serve to specify the location of the subject nominal (the Figure), whereas in (378), the postverbal locative suffixed PP determines the location, while the preverbal locative adverb provides additional specification of the location in a way that is often deictic.

(377) a. A macska kint maradt.
the cat outside stay.Past.3Sg
'The cat stayed outside.'

b. A kék tollak ott vannak.
the blue pen.Pl there be.3Pl
'The blue pens are there.'

(378) a. A macska kint maradt az utcá-n.
the cat outside stay.Past.3Sg the street-Sup
'The cat stayed out in the street.'

b. A kék tollak ott vannak az asztal-on.
the blue pen.Pl there be.3Pl the desk-Sup
'The blue pens are there on the desk.'

The use of *ott* in sentences such as (378b) contributes specification on the proximity (*here* vs. *there*) of the Figure, in addition to the lexically specified Ground in the postverbal part. In other cases, the adverb contributes semantic content concerning orientation, e.g. *up* vs. *down* in (379), in a way that is deictic in the sense that it is related to the vantage point of the speaker or some external point in space.

(379) a. A papírsárkány fenn maradt a tető-n.
the kite up stay.Past.3Sg the roof-Sup
'The kite stayed up on the roof.'

b. A fióka lenn maradt a tető-n(, de az anyja elrepült).
the nestling down stay.Past.3Sg the roof-Sup but the mother.Poss.3Sg away.flew.3Sg
'The nestling stayed down on the roof, but its mother flew away.'

There are a few locative adverbs the morphological make up of which is rather uncommon. They consist of the directional element *ide* 'to here' or *oda* 'to there' and one of the opposition pairs from above (380):

(380) a. ide-lent, ide-fent, ide-kint, ide-bent
here_to-down_at, here_to-up_at, here_to-outside_at, here_to-inside_at
'down here, up here, out here, in here'

b. oda-lent, oda-fent, oda-kint, oda-bent
there_to-down_at, there_to-up_at, there_to-outside_at, there_to-inside_at
'down there, up there, out there, in there'

The combination of the directional first morpheme and the locative second morpheme ends up with a locative meaning together, corresponding to the complex phrases 'down here', 'down there' an so on (381).

(381) Anna ide-bent / oda-kint maradt.
Anna here.to-inside.at / there.to-outside.at stay.Past.3Sg
'Anna stayed [in here] / [out there].'

It is also possible to adjoin two locative elements, ultimately resulting in the same meaning, but those two do not form a morphological unit (382):

(382) Anna [itt bent] / [ott kint] maradt.
Anna here_at inside_at / there_at outside_at stay.Past.3Sg
'Anna stayed [here, inside] / [there, outside].'

These adjoined locative adverbs in (382) can also appear separately in the clause, one may be preverbal and the other adjoined postverbally (383), which is not the case with the compound adverbs, as (384) is ungrammatical.

(383) Anna itt maradt bent.
Anna here_at stay.Past.3Sg inside_at
'Anna stayed in here.'

(384) *Anna ide maradt bent.
Anna here_to stay.Past.3Sg inside_at
Intended meaning: 'Anna stayed in here.'

2.3.1.3. Directional Ps

Ps with a directional meaning can be further classified as ones referring to goal (bounded path), (unbounded) path, or source. All directional elements involve some kind of path, but additionally goal-denoting ones involve an endpoint and source-denoting ones involve a point of origin. However, there are also Ps that only include the specification of the path without necessarily having an endpoint in their semantics; these are sometimes called route-denoting Ps (e.g., Zwarts 2005). As we will see, this distinction will be important in some of the subtypes of directional Ps. It is to be noted that the term directional is used in a broad sense here, covering all types of Ps that include a path in their reference.

2.3.1.3.1. Directional case suffixes

The case-markers that were listed in Section 2.3.1.2.1 as the group of locative suffixes have directional counterparts, both goal-denoting ones and ones referring to the source of the change of location.

Table 12: Directional case suffixes

	INSIDE / IN	SURFACE / ON	PROXIMITY / AT	ENDPOINT
GOAL	*Illative* *-ba, -be*	*Sublative* *-ra, -re*	*Allative* *-hoz, -hez, -höz*	*Terminative, Dative* *-ig, -nak/nek*
SOURCE	*Elative* *-ból, -ből*	*Delative* *-ról, -ről*	*Ablative* *-tól, -től*	*N/A*

The goal-denoting suffixes are the illative, the sublative, the allative and the terminative cases. The illative and the sublative suffixes have directional meanings where the endpoints of the movements are inside and on the surface of the Ground, respectively. The allative case refers to a direction to the vicinity of the Ground, which may or may not have an endpoint that is in contact with the Ground. The terminative suffix denotes the Ground as the endpoint of a path.

Remark 17. Note that the inessive and the illative suffixes are often syncretic in spoken language (but not in standard written Hungarian), as noted in Section 2.2.1.1: the illative form is often used for locative meanings, i.e., the illative suffix in (386) is acceptable for most speakers in the spoken register with a stative verb, expressing location.

PPs that include these case suffixes cannot be complements of static verbs like *stand* or *stay* (386), they can, however, appear with dynamic predicates, such as *tesz* 'put' as in (385).

(385) Lili [a fiók-ba] / [az asztal-ra] / [a fal-hoz] tette a táskát.
Lili the drawer-Ill / the table-Sub / the wall-All put.Past.DefObj.3Sg the bag.Acc
'Lili put the bag into the drawer / onto the table / next to the wall.'

(386) *A táska [a fiók-ba] / [az asztal-ra] / [a fal-hoz] maradt.
the bag the drawer-Ill / the table-Sub / the wall-All stay.Past.3Sg
Intended meaning: 'The bag stayed in(to) the drawer / onto the table / next to the wall.'

There are also three source-denoting case suffixes: the elative refers to movement from within the Ground object, the delative refers to movement from the surface of something, and the ablative means movement away from something; it is the least specific with respect to touching the point of origin.

Source denoting PPs can appear in neither of the test environments we have been using as complements of the verb: they cannot be used with stative verbs since they are directional, and they cannot be used with dynamic verbs like *put* since those require a goal PP as their complement, cf. (387).

(387) a. *A táska [a fiók-ból] / [az asztal-ról] / [a fal-tól] maradt.
the bag the drawer-Ela / the table-Del / the wall-Abl stay.Past.3Sg
Intended meaning: 'The bag stayed out of the drawer / off the table / from the wall.'

b. *Lili [a fiók-ból] / [az asztal-ról] / [a fal-tól] tette a táskát.
Lili the drawer-Ela / the table-Del / the wall-Abl put.Past.DefObj.3Sg the bag.Acc
Intended meaning: 'Lili put the bag out of the drawer / off the table / from the wall.'

In fact, source PPs are rarely complements: a source-denoting PP can be the complement of motion verbs such as *jön* 'come', *ered* 'originate' and *távolodik* 'move away from' (388) or a complement of the verb *van* 'be' when it has a lexical meaning 'to be made of something, to originate from something or a place' (389).

(388) a. Ez a levél Angliá-ból jött.
this the letter England-Ela come.Past.3Sg
'This letter came from England.'

b. A Duna a Fekete-erdő-ből ered.
the Danube the Black-Forest-Ela originate.3Sg
'The Danube originates in the Black Forest.'

c. A Tejút egyre távolodik a galaxis belsejé-től.
the Milky.Way continuously move_away_from.3Sg the galaxy inside.Poss-Abl
'The Milky Way is continuously moving away from the center of the galaxy.'

(389) a A cipőm bőr-ből van.
the shoe.Poss.1Sg leather-Ela is
'My shoes are made of leather.'

b. A láz a náthá-tól van.
the fever the cold-Abl is
'The fever is due to the cold.'

c. Mi mind Szeged-ről vagyunk.
we all Szeged-Del are
'We are all from Szeged.'

Source-denoting PPs are also completely grammatical when paired with a goal complement, as in (390a), but the same source PP cannot be the complement of the same verb on its own, (390b).

(390) a A tükör a padló-tól a mennyezet-ig ér.
the mirror the floor-Abl the ceiling-Ter reach.3Sg
'The mirror extends from the floor to the ceiling.'

b. *A tükör a padló-tól ér.
the mirror the floor-Abl reach.3Sg
Intended meaning: 'The mirror extends from the floor.'

PPs that are source-denoting in form can be complements in a non-spatiotemporal use as illustrated in Section 2.3.1.1.

The terminative case suffix can be used to refer to an end-point in space or time. We will see the temporal use in Section 2.3.2 (cf. (431)); its spatial use is illustrated in (390a) and (391).

(391) a. Mari a sarok-ig futott.
Mari the corner-Ter run.Past.3Sg
'Mari ran up to the corner.'

b. A medve a város-ig jutott.
the bear the city-Ter reach.Past.3Sg
'The bear got as far as the city.'

To a very limited extent, the dative case also has a goal denoting use (with motion verbs), expressing that the Figure has reached an endpoint at the Ground (392a,b). However, most of these sentences sound even more natural with the dative reduplicated and the duplicate acting as a verbal particle in the sentence (392a',b') (on duplicating Ps see Chapter 5 Section 5.2.3.5).

(392) a. Mari az üvegajtó-nak rohant.
Mari the glass.door-Dat run.Past.3Sg
'Mari ran into the glass door.'

a'. Mari neki-rohant az üvegajtó-nak.
Mari Dat.3Sg-run.Past.3Sg the glass.door-Dat
'Mari ran into the glass door.'

b. A labda a kerítés-nek ütközött.
the ball the fence-Dat clash.Past.3Sg
'The ball bumped into the fence.'

b'. A labda neki-ütközött a kerítés-nek.
the ball Dat.3Sg-clash.Past.3Sg the fence-Dat
'The ball bumped into the fence.'

There are also some set expressions with the dative case and a motion verb (393).

(393) a. világ-nak megy
world-Dat go
'to go / run away from home'

b. fal-nak megy
wall-Dat go
'to get fed up'

2.3.1.3.2. Directional case-like postpositions

The locative case-like Ps have directional counterparts: there are several goal-denoting directional case-like postpositions which also have source-denoting counterparts, and there are a few additional directional Ps that refer to an unbounded path. This latter group involves a direction that does not necessarily reach the Ground as its endpoint, so we cannot really say that they refer to a goal and their distribution is slightly different as well. A goal-denoting P always includes the meaning component of a path, but it is not true the other way around in these cases.

Table 13: Directional case-like postpositions

	CASE-LIKE P	MEANING
GOAL	*alá*	to under
	elé	to in front of
	fölé	to above
	köré	to around
	közé	to between
	mellé	to next to
	mögé	to behind
	után	after
PATH	*felé*	towards
	iránt	towards, in direction to

SOURCE	*alól*	from under
	elől	from in front of
	felől	from the direction of
	fölül	from above
	közül	from between
	mellől	from next to
	mögül	from behind

The directional Ps that denote the goal of the movement can appear with the change-of-location verb *tesz* 'put' (394).

(394) Ili [a pad alá] / [a fal mellé] / [a TV mögé] tesz egy dobozt.
Ili the bench under_to / the wall beside_to / the TV behind_to put.3Sg a box.Acc
'Ili puts a box under the bench / next to the wall / behind the TV.'

Applying this test to those two Ps that we labeled as referring to a path shows us that they cannot be used in this context (395). The reason for the ungrammaticality is that the verb needs a PP that is interpreted as a bounded path: putting something somewhere involves the meaning component that the Figure (which is being located) will end up in some spatial configuration with the Ground (the end location, the goal of the movement). This endpoint (the Ground) is not necessarily reached when we use the postpositions that refer to a simple path, and that is why they cannot be used with verbs like *put*. These Ps can still be used with motion verbs, however, as those only require them to involve a path (396).

(395) *Pál [az asztal felé] / [a fal iránt] tette a széket.
Pál the table towards / the wall towards put.Past.DefObj.3Sg the chair.Acc
Intended meaning: 'Pál put the chair towards the table / in direction of the wall.'

(396) Pál [az asztal felé] / [a fal iránt] futott.
Pál the table towards / the wall towards run.Past.3Sg
'Pál ran towards the table / in direction of the wall.'

The postposition *iránt* 'towards' also has a non-spatial, or only metaphorically spatial use, when it is used as a complement of *érdeklődik* 'be interested (in something)', or *lelkesedik* 'be enthusiastic (about something)' (397).

(397) a. Pál érdeklődik a fizika iránt.
Pál be_interested.3Sg the physics towards
'Pál is interested in physics.'

b. Mindenki nagyon lelkesedett a tervünk iránt.
everybody very be_enthusiastic.Past.3Sg the plan.Poss.1Pl towards
'Everyone was very enthusiastic about our plan.'

Source-denoting Ps cannot appear with verbs like *put*, either, since they do not include the endpoint, only the starting point of the movement, and that is not a suitable complement to these verbs (398).

(398) *Ili [a pad alól] / [a fal mellől] / [a TV mögül]
Ili the bench under_from / the wall beside_from / the TV behind_from
tesz egy dobozt.
put.3Sg a box.Acc
Intended meaning: 'Ili puts a box [from under the bench] / [from beside the wall] / [from behind the chair].'

Similarly to source-denoting case suffixes, source-denoting case-like postpositions mostly seem to be complements when they are not used spatiotemporally; however, there are fewer such cases with postpositions than with suffixes (399).

(399) Mari mindig érdeklődik a nagymamám felől.
Mari always inquire.3Sg the grandmother.Poss.1Sg from_direction_of
'Mari always inquires about my Grandmother.'

2.3.1.3.3. *Directional case-assigning postpositions*

There are not as many case-assigning Ps that are directional as there are locative ones. The directional ones have different semantics and some of them refer to a goal, i.e., to a bounded path, one that involves an endpoint, while some of them refer to an unbounded path, i.e., there is no inherent endpoint in their meaning, at least not in their postpositional use. There is also one source-denoting case-assigning postposition.

Table 14: Directional case-assigning postpositions

	CASE-ASSIGNING P	MEANING
GOAL	*végig*	along (to the end of)
	szembe	to opposite to
PATH	*át*	through, via, across, over
	keresztül	through, via, across
SOURCE	*szemből*	from opposite to

Applying the test of the ablility to complement change-of-state verbs of the *put* type is slightly more complicated than in the other cases, and there is only one of those Ps in Table 14 that can be the complement of *put* without the need to add anything else (400).

(400) Peti a színpad-dal szembe tette a székeket.
Peti the stage-Ins to_opposite_to put.Past.DefObj.3Sg the chair.Pl.Acc
'Peti put the chairs opposite the stage.'

All of the goal- and path-denoting case-assigning Ps have uses as a verbal particle as well, which influences their use in this context. As a postposition, *át* 'over, through' cannot be a VM with *put*, the full PP in (401) is not a proper VM, as it refers to an unbounded path, and the sentence seems to be missing an endpoint. However, as a particle (i.e., on its own in the preverbal position) *át* can be used with *put*-type verbs (402a) and it can also denote the endpoint of movement with motion verbs (402b), i.e., a goal is part of its meaning.

(401) *Lili [a kerítés-en át] tette a létrát.
Lili the fence-Sup over put.Past.DefObj.3Sg the ladder.Acc
Intended meaning: 'Lili put the ladder over the fence.'

(402) a. Lili át-tette a létrát a kerítés-en.
Lili over-put.Past.DefObj.3Sg the ladder.Acc the fence-Sup
'Lili put the ladder over the fence.'

b. Lili át-jött.
Lili over-come.Past.3Sg
'Lili came over.'

2.3.1.3.4. Directional particles

Particles are generally directional, almost without exception: they refer to a bounded path or an endpoint in an event. Hungarian has one particle, the telicizing element *meg*, which is not spatial any more, or at least its spatial use is very limited and non-productive (originally it was a directional particle).

There are also a few relatively newly gramaticalized particles that are not used spatially, although they do contain some directional morpheme formally. An often cited example for this is *tönk-re* '(V) to ruins' (see e.g., Forgács 2004), which contains the sublative case suffix but is only used to refer to endpoints in a non-spatial metaphorical or only telicizing sense.

(403) a. A bolt tönk-re ment.
the shop stump-Sub go.Past.3Sg
'The shop went bankrupt.'

b. A válság tönk-re tette a gazdaságot.
the crisis stump-Sub put.Past.DefObj.3Sg the economy.Acc
'The crisis wrecked the economy.'

Most particles have obviously directional as well as telicizing uses, where we use the term directional to refer to the fact that there is movement involved, so the particle has a spatial meaning (404).

(404) a. Ili ki-ment a kertbe. [directional]
Ili out-go.Past.3Sg the garden.Ill
'Ili went out into the garden.'

b. Ili ki-olvasta a könyvet. [telicizing]
Ili out-read.Past.DefObj.3Sg the book.Acc
'Ili has read the book from cover to cover.'

Importantly, however, there is a path covered in the telicizing use as well, as shown by the fact that we can add the modifier *félig* 'halfway' to the predicate (405).

(405) Ili fél-ig ki-olvasta a könyvet.
Ili half-Ter out-read.Past.DefObj.3Sg the book.Acc
'Ili is halfway done reading the book.'

Not all directional particles have a telicizing use in this sense. There are some particles that do not telicize the verbal predicate they are used with (Kiefer 2000b): the event in the next example is atelic, and the particle is simply directional (406).

(406) Mari tovább-gurította a labdát.
Mari further-rolled.3Sg the ball.Acc
'Mari passed / rolled the ball on.'

Table 15 below provides a list of directional particles. As mentioned in Section 2.2.3.1, there is no obvious exhaustive list of particles that could be given, but the items below are probably all considered particles in the literature.

Table 15: Directional particles

PARTICLE	MEANING
el	away
ki	out
fel	up
le	down
be	into
át	over, through
túl	over, beyond
össze	together
szét	apart
széjjel	apart
vissza	back
hátra	(to the) back
félre	aside, mis-
tovább	further

The semantic requirement for an item to be considered a particle is generally related to its use in a non-literal spatial sense, which would allow it to be used with a wider range of verbs than a strictly spatial complement (e.g., D. Mátai 1989, 1991, 1992 on the diachronic development of Hungarian verbal particles). At the other end of the spectrum, postpositions may be considered fully gramaticalized functional elements when they lose their spatial meaning (Roberts and Roussou 2003). The more general extended use applies to all the particles listed in the table (407).

(407) a. Pál el / be / vissza / félre tette a könyvet (a polc-ra).
Pál away / into / back / aside put.Past.DefObj.3Sg the book.Acc the shelf-Sub
'Pál put the book away / in / back / aside (on the shelf).'

b. ?Pál tovább-tette a könyvet (a polc-ra).
Pál further-put.Past.DefObj.3Sg the book.Acc the shelf-Sub
'Pál put the book further on (on the shelf).'

There is a use of *tovább* with the verb *tesz* 'put', where it means 'to pass on' or 'to move further on', and in this case it appears with a dative-marked beneficiary besides the accusative object, just like with *give*-type verbs, as in (408).

(408) Pál tovább-teszi a labdát Miki-nek.
Pál further-put.DefObj.3Sg the ball.Acc Miki-Dat
'Pál passes the ball on to Miki.'

Directional particles often co-occur with other directional PPs (that have case suffixes or postpositions as their P head) in the clause. In these cases the particle specifies an orientation, a specific direction as an additional semantic component to the directional meaning of the case or postposition. Comparing (409a) to (409b) and (410a) to (410b), the postverbal PPs are constant within the pairs but the different particles make the orientation of the paths different. There is a default combination, as in (409a), which shows that direction into the Ground naturally combines with a particle that also expresses orientation inward, but the movement into the Ground may also be oriented out of something at the same time, as in (409b). The expression still refers to a goal, only the vantage point of the speaker changes in the latter case. Similarly, a path onto something is often a path that is oriented upwards, (410a), but it can also be oriented downward if the Ground is lower than another vantage point that is involved, (410b).

(409) a. Mari be-vitte a dobozokat a garázs-ba.
Mari into-take.Past.DefObj.3Sg the box.Pl.Acc the garage-Ill
'Mary took the boxes into the garage.'

b. Mari ki-vitte a dobozokat a garázs-ba.
Mari out-take.Past.DefObj.3Sg the box.Pl.Acc the garage-Ill
'Mari took the boxes out to the garage.'

(410) a. A csiga fel-mászott a szék-re.
the snail up-climb.Past.3Sg the chair-Sub
'The snail climbed up on the chair.'

b. A csiga le-mászott a szék-re.
the snail down-climb.Past.3Sg the chair-Sub
'The snail climbed down on the chair.'

The particle *ki* 'out' is thus not a source-denoting particle: it specifies the orientation of the path that leads to the goal as one that leads from an inside vantage point to outside .

The particles *szét* and *széjjel* can both be translated as 'apart', and in some cases they are interchangeable (with individual preferences for one or the other) (411), but in other cases *szét* is slightly preferred (412), and in some metaphorical uses, only *szét* is possible (413).

(411) Mari szét- / széjjel-tépte a levelet.
Mari apart / apart-tear.Past.DefObj.3Sg the letter.Acc
'Mari tore the letter apart.'

(412) Mari szét- / ?széjjel-nézett, mielőtt átment az úton.
Mari apart / apart-look.Past.3Sg before over.go.Past.3Sg the road.Sup
'Mari looked around before she crossed the road.'

(413) Mari szét- / *széjjel-aggódta magát a vizsga előtt.
Mari apart / apart- worry.Past.DefObj.3Sg self.Acc the exam in_front_of
'Mari worried herself silly before the exam.'

2.3.1.3.5. *Directional adverbs*

The adverbs *ide* 'to here' and *oda* 'to there' are the directional counterparts of the locative *itt* 'here' and *ott* 'there', and while in many cases the directional counterpart of a locative adverb is considered to be a verbal particle, in these cases, they are still mostly regarded as adverbs, probably due to their deictic meanings (414).

(414) a. Anna ide-jött.
Anna here_to-come.Past.3Sg
'Anna came here.'

b. Anna oda-ment.
Anna there_to-go.Past.3Sg
'Anna went there.'

2.3.2. *Temporal Ps*

2.3.2.1. *Temporal postpositions*

Temporal Ps are those that refer to a point in time or some duration in time. There are a few P elements in Hungarian that are always temporal; these are listed in Table 16.

Table 16: Temporal postpositions

POSTPOSITION	MEANING
múlva / $^{\$}$*múltán*	in (X time), after (X time)
óta	since
tájban / $^{\%}$*tájt*	around (a point in time)

The temporal postposition *tájt* 'around' (lit. place.Loc) is the slightly less frequent equivalent of *tájban* 'around' (lit. place.Ine). There are also two further variants with morphologically more transparently possessive structures: *táján* 'around' (lit. place.Poss.Sup) and *tájékán* 'around' (lit. surroundings.Poss.Sup), which behave like postpositions to some extent but are transparently complex word forms, therefore we will discuss them among the borderline Ps in Section 2.4.2.1 point *II*.

The use of the regular postpositional forms *tájt* and *tájban* is quite restricted: they require their complement to refer to a certain time on the clock, usually measured in hours or other well-established points of time (e.g. noon, midnight), as in (415). If the time unit is smaller, their grammaticality gets slightly degraded, and if the time unit is of a different kind, they are ungrammatical (416).

(415) a. 6 óra tájban / tájt
6 hour around / around
'at around 6 o'clock'

b. negyed 10 tájban / tájt
quarter 10 around / around
'at around quarter past nine'

c. dél tájban / tájt
noon around / around
'at around noon'

(416) a. 6 óra 10 (perc) [(?)]tájban / tájt
6 hour 10 minute around / around
'at around 10 past 6'

b. húsvét *tájban / tájt
Easter around / around
'at around Easter'

c. múlt hét *tájban / *tájt
last week around / around
'at around last week'

d. január *tájban / [??]tájt
January around / around
'at around January'

The postposition *során* 'during' (lit. line.Poss.Sup) refers to time duration and thus needs a complement that denotes a sufficiently long time unit, as in (417). This is the reason why (417d) is ungrammatical; a point in time cannot be used to denote duration. If we compare (417d) and (417d'), the latter example is grammatical since here *6 óra* '6 hour / o'clock' does not refer to a point in time but to a period of 6 hours (as the modifier makes it explicit), therefore we can refer to something happening during that period.

(417) a. a múlt hét során
the last week during
'during last week'

b. a délelőtt során
the morning during
'during the morning'

c. (a) 2016(-os év) során
the 2016(-Adj year) during
'during (the year) 2016'

d. *6 óra során
6 hour during
Intended meaning: 'during 6 o'clock'

d'. a börtönben töltött 6 óra során
the prison.Ine spend.Part. 6 hour during
'during the 6 hours spent in prison'

Során requires a nominal complement, hence the contrast between (418a) and (418b).

(418) a. *tegnap során
yesterday during
Intended meaning: 'during yesterday'

b. [$_{NP}$ a tegnap-i nap] során
the yesterday-Attr day during
'during yesterday'

The postposition *múlva* 'in, after, later' refers to a point in time, which is temporally removed from an externally given time or event with the amount of time given in its complement. Any time unit is suitable as the complement, as (419) shows.

(419) a. 6 óra múlva
6 hour after
'after 6 hours / 6 hours later'

b. 8 perc múlva
8 minute after
'after 8 minutes / 8 minutes later'

c. 3 hét múlva
3 week after
'after 3 weeks / 3 weeks later'

d. 2 év múlva
2 year after
'after 2 years / 2 years later'

Finally, *óta* 'since, for' has a complement that refers either to a starting point or to a period of time and the PP expresses duration (420). Its use in the 'for x time' sense is slightly marked with some complements but is completely fine with others (421), a variation that is unclear at this point as it does not seem to depend on the time unit.

(420) a. 6 óra óta
6 hour since
'since 6 o'clock'

b. karácsony óta
Christmas since
'since Christmas'

c. tavaly óta
last_year since
'since last year'

(421) a. 3 év óta
3 year since
'for 3 years'

b. ?két hét óta
two week since
'for two weeks'

c. 6 nap óta
6 day since
'for 6 days'

d. ?5 perc óta
5 minute since
'for 5 minutes'

Instead of the strategy using *óta*, duration for a certain time period can also be expressed with a possessive construction, and this one is not semantically restricted with respect to its complement (422).

(422) a. 3 év-e
3 year-Poss
'for the past 3 years'

b. két het-e
two week-Poss
'for the past two weeks'

c. 6 nap-ja
6 day-Poss
'for the past 6 days'

c. 5 perc-e
5 minute-Poss
'for the past 5 minutes'

As noted in Section 2.2.2.2.2 point *V*, in connection with (153), we can find names and third person singular personal pronouns in the complement of *óta*, in which case the resulting phrase refers to the time period since the time (e.g. the life or reign) of that person, (423). It is also grammatical with nominals referring to events, again denoting the time period since the event.

(423) a. Napóleon óta
Napoleon since
'since (the time of) Napoleon'

b. a háború / költözés óta
the war / moving since
'since [the war] / [the moving]'

2.3.2.2. Temporal adverbs

The temporal suffix *-kor* attaches to various nouns to express a point in time (424). When referring to hours or hours plus minutes on the clock, it can also be used with just the numeral, without the temporal unit(s).

(424) a. 6 óra-kor
6 hour-Tmp
'at 6 o'clock'

a'. 6-kor
6-Tmp
'at 6'

b. 5 óra 20 perc-kor
5 hour 20 minute-Tmp
'at 20 minutes past 5 o'clock'

b'. 5:20-kor
5:20-Tmp
'at 5:20'

c. éjfél-kor
midnight-Tmp
'at midnight'

d. karácsony-kor
Christmas-Tmp
'at Christmas'

There are two other suffixes that create temporal adverbs somewhat productively: the distributive *-(V)nként* and the iterative *-(V)nta/-(V)nte.* The distributive suffix combined with a temporal unit expresses repetition distributed across time in the measures expressed by the noun it attaches to (425).

(425) a. 6 órá-nként
6 hour-Iter
'every 6 hours'

b. 5 év-enként
5 year-Iter
'every 5 years'

The iterative suffix -(*V)nta/-(V)nte* (also called distributive-temporal) is used with nouns referring to temporal units or points in time. Similarly to the temporal use of the distributive suffix, it also expresses repetition distributed across time in the measures given as its complement (426).

(426) a. 2 nap-onta
2 day-Iter
'every 2 days'

b. 5 év-ente
5 year-Iter
'every 5 years'

The syntactic distribution of these semi-productive suffixes is discussed in Section 2.2.4.1.2 *VI, VII, VIII.*

2.3.2.3. Temporal uses of locative Ps

Many of the primarily spatial Ps can also be used to refer to time. Among the case suffixes, we have the superessive, the inessive, the sublative, and the ablative. The superessive case is used with the days of the week, with exact dates and with the noun *hét* 'week' (427), while the inessive case is used with names of months or when referring to years or larger units, e.g. centuries, (428).

(427) a. szombat-on
Saturday-Sup
'on Saturday'

b. április 1-én
April 1st-Poss.Sup
'on 1st of April'

c. múlt hét-en
past week-Sup
'last week'

(428) a január-ban
January-Ine
'in January'

b. 2017-ben
2017-Ine
'in 2017'

c. a 20. század-ban
the 20th century-Ine
'in the 20th century'

The directional sublative suffix is used when something is to happen by a certain time, irrespective of what kind of time unit we are dealing with. Ablative case expresses the opposite: the complement refers to the starting point and the P expresses "direction" in time away from that starting point. The examples in (429) and (430) illustrate these two suffixes, respectively.

(429) a. 6 órá-ra
6 hour-Sub
'for / by 6 o'clock'

b. kedd-re
Tuesday-Sub
'for / by Tuesday'

c. holnap-ra
tomorrow-Sub
'for / by tomorrow'

d. jövő hét-re
coming week-Sub
'for / by next week'

e. január-ra
January-Sub
'for / by January'

f. 2017-re
2017-Sub
'for / by 2017'

g. a 20. század-ra
the 20th century-Sub
'by the 20th century'

(430) a. 6 órá-tól
6 hour-Abl
'from 6 o'clock'

b. kedd-től
Tuesday-Abl
'from Tuesday'

c. holnap-tól
tomorrow-Abl
'from tomorrow'

d. jövő hét-től
coming week-Abl
'from next week'

e. január-tól
January-Abl
'from January'

f. 2017-től
2017-Abl
'from 2017'

g. a 20. század-tól
the 20th century-Abl
'from the 20th century'

The semantically opposite meaning, i.e., when the complement refers to the end point of the time period is expressed by the terminative suffix *-ig* with all types of complements (431):

(431) a. 6 órá-ig
6 hour-Ter
'until 6 o'clock'

b. kedd-ig
Tuesday-Ter
'until Tuesday'

c. holnap-ig
tomorrow-Ter
'until tomorrow'

d. jövő hét-ig
coming week-Ter
'until next week'

e. január-ig
January-Ter
'until January'

f. 2017-ig
2017-Ter
'until 2017'

g. a 20. század-ig
the 20th century-Ter
'until the 20th century'

At the same time, the terminative suffix can also mark duration in its temporal use (432). Since *6 óra* can both mean the time on the clock and duration in hours, the example in (431a) and (432a) is ambiguous, as the different translations show. (432a') is an often used alternative of (432a).

(432) a. 6 órá-ig
6 hour-Ter
'for 6 hours'

a'. 6 óra hossz-á-ig
6 hour length-Poss-Ter
'for (the length of) 6 hours'

b. 2 hét-ig
2 week-Ter
'for 2 weeks'

Non-suffixal Ps that are primarily spatial can also be used to refer to temporal relations. When used temporally, the locative P *alatt* 'under' refers to duration for a certain period that is specified in the complement (433).

(433) a. Mari két perc alatt lefutotta a távot.
Mari two minute under down.run.Past.DefObj.3Sg the distance.Acc
'Mari ran the distance in two minutes.'

b. Mindenki megoldotta a feladatot fél óra alatt.
everyone Perf.solve.Past.DefObj.3Sg the task.Acc half hour under
'Everyone solved the task in half an hour.'

c. Innen egy nap alatt érsz el London-ba.
here_from one day under reach.2Sg away London-Ill
'You can reach London in a day from here.'

d. 5 év alatt épült fel az áruház.
5 year under be_built.Past.3Sg up the store
'The department store was built in 5 years.'

The two postpositions *előtt* 'before' and *után* 'after' are opposites when they are used to refer to time: both of them need to specify a point in time in their complement.

(434) a karácsony előtt / után
Christmas before / after
'before / after Christmas'

b. 1989 előtt / után
1989 before / after
'before / after 1989'

c. múlt év előtt / után
past year before / after
'before / after last year'

(435) a. tegnap-előtt
yeasterday-before
'the day before yesterday'

b. tavaly-előtt
last_year-before'
'the year before last year

c. ez-előtt, az-előtt
this-before that-before
'before this, before that'

(436) a. holnap-után
tomorrow-after
'the day after tomorrow'

b. ez-után az-után
this-after that-after
'after this, after that'

It is also possible to specify a length in time before or after which the Figure is placed in time, and then the measure phrase appears in the instrumental case (437):

(437) a. két nap-pal ez-előtt
two day-Ins this-before
'two days ago'

b. néhány nap-pal újév után
some day-Ins New.Year after
'a few days after New Year's'

The Ps *körül* 'around' and *felé* 'towards' are very similar when used temporally: they both need a point in time as their complement (438)-(439).

(438) a. 6 óra körül
6 hour around
'at around 6 o'clock'

b. 1989 körül
1989 around
'in around 1989'

c. újév körül
New.Year around
'at around New Year'

d. a 15. század körül
the 15th century around
'at around the 15th century'

(439) a. 6 óra felé
6 hour towards
'at around 6 o'clock'

b. 1989 felé
1989 towards
'in around 1989'

c. újév felé
New.Year towards
'at around New Year'

d. ?a 15. század felé
the 15th century towards
'by around the 15th century'

The postposition *között/közt* 'between' is used the same way temporally as when referring to spatial relations: it needs two points in time and specifies the time period between them (440).

(440) karácsony és újév között
Christmas and New.Year between
'between Christmas and New Year'

The case-assigning postpositions *át* 'over, through', *keresztül* 'across, through', as well as the locative *belül* 'inside', *felül* 'above', and *túl* 'beyond' are also used temporally and they refer to a period of time in relation to their complement (441).

(441) a. két nap-on át
two day-Sup over
'for two days'

b. két év-en keresztül
two year-Sup across
'for two years'

c. egy hét-en belül
one week-Sup inside
'within a week'

d. hat nap-on túl
six day-Sup beyond
'beyond six days'

2.3.3. Other: non-spatiotemporal Ps

2.3.3.1. Non-spatiotemporal case suffixes

There are a few suffixes that are case-markers but are not spatial or temporal in meaning:

Table 17: Non-spatiotemporal case suffixes

CASE NAME	CASE SUFFIX	MEANING
instrumental	*-val, -vel, -Cal, -Cel*	with something or somebody
translative(-essive)	*-vá, -vé, -Cá, -Cé*	into (expressing change of state)
causal(-final)	*-ért*	for (reason, aim)
essive-formal	*-ként*	as (role), in the capacity of

The instrumental case has two main uses: it marks the instrument or means of an action (the instrumental use), or it means accompaniment in an event (the comitative use). (442) illustrates each meaning with an example.

(442) a. Anna dugóhúzó-val nyitotta ki az üveget.
Anna corkscrew-Ins open.Past.DefObj.3Sg out the bottle.Acc
'Anna opened the bottle with a corkscrew.'

b. Anna Mari-val megy ma mozi-ba.
Anna Mari-Ins go.3Sg today cinema-Ill
'Anna is going to the cinema with Mari today.'

The translative(-essive) case suffix is used as a marker of resultative secondary predicates, it does not have a spatial meaning but is associated with change-of-state. It can be attached to nouns and to adjectives, as (443) and (444) show. The syntax of PPs as secondary predicates will be discussed in Chapter 4.

(443) Pál a kedvenc tanárom-má vált.
Pál the favorite teacher.Poss.1Sg-Tra become.Past.3Sg
'Pál became my favorite teacher.'

(444) A vihar ijesztő-vé vált.
the storm frightening-Tra become.Past.3Sg
'The storm got frightening.'

The causal(-final) *-ért* suffix can express the cause or reason in an event (445a) or the goal of an event (445b).

(445) a. Pált lopás-ért tartóztatták le.
Pál.Acc theft-Cau arrest.Past.DefObj.3Pl down
'Pál was arrested for theft.'

b. El-mentem kenyér-ért a bolt-ba.
away-go.Past.1Sg bread-Cau the shop-Ill
'I went to the shop for bread.'

Finally, the essive-formal is appears on NPs used as depictive secondary predicates, which express the role or state of a participant (446).

(446) a. Anna asszisztens-ként dolgozik.
Anna assistant-FoE work.3Sg
'Anna works as an assistant.'

b. Anna kutató-ként utazott az Antarktisz-ra.
Anna researcher-FoE travel.Past.3Sg the Antarctica-Sub
'Anna traveled to the Antarctica as a researcher.'

2.3.3.2. Non-spatiotemporal case-like postpositions

There are case-like postpositions that are not spatio-temporal. Those are listed here that do not have a spatial/temporal meaning synchronically, although they may have grammaticalized from spatial Ps.

Table 18: Non-spatiotemporal case-like Ps

CASE-LIKE P	MEANING
által	by
ellen	against
gyanánt	as, in the guise of
helyett	instead
miatt	because of
nélkül	without
szerint	according to
végett	in order to, due to

The interpretation of the Ps in Table 18 varies greatly but they express typical non-spatial relations such as cause or agent. Some of them are rather opaque (e.g. *miatt* 'because of', *szerint* 'according to'), even though they contain an obsolete spatial case-marker.

The postposition *által* 'by' is used with agentive arguments in standard Hungarian (447).

(447) a Mari által olvasott könyv
the Mary by read.Part book
'the book read by Mary'

Diachronically, *által* was a (superessive) case-assigning P and a verbal particle which had a directional meaning: 'via, through, across, over' (448). It still has this meaning dialectally, but in the standard language the case-assigning P *át* 'through, via, across, over' is used in this meaning (449).

(448) ezen nemes vármegyé-n által
this.Sup noble county-Sup via
'via this noble county'

(449) a vármegyé-n át
the county-Sup via
'via the county'

The standard meaning of postposition *végett* is 'in order to' (450), however, in spoken language and dialectally it is also used to express a reason ('due to'), as in (451).

(450) a félreértések elkerülése végett
the misunderstanding.Pl avoiding.Poss so_as_to
'so as to avoid [any] misunderstandings'

(451) %Juli a betegsége végett nem tudott iskolába menni.
Juli the illness.Poss.3Sg with_aim_of not could school.Ill go.Inf
'Juli could not go to school due to her illness.'

2.3.3.3. Non-spatiotemporal case-assigning postpositions

There are only a couple of case-assigning Ps with non-spatiotemporal meanings:

Table 19: Non-spatiotemporal case-assigning Ps

CASE-ASSIGNING P	MEANING
együtt	together with
képest	compared to, for

Együtt 'together with' has a comitative meaning, and may take a case-marked nominal that bears the instrumental/comitative case similarly to its English counterpart (452).

(452) A gyerekek Kati-val együtt érkeztek.
the children Kati-Ins together arrive.Past.3Pl
'The children arrived.together with Kati.'

The other non-spatial case-assigning P has a kind of standard-of-comparison meaning, as illustrated in (453):

(453) Mari-hoz képest mindenki gyors.
Mari-All compared_to everyone fast
'Everyone is fast compared to Mari.'

2.3.3.4. Non-spatiotemporal particles

As already mentioned earlier, there is one verbal particle that does not really have a spatial meaning in Modern Hungarian, and that is the particle *meg*, which largely functions as a telicizing element in the clause. However, in a couple of collocations it can still be understood as being used in its old meaning 'back' (454):

(454) Pál meg-adta a pénzt, amivel tartozott.
Pál Perf-give.Past.DefObj.3Sg the money.Acc which.Ins owe.Past.3Sg
'Pál returned (lit. gave back) the money that he owed.'

This is no longer productive in the language. If we have a sentence such as (455a), the meaning is not that the guests arrived back, it just means that they have arrived, the event of arriving has reached completion, and the same is true for (455b). (456a) is ungrammatical, it cannot mean that the guests went back to a place where they had been before; this meaning can be expressed using a different particle, namely, *vissza* 'back' (456b), and the verbal particle *el* 'away' (456c) can be used if the intended meaning was that they left (i.e., simple telicity by the particle).

(455) a. A vendégek meg-érkeztek.
the guests Perf-arrive.Past.3Pl
'The guests arrived.'

b. A vendégek meg-jöttek.
the guests Perf-come.Past.3Pl
'The guests arrived.'

(456) a. *A vendégek meg-mentek.
the guest.Pl Perf-went.3Pl
Intended meaning: 'The guests went back.'

b. A vendégek vissza-mentek.
the guests back-went.3Pl
'The guests went back.'

c. A vendégek el-mentek.
the guests away-went.3Pl
'The guests left (lit. went away).'

Chapter 4 will discuss the syntactic behavior and semantic contribution of particles in far more detail, here we only intended to introduce their basic semantic contribution.

2.3.3.5. Non-spatiotemporal adverbs

There are many adverbs that are neither spatial nor temporal. Several suffixes discussed in Sections 2.2.4.1.1 and 2.2.4.1.2 form such adverbs. Other non-spatial and non-temporal adverbs (e.g. manner adverbs and all the sentence-level adverbs) have an opaque morphological makeup (often with an obsolete spatial marker). These will be discussed in detail in Chapter 7. Furthermore, the volume on Adjectival Phrases will also deal with the *-n/-an/-en* suffix as it attaches to adjectives to form depictive secondary predicates, and the volume on Non-Finite and Semi-Finite Verb Phrases will describe the properties of the *-va/-ve* adverbial participles, which are not grammaticalized into simple manner PPs.

2.4. Where to draw the line: Borderline cases of postpositions

Taking stock of Ps, there is usually a core list of items everyone takes to be postpositional. There are, however, quite a few elements that some grammars list as postpositions, while others do not list them at all. This section discusses two groups of such borderline cases: the first one includes participial forms (Section 2.4.1), which show similarities to case-assigning Ps, while the second group has items of possessive origin (Section 2.4.2), which have some properties in common with case-like Ps. Kenesei *et al.* (1998) call the elements discussed below "transitional postpositions", referring to the fact that they are not fully grammaticalized members of the group of Ps. É. Kiss (1999, 2002), on the other hand, takes them to be participles and possessive phrases, respectively.

2.4.1. Participial postpositions

2.4.1.1. The inventory and form of participial postpositions

Participial postpositions comprise a verbal stem and the *-va/-ve* adverbial participial suffix (see the volume on Non-Finite and Semi-Finite Verb Phrases). The ordinary participial use of such forms is illustrated in (457).

(457) a. Pál [$_{\text{PartP}}$ az erkélyen ül-ve] olvas.
Pál the balcony.Sup sit-Part read.3Sg
'Pál is reading sitting on the balcony.'

b. A petíciót [$_{\text{PartP}}$ mindenki által aláír-va] küldtük el.
the petition.Acc everybody by under.write-Part send.Past.DefObj.1Pl away
'We sent the petition such that it was signed by everybody.'

Table 20 lists the participial forms that have sometimes been considered to be postpositions, i.e., to have grammaticalized from participial verbs into P elements. As already mentioned above, their status as participles or Ps is somewhat controversial in the literature. The major reason to regard them as members of the category of case-assigning Ps is that they obligatorily take an oblique case-marked complement.

Table 20: Participial postpositions

	P	MEANING	SUBCATEGORIZED CASE
TEMPORAL	*kezdve*	beginning from	ablative
	fogva	beginning from	ablative
OTHER	*fogva*	because of, due to	adessive
	nézve	regarding	sublative

I. Temporal Ps

The participle *kezd-ve* is made up of the verb *kezd* 'begin' and the adverbial participial suffix. Together they have a temporal interpretation, and the complement has to denote the starting point of the time interval (458).

(458) a. 1900-tól kezdve
1900-Abl begin.Part
'beginning from 1900'

b. január-tól kezdve
January-Abl begin.Part
'beginning from January'

c. tegnap-tól kezdve
yesterday-Abl begin.Part
'beginning from yesterday'

d. 6 órá-tól kezdve
6 hour-Abl begin.Part
'beginning from 6 o'clock'

Compare the garden variety participial use of *kezdve* in (459).

(459) a. [A kezelést kezd-ve] ne felejtsük el a fertőtlenítést.
the treatment.Acc start-Part not forget.Subj.1Pl away the disinfection.Acc
'When stating the treatment, let us not forget about disinfection.'

b. A szavakat [hátul-ról kezd-ve] /[az e betű-vel kezd-ve] tanulom.
the word.Pl.Acc back-Del start-Part / the e letter-Ins start-Part learn.DefObj.1Sg
'I learn the words [starting from the back of the list] / [starting with the letter E].'

The participial element *fog-va* contains the verb *fog* 'hold' and the adverbial participial suffix. Both the form of the complement and the fact that the complement has to refer to the starting point of the time period makes this construction similar to *kezdve,* and it is also used in the same contexts where *kezdve* is grammatical, as illustrated in (460).

(460) a. 1900-tól fogva
1900-Abl hold.Part
'beginning from 1900'

b. január-tól fogva
January-Abl hold.Part
'beginning from January'

c. tegnap-tól fogva
yesterday-Abl hold.Part
'beginning from yesterday'

d. 6 órá-tól fogva
6 hour-Abl hold.Part
'beginning from 6 o'clock'

The genuine participial use of *fogva* is illustrated in (461) for comparison.

(461) a. Pál [a kislánya kezé-t fog-va] sétál.
Pál the little.daughter hand.Poss-Acc hold-Part walk.3Sg
'Pál is walking holding his little daughter's hand.'

b. Pált [a lábá-nál fog-va] húzták ki a gödörből.
Pál.Acc the leg.Poss-Ade hold-Part pull.Past.DefObj.3Pl out the pit.Ela
'They pulled Pál out of the pit holding his legs.'

There are a couple of interesting combinations with this participial form. (462a) shows that the participial P-like element can have 'now' as its complement, however, the form is restricted, and it has to be the longer, transparently adverbial form *mostan* 'now'; the regularly used form *most* 'now' is ungrammatical. (462b) provides an example with more or less the same meaning. While the complement is a locative element, the temporal reading is still the more salient one (although the locative reading is available as well).

(462) a. mostan-tól / *most-tól fogva
now-Abl / now-Abl hold.Part
'beginning from now'

b. innen-től fogva
from_here-Abl hold.Part
'beginning from now / here'

II. Other Ps

Fogva also has a non-temporal use. In this use it means 'because of, due to' and it takes an adessive rather than an ablative complement (463).

(463) a törvény erejé-nél fogva
the law power.Poss-Ade hold.Part
'by the power of law'

The third P-like participial element is not temporal either: it consists of the verb *néz* 'look, regard' and the participial suffix and its complement carries the sublative suffix (464).

(464) mindenki-re nézve
everyone-Sub regard.Part
'regarding everyone'

The ordinary participial use of *nézve* is shown in (465).

(465) Ili [a kirakatok-at néz-ve] sétált.
Ili the shop_window.Pl-Acc look-Part walk.Past.3Sg
'Ili was walking looking at the shop windows.'

Finally, the temporal P *múlva* 'in / after (X time)' was originally also a participle, *múl-va* 'go.by-Part', but the morpheme boundary no longer seems transparent. *Múlva* is generally treated as a postposition. We also discussed it among case-like postpositions (Section 2.2.2.2.1 point *II*) and argued in detail that its properties are no longer compatible with a participial analysis.

2.4.1.2. Complementation

I. The form of the complement

As shown in the previous Section, participial Ps obligatorily take an oblique case-marked complement: *kezdve* (458) and temporal *fogva* (460), both meaning 'beginning from', take an ablative marked complement, causal *fogva* 'because of, due to' takes an adessive complement (463), and the complement of *nézve* 'regarding' bears the sublative case (464). The oblique marked complement is the major reason to regard these items as case-assigning Ps. As shown in (459a), (461a) and (465), in their genuine participial use these elements combine with an accusative object, and in this use they take oblique modifiers with cases different from the subcategorized case in their P use: (459b) and (461b).

II. PP-internal position with respect to the complement

Participial Ps always follow their complement.

(466) a. 1900-tól kezdve
1900-Abl start.Part
'starting from 1900'

a'. *kezdve 1900-tól
start.Part 1900-Abl
Intended meaning: 'starting from 1900'

b. január-tól fogva
January-Abl hold.Part
'beginning from January'

b'. *fogva január-tól
hold.Part January-Abl
Intended meaning: 'beginning from January'

c. ennél fogva
this.Ade hold.Part
'due to this'

c'. *fogva ennél
hold.Part this.Ade
Intended meaning: 'due to this'

d. az elnök-re nézve
the president-Sub look.Part
'regarding / for the president'

d'. *nézve az elnök-re
look.Part the president-Sub
Intended meaning: 'regarding / for the president'

Many case-assigning and all case-like Ps are also strictly postpositional (Section 2.2.2.3.2 point *II* and Section 2.2.2.2.2 point *II*), and all genuine participial phrases, including adverbial participles, are also strictly head-final.

III. Dropping the complement

Participial Ps must have an overt complement. In (467), the star means that the use of P without its complement is ungrammatical; it does not mean that the participial form itself is ill-formed.

(467) a. *kezdve
start.Part
Intended meaning: 'starting from'

b. *fogva
hold.Part
Intended meaning: 'beginning from'

c. *fogva
hold.Part
Intended meaning: 'due to'

d. *nézve
look.Part
Intended meaning: 'regarding / for'

As shown in Section 2.2.2.3.2 point *III*, some case-assinging Ps can be used without a complement, expressing (spatial or temporal) relation between the Ground and a deictic center of the utterance (468).

(468) a. A labda a vonal-on alul van. [case-assigning P]
the ball the line-Sup under be.3Sg
'The ball is under the line.'

b. A labda alul van.
the ball under be.3Sg
'The ball is down / [down there] (with respect to a reference point).'

This, however, does not characterize all case-assigning Ps, and case-like Ps cannot be used in this way either (Section 2.2.2.2.2 point *III*). *Kezdve* 'beginning with', *fogva* 'beginning with, due to' and *nézve* 'regarding' are based on transitive verbs; their garden variety participial uses thus take an accusative marked complement. These participles, however, can be used without an oblique phrase, as shown in (459a), (461a) and (465).

IV. The complement's demonstrative modifier

If the DP complement of the participial P has a demonstrative modifier, then the case selected by the P appears on the demonstrative, too (469).

(469) a. ettől az év-től fogva / kezdve [participial P]
this.Abl the year-Abl hold.Part / start.Part
'beginning from this year'

b. ennél az indok-nál fogva
this.Ade the reason-Ade hold.Part
'due to this reason'

c. erre a teljesítmény-re nézve
this.Sub and achievement-Sub look.Part
'regarding this achievement'

In this regard the case selected by partitive Ps has the same distribution as the case selected by case-assigning Ps (Section 2.2.2.3.2 point *IV*) and case suffixes not selected by a P (Section 2.2.1.2 point *IV*).

(470) a. ettől a ház-tól távol [case-assigning P]
this.Abl the house-Abl far_from
'far from this house'

b. ettől a ház-tól [case suffix]
this.Abl the house-Abl
'from this house'

V. Personal pronoun complements

If the complement of participial Ps is a personal pronoun, the case marker is followed by an agreement suffix (471). The personal pronoun itself can be dropped, as its reference is recoverable from the agreement.

(471) a. (én-)től-em kezdve [participial P]
I-Abl-1Sg begin.Part
'beginning from me'

b. (te-)rá-d nézve
you-Sub-2Sg regard.Part
'regarding you'

This is similar to what we see with ordinary case-assigning Ps and case suffixes (472).

(472) a. (én-)rajt-am kívül [case-assigning P]
I-Sup-1Sg ouside_of
'apart from me'

b (én-)rajt-am [case suffix]
I-Sup-1Sg
'on me'

Fogva in its temporal sense seems to always require a complement that expresses a 'location' in time, so its complement cannot be a personal pronoun (473). (The complement of *kezdve* can be a nominal which does not refer to a static point in time but to a source point in a spatial or temporal path, and so it allows for a pronominal complement, too (471a).)

(473) *én-től-em fogva
I-Abl-1Sg begin.Part
Intended meaning: 'beginning from me'

The causal use of *fogva* is also incompatible with a personal pronoun complement (474).

(474) *én-nál-am fogva
I-Ade-1Sg begin.Part
Intended meaning: 'because of me'

2.4.1.3. Separability of the P and its complement in the clause

Participial Ps are not separable from their complement; they must stay within the same constituent as their complement and cannot be P-stranded in constituent questions, for instance, cf. (475) and (476).

(475) a. Mikor-tól fogva kell elektronikusan pályázni? [participial P]
when-Abl hold.Part must.3Sg electronically apply.Inf
'From when does one have to apply electronically?'

b. Mikor-tól kezdve kell elektronikusan pályázni?
when-Abl start.Part must.3Sg electronically apply.Inf
'From when does one have to apply electronically'

c. Mi-nél fogva jelenthetjük ezt ki?
what-Ade hold.Part state.Mod.1Pl this.Acc out
'For what reason can we state this?'

d. Kik-re nézve káros ez?
who.Pl. look.Part harmful this
'For whom is this harmful?'

(476) a. *Mikor-tól kell elektronikusan pályázni fogva?
when-Abl must.3Sg electronically apply.Inf hold.Part
Intended meaning: 'From when does one have to apply electronically?'

b. *Mikor-tól kell kezdve elektronikusan pályázni?
when-Abl must.3Sg start.Part electronically apply.Inf
Intended meaning: 'From when does one have to apply electronically.'

c. *Mi-nél jelenthetjük fogva ezt ki?
what-Ade state.Mod.1Pl hold.Part this.Acc out
Intended meaning: 'For what reason can we state this?'

d. *Kik-re káros ez nézve?
who.Pl. harmful this look.Part
Intended meaning: 'For whom is this harmful?'

This makes participial Ps similar to some case-assigning postpositions: recall from Section 2.2.2.3.3 that some case-assigning Ps are also inseparable from their complement (and so are case-like Ps, cf. Section 2.2.2.2.3).

(477) a. Mi-n sétáltál át? [case-assigning P]
what-Sup walk.Past.2Sg through
'What did you walk through?'

b. ?Mi-vel van szemközt a posta?
what-Ins be.3Sg opposite_to the post.office
'What is the post office opposite to?'

c. *Mi-vel jött szemből a labda?
what-Sup come.Past.3Sg from_opposite_to the ball
Intended meaning: 'What is such that the ball came from opposite to it?'

However, this is not an argument for the P-status of these elements in itself, as subextraction from adverbial participial constituents is also disallowed.

2.4.1.4. *Combination with the Delative and Sublative case*

Participial Ps do not combine with the delative and the sublative case (478).

(478) a. *1900-tól kezdve-ről/re
1900-Abl start.Part-Del/Sub
Intended meaning: 'from / until beginning with 1900'

b. *január-tól fogva-ról/ra
January-Abl hold.Part-Del/Sub
Intended meaning: 'from / until beginning with January'

c. *ennél fogva-ról/re
this.Ade hold.Part-Del/Sub
Intended meaning: 'from / to therefore'

d. *az elnök-re nézve-ről/re
the president-Sub look.Part-Del/Sub
Intended meaning: 'from / to considering the president'

All case-assigning Ps and most case-like Ps also reject combination with these case suffixes (see Sections 2.2.2.2.4 and 2.2.2.3.4), and adverbial participles in general cannot be case-marked (with any case suffix) either.

2.4.1.5. N + participial Ps modifying a noun

PPs headed by participial Ps cannot function as noun modifiers. In the pre-N position they can be licensed by a verb in the present participial form (479).

(479) a. a [tavaly-tól fogva / kezdve] *(tart-ó) bojkott
the last_year-Abl hold.Part/ start.Part last-ing boycott
'the boycott that has been going on since last year'

b. a [megalapozatlan indok-nál fogva] *(történ-ő) átalakítás
the unsubstantiated reason-Ade hold.Part happen-ing reorganization
'the reorganization that happens for unsubstantiated reasons'

c. a [teljesítmény-re nézve] *(val-ó) hatás
the achievement-Sub look.Part be-ing effect
'the effect regarding / on the achievement'

Attributivization by *-i* is not compatible with participial Ps, however (480).

(480) a. *a [tavaly-tól fogva]-i bojkott
the last_year-Abl hold.Part-Attr boycott
Intended meaning: 'the boycott that has been going on since year'

a'. *a [tavaly-tól kezdve]-i bojkott
the last_year-Abl start.Part-Attr boycott
Intended meaning: 'the boycott that has been going on since year'

b. *a [megalapozatlan indok-nál fogva]-i átalakítás
the unsubstantiated reason-Ade hold.Part-Attr reorganization
Intended meaning: 'the reorganization that happens for unsubstantiated reasons'

c. *a [teljesítmény-re nézve]-i hatás
the achievement-Sub look.Part-Attr effect
Intended meaning: 'the effect regarding / on the achievement'

As described in Section 2.2.2.3.5, case-assigning Ps can be turned into N-modifiers either via a present participle or via *-i* attributivization (481).

(481) a. *a vonal-on felül minta [case-assigning P]
the line-Sup above pattern
Intended meaning: 'the pattern above the line'

b. a vonal-on felül-i minta
the line-Sup above-Attr pattern
'the pattern above the line'

c. a vonal-on felül levő minta
the line-Sup above be.Part pattern
'the pattern above the line'

Genuine adverbial participles, on the other hand, serve as modifiers of verb phrases and cannot be turned into N-modifiers either via the addition of a present participle or the *-i* attributivizer.

2.4.1.6. Modification

Degree modifiers precede the complement of participial Ps (482). They cannot intervene between the P and its complement and cannot follow the P either.

(482) a. pontosan / egészen / majdnem 1900-tól kezdve
exactly / completely / almost 1900-Abl start.Part
'starting [all the way] / almost from 1900'

a'. *1900-tól pontosan / egészen / majdnem kezdve
1900-Abl exactly / completely / almost start.Part
Intended meaning: 'starting [all the way] / almost from 1900'

a''.*1900-tól kezdve pontosan / egészen / majdnem
1900-Abl start.Part exactly / completely / almost
Intended meaning: 'starting [all the way] / almost from 1900'

b. pontosan / egészen / majdnem január-tól fogva
exactly / completely / almost January-Abl hold.Part
'beginning [all the way] / almost from January'

b'. *január-tól pontosan / egészen / majdnem fogva
January-Abl exactly / completely / almost hold.Part
Intended meaning: 'beginning [all the way] / almost from January'

b''.*január-tól fogva pontosan / egészen / majdnem
January-Abl hold.Part exactly / completely / almost
Intended meaning: 'beginning [all the way] / almost from January'

c. pontosan ennél (*pontosan) fogva (*pontosan)
exactly this.Ade exactly hold.Part exactly
'exactly due to this'

d. pontosan az elnök-re (*pontosan) nézve (*pontosan)
exactly the president-Sub exactly look.Part exactly
'regarding / for exactly president'

Many case-assigning Ps and all case-like Ps have this distribution, too (Sections 2.2.2.3.6 and 2.2.2.2.6 respectively). Genuine adverbial participles are also strongly head-final and do not allow modifiers to appear after the participial verb (483).

(483) az előadást pontosan kezd-ve (*pontosan) [participle]
the lecture.Acc exactly start-Part exactly
'starting the lecture on time'

They do, however, allow a degree modifier to intervene between the participle and its oblique modifier. (484) shows the adverbial participial use of *fogva*. Unlike in (482c), here it is possible for a semantically appropriate degree modifier to intervene between an adessive NP/DP modifier and *fogva*.

(484) Pált [a lábá-nál erősen fog-va] kilógatják az ablakon.
Pál.Acc the foot.Poss.3Sg-Ade strongly hold-Part out.hang.DefObj.3Pl the window.Sup
'They are hanging Pál out of the window, holding him strongly by his foot.'

Measure phrases are not compatible with participial Ps. In (485c,d) modification by measure phrases is expected to fail independently, too, due to the meaning of these Ps.

(485) a. *két nappal 1900-tól kezdve
two day.Ins 1900-Abl start.Part
Intended meaning: 'two days starting from 1900'

b. *két nappal január-tól fogva
two day.Ins January-Abl hold.Part
Intended meaning: 'two days starting from January'

c. *sokkal ennél fogva
much.Ins this.Ade hold.Part
Intended meaning: 'very much therefore'

d. *sokkal az elnök-re nézve
much.Ins the president-Sub look.Part
Intended meaning: 'as (very) much regards the president'

2.4.1.7. Conjunction reduction

Backward conjunction reduction is possible with participial Ps (486), similarly to case-like and case-assigning Ps (Sections 2.2.2.2.7 and 2.2.2.3.7).

(486) • Backward conjunction reduction

a. 1900-tól vagy 2000-től fogva / kezdve
1900-Abl or 2000-Abl hold.Part / start.Part
'beginning from 1900 or 2000'

b. korá-nál és beosztásá-nál fogva
age.Poss-Ade and rank-Ade hold.Part
'due to his age and rank'

c. az elnök-re és az osztályvezető-re nézve
the president-Sub and the department.leader-Sub look.Part
'regarding the president and the department leader'

Forward conjunction reduction cannot be tested with participial Ps. This test would require two different participial Ps which subcategorize for the same oblique case. There are only two Ps which take the same case: *kezdve* and *fogva* both take the ablative case. However, these are synonyms, thus coordinating PPs with them produces semantically anomalous phrases. (487a) and (487b) could be used in a question in a context in which the addressee did not hear clearly which P was used by the speaker.

(487) • Forward conjunction reduction

a. #1900-tól kezdve vagy 1900-tól fogva
1900-Abl start.Part or 1900-Abl hold.Part
'starting with 1900 or beginning with 1900'

b. #1900-tól kezdve vagy fogva
1900-Abl start.Part or hold.Part
'starting or beginning with 1900'

2.4.1.8. Combination with a verbal particle

Like other non-finite forms, adverbial participles can be formed from particle-verbs (488).

(488) a. az előadást el-kezd-ve [participle]
the lecture.Acc away-start-Part
'starting the lecture'

a'. az előadást meg-kezd-ve
the lecture.Acc Perf-start-Part
'starting the lecture'

b. a lábá-nál meg-fog-va
the foot.Poss.3Sg-Ade Perf-hold-Part
'holding him by his foot'

c. a kép-re rá-néz-ve
the picture-Sub onto-look-Part
'looking at the picture'

c'. a filmet meg-néz-ve
the movie.Acc Perf-look-Part
'having watched the movie'

Verbal particles cannot appear with participial Ps. (489) forms a minimal pair with (488a'). While the particle *meg* is perfectly compatible with the participle of 'start', it cannot occur with the transitional P *kezdve* 'beginning with'.

(489) *1900-tól meg-kezd-ve
1900-Abl Perf-start-Part
'starting from 1900'

Meg is also compatible with the participle of *fog* 'hold' (488b), but its presence forces a participial reading and excludes the P use, even in the presence of the adessive NP (490).

(490) ennél meg-fog-va
this.Ade Perf-hold-Part
'grabbing it by this' (Not: 'due to this')

Similarly, *rá* 'onto' can occur with the participle of *néz* 'look, regard' (488c), but this disallows the P reading even if the sublative NP is present (491).

(491) az elnök-re rá-néz-ve
the president-Sub onto-look-Part
'looking at the president' (Not: 'regarding the president')

2.4.1.9. Taking stock: participial Ps between participles and Ps

Participial Ps have some distributional properties which are shared with both case-assigning Ps and participles. They do not combine with the delative or the sublative case suffix and cannot be followed by degree (or other) modifiers. As these properties characterize both case-assigning Ps and adverbial participles, they are not revealing about the syntactic category of the forms discussed in this section.

The way participial Ps interact with personal pronoun complements and the appearance of demonstrative concord in their NP/DP complement does not shed light on their syntactic category either. These properties are solely due to the presence of the oblique case suffix and have no bearing on whether the lexeme selecting the oblique case is an adverbial participle or a P.

Some properties, however, firmly group participial Ps with case-assigning Ps rather than with ordinary adverbial participles. They have lost the participial verb's ability to take an accusative complement and a wide variety of optional oblique modifiers. Like case-assigning Ps, they must occur with an oblique NP headed by a particular (subcategorized) case suffix and compared to the participial verb, some have acquired a more specialized meaning (*fogva* means 'holding (with one's hands), taking' as an adverbial participle and 'beginning with, due to' as a transitional P; *nézve* means 'looking, regarding' in its adverbial participle use but as a transitional P it can only mean 'regarding, with respect to'). A further property that groups them with Ps is that they can be turned into prenominal N-modifiers by the addition of a present participial verb (crucially, this is not possible for genuine adverbial participles). The strict adjacency between the selected oblique NP/DP and the participial form (i.e. the impossibility of inserting a degree modifier into the position directly preceding the participle) also reinforces the similarity to postpositions, and the ban on the appearance of verbal particles further distances participial Ps from genuine adverbial participles. At the same time, the morpheme boundary between the verbal stem and the participial suffix has not become opaque for speakers. For these reasons, we may consider these forms to be transitional, in-between two categories, though closer to Ps than to participles.

2.4.2. *Possessive postpositions*

2.4.2.1. *The inventory and form of possessive postpositions*

In Section 2.2.2.2.1 point *III* we saw that the case-like Ps *helyett* 'instead of' and *gyanánt* 'as, by way of, in lieu of' originated in possessive structures but have become fully grammaticalized Ps and do not share the morpho-syntactic properties of possessed noun phrases any longer. However, some Ps originating in possessive constructions have not yet fully grammaticalized into Ps. These forms, listed in Table 21, may be regarded as transitional elements (Kenesei *et al.* 1998, in fact, call them transitional Ps). In this section we shall discuss their properties in detail, comparing them with garden variety case-like Ps with and without a possessive origin.

Table 21: Possessive postpositions

	POSSESSIVE P	MEANING
SPATIAL	*helyében*	in X's place/shoes
TEMPORAL	*táján*	around (a point in time)
	tájékán	around (a point in time)
	folyamán	during

	során	during
OTHER	*folytán*	owing to
	révén	by means of, through
	útján	by way of
	esetén	in case of
	nyomán	based on X, following X
	ellenére	despite
	részére	for (beneficient)
	számára	for (beneficient, experiencer)
	fejében	in exchange for

Possessive Ps are made up of a noun, the possessive suffix *-a/-e/-ja/-je* and a spatial case suffix.

(492) János hely-é-ben
János place-Poss-Ine
'in János' place / shoes'

If the complement of a possessive P is a personal pronoun, then (much like case-like Ps) the P agrees with the pronoun's person-number features. This agreement precedes the spatial case suffix (493).

(493) az én hely-em-ben, a te hely-ed-ben, az ő hely-é-ben
the I place-Poss.1Sg-Ine the you(Sg) place-Poss.2Sg-Ine, the he place-Poss.3Sg-Ine
'in my place / shoes, in your place / shoes, in his place / shoes'

This is the same morpheme order that we find in genuine possessive constructions (494).

(494) az én kez-em-ben, a te kez-ed-ben, az ő kez-é-ben
the I hand-Poss.1Sg-Ine the you(Sg) hand-Poss.2Sg-Ine, the he hand-Poss.3Sg-Ine
'in my hand, in your hand, in his hand'

In the case of oblique marked personal pronouns and case-like Ps with a personal pronoun complement, the case suffix (495) or case-like P (496) precedes the agreement, however (see Section 2.2.1.2 point *VB* and Section 2.2.2.2.2 point *V*).

(495) én-benn-em, te-benn-ed, ő-benn-e [case suffix]
I-Ine-Poss.1Sg you(Sg)-Ine-Poss.2Sg he-Ine-Poss.3Sg
'in me, in you(Sg), in him'

(496) én-mellett-em, te-mellett-ed, ő-mellett-e [case-like P]
I-next_to-Poss.1Sg you(Sg)-next_to-Poss.2Sg he-next_to-Poss.3Sg
'next to me, next to you(Sg), next to him'

In this respect possessive Ps are closer to ordinary possessive constructions than to case-like Ps.

I. Spatial Ps

The only spatial possessive P is *helyében* 'in X's place / shoes', which comprises the noun *hely* 'place', the possessive suffix and the inessive (*-ban/-ben*) case marker (497).

(497) Pál hely-é-ben otthon maradnék.
Pál place-Poss-Ine at_home stay.Cond.1Sg
'[If I were] in Pál's place / shoes, I would stay at home.'

As discussed in Section 2.2.2.2.1 point *III*, the case-like P *helyett* 'instead of' has a similar morphemic composition, but instead of the productive inessive case, it involves the obsolete *-(V)t* locative suffix (498).

(498) Pál helyett Katit hívom meg.
Pál instead_of Kati.Acc invite.DefObj.1Sg Perf
'I shall invite Kati instead of Pál.'

The meaning of the case-like *helyett* 'instead of' is less transparently compositional than that of the possessive *helyében* 'in X's place / shoes'. The morphemic composition of case-like *helyett* 'instead of' is also opaque to speakers, while the internal structure of *helyében* 'in X's places / shoes' is still transparent to a large degree.

II. Temporal Ps

The temporal elements *táján* and *tájékán* 'around (a point in time)' comprise the noun *táj* or *tájék*, both meaning 'region, country, land', the possessive suffix and the superessive (*-n/-on/-en/-ön*) case suffix (499).

(499) karácsony táj-á-n / tájék-á-n
Christmas area-Poss-Sup / area-Poss-Sup
'around Christmas'

These Ps are used as alternatives to the fully grammaticalized *tájban / tájt* 'around' discussed in Section 2.2.2.2.1 point *II* (500).

(500) a. 6 óra 10 perc ?táján / tájékán
6 hour 10 minute around / around
'at around 10 past 6'

b. húsvét táján / tájékán
Easter around / around
'at around Easter'

c. múlt hét táján / tájékán
last week around / around
'around last week'

d. január táján / tájékán
January around / around
'(in) around January'

In some contexts the possessive Ps *táján* and *tájékán* are not fully grammatical, however (501). In these cases the full-fledged Ps *tájban / tájt* 'around' can be used instead.

(501) a. 6 óra tájban / ?tájékán / ?táján
6 hour around / around / around
'at around 6 o'clock'

b. negyed 10 tájban / ?tájékán / ?táján
quarter 10 around / around / around
'at around quarter past nine'

c. dél tájban / *tájékán / *táján
noon around / around / around
'at around noon'

Folyamán and *során* both mean 'during'. They can be decomposed into the noun *folyam* 'course, river' or *sor* 'row, line, queue' the possessive suffix and the superessive (*-n/-on/-en/-ön*) case suffix. As Ps they refer to a temporal duration specified in their complement (502).

(502) a. a múlt év folyam-á-n
the past year course-Poss-Sup
'[in the course of] / during the past year'

b. a múlt év sor-á-n
the past year line-Poss-Sup
'during the past year'

The primarily spatial case-like P *alatt* 'under' can also be used in some temporal contexts, and in one such use, illustrated in (503b), its meaning is similar to that of *folyamán* and *során* 'during'.

(503) a. Mari két perc alatt lefutotta a távot.
Mari two minute under down.run.Past.DefObj.3Sg the distance.Acc
'Mari ran the distance in two minutes.'

b. I. István uralkodása alatt
1st István reign.Poss under
'during the reign of István the First'

b'. I. István alatt
1st István under
'under [the reign of] István the First'

In its temporal use, *alatt* 'under' takes a complement which i) refers to a temporal unit and has a numeral modifier (503a), ii) is a deverbal noun which refers to a period in time (503b) or iii) is a proper name which is understood, via metaphorical extension, to refer to a period in time (503b'). Nouns which refer to a temporal unit but have no numeral modifier can only be used with *folyamán* and *során* 'during', cf. (502) and (504).

(504) *a múlt év alatt
the past year under
Intended meaning: '[in the course of] / during the past year'

III. Other Ps

Non-spatial and non-temporal possessive Ps comprise a noun, the possessive suffix and the superessive (*-n/-on/-en/-ön*) or the sublative (*-ra/-re*) case marker.

A. Ps with the superessive case

Several Ps originate in a superessive marked possessed noun. *Folytán* 'owing to' is built on the deverbal nominal *folyt-* 'course, flowing' (505a), *révén* 'by means of, through' contains *rév* 'ferry' (505b), *útján* 'by way of' includes *út* 'road, way' (505c), *esetén* 'in case of' contains *eset* 'case' (505d) and *nyomán* 'based on X, following X' is built on *nyom* 'sign, track, evidence' (505e).

(505) a. [Szerencsés véletlen folyt-á-n] egymás mellé tudtunk ülni.
lucky coincidence course-Poss-Sup each_other to_next_to could.1Pl sit.Inf
'Due to a happy coincidence, we could sit next to each other.'

b. A projekt [nemzetközi együttműködés rév-é-n] valósul meg.
the project international cooperation ferry-Poss-Sup realize.3Sg Perf
'The project will be realized through international cooperation.'

c. A dokumtentumot [postai levél út-já-n] küldje be.
the document.Acc postal letter way-Poss.Sup send.Subj.3Sg in
'Send the document via post.'

d. [Tűz eset-é-n] csak a lépcső használható.
fire case-Poss-Sup only the stairs usable
'In case of fire only the stairs can be used.'

e. [Az új intézekedés nyom-á-n] javult a közbiztonság.
the new measure track-Poss-Sup improve.Past.3Sg the public.safety
'Following the new measures, public safety has improved.'

B. Ps with the sublative case

There are also possessive Ps which originate in a sublative marked possessed noun. *Részére* 'for (beneficient)' is built on *rész* (formerly: 'share, religious denomination' cf. Benkő 1976: 394, currently: 'part'); *számára* 'for (beneficient, experiencer)' contains *szám* (obsolete meaning: 'group, order or row of animates', see Benkő 1976: 669, glossed here as 'sake'; current meaning: 'number'); and *ellenére* 'despite' includes *ellen*, which has a nominal use ('enemy') and a case-like P use ('against'). These Ps are illustrated in (506).

(506) a. [Viszonteladók rész-é-re] kedvezményt biztosítunk.
distributor.Pl share-Poss-Sub discount.Acc provide.1Pl
'We offer a discount for distributors.'

b. Ez egy jó lehetőség [Európa szám-á-ra].
this a good opportunity Europe sake-Poss-Sub
'This is a good opportunity for Europe.'

c. [Az eső ellen-é-re] elmegyünk.
the rain against-Poss-Sub away.go.1Pl
'We'll go in spite of the rain.'

Részére 'for (beneficient)' and *számára* 'for (beneficient, experiencer)' are largely synonymous. In many cases either of them can be used. (506a), for instance, would also be grammatical with *számára*. However, if the complement refers to an abstract concept, then *számára* is highly preferred: (506b) would be odd with *részére*. Experiencers are also only compatible with *számára* (507).

(507) Ez kellemetlen volt Pál szám-á-ra / *rész-é-re.
this inconvenient was Pál sake-Poss-Sub / share-Poss-Sub
'This was inconvenient for Pál.'

In most cases both *részére* 'for (beneficient)' and *számára* 'for (beneficient, experiencer)' can be substituted with the dative suffix: (508) and (509).

(508) a. Viszonteladók-nak kedvezményt biztosítunk.
distributor.Pl-Dat discount.Acc provide.1Pl
'We offer a discount for distributors.'

b. Ez egy jó lehetőség Európá-nak.
this a good opportunity Europe-Dat
'This is a good opportunity for Europe.'

c. Ez kellemetlen volt Pál-nak.
this inconvenient was Pál-Dat
'This was inconvenient for Pál.'

(509) a. Pál szótárakat adományoz a könyvtár-nak.
Pál dictionary.Pl.Acc donate.3Sg the library-Dat
'Pál donates dictionaries to the library.'

b. Pál szótárakat adományoz a könyvtár szám-á-ra.
Pál dictionary.Pl.Acc donate.3Sg the library sake-Poss-Sub
'Pál donates dictionaries to the library.'

c. Pál szótárakat adományoz a könyvtár rész-é-re.
Pál dictionary.Pl.Acc donate.3Sg the library share-Poss-Sub
'Pál donates dictionaries to the library.'

C. Ps with the inessive case

The possessive P *fejében* 'in exchange for' comprises the noun *fej* 'head', the possessive suffix and the *-ban/-ben* inessive case suffix. The literal possessive use of *fejében* is shown in (510a), while the possessive P use is illustrated in (510b).

(510) a. Nehéz kitalálni, mi járhat Pál fej-é-ben. [possessive phrase]
difficult guess.Inf what go.Mod.3Sg Pál head-Poss-Ine
'It is difficult to guess what may be going on in Pál's head.'

b. Váltságdíj fej-é-ben elengedték a túszokat. [possessive P]
ransom head-Poss-Ine away.let.Past.DefObj.3Pl the hostage.Pl.Acc
'The hostages were let go in exchange for a ransom.'

Having shown the morphemic composition of possessive Ps, in the following sections we shall gloss them for the reader's convenience with their P meaning rather than as genuine possessive constructions, unless their internal make-up is relevant to the examples.

Remark 18. The reanalysis of possessive structures into possessive postpositions is a process that is still active in the language. In Table 21 we included the possessive Ps which are both semantically and grammatically different from their possessive phrase sources. There are further possessive phrases which can be considered to be at the initial phase of semantic bleaching. These include *alapján* 'based on', *árán* 'at the expense of', *ellenében* 'in return for', *érdekében* 'in order to', *kedvéért* 'for the sake of', *képében* 'in the form of', *keretében* 'in the framework of', *körében* 'in the sphere of', *környékén* 'around (temporal)', *magasságában* 'around (temporal)', *nevében* 'on behalf of', *szellemében* 'in the spirit of', *szemében* 'in the eyes of'.

2.4.2.2. Complementation

I. The form of the complement

In regular possessive constructions the possessor can be either unmarked or dative marked (511).

(511) a. Pál könyv-é-ben / könyv-é-n / könyv-é-re
Pál book-Poss-Ine / book-Poss-Sup / book-Poss-Sub
'in / on / onto Pál's book'

b. Pál-nak a könyv-é-ben / könyv-é-n / könyv-é-re
Pál-Dat the book-Poss-Ine / book-Poss-Sup / book-Poss-Sub
'in / on / onto Pál's book'

Common noun and proper name complements of possessive Ps must be morphologically unmarked, however; dative case on the complement is ungrammatical (512). (The definite article is required to follow dative possessors. With possessive Ps, neither the presence nor the absence of the definite article after a dative-marked complement improves grammaticality. This is shown by the parentheses around the article.)

(512) a. *6 órá-nak (a) táján / tájékán [temporal possessive P]
6 hour-Dat the around / around
Intended meaning: 'around 6 o'clock'

b. *Pál-nak (a) révén [other possessive P]
Pál-Dat the by_means_of
Intended meaning: 'through Pál'

Only the spatial possessive P *helyében* 'in the shoes of' allows a dative complement to some degree; but this is a highly marked option compared to the morphologically unmarked complement (513).

(513) ?(?)Pál-nak a helyében [spatial possessive P]
Pál-Dat the place.Poss.Ine
Intended meaning: '[in the shoes of] / [if I were] Pál'

This makes possessive Ps similar to case-like Ps, whose complement must also be unmarked. (514a) features *helyett* 'instead of', which has a possessive origin but has already fully grammaticalized into a case-like P, while (514b) involves *nélkül* 'under', which does not derive from a possessed noun. They pattern alike, and as shown in (512), possessive Ps pattern with them. (Inserting the definite article into the ungrammatical examples would not improve grammaticality here either.)

(514) a. Pál helyett [case-like P, with possessive origin]
Pál instead_of
'instead of Pál'

a'. *Pál-nak helyett
Pál-Dat instead_of
Intended meaning: 'instead of Pál'

b. Pál nélkül [case-like P, without possessive origin]
Pál without
'without Pál'

b'. *Pál-nak nélkül
Pál-Dat without
Intended meaning: 'without Pál'

II. PP-internal position with respect to the complement

Possessive Ps must follow their complement (515).

(515) a. Pál helyében [spatial possessive P]
Pál place.Poss.Ine
'in Pál's shoes / place'

a'. *helyében Pál
place.Poss.Ine Pál
Intended meaning: 'in Pál's shoes / place'

b. 6 óra táján / tájékán [temporal possessive P]
6 hour around / around
'around 6 o'clock'

b'. *táján / tájékán 6 óra
around / around 6 hour
Intended meaning: 'around 6 o'clock'

c. Pál révén [other possessive P]
Pál by_means_of
'through Pál'

c'. *révén Pál
by_means_of Pál
Intended meaning: 'through Pál'

This is expected on their analysis as possessive phrases and as case-like postpositions, too: a possessum must follow a morphologically unmarked possessor, and a case-like P also must follow its complement (516).

(516) a. Pál könyv-e [possessive phrase]
Pál book-Poss
'Pál's book'

a'. *könyv-e Pál
book-Poss Pál
Intended meaning: 'Pál's book'

b. Pál helyett [case-like P, with possessive origin]
Pál instead_of
'instead of Pál'

b'. *helyett Pál
instead_of Pál
Intended meaning: 'instead of Pál'

c. Pál nélkül [case-like P, without possessive origin]
Pál without
'without Pál'

c'. *nélkül Pál
without Pál
Intended meaning: 'without Pál'

III. Dropping the complement

Possessive Ps cannot be used intransitively. The stars in (517) mean that the lexical items in question cannot stand on their own; they do not mean that the forms themselves are ungrammatical.

(517) a. *táján / tájékán [temporal possessive P]
around / around

b. *révén [other possessive P]
by_means_of

c. *ellenére
in_spite_of

This follows from the fact that the possessive marker in these forms has not become opaque, and hence they must occur with a possessor. Only *helyében* 'in X's place/shoes', *részére* 'for' and *számára* 'for' occur without an overt complement (518), but in this case they are understood to have a *pro*-dropped third person singular complement. This is because pronominal third person singular possessors induce a phonologically zero agreement on the possessum (Bartos 1999), thus the forms in (518) are understood to have this zero agreement and a 3Sg possessor. A truly intransitive use is thus not possible for possessive Ps.

(518) a. a hely-é-ben
the place-Poss-Ine
'in his place / shoes'

b. (a) szám-á-ra
the share-Poss-Sub
'for him'

c. (a) rész-é-re
the share-Poss-Sub
'for him'

We will see in point *V* that possessive Ps other than *helyében* 'in X's place / shoes', *részére* 'for' and *számára* 'for' do not take pronominal complements in the first place, so they cannot be understood as Ps with a *pro*-dropped complement.

Common nouns with a possessive marker also must have a possessor (which may be *pro*-dropped), and case-like Ps, too, must occur with a complement (which again can be *pro*-dropped, see Section 2.2.2.2.2 point *V*).

IV. The complement's demonstrative modifier

If the possessive P's complement has a demonstrative modifier, then the P's complement must bear dative case, and dative must also appear on the demonstrative (519b,e).

(519) a. a dolgozó helyében [spatial possessive P]
the worker place.Poss.Ine
'in the place / shoes of the worker'

b. ennek a dolgozó-nak a helyében
this.Dat the worker-Dat the place.Poss.Ine
'in the place / shoes of this worker'

c. *ez a dolgozó helyében
this the worker place.Poss.Ine
Intended meaning: 'in the place / shoes of this worker'

d. az ajánlás nyomán [other possessive P]
the recommendation following
'[based on] / following the recommendation'

e. ennek az ajánlás-nak a nyomán
this.Dat the recommendation-Dat the following
'[based on] / following this recommendation'

f. *ez az ajánlás nyomán
this the recommendation following
Intended meaning: '[based on] / following this recommendation'

This is similar to what we see with real possessive constructions: possessors with a demonstrative modifier must be dative-marked; being morphologically unmarked is not compatible with having a demonstrative modifier (520b,c).

(520) a. a dolgozó lakása [possessive phrase]
the worker apartment.Poss
'the worker's apartment'

b. ennek a dolgozó-nak a lakása
this.Dat the worker-Dat the apartment.Poss
'this worker's apartment'

c. *ez a dolgozó lakása
this the worker apartment.Poss
Intended meaning: 'this worker's apartment'

Real case-like Ps, on the other hand, take an unmarked complement and they are copied onto the demonstrative modifier themselves: (521b, 522b) and Section 2.2.2.2.2 point *IV*.

(521) a. a dolgozó helyett [case-like P, with possessive origin]
the worker instead_of
'next to the worker'

b. e-helyett a dolgozó helyett
this-next_to the worker instead_of
'instead of this worker'

c. *ez a dolgozó helyett
this the worker instead_of
Intended meaning: 'instead of this worker'

d. *ennek a dolgozó-nak helyett
this.Dat the worker-Dat instead_of
Intended meaning: 'instead of this worker'

(522) a. a dolgozó nélkül [case-like P, without possessive origin]
the worker without
'without the worker'

b. e-nélkül a dolgozó nélkül
this-without the worker without
'without this worker'

c. *ez a dolgozó nélkül
this the worker without
Intended meaning: 'without this worker'

d. *ennek a dolgozó-nak nélkül
this.Dat the worker-Dat without
Intended meaning: 'without this worker'

V. Personal pronouns in the complement position

If the possessive P's complement is a personal pronoun, then the possessive marker between the nominal base and the case suffix shows agreement with the pronoun's number and person features (523).

(523) a. az én rész-em-re
the I share-1Sg-Sub
'for me'

b. a te rész-ed-re
the you(Sg) share-2Sg-Sub
'for you(Sg)'

c. az ő rész-é-re
the he share-3Sg-Sub
'for him'

d. a mi rész-ünk-re
the we share-1Pl-Sub
'for us'

e. a ti rész-etek-re
the you(Pl) share-2Pl-Sub
'for you(Pl)'

f. az ő rész-ük-re
the he share-3Pl-Sub
'for them'

This also characterizes genuine possessive constructions (524).

(524) a. az én könyv-em-re
the I book-1Sg-Sub
'onto my book'

b. a te könyv-ed-re
the you(Sg) book-2Sg-Sub
'onto your(Sg) book'

c. az ő könyv-é-re
the he book-3Sg-Sub
'onto his book'

d. a mi könyv-ünk-re
the we book-1Pl-Sub
'onto our book'

e. a ti könyv-etek-re
the you(Pl) book-2Pl-Sub
'onto your(Pl) book'

f. az ő könyv-ük-re
the he book-3Pl-Sub
'onto their book'

With case-like Ps the agreement appears after the obsolete locative, lative or source case suffix. In the examples in (525) we see the obsolete *-(Vt)t* locative case suffix.

(525) a. én-alatt-am
I-under-1Sg
'under me'

b. te-alatt-ad
you(Sg)-under-2Sg
'under you(Sg)'

c. ő-alatt-a
he-under-3Sg
'under him'

d. mi-alatt-unk
we-under-1Pl
'under us'

e. ti-alatt-atok
you(Pl)-under-2Pl
'under you(Pl)'

f. ő-alatt-uk
he-under-3Pl
'under them'

In both possessive phrases and possessive PPs, an overt personal pronoun must be preceded by the definite article, cf. (526) with (524a) and (523a).

(526) a. *én rész-em-re [possessive P]
I share-1Sg-Sub
Intended meaning: 'for me'

b. *én könyv-em-re [possessive phrase]
I book-1Sg-Sub
Intended meaning: 'onto my book'

In case-like PPs, on the other hand, a definite article preceding the personal pronoun complement leads to ungrammaticality (527).

(527) a. én-helyett-em [case-like P, with possessive origin]
I-instead_of-1Sg
'instead of me'

a'. *az én-helyett-em
the I-instead_of-1Sg
Intended meaning: 'instead of me'

b. én-nélkül-em [case-like P, without possessive origin]
I-without-1Sg
'without me'

b'. *az én-nélkül-em
the I-without-1Sg
Intended meaning: 'without me'

In possessive phrases, possessive PPs and case-like PPs alike, the personal pronoun complement can undergo *pro*-drop (528).

(528) a. rész-em-re, szám-om-ra [possessive P]
share-1Sg-Sub share-1Sg-Sub
'for me, for me'

b. a könyv-em-re [possessive phrase]
the book-1Sg-Sub
'onto my book'

c. helyett-em [case-like P, with possessive origin]
instead_of-1Sg
'instead of me'

d. nélkül-em [case-like P, without possessive origin]
without-1Sg
'without me'

In (528b) we can see that the article on the possessum is normally retained with pro-dropped possessors.

The article is also obligatory when the complement of *helyében* 'in X's place / shoes' is *pro*-dropped (529).

(529) a. a hely-em-ben
the place-1Sg-Ine
'in my place / shoes'

b. *hely-em-ben
place-1Sg-Ine
Intended meaning: 'in my place / shoes'

Részére and *számára* (both: 'for') are different, however. If they serve as a recipient, then the article may be retained (530a). When *számára* serves as an experiencer, however, then the article cannot appear (530b). (*Részére* cannot function as an experiencer at all.)

(530) a. Érkezett [(a) rész-em-re] / [(a) szám-om-ra] egy csomag.
arrive.Past.3Sg the share-1Sg-Sub / the share-1Sg-Sub a parcel
'A package has arrive for me.'

b. [(*A) szám-om-ra] ez kellemetlen volt.
the share-1Sg-Sub this inconvenient was
'This was inconvenient for me.'

This makes *helyében* PPs more similar to possessive constructions than *részére* or *számára* PPs. We will see below that other possessive Ps either do not allow a personal pronoun complement or the personal pronoun complement must be third person singular and overt, hence the issue of *pro*-drop is not relevant for other possessive Ps.

Possessive PPs with a third person plural pronoun complement exhibit an anti-agreement phenomenon: the pronoun must be formally singular (*ő* 'he' instead of *ők* 'they') and the plural feature of the pronoun is only reflected in the third person plural agreement on the P (523f). The same phenomenon can also be observed in case-like PPs (525f) and possessive phrases (524f); in both cases, the plurality of the pronoun is only indicated by the agreement on the P and the possessum, respectively.

Helyében 'in X's place/shoes', *részére* 'for' and *számára* 'for' may combine with any personal pronoun. The full paradigm for *részére* 'for' was shown in (523). There are possessive Ps, however, whose combination with personal pronouns is highly restricted: they only combine with third person singular pronouns. This group includes *révén* 'by means of, through' (531) and *nyomán* 'based on X, following X' (532).

(531) a. [az adatok] / Pál rév-é-n
the datum.Pl / Pál ferry-Poss-Sup
'by means of [the data] / Pál'

b. az ő rév-é-n
the he ferry-Poss-Sup
'by means of him'

c. *az én rév-em-en, *a te rév-ed-en
the I ferry-1Sg-Sup the you(Sg) ferry-2Sg-Sup
Intended meaning: 'by means of me, by means of you(Sg)'

d. *a mi rév-ünk-ön, *a ti rév-etek-en, *az ő rév-ük-ön
the we ferry-1Pl-Sup the you(Pl) ferry-2Pl-Sup the he ferry-3Pl-Sup
Intended meaning: 'by means of us, by means of you(Pl), by means of them'

(532) a. [az adatok] / Chomsky nyom-á-n
the datum.Pl / Chomsky trace-Poss-Sup
'[based on the data] / [following Chomsky]'

b. az ő nyom-á-n
the he trace-Poss-Sup
'following / [based on] his (work)'

c. *az én nyom-om-on, *a te nyom-od-on
the I trace-1Sg-Sup the you(Sg) trace-2Sg-Sup
Intended meaning: 'following me, following you(Sg)'

d. *a mi nyom-unk-on, *a ti nyom-otok-on, *az ő nyom-uk-on
the we trace-1Pl-Sup the you(Pl) trace-2Pl-Sup the he trace-3Pl-Sup
Intended meaning: 'following us, following you(Pl), following them'

Note that as full-fledged possessive constructions, with a literal nominal interpretation for *rév* 'ferry' and *nyom* 'trace, trail', the phrases in (531c,d) and (532) are fully grammatical: (533) and (534).

(533) a. az én rév-em-en, a te rév-ed-en
the I ferry-1Sg-Sup the you(Sg) ferry-2Sg-Sup
'on my ferry, on your(Sg) ferry'

b. a mi rév-ünk-ön, a ti rév-etek-en, az ő rév-ük-ön
the we ferry-1Pl-Sup the you(Pl) ferry-2Pl-Sup the he ferry-3Pl-Sup
'on our ferry, on your(Pl) ferry, on their ferry'

(534) a. az én nyom-om-on, a te nyom-od-on
the I trace-1Sg-Sup the you(Sg) trace-2Sg-Sup
'on my trace, on your(Sg) trace'

b. a mi nyom-unk-on, a ti nyom-otok-on, az ő nyom-uk-on
the we trace-1Pl-Sup the you(Pl) trace-2Pl-Sup the he trace-3Pl-Sup
'on our trace, on your(Pl) trace, on their trace'

The rest of the possessive Ps, that is, *táján* 'around (a point in time)', *tájékán* 'around (a point in time)', *folyamán* 'during', *során* 'during', *folytán* 'owing to', *útján* 'by way of', *esetén* 'in case of' and *ellenére* 'despite', do not take pronominal complements at all. (535) and (536) illustrate this with third person singular pronouns.

(535) a. húsvét táján [temporal possessive P]
Easter around
'around Easter'

a'. *az ő táján
the he around
Intended meaning: 'around him / [his time]'

b. húsvét tájékán
Easter around
'around Easter'

b'. *az ő tájékán
the he around
Intended meaning: 'around him / [his time]'

c. jövő hét folyamán
next week during
'during next week'

c'. *az ő folyamán
the he during
Intended meaning: 'around him / [his time]'

d. az eljárás során
the proceedings during
'during the proceedings'

d'. *az ő során
the he during
Intended meaning: 'during him / [his time]'

(536) a. szerencse folytán [other possessive P]
luck due_to
'due to luck'

a'. *az ő folytán
the he due_to
Intended meaning: 'due to him'

b. közvetítő útján
mediator by_way_of
'[by way of] / through a mediator'

b'. *az ő útján
the he by_way_of
Intended meaning: '[by way of] / through him'

c. válás esetén
divorce in_case_of
'in case of a divorce'

c'. *az ő esetén
the he in_case_of
Intended meaning: 'in case of him'

d. a hőség ellenére
the heat despite
'despite the heat'

d'. *az ő ellenére
the he despite
Intended meaning: 'despite him'

Note that postposition *folytán* 'as a consequence of, due to' does not combine with proper names either (537c).

(537) a. balszerencse folytán
misfortune due_to
'due to misfortune'

b. *az ő folytán
the he due_to
Intended meaning: 'due to him'

c. *Napóleon folytán
Napoleon due_to
Intended meaning: 'due to Napoleon'

Table 22 summarizes the combination of possessive postpositions with personal pronouns.

Table 22: Possessive postpositions and personal pronouns

	POSSESSIVE P	MEANING
ALL PRONOUNS	*helyében*	in X's place/shoes
	részére	for (beneficient)
	számára	for (beneficient, experiencer)
ONLY 3SG PRONOUNS	*révén*	by means of, through
	nyomán	based on X, following X
NO COMBINATION	*fejében*	in return for
	táján	around (a point in time)
	tájékán	around (a point in time)
	folyamán	during
	során	during
	folytán	owing to
	útján	by way of
	esetén	in case of
	ellenére	despite

VI. Demonstrative pronouns in the complement position

As shown in (511), possessors are unmarked or dative marked. A demonstrative pronoun that functions as a possessor, however, can only be dative marked (538).

(538) a. ennek a könyv-e [possessive phrase]
this.Dat the book-Poss
'the book of this'

b. *ez könyv-e
this book-Poss
Intended meaning: 'the book of this'

Demonstrative pronoun complements of possessive Ps also require dative marking (539).

(539) a. ennek $^{?}$(a) hely-é-ben [spatial possessive P]
this.Dat the place-Poss-Ine
'in the place / shoes of this'

a'. *ez hely-é-ben
this place-Poss-Ine
Intended meaning: 'in the place / shoes of this

b. ennek ($^{??}$a) táján [temporal possessive P]
this.Dat the around
'around this [time]'

b'. *ez táján
this around
Intended meaning: 'around this [time]'

c. ennek ($^{??}$a) számára [other possessive P]
divorce the for
'for this'

c'. *ez számára
this for
Intended meaning: 'for this'

Demonstrative pronoun complements of real case-like Ps resist dative case (540).

(540) a. e-helyett [case-like P, with possessive origin]
this-instead_of
'instead of this'

a'. *ennek (a) helyett
this.Dat the instead_of
Intended meaning: 'instead of this'

b. ez által [case-like P, without possessive origin]
this via
'via / [as a result of] this'

b'. *ennek (az) által
this.Dat the via
Intended meaning: 'via / [as a result of] this'

This parallel between possessive Ps and possessive constructions is not perfect, however. In ordinary possessive phrases the dative demonstrative pronoun must be followed by the definite article (542).

(541) ennek *(a) könyv-e [possessive phrase]
this.Dat the book-Poss
'the book of this'

The definite article is preferred but not obligatory with a demonstrative complement of *helyében* 'in X's place / shoes' (542), sharply ungrammatical with a demonstrative complement of *folytán* 'owing to' and *ellenére* 'in spite of' (543), and highly dispreferred with the demonstrative complement of the rest of the possessive Ps (544). Thus again *helyében* 'in X's place / shoes' is the most similar to genuine possessive constructions exemplified in (538).

(542) ennek $^{?}$(a) hely-é-ben
this.Dat the place-Poss-Ine
'instead of this'

(543) a. ennek (*a) folytán
this.Dat the owing_to
'owing to this'

b. ennek (*az) ellenére
this.Dat the despite
'in spite of this'

(544) a. ennek ($^{??}$a) táján / tájékán
this.Dat the around / around
'around this [time]'

b. ennek ($^{??}$a) során / folyamán
this.Dat the during / during
'for this'

c. ennek ($^{??}$a) révén
this.Dat the through
'[by means of] / through this'

d. ennek ($^{??}$az) útján
this.Dat the by_way_of
'by way of this'

e. ennek ($^{??}$az) esetén
this.Dat the in_case_of
'in case of this'

f. ennek ($^{??}$a) nyomán
this.Dat the following
'[based on] / following this'

g. ennek ($^{??}$a) számára / részére
divorce the for / for
'for this'

Demonstrative complements thus show that possessive Ps are truly in between possessive phrases and case-like Ps, not having identical properties to either of these.

As already shown in (512) and (523), common noun, proper name and personal pronoun complements of possessive Ps resist dative marking; these types of complements must be morphologically unmarked.

2.4.2.3. Separability of the P and its complement in the clause

A further test illustrating their partial P-status concerns the original possessor: when a dative-marked possessor is allowed to some extent (545b), separating the possessor from the rest of the phrase is still ungrammatical (545c).

(545) a. Pál hely-é-ben nem tenném ezt.
Pál place-Poss-Ine not do.Cond.1Sg this.Acc
'I wouldn't do this in Pál's shoes / place.'

b. $^{??}$Pál-nak a hely-é-ben nem tenném ezt.
Pál-Dat the place-Poss-Ine not do.Cond.1Sg this.Acc

c. *Pál-nak nem tenném ezt a hely-é-ben.
Pál-Dat not do.Cond.1Sg this.Acc the place-Poss-Ine

These illustrate the fact that the possessive structure is still slightly transparent, nevertheless we are not dealing with genuine possessives in these cases. We take this to mean that these possessors are no longer regular possessors, they have begun to grammaticalize into postpositions. However, they have not been reanalyzed as monomorphemic P heads yet.

2.4.2.4. Combination with the Delative and Sublative case

Possessive Ps do not combine with the delative or sublative case. Among all Ps, only some case-like Ps do (see Section 2.2.2.3.4).

(546) a. *Pál hely-é-ben-ről [spatial possessive P]
Pál place-Poss-Ine-Del
Intended meaning: 'from in Pál's shoes'

a'. *Pál hely-é-ben-re
Pál place-Poss-Ine-Sub
Intended meaning: 'to in Pál's shoes'

b. *pünkösd folyamán-ról [temporal possessive P]
Pentecost during-Del
Intended meaning: 'since during Pentecost'

b'. *pünkösd folyamán-ra
Pentecost during-Sub
Intended meaning: 'by during Pentecost'

c. *levél útján-ról [other possessive P]
letter by_way_of-Del
Intended meaning: 'from by way of a letter'

c'. *levél útján-ra
letter by_way_of-Sub
Intended meaning: 'to by way of a letter'

2.4.2.5. N + possessive P modifying a noun

As shown in Section 2.2.1.5, PPs headed by case suffixes can be turned into prenominal N-modifiers by the addition of a participial verb, while PPs containing case-like Ps and case-assigning Ps can function as prenominal N-modifiers if embedded under either a participle or the attributivizing *-i* suffix (Sections 2.2.2.2.5 and 2.2.2.3.5).

The combination of possessive Ps with *-i* is very limited. The following examples are based on naturally occurring examples on the web and in the Hungarian Gigaword Corpus (Oravecz, Váradi & Sass 2014). For possessive Ps not included in (547), we have not found any examples with *-i*.

(547) a. az eljárás során-i döntések
the procedure during-Attr decision.Pl
'the decisions during the procedure'

b. tagság lemondás folytán-i megszűnése
membership cancellation owing_to-Attr termination
'termination of membership due to cancellation'

c. rokoni kapcsolatok révén-i érvényesülés
relative.Attr realtionship.Pl through-Attr advancement
'advancement through / [by means of] relatives'

d. sajtó útján-i véleménynyilvánítás
media by_way_of-Attr opinion.expression
'expression of opinion via the media'

e. feljelentés nyomán-i intézekedés
report_to_police based_on-Attr measure
'measures [based on] / following a report to the police'

f. jó teljesítés esetén-i előrelépés
good performance in_case_of-Attr promotion
'promotion in case of good performance'

The attributivized forms in (547) mostly appear in official or legal contexts. The participial strategy is preferred over these forms (548), and is also available for possessive Ps which have no *-i* attributivized forms. Some examples of these are given in (549).

(548) a. az eljárás során hoz-ott döntések
the procedure during make-Part decision.Pl
'the decisions made during the procedure'

b. tagság lemondás folytán bekövetkez-ő megszűnése
membership cancellation owing_to occur-Part termination
'termination of membership due to cancellation'

c. rokoni kapcsolatok révén történ-ő érvényesülés
relative.Attr realtionship.Pl through happen-Part advancement
'advancement through / [by means of] relatives'

d. sajtó útján kiad-ott véleménynyilvánítás
media by_way_of publish-Part opinion.expression
'expression of opinion via the media'

e. feljelentés nyomán folytat-ott intézekedés
report_to_police based_on conduct-Part measure
'measures [based on] / following a report ot the police'

f. jó teljesítés esetén bekövetkez-ő előrelépés
good performance in_case_of occur-Part promotion
'promotion in case of good performance'

(549) a. a Pál számára / részére küldött levelek
the Pál for / for send-Part letter.Pl
'the letters sent to Pál'

b. az akarata ellenére kiad-ott állásfoglalás
the will.Poss.3Sg against publish-Part position.statement
'the position statement published against his will'

c. a karácsony tájt / tájékán zajl-ó események
the Christmas around / around happen-Part event.Pl
'the events happening around Christmas'

The fact that some possessive Ps can undergo *-i* attributivization shows that their morphemic composition, and especially the identity of the last morpheme as an ordinary case suffix is becoming more opaque and they are becoming more like postpositions (as already pointed out above, PPs headed by case suffixes are not compatible with *-i*, but PPs headed by case-like and case-assigning Ps are).

2.4.2.6. Modification

Possessive PPs can host degree modifiers, which must precede the P's complement (550).

(550) a. pontosan karácsony (*pontosan) folyamán (*pontosan) [temporal]
exactly Christmas exactly during exactly
'exactly during Christmas'

b. majdnem az akarata (*majdnem) ellenére (*majdnem) [other]
almost the will.Poss3Sg almost against almost
'almost against his will'

This is expected if possessive Ps are grammaticalizing into case-like Ps, as case-like Ps do not allow modifiers to intervene between the NP/DP and the P or to occur after the P either (see (551) for case-like Ps with and without possessive origin and Section 2.2.2.2.6).

(551) a. pontosan Pál (*pontosan) helyett (*pontosan)
exactly Pál exactly instead_of exactly
'exactly instead of Pál'

b. majdnem Pál (*majdnem) nélkül (*majdnem)
almost Pál almost without almost
'almost without Pál'

Possessive constructions, on the other hand, allow modifiers to intervene between the possessor and the possessum (NPs do not allow degree modifiers, however, so the relevant modifiers are numerals, classifiers and adjectives, as in (552)).

(552) a. Pál három cső zöld paprikája [possessive phrase]
Pál three Cl green pepper.Poss
'Pál's three green peppers'

Measure phrases are not compatible with possessive PPs (553).

(553) a. *sokkal / *kevéssel Pál hely-é-ben [spatial possessive P]
a_lot / a_bit Pál place-Poss-Ine
Intended meaning: '[a lot] / [a bit] in Pál's shoes'

b. *sokkal / *kevéssel 6 óra táján / tájékán [temporal possessive P]
a_lot / a_bit 6 hour around / around
Intended meaning: '[a lot] / [a bit] around 6 o'clock'

c. *sokkal / *kevéssel Pál révén [other possessive P]
a_lot / a_bit Pál through
Intended meaning: '[a lot] / [a bit] through Pál'

2.4.2.7. Conjunction reduction

Possessive PPs allow both forward and backward conjunction reduction: (554) and (555).

(554) • Backward conjunction reduction

a. Ili és Pál helyében [spatial possessive P]
Ili and Pál instead
'in the shoes of Ili and Pál'

b. karácsony vagy újév táján [temporal possessive P]
Christmas or New.Year around
'around Christmas or New Year's Eve'

c. Ili és Pál révén [other possessive P]
Ili and Pál through
'[by means of] / through Ili and Pál'

(555) • Forward conjunction reduction

a. karácsony táján vagy folyamán [temporal possessive P]
Christmas around or during
'around or during Christmas'

b. a ellenállás folytán vagy ellenére [other possessive P]
the resistance owing_to or despite
'owing to or despite the resistance'

Sections 2.2.2.2.7 and 2.2.2.3.7 have shown that both types of conjunction reductions are also possible with case-like and case-assigning Ps, and this is also an option for ordinary possessive phrases (556).

(556) a. Pál és Kati könyvei [backward conjunction reduction]
Pál and Kati book.Poss.Pl
'Pál and Kati's books'

b. Pál könyvei és lemezei [forward conjunction reduction]
Pál book.Poss.Pl and LP.Poss.Pl
'Pál's books and LPs'

2.4.2.8. Taking stock: possessive Ps between possessive NPs and Ps

The possessive construction has been and still is a relatively productive source of emerging postpositions. To the extent that the category of Ps can be extended, most of the new ones seem to originate in the type of syntactic environment illustrated here. When the emerging P-like elements i) lose the syntactic properties shared with genuine possessives (most prominently their ability to alternate with dative-marked possessors, the separability of that possessor, the loss of the article after a dative-marked demonstrative pronoun and they become compatible with the *-i* attributivizer) and ii) when their lexical content becomes bleached, we can talk about newly developed P items in the language.

We have also seen that *helyében* 'in X's place / shoes' is the least grammaticalized of the borderline cases discussed here: this is the only possessive P which a) allows lexical NP complements to bear dative case to some extent, b) requires the definite article if its complement is *pro*-dropped, and c) requires the definite article after a demonstrative pronoun complement. Its meaning is also perhaps the most transparent, least bleached of all the possessive Ps.

2.5. Bibliographical notes

Simonyi (1888, 1892, 1895) provides an early detailed description of what he calls adverbials (according to our terminology: various types of Ps and PPs) and provides historical insight as well. More recently, in descriptive works, case suffixes and the case system of Hungarian are comprehensively presented in Antal (1961), and Abondolo (1998), among others. A study of the inventory of Hungarian postpositions in the narrow sense is given in Sebestyén (1965).

The descriptive grammar *Hungarian* by Kenesei *et al.* (1998) briefly discusses the properties of case suffixes, postpositions, adverbs and particles, and introduces "transitional postpositions" (our possessive and participial postpositions), as well. The essive forms received special attention in de Groot (2017). The 3rd volume of the structuralist grammar of Hungarian (*Strukturális magyar nyelvtan 3.*) edited by Ferenc Kiefer is on morphology (Kiefer 2000c). Several chapters from the volume are important contributions to our understanding of word classes, inflection and derivation (Kenesei 2000, Kiefer and Ladányi 2000a, Laczkó 2000), of morphophonolgical (Rebrus 2000) and morphosyntactic (Bartos 2000) phenomena concerning the PP as defined here, and of particles (Kiefer and Ladányi 2000b).

Marácz (1986, 1989) gave the first generative syntactic analysis of postpositions, systematically distinguishing between case-like ("dressed") as case-assigning ("naked") postpositions. Postpositions were later analyzed in É. Kiss (2002 Chapter 8), Hegedűs (2006), Rákosi and Laczkó (2011), Rákosi (2012b). That postpositions and case suffixes are instantiations of the same category P is discussed in detail in Bartos (1999), Asbury *et al.* (2007), Spencer (2008), Trommer (2008). The morphosyntactic structure of Hungarian case suffixes and postpositions proper are featured in the dissertations by Asbury (2005), Dékány (2011), Hegedűs (2013). Spencer and Stump (2013) and Dékány (2018) focus specifically on the analysis of PP-internal agreement.

That Hungarian verbal particles are instantiations of the category P was first suggested in Horvath (1978). The syntactic properties of verbal particles have recently been analyzed, among others, by É. Kiss (2005, 2006a,b), Surányi (2009a,b,c), Hegedűs (2013), Hegedűs and Dékány (2017). Kiefer (2000b) gives a detailed semantic description of verbal particles, spatial and non-spatial alike.

For a historical overview, see Zsilinszky (1989) on postpositions, J. Soltész (1959) and D. Mátai (1989, 1991, 1992) on verbal particles. A generative syntactic analysis of the grammaticalization of postpositions in the broad sense is proposed by Hegedűs (2014, 2015).

Chapter 3
The internal syntax of PPs

Veronika Hegedűs and Éva Dékány

3.1. Introduction

In this chapter we discuss the internal syntax of postpositional phrases in the broad sense. We begin with the complementation possibilities of adpositions in Section 3.2, then in Section 3.3 we turn to the modifiers of PPs.

3.2. Complementation

This section discusses the complementation of adpositional phrases. First, we examine intransitive Ps in Section 3.2.1. In Section 3.2.2 we turn to postpositional heads that take a Noun Phrase complement. Postpositions with adjectival, adverbial and adpositional complements will be examined in Sections 3.2.3 through 3.2.5. Ps with a clausal complement will be the topic of Section 3.2.6. Finally, Section 3.2.7 will be dedicated to absolute PPs.

3.2.1. Intransitive Ps

Adpositional phrases that regularly appear in intransitive structures (i.e., without a complement) are adverbs and verbal particles. Examples involving a degree adverb, a manner adverb and a speaker-oriented adverb are given in (1).

(1) a. Ili *nagyon* magas.
Ili very tall
'Ili is very tall.'

b. Ili *gyorsan* futott.
Ili fast run.Past.3Sg
'Ili ran fast.'

c. Ili *szerencsére* otthon volt.
Ili luckily at_home be.Past.3Sg
'Luckily, Ili was at home.'

Verbal particles also often occur without a complement, as in (2) (but see Section 3.2.5 and Chapter 2 Section 2.2.3.4 point *I* for some exceptions).

(2) a. Ili be-jött.
Ili in-come-Past.3Sg
'Ili came in.'

b. Ili félre-tolta a könyvet.
Ili aside-push.Past.DefObj.3Sg the book
'Ili pushed the book aside.'

Pro-dropped and implicit complements will be discussed in Section 3.2.2.4.

3.2.2. Nominal complements

Case-like postpositions (Chapter 2 Section 2.2.2.2), the case suffixes required by case-assigning postpositions (Chapter 2 Section 2.2.2.3) and case suffixes occurring without an accompanying postposition (Chapter 2 Section 2.2.1) take nominal complements. The complement may be a definite Noun Phrase or indefinite Noun Phrase (with an indefinite article or a numeral / quantifier) without further ado. Bare

NP complements, however, are restricted. They are allowed only if i) the NP is focused or ii) it has a generic reading or iii) it forms a set phrase with the postposition.

Nominal complements with a determiner are referential. In (3), for instance, Ili works in the unique (and definite) hospital that is accessible to the discourse participants in the discourse situation.

(3) Ili a kórház-ban dolgozik.
Ili the hospital-Ine work.3Sg
'Ili works in the hospital.'

Nominal complements without a determiner are non-referential. In (4) there is no unique hospital in the discourse situation and *kórházban* does not refer to a specific building.

(4) Ili 'kórház-ban 'dolgozik.
Ili hospital-Ine work.3Sg
'Ili works in a hospital.'

While the determiner-less nominal in (4) is non-referential, it can be referred back to with a pronoun such as *ott* 'there' or *oda* 'to there' (5).

(5) a. Ili 'kórház-ban 'dolgozik, mert ott érzi jól magát.
Ili hospital-Ine work.3Sg because there feel.3Sg well self.Acc
'Ili works in a hospital, because that's where she likes it.'

b. Ili 'szakiskolá-ban 'tanul, mert csak oda vették fel.
Ili vocational.school-Ine study.3Sg because only there_to admit.Past.DefObj.3Pl up
'Ili is studying in vocational school because she didn't get admitted anywhere else.'

The referentiality of the complement influences its modifiability. Definite nominal complements may be freely modified by attributive adjectives (6).

(6) Ili a nagy kórház-ban dolgozik.
Ili the big hospital-Ine work.3Sg
'Ili works in the big hospital.'

Bare nominal complements allow adjectival modification if the adjective is focused, if the adjective plus noun unit has a generic or type reading, or if the adjective and the noun constitute a set phrase. (7a), with a bare noun modified by a focused adjective, is felicitous. (7c) is degraded, as the adjective plus noun unit cannot receive a generic or type interpretation here. If the adjective is not focused, the insertion of the indefinite article is necessary (7b).

(7) a. Ili "NAGY KÓRHÁZ-BAN dolgozik.
Ili big hospital-Ine work.3Sg
'It is a big hospital that Ili works in.'

b. Ili egy 'nagy 'kórház-ban 'dolgozik.
Ili a big hospital-Ine work.3Sg
'Ili works in a big hospital.'

c. *Ili 'nagy 'kórház-ban 'dolgozik.
Ili big hospital-Ine work.3Sg
Intended meaning: 'Ili works in a big hospital.'

In (8a) and (8b) the adjective is such that a type reading becomes available. Here it is not necessary to focus the adjective, i.e. to add focus stress to it, or to insert an indefinite article.

(8) a. Ili 'kertvárosi 'kórház-ban 'dolgozik.
Ili suburb.Attr hospital-Ine work.3Sg
'Ili works in a suburban hospital.'

b. Ili 'egyházi 'kórház-ban 'dolgozik.
Ili church.Attr hospital-Ine work.3Sg
'Ili works in a religious hospital.'

PPs inherit the referentiality of their nominal complement. For instance, adpositions with a referential complement can be topicalized, while those with a non-referential complement cannot. In (9) the PP with the definite NP complement can occur in the pre-focal topic position.

(9) [Az asztalra] / [Az asztal mellé] JÁNOS ült le.
the table-Sub / the table to_next_to János sit.Past.3Sg down
'It is JÁNOS that sat down onto / [next to] the table.'

This is not possible for the PP with the non-referential complement in (10).

(10) *[Asztalra] / [Asztal mellé] JÁNOS ült le.
table-Sub / table to_next_to János sit.Past.3Sg down
Intended meaning: 'It is JÁNOS that sat down onto / [next to] a table.'

(10) becomes grammatical if the PP is placed into the contrastive topic position, marked by the characteristic fall-rise intonation associated with this position, and, in writing, also by a comma (189b). Contrastive topics have no referentiality requirement (see the volume on Sentence Structure), so both bare nouns (189a) and PPs with bare noun complements (189b) are allowed here.

(11) a. [Asztal-t], JÁNOS vett.
table-Acc János buy.Past.3Sg
'As for buying a table, it is JÁNOS that did it.'

b. [Asztalra] / [Asztal mellé], JÁNOS ült le.
table-Sub / table to_next_to János sit.Past.3Sg down
'As for sitting down onto / [next to] a table, it was JÁNOS who did it.'

PPs are also transparent for agreement processes between their nominal complement and PP-external constituents. In (12) the dative-marked subject of the infinitive can trigger agreement on the infinitival verb. (See Tóth 2002 for arguments that in such examples *kell* is a monoargumental verb: the inanimate subject *tó* 'lake' cannot be an experiencer or holder of obligation in the main clause, controlling a PRO subject in the embedded clause; thus it must be a subject internal to the infinitival clause.)

(12) a. Nem kell a tó-nak befagy-ni-a.
not must the lake-Dat in.freeze-Inf-3Sg
'It is not the case that the lake will certainly freeze.'

b. Nem kell a tavak-nak befagy-ni-uk.
not must the lake.Pl-Dat in.freeze-Inf-3Pl
'It is not the case that the lakes will certainly freeze.'

Nominals embedded in PPs are also visible for binding purposes, as shown in (13), where co-reference between the children and the anaphor is possible.

(13) a. Beszélgettem a gyerekek-kel önmaguk-ról / egymás-ról.
talk.Past.1Sg the child.Pl-Ins self.3Pl-Del / each.other-Del
'I talked to the children about themselves / [each other].'

b. Tettem egy képet a gyerekek mellé önmaguk-ról.
put.Past.DefObj.1Sg a picture.Acc the child.Pl to_next_to self-Del
'I have put a picture of themselves next to the children .'

3.2.2.1. Referential DP complements

Any referential DP can occur in the complement position of a case suffix or case-like postposition that is semantically compatible with the meaning of the adposition in question (14).

(14) a. Pál a város-ban lakik.
Pál the city-Ine live.3Sg
'Pál lives in the city.'

b. Pál az ablak alatt hagyta a könyvet.
Pál the window under leave.Past.DefObj.3Sg the book.Acc
'Pál left the book under the window.'

In some cases the combination of the referential DP with a specific postpositional head requires metonymical extension of the nominal's meaning (15b,c).

(15) a. Az asztal alatt sok kacat volt.
the table under many bric_a_brac be_Past.3Sg
'There was a lot of bric-a-brac under the table.'

b. Mátyás alatt sok erőd épült.
Mátyás under many fortification be_built.3Sg
'Many fortifications were built during the reign of (King) Mátyás.'

c. Einstein óta nem volt ilyen felfedezés.
Einstein since not be_Past.3Sg such discovery
'There has not been such a discovery since Einstein('s work / time).'

Personal pronouns are also referential DPs. Some case suffixes and case-like postpositions do not take personal pronoun complements. These are discussed in Chapter 2 Section 2.2.1.2 point *V* and Section 2.2.2.2.2 point *V*.

3.2.2.2. Indefinite nominal complements with the indefinite article

Any nominal with the indefinite article can occur in the complement position of a case suffix or case-like postposition that is semantically compatible with the meaning of the adposition in question (16).

(16) a. Pál egy város-ban lakik.
Pál a city-Ine live.3Sg
'Pál lives in a city.'

b. Pál egy ablak alatt hagyta a könyvet.
Pál a window under leave.Past.DefObj.3Sg the book
'Pál left the book under a window.'

In the case of *alatt* 'under', the combination of a nominal with the indefinite article and a specific postpositional head may require metonymical extension of the nominal's meaning. Such examples often require an adjectival modifier, as in (17).

(17) A legtöbb vár egy jó király alatt épült.
the most castle a good king under be_built.3Sg
'Most fortifications were built during the reign of a good king.'

3.2.2.3. Bare nominal complements

A. Bare nominal complements of case suffixes

The non-spatial case suffixes exemplified in (18) can appear with bare nominal complements without further ado.

(18) a. Pál gyerek-ek-nek adott koncertet. [dative]
Pál child-Pl-Dat give.Past.3Sg concert.Acc
'Pál gave a concert to children.'

b. Ili kutyá-val ment sétálni. [instrumental]
Ili dog-Ins go.Past.3Sg walk.Inf
'Ili went for a walk with (her / a) dog.'

c. A báb lepké-vé változott. [translative(-essive)]
the pupa butterfly-TrE transform.Past.3Sg
'The pupa transformed into a butterfly.'

d. Tojás-ért megyek a szomszédba. [causal(-final)]
egg-Cau go.1Sg the neighbor's.Ill
'I am going to the neighbor's for eggs.'

e. Ili orvos-ként dolgozik. [essive-formal]
Ili doctor-FoE work.3Sg
'Ili works as a doctor.'

Bare nouns that denote a body part are fully grammatical as complements of spatial case suffixes, too. Note that the bare noun does not bear the possessive suffix *-ja/-je/-a/-e* (cf. N2.2.1.2.1.2), but there is an implied (though syntactically implicit) possessor: generic 'one' or 'man' for the body part in (19a) and the possessor of the subject in (19b).

(19) a. A víz boká-ig / térd-ig / nyak-ig ér. [terminative]
the water ankle-Ter / knee-Ter / neck-Ter reach.3Sg
'The water is ankle / knee / neck high.'

b. A hajad váll-ig / hátközép-ig / fenék-ig ér.
the hair.Poss.2Sg shoulder-Ter / back.middle-Ter / bottom-Ter reach.3Sg
'Your hair reaches [your shoulders] / [the middle of your back] / [your bottom].'

Further examples are given in (20).

(20) a. hát-ba vág [illative]
back-Ill slap.3Sg
'slap [sb] on the back'

b. térd-en rúg, kéz-en fog [superessive]
knee-Sup kick.3Sg hand-Sup take.3Sg
'kick [sb] on the knee, take by the hand'

c. derék-tól lefelé [ablative]
waist-Abl downward
'from the waist down'

An implicit possessor is also present in (21) due to the part-whole relation between the object noun and the complement of the terminative case; thus these examples are analogous to those in (19) and (20).

(21) a. Ili vég-ig / fél-ig el-olvasta a könyvet.
Ili end-Ter / half-Ter away-read.Past.DefObj.3Sg the book.Acc
'Ili has read the book completely / halfway.'

b. Ili sark-ig ki-tárta az ablakot.
Ili corner-Ter out-open.Past.DefObj.3Sg the window.Acc
'Ili opened the window completely.' (Lit. to corner)

c. Ili töv-ig nyomta a gázpedált.
Ili root-Ter push.Past.DefObj.3Sg the accelerator.pedal.Acc
'Ili pushed the accelerator pedal to the floor.' (Lit. to root)

Bare nouns are also grammatical in paired expressions of the form "N-ablative N-terminative", as in (22).

(22) A gyerekek tesiórán [fal-tól fal-ig] / [sarok-tól sarok-ig] futottak.
the child.Pl gym.class.Sup wall-Abl wall-Ter / corner-Abl corner-Ter run.Past.3Pl
'The children ran [from wall to wall] / [from corner to corner] during gym class.'

There are also some place-denoting nouns that form a set expression with the terminative case (23). These nouns have a unique reference and allow (but do not require) the definite article in (23).

(23) a. A fák (az) ég-ig érnek.
the tree.Pl the sky-Ter reach.3Pl
'The trees reach the sky.'

b. Ili (a) föld-ig hajolt.
Ili the ground-Ter bend.Past.3Sg
'Ili bent to the ground.'

If neither of the conditions discussed above hold, then the bare noun must be focused; otherwise it is ungrammatical.

(24) a. ?Ili SAROK-ig fut, nem híd-ig.
Ili corner-Ter run.3Sg not bridge-Ter
'Ili runs to a corner, not to a bridge.'

b. Ili *(a / egy) sarok-ig fut.
Ili the / a corner-Ter run.3Sg
Intended meaning: 'Ili runs to (the / a) corner.'

As for terminative PPs with a temporal reading, a bare noun complement is possible if the noun denotes a time of a day or mealtime (25a), if the bare noun denotes a specific point in time (25b, b') or if the bare noun and the terminative case form a set expression (25c). In these cases the event described in the verb phrase remains an activity: no telos is introduced, the PP simply marks the time when the activity was finished.

(25) a. Ili reggel-ig / est-ig / ebéd-ig / vacsorá-ig dolgozott.
Ili morning-Ter / evening-Ter / lunch-Ter / dinner-Ter work.Past.3Sg
'Ili worked until [the morning] / [the evening] / lunch(time) / dinner(time).'

b. Ili tegnap-ig / [múlt hét-ig] dolgozott.
Ili yesterday-Ter / last week-Ter work.Past.3Sg
'Ili worked until yesterday / [last week].'

b'. Ili má-ig / holnap-ig / [jövő hét-ig] dolgozik.
Ili today-Ter / tomorrow-Ter / next week-Ter work.3Sg
'Ili works until today / tomorrow / [next week].'

c. Ili orrvérzés-ig dolgozott.
Ili nose.bleeding-Ter work.Past.3Sg
'Ili worked ad nauseam.'

The temporal PPs with *-ig* discussed above refer to a point in time. However, terminative-marked nouns can also refer to a time-span. In this reading the bare noun must be plural marked (26).

(26) Ili perc-*(ek)-ig / het-*(ek)-ig / hónap-*(ok)-ig / év-*(ek)-ig várt.
Ili minute-Pl-Ter / week-Pl-Ter / monht-Pl-Ter / year-Pl-Ter wait.Past.3Sg
'Ili waited for minutes / weeks / months / years.'

There are two exceptions to this generalization, however. *Élethossz* 'lifespan' (lit. 'life length') and *életfogyt* 'lifespan' (lit. 'life-outrunning') are time-span denoting bare nouns which (presumably due to their meaning) do not combine with the plural marker under any circumstances. These nouns do combine with the terminative case maker, though (27). In fact, *élethossz* and *életfogyt* are only used in collocation with *-ig*; they are thus best characterized as bound stems.

(27) a. Ili szerint van élethossz-ig tartó szerelem.
Ili according_to be.3Sg lifespan-Ter lasting love
'Ili thinks there is such a thing as perpetual love.'

b. Ili életfogyt-ig kitartott az elvei mellett.
Ili lifespan-Ter stand_by.Past.3Sg the principle.Poss.Pl next_to
'Ili stood by her principles all her life.' (implication: she is not alive any more)

Spatial case suffixes can take a bare nominal complement under limited circumstances. These are the following: i) if the nominal has a generic or type interpretation (28d',e), ii) if the PP bears strong contrastive stress because it is focused (28a,b,c,d,f,g,h,i) and iii) in collocations and set phrases or when the case is subcategorized by a verb (28a',b',c', f', h', i').

(28) a. Pál SZÉK-EN ül. [superessive]
Pál chair-Sup sit.3Sg
'Pál is sitting on a CHAIR.'

a'. Pál szabadság-on van.
Pál holiday-Sup be.3Sg
'Pál is on holiday.'

b. Pál SZÉK-RE ült. [sublative]
Pál chair-Sub sit.Past.3Sg
'Pál sat down onto a CHAIR.'

b'. Pál szabadság-ra ment.
Pál holiday-Sub go.Past.3Sg
'Pál went on holiday.'

c. Pál SZÉK-RŐL kelt fel. [delative]
Pál chair-Del rise.Past.3Sg up
'Pál got up from a CHAIR.'

c'. Pál sárkány-ok-ról mesélt Ili-nek.
Pál dragon-Pl-Del tell_a_tale.Past.3Sg Ili-Dat
'Pál told Ili a tale about dragons.'

d. A kutya RÓKALYUK-BAN találta ezt a kölyköt. [inessive]
the dog fox.den-Ine find.Past.DefObj.3Sg this the puppy
'The dog found this puppy in a FOX DEN.'

d'. A bagoly odú-ban fészkel.
the owl cavity-Ine nest.3Sg
'Owls nest in cavities.'

e. A bagoly ODÚ-BA költözött. [illative]
the owl cavity-Ill move.Past.3Sg
'The owl has moved into a CAVITY.'

f. A kutya RÓKALYUK-BÓL hozta ezt a kölyköt. [elative]
the dog fox.den-Ela bring.Past.DefObj.3Sg this.Acc the puppy.Acc
'The dog brought this puppy from a FOX DEN.'

f'. A doboz fá-ból készült.
the box wood-Ela made_of.3Sg
'The box is made of wood.'

g. Ili TENGER-NÉL szeretne nyaralni. [adessive]
Ili sea-Ade would_like.3Sg holiday_make.Inf
'Ili would like to spend her holiday at the SEA(SIDE).'

h. Ili TENGER-HEZ szeretne utazni [allative]
Ili sea-All would_like.3Sg travel.Inf
'Ili would like to travel to the SEA(SIDE).'

h'. Ili férj-hez ment.
Ili husband-All go.Past.3Sg
'Ili got married.'

i. Az út KASTÉLY-TÓL indul. [ablative]
the road castle-Abl start.3Sg
'The road starts from a CASTLE.'

i'. ORVOS-TÓL kaptam a tanácsot.
doctor-Abl get.Past.1Sg the advice.Acc
'I got the advice from a DOCTOR.'

Some set collocations in which a spatial case suffix must take a bare nominal complement are shown in (29).

(29) a. Pál út-on van. [superessive]
Pál way-Sup be.3Sg
'Pál is on his way.'

b. A szekrény út-ban van. [inessive]
the cupboard way-Ine be.3sg
'The cupboard is in the way.'

In some cases the case-suffixed bare nominal has a special interpretation: there is a prototypical, conventionalized activity that one typically does at the location referred to. (30) shows some locative examples with the inessive case.

(30) Pál iskolá-ban / óvodá-ban / kórház-ban / börtön-ben /
Pál school-Ine / kindergarten-Ine / hospital-Ine / jail-Ine /
színház-ban / mozi-ban / ágy-ban van.
theatre-Ine / cinema-Ine / bed-Ine be.3Sg
'Pál is [at school] / [at kindergarten] / [in hospital] / [in jail] / [in the theatre] / [in the cinema] / [in bed].'

In (30), Pál is a student at school, a small child in kindergarten, a patient in the hospital, an inmate in jail, he watches a play at the theatre or a movie in the cinema or he is lying in bed. The reading that a conventionalized activity is taking place may (but does not have to) be lost when a determiner is used. In (31) Pál could be a parent or employee who happens to be in the school / kindergarten / hospital / jail / theatre / cinema building for any reason, and he may be sitting in bed, but the special conventionalized interpretation seen in (30) is also available. In other words, the bare nominals force the readings characteristic of conventionalized activities, while these readings are not the only options in (31).

(31) Pál [az iskolában] / [az óvodá-ban] / [a kórház-ban] /
Pál the school-Ine / the kindergarten-Ine / the hospital-Ine /
[a börtön-ben] / [a színház-ban] / [a mozi-ban] / [az ágy-ban] van.
the jail-Ine / the theatre-Ine / the cinema-Ine / the bed-Ine be.3Sg
'Pál is in [the school] / [the kindergarten] / [the hospital] / [the jail] / [the theater] / [the cinema] / [the bed].'

(32) shows that in combination with the copula, some bare nouns bearing the adessive case also give rise to the conventionalized reading; and so do some allative-marked bare nouns next to a motion predicate. The nouns in (32) refer to professionals who provide typical, regularly required service for their clients; there is some prototypical/conventionalized activity that one visits these professionals for. In (32a), for instance, Pál is a patient who is visiting the doctor to get a medical consultation or medical exam. Other nouns that can be used like this are shown in (32b,c).

(32) a. Pál [orvos-nál van] / [orvos-hoz ment].
Pál doctor-Ade be.3Sg / doctor-All go.Past.3Sg
'Pál [is at] / [went to] the doctor.'

b. Ili szerelő-nél / kozmetikus-nál / masszőr-nél / ügyvéd-nél van.
Ili repairman-Ade / beautician-Ade / massage_therapist-Ade / lawyer-Ade be.3Sg
'Ili is at the repairman / beautician / [massage therapist] / lawyer.'

c. Ili szerelő-höz / kozmetikus-hoz / masszőr-höz / ügyvéd-hez megy.
Ili repairman-All / beautician-All / massage_therapist-All / lawyer-All go.3Sg
'Ili is going to the repairman / beautician / [massage therapist] / lawyer.'

Some infelicitous examples are given in (33); these examples are unacceptable because there is no conventionalized activity associated with the professions they feature.

(33) a. *Ili politikus-nál / nővér-nél / sofőr-nél van.
Ili politician-Ade / nurse-Ade / driver-Ade be.3Sg
Intended meaning: 'Ili is at the / a politician / nurse / driver.'

b. *Ili politikus-hoz / nővér-hez / sofőr-höz ment.
Ili politician-All / nurse-All / driver-All go.Past.3Sg
Intended meaning: 'Ili went to the / a politician / nurse / driver.'

As before, the reading that a conventionalized activity is taking place may, but does not have to, be lost with a determiner: in (34) Pál could be at the doctor's house having a drink with him.

(34) Pál az [orvos-nál van] / [orvos-hoz ment].
Pál the doctor-Ade be.3Sg / doctor-All go.Past.3Sg
'Pál [is at] / [went to] the doctor's.'

The reading for the conventionalized activity also available with the illative and the sublative case in the collocations in (35):

(35) a. Pál iskolá-ba / óvodá-ba / egyetem-re jár.
Pál school-Ill / kindergarten-Ill / university-Sub attend.3Sg
'Pál attends school / kindergarten / university.'

b. Pál templom-ba jár.
Pál church-Ill attend.3Sg
'Pál regularly goes to church.'

Komlósy (1992: 513-514) has shown that the requirement that bare nouns give rise to a conventionalized reading is not specific to bare nouns within PPs: this is characteristic of all phrases that fulfill the verbal modifier role in the sentence, including bare objects. Compare (36a,b), which refer to a conventionalized activity with (36c), which does not.

(36) a. Pál fá-t vág.
Pál tree-Acc cut.3Sg
'Pál is cutting up wood [specifically for burning].'

b. Pál újság-ot olvas.
Pál newspaper-Acc read.3Sg
'Pál is reading a newspaper.'

c. *?Pál számlá-t olvas.
Pál bill-Acc read.3Sg
Intended meaning: 'Pál is reading a bill [to be paid].'

B. Bare nominal complements of case-like postpositions

Case-like postpositions with a spatial interpretation take bare nominal complements if the nominal has a generic or type interpretation, if the PP bears strong contrastive stress, and in idiomatic or set phrases. Some examples are given in (37).

(37) a. Ili KÖNYV ALÁ rejtette a papírt.
Ili book under_to hide.Past.DefObj.3Sg the paper.Acc
'It is under a book that Ili hid the paper.'

b. Ili NEHEZÉK ALATT tartja a papírt.
Ili paper_weight under_at keep.DefObj.3Sg the paper.Acc
'It is under a paperweight that Ili keeps the paper.'

c. Ili FÖLDKUPAC ALÓL húzta elő a fonalat.
Ili soil.pile under_from pull.Past.DefObj.3Sg out the thread.Acc
'It is from under a pile of soil that Ili pulled out the thread.'

(38) shows cases in which a specific case-like P takes a specific bare noun as a complement in a set phrase. In (38a) either the locative or the directional postposition is acceptable; individual speakers have preferences for one or the other P.

(38) a. Pál kéz alól / alatt vette a TV-t.
Pál hand under_from / under_at buy.Past.DefObj.3Sg the TV-Acc
'Pál bought the TV set [from a non-licensed vendor] / [on the black market].'

b. torony-iránt
tower-towards
'straight ahead, as the crow flies'

Of case-like postpositions with a temporal interpretation, *múlva* 'in (X time), after (X time)' and *óta* 'since' combine with plural bare nominal complements (136).

(39) a. Pál még órá-*(k) múlva is kint sétált.
Pál still hour-Pl after Emph outside walk.Past.3Sg
'Pál was walking outside even after hours had passed.'

b. Pál órá-*(k) óta nézi a TV-t.
Pál hour-Pl since watch.DefObj.3Sg the TV-Acc
'Pál has been watching TV for hours.'

The temporal case-like P *tájt/tájban* 'around (a point in time)' does not take bare nominal complements, unless nouns naming parts of the day and mealtimes are taken to be bare nominals (40). (These may perhaps be considered to be proper names, however.)

(40) a. Pál dél tájban megy az egyetem-re.
Pál noon around go.3Sg the university-Sub
'Pál goes to the university around noon.'

b. Pál vacsora tájban ér haza.
Pál dinner around get.3Sg home_to
'Pál gets home around suppertime.'

Case-like Ps with a non-spatial and non-temporal semantics take bare nominal complements under the same circumstances as spatial case suffixes: the case-marked P must be focused (41a,b) or must receive a generic / type interpretation (41c).

(41) a. FÖLDRENGÉS *MIATT* dőlt össze sok ház.
earthquake because_of fall.Past.3Sg together many house
'It is because of an earthquake that many houses collapsed.'

b. Pál [HITEL *NÉLKÜL*] / [GYEREK *NÉLKÜL*] / [BIZTOSÍTÁS *NÉLKÜL*] él.
Pál loan without / child without / insurance without live.3Sg
'Pál lives without a loan / child / insurance.'

c. Orvos *által* végzett beavatkozásainkra garanciát adunk.
doctor by performed procedure.Poss.Pl.Poss.1Pl.Sub guarantee.Acc give.1Pl
'A guarantee applies to our procedures performed by a doctor.'

3.2.2.4. Pro-dropped and implicit complements

Case suffixes (except for the morphologically unmarked nominative and the accusative suffix) allow their pronominal complement to be dropped (see Chapter 2

Section 2.2.1.2 point *V*). This is also true of case-like postpositions (see Chapter 2 Section 2.2.2.2.2 point *V*). In both cases, the person and number features of the dropped pronoun are recoverable from the agreement suffix that obligatorily appears on the adposition. Representative examples are given in (42).

(42) a. (Én-)nek-em minden cica tetszik.
I-Dat-1Sg every cat appeal.3Sg
'All cats appeal to me.'

b. A cica (én-)mellett-em alszik.
the cat I-next_to-1Sg sleep.3Sg
'The cat is sleeping next to me.'

Some case-assigning postpositions can also appear without a complement, as in (43b) (cf. Chapter 2 Section 2.2.3.2 point *III*).

(43) a. A labda a vonal-on alul van.
the ball the line-Sup under be.3Sg
'The ball is under the line.'

b. A labda alul van.
the ball under be.3Sg
'The ball is down there [wrt a contextually salient reference point].'

In this case the Ps express a (spatial or temporal) relation between the Ground and a deictic center of the utterance. It is therefore reasonable to assume that this is not a genuinely intransitive use: in these cases the case-assigning Ps take an implicit but syntactically represented complement. The same is true of case-assigning Ps that function as verbal modifiers and appear without an overt complement, cf. (44a) with a complement and (44b) without one.

(44) a. Ili a mező-n át sétált, amikor esni kezdett.
Ili the meadow-Sup through walk.Past.3Sg when rain.Inf start.Past.3Sg
'Ili was walking through the meadow when it started raining.'

b. Ili át-sétált.
Ili through-walk.Past.3Sg
'Ili walked over [to here / there].'

3.2.3. Adjectival complements

Postpositional heads typically take nominal complements. Some adverbial suffixes (which this book takes to be opaque P heads, cf. Chapter 1), however, regularly take adjectival complements. In addition, certain case suffixes also combine with adjectival complements either in a productive or in a restricted manner. Postpositions and verbal particles do not take adjectival complements.

VII. Adjectival complements of adverbial suffixes

Of the adverbial suffixes, the modal-essive suffix *-(V)n* (allomorphs: *-n/-on/-an/-en*) and the essive(-modal) suffix *-Vl* (allomorphs: *-ul/-ül*) take adjectival complements regularly (on these suffixes, see also Chapter 2 Section 2.2.4.1.1 points *II* and *III*). Examples of the modal-essive suffix are provided in (45).

(45) a. Kati szép-en / gyors-an / kitartó-an úszik.
Kati nice-ly / quick-ly / persistent-ly swim.3Sg
'Kati swims nicely / quickly / persistently.'

b. A kávét drágá-n vettem.
the coffee.Acc expensive-ly buy.Past.1Sg
'The coffee I bought was expensive (for that kind of coffee).'

c. A kávét feketé-n / keresű-n szeretem.
the coffee.Acc black-ly / bitter-ly like.1Sg
'I like coffee black / bitter.'

Examples of the essive(-modal) suffix are given in (46).

(46) a. Ili orosz-ul beszél.
Ili Russian-ly speak.3Sg
'Ili is speaking Russian.'

b. Ili jó-l oldotta meg a feladatot.
Ili good-ly solve.Past.DefObj.3Sg Perf the assignment.Acc
'Ili did the assignment well.'

Note that the essive(-modal) suffix may also take certain bare nouns as complement (47):

(47) a. Pál feleség-ül vette Ilit.
Pál wife-ly take.Past.DefObj.3Sg Ili.Acc
'Pál married Ili.' (Lit: Pál took Ili as wife.)

b. Ember-ül viselkedni nem mindig könnyű.
man-ly behave.Inf not always easy
'To behave in a way worthy of a man is not always easy.'

VIII. Adjectival complements of case suffixes

Hungarian has bare AP predicates only with copular (e.g. *van* 'be', *lesz* 'will be, become') and semi-copular verbs (e.g. *marad* 'remain, stay'):

(48) a. Te kedves vagy.
you(Sg) kind be.2Sg
'You(Sg) are kind.'

b. Pál kedves volt / lesz / maradt.
Pál kind be_Past.3Sg / will_be.3Sg / remain.Past.3Sg
'Pál was / [will be] / remained kind.'

Secondary AP predicates cannot be bare; they must be case-marked (with the translative(-essive), the sublative, the dative, the inessive or the illative case suffix, depending on the type of secondary predicate). That is, in order to form secondary predicates, adjectives must be embedded in a PP headed by a case suffix. In such cases we are thus dealing with AP complements of P heads.

A. Adjectival complements of the translative(-essive) case suffix

The translative(-essive) case suffix productively takes either bare nominal or adjectival complements (49).

(49) a. A fiú madár-rá változott.
the boy bird-TrE change.Past.3Sg
'The boy turned into a bird.' (Lit. changed into a bird)

a'. A fiú fiatal felnőtt-té cseperedett.
the boy young adult-TrE grow.Past.3Sg
'The boy grew up to be a young adult.' (Lit. grew into a young adult)

b. Az ég ijesztő-vé vált.
the sky threatening-TrE become.Past.3Sg
'The sky became threatening.'

b'. Kezelés után a bőr simá-vá válik.
treatment after the skin smooth-TrE become.3Sg
'After treatment the skin becomes smooth.'

The PP headed by the translative(-essive) case denotes the result state of a change and serves as a resultative secondary predicate in the clause. The state before the change has taken place can be expressed by a PP headed by the elative case (50).

(50) Ili kedves-ből ijesztő-vé változott.
Ili kind-Ela threatening-TrE change.Past.3Sg
'Ili changed from kind to threatening.'

With change of state predicates the PP headed by the elative case must always accompany the PP headed by the translative(-essive) case; it cannot occur on its own (51).

(51) *Ili kedves-ből változott.
Ili kind-Ela change.Past.3Sg
Intended meaning: 'Ili changed from [being] kind.'

While change of state predicates characteristically take the translative(-essive) case, in one idiomatic expression the illative case is used instead (52). Here, too, the state before the change can be expressed with an optional PP headed by the elative case.

(52) Ili át ment (kedves-ből) ijesztő-be.
Ili over go.Past.3Sg kind-Ela scary-Ill
'Ili turned (from kind to) scary.'

B. Adjectival complements of the sublative case suffix

Resultative secondary predicates are formed when the sublative case suffix takes an adjectival complement (53). This is an entirely productive process.

(53) a. Ili lapos-ra kalapálta a vasat.
Ili flat-Sub hammer.Past.DefObj.3Sg the iron.Acc
'Ili hammered the iron flat.'

b. Ili apró-ra vágta a diót.
Ili tiny-Sub cut.Past.DefObj.3Sg the walnut.Acc
'Ili cut the walnut into small pieces.'

C. Adjectival complements of the dative case suffix

A small group of verbs selects for a small clause complement in which the adjectival predicate must be dative marked. The verbs in question include *tart* 'consider (sb to be Adj)', *néz* 'take (sb to be Adj)', *gondol* 'think (of sb as Adj)', *vél* 'consider (sb to be Adj)', *tekint* 'consider (sb/sth to be Adj)', *tűnik* 'appear (to be Adj)' and *látszik* 'look/appear (to be Adj)'. The PP comprising the dative case and its adjectival complement serves as a secondary predicate next to these verbs. Some examples are given in (54).

(54) a. Ili okos-nak tartja Pált.
Ili clever-Dat consider.DefObj.3Sg Pál.Acc
'Ili considers Pál to be clever.'

b. Ili hülyé-nek nézi Pált.
Ili stupid-Dat take.DefObj.3Sg Pál.Acc
'Ili takes Pál to be stupid.'

c. Ili alkalmas-nak gondolja Pált.
Ili stupid-Dat think.DefObj.3Sg Pál.Acc
'Ili considers Pál to be capable.'

d. Ili egyenértékű-nek tekinti a megoldásokat.
Ili equivalent-Dat consider.DefObj.3Sg the solution.Pl.Acc
'Ili considers the solutions to be equivalent.'

Note that the dative suffix can also take a nominal complement as the secondary predicate in the small clause selected by one of the verbs listed above. This is shown in (55) for *néz* 'take (sb to be something)'.

(55) Ili orvos-nak nézte Pált.
Ili doctor-Dat take.Past.DefObj.3Sg Pál.Acc
'Ili took Pál to be a doctor.'

The dative suffix can also have an adjectival complement in the predicate cleft construction (see the volume on Sentence Structure).

(56) Szép-nek szép, de túl drága.
pretty-Dat pretty but too expensive
'As for [being] pretty, it is pretty, but it is too expensive.'

D. Adjectival complements of other case suffixes

Other case suffixes do not productively take adjectival complements, but they can occur with such complements in set collocations (57). In these examples the case-marked adjective functions as an argument of the verb.

(57) a. Ili feketé-be / piros-ba / fehér-be öltözött. [illative]
Ili black-Ill / red-Ill / white-Ill dress.Past.3Sg
'Ili dressed in all black / red / white.'

b. Ili feketé-ben / piros-ban / fehér-ben jár. [inessive]
Ili black-Ine / red-Ine / white-Ine walk.3Sg
'Ili is habitually dressed in all black / red / white.'

b'. Ili tilos-ban jár. [inessive]
Ili forbidden-Ine walk.3Sg
'Ili is doing something forbidden.'

3.2.4. *Adverbial complements*

The sublative and the delative case suffix can take certain locative adverbs as complements. Some examples are given in (58) and (59). This is not a productive pattern. (On the adverbs in (59b), see Chapter 2 Section 2.2.4.1.2 point *III*.)

(58) a. Ili távol-ra és közel-re is jól lát. [sublative]
Ili far-Sub and close-Sub too well see.3Sg
'Ili can see things well from afar and from up close.'

b. Ili [egymástól távol-ra] /[egymáshoz közel-re] ültet pár virágot.
Ili each_other.Abl far-Sub / each_other.All close-Sub plant.3Sg couple flower.Acc
'Ili plants some flowers [far apart] / [close to each other].'

(59) a. Ili távol-ról / közel-ről nézi a TV-t. [delative]
Ili far-Del / close-Del watch.DefObj.3Sg the TV-Acc
'Ili watches TV [from far away] / [up close].'

b. Ili bent-ről / kint-ről / lent-ről / fent-ről nézi a TV-t.
Ili inside-Del / outside-Del / down-Del / up-Del watch.DefObj.3Sg the TV-Acc
'Ili is watching TV [from inside] / [from the outside] / [from lower down] / [from up(stairs)].'

There are also collocations which do not represent a productive pattern, such as (60).

(60) késő-re jár (az idő)
late-Sub go.3Sg the time
'it is late, it is getting late'

3.2.5. *Adpositional complements*

Of adpositional heads, it is case-assigning postpositions (Chapter 2 Section 2.2.2.3) whose complement is adpositional by default. Verbal particles take adpositional complements only when the particle also functions as a case-assigning postposition. Among case suffixes, only the delative and the sublative case suffixes can have an adpositional complement and then only under restricted circumstances (see below and also Chapter 2 Section 2.2.2.2.4).

I. Adpositional complements of case-assigning postpositions

Case-assigning postpositions take PP complements headed by a superessive, allative or instrumental case suffix (61). The choice of the case suffix is determined by the individual postposition.

(61) a. Az erdő a kertítés-en túl kezdődik. [superessive complement]
the forest the fence-Sup beyond start.3Sg
'The forest starts beyond the fence.'

b. Az erdő a kertítés-hez közel kezdődik. [allative complement]
the forest the fence-All close_to start.3Sg
'The forest starts close to the fence.'

c. Az erdő a kertítés-sel szemben kezdődik. [instrumental complement]
the forest the fence-Ins opposite_to start.3Sg
'The forest starts opposite the fence.'

II. Adpositional complements of verbal particles

Some case-assigning postpositions can function as verbal particles. In this case they appear in the preverbal verb modifier position (in neutral sentences) and the PP that they subcategorize for may be dropped or may appear postverbally (62). The latter case can be thought of as involving a verbal particle taking an adpositional complement (cf. also Chapter 2 Section 2.2.3.4).

(62) Az ág túl-nyúlik (a kerítés-en).
the branch beyond-reach.3Sg the fence-Sup
'The branch goes beyond (the fence).'

III. Adpositional complements of case suffixes

Case suffixes normally do not take adpositional complements. The exceptions are the sublative and the delative case suffixes, which may, under very limited conditions, take a PP complement headed by a postposition expressing a location.

A. Adpositional complements headed by a case-like P

As discussed in Chapter 2 Section 2.2.2.2.1, many case-like Ps form semantically and morphologically related triplets. A P with the *-(Vt)t* locative suffix expresses static location at a position, a P with the *-á/-é* lative suffix expresses motion to a location, while a P with the *-(V)l* source suffix expresses motion away from a location (63).

(63) az asztal alatt / alá / alól
the table under_at / under_to / under_from
'under / [to under] / [from under] the table'

In special cases, motion to a location may be expressed by the combination of a locative (*-(Vt)t* marked) P and the sublative case instead of a lative marked P (64).

(64) a. a felszín alá tervezett garázs
the surface under_to designed garage
'the garage designed to be located under the surface'

b. ?a felszín alatt-ra tervezett garázs
the surface under_at-Sub designed garage
'the garage designed to be located under the surface'

Such combinations may become obligatory if the sublative case is subcategorized by a verb (65).

(65) a. A benzinfogyasztást ki lehet hozni 6 liter alatt-ra / alá.
the petrol.consumption.Acc out possible bring.Inf 6 liter under_at-Sub / under_to
'Petrol consumption can be reduced to under 6 liters.'

b. A játékban az asztal alatt-ra / *alá fogadtam.
the game.Ine the table under_at-Sub / under_to bet.Past.1Sg
'In the game I placed my bet on 'under the table' (being the correct solution).'

c. Ez a felszín alatt-ra / *alá nem vonatkozik.
this the surface under_at-Sub / under_to not concern.3Sg
'This does not concern (the area) under the surface.'

Similarly, in special cases motion away from a location may be expressed by the combination of a locative (*-(Vt)t* marked) P and the delative case instead of a *-(V)l* marked P (66).

(66) a. a felszín alól érkező hangok
the surface under_from coming sound.Pl
'the sounds coming from under the surface'

b. ?a felszín alatt-ról érkező hangok
the surface under_at-Del coming sound.Pl
'the sounds coming from under the surface'

Again, these unusual combinations may become obligatory if the verb subcategorizes for the delative case (67):

(67) A felszín alatt-ról / *alól még nem is beszéltünk.
the table under_at-Del / under_from yet not too speak.Past.1Pl
'We haven't even spoken about the area under the surface.'

The case-like Ps *előtt* 'in front of', *alatt* 'under' and *után* 'behind' may have temporal readings ('before', 'during' and 'after', respectively). In the temporal reading these Ps combine with the sublative or delative case suffix and the corresponding goal / source Ps are either degraded or outright ungrammatical (68), (69).

(68) • Case-like Ps with the sublative suffix

a. A szobrot a vaskor előtt-re / ?(?)elé datálják.
the sculpture.Acc the iron.age in_front_of-Sub / before_from date.3Pl
'The sculpture is dated (by experts) to be from before the Iron Age.'

b. A szobrot a vaskor alatt-ra / *alá datálják.
the sculpture.Acc the iron.age under_at-Sub / under_to date.3Pl
'The sculpture is dated (by experts) to be from the Iron Age.'

c. A szobrot a vaskor után-ra datálják.
the sculpture.Acc the iron.age behind_at-Sub date.3Pl
'The sculpture is dated (by experts) to be from after the Iron Age.'

(69) • Case-like Ps with the delative suffix

a. A szobor a vaskor előtt-ről / *elől származik.
the sculpture the iron.age in_front_of -Del / before_from be_from.3Sg
'The sculpture dates from before the Iron Age.'

b. A szobor a vaskor után-ról származik.
the sculpture the iron.age behind_at-Del be_from.3Sg
'The sculpture dates from after the Iron Age.'

Remark 1. Note that while *után* does have a spatial use, as in (i), it does not involve the *-(Vt)t* suffix, and it has no lative or *-(V)l* marked forms either.

(i) Ili Pál után baktat.
Ili Pál behind amble.3Sg
'Ili is ambling behind Pál.'

In contrast to the previous examples, in (70a) neither alternative is genuinely grammatical; this is because the availability of an alternative form with a case-marked noun (70b).

(70) • Case-like P blocked by case suffix

a. A szobor a vaskor *?alatt-ról / *alól származik.
the sculpture the iron.age under_at-Del / under_from be_from.3Sg
'The sculpture dates from the Iron Age.'

b. A szobor a vaskor-ból származik.
the sculpture the iron.age-Ela be_from.3Sg
'The sculpture dates from the Iron Age.'

B. Adpositional complements headed by a case-assigning P

In contrast to case-like postpositions, case-assigning Ps generally do not come in morphologically related triplets. The Ps that express a location but have no source or goal counterparts form goal and source PPs with the sublative and the delative case, respectively. (71) shows this for *túl* 'beyond'.

(71) a. A madár a folyó-n túl lakik.
the bird the river-Sup beyond live.3Sg
'The bird lives beyond the river.'

b. A madár a folyó-n túl-ra repült.
the bird the river-Sup beyond-Sub fly.Past.3Sg
'The bird flew (to the area) beyond the river.'

c. A madár a folyó-n túl-ról érkezett.
the bird the river-Sup beyond-Del arrive.Past.3Sg
'The bird came from (the area) beyond the river.'

3.2.6. Clausal complements

3.2.6.1. Finite clausal complements

Adpositions do not take finite clausal complements directly. Case suffixes and case-like postpositions can combine with a proleptic demonstrative pronoun *az* 'that' associated with a finite embedded clause in the clause-final position of the matrix clause, however, to the extent that the semantics of the P allows this. Case-assigning postpositions occur either with a PP complement or intransitively, but a proleptic pronoun (or a clause) is never a direct complement of such a postposition; their complement is always a PP headed by a case suffix. Verbal particles and the adverbial endings discussed in Chapter 2 Section 2.2.4.1 do not take finite clausal complements either.

I. Finite clausal complements of case suffixes

Almost all case suffixes may combine with a proleptic pronoun with a clausal associate (72). (The exceptions will be discussed shortly below, clauses and their associated pronouns will be discussed in detail in the volume on Finite Embedding.)

(72) a. Ili tudja (*az-t*), hogy Pál 8-ra jön. [accusative]
Ili know.3Sg that-Acc that Pál 8-Sub come.3Sg
'Ili knows that Pál comes at 8.'

b. Ili örül (*annak*), hogy Pál 8-ra jön. [dative]
Ili happy that.Dat that Pál 8-Sub come.3Sg
'Ili is happy that Pál comes at 8.'

b'. Ili *annak* szenteli az életét, hogy állatokat ment.
Ili that.Dat dedicate.3Sg the life.Poss.Acc that animal.Pl.Acc rescue.3Sg
'Ili dedicates her life to rescuing animals.'

c. Ili bízik *abban*, hogy Pál 8-ra jön. [inessive]
Ili hope.3Sg that.Ine that Pál 8-Sub come.3Sg
'Ili hopes that Pál comes at 8.'

d. Ili nem tehet *arról*, hogy kirúgták. [delative]
Ili not be_blamed_for.3Sg that.Del that out.fire.Past.3Pl
'Ili cannot be blamed for having been fired.'

e. Ili (*az-ért*) izgul, hogy Pál odaérjen 8-ra. [causal(-final)]
Ili that-Cau be_anxious.3Sg that Pál there.get.Subj.3Sg 8-Sub
'Ili is anxious for Pál to get there by 8.'

We use the term 'proleptic pronoun' in a way that is neutral with respect to word order, noting that it can also follow the associated clause (e.g. when the clause appears in the sentence-initial contrastive topic position). As shown in (72), in certain cases the proleptic pronoun can be dropped.

In the examples in (72) the proleptic pronoun is a demonstrative. In the postverbal position the proleptic pronoun can also be a dropped *pro*. This is shown in (73a) for the dative, in (73b) for the inessive and in (73c) for the delative.

(73) a. Ili örül *nek-i*, hogy Pál 8-ra jön. [dative]
Ili happy Dat-3Sg that Pál 8-Sub come.3Sg
'Ili is happy that Pál comes at 8.'

b. Ili bízik *benn-e*, hogy Pál 8-ra jön. [inessive]
Ili hope.3Sg Ine-3Sg that Pál 8-Sub come.3Sg
'Ili hopes that Pál comes at 8.'

c. Ili nem tehet *ról-a*, hogy kirúgták. [delative]
Ili not be_blamed_for.3Sg Del-3Sg that out.fire.Past.3Pl
'Ili cannot be blamed for having been fired.'

As detailed in Chapter 2 Section 2.2.1.2 point *V/B* and *V/E*, an oblique-marked personal pronoun has the form 'pronoun–oblique case–possessive agreement'. The pronoun itself can be dropped, leaving only the case suffix and the agreement suffix overt. This is shown for the third person singular pronoun *ő* 's/he' in (74).

(74) (ő-)benn-e, (ő-)ról-a, (ő-)től-e
he-Ine-3Sg he-Del-3Sg he-Abl-3Sg
'in him, from/about him, from him'

When the oblique pronoun refers to a [–human] noun, however, then the third person singular pronoun *ő* 's/he' must be dropped. Differently put, an overt *ő* 's/he' forces a [+human] interpretation (75). (In the examples below, *is* 'too' makes it possible for *ő* 's/he' to appear in a postverbal position; it does not influence the [+human] or [–human] interpretation.)

(75) a. Ili örült *ő-nek-i* is. [dative]
Ili be_happy.Past.3Sg he-Dat-3Sg too
'Ili was happy about him / her, too.'

a'. Ili örült *nek-i* is.
Ili be_happy.Past.3Sg Dat-3Sg too
'Ili was happy about him / her / it, too.'

b. Ili bízik *ő-benn-e* is. [inessive]
Ili trust.3Sg he-Ine-3Sg too
'Ili trusts in him / her, too.'

b'. Ili bízik *benn-e* is.
Ili trust.3Sg Ine-3Sg too
'Ili trusts in him / her / it, too.'

c. Ili sokat beszélt *ő-róla* is. [delative]
Ili lot.Acc speak.Past.3Sg he-Del.3Sg too
'Ili talked a lot about him / her, too.'

c'. Ili sokat beszélt *ról-a* is.
Ili lot.Acc speak.Past.3Sg Del-3Sg too
'Ili talked a lot about him / her / it, too.'

For this reason, the third person singular pronoun must also be dropped when used as a proleptic pronoun (76); that is, the proleptic pronoun comprises only the oblique case suffix and the agreement.

(76) a. Ili örül (*ő-)*nek-i*, hogy Pál 8-ra jön. [dative]
Ili be_happy.3Sg he-Dat-3Sg that Pál 8-Sub come.3Sg
'Ili is happy that Pál will come at 8.'

b. Ili bízik (*ő-)*benn-e*, hogy Pál 8-ra jön. [inessive]
Ili trust.3Sg he-Ine-3Sg that Pál 8-Sub come.3Sg
'Ili trusts that Pál will come at 8.'

c. Ili sokat beszélt (*ő-)*róla*, hogy kirúgták. [delative]
Ili lot.Acc speak.Past.3Sg he-Del.3Sg that out.fire.Past.3Pl
'Ili talked a lot about [the fact] that she has been fired.'

An overt accusative-marked personal pronoun cannot function as a proleptic pronoun either (77).

(77) Ili tudja (**ő-t*), hogy Pál 8-ra jön. [accusative]
Ili know.3Sg that-Acc that Pál 8-Sub come.3Sg
'Ili knows that Pál will come at 8.'

As for the accusative case suffix, it cannot appear in the pattern in (74), without an overt pronoun preceding it, under any circumstances. Therefore the grammatical version of (77) involves *pro*-drop of the entire inflected pronoun, that is, silence of both *ő* and the accusative case (78).

(78) Ili tudja, hogy Pál 8-ra jön.
Ili know.3Sg that Pál 8-Sub come.3Sg
'Ili knows that Pál will come at 8.'

In the preverbal field the proleptic pronoun appears either in the topic, distributive quantifier or focus position. In this case only the demonstrative can be used; the *pro* leads to ungrammaticality (Elekfi 1980, Kenesei 1992, Kenesei 1994, É. Kiss 2002: 231-232). This is shown with focused pronouns in (79).

(79) a. Ili AZ-T / *Ő-T tudja, hogy Pál 8-ra jön.
Ili that-Acc / he-Acc know.3Sg that-Acc Pál 8-Sub come.3Sg
'What Ili knows is that Pál will come at 8.'

b. Ili ANNAK / *NEK-I örül, hogy Pál 8-ra jön.
Ili that.Dat / Dat-3Sg happy that Pál 8-Sub come.3Sg
'What Ili is happy about is that Pál will come at 8.'

c. Ili ABBAN / *BENN-E bízik, hogy Pál 8-ra jön.
Ili that.Ine / Ine-3Sg hope.3Sg that Pál 8-Sub come.3Sg
'What Ili hopes is that Pál will come at 8.'

d. Ili ARRÓL / *RÓL-A beszélt, hogy kirúgták.
Ili that.Ine / Ine-3Sg speak.Past.3Sg that out.fire.Past.3Pl
'What Ili talked about is that she has been fired.'

That personal pronouns as proleptic pronouns are restricted to the post-verbal field stems from the fact that forms without an overt *ő*, such as *neki*, *benne* and *róla* as proleptic pronouns are weak, and weak pronouns cannot be focused.

Probably due to their meanings, the translative(-essive) *-vá/-vé* and the essive-formal *-ként* do not take clausal complements, therefore they do not occur in the [[proleptic *az* 'that'+case] … clausal associate] construction where the clausal associate would be the semantic complement of the case suffix.

Remark 2. The translative(-essive) *-vá/-vé* and the essive-formal *-ként* can combine with an *az* 'that' that is associated with a clause, however, these are always relative clauses, which are (with the exception of some free relatives) not complements, see the volume on Finite Embedding. In (i) the associate clause is a correlative clause. As argued by Lipták (2008, 2012), Hungarian correlatives are base-generated topics; thus there is no complementation relation between the oblique case and the clause (or between the demonstrative and the clause).

(i) a. [Aki akart lenni], Ili az-zá vált.
rel.who want.Past.3Sg be.Inf Ili that-TrE become.Past.3Sg
'Ili has become who she wanted to be.'

b. [Ahogy teljesítettek], Ili ak-ként jutalmazta
rel.how deliver.Past.3Pl Ili that-FoE reward.Past.DefObj.3Sg
a beosztottakat.
the employee.Pl.Acc
'Ili rewarded the employees commensurate with their achievements.'

A demonstrative with a translative(-essive) or essive-formal case can also function as the head of the relative clause (leading to a so-called light-headed relative clause, cf. Citko 2004). This is illustrated in (ii), with an extraposed relative clause. There is no selection between the oblique case and the clause here either: the case selects for the referential demonstrative pronoun and we are not dealing with a proleptic pronoun. The relative clause itself is an adjunct of the pronoun (see the volume on Finite Embedding).

(ii) a. Ili az-zá vált, [aki akart lenni].
Ili that-TrE become.Past.3Sg rel.who want.Past.3Sg be.Inf
'Ili has become who she wanted to be.'

b. Ili ak-ként jutalmazta a beosztottakat,
Ili that-FoE reward.Past.DefObj.3Sg the employee.Pl.Acc
[ahogy teljesítettek].
rel.how deliver.Past.3Pl
'Ili rewarded the employees commensurate with their achievements.'

II. Finite clausal complements of case-like postpositions

Case-like Ps can combine with a proleptic *az* 'that' associated with a finite clause under limited circumstances. The pattern is always felicitous with the temporal reading of those Ps that also have a spatial reading, e.g. *alatt* 'under, during', *körül* 'around', *mellett* 'next to', *előtt* 'in front of, before', *után* 'behind, after' (80b).

(80) a. Sok mindent láttam az-alatt, hogy katona voltam.
much everything.Acc see.Past.3Sg that-under that solider be.Past.1Sg
'I saw a lot while I was a soldier.'

b. Választani kell aközött, hogy maradjak vagy hogy menjek.
choose.Inf must that.between that stay.Subj.1Sg or that go.Subj.1Sg
'I have to choose between staying and going.'

The case of *mellett* 'next to' is special in the sense that *amellett* 'next to that' has assumed the broader reading 'in addition to' (81).

(81) a. Amellett, hogy tanul, rendszeresen edz is.
that.next_to that study.3Sg regularly work_out.3Sg too
'In addition to studying, he regularly works out, too.'

b. Amellett, hogy igaza van, még udvarias is.
that.next_to that right.Poss be.3Sg also polite too
'In addition to being right, he is also polite.'

Moreover, while directional case-like Ps normally do not combine with proleptic pronouns of clauses, the lative-marked *mellé* 'to next to' does, also with the meaning 'in addition to' (82).

(82) Amellé, hogy megírok egy könyvet, más munkát nem vállalok.
that.to_next_to that Perf.write.1Sg a book.Acc other work.Acc not undertake.1Sg
'I do not undertake any tasks beyond writing a book.'

Directional (goal or source) case-like postpositions can combine with a proleptic pronoun if the postposition is part of a collocation or set phrase, as in (83), for instance.

(83) a. kihúzza magát valami alól
out.pull self.Acc something under_from
'back out of something'

b. Ili kihúzta magát az-alól, hogy ebédet főzzön.
Ili out.pull.Past.DefObj.3Sg self.Acc that-under_from that lunch.Acc cook.Subj.3Sg
'Ili backed out of cooking lunch.'

Of case-like Ps that have only a temporal reading, only *óta* 'since' is clearly grammatical with proleptic *az* 'that' (84).

(84) Sok mindent láttam az-óta, hogy katona voltam.
lot everything.Acc see.Past.3Sg that-since that solider be.Past.1Sg
'I saw a lot since I was a soldier.'

Múlva 'since' and *tájban* '(temporal) around' are ungrammatical with both unmarked and dative marked proleptic pronouns; they do not combine with a proleptic pronoun at all (85).

(85) a. *Sok mindent láttam a-múlva, hogy katona voltam.
lot everything.Acc see.Past.3Sg that-after that solider be.Past.1Sg
Intended meaning: 'I have seen a lot since I was a soldier.'

a'. *Sok mindent láttam annak múlva, hogy katona voltam.
lot everything.Acc see.Past.3Sg that.Dat after that solider be.Past.1Sg
Intended meaning: 'I have seen a lot since I was a soldier.'

b. *?Sok mindent láttam a-tájban, hogy katona voltam.
lot everything.Acc see.Past.3Sg that-around that solider be.Past.1Sg
Intended meaning: 'I saw a lot around the time when I was a soldier.'

b'. *Sok mindent láttam annak tájban, hogy katona voltam.
lot everything.Acc see.Past.3Sg that.Dat around that solider be.Past.1Sg
Intended meaning: 'I saw a lot around the time when I was a soldier.'

Most case-like Ps with a non-spatial and non-temporal reading (the 'other' group in Chapter 2 Table 4) can take a proleptic pronominal complement associated with a finite clause (86).

(86) a. Az-által, hogy időben indult, nem késett el.
that-by that time.Ine start.Past.3Sg not be_late.Past.3Sg away
'Thanks to the fact that he started early, he was not late.'

b. Szomorú vagyok a-miatt, hogy elkéstél.
sad be.1Sg that-because_of that away.be_late.Past.3Sg
'I am sad because you were late.'

However, *gyanánt* 'as, in the guise of' does not combine with a proleptic pronoun (87).

(87) Tulipánt ültettek *annak / *az gyanánt, hogy
tulip.Acc plant.Past.3Pl that.Dat / that in_guise_of that
[szépítsék a kertet] / [bosszantsák a szomszédot].
beautify.Subj.3Pl the garden.Acc / annoy.Subj.3Pl the neighbour.Acc
'They planted tulips to [beautify the garden] / [annoy the neighbor].'

3.2.6.2. Non-finite clausal complements

Of non-finite clauses, infinitives, -ÁS nominalizations and -T nominalizations can appear in nominal positions. Of these non-finite clauses, infinitives cannot appear in the complement position of either case suffixes or case-like postpositions (88).

(88) a. *Örülök (a) [telefonál-ni]-*nak*.
rejoice.1Sg the phone-Inf-Dat
Intended meaning: 'I am happy about the phone call.'

b. *[Telefonál-ni] *mellett* enni is akarok.
phone-Inf next_to eat.Inf too want.1Sg
Intended meaning: 'In addition to making a phone call, I also want to eat.'

-ÁS nominalizations, discussed in detail in N1.3.1.2, Szabolcsi and Laczkó (1992), Laczkó (1995, 1997, 2000, 2009, 2010, 2015) and Kenesei (2005), regularly combine with case suffixes (89).

(89) Örülök [az utcára vonul-ás]-*nak*.
rejoice.1Sg the street.Sub march-Nmn-Dat
'I am happy about the marching to the street.'

They also combine with case-like Ps that i) have both a spatial and a temporal reading, as in (90a), ii) have a temporal-only reading (except for *múlva* 'after X time', which only takes complements that denote a time-period), as in (90b), and also iii) case-like Ps with a non-spatial and non-temporal reading, as in (90c).

(90) a. [Az utcára vonul-ás] *mellett* mást is kell tennünk.
the street.Sub march-Nmn next_to other.Acc too must do.Inf.1Pl
'In addition to marching to the street, we also have to do something else.'

b. [Az utcára vonul-ás] *óta* megváltoztak a dolgok.
the street.Sub march-Nmn since Perf.change.Past.3Pl the thing.Pl
'Things have changed since the marching to the street.'

c. [Az utcára vonul-ás] *nélkül* nem változtak volna a dolgok.
the street.Sub march-Nmn without not change.Past.3Pl be.Cond the thing.Pl
'Things would not have changed without the marching to the streets.'

-T nominalizations that correspond to English gerunds, discussed at length in N1.3.1.4 and in the volume on Non-Finite and Semi-Finite Verb Phrases, Radics (1992), Tóth (2011) and Dékány (2014), obligatorily show agreement with the subject's person and number, and are not productive any more. They can be the complements of case suffixes, especially when the case is subcategorized by the matrix verb (91a), or when the case-marker is the inessive (91b,c). The inessive on these nominalizations expresses that the event in the matrix clause and the embedded clause are cotemporaneous.

(91) a. [Ott-jár-t-unk]-*nak* nem örültek a helyiek.
there-go-Nmn-1Pl-Dat not rejoice.Past.3Pl the local.Pl
'The locals were not happy about our going there.'

b. [Arrafelé jár-t-unk]-*ban* sok helyi embert megismertünk.
there.towards go-Nmn-1Pl-Ine many local person.Acc Perf.know.Past.1Pl
'We got to know many local people when we went there.'

c. A sas [röp-t-é]-*ben* kapta el a galambot.
the eagle fly-Nmn-3Sg-Ine catch.Past.3Sg away the dove.Acc
'The eagle caught the dove while flying.' (Either the eagle or the dove was flying; or both.)

-T nominalizations also combine with case-like Ps that have a temporal reading (92).

(92) [Ott-jár-t-unk] *előtt* / *alatt* / *után* / *óta* lettem beteg.
there-go-Nmn-1Pl in_front_of / under / after / since become.Past.1Sg sick
'I became sick before / during / after / since our going there.'

3.2.7. *Absolute PPs*

In this section we turn to absolute PPs, that is, constructions in which the complement of P is a small clause that comprises a subject nominal and a predicate. Absolute constructions are headed by Ps corresponding to 'with' and 'without', as in the English examples in (93). In these examples 'John' is the subject nominal and 'on the team' is the predicate.

(93) a. With [John on the team], we will have no difficulties.
b. Without [John on the team], we will have major difficulties.

I. Absolute -val/-vel *'with' PPs*

The meaning 'with' is expressed in Hungarian by the instrumental case suffix *-val/-vel.* (The first consonant of the suffix undergoes assimilation to the consonant of consonant-final stems, cf. Chapter 2 Section 2.2.1.1 point *II*). This P can take a small clause complement comprising an NP/DP subject and a spatial PP predicate. In this scenario the instrumental ending appears suffixed to the subject nominal of the small clause (94).

(94) a. [János-*sal* a csapat-ban] biztosan nyerni fogunk.
János-Ins the team-Ine surely win.Inf will.1Pl
'With John on the team, we will surely win.'

b. A díjátadón [a feleségé-*vel* az oldalá-n] jelent meg.
the award.ceremony.Sup the wife.Poss-Ins the side.Poss-Sup appear.Past.3Sg Perf
'He came to the award ceremony with his wife (by his side).'

c. A sztárvendégek [Cher-*rel* az él-en] nagy csalódást okoztak.
the star.guest.Pl Cher-Ins the lead-Sup huge disappointment cause.Past.3Pl
'The guest stars, with Cher in the lead, caused a huge disappointment.'

While the case takes the whole small clause as its complement, it cannot appear suffixed to the clause (95).

(95) *[János a csapat-ban]-*nal* biztosan nyerni fogunk.
János the team-Ine-Ins surely win.Inf will.1Pl
Intended meaning: 'With John on the team, we will surely win.'

The predicate of the small clause can only be adpositional, as in (94); adjectival and nominal predicates lead to ungrammaticality (96).

(96) a. *[János beteg]-*gel* nem fogunk nyerni.
János sick-Ins not will.1Pl win.Inf
Intended meaning: 'With John (being) sick, we will not win.'

a'. *[János-*sal* beteg] nem fogunk nyerni.
János-Ins sick not will.1Pl win.Inf
Intended meaning: 'With John (being) sick, we will not win.'

b. *[János orvos]-*sal* van a csapatban egészségügyi dolgozó.
John doctor-Ins be.3Sg the team.Ine health.care.Attr worker
Intended meaning: 'With John being a doctor, there is a healthcare worker on the team.'

b'. *[János-*sal* orvos] van a csapatban egészségügyi dolgozó.
John-Ins doctor be.3Sg the team.Ine health.care.Attr worker
Intended meaning: 'With John being a doctor, there is a healthcare worker on the team.'

Moreover, not all adpositional predicates are felicitous. While predicates headed by case suffixes and postpositions are acceptable, adverbs (which Chapter 2 Section 2.2.4 argued are also PPs) are not. Compare (94a) and (97).

(97) *[János-*sal* otthon] nem fogunk nyerni.
János-Ins at_home not will.1Pl win.Inf
Intended meaning: 'With John at home, we will not win.'

As shown in the previous examples, the absolute *-val/-vel* 'with' PPs are used adverbially: they refer to some accessory circumstance under which the event denoted by the verb takes place. Given that the head of the absolute *-val/-vel* 'with' PP is the case suffix, and PPs headed by case suffixes do not function as prenominal attributive modifiers of Ns (98a) (cf. also Chapter 2 Section 2.2.1.5), absolute *-val/-vel* 'with' PPs have no prenominal attributive use either (98b).

(98) a. *a [cukor-*ral*] kávé
the sugar-Ins coffee
Intended meaning: 'the coffee with sugar'

b. *a [János-*sal* a csapat-ban] terv
the János-Ins the team-Ine plan
Intended meaning: 'the plan with John on the team'

II. Absolute nélkül *'without' PPs*

The meaning 'without' is expressed in Hungarian by the case-like postposition *nélkül*. This P does not take a small clause predicate, in other words, absolute 'without' PPs do not exist in Hungarian. *Nélkül* cannot appear outside of a small clause (99a), nor can it be linearized on the subject nominal of the small clause (99b).

(99) a. *[János a csapat-ban] nélkül nem fogunk nyerni.
János the team-Ine without not will.1Pl win.Inf
Intended meaning: 'Without John on the team, we will not win.'

b. *[János nélkül a csapat-ban] nem fogunk nyerni.
János without the team-Ine not will.1Pl win.Inf
Intended meaning: 'Without John on the team, we will not win.'

In case the small clause predicate is nominal or adjectival, placing *nélkül* on the subject nominal has no ameliorating effect (100).

(100) a. *[János beteg] nélkül nyerni fogunk.
János sick without win.Inf will.1Pl
Intended meaning: 'Without John (being) sick, we will win.'

a'. *[János nélkül beteg] nyerni fogunk.
János without sick win.Inf will.1Pl
Intended meaning: 'Without John (being) sick, we will win.'

b. *[János orvos] nélkül nincs a csapatban egészségügyi dolgozó.
John doctor without not_be.3Sg the team.Ine health.care.Attr worker
Intended meaning: 'Without János being a doctor, there is no healthcare worker on the team.'

b'. *[János nélkül orvos] nincs a csapatban egészségügyi dolgozó.
János without doctor not_be.3Sg the team.Ine health.care.Attr worker
Intended meaning: 'Without János being a doctor, there is no healthcare worker on the team.'

3.3. Modification

We will now turn to the modification possibilities of PPs, and will proceed as follows. Section 3.3.1 will discuss the modifiers that can be found with spatial (locative or directional) and temporal PPs. We will cover modifiers of PPs that are neither spatial nor temporal in Section 3.3.2, and finally we will examine the modification possibilities with comparative and superlative formation in Section 3.3.3.

3.3.1. Modification of spatial and temporal postpositions

Depending on their meaning, spatial PPs combine with different modifiers but a shared property is that both locative and directional ones allow for modifiers expressing orientation and distance, as well as measure phrases. Temporal PPs are not different in this respect. Categorially, these modifiers are quite uniform in Hungarian since they are all PPs themselves, i.e., we do not find simple NPs or APs as modifiers; they are either adorned with an adverbial suffix (mostly *-n/-an/-en*) or a case suffix (sublative or instrumental).

The most general modifiers that can combine with spatial (locative and directional) and temporal Ps as well are *pontos-an* 'precisely, exactly' and *épp-en* 'right', which have the adverbial *–n/-an/en* suffix (Kenesei *et al.* 1998). There are various other adverbs used as modifiers that are limited in their distribution to varying degrees. Furthermore, there are two types of measure phrases (one with the instrumental suffix and one with the sublative suffix) that are used to modify spatial and temporal PPs.

This section will first look at the general word order properties of PPs with modifiers in Section 3.3.1.1, and then Sections 3.3.1.2 through 3.3.1.9 will discuss the modifiers in more detail.

3.3.1.1. Word order properties

Modifiers precede the complement of case-suffixes and case-like postpositions, as illustrated in (101)-(104).

(101) A virágos [*pontosan* az-on a sark-on] van. [locative case suffix]
the florist exactly that-Sup the corner-Sup be.3Sg
'The florist is right on that corner.'

(102) A kutya ki-szaladt, [*egyenesen* a kert-be]. [directional case suffix]
the dog out-run.Past.3Sg straight.ly the garden-Ill
'The dog ran out, straight into the garden.'

(103) A busz [*épp(en)* a kapu előtt] áll meg. [locative case-like P]
the bus right.ly the gate in_front_of stop.3Sg Perf
'The bus stops right in front of the gate.'

(104) Anna [*közvetlenül* az iskola mellé] költözött. [directional case-like P]
Anna immediately the school to_next_to move.Past.3Sg
'Anna moved right next to the school.'

The modifier may never intervene between the complement and the P with case-like postpositions (105)-(106).

(105) *A busz [a kapu *éppen* előtt] áll meg.
the bus the gate right.ly in_front_of stop.3Sg Perf
Intended meaning: 'The bus stops right in front of the gate.'

(106) *Anna [az iskola *közvetlenül* mellé] költözött.
Anna the school immediately to_next_to move.Past.3Sg
Intended meaning: 'Anna moved right next to the school.'

However, with case-assigning postpositions, there are two possible word orders: the modifier may precede the complement of the case-assigning P (107a), and it may also intervene between the complement and the case-assigning P (107b) (see also Dékány & Hegedűs 2015).

(107) a. Az út [*egészen* az erdő-höz közel] fog vezetni.
the road completely the forest-All close_to will.3Sg lead.Inf
'The road will lead very close to the forest.'

b. Az út [az erdő-höz *egészen* közel] fog vezetni.
the road the forest-All completely close_to will.3Sg lead.Inf
'The road will lead very close to the forest.'

The order in (107b), however, is dispreferred with *alul* 'below' and *innen* 'on this side of' and it is ungrammatical with *felül* 'above' (108).

(108) a. A művész aláírása [*közvetlenül* a vonal-on alul] látható.
the artist signature.Poss directly the line-Sup below visible
'The artist's signature can be seen directly below the line.'

a.' ?A művész aláírása [a vonal-on *közvetlenül* alul] látható.
the artist signature.Poss the line-Sup directly below visible
'The artist's signature can be seen directly below the line.'

b. A labda [*közvetlenül* a vonal-on innen] esett le.
the ball directly the line-Sup this_side fall.Past.3Sg down
'The ball fell down right on this side of the line.'

b.' ?A labda [a vonal-on *közvetlenül* innen] esett le.
the ball the line-Sup immediately this_side fall.Past.3Sg down
'The ball fell down right on this side of the line.'

c. A művész aláírása [*közvetlenül* a vonal-on felül] látható.
the artist signature.Poss directly the line-Sup above visible
'The artist's signature can be seen directly above the line.'

c'. *A művész aláírása [a vonal-on *közvetlenül* felül] látható.
the artist signature.Poss the line-Sup directly above visible
Intended meaning: 'The artist's signature can be seen directly above the line.'

The word order possibilities are determined by the fact that case-like postpositions (just like case suffixes) cannot be separated from their complement at all (Chapter 2 Sections 2.2.2.2.6 and 2.2.2.2.3), while case-assigning postpositions are morphologically more independent and can be separated from their complement to some extent (Chapter 2 Sections 2.2.2.3.6 and 2.2.2.3.3).

It can be tested whether the modifier is really a modifier of the PP and not of a larger constituent, by trying to dislocate the full modified PP, i.e., to have the phrase including the modifier as a contrastive topic or as a preverbal focus (e.g. with the focus particle *csak* 'only'):

(109) [Pontosan az-on a sark-on], sosem volt virágbolt.
exactly that-Sup the corner-Sup never was florist
'There's never been a florist right on that corner.'

(110) a. Az utat [csak egyenes-en az erdő-n át] tudták megépíteni.
the road.Acc only straight.ly the forest-Sup through could.3Pl Perf.build.Inf
'The road could only be built straight through the forest.'

b. Az utat [csak az erdő-n egyenes-en át] tudták megépíteni.
the road.Acc only the forest-Sup straight.ly through could.3Pl Perf.build.Inf
'The road could only be built straight through the forest.'

Applying this test highlights that the modification of verbal particles is not a straightforward issue. So far, they have been conspicuously missing from our examples and that is because they are not modified on their own. Consider the sentence in (111a), which contains the particle *ki* 'out' preverbally and the modifier *egyenesen* 'straight'. Based on this sentence, we can come up with the grammatical PP-with-DP constructions shown in (112). These sentences show that the modifier and the particle form a constituent, and they suggest that either the particle and the case suffixed PP together or the particle on its own can be modified. However, we also have (111b), where the same particle appears but it cannot be used on its own with the PP-with-DP construction in (113). The reason for this is that in the latter example there is no other directional element. As Chapter 2 Section 2.3.1.3.4 has shown, particles in their telicizing use involve a path in their meaning, but this path on its own does not seem to be suitable for modification. If there is a more lexical directional element or the particle is used in its literal directional sense, modification becomes possible, since then the modifier can be semantically related to the full phrase.

(111) a. János egyenesen ki-vitte az üres üvegeket a kukába.
János straight.ly out-take.Past.DefObj.3Sg the empty bottle.Pl.Acc the trash.Ill
'John took the empty bottles straight out to the trashcan.'

b. Az igazgató egyenesen ki-mondta a véleményét.
the director straight.ly out-say.Past.DefObj.3Sg the opinion.Poss.3Sg.Acc
'The director stated his opinion straight out.'

(112) a. Egyenesen ki a kuká-ba az üres üvegek-kel!
straight.ly out the trash-Ill the empty bottle.Pl-Ins
'Straight to the trashcan with the empty bottles!'

b. Egyenesen ki az üvegek-kel!
straight.ly out the bottle.Pl-Ins
'Straight out with the bottles!'

(113) *Egyenesen ki az igazgató véleményé-vel!
straight.ly out the director opinion.Poss-Ins
Intended meaning: 'Straight out with the director's opinion!'

A similar conclusion can be drawn if we try to have the modifier and the particle as a contrastive topic together, as one constituent. The only modifier that seems to work to some extent is *egyenesen* 'straight', however, even that is limited to the straigthforwardly directional, semantically more transparent use of particles. In other instances, the same modifier can be a modifier of the VP in which the particle happens to be the first element in a neutral sentence with straight word order, e.g. (114c).

(114) a. Mari egyenesen haza-vitte a gyerekeket.
Mari straight.ly home_to-take.Past.DefObj.3Sg the kid.Pl.Acc
'Mari took the kids straight home.'

b. Egy galamb egyenesen be-repült az ablak-on.
a pigeon straight.ly into-fly.Past.3Sg the window-Sup
'A pigeon flew straight in through the window.'

c. Mari egyenesen fel-háborodott a feltételezések-en.
Mari straight.ly up-got_indignant the assumption.Pl-Sup
'Mary became downright indignant about the assumptions.'

(115) a. [Egyenesen haza], csak Mari vitte a gyerekeket.
straight.ly home_to only Mari take.Past.DefObj.3Sg the kid.Pl.Acc
'It was only Mari who took the kids straight home.'

b. ?[Egyenesen be], csak egy galamb repült az ablak-on.
straight.ly into only one pigeon fly.Past.3Sg the window-Sup
'Only one pigeon flew straight in through the window.'

c. *[Egyenesen fel], csak Mari háborodott a feltételezések-en.
straight.ly up only Mari got_indignant the assumption.Pl-Sup
Intended meaning: 'Only Mari became downright indignant about the assumptions.'

When such modifiers do not belong only to the PP, they often have a considerably different meaning, as is the case in (114c) and in the examples in (116). In these sentences, we are dealing with the modification of a larger syntactic unit and these will not be discussed in this chapter (see Chapter 7).

(116) a. Ili éppen el-érte a buszt.
Ili just away-reach.Past.DefObj.3Sg the bus.Acc
'Ili just managed to catch the bus.'

b. Pál pontosan fel-mérte a helyzetet.
Pál exactly up-measure.Past.DefObj.3Sg the situation.Acc
'Pál gauged the situation accurately.'

In the following sections we will look at the individual modifiers in more detail but will leave particles out of the discussion for the reasons illustrated here.

3.3.1.2. Pontosan *'precisely, exactly'*

The modifier *pontosan* 'precisely, exactly' can appear with Ps referring to points or well-defined regions. It can be used modifying locative and directional case suffixes, case-like and case-assigning postpositions, as well as adverbs, as illustrated in (117) and (118), respectively.

(117) a. pontosan a sarok-nál [locative case suffix]
exactly the corner-Ade
'right at the corner'

b. pontosan a ház felett [locative case-like P]
exactly the house above_at
'right above the house'

c. pontosan a ház-zal szemben [locative case-assigning P]
exactly the house-Ins opposite
'exactly opposite the house'

d. pontosan itt [locative adverb]
exactly here_at
'right here'

(118) a. pontosan a sarok-tól [directional case suffix]
exactly the corner-Abl
'right from the corner'

b. pontosan a ház fölé [directional case-like P]
exactly the house above_to
'right (to) above the house'

c. pontosan a ház-zal szembe [directional case-assigning P]
exactly the house-Ins to_opposite_to
'exactly (to) opposite the house'

d. pontosan ide [directional adverb]
exactly here_to
'right here'

However, this modifier cannot be used with all spatial Ps. The examples in (119) show that it cannot modify locative PPs that refer to a region which is not well-defined enough for the Figure to be precisely at that point or in that region.

(119) a. *pontosan a ház-hoz közel
exactly the house-All close_to
Intended meaning: 'right close to the house'

b. *pontosan a folyó-n túl
exactly the river-Sup beyond
Intended meaning: 'right beyond the river'

c. *pontosan benn (a konyhá-ban)
exactly inside the kitchen-Ine
Intended meaning: 'right in(side) the kitchen'

d. *pontosan fenn (a padlás-on)
exactly up the attic-Sup
Intended meaning: 'right up in the attic'

(120) provides examples where the modified PPs are constituents (in focus or contrastive topic), and they are ungrammatical.

(120) a. *A repülő [pontosan a folyó-n túl] szállt le.
the plane exactly the river.Sup beyond fly.Past.3Sg down
Intended meaning: 'The plane landed exactly beyond the river.'

b. *A busz [pontosan a ház-hoz közel] áll meg.
the bus exactly the house-All close_to stop.3Sg Perf
Intended meaning: 'The bus stops right close to the house.'

c. *[Pontosan benn (a konyhá-ban)], csak kevesen akartak maradni.
exactly inside the kitchen-Ine only few want.Past.3Pl stay.Inf
Intended meaning: 'Only few people wanted to stay right inside (in the kitchen).'

d. *[Pontosan fenn (a padlás-on)], egy üres dobozt se találtunk.
exactly up the attic-Sup one empty box.Acc not_even find.Past.1Pl
Intended meaning: 'We didn't even find one empty box right up (in the attic).'

Pontosan is also the most general modifier of temporal Ps, as well as of primarily spatial Ps in their temporal use. With strictly time-denoting Ps, it can modify points and periods in time, as shown in (121a,b). Similarly to the restriction on its use with spatial Ps, if it modifies a PP referring to a time period, the period has to be well-defined so that we can refer to exactly that period (121c,c').

(121) a. pontosan dél óta
exactly noon since
'exactly since noon'

b. pontosan [10 perc] / [1 óra] / [2 hét] / [5 év] múlva
exactly 10 minute / 1 hour / 2 week / 5 year after
'after exactly 10 minutes / 1 hour / 2 weeks / 5 years'

c. pontosan 2 hét alatt
exactly 2 week under
'exactly in 2 weeks'

c'. *pontosan hetek alatt
exactly week.Pl under

This modifier semantically clashes with the temporal postposition *tájban/tájt* 'around' since being at around some point in time and at exactly a certain point in time are incompatible. It is not completely ungrammatical, however, if one regards being at around a point in time as a "region", as then we can refer to exactly that region (i.e., period in time), with (122) then being acceptable but pragmatically marked (as it goes against the Gricean Maxim of Quantity).

(122) #pontosan 6 óra tájban / tájt
exactly 6 hour around / around
'exactly at around 6 o'clock'

The temporal suffix *-kor* is fully compatible with *pontosan*, (123). The modifier is also compatible with those spatial case suffixes that have a temporal meaning (124) if their complement refers to a unit in time that matches the requirement of being a point or a well-defined period or can be interpreted as such.

(123) pontosan fél 9-kor
exactly half 9-Tmp
'exactly at half past 8'

(124) a. pontosan április 1-én
exactly April 1st-Poss.Sup
'exactly on April 1'

b. pontosan dél-ben
exactly noon-Ine
'exactly at noon'

c. pontosan 12-re
exactly 12-Sub
'by exactly 12 o'clock'

d. pontosan 12-től
exactly 12-Abl
'from exactly 12 o'clock'

(125) a. pontosan húsvét előtt
exactly Easter before
'right before Easter'

b. pontosan két nap alatt
exactly two day under
'in exactly two days'

c. pontosan 6 hét után
exactly 6 week after
'exactly after 6 weeks'

Pontosan is sometimes used in a shorter, truncated form *pont*, literally meaning 'dot', and its use and meaning is generally the same as that of the regular long form (126).

(126) a. A busz pont a házunk előtt áll meg.
the bus right the house.Poss.1Pl in_front_of stop.3Sg Perf
'The bus stops right in front of our house.'

b. Mari pont 6 óra-kor ért haza.
Mari exactly 6 hour-Tmp reach.Past.3Sg home_to
'Mary got home exactly at 6.'

Remark 3. It is interesting to note that while the truncated form *pont* 'precisely, exactly' generally seems to alternate with the full adverb form *pontosan*, with the short version being a variant used typically in spoken language, sentences such as (i), have two meanings, and with the second meaning given below (i) only the truncated adverb form is possible.

(i) Miért pont az ablak elé ültettél fát?
why exactly the window before_to plant.Past.2Sg tree.Acc
'Why did you plant a tree right in front of the window?'
'Why did you plant a tree in front of the window and not somewhere else?'

In this use, the truncated form *pont* seems to function as a focus modifier and not a degree modifier of the PP.

3.3.1.3. Épp(en) *'right'*

The adverbial modifier *éppen* 'right, just' expresses the lack or minimality of distance – both spatial and temporal – between the Figure and the Ground. Its form is often truncated to *épp*, without any change in meaning or use. It can co-occur with locative and directional Ps alike (127)-(128).

(127) a. épp(en) az iskolá-nál [locative case suffix]
right the school-Ade
'right at the school'

b. épp(en) az iskola előtt [locative case-like P]
right the school in_front_of
'right in front of the school'

c. épp(en) az iskolá-val szemben [locative case-assigning P]
right the school-Ins opposite_to
'right opposite the school'

d. épp(en) ott [locative adverb]
right there_at
'right there'

(128) a. épp(en) az iskolá-hoz [directional case suffix]
right the school-All
'right to the school'

b. épp(en) az iskola elé [directional case-like P]
right the school before_to
'right (to) in front of the school'

c. épp(en) az iskolá-val szembe [directional case-assigning P]
right the school-Ins to_opposite_to
'right opposite the school'

d. épp(en) oda [directional adverb]
right there_to
'right there'

This modifier is compatible with some of the Ps with which *pontosan* 'exactly' does not co-occur (compare (129a)-(129b) with (120a)-(120b)). However, *éppen* 'right' (similarly to *pontosan* 'exactly') does not seem to work with the spatial adverbs that are not deictic (compare (129c)-(129d) with (120c)-(120d)).

(129) a. A repülő [éppen a folyó-n túl] szállt le.
the plane right the river.Sup beyond fly.Past.3Sg down
'The plane landed right beyond the river.'

b. A busz [éppen a ház-hoz közel] áll meg.
the bus right the house-All close_to stop.3Sg Perf
'The bus stops right close to the house.'

c. *[Éppen benn (a konyhá-ban)], csak kevesen akartak maradni.
right inside the kitchen-Ine only few want.Past.3Pl stay.Inf
Intended meaning: 'Only few people wanted to stay right inside (in the kitchen).'

d. *[Éppen fenn (a padlás-on)], egy üres dobozt se találtunk.
right up the attic-Sup one empty box.Acc not_even find.Past.1Pl
Intended meaning: 'We didn't even find one empty box right up (in the attic).'

There is also a set expression with *épp(en)*, shown in (130), which involves the deictic adverb *itt* 'here':

(130) Épp(en) (itt az) ideje (ennek).
right here the time.Poss (this.Dat)
'It's high time (for this).'

This modifier is also used with temporal PPs (131). The phrase expresses being right at a point or period of time. The complement of the P can be any time unit.

(131) a. épp(en) 6 óra-kor
right 6 hour-Tmp
'right at 6 o'clock'

b. épp(en) 10 perc múlva
right 10 minute after
'after exactly 10 minutes'

c. épp(en) éjfél óta
right midnight since
'since (exactly at) midnight'

d. épp(en) 10 óra tájban / tájt
right 10 hour around / around
'right around 10 o'clock'

Éppen also modifies spatial Ps in their temporal use, without any restrictions:

(132) a. épp(en) április 1-én
right April 1st-Poss.Sup
'right on April 1'

b. épp(en) dél-ben
right noon-Ine
'right at noon'

c. épp(en) 12-re
right 12-Sub
'right by 12 o'clock'

d. épp(en) 12-től
right 12-Abl
'right from 12 o'clock'

(133) a. épp(en) húsvét előtt
right Easter before
'right before Easter'

b. épp(en) két nap alatt
right two day under
'right in two days'

c. épp(en) 6 hét után
right 6 week after
'right after 6 weeks'

Pontosan 'exactly' and *éppen* 'right' are the two general PP-modifiers that are compatible with the most PPs with respect to both semantic compatibility and formal compatibility.

3.3.1.4. Közvetlenül *'directly'*, mindjárt *'right away'*, rögtön *'immediately'*

There are two types of modifiers expressing distance: they can formally be simple modifiers or measure phrases. We will turn to measure phrases in Section 3.3.1.9;

and discuss the simple modifiers *közvetlenül* 'directly, immediately', *mindjárt* 'soon, right away', and *rögtön* 'immediately, right' in this section. These modifiers are used to refer to the smallest distance, namely, when something is or ends up located in the closest vicinity of the Ground.

The modifier *közvetlenül* 'directly, immediately, right' is used to modify spatial PPs without restrictions. (134) shows its combinations with locative PPs, and (135) shows that it can also modify directional PPs.

(134) a. közvetlenül az ajtó-nál [locative case suffix]
directly the door-Ade
'directly at the door'

b. közvetlenül a ház mögött [locative case-like P]
directly the house behind_at
'directly behind the house'

c. közvetlenül a város-on kívül [locative case-assigning P]
directly the city-Sup outside_of
'directly outside of the city'

d. közvetlenül itt [locative adverb]
directly here_at
'directly here'

(135) a. közvetlenül az ajtó-hoz [directional case suffix]
directly the door-All
'directly to the door'

b. közvetlenül a ház mögé [directional case-like P]
directly the house to_behind
'directly(to) behind the house'

c. közvetlenül a belváros-on át [directional case-assigning P]
directly the downtown-Sup through
'directly through the downtown'

d. közvetlenül ide [directional adverb]
directly here_to
'directly here'

This modifier cannot co-occur with strictly temporal PPs at all, regardless of whether they refer to a point or period of time (136).

(136) a. *közvetlenül fél 9-kor
directly half 9-Tmp
Intended meaning: 'exactly at half past 8'

b. *közvetlenül 1 óra múlva
directly 1 hour after
Intended meaning: 'exactly after an hour'

c. *közvetlenül karácsony óta
directly Christmas since
Intended meaning: 'exactly since Christmas'

d. *közvetlenül 6 óra tájban / tájt
directly 6 hour around / around
Intended meaning: 'exactly around 6 o'clock'

It has a very limited use with some spatial Ps referring to time (137): only *után* 'after' and *előtt* 'before' can be modifed by *közvetlenül* 'directly' (137a)-(137b). These take complements that refer to points in time, but Ps that refer to a time period with a primarily locative or directional P in them are incompatible with *közvetlenül* 'directly' (137c)-(137e), similarly to the strictly temporal PPs in (136).

(137) a. közvetlenül karácsony után
directly Christmas after
'right after Christmas'

b. közvetlenül 5 óra előtt
directly 5 hour before
'right before 5 o'clock'

c. *közvetlenül karácsony körül
directly Christmas around
Intended meaning: 'right around Christmas'

d. *közvetlenül egy hét-en belül
directly one week-Sup inside
Intended meaning: 'right within a week'

e. *közvetlenül 5 órá-n át
directly 5 hour-Sup through
Intended meaning: 'exactly for 5 hours'

There are two other modifiers with a very similar meaning: *mindjárt* 'soon' and *rögtön* 'immediately'. In the sentence, they are temporal, aspectual adverbials (see Chapter 7). When they are modifiers within the PP, their original temporal meaning seems to be extended to refer to a very small distance in space. Similarly to the related *közvetlenül* 'directly', they can be used with locative PPs (138), however, their use is restricted with directional PPs, as (139a,b) vs. (139c,d) show. While (139c) may be ungrammatical because the meaning of *át* 'through' as a postposition does not involve an endpoint, the directional P in (139d) is an adverb with a goal meaning, so the lack of an endpoint in (139c) cannot fully explain the ungrammaticality.

(138) a. mindjárt / rögtön az ajtó-nál [locative case suffix]
soon / immediately the door-Ade
'immediately at the door'

b. mindjárt / rögtön a ház mögött [locative case-like P]
soon / immediately the house behind_at
'immediately behind the house'

c. mindjárt / rögtön a város-on kívül [locative case-assigning P]
soon / immediately the city-Sup outside
'immediately outside the city'

d. mindjárt / rögtön ott [locative adverb]
soon / immediately there_at
'immediately there'

(139) a. mindjárt / rögtön az ajtó-hoz [directional case suffix]
soon / immediately the door-All
'right to the door'

b. mindjárt / rögtön a ház mögé [directional case-like P]
soon / immediately the house behind_to
'right (to) behind to house'

c. *mindjárt / *rögtön a belváros-on át [directional case-assigning P]
soon / immediately the downtown-Sup through
Intended meaning: 'right through the downtown area'

d. ??mindjárt / ??rögtön oda [directional adverb]
soon / immediately there_to
Intended meaning: 'right there'

Perhaps due to the fact that *mindjárt* 'right' and *rögtön* 'immediately' are originally temporal adverbs, they are compatible with some of the strictly temporal PPs. The distribution is semantically restricted, since these modifiers are perfectly good with temporal PPs referring to points in time but are degraded or ungrammatical with temporal PPs that refer to time periods.

(140) a. mindjárt / rögtön fél 9-kor
soon / immediately half 9-Tmp
'right at half past 8'

b. mindjárt / rögtön 1 óra múlva
soon / immediately 1 hour after
'immediately after an hour'

c. ??mindjárt / ??rögtön karácsony óta
soon / immediately Christmas since
Intended meaning: 'right since Christmas'

d. *mindjárt / *rögtön az elmúlt 2 hét alatt
soon / immediately the past 2 week under
Intended meaning: 'right during the past 2 weeks'

e. mindjárt / rögtön 6 óra tájban / tájt
soon / immediately 6 hour around / around
'immediately around 6 o'clock'

These two modifiers are generally used when the event takes place slightly later than some other event. Therefore (141a) is grammatical, (141b) is used only when we actually mean some time after Christmas, (141c) is degraded. Perhaps related to the 'slightly later' meaning component, these modifiers are not used with PPs that refer to time periods (141d,e).

(141) a. mindjárt / rögtön karácsony után
soon / immediately Christmas after
'immediately after Christmas'

b. mindjárt / rögtön karácsony körül
soon / immediately Christmas around
'right around Christmas'

c. ??mindjárt / ??rögtön 5 óra előtt
soon / immediately 5 hour before
Intended meaning: 'immediately before 5 o'clock'

d. *?mindjárt / *?rögtön egy hét-en belül
soon / immediately one week-Sup inside
Intended meaning: 'right within a week'

e. *mindjárt / *rögtön 5 órá-n át
soon / immediately 5 hour-Sup through

Remark 4. There is a further modifier that refers to a point in time slightly later than another one, but it is even more restricted. The adverb *azonnal* 'immediately' can be used as a PP-modifier only with the postposition *után* 'after':

(i) a. azonnal 6 óra után
immediately 6 hour after
'immediately after 6 o'clock'

b. azonnal a születésnapja után
immediately the birthday.Poss.3Sg after
'immediately after his birthday'

The use of this adverb as a modifier in a PP is very literal, and so its distribution is rather limited, contrary to the slightly more general use of the other modifiers with a similar meaning.

3.3.1.5. Messze *'far'*

The adverb *messze* 'far' expresses distance and can be the modifier of spatial PP in general: both locative PPs (142) and directional PPs are compatible with it, except for the deictic directional adverb, which is ungrammatical with this modifier (143).

(142) a. messze az erdő-ben [locative case suffix]
far the forest-Ine
'far in the forest'

b. messze a ház mögött [locative case-like P]
far the house behind_at
'far behind the house'

c. messze a város-on túl [locative case-assigning P]
soon the city-Sup beyond
'far beyond the city'

d. messze kinn [locative adverb]
far outside
'far outside'

(143) a. messze az erdő-be [directional case suffix]
far the forest-Ill
'far into the forest'

b. messze a ház mögé [directional case-like P]
far the house behind_to
'(to) far behind to house'

c. messze az út-on végig [directional case-assigning P]
far the road-Sup along
'far along the road'

d. *messze oda [directional adverb]
far there_to
Intended meaning: '(to) far there'

It never co-occurs with any of the strictly temporal PPs (irrespective of their reference to points or periods in time) as illustrated in (144) with a few examples, but it is compatible with some spatial PPs in their temporal use (145). This may be due to its very transparent spatial meaning, which requires the PP to have a reference to points in space (metaphorically, time) from which the distance can be measured.

(144) a. *messze fél 9-kor
far half 9-Tmp

b. *messze 1 óra múlva
far 1 hour after

(145) a. messze karácsony után
far Christmas after
'far after Christmas'

b. messze 5 óra előtt
far 5 hour before
'far before 5 o'clock'

c. *messze karácsony körül
far Christmas around

d. *messze egy hét-en belül
far one week-Sup inside

e. *messze 5 órá-n át
far 5 hour-Sup through

3.3.1.6. Egyenesen *'straight'*

Limited in its use to spatial, directional PPs, we find *egyenesen* 'straight' as the modifier expressing orientation (146). This modifier cannot be used with locative PPs (147).

(146) a. egyenesen az erdő-be [directional case suffix]
straight.ly the forest-Ill
'straight into the forest'

b. egyenesen az ágy alá [directional case-like P]
straight.ly the bed under_to
'straight under the bed'

c. egyenesen az erdő-n át [directional case-assigning P]
straight.ly the forest-Sup through
'straight through the forest'

d. egyenesen oda [directional adverb]
straight.ly there_to
'straight there'

(147) a. *egyenesen az erdő-ben [locative case suffix]
straight.ly the forest-Ine
Intended meaning: 'straight in the forest'

b. *egyenesen az ágy alatt [locative case-like P]
straight.ly the bed under_at
Intended meaning: 'straight (at) under the bed'

c. *egyenesen az erdő-n belül [locative case-assigning P]
straight.ly the forest-Sup inside
Intended meaning: 'straight through the forest'

d. *egyenesen ott [locative adverb]
straight.ly there_at
Intended meaning: 'straight there'

Egyenesen is not used with PPs expressing temporal meanings, as it seems to literally relate to the path meaning component of directional spatial PPs. This is illustrated by the difference between (146a,c) and (148a,b), where the PPs modified by *egyenesen* 'straight' contain the same case-assigning P *át* 'through' with a spatial meaning and with a temporal meaning, respectively, and the latter is ungrammatical.

(148) a. *egyenesen 5 órá-ra
straight.ly 5 hour-Sub
Intended meaning: 'straight for 5 o'clock'

b. *egyenesen 3 héten át
straight.ly 3 week-Sup through
Intended meaning: 'straight through 3 weeks'

3.3.1.7. Magasan *'high' and* mélyen *'deep'*

There are a couple of modifiers that only combine with certain spatial postpositions. The modifier *magasan* 'high(ly)' only combines with Ps meaning 'above' (both locative and directional), as in (149), while *mélyen* 'deeply' only appears with Ps meaning 'under' (both locative and directional) (150).

(149) a. A repülő magas-an a hegyek fölött / fölé repült.
the plane high-ly the mountain.Pl above_at / above_to fly.Past.3Sg
'The plane flew high [above the mountains] / [(to) above the mountains].'

b. A repülő magas-an a hegyek fölül kezdett ereszkedni.
the plane high-ly the mountain.Pl above_from start.Past.3Sg descend.Inf
'The plane started descending from high above the mountains.'

(150) a. A vezeték mély-en a föld alatt / alá vezetett.
the pipe deep-ly the ground under_at / under_to run.Past.3Sg
'The pipe ran deep [under the ground] / [(to) under the ground].'

b. A vezeték mély-en a föld alól hozott fel tiszta vizet.
the pipe deep-ly the ground under_from bring.Past.3Sg up clean water.Acc
'The pipe brought up clean water from deep under the ground.'

3.3.1.8. Other degree modifiers

There are also a few modifiers that express approximation or close degree on a scale. Among these modifiers, we find *olyan*, literally meaning 'such, so', but here used in the sense of 'approximately, about. around' and *alig* 'barely', which are both restricted to some temporal PPs. We also have *úgy* 'so', *nagyjából* 'roughly, by and large', and *körülbelül* 'about', which are very similar both in their semantics and in their distribution with spatial and temporal PPs.

The modifier *olyan* 'such, so' is compatible with temporal PPs that refer to a point in time (151a)-(151c), but gets degraded to various degrees when it is used to refer to a time period (151d)-(151f).

(151) a. olyan 6 óra-kor
such 6 hour-Tmp
'approximately at 6 o'clock'

b. olyan 10 óra tájban /tájt
such 10 hour around / around
'approximately around 10 o'clock'

c. olyan 10 perc múlva
such 10 minute after
'after about 10 minutes'

d. ?olyan éjfél óta
such midnight since
'since about midnight'

e. ?olyan egy hét óta
such one week since
'for about a week'

f. *olyan az ünnepek alatt
such the holidays under
Intended meaning: 'approximately during the holidays'

Olyan 'such' is compatible with various spatial PPs used to refer to time, but the P's NP complement has an influence on whether the combination with *olyan* is acceptable or not (152).

(152) a. olyan 5 óra előtt / után / körül / felé / ?alatt [case-like P]
such 5 hour before / after / around / towards / under
'approximately before / after /around / around / under 5 o'clock'

b. olyan karácsony ??előtt / ??után / körül / felé / *alatt. [case-like P]
such Christmas before / after / around / towards / under
'approximately before / after /around / around / under Christmas'

c. olyan két hét-en belül / át [case-assigning P]
such two week-Sup inside / through
'for around two weeks'

d. olyan 5 órá-ra [case suffix]
such 5 hour-Sub
'for around 5 hours / by 5 o'clock'

A few spatial PPs are ungrammatical when modified by *olyan* 'such' in their temporal use (153).

(153) a. *olyan április 1-én
such April 1st-Poss.Sup
Intended meaning: 'approximately on April 1'

b. *olyan múlt hét-en
such last week-Sup
Intended meaning: 'approximately last week'

c. *olyan január-ban
such January-Ine
Intended meaning: 'approximately in January'

This modifier is not compatible with a spatial meaning at all; the examples in (154) serve to illustrate this.

(154) a. *olyan a sarok-nál / sarok-hoz / a sarok-tól [case suffix]
such the corner-Ade / corner-All / the corner-Abl
Intended meaning: 'approximately at / to / from the corner'

b. *olyan [a ház előtt] / [a ház elé] / [a ház elől] [case-like P]
such the house in_front_of / the house to_front / the house from_front
Intended meaning: 'approximately at/to/from in front of the house'

c. *olyan [a sark-on túl] / [az erdő-n át] [case-assigning P]
such the corner-Sup beyond / the forest-Sup through
Intended meaning: 'approximately [beyond the corner] / [through the forest]'

d. *olyan itt / ide [adverb]
such here_at / here_to
Intended meaning: 'approximately here / (to) here'

The distribution of *alig* 'barely' is even more restricted: it can only modify the temporal PPs with *múlva* 'after' and *óta* 'since', as (155) shows, and only *előtt* 'before' and *után* 'after' are compatible with it from among the spatial Ps that can be used temporally (156).

(155) a. alig 10 perc múlva
barely 10 minute after
'in barely 10 minutes'

b. alig egy hét óta
barely one week since
'barely for a week'

c. ?alig éjfél óta
barely midnight since
'barely since midnight'

d. *alig 6 óra-kor
barely 6 hour-Tmp
Intended meaning: 'barely at 6 o'clock'

e. *alig 10 óra tájban / tájt
barely 10 hour around / around

(156) a. alig 5 óra előtt
barely 5 hour before
'barely before 5 o'clock'

b. alig karácsony után
barely Christmas after
'barely after Christmas'

c. *alig április 1-én
barely April 1st-Poss.Sup
Intended meaning: 'almost on April 1'

d. *alig az ünnepek alatt
barely the holidays under
Intended meaning: 'almost during the holidays'

The sentences in (157) illustrate the indended temporal meanings with spatial Ps in context:

(157) a. Ma alig 8 óra előtt estem be a suli-ba.
today barely 8 hour before fall.Past.1Sg into the school-Ill
'Today I got to the school barely before 8 o'clock.'

b. Alig karácsony után már elkezdődtek a leárazások.
barely Christmas after already start.Past.3Pl the sale.Pl
'Sales already started barely after Christmas.'

Alig 'barely' is never used with spatial meanings, regardless of the locative or directional semantics of the P involved.

(158) a. *alig [a sarok-nál] / [a sarok-hoz] / [a sarok-tól] [case suffix]
barely the corner-Ade / the corner-All / the corner-Abl
Intended meaning: 'approximately at / to / from the corner'

b. *alig [a ház előtt] / [a ház elé] / [a ház elől] [case-like P]
barely the house in_front_of / the house to_front / the house from_front
Intended meaning: 'approximately in front of the house / to in front of the house / from in front of the house'

c. *alig [a sark-on túl] / [az erdő-n át] [case-assigning P]
barely the corner-Sup beyond / the forest-Sup through
Intended meaning: 'barely [beyond the corner] / [through the forest]'

d. *alig itt / ide [adverb]
barely here_at / here_to
Intended meaning: 'barely here / (to) here'

There are three more modifiers that express approximation with a roughly identical meaning and distribution: these are *úgy* 'so', *nagyjából* 'roughly, by and large', and *körülbelül* 'approximately' (which has the abbreviation *kb.* 'c(irca)'). They can be used as modifiers of temporal PPs (159).

(159) a. úgy / nagyjából / körülbelül 6 óra-kor
so / roughly / approximately 6 hour-Tmp
'approximately at 6 o'clock'

b. úgy / nagyjából / körülbelül 10 óra tájban / tájt
so / roughly / approximately 10 hour around / around
'approximately around 10 o'clock'

c. úgy / nagyjából / körülbelül 10 perc múlva
so / roughly / approximately 10 minute after
'after approximately 10 minutes'

d. úgy / nagyjából / körülbelül éjfél óta
so / roughly / approximately midnight since
'approximately since midnight'

e. úgy / nagyjából / körülbelül egy hét óta
so / roughly / approximately one week since
'for approximately a week'

Furthermore, they can be modifiers of spatial PPs in their temporal use (160):

(160) a. úgy / nagyjából / körülbelül 5 óra előtt
so / roughly / approximately 5 hour before
'about / roughly / approximately before 5 o'clock'

b. úgy / nagyjából / körülbelül karácsony után
so / roughly / approximately Christmas after
'about / roughly / approximately after Christmas'

c. úgy / nagyjából / körülbelül április 1-én
so / roughly / approximately April 1st-Poss.Sup
'about / roughly / approximately on April 1'

d. úgy / nagyjából / körülbelül az ünnepek alatt
so / roughly / approximately the holidays under
'about / roughly / approximately during the holidays'

They are also productively used with spatial PPs, both with locative meanings and with directional ones:

(161) • Locative PPs

a. úgy / nagyjából / körülbelül a sarok-nál [case suffix]
so / roughly / approximately the corner-Ade
'about / roughly / approximately at the corner'

b. úgy / nagyjából / körülbelül a ház előtt [case-like P]
so / roughly / approximately the house in_front_of
'about / roughly / approximately in front of the house'

c. úgy / nagyjából / körülbelül a ház-zal szemben [case-assigning P]
so / roughly / approximately the house-Ins opposite
'about / roughly / approximately opposite the house'

d. úgy / nagyjából / körülbelül ott [adverb]
so / roughly / approximately there_at
'about / roughly / approximately there'

(162) • Directional PPs

a. úgy / nagyjából / körülbelül a sarok-hoz [case suffix]
so / roughly / approximately the corner-All
'roughly / approximately to the corner'

b. úgy / nagyjából / körülbelül a ház elé [case-like P]
so / roughly / approximately the house to_front
'roughly / approximately (to) in front of the house '

c. úgy / nagyjából / körülbelül a ház-zal szembe [case-assigning P]
so / roughly / approximately the house-Ins opposite_to
'roughly / approximately (to) opposite the house'

d. úgy / nagyjából / körülbelül oda [adverb]
so / roughly / approximately there_to
'about / roughly / approximately there'

3.3.1.9. Measure phrases as modifiers

PPs can also be modified by measure phrases, which specify a certain numeric measure relating to the distance between the Figure and the Ground. There are two types of measure phrases in Hungarian PPs: one is an instrumental-marked measure, the other bears the sublative case and has a slightly more complex internal structure.

The measure phrase that bears instrumental case refers to the distance from a certain point in space. It cannot be used with spatial case suffixes: neither locative, nor directional case-suffixes are grammatical with it (163). However, both locative and directional case-like and case-assigning postpositions can take it as their modifier if they are semantically compatible (164).

(163) a. *két méter-rel az erdő-ben
two meter-Ins the forest-Ine
Intended meaning: 'two meters in the forest'

b. *két méter-rel az erdő-be
two meter-Ins the forest-Ill
Intended meaning: 'two meters into the forest'

c. *két méter-rel az erdő-ből
two meter-Ins the forest-Ela
Intended meaning: 'two meters out of the forest'

(164) a. két méter-rel [a ház mögött] / [a föld alatt]
two meter-Ins the house behind_at / the ground under_at
'two meters [behind the house] / [under the ground]'

b. két méter-rel [a ház mögé] / [a föld alá]
two meter-Ins the house behind_to / the ground under_to
'(to) two meters [behind the house] / [under the ground]'

c. két méter-rel [a ház mögül] / [a föld alól]
two meter-Ins the house behind_from / the ground under_from
'from two meters [behind the house] / [under the ground]'

d. két méter-rel [a vonal-on belül] / [a határ-on túl]
two meter-Ins the line-Sup inside / the border-Sup beyond
'two meters [inside the line] / [beyond the border]'

Some case-like and case-assigning Ps are incompatible with the instrumental-marked measure phrase due to their meaning. These are listed in (165).

(165) a. *két kilométer-rel a város körül
two kilometer-Ins the city around
Intended meaning: 'two kilometers around the city'

b. *két kilométer-rel a város felé
two kilometer-Ins the city towards
Intended meaning: 'two kilometers towards the city'

c. *két kilométer-rel a város felől
two kilometer-Ins the city from_direction_of
Intended meaning: 'at two kms distance from the direction of the city'

d. *két kilométer-rel a városok között
two kilometer-Ins the city.Pl between
Intended meaning: 'at two kms distance between the cities'

e. *két kilométer-rel a város köré
two kilometer-Ins the city to_around
Intended meaning: 'to two kilometers around the city'

f. *két kilométer-rel a város-hoz közel
two kilometer-Ins the city-All close_to
Intended meaning: 'as close as two kilometers (away) from the city'

g. *két méter-rel Anná-val szembe
two meter-Ins Anna-Ins to_opposite
Intended meaning: 'to two meters opposite Anna'

This modifier is syntactically rather free: it can appear both on the left edge and on the right edge of the PP it modifies, and it can be separated from the PP as well (166). This is only typical of measure phrases, distinguishing them further from simpler modifiers that we discussed in previous sections.

(166) a. Az almafát [10 méter-rel a ház mögött] ültettük el.
the apple.tree.Acc 10 meter-Ins the house behind_at plant.Past.DefObj.1Pl away
'We planted the apple tree 10 meters behind the house.'

b. Az almafát [a ház mögött 10 méter-rel] ültettük el.
the apple.tree.Acc the house behind_at 10 meter-Ins plant.Past.DefObj.1Pl away
'We planted the apple tree 10 meters behind the house.'

c. Az almafát [a ház mögött] ültettük el [10 méter-rel].
the apple.tree-Acc the house behind_at plant.Past.DefObj.1Pl away 10 meter-Ins
'We planted the apple tree 10 meters behind the house.'

The other measure phrase involves the sublative case on the modifier itself and the ablative case on the Ground:

(167) a. két méter-re a ház-tól
two meter-Sub the house-Abl
'two meters from the house'

b. 5 kilométer-re a határ-tól
5 kilometer-Sub the border-Abl
'5 kilometers from the border'

c. két órá-ra a város-tól
two hour-Sub the city-Abl
'two hours from the city'

Similarly to the other measure phrase, we find word order variants here, too. The ablative marked phrase can either precede or follow the sublative measure (168a) and (168b), and the measure can be separated as well, especially if it is focused as in (168c).

(168) a. [10 méter-re a ház-tól] parkoltuk le az autót.
10 meter-Sub the house-Abl park.Past.DefObj.1Pl down the car.Acc
'We parked the car 10 meters from the house.'

b. [A ház-tól 10 méter-re] parkoltuk le az autót.
the house-Abl 10 meter-Sub park.Past.DefObj.1Pl down the car.Acc
'We parked the car 10 meters from the house.'

c. [10 méter-re] parkoltuk le az autót [a ház-tól].
10 meter-Sub park.Past.DefObj.1Pl down the car.Acc the house-Abl
'We parked the car 10 meters from the house.'

The ablative can be left out of the sentence and the sentence is still grammatical, but the ablative without the measure phrase is ungrammatical

(169) a. 10 méter-re parkoltuk le az autót.
10 meter-Sub park.Past.DefObj.1Pl down the car.Acc
'We parked the car 10 meters away.'

b. *A ház-tól parkoltuk le az autót.
the house-Abl park.Past.DefObj.1Pl down the car.Acc
Intended meaning: 'We parked the car (some distance) away from the house.'

In sum, these measure phrases share the property of having the syntactic freedom to appear in various word orders, but they are different in that the instrumental marked measure is a modifier within its PP, while the sublative marked measure can be supplemented with an ablative base but it need not be.

3.3.2. Modification of non-spatial/non-temporal PPs

Non-spatiotemporal PPs can be modified with degree modifiers, which are generally adverbs and most often involve the *-n/-an/-en* suffix (170).

(170) a. A levest [teljes-en hideg-en] hozták ki.
the soup.Acc completely cold-ly bring.Past.DefObj.3Pl out
'The soup was served completely cold.'

b. A vihar [nagyon ijesztő-vé] vált.
the storm very frightening-Tra became.3Sg
'The storm became very frightening.'

c. A hírt mindenki [kivételes-en rossz-ul] fogadta.
the news.Acc everyone exceptional-ly bad-ly receive.Past.DefObj.3Sg
'Everyone received the news exceptionally badly.'

There are also modifiers that are adjectival and this is not just a result of optionally dropping an adverbial suffix. While the expressions in (171) and (172) with an adjectival modifier do not differ in meaning from the similar phrases that contain the adverbial form of the modifier, it is not the case with (173), where the adverbial modifier is not an option, only the adjectival one is grammatical. These modifiers are discussed as degree quantifiers in N2.6.2.3.1 and N2.6.2.6).

(171) a. nagy boldogan
big happily
'very happily'

b. nagyon boldogan
very happily
'very happily'

(172) a. szép komótosan
nice unhurriedly
'fairly unhurriedly'

b. szép-en komótosan
nice-ly unhurriedly
'fairly unhurriedly'

(173) a. jó nehezen
good difficult.ly
'with great difficulty'

b. *jól nehezen
well difficult.ly
Intended meaning: 'with great difficulty'

These adverbial modifiers are also discussed in Chapter 2 Section 2.2.4.2.

We must also mention here the modifier *totál* 'completely, absolutely', used in colloquial spoken language as an equivalent of *teljesen* 'completely'. The syntactic category of *totál* is not obvious at first sight as it does not bear any of the adverb suffixes discussed in Chapter 2 Section 2.2.4.1, nor does it bear the attributivizer suffix *-i*, contrary to other, similar modifiers, such as *állati* 'extremely, lit. animal-Attr'. However, its distribution is the same as that of *teljesen* 'completely' except for its restriction to the colloquial register.

(174) a. totál mérgesen
total angrily
'absolutely angrily'

b. teljes-en mérgesen
complete-ly angrily
'completely angrily'

Other adverbs which do not bear a (productive or unproductive) suffix are discussed in Chapter 2 Section 2.2.4.3.

3.3.3. Comparative/superlative formation

Those locative adverb Ps that are formed with the locative *-nn* and *-nt* suffixes have a comparative form, as discussed already in Chapter 2 Section 2.2.4.1.2 point *III*. Some particles that are very transparently directional also have comparative forms. These comparative forms can be used together with degree modifiers, the same way comparative adjectives can. The measure phrase used as the modifier is marked with instrumental case, it is the same as was discussed in Section 3.3.1.9. In (175) we provide examples of such comparative adverbs with measure phrases.

(175) a. két méter-rel ki-jjebb / kint-ebb / %kinn-ebb
two meter-Ins out-Comp / outside-Comp / outside-Comp
'at / to two meters more outside'

b. két méter-rel bent-ebb / bel-jebb / %benn-ebb
two meter-Ins inside-Comp / in-Comp / inside-Comp
'at / to two meters more inside'

c. sok-kal lent-ebb / le-jjebb / %lenn-ebb
much-Ins down-Comp / down-Comp / down-Comp
'(at / to a) much lower (place)'

d. sok-kal fent-ebb / fel-jebb / %fenn-ebb
much-Ins up-Comp / up-Comp / up-Comp
'(at / to a) much higher (place)'

e. 10 méter-rel visszá-bb
10 meter-Ins back-Comp
'10 meters back'

f. 10 méter-rel hátrá-bb / hátr-ébb
10 meter-Ins back-Comp / back-Comp
'10 meters back' (locative or directional)

With non-spatial adverbs, the comparative marker attaches to the adjectival stem to which the adverb suffix is added, the order is fixed (176), and it is the comparative suffix that makes it possible to include a measure phrase with various non-spatial adverbs (177).

(176) a. gyors-abb-an
quick-Comp-ly
'quicker'

b. szerencsétlen-ebb-ül
unlucky-Comp-ly
'more unluckily'

(177) a. sok-kal ritká-bb-an
much-Ins rare-Comp-ly
'much more rarely'

b. *sok-kal ritká-n
much-Ins rare-ly

3.4. Bibliographical notes

When it comes to the complementation of postpositions, generally Noun Phrases and pronominal complements are described in the literature. Nominal complements and their word order possibilities with respect to the P head are discussed by Marácz (1989), É. Kiss (2002, Chapter 8), Asbury (2008), and the variation in PP-internal word order is studied in more detail by Dékány and Hegedűs (2015). The fact that PPs can also be complements of P heads is described by Hegedűs (2006, 2013), Dékány (2011); while Dékány and Hegedűs (2015) discuss potentially intransitive uses of (case-assigning) postpositions.

Ürögdi (2006) described and analyzed predicate fronting involving the dative case suffix, while predicate clefts in more general (involving verbal particles) are discussed in Vicente (2007). Clausal complements of Ps, or rather the lack thereof and the properties of the proleptic pronoun with clausal complements in general, are described and analyzed in Kenesei (1992, 1994), Lipták (2008, 2012), Den Dikken (2018).

As far as modifiers are concerned, the fact that case-like postpositions and case-assigning postpositions are different in their word order properties is well-known from Marácz (1986, 1989), É. Kiss (2002, Chapter 8), and Dékány (2011), among others.

Chapter 4
Predicative PPs

Katalin É. Kiss

4.1. Introduction

Predicative PPs typically function as secondary predicates, predicated of the internal argument of the verbal predicate: the object of transitive verbs and the subject of unaccusative verbs. Their use as primary predicates is limited; it is mostly restricted to PPs expressing place and time. PPs used as primary predicates – unlike nominal primary predicates – require the presence of the copula, the equivalent of the verb 'be'.

(1) a. A gyerekek *otthon* vannak.
the children at_home are
'The children are at home.'

b. A konferencia *május-ban* lesz.
the conference May-Ine be.Fut.3Sg
'The conference will be in May.'

If we analyze the *be*-verb in (1a,b) as a verb of existence, then this type of PPs, too, can be assimilated to the class of PPs functioning as secondary predicates, predicating a condition (place, time, state, etc.) of the theme argument of the verb.

The prototypical secondary predicate PP, providing information about the internal argument of the verb and forming a complex predicate with it, is the verbal particle. The verbal particle is selected by the verb and constitutes a lexical unit with it. It may change the argument structure of the base verb. For example, *jár* 'walk' is intransitive; *be-jár* 'in-walk', however, is transitive when it means 'tour something'. Or *olvas* 'read' takes an accusative complement; but *rá-olvas* 'on-read', when meaning 'cast a spell', subcategorizes for a sublative-marked noun phrase.

The verb modifier can not only be represented by a verbal particle (2a), (3a), (4a), but it can also be an NP (2b), AP (2c) or DP (3b) supplied with an oblique case morpheme. It might also be a DP (4b) or an NP (4c) supplied with a postposition. Secondary predicates forming a complex predicate with the verb are called verb modifiers. They have a designated position in Hungarian sentence structure: in neutral clauses (i.e., in clauses containing no focus, interrogative, negative, or imperative operator triggering verb movement), they immediately precede the verb. The 'verb modifier–verb' string is interpreted as a semantic unit and constitutes a single phonological word.

(2) a. János *össze*-tépte a levelet.
János up-tore the letter.Acc
'János tore the letter up.'

b. János *darabok-ra* tépte a levelet.
János pieces-Sub tore the letter.Acc
'János tore the letter into pieces.'

c. Mari *simá-ra* vasalta a lepedőt.
Mari smooth-Sub ironed the sheet.Acc
'Mari ironed the sheet smooth.'

(3) a. János *be*-vitte a számítógépét.
János in-took the computer.Poss.3Sg.Acc
'János took in his computer.'

b. János *az irodá-ba* vitte a számítógépét.
János the office-Ill took the computer.Poss.3Sg.Acc
'János took his computer to the office.'

(4) a. A csatár *fölé* rúgta a labdát.
the forward above kicked the ball.Acc
'The forward kicked the ball above [the goal].'

b. A csatár *a kapu fölé* rúgta a labdát.
the forward the goal above kicked the ball.Acc
'The forward shot the ball above the goal.'

c. A fóka *víz alá* merült.
the seal water under dived
'The seal dived under water.'

Most verb modifiers, e.g., those in (2)-(4), have a resultative or terminative function, and they are a concomitant of telic achievement and accomplishment predicates. There are also locative verb modifiers, which occur with atelic predicates expressing existence or spatial configuration:

(5) a. János *bent* tartja a számítógépét.
János in keeps the computer.Poss.3Sg.Acc
'János keeps his computer in there.'

b. János *az irodá-ban* tartja a számítógépét.
János the office-Ine keeps the computer.Poss.3Sg.Acc
'János keeps his computer in the office.'

Some verbs take a stative verb modifier, represented by an adjective or a nominal marked by an essive-formal or dative case ending:

(6) a. *Helytartó-ként* viselkedik.
procurator-FoE behave.3Sg
'He behaves like a procurator.'

b. Jánost *okos-nak* tartják.
János.Acc smart-Dat consider.DefObj.3Pl
'János is considered to be smart.'

Despite their semantic and prosodic, and often also lexical, unity, the verb modifier and the verb are syntactically independent constituents. Although a resultative or terminative verbal particle and the verb immediately following it are (misleadingly) spelled as one word according to Hungarian spelling conventions (7a), they often split. Operators, among them the negative particle (7b) and the exhaustive focus (7c), attract the verb into a position preceding the verbal particle. The particle and the verb can also be separated by intervening constituents both in the case of the 'verb...particle' order (7d) and in the case of the 'particle ...verb' order (7e). As illustrated by (7f), a verbal particle originating in the finite (or non-finite) complement clause of the modal verbs *kell* 'must' and *szabad* 'may' can land in the position preceding the matrix modal, crossing the finite complementizer on the way. (For perspicuity's sake, the verbal particle and the verb immediately following will be separated by a hyphen from now on. The verbal particle *meg*, which is void of any lexical content, is glossed as 'Perf', signaling its telicizing-perfectivizing role.)

(7) a. János *meg-érkezett.*
János Perf-arrived
'János arrived.'

b. János nem *érkezett meg.*
János not arrived Perf
'János did not arrive.'

c. Hét-ig KÉT VENDÉG *érkezett meg.*
seven-Ter two guest arrived Perf
'It was two guests who arrived by seven.'

d. János nem *érkezett* idő-ben *meg* tegnap.
János not arrived time-Ine Perf yesterday
'János did not arrive in time yesterday.'

e. János hamarosan *meg* is *érkezett.*
János soon Perf Prt arrive.Past.3Sg
'János, as expected, soon arrived.'

f. János hamarosan *meg* kell, hogy *érkezzen.*
János soon Perf must that arrive.Subj.3Sg
'János must soon arrive.'

Depictives are secondary predicates that can cooccur with a verb modifier. They need not immediately precede the verb and do not form a complex predicate with it. They are predicated of the object or the subject:

(8) Péter *beteg-en* meg-látogatta Marit.
Péter sick-Adv Perf-visited Mari.Acc
'Péter visited Mari sick.'

This chapter is organized as follows: Section 4.2 introduces PPs used as primary predicates. Section 4.3 discusses telicizing, i.e., resultative and terminative, verb modifiers. Section 4.4 deals with atelic verb modifiers, among them locative verb modifiers, and stative verb modifiers represented by an NP or AP bearing essive or dative case. Section 4.5 describes the syntax of verb modifiers. Section 4.6 provides an analysis of depictive adjectives, i.e., APs bearing oblique case. Section 4.7 is a summary.

4.2. PPs used as primary predicates

PPs expressing place and time, and rarely also PPs of other types, e.g. those expressing a beneficiary, cause, purpose or state, can serve as primary predicates. A

PP functioning as a primary predicate – unlike a 3rd person nominal predicate in present indicative – requires the presence of the copula:

(9) a. A kulcs *a lábtörlő alatt* volt.
the key the doormat under was
'The key was under the doormat.'

b. A hangverseny *öt-kor* lesz.
the concert five-Tmp be.Fut.3Sg
'The concert will be at five.'

c. Az ajándék *nek-ed* van.
the present Dat-2Sg is
'The present is for you.'

d. A késedelem *Péter miatt* volt.
the delay Péter because_of was
'The delay was because of Péter.'

e. Mind-ez *ért-etek* volt.
all-this Cau-2Pl was
'All this was for you/in your interests.'

f. A gyerekek *jól* vannak.
the children well are
'The children are well.'

The predicative PPs in (9a-f) do not form a homogeneous class syntactically. Locative and stative adverbs behave like verb modifiers; under predicate negation, they stand behind the negated verb (which is fused into a single negative existential verb in 3rd person present indicative) – see (10a,b). The PPs expressing time, beneficiary, cause and purpose behave like preverbal foci; they immediately follow the negative particle, preceding the verb (10c-f).

(10) a. A kulcs nem volt *a lábtörlő alatt.*
the key not was the doormat under
'The key wasn't under the doormat.'

b. A gyerekek nincsenek *jól.*
the children aren't well
'The children aren't well.'

c. A hangverseny nem *öt-kor* lesz.
the concert not five-Tmp be.Fut.3Sg
'The concert won't be at five.'

d. Az ajándék nem *nek-ed* van.
the present not Dat-2Sg is
'The present isn't for you.'

e. A késedelem nem *Péter miatt* volt.
the delay not Péter because_of was
'The delay wasn't because of Péter.'

f. Mind-ez nem *ért-etek* volt.
all-this not Cau-2Pl was
'All this wasn't for your sake.'

The copula accompanying a PP predicate can occasionally be ellipted. Corpus investigations show that it tends to be omitted in presentative sentences containing the locatives *hol* 'where' (11a), *itt* 'here'(11b) and *ott* 'there' (11c).

(11) a. *Hol* a kulcs?
where the key
'Where is the key?'

b. *Itt* a tavasz.
here the spring
'Spring is here.'

c. *Ott* a busz.
there the bus
'The bus is there.'

Ellipsis rarely occurs with PP predicates having lexical content as well. Such sentences, unlike those involving *itt, ott*, or *hol*, are somewhat marked; they give the impression of telegraphic style – as is indicated by the fact that although the subject of such sentences is a topic, it typically lacks a determiner:

(12) a. Kulcs *a lábtörlő alatt.* Ebéd *a hűtő-ben.*
key the doormat under lunch the fridge-Ine
'The key is under the doormat. The lunch is in the fridge.'

b. Nyitás *tíz-kor.* Zárás *hat-kor.*
opening ten-Tmp closing six-Tmp
'Opening is at ten. Closing is at six.'

4.3. Telicizing PPs

4.3.1. The telicizing function

As shown by Vendler (1967), predicates form four classes on the basis of their aspectual properties: states, processes, accomplishments and achievements. (For a finer classification, see Kiefer (2006).) States and processes are atelic, i.e. they do not have an inherent endpoint. They differ in that states are static whereas processes are dynamic, denoting a change of state or change of location of their internal argument. Accomplishments and achievements are telic, i.e. they have an inherent endpoint; they denote not only a change of state or change of location of their internal argument, but also the new state it achieves as a result of the change. (Psychological accomplishments are different in certain respects, as will be discussed below.) Where accomplishments and achievements differ is that accomplishments are incremental, whereas achievements occur instantaneously. Hungarian is a language which systematically distinguishes telic predicates from atelic ones. Telicity is marked iconically in that complex telic events are expressed by complex predicates consisting of a verb denoting the change, and a resultative or terminative verb modifier, i.e. a PP denoting the resultant state of the internal argument (É. Kiss 2005; 2006a,b).

Accomplishment verbs expressing a telic change of state are derived from process verbs (13a), (14a) by the addition of a resultative or terminative PP. The verb corresponds to the process component and the PP corresponds to the resultant state component of the complex event. (Telic predicates in the present tense, like that in (13b), refer to the future in the default case.)

(13) a. Anya főzi az ebédet.
Mother cooks the lunch.Acc
'Mother is cooking the lunch.'

b. Anya *meg*-főzi az ebédet.
Mother Perf-cooks the lunch.Acc
'Mother will cook the lunch.'

(14) a. Az ebéd főtt.
the lunch cooked
'The lunch was cooking.'

b. Az ebéd *meg*-főtt.
the lunch Perf-cooked
'The lunch (has) cooked.'

In the case of achievement predicates, the change of the internal argument is simultaneous with the attainment of the resultant state, hence the correspondence between the verb and the process phase, and between the resultative PP and the resultant state is less transparent, e.g.:

(15) a. János *meg*-találta a gyűrűt.
János Perf-found the ring.Acc
'János found the ring.'

b. János *fel*-ébredt.
János up-woke
'János woke up.'

4.3.2. Resultative verb modifiers

4.3.2.1. Types of resultative verb modifiers

The resultative PP is a verbal particle in the default case (16b), but it can also be a case-marked NP (16c), AP (16d) or DP (16e). The verbal particle, which has minimal descriptive content, expresses that the internal argument has reached the state resulting from the activity denoted by the verb; it has been totally affected. A case-marked resultative NP, AP or PP, however, also specifies the nature of the resultant state.

(16) a. János vágta a fát.
János cut the wood.Acc
'János was cutting the wood.'

b. János *fel*-vágta a fát.
János up-cut the wood.Acc
'János cut the wood up.'

c. János *25 centis darabok-ra* vágta a fát.
János 25 cm.Adj pieces-Sub cut the wood.Acc
'János cut the wood into 25 cm pieces.'

d. János *vékony-ra* vágta a fát.
János thin-Sub cut the wood
'János cut the wood thin.'

e. János *a szükséges méret-re* vágta a fát.
János the necessary size-Sub cut the wood.Acc
'János cut the wood to the necessary size.'

The verbal particle can also modify the lexical meaning of the base verb, as is shown by (17).

(17) Éva *közbe-vágott.*
Éva into-cut
'Éva interrupted.'

The verbal particle and the verb often form a lexical unit, the meaning of which can be partly or fully non-compositional (18d,e,f).

(18) a. Mari *fel-vágta* a petrezselymet.
Mari up-cut the parsley.Acc
'Mari cut the parsley up.'

b. Péter *rá-vágott* az asztal-ra az öklé-vel.
Péter upon-cut the table-Sub the fist.Poss.3Sg-Ins
'Péter struck at the table with his fist.'

c. Éva *vissza-vágott.*
Éva back-cut
'Éva riposted.'

d. A kritikus *le-vágta* a darabot.
the critic down-cut the play.Acc
'The critic ran down the play.'

e. A csaló mindenkit *át-vágott.*
the swindler everybody.Acc through-cut
'The swindler deceived everybody.'

f. Éva *fel-vág.*
Éva up-cuts
'Éva puts on airs.'

The most common, and also the oldest, resultative verbal particle is *meg*. This has grammaticalized from *mög-é/meg-é* 'back-Lative', originally a case-marked nominal; but except for a few cases such as *meg-tér* 'return', *meg-ad* 'give back', it has lost its descriptive content; it only means that the action denoted by the verb has reached its natural endpoint:

(19) a. János ette az almát.
János ate the apple.Acc
'János was eating the apple.'

b. János *meg*-ette az almát.
János Perf-ate the apple.Acc
'János ate/has eaten the apple (up).'

The set of most frequent verbal particles also include *el* 'off' (20), *ki* 'out' (21), *be* 'in' (22), *le* 'down' (23), and *fel* 'up' (24).

(20) a. János olvassa a könyvet.
János reads the book.Acc
'János is reading the book.'

b. János *el*-olvassa a könyvet.
János off-reads the book
'János will read the book.'

(21) a. Éva mosta a szennyest.
Éva washed the laundry.Acc
'Éva was washing the laundry.'

b. Éva *ki*-mosta a szennyest.
Éva out-washed the laundry
'Éva (has) washed the laundry.'

(22) a. A tulajdonos éppen zárja a boltot.
the owner just closes the shop.Acc
'The owner is just closing the shop.'

b. A tulajdonos mindjárt *be*-zárja a boltot.
the owner soon in-closes the shop.Acc
'The owner will soon close the shop.'

(23) a. János nyírja a füvet.
János mows the grass.Acc
'János is mowing the grass.'

b. János *le*-nyírja a füvet.
János down-mows the grass.Acc
'János will mow the grass.'

(24) a. Az építész mérte a házat.
the architect measured the house
'The architect was measuring the house.'

b. Az építész *fel*-mérte a házat.
the architect up-measured the house.Acc
'The architect (has) measured the house.'

Resultative NPs, APs and DPs are supplied with a lative (sublative (25), illative (25b), allative (25c), or translative (25d)) case morpheme.

(25) a. A hús *puhá-ra* főtt.
the meat tender-Sub cooked
'The meat cooked tender.'

b. *Kettő-be* hajtottam a papírt.
two-Ill folded.1Sg the paper.Acc
'I folded the paper into two.'

c. A beteg *magá-hoz* tért.
the patient himself-All returned
'The patient came round.'

d. A boszorkány *béká-vá* változtatta a királyfit.
the witch frog-TrE changed the prince.Acc
'The witch changed the prince into a frog.'

4.3.2.2. The subject of resultative secondary predication

Since a resultative PP is predicated of the internal argument, it can only occur with verbs taking an internal argument – either as their subject (25a,c) or as their object or adverbially case-marked complement (25b,d). Optionally transitive verbs take a verbal particle only in their transitive use (26)-(27).

(26) a. János olvasott.
János read
'János was reading.'

b. *János *el*-olvasott.
János off-read
'János read.'

c. János *el*-olvasott egy krimit.
János off-read a crime_story.Acc
'János read a crime story.'

(27) a. János nyert.
János won

b. *János *meg*-nyert.
János Perf-won

c. János *meg*-nyerte a meccset.
János Perf-won the match.Acc
'János won the match.'

Unergative verbs, whose only argument is an external argument, take no resultative secondary predicate:

(28) Éva telefonál / dolgozik / kiabál / sír.
Éva telephones / works / shouts / cries
'Éva is telephoning / working / shouting / crying.'

In fact, unergative verbs can also be telicized with a resultative element – if they are provided with a non-thematic object (usually a reflexive pronoun or a body part coindexed with the subject):

(29) a. Péter *beteg-re* dolgozta *magát.*
Péter sick-Sub worked himself.Acc
'Péter worked himself sick.'

b. Péter *rekedt-re* kiabálta *magát.*
Péter hoarse-Sub shouted himself.Acc
'Péter shouted himself hoarse.'

c. Péter *ki*-sírta *a szemét.*
Péter out-cried the eye.Poss3Sg.Acc
'Péter cried his eyes out.'

Unergative verbs may also allow a temporal or locative pseudo-object, e.g.:

(30) a. Éva *át*-aludta *a délután-t.*
Éva through-slept the afternoon-Acc
'Éva slept through the afternoon.'

b. Péter *le*-futotta *a maraton-t.*
Péter down-ran the marathon-Acc
'Péter ran the marathon.'

Complex predicates do not tolerate a nonspecific, bare singular or bare plural internal argument. It is presumably the predication relation between the internal argument and the verb modifier that requires that the internal argument be specific, i.e. it be associated with an existential presupposition. In the presence of a non-specific internal argument, no predicative PP is licensed (31a)–(32a); the nonspecific internal argument itself appears in the preverbal position (31b)–(32b).

(31) a. *Mari *ki*-mosott *ágyneműt.*
Mari out-washed bed.linen.Acc

b. Mari *ágyneműt* mosott.
Mari bed.linen.Acc washed
'Mari was washing bed-linen.'

(32) a. *Mari *el*-olvasott *verseket.*
Mari off-read poems.Acc

b. Mari *verseket* olvasott.
Mari poems.Acc read
'Mari was reading poems.'

The internal argument of a complex predicate must be either a definite or a specific indefinite noun phrase. (Specific indefinites refer to a subset of a previously introduced set, whereas nonspecific indefinites introduce a new referent into the domain of discourse.). Overt indefinite determiners, among them *egy* 'a/an', *két* 'two', *három* 'three', etc., *néhány* 'some', *kevés* 'few, little', *sok* 'many, much', can have either a specific or a nonspecific interpretation. In the presence of a resultative

PP, however, the indefinite internal argument of a resultative construction can only be assigned a specific reading – as happens in the second sentence of (33a), where *egy lányt* 'a girl.Acc' is understood as one of the two students mentioned in the first sentence. If the resultative element is dropped, the subset reading of the internal argument is not enforced, and the text becomes incoherent (33b).

(33) a. Az állás-ra két diák jelentkezett. Tegnap *meg-hallgattunk* egy lányt.
the job-Sub two student applied yesterday Perf-listen.Past.1Pl a girl.Acc
'Two students applied for the job. Yesterday we interviewed a girl.'

b. #Az állás-ra két diák jelentkezett. Tegnap *hallgattunk* egy lányt.
the job-Sub two student applied yesterday listen.Past.1Pl a girl.Acc
'Two students applied for the job. Yesterday we were listening to a girl.'

A special type of telic predicates, those denoting coming into being or creation, select a nonspecific internal argument, and consequently they take no verb modifier. They are discussed in detail in Chapter 6.

4.3.2.3. Resultative psychological verbs

Psychological verbs denoting the psychological or cognitive state of a nominative-marked experiencer, such as *szeret* 'like, love', *utál* 'hate', *gyűlöl* 'hate', *irigyel* 'envy', *sajnál* 'be sorry', *lát* 'see', *hall* 'hear', can form a complex predicate with the verbal particle *meg*, yielding *meg-szeret* 'come to like', *meg-utál* 'come to hate', *meg-gyűlöl* 'come to hate', *meg-irigyel* 'become envious of', *meg-sajnál* 'come to feel sorry', *meg-lát* 'come to see', *meg-hall* 'come to hear'.

(34) a. János mindig szerette a nyelvészetet.
János always liked the linguistics.Acc
'János always liked linguitics.'

b. A kurzus végére János meg-szerette a nyelvészetet.
the course end.Poss.Sub János Perf-liked the linguistics.Acc
'By the end of the course, János came to like linguistics.'

In these cases, the base verb denotes the end state of the experiencer, and the verbal particle evokes the preceding durative preparatory phase (Eszes 2006).

4.3.3. Terminative verb modifiers

4.3.3.1. Types of terminative verb modifiers

Accomplishment and achievement predicates expressing a delimited change of location consist of a verb of motion, and a terminative verb modifier. The verb denotes the type of movement carried out by the moving individual, represented by the internal argument, and the verb modifier denotes its end location, where its movement is terminated. The preverbal verb modifier can be a verbal particle (35a), or a lexical noun phrase supplied with an oblique case ending (35b) or a verbal particle doubling a postverbal lexical noun phrase supplied with an oblique case ending (35c). Some analyses of the construction in (35c) (e.g. Surányi 2009a,c) treat the noun phrase bearing oblique case and the verbal particle doubling it as a unit, sharing the secondary predicate function. In more traditional approaches, the postverbal noun phrase is the goal argument of the verbal particle + verb complex.

(35) a. A csatár *be*-gurította a labdát.
the forward into-rolled the ball.Acc
'The forward rolled the ball in.'

b. A csatár *a kapu-ba* gurította a labdát.
the forward the goal-Ill rolled the ball.Acc
'The forward rolled the ball into the goal.'

c. A csatár *be*-gurította a labdát *a kapu-ba.*
the forward into-rolled the ball.Acc the goal-Ill
'The forward rolled the ball into the goal.'

The terminative verb modifier can also be a postpositional phrase (36a), or, rarely, also a bare postposition with an implicit complement (36b). Terminative postpositional phrases can display splitting, instead of doubling, in which case the postposition stands alone in the position of the verb modifier, while its complement appears postverbally, bearing dative case (which is a relic of the phase when the postposition was the case-marked head noun of a possessive construction, and the complement DP was its possessor) (36c).

(36) a. A csatár *a kapu fölé* rúgta a labdát.
the forward the goal above kicked the ball.Acc
'The forward kicked the ball above the goal.'

b. A csatár *fölé* rúgta a labdát.
the forward above kicked the ball.Acc
'The forward kicked the ball above.'

c. A csatár *fölé* rúgta a labdát *a kapu-nak.*
the forward above kicked the ball.Acc the goal-Dat
'The forward kicked the ball above the goal.'

When the complement of P is a personal pronoun, P bears an agreement morpheme, and the pronoun itself is usually dropped:

(37)

(én) fölé-m I above-1Sg 'above me'	(mi) fölé-nk we above-1Pl 'above us'
(te) fölé-d you above-2Sg 'above you$_{sg}$'	(ti) fölé-tek you above-2Pl 'above you$_{pl}$'
(ő) fölé (s)he above.3Sg 'above him/her'	(ő) fölé-jük they above-3Pl 'above them'

Remark 1. In fact, the 3rd person plural personal pronoun is *ők*, with *-k* representing the plural morpheme. The lack of *-k* is interpreted by native speakers as a phonological accident; an *ő* eliciting 3rd person plural agreement is interpreted as 'they'.

If the postposition has a pronominal complement, pattern (36c), the separation of the postposition and the pronominal is impossible:

(38) a. A csatár *(én) fölé-m* rúgta a labdát.
the forward I above-1Sg kicked the ball
'The forward kicked the ball over me.'

b. *A csatár *fölé / fölé-m* rúgta a labdát *(én-)nek-em.*
the forward above / above-1Sg kicked the ball I-Dat-1Sg

Postpositions which have become oblique case endings with front- and back-vowel allomorphs (e.g., *ház-hoz* 'house-to'; *kert-hez* 'garden-to') also behave like invariant independent postpositions when their complement is a (mostly dropped) personal pronoun:

(39)

(én) hozzá-m I All-1Sg 'to me'	(mi) hozzá-nk we All-1Pl 'to us'
(te) hozzá-d you All-2Sg 'to you$_{sg}$'	(ti) hozzá-tok you All-2Pl 'to you$_{pl}$'
(ő) hozzá (s)he All.3Sg 'to him/her'	(ő) hozzá-juk they All-3Pl 'to them'

For example:

(40) A csatár *(én) hozzá-m* gurította a labdát.
the forward I All-1Sg rolled the ball.Acc
'The forward rolled the ball to me.'

Motion can also be interpreted in the temporal dimension. The delimited motion of time is also expressed by a delimiting verb modifier represented by a verbal particle (41a), or a full PP (41b), or by a particle doubling a full PP (41c).

(41) a. Az előadás *el*-húzódott.
the performance away-dragged
'The performance dragged on.'

b. Az előadás *öt-ig* húzódott.
the performance five-Ter dragged
'The performance dragged until five.'

c. Az előadás *el*-húzódott *öt-ig.*
the performance away-dragged five-Ter
'The performance dragged on until five.'

The omission of the terminative verb modifier from an accomplishment predicate yields a process interpretation.

(42) a. A labda gurult.
the ball rolled
'The ball was rolling.'

b. János futott.
János ran
'János was running.'

We also obtain a process interpretation if the verbal particle is present but is not preposed into preverbal position. In such cases, the particle does not form a complex predicate with the verb; it is understood as an element denoting direction. For example:

(43) Amikor le-fújták a meccset, a labda (épp) gurult *be a kapu-ba.*
when off-called.3Pl the match.Acc the ball (just) rolled into the goal-Ill
'When the match was called off, the ball was (just) rolling into the goal.'

In the case of achievements denoting a change of location, the momentary motion and the attainment of the end location are practically simultaneous, hence cutting off the end location is usually not possible (44a), but the progressive interpretation can, nevertheless, be evoked by leaving the particle in postverbal position (44b):

(44) a. *Éva tette a könyvet.
Éva put the book.Acc

b. Éva éppen tette *fel* a könyvet *a polc-ra*, amikor meg-fájult a dereka.
Éva just put up the book.Acc the shelf-Sub when Perf-ached the back.Poss.3Sg
'Éva was just putting the book up on the shelf when her back started to ache.'

4.3.3.2. The subject of terminative predication

A terminative verb modifier is, in most cases, a secondary predicate predicated of the internal argument, whether it is an object, as in (35a-c) and (36a-c) above, or a subject, as in (45a-c) below.

(45) a. A labda *be*-gurult.
the ball in-rolled
'The ball rolled in.'

b. A labda *a kapu-ba* gurult.
the ball the goal-Ill rolled
'The ball rolled into the goal.'

c. A labda *be*-gurult *a kapu-ba.*
the ball in-rolled the goal-Ill

In the case of internally controlled motion events, the causer and the executor of motion is one and the same individual. When verbs of internally controlled motion express a manner of motion, as in (46a), they behave as unergatives, i.e., their only argument is analyzed as an external argument. In lack of an internal argument, these verbs do not combine with a terminative or resultative verb modifier, unless they also take a non-thematic internal argument (46b).

(46) a. Mari futott.
Mari ran
'Mari was running.'

b. Mari *ki*-futotta *magá-t.*
Mari out-ran herself-Acc
'Mari ran [until she had enough].'

Some motion verbs take a 'route' or 'path' pseudo-object together with a verb modifier:

(47) a. Péter *le*-futotta *a maratoni táv-ot.*
Péter down-ran the marathon.Attr distance-Acc
'Péter ran the marathon.'

b. Péter *be*-járta *a város-t.*
Péter in-walked the city-Acc
'Péter walked [all over] the city.'

When internally controlled motion verbs express directed motion, they behave as unaccusatives, i.e.,their subject is analyzed as an internal argument, which can license a verb modifier:

(48) a. János *el*-futott.
János off-ran
'János ran off.'

b. János *a bolt-ba* futott.
János the store-Ill ran
'János ran to the store.'

c. János *el*-futott *a bolt-ba.*
János off-ran the store-Ill
'János ran off to the store.'

(49) a. János *fel*-ért.
János up-arrived
'János arrived.'

b. János *a csúcs-ra* ért.
János the peak-Sub arrived
'János arrived at the peak.'

c. János *fel*-ért *a csúcs-ra.*
János up-arrived the peak-Sub
'János arrived up at the peak.'

Semelfactives, i.e., verbs expressing a momentary motion or emission, can also take a verb modifier (a verbal particle in most cases):

(50) a. *Fel*-villant a fény.
up-flashed the light
'The light flashed.'

b. *Fel*-harsant egy kürtjel.
up-blared a horn_signal
'A horn signal blared.'

c. *Meg*-mozdult a bokor.
Perf-stirred the bush
'The bush stirred.'

d. A gyerek *fel*-kiáltott.
the child up-cried
'The child cried out.'

Similarly to resultatives, terminative verb modifiers can only be predicated of a definite or a specific indefinite internal argument. If the internal argument of a verb of motion or emission is nonspecific, no terminative verb modifier is licensed and the nonspecific internal argument itself appears in the verb modifier position:

(51) a. *A csatár *be*-gurított labdát a kapu-ba
the forward in-rolled ball.Acc the goal-Ill

b. A csatár *labdát* gurított a kapuba.
the forward ball.Acc rolled the goal-Ill
'The forward rolled a ball into the goal.'

(52) a. **Fel*-villant fény.
up-flashed light

b. *Fény* villant.
light flashed
'A light flashed.'

4.3.3.3. Directional verb modifiers

In some cases, the internal argument representing the moving object whose path the verbal particle terminates remains implicit, e.g.:

(53) a. A vadász *rá*-lőtt a nyúl-ra.
the hunter on-shot the rabbit-Sub
'The hunter shot at the rabbit.'

b. A dühös autós *rá*-szólt a gyalogos-ra.
the angry driver on-spoke the pedestrian-Sub
'The angry driver called to the pedestrian.'

c. Az anya *rá*-nézett a gyerek-re.
the mother on-looked the child-Sub
'The mother looked at the child.'

In (53a), the implicit moving object is obviously a bullet. In the case of (53b) and (53c), no internal argument has been ellipted; the moving objects (words in the case of (53b), and looks in the case of (53c)), can only be reconstructed on the conceptual level. In such cases, the verbal particle is not a secondary predicate predicated of the implicit argument. Even if we reconstruct an internal argument, the verbal particle does not predicate its end location. If the hunter shoots at the rabbit, the bullet does not necessarily hit it; the verbal particle merely indicates the direction of movement. A directional particle does not necessarily telicize the base verb, e.g.:

(54) A bokor ágai egész nyáron *ki*-hajlanak *az utcá-ra.*
the bush branch.Poss.Pl whole summer.Sup out-lean the street-Sub
'The branches of the bush lean onto the street the whole summer.'

4.4. Atelic verb modifiers

4.4.1. Locative verb modifiers

In Hungarian, verbs of existence and spatial configuration can form complex predicates with locative verb modifiers. The relation of the verb of existence or spatial configuration and the locative element is similar to the relation of the verb of movement and the terminative verb modifier in accomplishment predicates. Compare the complex predicates expressing terminated movement in (55) and (57) with their counterparts expressing existence in a given location in (56) and (58).

(55) a. János *ki*-tette a képet.
János out-put the picture.Acc
'János put out the picture.'

b. János *a kirakat-ba* tette a képet.
János the shop_window-Ill put the picture.Acc
'János put the picture into the shop window.'

c. János *ki*-tette a képet *a kirakat-ba.*
János out-put the picture.Acc the shop_window-Ill
'János put the picture into the shop window.'

(56) a. A kép *kint* van.
the picture outside is
'The picture is out there.'

b. A kép *a kirakat-ban* van.
the picture the shop_window-Ine is
'The picture is in the shop window.'

c. A kép *kint* van *a kirakat-ban.*
the picture outside is the shop_window-Ine
'The picture is in the shop window.'

The verb *fekszik* 'lie' in (57) and (58) is lexically ambiguous, it can mean both movement and spatial position; however, it is disambiguated by the verb modifier. When combined with the directional-terminative *oda* 'to there' or with a PP headed by the directional *elé* 'to before', it means directed movement and when combined with the locative *ott* 'there' or with a PP headed by the locative *előtt* 'in front of', it means position:

(57) a. A kutya *oda*-feküdt.
the dog to_there-lay
'The dog lay there.'

b. A kutya *a küszöb elé* feküdt.
the dog the threshold to_before lay
'The dog lay down before the threshold.'

c. A kutya *oda*-feküdt *a küszöb elé.*
the dog to_there-lay the threshold to_before
'The dog lay down before the threshold.'

(58) a. A kutya *ott* fekszik.
the dog there lies
'The dog is lying there.'

b. A kutya *a küszöb előtt* fekszik.
the dog the threshold before lies
'The dog is lying before the threshold.'

c. A kutya *ott* fekszik *a küszöb előtt.*
the dog there lies the threshold before
'The dog is lying before the threshold.'

In (56) and (58), the verb expresses the existence and the spatial configuration of the internal argument, whereas the locative verb modifier predicates its location. The verb forming a complex predicate with a locative verb modifier can also be transitive:

(59) a. János *bent* tartja a számítógépét.
János in keeps the computer.Poss.3Sg.Acc
'János keeps his computer in there.'

b. János *az irodá-ban* tartja a számítógépét.
János the office-Ine keeps the computer.Poss.3Sg.Acc
'János keeps his computer in the office.'

c. János *bent* tartja a számítógépét *az irodá-ban.*
János in keeps the computer.Poss.3Sg.Acc the office-Ine
'János keeps his computer in the office.'

(60) a. János *ott* hagyta a kalapját.
János there left the hat.Poss.3Sg.Acc
'János left his hat there.'

b. János *a fogas-on* hagyta a kalapját.
János the rack-Sup left the hat.Poss.3Sg.Acc
'János left his hat on the rack.'

c. János *ott* hagyta a kalapját *a fogas-on.*
János there left the hat.Poss.3Sg.Acc the rack-Sup
'János left his hat on the rack.'

In non-prototypical cases, the locative PP can also combine with an activity verb as in (61a-c). These sentences express existence in a particular way in a given location; they would be appropriate answers to the question *Where is János?*.

(61) a. János *lent* dolgozik.
János down works
'János is working down there.

b. János *a kert-ben* dolgozik.
János the garden-Ine works
'János is working in the garden.'

c. János *lent* dolgozik *a kert-ben.*
János down works the garden-Ine
'János is working down in the garden.'

As shown by the above examples, the locative PP functioning as a secondary predicate can be a sole verbal particle, a preverbal case-marked noun phrase, a postpositional phrase, or a verbal particle doubling a case-marked noun phrase or postpositional phrase. Whereas the terminative case endings are represented by a productive illative, sublative, allative or translative case suffix, and the terminative particles and postpositions involve an obsolete (*-a/e*) lative morpheme, the locative case endings are represented by a productive inessive, superessive or adessive case suffix, and the locative particles and postpositions involve an obsolete (*-t/tt*) locative morpheme.

The locative element of the complex predicate predicates the location of a definite or specific indefinite noun phrase functioning as the subject in intransitive sentences and the object in transitives. In the presence of a bare singular or bare plural internal argument, which has no specific interpretation, no locative verb modifier is licensed; the nonspecific internal argument appears in the position of the verb modifier:

(62) a. %*Kint* van *kép* a kirakat-ban.
outside is picture the shop_window-Ine

b. *Kép* van a kirakat-ban.
picture is the shop_window-Ine
'There is a picture in the shop window.'

Remark 2. (62a) is only acceptable if *kint* is not a verb modifier but a focus, with the rest of the sentence destressed.

(63) a. *János *ott* hagyott fontos iratot a páncélszekrény-ben.
János there left important paper.Acc the safe-Ine

b. János *fontos iratot* hagyott a páncélszekrény-ben.
János important paper.Acc left the safe-Ine
'János left some important paper in the safe.'

4.4.2. Stative verb modifiers

A set of verbs select a dative- (64) or essive-formal marked (65) noun phrase or adjective phrase which functions as a secondary predicate, attributing a state to the internal argument of the verb. The essive-formal marked noun phrase can also be replaced by a PP headed by *gyanánt* 'as' (66a), or by a manner adverb (66b,c). The internal argument functioning as the subject of the dative- or essive-formal marked predicate is the grammatical subject in (64a) and (66b), the accusative object in (64b-e), (65b) and (66a), and an oblique (instrumental) object in (66c). Essive-formal marked verb modifiers can also be predicated of an agent subject (66a). The secondary predicate occupies the verb modifier position and forms a complex predicate with the verb.

(64) a. Éva *boldog-nak* látszik.
Éva happy-Dat seems
'Éva seems happy.'

b. Évát *orvos-nak* hitték / vélték.
Éva.Acc doctor-Dat believe.Past.3Pl / assume.Past.3Pl
'Éva was believed/assumed to be a doctor.'

c. Péter *az intézet igazgatójá-nak* gondolta Évát.
Péter the institute director.Poss-Dat thought Éva.Acc
'Péter thought Éva to be the director of the institute.'

d. Évát *lelkiismeretes-nek* tartják / tekintik.
Éva.Acc conscientious-Dat hold.3Pl / consider.3Pl
'Éva is held/considered to be conscientious.'

e. Péter *szép-nek* látta Évát.
Péter beautiful-Dat saw Éva.Acc
'Péter sees Éva beautiful.'

(65) a. Péter *felelős vezető-ként* cselekedett.
Péter responsible leader-FoE acted
'Péter acted as a responsible leader.'

b. Évát *gyerek-ként* kezelik.
Éva.Acc child-FoE treat.3Pl
'Éva is treated as a child.'

(66) a. Éva *váza-ként / váza gyanánt* használta az üveget.
Éva vase-FoE / vase for used the bottle.Acc
'Éva used the bottle as/for a vase.'

b. Éva *gyerek-ként / rosszul* viselkedett.
Éva child-FoE / naughtily behaved
'Éva behaved [as a child]/ naughtily.'

c. Évá-val *gyerek-ként / jól* bánnak.
Éva-Ins child-FoE / well treat.3Pl
'Éva is treated [as a child] / well.'

The different nominal/adjectival/adverbial secondary predicate + verb complexes in (64)-(66) show different degrees of lexical, semantic and prosodic unity. Nevertheless, their predicative PPs share the syntactic behavior of resultative, terminative and locative verb modifiers. An immediately preverbal constituent could, in principle, not only be a verb modifier but also a focus. Under negation, however, a focus precedes the verb, whereas the verb modifier follows it. The predicative PPs in (64)-(66) can follow the negated verb, which indicates that they are verb modifiers. (Like all verb modifiers, they can also be focused – as will be discussed in Chapter 4 Section 4.5.2).

(67) a. Éva *nem* látszik *boldog-nak.*
Éva not seems happy-Dat
'Éva does not seem to be happy.'

b. Évát *nem* hitték / vélték *orvos-nak.*
Éva.Acc not believe.Past.3Pl / assume.Past.3Pl doctor-Dat
'Éva was not believed/assumed to be a doctor.'

c. Péter nem gondolta Évát az intézet igazgatójá-nak.
Péter not thought Éva.Acc the institute director.Poss-Dat
'Péter did not think Éva to be the director of the institute.'

d. Évát *nem* tartják / tekintik *lelkiismeretes-nek.*
Éva.Acc not hold.3Pl / consider.3Pl conscientious-Dat
'Éva is not held/considered to be conscientious.'

e. Péter *nem* látta *szép-nek* Évát.
Péter not saw beautiful-Dat Éva.Acc
'Péter didn't see Éva beautiful.'

(68) a. Péter *nem* cselekedett *felelős vezető-ként.*
Péter not acted responsible leader-FoE
'Péter did not act as a responsible leader.'

b. Évát *nem* kezelik *gyerek-ként.*
Éva.Acc not treat.3Pl child-FoE
'Éva is not treated as a child.'

(69) a. Éva *nem* használta *váza-ként* / *váza gyanánt* az üveget.
Éva not used vase-FoE / vase for the bottle.Acc
'Éva did not use the bottle as / for a vase.'

b. Éva *nem* viselkedett *gyerek-ként* / *rosszul.*
Éva not behaved child-FoE / naughtily
'Éva did not behave [as a child] / naughtily.'

c. Évá-val *nem* bánnak *gyerek-ként* / *jól.*
Éva-Ins not treat.3Pl child-FoE / well
'Éva is not treated [as a child] / well.'

Remark 3. *Mint* 'as' is an alternative of the postposition *gyanánt* with ill-understood syntactic properties. It appears to be a preposition, however, a *mint*-phrase, unlike a PP headed by *gyanánt*, is negated as a focus; it immediately follows the negative particle, i.e. it is not a verb modifier. Compare with (66a) and (69a):

(i) Éva *mint vázát* használta az üveget.
Éva like vase.Acc used the bottle.ACC
'Éva used the bottle as a vase.'

(ii) Éva *nem mint vázát* használta az üveget.
'Éva didn't use the bottle as a vase.'

Interestingly, the *mint*-phrase agrees in case with the argument that it is predicated of:

(iii) Évá-val mint a jövendő igazgató-val beszéltek.
Éva-Ins like the future director-Ins speak.Past.3Pl
'They spoke with Éva as the future director.'

A *mint*-phrase can also be predicated of an agent.

Stative verb modifiers, too, can only be predicated of a definite or specific indefinite noun phrase:

(70) a. ??Éva *lelkiismeretes-nek* tart egyetemi hallgatókat.
Éva conscientious-Dat holds university students.Acc
'Éva holds [some] university students to be conscientious.'

b. Éva *lelkiismeretes-nek* tartja az egyetemi hallgatókat.
Éva conscientious-Dat holds the university students.Acc
'Éva holds university students [in general] to be conscientious.'

(71) a. *Gyerekek *jól* viselkedtek.
children well behaved
'[Some] children behaved well.'

b. A gyerekek *jól* viselkedtek.
the children well behaved
'The children [in general] behaved well.

4.5. The syntax of verb modifiers

4.5.1. Neutral sentences

4.5.1.1. Default verb modifier – verb order

In neutral sentences, i.e., in sentences containing no focus, no negation, and no imperative or optative operator, the secondary predicate forming a complex predicate with the verb occupies the immediately preverbal verb modifier position. In topicless, thetic sentences, the verb modifier position is usually the clause-initial slot (72a), whereas in topic–comment constructions, it is usually the initial slot of the comment (72b):

(72) a. *Meg*-érkezett néhány vendég.
Perf-arrived some guest
'Some guests arrived.'

b. [TOPIC A vendégek] [COMMENT *meg*-érkeztek].
the guests Perf-arrived
'The guests arrived.'

Both in thetic sentences and in the comment of topic–comment structures, the verb modifier + verb complex can be preceded by quantifier expressions and by adverbial adjuncts, e.g.:

(73) a. Minden szállodá-ba idejé-ben *meg*-érkeztek a vendégek.
every hotel-Ill time-Ine Perf-arrived the guests
'The guests arrived at every hotel in time.'

b. [TOPIC A vendégek] [COMMENT minden szállodá-ba idejé-ben *meg*-érkeztek].
the guests every hotel-Ill time-Ine Perf-arrived
'The guests arrived at every hotel in time.'

The preverbal verb modifier position of the secondary predicate is a condition of complex predicate formation in semantics. A resultative or terminative verbal particle and a process verb yield a telic accomplishment or achievement interpretation if the verb follows the verb modifier as in (74a,b). The viewpoint aspect of such clauses is perfective, i.e., if the sentence is in the past, it is understood as an event completed before the speech time (or before a past reference time), and if the verb is in the present tense, it is understood as an event to be completed in the future:

(74) a. Péter *fel*-ment a lépcső-n.
Péter up-went the stair-Sup
'Péter went upstairs.'

b. Péter *fel*-megy a lépcső-n.
Péter up-goes the stair-Sup
'Péter will go upstairs.'

4.5.1.2. Verb – verb modifier order

The resultative or terminative PP can also follow the verb; in that case, however, the postverbal PP, whether a verbal particle or a full PP, does not predicate the resultant state of the internal argument; it is a directional element, assigned a stress of its own. No complex predicate formation takes place and the sentence is understood as a process in progress:

(75) Péter (éppen) ment *fel* a lépcső-n, amikor észrevettem.
Péter just went up the stair-Sup when notice.Past.DefObj.1Sg
'Péter was (just) going upstairs when I noticed him.'

(76)–(77) describe accomplishments in progress, without the result state of the internal argument attained. A verbal particle which merely telicizes the base verb, i.e., which merely adds an endpoint to it without completing or modifying its meaning in any other respect, is usually omitted in such cases:

(76) Péter éppen ette (??*meg*) az ebédjét, amikor csengettek.
Péter just ate Perf the lunch.Poss.3Sg.Acc when ring.Past.3Pl
'Péter was just eating (up) his lunch when the bell was rung.'

The directional adjunct status of postverbal particles in progressive sentences can be emphasized by the suffix *-fele* '-wards' (the construction has a dialectal flavor):

(77) Péter éppen ment *el(fele)* hazul-ról, amikor észrevettem.
Péter just went away(wards) home-Del when notice.Past.DefObj.1Sg
'Péter was just leaving home when I noticed him.'

4.5.1.3. Interrupted verb modifier – verb order

In sentences displaying the default 'verb modifier – verb' order, the verb modifier and the verb can be separated by an intervening emphatic particle (*is*):

(78) János meg-ígérte, hogy öt-kor meg-érkezik, és *meg is érkezett.*
János Perf-promised that five-Tmp Perf-arrive.3Sg and Perf Emph arrived
'János promised to arrive at five, and arrive he did (at five).'

The verb modifier and the verb can also be separated in neutral infinitival constructions involving a temporal or modal finite verb and in neutral *-va/ve* participle constructions involving a finite copula, where the verb modifier of the non-finite verb lands in front of the finite verb:

(79) a. János *fel* fog *ébredni.*
János up will wake.Inf
'János will wake up.'

b. Éva *ropogós-ra* akarja *sütni* a kalácsot.
Éva crispy-Sub wants bake.Inf the cake.Acc
'Éva wants to bake the cake crispy.'

c. A kalács *meg* van *sül-ve.*
the cake Perf is bake-Part
'The cake has been baked.'

This type of verb modifier raising is elicited by the stress-avoiding nature of the verbs involved. An auxiliary or the copula cannot bear phrasal stress, which is assigned to the left edge of projections in Hungarian. The verb modifier selected by the non-finite lexical verb is raised into pre-auxiliary position to pick up the phrasal stress assigned to the verbal projection of the matrix clause. If the non-finite verb has no verb modifier, the non-finite verb itself moves into the pre-auxiliary position:

(80) a. Éva *főzni* fog / akar.
Éva cook.Inf will / wants
'Éva will/wants to cook.'

b. A pad *fest-ve* van.
the bench paint-Part is
'The bench is painted.'

In non-neutral sentences, where the phrasal stress of the extended verbal projection is borne by a focus or a negative particle, this phonological constraint is not evoked and no verbal participle raising or verb raising takes place:

(81) a. János ÖT-KOR fog *fel-ébredni.*
János five-Tmp will up-wake.Inf
'János will wake up at five.'

b. Éva nem akarja *ropogós-ra sütni* a kalácsot.
Éva not wants crispy-Sub bake.Inf the cake.Acc
'Éva doesn't want to bake the cake crispy.'

The impersonal modals *kell* 'need' and *szabad* 'may' can attract the verbal particle of their complement clause also across a finite complementizer (82a,b).

(82) a. Éva idejében *fel* kell, hogy *ébredjen.*
Éva time.Ine up needs that wake.Subj.3Sg
'It is necessary that Éva wake up in time.'

b. *Be* szabad, hogy *menjünk* a kórterem-be?
in may that go.Subj.1Pl the ward-Ill
'Is it allowed that we enter the ward?'

The raising of a verbal particle across a complementizer is fully grammatical only if the matrix predicate, the complementizer, and the embedded verb are adjacent. (This construction is analyzed as a borrowing of the Balkan subjunctive by É. Kiss 2009c.) Compare with (82a,b):

(83) a. *Éva idejében *fel* kell, hogy minden nap *ébredjen.*
Éva time.Ine up needs that every day wake.Subj.3Sg
'It is necessary that Éva wake up in time every day.'

b. **Be* szabad szerint-ed, hogy *menjünk* a kórterem-be?
in may according_to-2Sg that go.Subj.1Pl the ward-Ill
'Is it allowed according to you that we enter the ward?'

The raising of a verb modifier represented by a case-marked noun phrase or a full PP (i.e., a verb modifier with some descriptive content) across a finite complementizer is allowed by a wider range of matrix predicates. The expressions landing in front of the matrix verb, especially if they are referential as in (84c) and (84e), can also be interpreted as contrastive foci. Verb modifier extraction is easier from subjunctive clauses (84a-c) than from indicative complements (84d-e).

(84) a. Éva *ropogós-ra* akarja, hogy süssem a kalácsot.
Éva crispy-Sub wants that bake.Subj.1Sg the cake.Acc
'Éva wants me to bake the cake crispy.'

b. Péter *mozi-ba* szeretné, hogy menjünk.
Péter movies-Ill want.Cond.3Sg that go.Subj.1Pl
'Péter wants us to go to the movies.'

c. *Az otthoni címem-re* kérem, hogy küldjétek a levelet.
the home address.Poss.1Sg-Sub ask.1Sg that send.Subj.2Pl the letter.Acc
'I ask for the letter to be sent to my home address.'

d. ?Péter *mozi-ba* mondta, hogy megy.
Péter cinema-Ill said that goes
'Péter said that he goes to the cinema.'

e. ?János *az otthoni címem-re* ígérte, hogy küldi a levelet.
János the home address.Poss.1Sg-Sub promised that sends the letter.Acc
'Péter promised to send the letter to my home address.'

A secondary predicate with referential content can undergo regular topicalization:

(85) *Az irodá-ba* PIZZAFUTÁR vitte az ebédet.
the office-Ill pizza.deliverer took the lunch.Acc
'To the office, the lunch was taken by a pizza deliverer.'

A verbal particle preposed into topic position can only be pronounced and interpreted as a contrastive topic:

(86) *Fel* JÁNOS vitte a biciklit, *le* PÉTER.
up János carried the bicycle.Acc down Péter
'Upstairs, the bicycle was carried by János, downstairs, by Péter.'

4.5.2. Non-neutral sentences

4.5.2.1. Sentences with focus and/or negation

In sentences containing a focus or a negative particle, the verb modifier – verb order is reversed. (Interrogative *wh*-phrases, like that in (87a), occupy the focus position in Hungarian.)

(87) a. KI *festette be* a kerítést?
who painted in the fence.Acc
'Who painted up the fence?'

b. János A KERÍTÉST *festette be.*
János the fence.Acc painted in
'It was the fence that János painted up.'

c. János nem *festette be* a kerítést.
János not painted in the fence.Acc
'János didn't paint up the fence.'

d. János *be-festette* a kerítést.
János in-painted the fence.Acc
'János painted up the fence.'

Movement into the focus position in the left periphery of the comment (87a,b) as well as negation (87c) elicit verb preposing across the verb modifier. Evidence for verb movement is provided by the fact that the adverbial adjuncts preceding the extended verbal projection in neutral sentences (88a) surface postverbally in the case of focusing and/or negation (88b,c):

(88) a. János ″nagyon össze-veszett Mari-val.
János very_much out-fell Mari-Ins
'János fell out with Mari greatly.'

b. JÁNOS *veszett* nagyon *össze* Mari-val.
'It was János who fell out with Mari very much.'

c. János nem *veszett* nagyon *össze* Mari-val.
János not fell very_much out Mari -Ins
'János didn't fall out with Mari very much.'

d. %Nagyon JÁNOS *veszett össze* Mari-val.
very_much János fell out Mari-Ins

e. %János nagyon ″nem *veszett össze* Mari-val.
János very_much not fell out Mari-Ins

(88d,e) are ungrammatical with regular prosody. However, they can be acceptable if *nagyon* is pronounced as a contrastive topic, with a fall rise intonation. (88e) can also be saved by interpreting *nagyon* as an intensifier of the negative particle.

The focus and the negative particle can be present simultaneously. The negative particle can either precede or follow the focus, or can be present in both positions simultaneously. In each of these cases, the verb occupies the same position, preceding the extended verbal projection and following the focus and the negative particle(s). This indicates that Hungarian verb movement is unlike Germanic verb second; the verb only moves to the left edge of the neutral field; it does not enter the operator section.

(89) a. János ″nem A KERÍTÉST *festette be*.
János not the fence.Acc painted in
'It wasn't the fence that János painted up.'

b. János A ″KERÍTÉST nem *festette be*.
'It was the fence that János didn't paint up.'

c. János nem a ″KERÍTÉST nem *festette be*.
'It wasn't the fence that János didn't paint up.'

In the marked negative constructions below, the negative particle intervenes between the verbal particle and the verb:

(90) a. János *be* nem *festené* a kerítést!
János in not paint.Cond.3Sg the fence.Acc
'János wouldn't paint up the fence.'

b. *Meg* nem *mondom*, mi történt.
Perf not tell.1Sg what happened
'I can't tell what happened.'

c. Várok, amíg *meg* nem *érkezik* mindenki.
wait.1Sg until Perf not arrives everybody
'I will wait until everybody arrives.'

d. egy [be nem fejezett] / [nem be-fejezett] dolgozat
an in not completed / not in-completed paper
'a paper not completed'

e. Jó volna [nem meg-buk-ni] /[nem buk-ni meg] / [meg nem buk-ni]
good be.Cond.3Sg not Perf-fail-Inf / not fail-Inf Perf / Perf not fail-Inf
'It would be good not to fail.'

In finite clauses, the optional 'verbal particle - negative particle - verb' order has assumed a special modal value; (90a) seems to contain an implicit *will*, whereas (90b) seems to contain an implicit *can*. The 'verb modifier - negative particle - verb' order is the unmarked option in subordinate clauses introduced by *amíg* 'until' (90c), although the regular 'negative particle - verb - verb modifier' order is also possible. In head-final participial relatives, either the 'verb modifier - negative particle - verb' order or the 'negative particle - verb modifier - verb' order is possible (90d). Other types of non-finite clauses allow not only these two options but also the standard 'negative particle - verb - verb modifier' order (90e).

4.5.2.2. Imperative and optative sentences

The verb precedes the verb modifier in imperative sentences (91):

(91) a. *Állj* *fel*!
stand.Subj.2Sg up
'Stand up!

b. *Legyen* *kint* a kép a kirakat-ban?
be.Subj.3Sg outside the picture the shop_window-Ine
'Shall the picture be in the shop window?'

c. Tekintsd tárgytalan-nak az ügyet!
consider.Subj.2Sg void-Dat the matter
'Consider the matter void!'

d. Ne álljatok fel!
not stand.Subj.2Pl up
'Don't stand up!'

e. Ne *legyen* *kint* a kép a kirakat-ban!
not be.Subj.3Sg outside the picture the shop_window-Ine
'The picture shall not be in the shop window!'

f. Ne nézd hülyé-nek!
not take.Subj.DefObj.2Sg fool-Dat
'Don't take him for a fool!'

Rarely, the 'verb modifier - (*ne*) V' order occurs in imperative sentences as well. This order has also assumed a special pragmatic value in the case of imperatives; it is used if the propositional basis of the imperative sentence is contextually or situationally given, that is, if it is a possibility under discussion (Varga 2013).

(92) a. *El ne késs* nekem!
off not be.late.Subj.2Sg Dat.1Sg
'Don't be late on me!'

b. Aztán *be-add* a pályázatot határidő-re!
then in-give.Subj.2Sg the application.Acc deadline-Sub
'Do submit the application by the deadline!'

In optative sentences, the 'verb modifier - verb' order and the 'verb - verb modifier' order are equally possible:

(93) a. (Bár-)csak *meg-látogatna* minket!
if-only Perf-visit.Cond.3Sg us
'If only he would visit us!'

b. (Bár-)csak *látogatna meg* minket!

4.5.2.3. The postverbal position of the verb modifier

In sentences involving a 'verb – (…) verb modifier' order, the word order position of the verb modifier is determined by the fact that the order of major constituents in the postverbal section of the Hungarian sentence is free, but the optimal order is that obeying Behaghel's Law of Growing Constituents (Behaghel 1932). That is, the phonologically heavier a constituent is, the closer it will be to the end of the clause, and the lighter it is, the closer it will be to the verb. Hence a postverbal verbal particle is likely to stand right-adjacent to the verb, except when it is two-syllabic and the postverbal constituents also include short, unstressed elements, e.g. personal pronouns. Thus the word order variants in (94a,b) are equally unmarked, but (95a) is preferred to (95b):

(94) a. János nem *veszett össze* vel-ük.
János not fell out Ins-3Pl
'János didn't fall out with them.'

b. János nem *veszett* velük *össze*.

(95) a. Éva nem *találta meg* az elveszett karkötőt.
Éva not found Perf the lost bracelet.Acc
'Éva did not find the lost bracelet.'

b. ??Éva nem *találta* az elveszett karkötőt *meg*.

In a type of non-neutral sentences, the verb modifier itself is focused. Since both the default position of the verb modifier and the position of the focus is immediately preverbal, and since both the verb modifier and the focus bear primary stress with the subsequent verb destressed, the focus position and focus function of a verb modifier is usually made clear contextually by an explicit contrast:

(96) Péter *FEL* ment a lépcső-n, nem *LE*.
Péter up went the stairs-Sup not down
'Péter went upstairs, not downstairs.

The assumption that the verbal particle in (96) has moved to the focus position in the left periphery of the comment, also taking the verb along, is supported by the fact that their position relative to manner adverbs has changed; whereas the 'verb modifier - verb' complex of a neutral sentence is preceded by a manner adverb (97a), the focused 'verb modifier – verb' complex is followed by it (97b).

(97) a. Péter *lassan fel-ment* a lépcső-n.
Péter slowly up-went the stair-Sup
'Péter slowly went upstairs.'

b. Péter *FEL-ment lassan* a lépcsőn, nem *LE*.

When a resultative or terminative verb modifier is focused, the sentence is aspectually ambiguous; it can be understood as an accomplishment with the result state attained (98a) or as a process in progress (98b) – presumably because the basis of focus movement can be either the telic, perfective pattern in (74) or the progressive pattern in (75).

(98) a. Péter *FEL-ment* a lépcső-n 30 másodperc alatt, nem *LE* (*ment*).
Péter up-went the stair-Sup 30 seconds in not down went
'In 30 seconds, János went up the stairs, not down.'

b. Péter *FEL-ment* a lépcső-n, nem *LE*, amikor a lábát törte.
Péter up-went the stair-Sup not down when the leg.Poss.3Sg.Acc broke
'Péter was going up the stairs, not down, when he broke his leg.'

4.6. Depictives

Not all predicative PPs form a complex predicate with the verb. Adjectives supplied with the morphemes *-an/en* and *-ul/ül*, the so-called depictives, are secondary predicates predicating a property of the subject or the object without semantically incorporating into the verb. Depictives are not selected by the primary predicate or by any sentence constituent, and from this perspective, they are adjuncts. Accordingly, they also figure in Section 7.3.4 of the chapter discussing PPs functioning as adjuncts. The distribution of *-an/en* and *-ul/ül* is lexically determined; *-an/en* is the default variant; *-ul/ül* can be productively combined with adjectives derived by the suffix *-tlan/tlen*, and with adjectives denoting languages.

(99) a. Az orvos részeg-en vizsgálta meg a beteget.
the doctor drunken-ly examined Perf the patient.Acc
'The doctor examined the patient drunk.'

b. Az orvos *ügyetlen-ül* vizsgálta meg a beteget.
the doctor clumsy-ly examined Perf the patient.Acc
'The doctor examined the patient clumsily.'

c. Az orvos *meztelen-ül* vizsgálta meg a beteget.
the doctor naked-ly examined Perf the patient.Acc
'The doctor examined the patient naked.'

d. Péter *német-ül* olvasta a regényt.
Péter German-ly read the novel.Acc
'Péter read the novel in German.'

Hungarian grammars treat *-an/en* and *-ul/ül* as derivational suffixes deriving adverbs from adjectives (see Chapter 2 Section 2.2.4.1.1). However, *-an/en* is clearly cognate with the superessive case ending *-on/en/ön*, and *-ul/ül* is clearly cognate with the shared *-l* element of the elative suffix *-ból/ből*, the delative *-ról/ről*, and the ablative *-tól/től*, hence it seems justified to analyze adjective + *-an/en* or *-ul/ül* complexes as PPs (as proposed by Kádár 2009).

Whether the depictive PP is predicated of the subject or the object of the clause is pragmatically determined. (99a) is ambiguous in this respect out of context; in (99b), the depictive is understood to be predicated of the subject, whereas in (99c,d) it is understood to be predicated of the object.

The preferred position of depictives is the preverbal focus position, as illustrated in (99a-d). In (99a-c), the focus position of the depictive is shown by the fact that it has elicited verb movement across the verb modifier. In the case of (99d), which contains no verb modifier, the focus position of the depictive becomes evident under negation: whereas a verb modifier is preceded by a negated verb, a focus remains preverbal, as is the case in (100).

(100) János nem *német-ül* olvasta a regényt.
János not German-ly read the novel.Acc
'János didn't read the novel in German.'

A depictive is slightly marked (but not ungrammatical) in positions other than focus, e.g.:

(101) a. ?Az orvos *részeg-en* meg-vizsgálta a beteget.
the doctor drunken-ly Perf-examined the patient.Acc
'The doctor examined the patient drunk.'

b. ?Az orvos meg-vizsgálta a beteget *részegen*.

The different word order variants do not disambiguate the sentence – although the topic-oriented interpretation is more likely in the case of the high depictive in (101a) than in the case of the low depictive in (101b).

The fact that depictives do not occupy the position of the verb modifier is in accordance with the semantic intuition that they are not incorporated into the verb semantically, i.e., they do not form a complex predicate with it.

4.7. Summary

Predicative PPs can function as secondary predicates forming a complex predicate with the verb. As such they occupy the immediately preverbal position in neutral sentences, reserved for a heterogeneous class of predicative elements known as verb modifiers, where they are both semantically and prosodically incorporated into the verb. The predicative PP semantically incorporated into the verb is in most cases a verbal particle, but it can also be represented by an AP, NP or DP supplied with an oblique case ending or a postposition. Verbal particle + V complexes usually form a lexical unit, as well.

Verb modifiers play a resultative or terminative role in the default case. They combine with activity and process verbs; they predicate the resultant state or resultant location of the internal argument, thereby telicizing the base verb. A small subset of predicative PPs denote location; they form complex predicates with verbs of existence and spatial configuration.

In syntax, verb modifiers are independent constituents. In sentences containing a focus and/or negation, as well as in imperative and optative sentences, the verb is raised on its own, leaving the verb modifier behind. The verb modifier and the verb can be separated by intervening elements both in the case of 'verb modifier, verb' order, and in the case of 'verb, verb modifier' order. The 'verb modifier - verb' string can be broken up by an intervening emphatic particle, or by particle movement into topic position, or into the verb modifier position of a higher clause. The word order of major constituents in the postverbal section of the Hungarian sentence is syntactically free, but the optimal order is determined by Behaghel's Law of Growing Constituents. That is, monosyllabic verb modifiers, among them verbal particles, tend to be right-adjacent to the verb, but longer verb modifiers may drift away from it.

Depictives are case-marked adjectives (AP+P complexes). They predicate a property of the subject or object of the clause without forming a complex predicate with the verb.

4.8. Bibliographical notes

The claim that the verbal particle+verb string, forming one unit semantically, prosodically and orthographically, is the sequence of two independent elements in syntax, was first put forth by Brassai (1863-65), then revived by É. Kiss (1977). The categorial status, the structural position, and the function of verbal particles and of verb modifiers, in general, has been a much discussed issue in the past decades – see, e.g., Ackermann (1984), Komlósy (1994), É. Kiss (2002; 2006a,b,c), Kiefer and Ladányi (2000b), Kiefer (2006), Kiefer and Németh (2012), Csirmaz (2006b), Surányi (2009a,c), Hegedűs (2014), etc. The issue of 'particle climbing' in non-finite constructions has been analyzed in various theoretical frameworks by Farkas and Sadock (1989), Koopman and Szabolcsi (2000), and in chapters of É. Kiss and Van Riemsdijk (eds.) (2004), among them Szendrői (2004). The syntactic behavior of dative-marked secondary predicates was studied by Ürögdi (2006). Kalivoda (2018, 2020) studies Hungarian verbal particles in a corpus-driven fashion.

Chapter 5
PPs used as arguments

György Rákosi

5.1. Introduction

This chapter discusses the grammar of PPs selected by a verb, an adjective, or a noun in Hungarian. We provide an overview of how PPs are licensed and how they contribute to structure building, with a primary focus on the verb phrase and a subsequent inquiry into PP complements in adjectival phrases and noun phrases. Section 5.2 provides an inventory of PP types that are directly selected by the verb and PPs that are licensed in particle verb constructions. Section 5.3 introduces a distinction between core arguments and non-core arguments of the verb. After a systematic comparison of these two types of PP complements, we illustrate this divide via detailed case studies taken from the domain of PPs marked by dative case, instrumental case, and ablative case, as well as an outlook on other PP varieties. PP complements of adjectives and nouns are discussed in Section 5.4 and Section 5.5, respectively.

What constitutes the focus of attention in this chapter are often referred to in the pertinent literature as **participant PPs**. The fundamental objective of this chapter is to describe the major modes of composition between such PPs and the heads that select them. PP complements that have a predicative function are discussed in Chapter 4 of this volume, and Chapter 7 provides a thorough inventory of adjunct PP types in Hungarian.

5.2. PPs and verbal particles

5.2.1. Introductory remarks

A PP complement can be selected either directly by the verb or by the complex of the verb and a verbal particle, if there is one. This second mode of composition is a characteristic feature of the Hungarian verb phrase. The verbal particle typically bears a telicizing function, and its presence may induce changes in the argument structure and in the subcategorization frame of the verb (see Chapter 4 of this volume for a more detailed discussion of this function of particles). Consider (1) for illustration.

(1) a. Kati [az asztal-on]/ [az asztal alatt] ült.
Kati the table-Sup / the table under sit.Past.3Sg
'Kati was sitting [on the table] / [under the table].'

b. Kati rá-ült [az asztal-ra] / [*az asztal alá].
Kati onto-sit.Past.3Sg the table-Sub / the table to.under
'Kati sat [onto the table] / [*under the table].'

The verb *ül* 'sit' selects for a locative PP complement with no specific formal restrictions on the choice of the locative marker (1a). In the particle verb construction represented by (1b), the PP complement may only bear the goal-denoting case marker that the particle itself spells out (see 5.2.3.5 below for more on this construction), and the particle-verb complex is interpreted as an achievement predicate.

Though most particles generally telicize the verb that they combine with, the aspectual properties of particle verbs are somewhat less predictable in the case of particle-verb combinations that are not transparent semantically. While the motion verb in (2a) is telic in the presence of the particle *be* 'into', when the same verb plus particle combination is interpreted non-compositionally as a dative experiencer verb, it denotes a state (2b).

(2) a. Kati be-jön a szobá-ba.
Kati into-come.3Sg the room-Ill
'Kati comes into the room.'

b. Kati be-jön Feri-nek.
Kati into-come.3Sg Feri-Dat
'Feri likes Kati.'

Notice that the subcategorization frame of the complex verb is also different in the two cases. The motion verb takes a directional PP complement (1a), and the experiencer verb requires a dative experiencer (2b).

Our goal in this section is to provide an overview of the **syntactic constructions** in which PP complements of verbs occur, with or without a particle. The influence of the particle on the aspectual composition and the complement structure of the verb phrase receives occasional commentary when it is systematic. A more comprehensive inventory of argument structure alternations involving argument PPs is available in the volume on Verb Phrases.

5.2.2. PPs directly selected by the verb

Finite verbs can only select PPs as their **internal** arguments in Hungarian. This does not entail, nevertheless, that PP complements always appear in the postverbal field in neutral sentences. The primary aim of this section is to provide a summary of the default surface realization patterns of argument PPs in neutral sentences in Hungarian, as conditioned by the type of the verbal predicate. We discuss two-place predicates first, and then we turn to a brief inquiry into predicates of higher arity in the light of the results of this introductory discussion. This subsection focuses on verbs that do not combine with verbal particles. Particle verbs are discussed separately in Subsection 5.2.3.

The canonical spell-out position of PP complements of dyadic verbs is in the postverbal field in neutral sentences. Thus (3a) below can be a neutral sentence in response to a question inquiring about what happened. The preverbal, inessive case-marked PP either receives sentential accent and is interpreted as the focus of the clause (3b), or it is a topic (3c).

(3) a. A bíróság döntött Péter ügyé-ben.
the court decide.Past.3Sg Péter case.Poss-Ine
'The court has made a decision in Péter's case.'

b. A bíróság PÉTER ÜGYÉ-BEN döntött.
the court Péter case.Poss-Ine decide.Past.3Sg
'It is in Péter's case that the court has made a decision.'

c. A bíróság Péter ügyé-ben már döntött.
the court Péter case.Poss-Ine already decide.Past.3Sg
'As for Péter's case, the court has already made a decision (in it).'

The complement of the adposition is a definite noun phrase in these examples, as is in most examples below. This is so to ensure that the examples instantiate the canonical word order. Non-specific noun phrase objects occupy the preverbal verb modifier position in neutral sentences (see Chapter 4), and PPs with non-specific noun phrase complements may also target this position. In such cases, the non-specific feature of the noun phrase percolates up to the PP and it triggers the movement of the whole PP into the verb modifier position. Thus the PP in (4) can be a non-focussed verb modifier, unlike the definite PP in (3b), which cannot.

(4) A bíróság kényes ügyek-ben döntött.
the court sensitive case.Pl-Ine decide.Past.3Sg
'The court has made a decision in sensitive cases.'

Some verbs require their PP complements to occupy the verb modifier position even when the noun phrase complement of the adposition is specific. We turn to such examples below after a discussion of the dominant pattern that (3) represents.

The most frequent type of adpositions that are subcategorized for by verbs are case suffixes. This is non-surprising given that the ability to occur on subcategorized arguments of the verb has been argued to be a defining property of **case suffixes** (see Chapter 2). We list some examples for such subcategorized case markers from the spatial domain in (5)-(7).

(5) • Case suffixes on PP complements: locatives

a. A magyar történelem bővelkedik furcsaságok-ban.
the Hungarian history abound.3SG oddity.Pl-Ine
'Hungarian history abounds with oddities.'

b. Ez nem Pál-on múlik.
this not Pál-Sup pass.3Sg
'This is not up to Pál.'

(6) • Case suffixes on PP complements: sources

a. János régóta gondoskodik a nagymamájá-ról.
János for_long look_after the grandmother.Poss.3Sg-Del
'János has long been looking after his grandmother.'

b. Éva is részesült a jutalom-ból.
Éva too receive_a_share_of.Past.3sg the reward-Ela
'Éva also received a share of the reward.'

c. Feri fél a pókok-tól.
Feri fear.3Sg the spider.Pl-Abl
'Feri is afraid of spiders.'

(7) • Case suffixes on PP complements: goals

a. Mihály ragaszkodik a korábbi álláspontjá-hoz.
Mihály adhere.Past.3Sg the former opinion.Poss.3Sg-All
'Mihály adheres to his former opinion.'

b. Kati számít Feri-re.
Kati count.on.3Sg Feri-Sub
'Kati counts on Feri.'

c. János gratulált Feri-nek.
János congratulate.Past.3Sg Feri-Dat
'János congratulated Feri.'

As these examples testify, PP complements can bear different types of case morphology.

Remark 1. The categories **locative**, **source** and **goal** refer to the primary spatial readings of the case suffixes, and they do not necessarily describe the semantic contribution of these elements in the examples above (5)-(7). We continue using these terms here to refer sometimes only to **the morphological form** of the adposition rather than to its actual meaning.

The verbs in these examples tend to be lexical items that have relatively rich descriptive content, and they receive sentential stress.

There are relatively few verbs in this group that require their PP complements to be headed by a postposition. The following two sentences contain two relevant examples with the PP occupying a postverbal position in neutral sentences.

(8) • PPs headed by a subcategorized postposition

a. Feri menekül Éva elől.
Feri flee.3Sg Éva away_from
'Feri is running away from Éva.'

b. János aggódik Kati miatt.
János worry.3Sg Kati because_of
'János worries about Kati.'

Both adpositions in (8) are case-like postpositions, and case-assigning postpositions are unusual in this construction type. A case-assigning postposition may also act as a verbal particle when selected by the verb, and its complement is in fact licensed as the complement of the particle verb complex. We discuss such examples in Section 5.2.3.3.

Another set of dyadic verbs taking PP complements tend to be stress-avoiding, and many items in this group have relatively weak semantic content (see Komlósy 1992 and 1994 for a detailed discussion). The PP complement of these verbs occupies a preverbal verb modifier position in neutral sentences. (9) is illustrative of this pattern.

(9) a. Éva a mamá-ra gondolt.
Éva the mum-Sub think.Past.3Sg
(i) 'Éva thought of Mum.'
(ii) 'It is Mum that Éva thought of.'

b. Éva gondolt a mamá-ra.
Éva think.Past.3Sg the mum-Sub
(i) *'Éva thought of Mum.'
(ii) 'It is Éva that thought of Mum.'
(iii) 'Éva did think of Mum.'

The word order shown in (9b) is only grammatical if the subject DP is focussed (9bii), or in a verum focus construal with the verb bearing sentential stress (9biii). Unlike in the previous set of examples (5)-(8), the subject argument in this construction (9b) cannot be interpreted as the topic of a neutral sentence (9bi). (9a) has two interpretations: the preverbal PP is either a verb modifier (9ai) or it is interpreted as the focus of the clause (9bii). The two readings are differentiated by two distinct intonational patterns.

(9a) is thus different from (3b), which we repeat as (10):

(10) A bíróság Péter ügyé-ben döntött.
the court Péter case.Poss-Ine decide.Past.3Sg
'It is in Péter's case that the court has made a decision.'

The preverbal PP can only be interpreted as focus in the construction type represented by (10), disregarding for now the possibility that it can also be a (contrastive) topic. Preverbal focus is exhaustive in Hungarian, and (10) is only true if there is no other case that the court decided on in the event described by the sentence. The PP thus cannot be assumed to be a verb modifier, since in that case it would not necessarily have an exhaustive interpretation. The lack of exhaustivity is, however, an option for the interpretation of the preverbal PP in (9a). A standard test to establish this involves the comparison of (9a) and (11).

(11) Éva a mamá-ra és a papá-ra gondolt.
Éva the mum-Sub and the dad-Sub think.Past.3Sg
(i) 'Éva thought of Mum and Dad.'
(ii) 'It is Mum and Dad that Éva thought of.'

(11) contains a coordinate PP with the PP of (9a) being one of the conjuncts. If (11) is true, (9a) can still be true, and the two respective propositions are in fact mutually compatible. This may only be so if the PP is not necessarily interpreted exhaustively in either sentence. If (9a) necessarily expressed an exhaustive statement about *Mum*, then its truth would not follow from (11). Consequently, the preverbal PP in (9a) does not have to be a focussed constituent. The sentence is grammatical with neutral prosody, and the preverbal PP occupies a verb modifier position in this case.

The following examples contain other verbs that pattern up with *gondol* 'think of' in this respect.

(12) • Verbs licensing preverbal PPs as verb modifiers

a. A filozófia a csodálkozás-ból ered.
the philosophy the astonishment-Ela originate.3Sg
'Philosophy originates from astonishment.'

b. Kati ebből él.
Kati this.Ela live.3Sg
'Kati makes a living by doing this.'

c. Mindez Feri-re vall.
all.this Feri-Sub bespeak.3Sg
'All this sounds like Feri.'

d. A falu ma Romániá-hoz tartozik.
the village today Romania-All belong_to.3Sg
'Today the village belongs to Romania.'

e. A parti másnap reggel-ig tartott.
the party next.day morning-Ter last.Past.3Sg
'The party lasted till the next morning.'

f. Ez az út Miskolc felé vezet.
this the road Miskolc towards lead.3Sg
'This road goes towards Miskolc.'

g. Az összeesküvés a király ellen irányult.
the conspiracy the king against is_directed_against.Past.3Sg
'The conspiracy was directed at the king.'

These verbs are all stress-avoiding, and their PP complement occupies the verb modifier position in neutral sentences. The head of these PPs is either a case suffix (12a-e) or a case-like postposition (12f-g). There are no thematic restrictions on the type of the adposition that can head a verb modifier PP: source-type markers (12a-b) are acceptable just as well as goal-type markers (12c-d,f-g), alongside temporal PPs, such as the terminative PP in (12e) and other types not discussed here. It is also noteworthy that the adposition takes a definite noun phrase complement in each of the examples above. Verbs in this group require their PP argument to occupy the verb modifier position in neutral sentences irrespective of the type of the noun phrase that the P-head selects.

Remark 2. The verbs discussed here ((9), (12)) may superficially look like the Definiteness Effect verbs discussed in Chapter 6. Definiteness Effect verbs require the presence of a preverbal PP if their internal argument is specific and if the clause contains no preverbal focus constituent. The example in (i) contains a Definiteness Effect verb, and (ii) illustrates the construction that we are discussing:

(i) A gyerek *(a kórház-ban) született.
the child the hospital-Ine be_born.Past.3Sg
'The child was born in the hospital.'

(ii) A gyerek *(a kórház-ra) gondolt.
the child the hospital-Sub think.Past.3Sg
'The child thought of the hospital.'

The PP is obligatory in both sentences if the subject is a definite noun phrase. If, however, the subject is an indefinite noun phrase, the PP is optional in the case of Definiteness Effect verbs (iii):

(iii) Két gyerek (a kórház-ban) született.
two child the hospital-Ine be_born.Past.3Sg
'Two children were born (in the hospital).'

(iv) Két gyerek *(a kórház-ra) gondolt.
two child the hospital-Sub think.Past.3Sg
'Two children thought of the hospital.'

There is no change in the status of the PP in (iv). Such stress-avoiding verbs, like *gondol* 'think of', subcategorize for PP-arguments with designated morphological markers. This PP is an obligatory argument, unlike the adjuncts that surface by Definiteness Effect verbs under the conditions discussed in Chapter 6.

The verbs that we have overviewed so far are two-place predicates with an internal PP argument, and they do not combine with verbal particles. They fall into two groups depending on whether their PP-complement occupies a verb modifier position in neutral sentences or not. If the verb is richer in its semantics, it will typically not strive to avoid receiving sentential stress, and its PP-complement occupies a postverbal position. An immediately preverbal PP is interpreted as focus in these constructions, and it receives the accompanying focus intonation.

These observations carry over to three-place verbal predicates, too. Since our immediate aim here is to probe into the patterns that characterize the core syntax of PP complements in Hungarian, we restrict this brief discussion to verbs that take an object and an internal PP argument. Triadic verbs of this kind show the same basic divide that we have observed above. Consider the following examples.

(13) • Triadic verbs: postverbal PPs in neutral contexts

a. János figyelmeztette Kati-t a veszély-re.
János warn.Past.3Sg Kati-Acc the danger-Sub
'János warned Kati of the danger.'

b. Az orvos tájékoztatta a beteg-et a lehetőségek-ről.
The doctor inform.Past.3Sg the patient-Acc the alternative.Pl-Del
'The doctor informed the patient about the alternatives.'

(14) • Triadic verbs: preverbal PPs in neutral contexts

a. A tudós a kísérleti adatok-ra alapozta az elmélet-é-t.
the scientist the experimental data-Sub base.Past.3Sg the theory-Poss-Acc
'The scientist based his theory on experimental data.'

b. A szónok maga mellé állította a tömeg-et.
the speaker himself to_next_to make_stand.Past.3Sg the crowd-Acc
'The speaker made the crowd stand by his side./The speaker won over the crowd.'

The two verbs in (13) license a PP argument in the postverbal field in neutral contexts. (14) contains examples in which the PP – even in the presence of a definite noun phrase complement – is in the verb modifier position in a discourse-neutral setting. The PPs are headed by a case suffix ((13) and (14a)) or by a case-like postposition (14b).

If the object is a non-specific noun phrase, then it outcompetes the PP-complement for the verb modifier position in neutral sentences. In other words, the PP-complement will appear postverbally in these cases, as in the following two examples.

(15) • Triadic verbs: bare noun phrase objects

a. A szónok tömegek-et állított maga mellé.
the speaker crowd.Pl-Acc make_stand.Past.3Sg himself to_next_to
'The speaker made crowds (of people) stand by his side'

b. Az elnök tudomás-t szerzett a terv-ről.
the president knowledge-Acc gain.Past.3Sg the plan-Del
'The president came to know about the plan.'

(15a) is a variant of (14b) with a bare plural object. The non-specific object occupies the preverbal position, and the PP stays in the postverbal field. (15b) is a similar construction, which includes a bare singular that forms a slightly idiomatic complex predicate with the verb (*tudomást szerez* 'gain knowledge of'). Such examples abound in Hungarian, so (15b) is representative of a frequent mode of complex verb formation.

Another prominent complex predicate formation process is the combination of the verb and a verbal particle. In the next Subsection, we investigate particle verb constructions that typically license PP complements. Viewed from the vantage point of the observations we have made above, verbal particles instantiate another strategy that makes it possible, as it were, for PP complements to stay in the postverbal zone in neutral sentences. We now turn to a discussion of the most frequent particle verb constructions in Hungarian.

5.2.3. PP complements in particle verb constructions

5.2.3.1. Particle verbs and verbal particles

We distinguish here four different formal types of particle verb constructions that can host PP complements. (16) illustrates these.

(16) • Particle verb constructions with PP complements in Hungarian

a. János fel-néz Kati-ra. [adverbial particle]
János up-look.3Sg Kati-Sub
'János looks up to Kati.'

b. János át-néz Kati-n. [case-assigning postposition as particle]
János through-look Kati-Sup
'János looks through Kati.'

c. Kati utána-nézett az információ-nak. [case-like postposition as particle]
Kati after-look the information-Dat
'Kati checked up on the solution.'

d. Kati rá-nézett János-ra. [particle cognate with a case suffix]
Kati onto-look.Past.3Sg János-Sub
'Kati looked onto János.'

Each of these constructions have their own distinguishing properties, which we discuss respectively in the following four subsections.

In principle, the above particle verb constructions are in free variation with PP complements that occur in the company of "bare", particleless verbs. So (17a) and (17b) are equally grammatical:

(17) a. János fel-ugrott a szék-re
János up-jump.Past.3Sg the chair-Sub
'János jumped up onto the chair.'

b. János a szék-re ugrott.
János the chair-Sub jump.Past.3Sg
'John jumped onto the chair.'

In a descriptive sense, the sublative-marked PP is the complement of the particle verb in (17a) and of the verb in (17b). The PP occupies the preverbal position in the absence of the particle in (17b), which, if present, outcompetes the PP for this position in neutral sentences in the case of this particular verb. Semantic differences are easy to attest between the two members of such contrastive pairs, even if it is not always straightforward to predict them. This is certainly not the case in (17), where the particle in the first sentence provides information about the upward directionality of the movement, a contextual parameter that is simply left unspecified in the second. In other words, (17b) is true either if János jumps up, down or across onto the chair, whereas (17a) is only compatible with the first of these possible scenarios. (For an alternative approach that treats the particle and the PP as forming one underlying constituent and sharing a secondary predicate function, see Chapter 4.)

The apparent free variation between these two modes of structure building might be absent in less compositional cases, where the semantic contribution of the particle is less predictable.

(18) a. Judit *(rá-)jött a megoldás-ra.
Judit onto-came.3Sg the solution-Sub
'Judit figured out the solution.'

b. Ez még rá-ér.
this still onto-reach.3Sg
'This can still wait.'

The particle is obligatory in (18a), or else the targeted idiomatic meaning of the verbal predicate is totally lost. In (18b), the particle forms an idiomatic complex with the verb, and this particular interpretation is only available if no accompanying PP complement is present. There are also examples where the particle is optional, but unlike in the case of the variation in (17), its presence or the absence does not seem to change the descriptive semantics of the VP:

(19) A leírás (rá-)illik Feri-re.
the description (onto-)fit.3Sg Feri-Sub
'The description fits Feri.'

This variation in the distribution of particles and PP complements is, to some extent, non-predictable, even if we can detect several factors that motivate the observed data patterns. As discussed in detail in Chapter 4 of this volume, directional verbal particles typically have a telicizing function, and the particle evidently has this function in (18a). It is less obvious in what sense the particle in (19) may have a telicizing function (see Chapter 4 for a pertinent discussion). Our concern here, however, is not a detailed investigation of these factors, but a summary overview of the particle verb constructions that include PPs.

One final note about the term **verbal particle** is in order here before we embark on this description. Chapter 2 Section 2.2.3 of this volume provides a comprehensive survey of verbal particles in Hungarian. Here we would like to highlight some illustrative differences between the grammar of verbal particles and PP complements. As we noted in Section 5.2.2 above, source type directional PPs may occupy the preverbal verb modifier position in neutral sentences. Most verbal particles are directionals of the goal or of the path type, though we find some locative items among them, too. But source markers cannot be used as verbal particles, a possible reflex of a universal constraint on sources that bans them from entering complex predicate formation processes (see É. Kiss 1998 and Surányi 2009b on the Hungarian data). Consequently, whereas the illative case marker can be used as a particle, duplicating the case morphology of the PP (20a), the elative case marker cannot participate in this construction (20b). To express the intended meaning, the goal-denoting particle *ki* 'out' can be used in this context, together with an elative case marked PP denoting the starting point of the movement (20c).

(20) a. Feri bele-mászott a ládá-ba.
Feri into-climb.Past.3Sg the box-Ill
'Feri climbed into the box.'

b. *Feri belőle-mászott a ládá-ból.
Feri out_from-climb.Past.3Sg the box-Ela
Intended meaning: 'Feri climbed out of the box.'

c. Feri ki-mászott a ládá-ból.
Feri out-climb.Past..3Sg the box-Ela
'Feri climbed out of the box.'

Note furthermore that the neutral order in each of the four constructions introduced above is the one where the particle occupies the preverbal slot, and the PP is in the postverbal field.

(21) a. János fel-néz Kati-ra.
János up-look.3Sg Kati-Sub
'János looks up to Kati.'

b. János KATI-RA néz fel.
János Kati-Sub look.3Sg up
'It is Kati that János looks up to.'

The inverse order of the two requires the PP to be interpreted as the focus of the clause (21b).

Remark 3. There are a few exceptions to this overall pattern (see Komlósy 1992: 341). One is given below:

(i) A vizsga két rész-ből tevődik össze.
the exam two part-Ela consist_of.3Sg together
'The exam consists of two parts.'

(ii) *A vizsga két rész-ből össze-tevődik.
the exam two part-Ela together-consist_of.3Sg

The particle verb *összetevődik* 'consist of' requires the elative-marked PP in the preverbal slot, and the particle follows the verb in neutral contexts (i). The usual particle+verb order is in fact ungrammatical in this case (ii). *Elhelyezkedik* 'is located' is another similar example:

(iii) Ezek a létesítmények több tagállam-ban helyezked-nek el.
these the facility.Pl several member_state-Ine be_located-3Pl away
'These facilities are located in several member states.'

(iv) *Ezek a létesítmények több tagállam-ban el-helyezked-nek.
these the facility.Pl several member_state-Ine away-be_located-3Pl

The particle el 'away' is in the postverbal field in neutral sentences since a locative PP occupies the preverbal verb modifier position.

As we have seen above, the verbal particle outcompetes the PP for the verb modifier position in the usual case. Another context where this difference manifests itself is nominalizations of particle verb constructions (see Section 5.5 and Chapter 4 for more on nominalizations). The particle directly combines with the nominalized head, and the PP argument itself is introduced as the complement of the participial form of the copula (22a). If we switch the respective positions of the particle and the PP, the result is entirely ungrammatical.

(22) a. a hegy-re való fel-mászás
the mountain-Sub being up-climbing
'the climbing up to the mountain'

b. *a fel való hegy-re mászás
the up being mountain-Sub climbing
Intended meaning: 'the climbing up to the mountain'

These observations highlight a substantial difference between verbal particles and PP complements, illustrating the fact that the former have a much stronger drive to form a complex with the verb than the latter.

Remark 4. One might be tempted to conclude on these grounds that particles are mere P-heads, and they do not project a PP. An argument against this view has been constructed on the basis of bridge verbs that show strong clause union effects even with finite complement clauses (see Koopman & Szabolcsi 2000). In particular, some modal verbs can attract the verbal particle of the verb in their finite complement clauses across the complementizer (see also Chapter 4):

(i) Rá kell, hogy jöjj a megoldás-ra.
onto must that come.Subj.2Sg the solution-Sub
'You must figure out the solution.'

Since such movement across finite clause boundaries can only target phrases, but not heads, the raised particle in (i) must be a PP.

5.2.3.2. Particle verb constructions: adverbial particles

A handful of directional particles that we call **adverbial particles** constitute a special subclass of verbal particles. Prominent members of this class are listed in (23).

(23) • Adverbial particles

ki	be	le	fel	el	vissza
'out'	'into'	'down'	'up'	'away'	'back'

As discussed in Chapter 2 of this volume, these are locative adverbs used as particles (with the exception of *el* 'away' and *vissza* 'back'), and they have comparative and superlative forms (with the exception of *el*).

These particles participate in complex predicate formation with the verb, and the resulting particle verb often selects for a PP argument. The particles themselves introduce no specific constraint on the form and the type of the PP, and the P-head itself is always selected by the particle verb complex. Some examples involving source-type PPs are listed in (24), and others including goal PPs are in (25).

(24) a. Feri ki-lépett a szövetkezet-ből.
Feri out-step.Past.3Sg the cooperative-Ela
'Feri quit the cooperative.'

b. Kati be-számolt a konferenciá-ról.
Kati in-count.Past.3Sg the conference-Del
'Kati reported on her conference experiences.'

c. Le-maradt-am a hírek-ről.
down-stay.Past-1Sg the news-Del
'I missed the news.'

d. János el-állt a szerződés-től.
János away-stand.Past.3Sg the contract-Abl
'János retracted from the contract.'

e. Kati vissza-riadt a felelősség-től.
Kati back-startle.Past.3Sg the responsibility-Abl
'Kati shrank back from the responsibility.'

(25) a. Éva ki-nézett a meccs-re.
Éva out-look.Past.3Sg the match-Sub
'Éva went out to take a look at the match.'

b. Kati be-költözött az új lakás-ba.
Kati in-move.Past.3Sg the new flat-Ill
'Kati moved in to the new flat.'

c. János le-nézett a kocsmá-ba.
János down-look.Past.3Sg the pub-Ill
'János went down to the pub to spend some time there.'

d. János fel-néz Kati-ra.
János up-look.3Sg Kati-Sub
'János looks up to Kati.'

e. El-jutott Feri-hez is a hír.
away-reach.Past.3Sg Feri-All too the news
'The news reached Feri, too.'

f. Kati vissza-emlékezett a kezdet-re.
Kati back-remember.Past.3Sg the beginning-Sub
'Kati recalled the beginning.'

The verbs in most of these examples either do not by themselves subcategorize for the PPs, or their meaning is different in the absence of the particle. The presence of the particle is therefore essential.

Adverbial particles also have uses in which they do not associate with PP complements. In (26a), for example, the particle is a telic marker, and it measures the event out by predicating that the referent of the object DP, the whole book was read. This function of the particle is discussed in detail in Chapter 4. The same particle *el* 'away' may have another aspectual value in particle verb complexes when it makes the verbal event durative (26b). According to Kiefer (2009: 252), this particle has a delimitative-perfective meaning: the activity is temporally delimited, but the VP is not telic. Note that there is no VP-internal complement in (26b).

(26) a. János el-olvasta a könyv-et.
János away-read.3Sg the book-Acc
'János read the (whole) book.'

b. Feri el-borozgatott.
Feri away-sip_wine.Past.3Sg
'Feri was sipping wine.'

The dominant aspectual contribution of adverbial particles is telicity (and perfectivity, see Chapter 4), and this holds of most of the examples in (24) and (25). But, as we have seen before, the attested aspectual structure of the particle verb complex is not necessarily predictable in non-compositional combinations. (25d), for example, is the description of the mental state of the subject referent on the experiencer reading of the particle verb.

5.2.3.3. Case-assigning postpositions as particles

A subset of case-assigning Ps can be used as verbal particles. These are the same case-assigning Ps that allow P-stranding (see Chapter 2).

(27) • Case-assigning Ps used as particles

át	belül	keresztül	közel	végig
'across, through'	'inside of'	'through'	'close to'	'all along'
szembe	túl			
'to opposite, against'	'beyond, over'			

When used as adpositions, these Ps subcategorize for superessive, allative or instrumental case on their noun phrase complement. As particles, they require the same case morphology on the PP argument of the particle verb complex. (28) contains relevant examples, with one spatial PP example for each respective adposition given on the right for comparison.

(28)	a.	Át-lát-ok az orvosok-on. through-see-1Sg the doctors-Sup 'I can see through the doctors.'	a mező-n át the meadow-Sup across 'across the meadow'
	b.	Ő közel került hozzám lelkileg. (s)he close_to get.Past.3Sg All.1Sg spiritually 'She got close to me spiritually.'	a ház-hoz közel the house-All close.to 'close to the house'
	c.	Feri keresztül-ment sok minden-en. Feri through-go.Past.3Sg many everything-Sup 'Feri went through a great deal.'	az erdő-n keresztül the forest-Sup through 'through the forest'
	d.	Éva szembe-fordult korábbi barátai-val. Éva against-turn.Past.3Sg former friend.Poss.Pl.3Sg-Ins 'Éva turned against her former friends.'	a nap-pal szembe the sun-Ins against 'against the sun'
	e.	Feri túl-lépett végre a kudarcok-on. Feri over-step.3Sg finally the failure.Pl-Sup 'Feri finally got over the failures.'	a hegy-en túl the hill-Sup over 'over the hill'
	f.	Végig-megy-ek az út-on. all.along-go-1Sg the road-Sup 'I go all the way through on this road.'	az utcá-n végig the street-Sup all.along ' all along the street '

These particles, like the adverbial particles discussed in the previous section, also have uses in which they do not take PP associates. Since these are not directly relevant for our overview of PP arguments, we do not discuss such examples here.

5.2.3.4. Case-like postpositions as particles

Directional and locative case-like postpositions can function as verbal particles. Some of them are listed in (29) below (see Chapter 2 for a detailed inventory).

(29) • Case-like Ps used as particles

alá	elé	fölé	mellé	mögé
'to under'	'to in front of'	'to above'	'to next.to'	'to behind'
alatta	mellette	utána		
'under'	'next to'	'after'		

The directional particles end in the now obsolete lative marker *-é*, and they also function as PPs with 3Sg pronominal complements. The locative particles more transparently spell out the 3Sg agreement morphology, as is clear from the comparison of *után* 'after' and *utána* 'after it/him/her'. So these particles are identical in form to case-like Ps with 3Sg pronominal complements (where the pronoun complement is *pro*-dropped and the agreement morphology on the adposition itself spells out its person and number features). Consider the singular paradigm of the postposition *alatta* 'under' (30) for illustration. (30c) contains the 3Sg form.

(30) a. Éva alattam maradt
Éva under.1Sg stay.Past.3Sg
'Éva stayed under me.'

b. Éva alattad maradt.
Éva under.2Sg stay.Past.3Sg
'Éva stayed under you.'

c. Éva alatta maradt.
Éva under.3Sg stay.Past.3Sg
'Éva stayed under it/him/her.'

This construction is to be compared with the particle verb construction in (31d).

When these Ps are used as verbal particles, the particle verb can take a dative-marked complement headed by a lexical noun. The examples in (31) illustrate this construction.

(31) a. János alá-vetette magá-t az akarat-om-nak.
János to_under-throw.Past.3Sg himself-Acc the will-Poss.1Sg-Dat
'János deferred himself to my will.'

b. Elé-lépt-em a vonat-nak.
to_in_front_of-step.Past-1Sg the train-Dat
'I stepped out in front of the train'.

c. Éva utána-nézett a személyzet-nek.
Éva after-look.Past.3Sg the staff-Dat
'Éva checked up on the staff.'

d. Az infláció alatta maradt a várakozások-nak.
the inflation under stay.Past.3Sg the expectation.Pl-Dat
'The inflation rate stayed lower than expected.'

These particles share some properties that distinguish them from PPs that include true pronominal complements. Since the same issue arises with the duplicating particles discussed in the next section, we provide arguments there against the assumption that these inflecting particles are pronominal in the sense of taking referential pronoun complements.

When the dative complement is plural with animate referents, and the particle is used in its primary spatial meaning, then a subset of native speakers can also accept plural morphology on the particle (that is, this particle is identical in form to the inflected postposition with a *pro*-dropped 3Pl complement). But the singular form is just as acceptable in these cases, too, and it is actually the preferred option in the standard.

(32) a. Feri utána-futott a rendőrök-nek.
Feri after-run.Past.3Sg the policeman.Pl-Dat
'Feri ran after the policemen.'

b. %Feri után-uk futott a rendőrök-nek.
Feri after-3Pl run.Past.3Sg the policeman.Pl-Dat
'Feri ran after the policemen'.

The plural variety of the particle is much worse if the dative complement is not animate and if the particle-verb combination is more idiomatic. It is absolutely ungrammatical if neither condition is met, and therefore (31d) has no alternative with the plural form of the particle:

(33) *Az infláció alatt-uk maradt a várakozások-nak.
the inflation under-3Pl stay.Past.3Sg the expectation.Pl-Dat
Intended meaning: 'The inflation rate stayed lower than expected.'

We discuss this agreement pattern in more detail in the next subsection, since these effects are more pronounced in the case of duplicating particles.

5.2.3.5. Case suffixes as duplicating particles

A subset of the case suffixes can also function as verbal particles in Hungarian (see Chapter 2 for an in-depth discussion of case suffixes). The following list is a comprehensive survey of all particles in this group, with the first five items being directional, and the last three being locatives.

(34) • Case suffixes used as duplicating particles

bele	érte	hozzá	neki	rá	benne	rajta	vele
'into'	'for'	'to'	'to'	'onto'	'in'	'on'	'with'

It is only a subset of native speakers who use the particle based on the causal-final case suffix (*érte* 'for') or the one based on the instrumental suffix (*vele* 'with'), and, consequently, (35b) below is not acceptable for everyone. As in the case of the particles derived from case-like postpositions, the particles in this group too are formally identical to the 3Sg pronominal form of the case-marker (with the pronoun complement itself being *pro*-dropped). The particle-verb complex requires the same case morphology on the PP complement that the particle itself spells out, hence the term **duplicating particle**. Some examples are given in (35), and notice that in some cases the phonological form that the case suffix has when it takes a noun complement might be substantially different from how the same suffix is spelled out as a particle (which, in its turn, is phonologically identical to a case suffix bearing a pronoun complement). See examples (35a) and (35d) as illustration for such phonological divergence.

(35) a. Kati bele-nyugodott a döntés-be.
Kati into-become_resigned.to the decision-Sub
'Kati resigned herself to the decision.'

b. %Érte-megy-ek a gyerekek-ért az óvodá-ba.
for-go-1Sg the child.Pl-Caus the kindergarten-Sub
'I go to collect the children from the kindergarten'.

c. Feri is hozzá-szokott a gondolat-hoz.
Feri too to-get_used_to.Past.3Sg the thought-All
'Feri too got used to the thought.'

d. A katonák rajta-ütöttek az ellenség-en.
the soldier.Pl on-hit.Past.3Sg the enemy-Sup
'The soldiers took the enemy by surprise.'

The superficial appearances are that the particle is a P with some sort of a weak pronominal element in this construction, but it becomes clear on closer inspection that this is far from obviously so.

We note first that the pronominal complement of the case marker can never be spelled out in the duplicating construction. So while we have (36a), (36b) is ungrammatical if the pronoun is overt:

(36) a. Én ő-hozzá mentem feleség-ül.
I (s)he-All.3Sg go.Past.3Sg wife-Adv
'It is him that I married.'

b. Én (*ő-)hozzá mentem Feri-hez feleség-ül.
I (s)he-to go.Past.3Sg Feri-All wife-Adv
'I married Feri'.

The particle does not change its form in standard Hungarian if the PP complement is plural. Nevertheless, the agreeing, plural form is also available for some speakers as an alternative (with varying judgements reported in the pertinent literature, see Rákosi 2014 for an overview). As is the case with particles derived from case-like Ps (see (32) and (33)), the plural particle is only available if the noun phrase complement of the adposition has animate reference. Compare the standard (37a) and its plural variant (37b).

(37) a. Feri rá-rivallt a gyerekek-re.
Feri onto-yell.Past.3Sg the child.Pl-Sub
'Feri yelled at the children.'

b. %Feri rájuk-rivallt a gyerekek-re.
Feri onto.3Pl-yell.Past.3Sg the child.Pl-Sub
'Feri yelled at the children.'

That this variation is more substantial for speakers accepting both varieties than variation in the spellout of number features is suggested by at least the following consideration. If the PP complement is an anaphor, then the plural particle is ungrammatical even for speakers who otherwise accept it in (37b):

(38) a. A gyerekek rá-rivalltak egymás-ra
the child.Pl onto-yell.Past.3Pl each.other-Sub
'The children yelled at each other.'

b. *A gyerekek rájuk rivalltak egymás-ra.
the child.Pl onto.3Pl yell.Past.3Pl each.other-Sub
Intended meaning: 'The children yelled at each other.'

If the plural particle is a pronominal element, then its presence simply induces a locality violation: a pronoun cannot have a coreferring antecedent in the same clause. Since (38a) is grammatical for all speakers, we can conclude that the particle *rá* 'onto' is not a PP with a pronoun complement in the duplicating construction. It is certainly not marked for NUMBER, though it may be specified for PERSON.

The issue is further complicated by the fact that though pronominal PPs normally do not participate in the duplicating construction, they may occasionally do so under special circumstances. If the pronoun receives a discourse function (by, for example, appearing with the discourse particle *is* 'too'), then both the particle and the pronoun complement can be spelled out simultaneously. This is an option for practically all speakers in third person (39a-a'), irrespective of whether the pronominal PP is postverbal or in the preverbal field. Judgements are more complex in first or second person. The default form of the particle is acceptable for some speakers if the pronominal PP is postverbal (39b), but not when it is preverbal (39b'). The agreement features of the pronoun complement can also be copied onto the particle, with the result being subject to variable acceptability when the PP is postverbal (39c). The construction is generally judged acceptable if the pronominal PP is preverbal (39c').

(39) a. Én rá-néztem ő-rá is.
I onto-look.Past.3Sg (s)he-Sub.3Sg too
'I did look at him, too.'

a'. Én ő-rá is rá-néztem.
I (s)he-Sub.3Sg too onto-look.Past.3Sg
'I looked at him, too.'

b. %Én rá-néztem te-rád is.
I onto-look.Past.3Sg you-Sub.2Sg too
'I did look at you, too.'

b'. *Én te-rád is rá-néztem.
I you-Sub.2Sg too onto-look.Past.3Sg
intended meaning: 'I looked at you, too.'

c. %Én rád-néztem te-rád is.
I onto.2Sg-look.Past.3Sg you-Sub.2Sg too
'I did look at you, too.'

c'. Én te-rád is rád-néztem.
I you-Sub.2Sg too onto.2Sg-look.Past.3Sg
'I looked at you, too.'

Thus in non-third persons the fully agreeing variety is preferred, but only if the pronominal PP is preverbal (39c'), or else there is no optimal solution (39b-c).

5.3. Core and non-core PP arguments

5.3.1. Two types of participant PPs: an overview

A prototypical PP argument is both selected and subcategorized for by the verb. We regard such PPs as **core arguments** of the verb. Consider (40) for illustration.

(40) a. Mindez *(Péter-re) vall.
all.this Péter-Sub bespeak.3Sg
'All this sounds like Péter.'

b. *Mindez Péter-hez vall.
all.this Péter-All bespeak.3Sg
Intended meaning: 'All this sounds like Péter.'

(40a) shows us that the sublative PP is obligatory in this use of the verb, and (40b) illustrates that the morphological coding of this PP is lexically determined; no other adposition can substitute for the sublative case that the verb requires. With other verbal predicates, PP arguments may also be left implicit in facilitating discourse settings. (41) features a dative experiencer verb, and (41b) specifically shows that such PP omission is licit in this case.

(41) a. Nagyon tetszett nekem a film.
very_much appeal.Past.3Sg Dat-1Sg the movie
'I very much liked the movie.'

b. Nagyon tetszett a film. Jó, hogy elment-ünk.
very_much appeal.Past.3Sg the movie good that away.go.Past-1Pl
'I very much liked the movie. It is good that we went.'

c. *Nagyon tetszett számomra a film.
very_much appeal.Past.3Sg for.me the movie
'*The movie very much appealed for me.'

The verb *tetszik* 'appeal, like' expresses a relation between a subject matter of emotion and an individual who is construed as the attitude holder. This attitude holder is the speaker both in (41b) and (41b), irrespective of whether the 1Sg dative argument is spelled out or not. The existence of such a specific attitude holder (or a group of them) is entailed in each use of this verbal predicate. In this semantic sense, the dative argument of *tetszik* 'appeal to, like' is never optional, and we regard it as a core argument. Its morphology is not subject to variation, as is typical of participant PPs selected as core arguments of the verb. This is the reason why (41c) with an alternative adposition fails.

Many other PPs that express different participants of the verbal event do not have these properties, and we can regard them as non-core arguments of the verb. These PPs are optional (they are not entailed by the predicate), and the semantics of their P-head quite transparently frames the interpretation of the PP, describing the nature of the contribution that the referent of the PP makes to the verbal event. The verb *dolgozik* 'work', for example, can combine with several participant PPs of this kind.

(42) • Non-core arguments of the verb *dolgozik* 'work'

a. Éva Kati-nak dolgozik.
Éva Kati-Dat work.3Sg
'Éva works for Kati.'

b. Éva Kati-nál dolgozik.
Éva Kati-Ade work.3Sg
'Éva works at Kati's place.'

c. Éva Kati-ért dolgozik.
Éva Kati-Cau work.3Sg
'Éva works for (the benefit of) Kati.'

d. Éva Kati-val dolgozik.
Éva Kati-Ins work.3Sg
'Éva works with Kati.'

e. Éva az új darab-on dolgozik.
Éva the new play-Sup work.3Sg
'Éva is working on the new play.'

The dative PP in (42a) can be interpreted as a proper recipient – Kati will receive what Éva creates –, and we can alternatively construe Kati also as the employer. The adessive PP in (42b) either describes the location of the working event, or, by implicature, it can also identify Kati as Éva's employer. The causal-final suffix on the PP in (42c) denotes a beneficiary, and the instrumental suffix in (42d) is a device to present Kati as Éva's associate during the work. Finally, the superessive case morphology in (42e) allows us to express the target of Éva's working activity.

This section probes into the nature of these two distinct types of coding of participant PPs in Hungarian. In particular, we focus on representative construction types where the same case morphology turns up both in the core and the non-core argument domain on PPs that have converging semantic-conceptual types and non-identical grammatical properties. One important correlate of this divide is that the case morphology that is used on arguments may be in competition with other morphological devices in the non-core domain. We have seen in (41) above that dative experiencer arguments can only be marked with dative case. But there are verbal predicates that license such experiencers optionally, and then dative is not the only possible coding tool:

(43) a. Ez nem jelent semmi-t.
this not mean.3Sg nothing-Acc
'This does not mean anything.'

b. Ez nem jelent semmi-t nek-em.
this not mean.3Sg nothing-Acc Dat-1Sg
'This does not mean anything to me.'

c. Ez nem jelent semmi-t számomra.
this not mean.3Sg nothing-Acc for.me
'This does not mean anything for me.'

The holder of the mental state described by the verb *jelent* 'mean' may either be coded with dative case (43b) or with the postposition *számára* 'for' (43c), and both sentences can be true under the same conditions. But it is also an option not to name such a participant and not to imply that there is one specific attitude holder in the discourse. (43a) can be used as an objective description, without any specific experiencer(s) in mind. In other words, (43a) is a construction where the experiencer is not represented at any relevant level of linguistic representation. Thus the PP in (43b) and (43c) is genuinely introduced into the construction, and this PP is a non-core argument in our terms (see Section 5.3.2 below for more on this).

Remark 5. What we call here *non-core arguments* are thus optional complements of the verb. They are optional in the strong sense of the word, since they are not included in the core argument list of the verb. We could alternatively consider them adjuncts for this reason (see also Chapter 7). Since a more fine-grained representation of the syntax of these constructions lies beyond the reach of our primarily descriptive goals, we continue referring to these optional participant PPs as non-core argument PPs. This is also in line with the more traditional approach to the description of argument structure phenomena, where such PPs are regularly discussed as arguments.

The different types of adpositions identified in Chapter 2 of this volume are not created equal inasmuch as they do not have the same potential to be used in the argument domain. The less grammaticalized, borderline cases of postpostions discussed in Section 2.4 are never subcategorized for. *Számára* 'for' is one of these, and it is only found outside of the core argument domain in cases like (43) above, where it is never the sole morphological option. It can often be replaced by a dative PP without changing the propositional meaning of the clause. Case-like Ps, and to a lesser degree, case-assigning Ps are attested in the subcategorization frames of certain verbs. Even if they do not contribute their basic (spatial) meaning, they may have a recognizable function across different occurrences, as in the following examples:

(44) • The case-like postposition *mellett* 'next to' on non-spatial arguments

a. A változás mellett döntött-em.
the change next_to decide.Past-1Sg
'I decided on change.'

b. Kiállt-am János mellett.
stand.Past-1Sg János next.to
'I stood by János.'

c. Kati Klára mellett szólt a gyűlés-en
Kati Klára next.to speak.Past.3Sg the meeting-Sup
'Kati spoke for Klára at the meeting.'

In each of these three examples, the agent performs an action targeted at facilitating the realization of a certain cause. This conceptual content is relatively consistently represented by the case-like postposition *mellett* 'next to'. But this pattern is restricted to a handful of verbs at most. We cannot productively supplement any potential verbal candidate with this postposition to arrive at the meaning characterized above.

More productive patterns in argument realization are much more likely to employ case suffixes, the most grammaticalized type of adpositions. We discuss here three such productive argument realization patterns: the expression of participant phrases marked by dative case, instrumental (or comitative) case, and ablative case. The discussion involves a systematic comparison of core and non-core arguments marked by the same case morphology and belonging to the same broader conceptual type. The case marker is the sole option in the core argument domain, but it is in competition with postpositional P-markers in the non-core argument domain. Time and space denoting argument PPs merit closer attention on their own right, and we conclude the discussion of verbal argument PPs with some remarks on these PP types.

5.3.2. Dative case and its competitors: recipients and experiencers

5.3.2.1. Recipients

Dative case functions as the primary means of marking recipients in Hungarian. Dative-marking on recipient arguments normally implies that the transmission described by the verb is successful. In the examples in (45) below, this means that Péter receives the ten-dollar sum (45a), Péter hears and processes the joke (45b), or the greeting probably goes through to Péter (45c). In other words, the dative participant usually becomes a possessor at the end of the event (albeit in a more figurative sense of the word in (45b) and (45c): the message comes to the possession of Péter). This is the normal course of events, since (45c), for example, can also be true if Péter misses the greetings. But it is still presupposed that the dative participant is a potential recipient, and (45c) is not felicitous in a context in which Péter is asleep or unconscious.

(45) • Dative-marked recipient arguments

a. János adott 10 dollár-t Péter-nek.
János give.Past.3Sg 10 dollar-Acc Péter-Dat
'János gave Péter 10 dollars.'

b. Kati mondott Péter-nek egy vicc-et.
Kati tell.Past.3Sg Péter-Dat a joke-Acc
'Kati told Péter a joke.'

c. Kati hangosan köszönt Péter-nek.
Kati loudly greet.Past.3Sg Péter-Dat
'Kati said hello to Péter in a loud voice.'

Most of the verbs with dative recipient arguments do not necessarily denote movement in the true physical sense of the word. (45a) is true, for example, if János transfers the money to Péter's bank account.

Remark 6. Genuinely spatial uses of dative morphology are also frequent. In example (i) and (ii), the dative PP is interpreted as a spatial goal, as it denotes the endpoint of movement:

(i) Az autó a fal-nak ütközött.
the car the wall-Dat bump.Past.3Sg
'The car bumped into the wall.'

(ii) Judit-nak dobt-am a labdá-t.
Judit-Dat throw.Past-1Sg the ball-Acc
'I threw the ball to Judit.' or 'I threw the ball at Judit.'

In a few examples, the dative PP expresses a direction, that is, it refers to a potential endpoint along a path. This endpoint is not necessarily reached.

(iii) A hajó észak-nak / [észak felé] tartott.
the ship north-Dat / north towards head.Past.3Sg
'The ship headed towards the north.'

(iv) %Miskolc-nak / [Miskolc felé] megyünk.
Miskolc-Dat / Miskolc towards go.1Pl
'We are going in the direction of Miskolc.'

The case-like postposition *felé* 'towards' is the unmarked choice in standard Hungarian both in (iii) and in (iv). The dative version of (iv) is distinctively dialectal. The apparent scarcity of directional uses indicates that dative-marking on goals and recipients requires the completion of the movement described by the verb in the prototypical case.

Recipients can also be expressed with the postpositions *részére* 'for him/her' and *számára* 'for him, her' (see Chapter 2 Section 2.4 of this volume for more on these). Verbs that do not entail a transfer of possession, and which therefore do not take recipient arguments, generally allow the insertion of a non-core recipient argument if such an extra participant can be included in the event denoted by the verb. (46) is an example.

(46) a. Az iskola külön asztal-t foglalt a tanár-ok számára / részére.
the school separate table-Acc reserve.Past.3Sg the teacher-Pl for / for
'The school reserved a separate table for the teachers.'

b. Az iskola külön asztal-t foglalt a tanár-ok-nak.
the school separate table-Acc reserve.Past.3Sg the teacher-Pl-Dat
'The school reserved a separate table for the teachers.'

There appears to be no strong truth-conditional difference at first sight between the dative version (46b) and the postpositional varieties (46a) of this sentence. These PPs are nevertheless not equivalent, as becomes evident in other contexts.

Note first that neither postposition can appear in argument positions (47c). (47a) does not contradict this claim since this sentence must be interpreted with an implicit (dative) recipient argument, someone who directly receives the money, and the overt PP itself denotes a secondary recipient. This secondary recipient, János, will become the ultimate possessor of the 10 dollar sum once it is handed over to him. (47b) explicitly spells this scenario out with an overt dative argument and the non-core secondary recipient PP marked by either of the two postpositions.

(47) a. Péter át-adott 10 dollár-t János részére / számára.
Péter over-give.Past.3Sg 10 dollar-Acc János for / for
'Péter gave over 10 dollars for János.'

b. Péter át-adott 10 dollár-t az alapítvány-nak
Péter over-give.Past.3Sg 10 dollar-Acc the foundation-Dat
János részére / számára.
János for / for
'Péter gave over 10 dollars to the charity foundation for John.'

c. *Kati hangosan köszönt Péter részére / számára.
Kati loudly greet.Past.3Sg Péter for / for
Intended meaning: 'Kati said hello to Péter in a loud voice.'

The postposition *részére* 'for him/her' is not acceptable in contexts in which no obvious recipient is present and transfer of possession does not obviously take place, whereas dative case and the postposition *számára* 'for him/her' are compatible with such contexts.

(48) Talált-am nek-ed / számodra / ??részedre egy érdekes hír-t.
find.Past-1Sg Dat-2Sg / for.2Sg / for.2Sg an interesting news-Acc
'I found an interesting piece of news for you.'

The interpretation of the dative PP and the PP headed by *számodra* 'for you' may have beneficiary overtones in (48) and in other contexts as well. Nevertheless, beneficiaries that are not construed as recipients are usually expressed by alternative P-markers, with the causal-final suffix being a prime vehicle for this function. Thus whereas the dative or the postposition in (49a) identify an extra participant who is the receiver of the song in some sense of the word (the song might be dedicated to this person, or this person will perform the song), (49b) only conveys the message that the addressee will somehow benefit from this song. For example, it will help raise public awareness towards a particular cause that benefits the addressee.

(49) a. Írt-am nek-ed / számodra egy dal-t.
write.Past Dat-2Sg / for.2Sg a song-Acc
'I wrote a song to/for you.'

b. Írt-am ért-ed egy dal-t.
write.Past-1Sg Cau-2Sg a song-Acc
'I wrote a song for (the benefit of) you.'

The verb *write* is a two-place predicate, and it does not entail the existence of either a recipient or a beneficiary. One can just simply write a song without having anybody else in mind who will receive or benefit from this song in some way. But it is an option to introduce an extra participant of this kind, and then we see the morphological variation that (49) attests, with concomitant fine-grained variation in the interpretation of the PP. If a recipient argument is entailed by the verb, as in the examples in (45), then the verb typically subcategorizes for dative case on this argument, and no other adposition is grammatical.

Thus the data that we have surveyed in this subsection illustrate the typical distribution of case morphology and postpostional P-markers across complements of the verb: dative case is used on recipient arguments, whereas secondary recipients and beneficiaries, qua non-core arguments, are either expressed as dative or as postpositional PPs. Dative case is a heavily grammaticalized element of the large set of adpositions, but the postpostions *részére* 'for him' and *számára* 'for him' are less so. As discussed in Chapter 2 of this volume, many adpositions originate as possessive constructions, and this possessive character is especially visible with the two postpositions discussed in this section (see also Section 2.4). One manifestation of this is the optional use of the definite article by the pronominal forms of these adpositions.

Remark 7. Pronominal possessors and the definite article are not in complementary distribution in Hungarian. In fact, the article is obligatory if the pronominal possessor is overt:

(i) az én apám-nak
the I father.Poss.1Sg-Dat
'to my father'

The article can often be dropped in spoken registers if the possessum is uniquely identifiable through the possessor. The possessor is typically inalienable in this case, see (50a) in the main text below. Note that possessive postpositions *részére* 'for him' and *számára* 'for him' are inalienable possessive constructions historically.

Consider the data in (50) for illustration.

(50) • Variation in article use

a. Vett-em egy kabát-ot (az) apám-nak.
buy.Past-1Sg a coat-Acc the father.Poss.1Sg-Dat
'I bought a coat for my father.'

b. Vett-em egy kabát-ot (a) részére / számára.
buy.Past-1Sg a coat-Acc the for.3Sg / for.3Sg
'I bought a coat for him.'

c. Vett-em egy kabát-ot (*a) nek-i.
buy.Past-1Sg a coat-Acc the Dat-3Sg
'I bought him a coat.'

If the pronominal possessor is not spelled out, the definite article is often optional in the possessive noun phrase with inalienable possessums. The kinship term in (50) is inalienably possessed, and the article can be omitted. The pronominal postpositions *részére* and *számára* 'for him' usually appear without a definite article, but they are just as grammatical in its presence (50b). The dative-marked form of a pronoun, however, is not compatible with the definite article, instructing us that the grammaticalization process has gone much further in the case of the case marker than in the case of the postpositions in (50b).

Remark 8. Another interesting difference between dative case and these two postpositions concerns the selectional restrictions that they impose on their complements. Dative case shows essentially no such restrictions, and anything that can be conceived of as a recipient in some sense can be marked with dative case.

(i) Faragt-am egy új láb-at [a kalóz-nak] / [a kutyá-nak] / [a szék-nek].
carve.Past-1Sg a new leg-Acc the pirate-Dat / the dog-Dat / the chair-Dat
'I carved a new leg for the pirate / for the dog / for the chair.'

Of the two postpositions, *számára* 'for him' is acceptable for most speakers with referents higher up on the animacy scale, but *részére* 'for him' is preferably used only to pick human participants.

(ii) Faragt-am egy új láb-at [a kalóz] / [a kutya] /
carve.Past-1Sg a new leg-Acc the pirate / the dog /
[*a szék] számára
the chair for.3Sg
'I carved a new leg [for the pirate] / [for the dog] / [for the chair].'

(iii) Faragt-am egy új láb-at [a kalóz] / [?a kutya] /
carve.Past-1Sg a new leg-Acc the pirate / the dog /
[*a szék] részére
the chair for.3Sg
'I carved a new leg for the pirate / for the dog / for the chair.'

These semantic restrictions are not specific to the contexts discussed in this subsection, but they generally characterize the use of these postpositions (see also the next subsection for pertinent data).

5.3.2.2. Dative experiencers

Experiencers represent another domain where dative case is used in Hungarian. Verbs can either take dative experiencers as core arguments (51), or as non-core arguments (52).

(51) • Dative experiencer arguments

a. Az ilyesmi tetszik János-nak.
the such_thing appeal.3Sg János-Dat
'János likes such things.'

b. Az ilyesmi derogál János-nak.
the such_thing is_below_dignity John-Dat
'Such things are below János's dignity.'

c. Hirtelen be-ugrott a megoldás János-nak.
suddenly in-jumped.3Sg the solution János-Dat
'The solution suddenly clicked for János.'

d. Be-jön nek-em ez az életmód.
in-come.3Sg Dat-1Sg this the life_style
'I like this lifestyle.'

(52) • Non-core dative experiencer PPs

a. Ez a város nagyon megfelel Feri-nek.
this the town very_much suit.3Sg Feri-Dat
'This town is very much suitable for Feri.'

b. Egyedül te számítasz nek-em.
only you matter.2Sg Dat-1Sg
'Only you matter to me.'

c. Feri-nek kell egy új kabát.
Feri-Dat need.3Sg a new coat
'Feri needs a new coat.'

d. Bevált az új rendszer mindenki-nek.
worked_well.3Sg the new system everyone-Dat
'This new system has worked well for everyone.'

Verbs in the first group (51) denote mental states of specific individuals, who have the respective dispositions towards a certain subject matter that the nominative subject refers to. Verbs in the second group can also express an individualized relation of this kind, but they are also capable of assigning a more objective construal to the subject matter argument, where the role of specific experiencers is backgrounded or it is missing altogether.

The two types of dative PPs differ accordingly. Both types are optional in the syntactic sense, since even dative experiencer arguments can be omitted in Hungarian in facilitating discourse contexts (see also 5.3.1). But dative experiencer arguments are always entailed, and in the absence of an overt spellout, they are interpreted as specific implicit arguments. In the usual case, a dative experiencer verb without an overt dative PP makes a claim about the speaker's attitudes (53a). Verbs licensing non-core dative experiencer arguments may actually be interpreted without any reference to such an implicit experiencer or a group of them. (53b) is a well-formed description of a property of the subject argument – the prominent property of the system that it has worked well –, and this statement is not particularized to the mental state of any specific groups of speakers.

(53) • Optionality

a. Be-jön ez az életmód.
in-come.3Sg this the life_style
'I like this lifestyle.'

b. Bevált az új rendszer.
worked_well.3Sg the new system
'This new system has worked well.'

Another semantic difference between the two types of dative PPs concerns the availability of non-experiencer readings only in the second group. Dative arguments of dative experiencer verbs must be interpreted as experiencers (54a), whereas this is not necessary in the case of non-core dative experiencer PPs (54b).

(54) • Non-experiencer readings

a. #Az ilyesmi derogál János-nak akkor is, ha nem tud ról-a.
the such_thing is_below_dignity János-Dat then too if not know.3Sg Del-3Sg
'Such things are below János's dignity, even if he does not know about it.'

b. Ez a város nagyon megfelel Péter-nek akkor is, ha
this the town very_much suit.3Sg Péter-Dat then too if
nem tud róla.
not know.3Sg Del-3Sg
'This town is very much suitable for Péter, even if he does not know about it.'

It follows from this that the dative arguments of experiencer verbs must refer to human beings (55a). Interestingly, this is not required in the case of verbs that take optional dative experiencer PPs (55b).

(55) • Non-experiencer readings

a. #Az ilyesmi derogál ennek a fafaj-nak.
the such_thing is_below_dignity this.Dat the tree_species-Dat
'#Such things are below the dignity of this tree species.'

b. Ez a város nagyon megfelel ennek a fafaj-nak.
this the town very_much suit.3Sg this.Dat the tree_species-Dat
'This town is very much suitable for this tree species.'

(55b) obviously does not describe the mental states of these trees, but their propensity to grow well in this particular habitat.

There is no competitor for dative case in the argument domain, but the postposition *számára* 'for him' is an alternative marker on non-core experiencer arguments. In fact, both types of adpositions license both the experiencer and the non-experiencer reading in the latter case, though *számára* might be more geared towards the non-experiencer reading in some contexts. So, other things being equal, the choice of the dative case in (56b) is the preferred vehicle to host the experiencer reading. The postposition *számára* 'for him' is preferred when others decide about Feri's fate, and he might not even know about the town at the time of speaking.

(56) • Morphological variation

a. Hirtelen be-ugrott a megoldás János-nak / [*János számára].
suddenly in-jumped.3Sg the solution János-Dat / János for
'The solution suddenly clicked for János.'

b. Ez a város nagyon megfelel Feri-nek / [Feri számára].
this the town very_much suit.3Sg Feri-Dat / Feri for
'This town is very much suitable for Feri.'

We noted above (see Remark 8) that whereas dative case imposes no selectional restrictions on its complement, *számára* 'for him' may only take noun phrases that refer to entities higher up on the animacy scale. Flowers may represent a borderline case in this respect (57a), but the postposition is only a slightly acceptable choice at best when we are discussing clothes (57b).

(57) • Animacy restrictions

a. Ez a víz megfelel [a virág-ok-nak] / [?a virág-ok számára].
this the water suit.3Sg the flower-Pl-Dat / the flower-Pl for
'This water is suitable for flowers.'

b. Ez a víz megfelel [a ruhá-k-nak] / [??/*a ruhá-k számára].
this the water suit.3Sg the clothes-Pl-Dat / the clothes-Pl for
'This water is suitable for the clothes.'

Such idiosyncratic referential constraints do not nevertheless disturb the emerging picture, which once again depicts competition between a case marker and a postposition only in the non-core argument domain, with dative case being the sole option in the case of experiencer PPs selected as arguments of the verb.

5.3.3. Instrumental case: comitatives and instruments

5.3.3.1. Comitatives

Instrumental case is the primary morphology used in comitative and instrumental PPs. We discuss these two distinct functions in these two consecutive subsections, starting with comitatives. Comitative PPs denote participants who accompany the agent (expressed as the subject argument), and who are themselves intentional agents playing a causal role in the unfolding of the event denoted by the verb. We argue here that comitative PPs fall into two major categories: they can be the core arguments of causative and reciprocal verbs, and they are also licensed as non-core comitative PPs by agentive verbs in general.

Hungarian has productive causative morphology that expands the argument structure of the input verb by adding an agent to it. This new argument is expressed as the subject of the causativized verb, and it denotes a participant who is causally responsible for initiating the event described by the verbal stem. The original agent of this event (the subject argument of the input verb) bears instrumental case if the input verb is transitive. In the examples below, (58a) and (58b) are the input transitive constructions, and (58a') and (58b') are the causativized varieties, respectively.

(58) • Causative verbs: transitive inputs

a. A diák-ok meg-ír-t-ák a teszt-et.
the student-Pl Perf-write-Past-3Pl the test-Acc
'The students wrote the test.'

a'. A tanár meg-ír-at-t-a a diák-ok-kal a teszt-et.
the teacher Perf-write-Caus-Past-3Sg the student-Pl-Ins the test-Acc
'The teacher had the students write the test.'

b. Az autószerelő meg-javít-ott-a a kocsi-m-at.
the car_mechanic Perf-repair-Past-3Sg the car-Poss.1Sg-Acc
'The car mechanic repaired my car.'

b'. Meg-javít-tat-t-am a kocsi-m-at az autószerelő-vel.
Perf-repair-Caus-Past-1Sg the car-Poss.1Sg-Acc the car_mechanic-Ins
'I had my car repaired by the car mechanic.'

The PP in the causative sentences denotes a secondary agent, as it were: a participant who is the immediate agent of the respective writing and repairing events, but who acts under the subject argument's influence. If the input verb is intransitive, then the causativized version is usually a transitive verb, expressing the input agent as the object of the clause. The demoted agent can nevertheless also be expressed alternatively as an instrumental PP in certain cases, and we may find minimal pairs of the following kind:

(59) • Causative verbs: intransitive input

a. Miért dolgoz-tat-od ez-t az ember-t?
why work-Caus-2Sg this-Acc the person-Acc
'Why do you make this person work?'

b. Miért dolgoz-tat-sz ez-zel az ember-rel?
why work-Caus-2Sg this-Ins the person-Ins
'Why do you have this person work? / Why do you employ this person to work?'

Accusative marking on the demoted agent implies that this person is directly controlled by the addressee. The alternative construction with instrumental case is used when the agent of the working event is free(r) to act on his or her own, and the subject of the causativized verb (the addressee in (59b)) has no direct control over this process beyond initiating it.

Instrumental marking also spells out this comitative, secondary agent role in reciprocal verb constructions. The core set of reciprocal verbs are derived from transitive verbs, and they denote events in which the individuals denoted by the subject and the instrumental PP act in a more or less symmetrical manner. Consider (60) for illustration:

(60) • Reciprocal verbs derived from transitive verbs

a. Kati meg-csókol-t-a Péter-t.
Kati Perf-kiss-Past-3Sg Péter-Acc
'Kati kissed Péter.'

a'. Kati csókol-óz-ott Péter-rel.
Kati kiss-Rec-Past.3Sg Péter-Ins
'Kati was involved in a mutual kissing activity with Péter.'

b. Kati ver-i Péter-t.
Kati beat-3Sg Péter-Acc
'Kati beats Péter.'

b'. Kati ver-eked-ik Péter-rel.
Kati beat-Rec-3Sg Péter-Ins
'Kati is exchanging blows with Péter.'

The transitive sort of kissing is asymmetric, Péter need not kiss Kati back (60a). This cannot be the case with the reciprocal version (60a'), where both participants are involved in the event to the same extent. The transitive verb *ver* 'beat' is also unidirectional in terms of the causal influence of one participant over the other (60b), unlike (60b'), where the blows are necessarily reciprocated.

The set of reciprocal verbs derived from transitive inputs is relatively small, but any verbal predicate describing potentially symmetric events requiring a partner may be used in the comitative construction represented by the primed-examples in (60). Some relevant examples are listed in (61).

(61) • Verbs of social interaction

a. Kati beszélget Évá-val.
Kati talk.3Sg Éva-Ins
'Kati is conversing with Kate.'

b. Kati küzd Évá-val.
Kati fight.3Sg Éva-Ins
'Kati is fighting with Éva.'

c. Kati sakkozik Évá-val.
Kati play_chess.3Sg Éva-Ins
'Kati is playing chess with Éva.'

These comitative PPs denote participants who act as partners in the social activity described. Verbs of social interaction that allow for non-symmetric construals may take other adpositional markers to indicate the lack of symmetry. (62) is to be compared to (61b) in this respect.

(62) Kati küzd Éva ellen.
Kati fight.3Sg Éva against
'Kati is fighting against Éva.'

Remark 9. Many verbs of social interaction are complexes formed with the particle *össze* 'together' or with the particle *együtt* 'together'. The former often implies some directionality, in the sense that the two participants come to occupy the same location during the event (albeit in a metaphorical sense in examples like (ii)).

(i) Géza össze-költözött Adrienn-nel.
Géza together-move.Past.3Sg Adrienn-Ins
'Géza moved in together with Adrienn.'

(ii) Géza össze-fogott Adrienn-nel.
Géza together-hold.Past.3Sg Adrienn-Ins
'Géza joined forces with Adrienn.'

Együtt 'together' is a case-assigning postposition that requires instrumental case on its complement. It functions as a verbal particle with many verbs of social interaction, and the resulting particle-verb complex takes a comitative argument bearing instrumental case.

(iii) Péter együtt-működik Bélá-val.
Péter together-operate.3Sg Béla-Ins
'Péter cooperates with Béla.'

(iv) Kati együtt-maradt Péter-rel.
Kati together-stay.Past.3Sg Péter-Ins
'Kati stayed together with Péter.'

We note that the comitative construction discussed here is one of the two alternative syntactic realizations of symmetric verbs. The participants of these events can also be expressed via a plural subject argument without an accompanying comitative PP. Below are such alternatives to two of the comitative constructions from the main text ((60a') and (61b)).

(v) Kati és Péter csókol-óz-t-ak.
Kati and Péter kiss-Rec-Past.3Pl
'Kati and Péter were involved in a mutual kissing activity.'

(vi) Kati és Éva küzd-enek.
Kati and Éva fight-3Pl
'Kati and Éva are fighting.'

We refer the reader to the volume on Verb Phrases for a discussion of semantic differences between the comitative construction and this plural subject construction.

The instrumental PPs of causative verbs and of verbs of social interaction form one natural class that we regard here as **comitative arguments**. They contrast with non-core comitative arguments, which are optional participants that can freely be inserted into clauses if the event denoted can contain individuals who accompany the subject argument.

(63) • Optional comitative PPs

a. Kati level-et írt Évá-val.
   Kati letter write.Past.3Sg Éva-Ins
   'Kati wrote a letter with Éva'

b. Kati Évá-val tanul.
   Kati Éva-Ins study.3Sg
   'Kati is studies with Éva.'

c. Kati haza-megy Évá-val.
   Kati home-go.3Sg Éva-Ins
   'Kati goes home with Éva.'

The referent of this comitative PP normally performs the same activity that the subject argument does, though in some cases it might be interpreted to take on a less active role. (63c), for example, allows for a reading where Éva is carried home by Kati, and she does not perform a movement activity herself.

The differences between these non-core PPs and core comitative PPs are systematic. The PPs in (63) are all optional, and if they are not present in the clause, then the existence of the respective participants is not entailed. We do not need a partner for writing a letter, sleeping or going home. True comitative arguments, however, are obligatory, in certain cases even in the strict syntactic sense of the word. The comitative PP cannot be dropped in the following causative (64a) and reciprocal verb (64b) constructions.

(64) • Obligatory comitative arguments

a. Én *(vel-ük) dolgoz-tat-ok.
   I Ins-3Pl work-Caus-1Sg
   'As for me, I employ them (for such jobs).'

b. Kati *(Évá-val) talál-koz-ott.
   Kati Éva-Ins find-Rec-Past.3Sg
   'Kati met Éva.'

The comitative argument may remain implicit in the case of other verbs in these two groups, but its existence is still entailed.

(65) • Implicit comitative arguments

a. A tanár meg-ír-at-t-a a dolgozat-ot.
   the teacher Perf-write-Caus-Past-3Sg the test-Acc
   'The teacher had the test written (by someone/some individuals).'

b. Kati csókol-óz-ott.
   Kati kiss-Rec-Past.3Sg
   'Kati was involved in a mutual kissing activity (with someone).'

Instrumental case is not the sole option in the case of non-core comitatives, which may also be marked by other means. Such PPs can be headed by the case-assigning postposition *együtt* 'together' – which requires instrumental case on its complement (66a) –, or they can be expressed through a periphrastic phrase like *társaságában* 'in the company of'.

(66) • Non-core comitatives: variation in form
a. Kati Évá-val együtt tanul.
Kati Éva-Ins together study.3Sg
'Kati is studying together with Éva.'
b. Kati haza-megy Éva társaság-á-ban.
Kati home-go.3Sg Éva company-Poss-Ine
'Kati goes home in the company of Éva.'

No such variation is licit if the comitative PP is a core argument:

(67) • Core comitatives: only instrumental case
a. *Én vel-ük együtt dolgoz-tat-ok.
I Ins-3Pl together work-Caus-1Sg
Intended meaning: 'As for me, I employ them (for such jobs).'
b. *Kati Éva társaság-á-ban talál-koz-ott.
Kati Éva company-Poss-Ine find-Rec-Past.3Sg
Intended meaning: 'Kati met Éva.'

Another interesting difference between core and non-core comitative PPs concerns the acceptability of instrumental-case marked reciprocal anaphors. If the subject is a plural noun phrase, then the comitative PP can host the anaphor both in causative (68a) and reciprocal constructions (68b), but the reciprocal anaphor is ungrammatical in Hungarian in non-core comitative PPs (68c).

(68) • Comitative reciprocal anaphors
a. A tanár-ok meg-ír-at-t-ák egymás-sal a teszt-et.
the teacher-Pl Perf-write-Caus-Past-3Pl each_other-Ins the test-Acc
'The teacher had each other write the test.'
b. Kati és Jani csókol-óz-t-ak egymás-sal.
Kati and Jani kiss-Rec-Past.3Pl each_other-Ins
'Kati and Jani were involved in a mutual kissing activity with each other.'
c. *Kati és Éva level-et írt-ak egymás-sal.
Kati and Éva letter-Acc write.Past-3Pl each_other-Ins
Intended meaning: 'Kati and Éva wrote a letter with each other'

These differences all support the argument analysis of instrumental PPs in causative and reciprocal constructions, which are selected and subcategorized for by the verb, unlike non-core comitative PPs, which are not and which show a less constrained grammatical behaviour.

5.3.3.2. Instrument PPs

While the grammatical differences between core and non-core occurrences of comitative PPs are quite prominent, it is less easy to make the same distinction in the domain of instrument PPs. The examples in (69) below illustrate constructions in which instrument PPs are used.

(69) • Instrument PPs

a. A diák-ok virág-ok-kal díszített-ék a táblá-t az iskolá-ban.
the students-Pl flower-Pl-Ins decorate-3Pl the board-Acc the school-Ine
'The students decorated the board with flowers in the school.'

b. Meg-tölt-ött-em a hordó-t víz-zel.
Perf-fill-Past-1Sg the barrel-Acc water-Ins
'I filled the barrel with water.'

c. Az orvos gyógynövény-ek-kel gyógyított-a meg a beteg-et.
the doctor herb-Pl-Ins cure.Past-3Sg Perf the patient-Acc
'The doctor cured the patient with herbs.'

d. Ez-zel a tol-lal írt-am a vers-e-i-m-et.
this-Ins the pen-Ins write.Past-1Sg the poem-Poss-Pl-1Sg-Acc
'I wrote my poems with this pen.'

e. János kalapács-csal tört-e össze a jeg-et.
János hammer-Ins break.Past-3Sg apart the ice-Acc
'János smashed the ice into pieces with a hammer.'

f. Jobban lát-ok az új szemüveg-gel.
better see-1Sg the new glasses-Ins
'I can see better with the new glasses.'

Examples (69d-f) contain optional instrument PPs that are prototypical representatives of this conceptual category. We can use our own body when we smash things and, consequently, instruments are not obligatory participants of breaking events in general. We can also visualize the world around without the help of glasses or other machinery. In a similar manner, one can imagine writing activities in which the human agent uses only his or her fingers to create characters (in the sand, for example), and therefore external instruments are not a conceptual necessity in this case either. On the other hand, the existence of the instrument-marked argument is entailed in examples (69a-c). We need to use some material when we decorate or fill a target location, and curing processes also generally involve some sort of a secondary agent that creates the curative effect. Admittedly, these PPs are less prototypical instances of what we normally consider instruments. The water in (69b), for example, is not a device causally facilitating the filling event to go through, but it is the entity that moves from one position to another. Nevertheless, the three examples in (69a-c) are more obviously core arguments of the verb, the existence of the PP argument is entailed in each case.

One prominent difference between the two groups of verbs concerns the availability of alternations targeting the instrument-marked PP. If this PP is a core argument, then it can also be expressed as the subject of the verb in an alternative argument realization pattern (70a-c). This is usually not an option for non-core instrument PPs (70d-f) in episodic contexts.

(70) • Instrument subjects

a. Virág-ok díszített-ék a táblá-t az iskolá-ban.
flower-Pl decorate-3Pl the board-Acc the school-Ine
'Flowers decorated the wall in the school.'

b. A víz meg-tölt-ötte a hordó-t.
the water Perf-fill-Past-3Sg the barrel-Acc
'The water filled the barrel.'

c. A gyógynövény-ek meg-gyógyított-ák a beteg-et.
the herb-Pl Perf-cure.Past-3Pl the patient-Acc
'The herbs cured the patient.'

d. ??Ez a toll írt-a a vers-e-i-m-et.
this the pen write.Past-3Sg the poem-Poss-Pl-1Sg-Acc
'??This pen wrote my poems.'

e. ?A kalapács össze-tört-e a jeg-et.
the hammer apart-break.Past-3Sg the ice-Acc
'The hammer smashed the ice into pieces.'

f. *Az új szemüveg jobban lát.
the new glasses better see-3Sg
'*The new glasses can see better.'

Non-core instrument PPs can be paraphrased with periphrastic descriptions like *segítségével* 'with the help of', *használatával* 'using' or *alkalmazásával* 'using, with the application of' (71c-d). This is not possible in the case of *díszít* 'decorate' (71a) or *megtölt* 'fill', though such a paraphrase is possible for *meggyógyít* 'cure' (71b).

(71) • Instrument PPs: modifying the adposition

a. *A diák-ok virág-ok segítség-é-vel díszített-ék a táblá-t
the student-Pl flower-Pl help-Poss-Ins decorate.Past-3Pl the board-Acc
az iskolá-ban.
the school-Ine
'*The students decorated the board with the help of flowers in the school.'

b. Az orvos gyógynövény-ek segítség-é-vel gyógyított-a meg a beteg-et.
the doctor herb-Pl help-Poss-Ins cure.Past-3Sg Perf the patient-Acc
'The doctors cured the patient with the help of herbs.'

c. János kalapács segítség-é-vel tört-e össze a jeg-et.
János hammer help-Poss-Ins break.Past-3Sg apart the ice-Acc
'János smashed the ice into pieces with the help of a hammer.'

d. Jobban lát-ok az új szemüveg segítség-é-vel.
better see-1Sg the new glasses help-Poss-Ins
'I can see better with the help of the new glasses.'

Thus the difference between core and non-core instrument PPs is less pronounced than in the case of comitatives, and we seem to be dealing with a cline in this case rather than an absolute dichotomy.

5.3.4. Ablative case and the coding of causes

Causality plays an important role in how we see and describe events of the world, and languages employ intricate machinery to represent causal relations. Hungarian is no exception to this. In this subsection, we describe one prominent pattern in representing causes in the clause: the use of ablative case and cause-denoting postpositions. In this domain, too, these PPs are core arguments of some verbs, and they function as non-core cause arguments elsewhere.

Ablative causes are selected as arguments of a good number of subject experiencer verbs. One group of these verbs are non-derived subject experiencers from the broad set where the English *love* and *hate* belong. What makes this subset special in Hungarian is that their internal argument is a PP, rather than an accusative object. This PP denotes the cause that triggers the respective mental state in the experiencer (72).

(72) • Ablative arguments of non-derived subject experiencers.

Kati fél / retteg / szenved / pánikol a pók-ok-tól.
Kati fear.3Sg / dread.3Sg / suffer.3Sg / panic.3Sg the spider-Pl-Abl
'Kati is afraid of / dreads / suffers because of / panics over spiders.'

Another group of subject experiencers are derived from object experiencer verbs of the *frighten*-type (73). In the subject experiencer version, the cause of the emotional response is expressed as an ablative PP (73b).

(73) • Ablative arguments of derived subject experiencers

a. Kati-t meg-hat-ják / meg-ijeszt-ik / meg-lep-ik a pók-ok.
Kati-Acc Perf-move-3Pl / Perf-frighten-3Pl / Perf-surprise-3Pl the spider-Pl
'Spiders move / frighten / surprise Kati.'

b. Kati meg-hatód-ik / meg-ijed / meg-lepőd-ik a pók-ok-tól.
Kati Perf-be_moved-3Sg / Perf-be_frightened.3Sg / Perf-be_surprised-3Sg the spider-Pl-Abl
'Kati is moved / frightened / surprised by spiders.'

Ablative marking is the dominant pattern across experiencer verbs that entail the existence of a primary cause of the mental state. A few atelic verbs in the object experiencer group, nevertheless, have a subject experiencer alternate which comes with a PP that denotes a target of emotion, rather than a pure cause. Ablative marking is not possible in these cases, and an alternative postposition is used instead. (74) contains two relevant examples.

(74) • Postpositional PPs in derived subject experiencer constructions

a. Kati-t aggaszt-ják / érdekl-ik a pók-ok.
Kati-Acc worry-3Pl / interest-3Pl the spider-Pl
'Spiders worry / interest Kati.'

b. Kati aggód-ik [a pók-ok miatt] / [*a pók-ok-tól].
Kati be_worried-3Sg the spider-3Pl because_of / the spider-3Pl-Abl
'Kati is worried about the spiders.'

c. Kati érdeklőd-ik [a pók-ok iránt] / [*a pók-ok-tól].
Kati be_interested-3Sg the spider-3Pl towards / the spider-3Pl-Abl
'Kati is interested in spiders.'

This PP expressing a target of emotion can be regarded as a secondary, less direct cause that is used instead of the ablative when a direct cause is not compatible with the verbal event.

Ablative causes are also compatible with anticausative verbs. This is a large group of derived verbal predicates, which do not entail the presence of a causer but which are compatible with one. The ablative PP functions as a non-core argument in this case. Anticausative verbs are derived from transitive verbs whose subject is either an agent or a non-agentive cause.

(75) • The causative-anticausative alternation
a. Kati / [A huzat] be-tört-e az ablak-ot.
Kati / the draught in-break.Past-3Sg the window-Acc
'Kati / [The draught] broke the window.'
b. Az ablak be-tört (a huzat-tól /*Kati-tól).
the window in-break.Past.3Sg the draught-Abl / Kati-Abl
'The window broke from [the draught] / *Kati.'

The ablative is optional in the intransitive version, and one may decide to augment this description with the inclusion of a causer, or leave it out altogether. The insertion of the ablative phrase in anticausatives is a productive pattern, unlike in English, where the corresponding *from*-phrases often have a marked character. A strong constraint on these PPs is that they cannot denote agents, hence the ungrammaticality of *Katitól* 'from Kati' in (75b).

Remark 10. The constraint against agents is not specific to ablative case itself, but is a property of the anticausative construction. This case marker could function as an adposition marking *by*-phrases in passive constructions in earlier stages of Hungarian. It has been replaced by the case-like postposition *által* 'by' in this use, though some speakers still find ablative case an alternative in participial constructions:

(i) %Testőrök-től / [Testőrök által] körülvé-ve,
bodyguards-Abl / bodyguards by surround-Part,
az elnök elhagyt-a a palotá-t.
the president left-3Sg the palace-Acc
'Surrounded by bodyguards, the president left the palace.'

Ablative case is not necessarily the only option in the intransitive construction represented by (75b), since other adpositions are also available to express causes. The variation in the choice of the adposition correlates with the nature of the causal chain that is described. Consider the following sentences for illustration:

(76) • Cause-PPs in anticausatives
a. Az ablak be-tört a szél-től.
the window in-break.Past.3Sg the wind-Abl
'The window broke from the wind.'

b.

Az	ablak	be-tört	a	szél	miatt.
the	window	in-break.Past.3Sg	the	wind	because_of

'The window broke because of the wind.'

c.

Az	ablak	be-tört	a	szél-ben.
the	window	in-break.Past.3Sg	the	wind-Ine

'The window broke in the wind.'

The ablative in (76a) denotes a direct cause, whereas the case-like postposition *miatt* 'because of' can be used to code any indirect causal relation between the breaking of the window and the wind (76b). Thus (76b) may be true if the wind pushed something against the window, which then broke it. (76a) is not considered true in such situations. The inessive PP in (76c) is not a primary cause marker, it is only through extra reasoning that we establish a causal relation between the breaking of the window and the wind. This relation does not have to be a direct causal relation, either.

Anticausative PPs are therefore non-core arguments of decausativized transitive verbs. They are not entailed by the intransitive verb, and their adposition is not selected by the verb. They contrast with the subject experiencers surveyed above, which do entail the existence of a cause, and which only license a specific adpositional marker to express it. The difference between the two types of ablative PP is especially clear if their complement is the reflexive anaphor. The ablative PP in the anticausative construction has the idiosyncratic meaning 'by itself, without any external cause'.

(77) • Anticausatives and a reflexive PP

a.

Az	ablak	magá-tól	be-tört.
the	window	itself-Abl	in-break.Past.3Sg

'The window broke by itself.'

b.

Az	ablak	magá-tól	ki-nyílt.
the	window	itself-Abl	out-open.Past.3Sg

'The window opened by itself.'

We may actually regard these examples as arguments for the default non-causal nature of anticausative descriptions. In contrast, these PPs do not have this idiosyncratic reading with experiencer verbs:

(78) • Subject experiencers and a reflexive PP

a.

Feri	magá-tól	fél.
Feri	himself-Abl	fear.3Sg

'Feri is afraid of himself.'

b.

Feri	magá-tól	ijedt	meg.
Feri	himself-Abl	frighten.Past.3Sg	Perf

'Feri got frightened of himself.'

The two examples in (78) both describe a binary relation between an experiencer and a cause, which happen to coincide in the event under description. In other words, whereas the events described in (78) require the conceptualization of a cause, the events denoted by (77) do not. The variation that we have surveyed here can be once again regarded as variation in coding causes as core argument PPs by a selected group of verbs, or as non-core arguments elsewhere.

5.3.5. Spatiotemporal PPs in the argument domain

Temporal and spatial PPs internal to the verb phrase can be selected by their verbal predicates as core or as non-core arguments, and as a group, they have some characteristic properties that distinguish them from other PP types which deserve particular attention. This section gives an overview of these properties.

Even if such PPs are listed among the arguments of a verbal predicate, it is barely the case that a designated adposition is required in their heads. One pertinent exception is the verb *telik* 'takes a certain amount of time', which takes a PP headed by illative case to measure out the runtime of the event under discussion:

(79) • Temporal argument with designated morphology
[Sok idő-be] / [Három hét-be] / [Négy órá-ba] telt, amíg végezt-ünk.
much time-Ill / three week-Ill / four hour-Ill took.3Sg till finsih.Past-1Pl
'It took us [a lot of time] / [three weeks] / [four hours] to finish.'

The noun phrase complement of this PP can be an expression that denotes a time interval, but irrespective of the choice of the noun, the P-head must be the illative case marker. The dominant pattern in this domain, however, is that the verb only selects the semantic type of the PP and any adposition is licensed that is compatible with this type. Consider the following two examples for illustration.

(80) • Temporal and spatial argument PPs showing morphological variation
a. János Győr-ben / [a ház mellett] / [a kerítés-en kívül] maradt.
János Győr-Ine / the house next.to / the fence-Sup outside stay.Past.3Sg
'János stayed [in Győr] / [next to the house] / [outside of the fence].'
b. Az előadás hét-kor / [a jövő hét-en] / május-ban kezdőd-ik.
the lecture seven-Tmp / the next week-Sup / May-Ine start-3Sg
'The lecture starts [at seven] / [next week] / [in May].'

The locative PP argument in (80a) can be spelt out by any of the locative adpositions, and the temporal PP argument in (80b) is likewise subject to morphological variation. We may also add to this that some verbal predicates that require a temporal or a spatial argument are compatible with either type (without any obvious change in the meaning and the grammatical properties of the verb itself).

(81) a. A középkor-ból származ-ik ez a szokás.
the Middle_Ages-Ela originate-3Sg this the custom
'This custom originates from the Middle Ages.'
b. Görögország-ból származik ez a szokás.
Greece-Ela originate-3Sg this the custom
'This custom originates from Greece.'

c. *Ez a szokás származik.
this the custom originates
'*This custom originates.'

The obligatory PP argument of *származik* 'originates' may denote a temporal or a spatial source, and the construction is grammatical as long as one such PP is present.

As discussed in Section 5.2 of this chapter, argumental PPs frequently occur in particle verb constructions in Hungarian. Thus locative and directional argument PPs are licensed both in the absence (82a) and the presence (82b) of a verbal particle by default. If neither the PP nor the particle is present, the sentence is ungrammatical if the verb selects an obligatory spatial PP (82c). Note that the PP is still optional in the presence of the particle (82b).

(82) • Verbal particle and a directional PP

a. Az asztal-ra tett-em a könyvet.
the table-Sub put.Past-1Sg the book-Acc
'I put the book on the table.'

b. Le-tett-em a könyv-et (az asztal-ra).
down-put-1Sg the book-Acc the table-Sub
'I put the book down (on the table).'

d. *Tettem a könyv-et
put.Past-1Sg the book-Acc
'*I put the book.'

Temporal PPs are in principle more likely to be omissible even when they serve as core arguments. The pattern in (83) is analogous to what we see in (82), except that the construction without the particle and the PP is only marked, but not totally ungrammatical.

(83) • Verbal particle and a temporal PP

a. A megbeszélés-t este hat-ra halasztott-ák.
the meeting-Acc evening six-Sub postpone.Past-3Pl
'The meeting has been postponed to six in the evening.'

b. A megbeszélés-t el-halasztott-ák (este hat-ra).
the meeting-Acc away-postpone.Past-3Pl evening six-Sub
'The meeting has been postponed (to six in the evening).'

c. ?(?)A megbeszélés-t halasztott-ák.
the meeting-Acc postpone.Past-3Pl
'The meeting has been postponed.'

The omission of these PPs is in fact a widely available option in the right discourse setting, when the relevant spatiotemporal parameter of the verbal eventuality is identifiable in the context of use.

(84) • Implicit spatiotemporal arguments

a. János *(itt) lak-ik.
   János here live-3Sg
   'János lives *(here).'

b. János (itt) marad.
   János here stay.3Sg
   'János stays (here).'

c. Az előadás (most) kezdőd-ik.
   the lecture now start-3Sg
   'The lecture is starting (now).'

d. (Még) Tart az előadás.
   still go_on.3Sg the lecture
   'The lecture is (still) going on.'

The verb *lakik* 'live' requires the spellout of a locative PP argument even if we could in principle accommodate the eventuality within the frame associated with the speech situation (84a). But such omission is possible with many other verbs, including *marad* 'stay' (84b). Most temporal PP arguments can stay implicit, as they can be generally given a specific value from the context. The most prominent and most easily available reference point is the speech time, as is the case in (84c) and (84d).

This raises the issue of how we can distinguish core spatial and temporal PP arguments from optional VP-internal spatiotemporal PPs. The division is not always easy to draw, given that many spatiotemporal argument PPs can be omitted, and any eventuality can in principle be anchored both in time and space. In other words, a spatiotemporal frame is present for every eventuality and the relevant parameters can be explicitly spelled out. This issue is discussed in more detail in Chapter 7 of this volume, and we only note here that tests that are sensitive to argumenthood support the argument status of only those spatiotemporal PP types that we have discussed above. Consider (85) for illustration.

(85) • Spatiotemporal arguments: the paraphrase test

a. Kati a koli-ban lak-ik Pécs-en, és Feri is az-t tesz-i
   Kati the dorm-Ine live-3Sg Pécs-Sup and Feri too that-Acc do.3Sg
   (*a szállodá-ban).
   the hotel-Ine
   'Kati lives in the dorm in Pécs, and Feri too does the same thing (*in the hotel).'

b. Kati a koli-ban lak-ik Pécs-en, és Feri is az-t tesz-i (Győr-ben).
   Kati the dorm-Ine live-3Sg Pécs-Sup and Feri too that-Acc do.3Sg Győr-Ine
   'Kati lives in the dorm in Pécs, and Feri too does the same (in Győr).'

This test builds on the observation that the transitive construction *azt teszi* 'does that' acts as a pro-VP element that necessarily includes (PP) arguments in its scope, but it only optionally stands for VPs extended with a non-argumental PP. This is why the PP is ungrammatical in (85a), since this would spell out an argument of the target verb *lakik* 'lives'. Without this PP, the sentence either means that Feri also lives in the dorm (in a location that is left unspecified), or that Feri also lives in the dorm in Pécs. With this PP, the sentence should mean that Feri too lives in Pécs, but in a hotel, rather than a dorm. This is the reading that is unavailable. (85b) shows that the frame adverbial identifying the town is indeed not a core argument since it is compatible with the pro-VP construction.

5.4. Core and non-core PP arguments of adjectives

5.4.1. Introduction

This section investigates PP complements of adjectives and their contribution to the construction of the adjectival phrase. We make the assumption that adjectives can take PP arguments and that the distinction between core and non-core argument PPs is applicable to PP complements of adjectives, too. This is not necessarily an uncontroversial claim, but for the purposes of this chapter, we follow most of the pertinent literature in assuming that adjectives have argument structure and they bear important similarities to verb phrases in this respect. The discussion centres on adjectives that are either non-derived or that are not derived via a productive morphological process. These form the core group of adjectives in Hungarian, and here we focus on argument realization patterns that are characteristic of this domain.

Subsection 5.4.2 discusses the basic issues, and 5.4.3 offers an overview of the most important patterns of PP complementation in APs and an inventory of the case suffixes that are most frequently employed in this domain. Subsection 5.4.4 investigates PP complements that appear in comparative and superlative constructions.

5.4.2. Complementation in the AP

5.4.2.1. Core and non-core PP arguments of adjectives

Our understanding of what makes a PP complement a prototypical argument of the adjective is the same as what we pursued in the case of verbs in Section 5.3: a prototypical PP argument is both selected and subcategorized for by an adjectival head. In other words, the adjective necessarily describes a relation between the referent of this PP and another individual (typically the subject of the clause in predicative uses) and the morphosyntactic form of this PP is determined by the adjective. In comparison to the verbal domain, the number of adjectives that take argument PPs in this sense seems to be relatively small, and most participant PPs that appear in adjectival phrases are better regarded as non-core arguments in our terms. In this subsection, we discuss the key dimensions of the variation that we can observe in adjectival phrases in this respect. We illustrate our points with examples in which the adjective is used predicatively. The syntax of PP complements in attributive and predicative constructions is briefly discussed in Subsection 5.4.2.2.

The adjectives listed in (86) all denote a binary relation and they require the spellout of a PP argument. The adjective also dictates the choice of the adposition: it must be sublative case in (86a) and (86b), allative case in (86c), and inessive case in (86d).

(86) • PP arguments of adjectives

a. Sára képes *(a változás-ra).
Sára capable the change-Sub
'Sára is capable of change.'

b. Sára hajlandó *(a kompromisszum-ra).
Sára willing the compromise-Sub
'Sára is ready for a compromise.'

c. Sára hasonló *(hozzám).
Sára similar All.1Sg
'Sára is similar to me.'

d. Sára biztos *(a siker-ben).
Sára certain the success-Ine
'Sára is positive about success.'

While the relational nature of these adjectives is a necessary feature of their semantics, the PP may be omitted in contexts that license its ellipsis. Therefore the judgements concerning the omission of the PP in the examples in (86) are relative to default discourse settings. In contrast, the following examples represent contexts where the PP argument can be left implicit.

(87) • PP argument omission

a. Sokan képtelenek a változás-ra, Sára viszont képes.
many incapable.Pl the change-Sub Sára but capable
'Many are incapable of change, but Sára is capable.'

b. Most mások a körülmények, de a helyszín alapvetően hasonló.
now different.Pl the circumstance.Pl but the venue fundamentally similar
'The circumstances are different now, but the venue is essentially similar.'

This implicit argument is identical to the PP argument *a változásra* 'for the change' in the first clause in (87a). In the case of (87b), however, the comparison is with a previous venue, which is not explicitly mentioned in the sentence. Still, the omission of the PP argument is an option in the second clause in (87b). Such examples do not refute the point that the adjectives listed in (86) take **PP arguments**, since the omission of this PP is a restricted option, and the adjective entails the relevant semantic role even in elliptical contexts.

Some of the adjectives in this group may undergo specific argument structure alternations. Under the assumption that such alternations target **arguments**, this supports the view that the PPs in question are arguments themselves. *Hasonló* 'similar', for example, which denotes a relation that can be interpreted as symmetric with respect to its two arguments, can be inserted into two different syntactic constructions. It takes a PP argument in the construction that we have seen above in (86c), and which we repeat here as (88a), but roughly the same state of affairs can be expressed by using a plural subject without an accompanying allative PP (88b). The denotation of this plural PP is the union of the denotation of the subject and the PP argument in (88a), and these two constructions are alternative syntactic realizations of the same underlying adjectival concept.

(88) a. Sára hasonló hozzám.
Sára similar All.1Sg
'Sára is similar to me.'

b. Én és Sára hasonlóak vagyunk.
I and Sára similar be.1Pl
'I and Sára are similar.'

The existence of this alternation may be viewed as additional evidence supporting the argument status of the allative PP in (88a). Another type of alternation that results in the promotion of a PP argument to the subject position is represented in (89).

(89) a. Sára biztos a siker-ben.
Sára certain the success-Ine
'Sára is positive about success.'

b. Biztos a siker.
certain the success
'Success is assured.'

The adjective *biztos* 'certain' takes an experiencer subject and a PP that denotes the subject matter of the respective mental state ((87d) is repeated as (89a)). But in an alternative diathesis, no experiencer argument is present and the predicate asserts the probability of the event denoted by the subject. Once again, the alternation targets a PP complement that is re-expressed, as it were, as a subject argument in the alternative construction represented by (89b). This implies within our set of assumptions that the PP in (89a) is indeed an argument of the adjective *biztos* 'certain'.

It is less obvious in many other cases that a PP complement of an adjective is an argument. Consider the following pair:

(90) • PP argument omission

a. Béla féltékeny (Sándor-ra).
Béla jealous Sándor-Sub
'Béla is jealous of Sándor.'

b. Béla mérges (Sándor-ra).
Béla angry Sándor-Sub
'Béla is angry with Sándor.'

Both adjectives denote a particular mental state of the subject experiencer, and the target of this mental state is expressed as a sublative-marked PP complement. The PPs can be omitted under relatively neutral discourse conditions in both cases, yet their relation to the adjectival head does not seem to be identical. While it is possible to deny the existence of a particular target of emotion in the case of *mérges* 'angry' (91b), (91a) is semantically ill-formed, suggesting that *féltékeny* 'jealous' describes a mental state that must include a target.

(91) • Denying the existence of a specific target of emotion

a. #Béla konkrétan nem féltékeny senki-re, csak úgy egyszerűen féltékeny.
Béla specifically not jealous nobody-Sub just so simply jealous
'#Béla is not jealous of anyone specifically, he is just simply jealous.'

b. Béla konkrétan nem mérges senki-re, csak úgy egyszerűen mérges.
Béla specifically not angry nobody-Sub just so simply angry
'Béla is not angry with anyone specifically, he is just simply angry.'

Consequently, the sublative PP complement of *mérges* 'angry' is a non-core argument. Another piece of evidence for the optional nature of this PP comes from verbalizations of the respective adjectival roots. Both *féltékeny* 'jealous' and *mérges* 'angry' can take the same verbalizing inflection, with the resulting verbs denoting activities in which the experiencer subject is behaving in a manner described by the adjective. Crucially, the sublative PP is grammatical in the former case, but not in the latter.

(92) • Target of emotion PPs by deadjectival activity verbs

a. Béla féltékeny-ked-ik a feleség-é-re.
Béla jealous-Vrb-3Sg the wife-Poss.3Sg-Sub
'Béla is being jealous of his wife.'

b. Béla mérges-ked-ik (*a feleség-é-re).
Béla angry-Vrb-3Sg the wife-Poss.3Sg-Sub
'Béla is being angry (with his wife).'

In other words, *féltékenykedik* 'be jealous' takes a target of emotion PP, but *mérgeskedik* 'be angry' cannot take one. Under the assumption that that the respective adjectival and verbal entries spell out the same root concept, we can conclude that *féltékeny* 'jealous' is stored as a relational term with a PP argument in the lexicon of Hungarian, whereas *mérges* 'angry' is not necessarily relational and the optional PP argument that may appear in the adjectival construction is a non-core argument.

The two adjectives just discussed share the property that they require sublative case on their complement, and they differ in whether they entail the existence of the participant denoted by this PP or not. It is also a possible scenario that an adjectival head entails the existence of a PP argument without specifying its morphosyntactic form. Two such examples are *őshonos* 'indigenous' and *ismerős*, which means 'familiar' and which is also used with the special meaning 'familiar with a place'. Both of these adjectives describe a relation between the subject argument and a location, but they do not subcategorize for a specific morphosyntactic marker on this PP.

(93) a. Ez a virág nem őshonos itt / [ebben az erdő-ben] / Magyaroszág-on / Európá-ban.
this the flower not indigenous here / this.Ine the forest-Ine / Hungary-Sup / Europe-Ine
'This flower is not indigenous here / to this forest / to Hungary / to Europe.'

b. Ismerős vagyok [ebben a város-ban] / Pécs-en / Magyarország-on.
familiar am this.Ine the town-Ine / Pécs-Sup / Hungary-Sup
'I am familiar with [this town] / Pécs / Hungary.'

The PP complement spells out a location in both cases, but the choice of the adposition depends solely on the nature of the noun phrase complement of this P head.

Most participant PPs that we discuss in Section 5.4.3 below are optional semantically, and thus we treat them as non-core arguments of the adjective. It seems to be a relatively marked option for an adjectival head to require the spellout of a PP complement, though, as we have seen above, this is attested in the adjectival domain just as well as in the case of verbs. The argument structure properties of adjectives may resemble those of verbs in some other respects, too. A few adjectives, for example, can select two PP complements:

(94) • Adjectives selecting two PPs

a. Hálás vagyok neked a segítség-ért.
grateful am Dat.2Sg the help-Cau
'I am grateful to you for your help.'

b. Béla adós Kati-nak 100 euró-val.
Béla indebted Kati-Dat 100 Euro-Ins
'Béla owes Kati 100 Euros.'

The dative-marked PP expresses a recipient in the above examples. An extra PP in the causal-final case spells out the reason for the speaker's being grateful in (94a), and a PP in instrumental case specifies the amount Béla owes to Kati in (94b). These adjectives are akin in conceptual content to the recipient argument-taking verbs discussed in 5.3.2.1. One prominent grammatical difference between verbs and adjectives is that adjectives cannot assign accusative case to their complements in Hungarian, so the non-subject arguments of an adjective are always realized as PPs.

If the adjective subcategorizes for a specific morphology on its PP complement, then this will typically be a case-marker. This is another characteristic feature of adjectives that they share with verbs (see 5.3). Nevertheless, case morphology is not the sole option, and we can occasionally find case-like postpositions (95a-b), case assigning postpostions (95c), as well as less grammaticalized possessive postpositions (95d) on participant PPs licensed by adjectival heads.

(95) • Variation in the morphosyntactic type of the PP

a. Jenő ideges a veszteség-ek miatt.
Jenő worried the loss-Pl because_of
'Jenő is worried about the losses.'

b. Éva közömbös a politika iránt.
Éva indifferent the politics towards
'Éva is indifferent to politics.'

c. Feri ellenséges velem szemben.
Feri hostile Ins.1Sg opposite_to
'Feri is hostile to me.'

d. Sára nagyon fontos számomra.
Sára very important for.me
'Sára is very important for me.'

Thus adjectives manifest the whole array of morphological variation on the head of their PP complements in a distributional pattern that is largely reminiscent of the verbal domain.

5.4.2.2. On the syntax of PP complements in APs

When adjectives are used predicatively, the adjective itself typically occupies the preverbal verb modifier position, and the PP complement follows the copula in neutral sentences. Since the copula has a zero form in third person in present tense, we use here past tense clauses for the purposes of illustration.

(96) • PP complements in neutral sentences

a. Kati eléggé barátságos volt Feri-vel.
Kati quite friendly was.3Sg Feri-Ins
'Kati was quite friendly with Feri.'

b. A középkori Magyarország gazdag volt arany-ban.
the medieval Hungary rich was.3Sg gold-Ine
'Medieval Hungary was rich in gold.'

The PP can also assume a discourse function, and then it occupies a preverbal position. It is the focus of the clause in (97a), and it is a quantifier phrase in (97b). The adjective, as any other verb modifiers would do, follows the copula if the PP is focused (97a).

(97) • PP complements in discourse functions

a. Kati FERI-VEL volt barátságos.
Kati Feri-Ins was.3Sg friendly
'It is Feri that Kati was friendly with.'

b. Kati Feri-vel is barátságos volt.
Kati Feri-Ins too friendly was.3Sg
'Kati was friendly with Feri, too.'

The PP complement and the predicative adjective do not make up a constituent, or do so only very rarely. (98) is an example for this latter option, where the two occupy the focus position together, indicating that they indeed form a constituent. The adjectival head must strictly follow the PP complement in this case, hence the ungrammaticality of (98b).

(98) • PP complements inside the predicative AP

a. CSAK VELEM EGYKORÚ lehet az, aki-hez férj-hez megy-ek.
only Ins.1Sg of.the.same.age can.be.3Sg that who-All husband-All go-1Sg
'Who I marry can only be of the same age as me.'

b. *CSAK EGYKORÚ VELEM lehet az, aki-hez férj-hez megy-ek.
only of.the.same.age Ins.1Sg can.be.3Sg that who-All husband-All go-1Sg
Intended meaning: 'Who I marry can only be of the same age as me.'

This ordering restriction attests to the strict head-final nature of the Hungarian AP.

This feature is also manifest in attributive constructions. PP complements always precede the adjective if it is used attributively ((99a) vs. (99b)), and they also precede any degree modifiers of the head ((99c) vs. (99d)). Such a complex AP always precedes the noun that it modifies in Hungarian, which is once again in line with the fact that Hungarian is a head final language historically, and it still shows head final tendencies in many pockets of its grammar.

(99) • Ordering restrictions in attributive constructions

a. a Feri-vel barátságos lány
the Feri-Ins friendly girl
'the girl friendly with Feri'

b. *a barátságos Feri-vel lány
the friendly Feri-Ins girl
intended meaning: 'the girl friendly with Feri'

c. a Feri-vel nagyon barátságos lány
the Feri-Ins very friendly girl
'the girl very friendly with Feri'

d. *a nagyon Feri-vel barátságos lány
the very Feri-Ins friendly girl
intended meaning: 'the girl very friendly with Feri'

If an attributive adjective has several PP complements, then their ordering is relatively free, with several factors influencing what counts as the most natural order. These factors include the syntactic category of the noun phrase complement of the P-head, the phonological weight of the PP, the relation between the PP and the adjectival head (core argument, non-core argument or adjunct), as well as the discourse function of the respective PPs and the scope relations among them, if these play a semantically relevant role. Since a detailed investigation of these factors is not relevant for our current purposes, we refer the reader to the volume on the Adjectival Phrase for a more in-depth discussion of these ordering facts.

5.4.3. Core and non-core PP arguments of adjectives: an inventory of the most frequent patterns

5.4.3.1. Agentive adjectives

Agentive adjectives describe a property of a human subject who behaves in the particular manner described by the adjective in his or her treatment of typically another human being. It is possible to paraphrase such examples switching to a verbal construction containing the adverb derived from the respective adjective. (100) is a relevant minimal pair: *barátságos* 'friendly' is the adjective (100a), and *barátságosan* 'in a friendly manner' is the adverb derived from it (100b).

(100) • Agentive adjectives and adverbs

a. Sára barátságos Kati-val.
Sára friendly Kati-Ins
'Sára is friendly with Kati.'

b. Sára barátságos-an viselked-ik Kati-val.
Sára friendly-Adv behave-3Sg Kati-Ins
'Sára behaves with Kati in a friendly manner.'

The other party involved in this interaction is denoted by an instrumental case-marked PP in both constructions.

Some representatives of this group of adjectives are listed in (101).

(101) • **Agentive adjectives**

agresszív 'agressive', *barátságos* 'friendly', *bizalmas* 'confidential', *bizalmatlan* 'distrustful', *bőkezű* 'generous', *ellenséges* 'hostile', *igazságos* 'just', *igazságtalan* 'unjust', *intoleráns* 'intolerant', *irgalmas* 'merciful', *jóságos* 'kind, warm-hearted', *kedves* 'kind, nice', *kíméletes* 'tactful', *korrekt* 'fair', *óvatos* 'cautious', *őszinte* 'honest', *rendes* 'decent, kind', *szívélyes* 'cordial', *tapintatlan* 'indiscreet', *toleráns* 'tolerant', *türelmes* 'patient', *udvarias* 'polite', *udvariatlan* 'impolite', *utálatos* 'mean', etc.

These adjectives are agentive in the sense that the referent of their subject argument does not only act in a particular manner, but he or she either intends to act in such a manner or at least this manner is an aspect of the underlying activity that is in principle under the control of this participant. Those adjectives that imply some degree of enmity may optionally license the case-assigning P *szemben* 'opposite to' on their complement PP. This adposition itself takes noun phrase complements in instrumental case.

(102) • Agentive adjectives denoting some type of enmity

a. Péter aggresszív Sándor-ral (szemben).
Péter aggressive Sándor-Ins opposite_to
'Péter is aggressive with/against Sándor.'

b. Éva nagyon óvatos velem (szemben).
Éva very cautious Ins.1Sg opposite_to
'Éva is very cautious with me.'

c. Bálint mindenki-vel (szemben) ellenséges.
Bálint everyone-Ins opposite_to hostile
'Bálint is hostile to everyone.'

Whether these adjectives select plain instrumental case on their PP complement or the postpostion *szemben* 'opposite to', the construction implies that both the subject participant and the participant denoted by the PP interact with each other. This interaction does not have to be symmetric: being friendly or cautious with someone does not entail the same manner of behavior in the reverse direction. Nevertheless, being friendly or cautious with someone does normally mean that the two parties interact to some extent.

When this feature is absent or backgrounded, the PP complement of the adjective may also be marked by allative case. Many of the adjectives listed in (103) are compatible both with instrument or allative PPs:

(103) • Agentive adjectives taking instrument or allative PPs

a. János mindig kedves / barátságos mindenki-vel.
János always kind / friendly everyone-Ins
'János is always kind/friendly with everyone.'

b. János mindig kedves / barátságos mindenki-hez.
János always kind / friendly everyone-All
'János is always kind/friendly to everyone.'

The allative variety (103b) may imply the lack of a true interaction between the subject and the PP participants, whereas the choice of instrument case (103a) biases the description towards a more interactive construal. When this is not an option, allative case is the more natural choice:

(104) Ez a környezet nem igazán barátságos hozzájuk / ??velük.
this the environment not really friendly All.3Pl / Ins.3Pl
'This environment is not really friendly [to them] / [??with them].'

The agentive adjectives *hűséges* 'faithful, loyal' and *hűtlen* 'unfaithful' can only take allative case. These describe manners of behavior that are potentially controllable, but they do not make reference to any interaction with the referent of the PP. This is arguably the reason for their inability to take instrumental case-marked PPs.

(105) Péter hűséges / hűtlen Évához / *Évá-val.
Péter faithful / unfaithful Éva-All / Éva-Ins
'Péter is faithful / unfaithful [to Éva] / [*with Éva].'

The adjective *engedelmes* 'obedient' has a PP argument which is either in allative or dative case:

(106) Ő engedelmes hozzám / nekem.
He obedient All.1Sg / Dat.1Sg
'He is obedient to me.'

Dative case is the more usual choice here, and it is picked when the PP participant exercises explicit control over the subject argument.

5.4.3.2. Adjectives describing mental states

Mental state adjectives describe a particular psychological or mental state of a designated experiencer argument. We discuss here several groups of adjectives which either necessarily or optionally manifest this psychological reading.

Subject experiencer adjectives select a human subject whose mental state they describe, and a PP complement which is interpreted as a target or a subject matter of emotion. We list some representative members of this group in (107) below. Most subject experiencer adjectives take a PP in sublative case (107a), whereas others require illative case (107b), or the case-like postposition *miatt* 'because of' (107c) or *iránt* 'towards' (107d).

(107) • Subject experiencer adjectives: target or subject matter of emotion PP complements

a. **sublative case**
büszke 'proud', *dühös* 'furious, vexed', *féltékeny* 'jealous', *hajlamos* 'susceptible to, inclined to', *hajlandó* 'willing', *haragos* 'angry', *képes* 'able', *képtelen* 'unable', *kíváncsi* 'curious, inquisitive', *mérges* 'angry', etc.

b. **illative case**
szerelmes 'in love'

c. ***miatt*** 'because of'
bosszús 'vexed', *frusztrált* 'frustrated', *ideges* 'nervous, worried', *nyugtalan* 'troubled, agitated', etc.

d. ***iránt*** 'towards'
közömbös 'indifferent'

Sublative case is the usual choice when the PP is interpreted as the target of the respective mental state, though *szerelmes* 'in love' requires illative case. (108) shows two respective examples.

(108) a. Nagyon dühös vagyok rád.
very vexed am Sub.2Sg
'I am very vexed with you.'

b. Szerelmes vagyok beléd.
in.love am Ill.2Sg
'I am in love with you.'

A subject matter of emotion is typically expressed with *miatt* 'because of', and *közömbös* 'indifferent' requires the case-like postposition *iránt* 'towards'.

(109) a. Péter ideges volt a vizsga miatt.
Péter worried was.3Sg the exam because_of
'Péter was worried about the exam.'

b. János közömbös mások érzés-e-i iránt.
János indifferent others feeling-Poss-Pl towards
'János is indifferent to other people's feelings.'

The distribution of sublative case and the postposition *miatt* 'because of' is somewhat more complicated than what the overview in (107) suggests, since many adjectives that normally take sublative PPs may also combine with a PP headed by *miatt*, and vice versa, for some of the adjectives that usually take *miatt*, sublative case is also an option. It is in fact possible for the two types of PPs to co-occur, and then the sublative PP is an obvious target of emotion, whereas the PP with *miatt* denotes a subject matter of emotion that is interpreted as a(n indirect) cause. (110) is one such example.

(110) Sára mérges a tanár-ra a vizsga miatt.
Sára angry the teacher-Sub the exam because_of
'Sára is angry with the teacher about the exam.'

Thus subject experiencer adjectives show variation in the choice of the adposition in their PP complement, and this variation is concomitant with subtle differences in the interpretation of this PP.

A small group of subject experiencer adjectives require inessive complements:

(111) • Subject experiencer adjectives taking inessive PPs
a. Biztos / Bizonytalan voltam az útvonal-ban.
certain / uncertain was.1Sg the route-Ine
'I was certain/uncertain about the route.'
b. Elvira jártas volt az ámítás művészet-é-ben.
Elvira practiced was.3Sg the deception art-Poss.3Sg-Ine
'Elvira was practiced at the art of deception.'

This inessive PP describes an entity or a domain that is profiled in a designated state of mind of the subject experiencer.

Evaluative and modal adjectives take dative complements that can be interpreted as experiencers. A representative list of such dative experiencer adjectival predicates is given in (112).

(112) • Dative experiencer predicates: evaluative and modal adjectives
a. **evaluative adjectives**
elég 'enough', *fontos* 'important', *hasznos* 'useful', *jó* 'good', *kellemes* 'pleasant', *kellemetlen* 'unpleasant', *kényelmes* 'comfortable', *kínos* 'embarrassing', *kockázatos* 'risky', *korai* 'early', *könnyű* 'easy', *nehéz* 'difficult, heavy', *nyilvánvaló* 'evident', *rossz* 'bad', *sürgős* 'urgent', *tanácsos* 'advisable', *veszélyes* 'dangerous', etc.
b. **modal adjectives**
illendő 'proper, becoming', *kötelező* 'obligatory', *lehetetlen* 'impossible', *lehetséges* 'possible', *muszáj* 'necessary', *szabad* 'permitted', *szükséges* 'necessary', *szükségtelen* 'unnecessary', *tilos* 'forbidden', etc.

The dative PPs these adjectives license pattern with the non-core dative PPs that we discussed in Section 5.3.2.2, and they provide a clear illustration for what we call here non-core argument PPs within the adjectival domain.

Remark 11. Each of the adjectival predicates listed in (112) may appear in three different syntactic constructions. They either select a nominative DP subject (i), an infinitival complement (ii), or a finite *that*-clause (iii).

(i) János-nak fontos a vizsga. [DP-subject]
János-Dat important the exam
'The exam is important to/for János.'

(ii) János-nak fontos le-vizsgáz-ni-a. [infinitival complement]
János-Dat important down-exam-Inf-3Sg
'It is important for János to take the exam.'

(iii) János-nak fontos, hogy le-vizsgáz-z-on [*that*-clause complement]
János-Dat important that down-exam-Subj-3Sg
'It is important for János that he take the exam.'

We focus on the first of these constructions here, since it provides a comprehensive illustration of the grammar of the dative PP. The clausal constructions (ii)-(iii) are discussed in detail in the volume on Non-Finite and Semi-Finite Verb Phrases.

Note first of all that the PP is genuinely optional with these predicates. The adjectives in the examples in (113) each assign some property to the subject argument without the involvement of any reference to another participant. In other words, these examples represent the non-relational use of these adjectives.

(113) • Evaluative and modal adjectives without a PP

a. Nagyon könnyű volt a vizsga.
very easy was.3Sg the exam
'The exam was very easy.'

b. Jó a nyakkendő-d.
good the tie-Poss.2Sg
'Your tie is good.'

c. Minden lehetséges.
everything possible
'Everything is possible.'

b. Tilos az ásítás.
forbidden the yawning
'Yawning is forbidden.'

When the dative PP is introduced, its referent does not have to be construed as an experiencer. Thus, for example, (114a) is ambiguous. It may describe Éva's attitudes towards the exam, thereby representing her mental state. But (114a) may also be true if Éva does not consider the exam important at all, and it is in fact somebody else's evaluation of the situation that the sentence describes. The adjective is relational in this case too, but this relation is not a representation of Éva's mental state.

(114) • Experiencer and non-experiencer readings

a. Évá-nak fontos volt ez a vizsga.
Éva-Dat important was.3Sg this the exam
'This exam was important to Éva.'

b. A fokhagyma jó a hangszalag-ok-nak.
the garlic good the vocal_cord-Pl-Dat
'Garlic is good for the vocal cords.'

That these adjectives do not necessarily require their non-core PP argument to be an experiencer is further shown by the example in (114b), in which the noun phrase complement of the adposition is not animate.

Finally, dative case is not the sole option on the PP complement of evaluative and modal predicates, since the case-like postposition *számára* 'for' is a frequent alternative. The observations that we made in Section 5.3.2 concerning the non-core

PP arguments of experiencer verbs also apply here: the postposition *számára* 'for' is more likely to be used with non-experiencer interpretations (though this is only a bias, rather than an absolute rule), and it requires in standard Hungarian its noun phrase complement to be animate.

(115) • Dative case in competition with the postposition *számára* 'for'

a. Évá-nak / [Éva számára] fontos volt ez a vizsga.
Éva-Dat / Éva for important was.3Sg this the exam
'The exam was important to/for Éva.'

b. A fokhagyma jó [a hangszalagok-nak] / [??a hangszalagok számára].
the garlic good the vocal-cord.Pl-Dat / the vocal_cord.Pl for
'Garlic is good for the vocal cords.'

Thus, other circumstances being equal, dative case in (115a) will typically single out Éva as an experiencer participant, whereas the non-experiencer reading is more available with the postpostion *számára* 'for'. In (115b), the postposition is a marked option at best, since most speakers do not find inanimate complements acceptable with this adposition.

Remark 12. The evaluative adjectives listed in (112) all denote properties that are typically or usually subject to negotiation. Whether an individual is described as good, pleasant or important may vary from one model of evaluation to another. In this respect, properties like being tall, deep or shiny are more objective and whether they hold of an individual or not is less of a matter of negotiation. Nevertheless, any adjectival predicate that can be interpreted as evaluative in some loose sense of the term may take dative PP complements in appropriate contexts:

(i) János-nak / [János számára] túl mély ez a tó.
János-Dat / János for too deep this the lake
'This lake is too deep to/for János.'

The difference between core evaluative predicates (112) and evaluative uses of primarily non-evaluative adjectives (i) is that the latter require strong contextual support. Degree modification on the adjective is a frequent trigger, and the PP in (i) would certainly be less felicitous in the absence of *túl* 'too'. In any other respect, these PPs are like the PPs discussed in the main text above. They are optional, they are in competition with PPs headed by the case-like postposition *számára* 'for', and they may or may not denote a participant whose mental state is described.

5.4.3.3. Symmetric adjectives

Symmetric adjectives denote a relation between two arguments that are reversible without necessarily changing the truth conditions of the proposition expressed by the sentence. If, for example, street A is parallel with street B, then street B is also parallel with street A. A list of such Hungarian adjectives is given in (116).

(116) • **Symmetric adjectives**

arányos 'proportional', *azonos* 'identical', *egyenrangú* 'of the same rank, equal', *egyidejű* 'simultaneous', *egyidős* 'of the same age', *egyívású* 'of the same age/generation' or 'like-minded', *egykorú* 'of the same age', *párhuzamos* 'parallel', etc.

A relatively productive pattern in this group is the application of the prefix *egy-*, which is identical in form and is historically a derivative of the numeral *egy* 'one'. Such adjectives have a nominal root (like *idő* 'time' in *egyidős* 'of the same age') that takes adjectivizing morphology plus the prefix *egy-*.

Symmetric adjectives have two different diatheses (see also 5.4.2.1). In the first construction (117a), the two members of the symmetric relation are expressed as two distinct arguments, with the second argument bearing instrumental case. In the alternative construal, these two semantic arguments are expressed as a single syntactic argument, the plural subject (117b).

(117) • Symmetric adjectives in two syntactic constructions

a. Kati egyidős Bélá-val.
Kati of_the_same_age Béla-Ins
'Kati is of the same age as Béla.'

b. Kati és Béla egyidősek.
Kati and Béla of_the_same_age
'Kati and Béla are of the same age.'

This alternation is characteristic of every symmetric adjective.

Symmetry is not necessarily entailed upon every use of these adjectives. If one member of the relation is more naturally profiled than the other, then the two arguments often cannot be flipped. (118) below contains a relevant example.

(118) • Lack of symmetry

a. A biztosítási díj a kockázat mérték-é-vel arányos.
the insurance fee the risk extent-Poss-Ins proportional
'The insurance fee is proportional to the extent of the risk.'

b. #A kockázat mértéke a biztosítási díj-jal arányos.
the risk extent-Poss the insurance fee-Ins proportional
'#The extent of the risk is proportional to the insurance fee.'

While the insurance fee and the extent of the risk are mutually proportional in the mathematical sense of the term, (118b) sounds unnatural. The reason is that the insurance fee is calculated relative to the extent of the risk, which makes the former the prominent figure of the discussion and thus a natural candidate for subjecthood. It is for similar reasons that the very adjective *hasonló* 'similar' takes allative, rather than instrumental case-marked complements. Though *hasonló* also undergoes the alternation that is characteristic of symmetric adjectives (see the examples in (88) and the discussion around them), it frequently compares one entity to another in a non-reversible manner, as in the following simile:

(119) a. A menny-ek országa hasonló a mustármag-hoz.
the heaven-Pl country-Poss similar the mustard_seed-All
'The kingdom of heaven is like a grain of mustard seed.'

b. #A mustármag hasonló a menny-ek ország-á-hoz.
the mustard_seed similar the heaven-Pl country-Poss-All
'#The grain of mustard seed is similar to the kingdom of heaven.'

This tendency to be involved in the comparison of non-equally prominent entities is the underlying reason why *hasonló* 'similar' requires allative, rather than instrumental case on its PP argument.

5.4.3.4. Cause PPs licensed by adjectives

The cause PPs of verbs that we discussed in Section 5.3.4 also occur in the adjectival domain. They can be added relatively freely to any adjective if the relevant state of affairs denoted by the AP can be conceptualized as the result of some prominent cause in the outside world. Ablative case is used to introduce direct causes (120), and the case-like postposition *miatt* 'because of' is chosen if the real-world causal chain is more complex and the cause under description is only indirectly related to the coming about of the result state denoted by the adjective (121).

(120) • Direct causes: ablative case

a. A disznótorok-tól volt hangos a december.
 the pig_slaughter.Pl-Abl was.3Sg loud the December
 'December was loud with pig slaughters.'

b. A palack büdös volt a poshadt víz-től.
 the bottle smelly was.3Sg the foul water-Abl
 'The bottle was smelly from the foul water.'

c. A tér piros volt a vértől.
 the square red was.3Sg the blood-Abl
 'The square was red with blood.'

(121) • Indirect causes: the postposition *miatt* 'because of'

a. A takarítás nem csak a baktériumok miatt fontos.
 the cleaning not only the bacteria because_of important
 'Cleaning is important not only because of bacteria.'

b. Filmforgatás miatt tilos a parkolás.
 film_shooting because_of forbidden the parking
 'Parking is forbidden because of the shooting of a movie.'

c. A nehéz gazdasági helyzet miatt gyenge a kormány.
 the tough economic situation because_of weak the government
 'The government is weak because of the tough economic situation.'

Of the two adpositions, it is the postposition *miatt* 'because of' that has a wider distribution. We may in principle replace ablative case with *miatt* in the examples in (120), and this will allow us to interpret the PPs as less direct causes. (120a), for example, is true if it is the noise of the pig slaughtering activities - still a common festive event in Hungary – which makes December a loud month. If we switch to the postposition *miatt*, then this reading is less prominent or need not be the only option.

(122) A disznótorok miatt volt hangos a december.
 the pig_slaughter.Pl because of was.3Sg loud the December
 'It is because of the pig slaughters that December was loud.'

(122) may be true if, for example, it is the cleaning up after the festive pig killing or the afterparty that is loud, and the actual event itself does not generate a significant level of noise. Ablative case is no option in the situations described in (121), because the PP introduces an indirect cause in each case.

Ablative case is also used to introduce special, agentive causers by a handful of evaluative adjectives.

(123) • Ablative case on agents

Ez gyerekes / kedves / kegyetlen / szép / szemét volt tőled.
this childish / kind / cruel / nice / distasteful was Abl.2Sg
'This was childish / kind / cruel / nice / distasteful of you.'

The evaluative adjectives discussed in 5.4.3.2 describe the attitudes of the individuals denoted by their dative complements. The adjectives listed in (123) describe the speaker's perspective by default, and the ablative PP introduces an agent participant whose behavior is evaluated in the speaker's model of the world.

5.4.3.5. *Miscellaneous PP complements in APs*

In the previous sections, we have surveyed PP complementation patterns that are relatively productive in adjectival phrases. Here we add further examples of a more idiosyncratic nature to illustrate the depth of morphological variation in the coding of these PPs.

We have already pointed it out that if a particular adposition is selected on PP arguments of an adjective, then it is typically a case marker. The examples in (124) illustrate this typical case.

(124) • Varying case morphology on PP complements of adjectives

a. Éva elválaszthatatlan / független Kati-tól. [ablative]
Éva inseparable / independent Kati-Abl
'Éva is [inseparable from] / [independent of] Kati.'

b. Ez a trükk méltó / méltatlan hozzád. [allative]
this the trick worthy / unworthy All.2Sg
'This trick is worthy / unworthy of you.'

c. Éva nem alkalmas a tanár-i pályá-ra. [sublative]
Éva not suitable the teacher-Attr career-Sub
'Éva is not suitable for a teaching career.'

d. Ekkor már terhes / elégedett voltam a gyerek-ünk-kel. [instrumental]
then already pregnant / satisfied was.1Sg the child-Poss.1Pl-Ins
'Then I was already pregnant / satisfied with our second child.'

e. Vad-ban gazdag / szegény ez a táj. [inessive]
game-Ine rich / poor this the land
'This land is rich / poor in game.'

We find source-type case markers (124a), directionals (124b-c), as well as instrumentals (124d) and locatives (124e) in this selection, indicating that there is no general semantic or conceptual constraint on the type of adposition selected by adjectives. Postpositions are also an option, and (125) contains some examples where the P-head of the complement PP is not a case marker.

(125) • Postpositional complements of adjectives

a. Géza elfogulatlan Katival szemben.
   Géza unbiased Kati-Ins opposite_to
   'Géza is unbiased towards Kati.'

b. A kormány iránt lojális tudósok kaptak csak ösztöndíj-at.
   the government towards loyal scientist.Pl received.3Pl only scholarship-Acc
   'Only scientists loyal to the government received a scholarship.'

c. Éva meglehetősen tájékozott a korszak-kal kapcsolat-ban.
   Éva considerably versed the era-Ins connection-Ine
   'Éva is considerably well-versed in the era.'

The PP argument of these adjectives is headed by the case-assigning postposition *szemben* 'opposite to' in (125a), by the case-like postposition *iránt* 'towards' in (125b), or by the less grammaticalized adpositional element *kapcsolatban* 'in connection with' in (125c).

5.4.4. PP complements in comparative and superlative constructions

We have so far investigated constructions in which adjectives occur in their base form, and take one or two PP complements as their arguments or as their non-core arguments. The participants these PPs denote populate the space that the conceptual content of the adjective describes. In this section, we inquire into PP-types that are introduced in APs as a consequence of comparative or superlative morphology on the adjectival head.

Comparatives license two such extra PP complement types. PPs headed by adessive case denote the second member of the relation that the comparative adjective describes, the standard of comparison (126). PPs headed by instrumental case measure the degree of difference between two members of this relation. The instrumental PP in (127), for example, asserts the age gap between Kati and somebody else in terms of years.

(126) • Comparative constructions: adessive PPs

a. Kati fiatal-abb volt Évá-nál.
   Kati young-Comp was.3Sg Éva-Ade
   'Kati was younger than Éva.'

b. a Kati-nál fiatal-abb lány
   the Kati-Ade young-Comp girl
   'the girl younger than Kati'

(127) • Comparative constructions: instrumental PPs

a. Kati fiatal-abb volt 5 év-vel.
   Kati young-Comp was.3Sg 5 year-Inst
   'Kati was 5 years younger.'

b. az 5 év-vel fiatal-abb lány
the 5 year-Inst young-Comp girl
'the girl 5 years younger'

Neither of these two PP types is obligatory syntactically, and they can co-occur. When the comparative adjective is used predicatively, these PP complements are normally extracted from the AP and they can in principle occupy any syntactic position available for PPs. We illustrate this with a focused instrumental PP in (128a), and a contrastively topicalized adessive PP in (128b).

(128) • Adessive and instrumental PPs with predicative comparative adjectives
a. 5 ÉV-VEL volt fiatal-abb Kati Sándor-nál.
5 year-Ins was.3Sg young-Comp Kati Sándor-Ade
'It was by 5 years that Kati was younger than Sándor.'
b. Sándor-nál bezzeg fiatal-abb volt Kati 5 évvel.
Sándor-Ade as.for young-Comp was.3Sg Kati 5 year-Ins
'As for Sándor, Kati was 5 years younger than him.'

When the comparative adjective is used attributively, the instrumental PP normally occurs closer to the adjectival head, following the adessive PP (129a). The inverse order is marked (129b).

(129) • Adessive and instrumental PPs with attributive comparative adjectives
a. a Kati-nál 5 év-vel fiatal-abb lány
the Kati-Ade 5 year-Ins young-Comp girl
'the girl 5 years younger than Kati'
b. ??az 5 év-vel Kati-nál fiatal-abb lány
the 5 year-Ins Kati-Ade young-Comp girl
'the girl 5 years younger than Kati'

The PP complements must precede the adjectival head in the attributive construction, as (129) shows.

When the argument structure of the adjective contains an argumental PP, then it can co-occur with the two PP-types that are licensed in the comparative construction. The instrumental PP measuring the degree of difference tends to form a constituent with the head (especially if it does not denote a specific degree, as in (130) below), but the adessive PP and the PP argument of the adjectival head are normally extracted.

(130) Kati-nál Éva sok-kal féltékény-ebb volt Sárá-ra.
Kati-Ade Éva much-Ins jealous-Comp was.3Sg Sára-Sub
'As for Kati, Éva was much more jealous of Sára than her.'

The degree-term is also left-adjacent to the comparative adjective in the attributive construction, and the adessive PP and the target of emotion argument of the adjective precede it in either of the two possible orders:

(131) a. a Kati-nál Sárá-ra sok-kal féltékény-ebb lány
the Kati-Ade Sára-Sub much-Ins jealous-Comp girl
'the girl much more jealous of Sára than Kati'

b. a Sárá-ra Kati-nál sok-kal féltékeny-ebb lány
the Sára-Sub Kati-Ade much-Ins jealous-Comp girl
'the girl much more jealous of Sára than Kati'

These ordering facts are characteristic of the attributive construction in general. All the PP types discussed here precede the adjectival head, and the degree modifier is closer to the head than any other participant PPs licensed in the comparative construction.

Remark 13. Adessive case is the standard morphology on the comparison PP in comparative constructions. But it is not the sole option, as many speakers opt for ablative case in the same function. This is especially so if this PP is pronominal.

(i) %Kati fiatal-abb volt tőlem.
Kati young-Comp was.3Sg Abl.1Sg
'Kati was younger than me.'

(ii) %a tőlem fiatal-abb lány
the Abl.1Sg young-Comp girl
'the girl younger than me'

This use of the ablative case is essentially the regional colloquial standard for many speakers in the Eastern part of Hungary, and for many others it is a more or less free substitute for adessive case. Another instance of variation in this function is the doubling of the adessive case morpheme on pronominal PPs in comparative constructions.

(iii) %a nál-am-nál sok-kal fiatal-abb lány
the Ade-1Sg-Ade much-Ins young-Comp girl
'the girl much younger than me'

This doubling construction is restricted both in terms of register and its distribution, and it is definitely recognized as dialectal. It is much more marked in this respect than the ablative construction in (i) and (ii), and it clearly does not have the status of a regional standard.

Superlative constructions require a domain which they quantify over, making the assertion that only one individual (or a group of them) has the relevant property to a maximal degree within this domain. Thus, unlike in the case of comparatives, a designated individual is not compared to another one, but it is singled out as a member of a larger group. It is not compulsory to make explicit reference to this group, and if we do so, we can in principle select any appropriate adposition for the purpose:

(132) • Domain PPs in superlative constructions

a. Sára a leg-magas-abb az osztály-ban.
Sára the Sprl-tall-Comp the class-Ine
'Sára is the tallest in the class.'

b. Éva volt a leg-okos-abb közöttünk.
Éva was.3Sg the Sprl-tall-Comp among.1Pl
'Éva was the cleverest among us.'

c. Feri volt a leg-jobb a verseny-en.
Feri was.3Sg the Sprl-good.Comp the competition-Sup
'Feri was the best at the competition.'

The domain PP is headed by inessive case in (132a), by a case-like postposition in (132b) and by superessive case in (132c).

5.5. PP complements in noun phrases

5.5.1. Introductory remarks

Nouns have argument structure if they inherit one from their verbal or adjectival root. (133) and (134) provide an example for each scenario.

(133) • Deverbal nominalization
a. Kati találkozott *(Évá-val)
Kati met.3Sg Éva-Ins
'Kati met Éva.'
b. Kati találkoz-ás-a *(Évá-val)
Kati meet-Nmn-Poss.3Sg Éva-Ins
'Kati's meeting with Éva'

(134) • Deadjectival nominalization
a. Lajos hű *(a párt-hoz).
Lajos loyal the party-All
'Lajos is loyal to the party.'
b. hű-ség (a párt-hoz)
loyal-Nmn the party-All
'loyalty to the party.'

The deverbal noun *találkozás* 'meeting' may denote a complex event (133b), including each of the two participant PPs that are necessary in the verbal construction, too (133a). The deadjectival noun *hűség* 'loyalty' takes an allative PP complement (134b) that is similar to the allative PP argument of the adjective (134a). The difference in this case is that the allative PP does not need to be spelled out in the nominal construction.

What is remarkable about the obligatory nature of the comitative PP in the complex event nominalization example in (135b) is that it is not obviously the result of some underlying semantic or conceptual need. To recognize this, it is enough to compare *találkozás* 'meeting' with the noun *meeting*, which is a recent loan in colloquial Hungarian in the sense of 'business meeting'.

(135) a. Holnap lesz Kati első meeting-je (az igazgató-val).
tomorrow be.Fut.3Sg Kati first meeting-Poss the director-Ins
'Kati's first meeting (with the director) will take place tomorrow.'
b. Holnap lesz Kati első találkoz-ás-a *(az igazgató-val).
tomorrow be.Fut.3Sg Kati first meeting-Nmn-Poss the director-Ins
'Kati's first meeting with the director will take place tomorrow.'

Both nouns denote a meeting event with two participants, but only the deverbal *találkozás* 'meeting' requires the spellout of the comitative PP in this construction where the agent is spelled out as the possessor of the nominalized head. It is therefore the grammatical properties of the construction that may dictate the spellout of participant PPs in the case of deverbal nominalizations.

This section provides an overview of how PP complements are licensed in noun phrases. In Section 5.5.2, we investigate non-event nouns first. We regard both deverbal and deadjectival nouns as event nominalizations, extending the meaning of the term *event* to states to cover denotations typical of deadjectival nouns and stative verbs. We focus on deverbal nominalizations for expository purposes, since they provide the best illustration of the constraints governing the grammar of complement PPs in noun phrases. In Section 5.5.3, we discuss simple and complex event nominalizations. Our aim here is to revisit these phenomena from the special perspective of the grammar of PP complements in noun phrases. We refer the readers to the volume on Nouns and Noun Phrases for more comprehensive discussions of nominalization constructions in Hungarian.

5.5.2. Simple nouns and PP complements

Nouns, in principle, may take any kind of complements that are compatible with their lexical-conceptual content. Some examples are listed in (136) below.

(136) a. Lány gyöngy fülbevaló-val
girl pearl earring-Ins
'Girl with the pearl earring'

b. Dal a boldogság-ról
song the happiness-Del
'Song about happiness'

c. Nyár a hegy-en
summer the hill-Sup
'Summer on the hill'

d. Ház a sziklák alatt
house the rock.Pl under
'House under the rocks'

The PP complement is headed by a case marker in (136a-c), and by a postposition in (136d). The instrumental PP in (136a) denotes an attribute of the girl, the delative PP describes the topic of the song in (136b), and the PPs in (136c-d) associate the referent of the noun head with a respective location.

The examples in (136) are all conspicuously titles. This is so because unlike in English, PP complements of nouns in Hungarian prefer not to stay in the post-head zone. Titles represent the primary context where this configuration is the most natural. If the complex noun phrase is embedded in a clausal structure (especially in a clause-final position), then the post-head position for the complement PP is acceptable if the head noun is nominative or accusative (137a-b). If the head noun is the complement of an adposition, then this construction is usually ungrammatical.

(137) • Post head complement PPs in noun phrases

a. Tetszik nekem egy új könyv Bélá-ról.
appeal.3Sg Dat.1Sg a new book Béla-Del
'I like a new book about Béla.'

b. Olvast-am egy új könyv-et Bélá-ról.
read.Past-1Sg a new book-Acc Béla-Del
'I read a new book about Béla.'

c. *Bízom egy új könyv-ben Béláról.
trust.1Sg a new book-Ine Béla-Del
'I trust in a new book about Béla.'

d. *Kitart-ok egy új könyv mellett Bélá-ról.
out.stand-1Sg a new book next.to Béla-Del
'I stand by a new book about Béla.'

In other words, if the complex noun phrase itself is embedded in a PP, then the PP complement of the noun head cannot stay in the post-head zone. The divide that we see in (137) does not disappear if the complement PP is extracted into positions outside of complex noun phrase (though even the good examples get somewhat worse):

(138) • Extraction possibilities for PP complements

a. ?Béláról tetszik nekem egy új könyv.
Béla-Del appeal.3Sg Dat.1Sg a new book
'As for Béla, I like a new book about him.'

b. ?Bélá-ról talál-am egy új könyv-et.
Béla-Del find.Past-1Sg a new book-Acc
'As for Béla, I found a new book about him.'

c. *Béláról bízom egy új könyv-ben.
Béla-Del trust.1Sg a new book-Ine
Intended meaning: 'As for Béla, I trust in a new book about him.'

d. *Bélá-ról kitartok egy új könyv mellett.
Béla-Del out.stand.1Sg a new book next_to
Intended meaning: 'As for Béla, I stand by a new book about him.'

In practice, speakers tend to avoid populating the complement zone of simple (non-eventive) noun phrases, and even (137a-b) and (138a-b) have a somewhat marked character. The preferred alternative, in compliance with the head-final tendencies of Hungarian, is to insert these complement PPs into the pre-head zone of the noun phrase. This phenomenon is known as **attributivizing** in the pertinent literature on Hungarian. There are essentially two ways for complement PPs to survive in pre-head positions: they can take on adjectivizing morphology, or they can be embedded in participial clauses. In the rest of this section, we discuss these two manners of structure building with a focus on non-eventive noun-heads.

The derivational suffix *-i* can productively create adjectival phrases out of most postpositional or adverbial phrases (see Chapter 2 for the details). It cannot, however, be used on case-marked nouns, compare (139a) and (139b). The only morphological option in this latter case is to drop the case marker, and try using a denominal adjectivalizing suffix. This happens in (139c), where the noun stem takes the adjectival suffix -*(V)s*.

(139) • PP complements attributivized by derivational morphology

a. a sziklák alatt-i ház
the rock.Pl under-Attr house
'the house under the rocks'

b. *a gyöngy fülbevaló-val-i lány
the pearl earring-Ins-Attr girl
Intended meaning: 'the girl with the pearl earring'

c. a gyöngy fülbevaló-s lány
the pearl earring-Adj girl
'the girl with the pearl earring'

(139c) in fact involves a conversion from a PP to a noun phrase through the loss of the case suffix, and it cannot be regarded as a productive attributivizing device. Nevertheless, it is representative of a syntactic construction that is used to host non-argumental modifiers of the noun head in the pre-head zone in Hungarian.

The other productive possibility to license PP complements of noun heads in the pre-head zone is to embed them in a participial phrase headed by some semantically appropriate verbal root. This is the only productive option if the PP is headed by a case marker (140a-c), and a competitor to -*i*-suffixation in the case of postpositions (140d).

(140) • PP complements embedded in participial constructions

a. az Évá-nak írt levél
the Éva-Dat write.Part letter
'the letter written to Éva'

b. a Bélá-ról szóló könyv
the Béla-Del tell.Part book
'the book about Béla'

c. a gyöngy fülbevaló-val le-festett lány
the pearl earring-Ins down-paint.Part girl
'the girl painted with the pearl earring'

d. a sziklák alatt levő ház
the rock.Pl under be.Part house
'the house under the rocks'

The productive participial form of the copula *van* 'is' is *levő* 'being' (*lévő* is an alternative phonological form of this participle, felt to be a slightly archaic variant by most native speakers). This is the typical choice for the participle functioning as an attributivizer with locative and temporal PP complements. (141) is another illustration for its use.

(141) a. A hűtő jó állapot-ban van.
the fridge good condition-Ine is
'The fridge is in a good condition.'

b. a jó állapot-ban levő hűtő
the good condition-Ine be.Part fridge
'the fridge that is in a good condition'

The copular verb of the finite clause (141a) corresponds to the participle *levő* in the noun phrase paraphrase (141b).

5.5.3. Event nominalizations and PP complements

It is customary to distinguish at least two different types of event nominals. The arguments or adjuncts of the verb or adjective that has a nominal counterpart do not necessarily need to be expressed in the case of simple event nominalizations. (142) contains some examples. The expression of the PP always remains an option in these cases, even if the relevant participant is entailed by the use of the noun.

(142) • Simple event nominals

a. verseny (az idő-vel)
race the time-Ins
'race with time'

b. képesség (a megértés-re)
ability the understanding-Sub
'ability for understanding'

c. János verseng-és-e-i (Kati-val)
János rival-Nmn-Poss-Pl Kati-Ins
'János's rivalries (with Kati)'

The noun *verseny* 'race' is input to the formation of the pertinent verb *versenyez* 'compete', *képesség* 'ability' is the noun derived from the adjective *képes* 'able', and *versengés* 'rivalry' is derived from the verb *verseng* 'rival' with the deverbal nominalizer suffix *-Ás*.

This latter suffix productively creates complex event nominals from verbs. Complex event nominals inherit the argument structure of the input verb, and therefore the argumental PPs of the verb are also present in these nominalizations.

(143) • Complex event nominalization

a. A tanár figyelmeztette a gyerek-ek-et a veszély-re.
the teacher warn.Past.3Sg the child-Pl-Acc the danger-Sub
'The teacher warned the children of danger.'

b. a gyerek-ek figyelmeztet-és-e a veszély-re a tanár által
the child-Pl warn-Nmn-Poss.3Sg the danger-Sub the teacher by
'the warning of the children by the teacher of the danger'

Here we give a short overview of how the two types of event nominals differ in the expression of complement PPs from the non-eventive nominals we have surveyed in the previous subsection. The interested reader will find a more detailed discussion of event nominalizations in the volume on Nouns and Noun Phrases.

The PP complements of event nominals are also preferably attributivized, other factors being equal (see also below). In the case of these, a special participial form of the copula is used to create a syntactic environment in which these PPs survive in a pre-head position. This element is *való*, which is in fact an empty formative, rather than a productive form of the copula. As we have seen above in the discussion of (140d), the productive form of the copula is *levő* 'being'. *Való*-participle formation is an option in the case of each of the event nominals in (142) and (143):

(144) • *Való*-nominalizations

a. az idő-vel való verseny
   the time-Ins being race
   'race with time'

b. a megértés-re való képesség
   the understanding-Sub being ability
   'ability for understanding'

c. János Kati-val való verseng-és-e-i
   János Kati-Ins being rival-Nmn-Poss-Pl
   'János's rivalries with Kati'

d. a gyerekek-nek a tanár által a veszély-re való figyelmeztet-és-e
   the children.Pl-Dat the teacher by the danger-Sub being warn-Nmn-Poss
   'the warning of the children by the teacher of the danger'

Való could also be replaced by any contextually appropriate verbal participle in analogy with the examples we have listed in (140). But the *való*-construction is restricted to event nominals, and it is not available for the non-eventive nominals in (140).

An interesting contrast can be observed among event nominals if both the adjectivalizer suffix *-i* (see the previous subsection) and the *való*-construction are available. Consider the following example for illustration.

(145) a. János ebéd után rohangált.
   János lunch after ran.3Sg
   (i) 'János was running about after lunch.'
   (ii) 'János was running after lunch.' (i.e. János was busy getting lunch somehow).

b. János ebéd után-i rohangál-ás-a
   János lunch after-Attr run-Nmn-Poss
   (i) 'János's running about after lunch'
   (ii) 'János's running after lunch'

c. János ebéd után való rohangál-ás-a
   János lunch after being run-Nmn-Poss
   (i) *'János's running about after lunch'
   (ii) 'János's running after lunch'

The PP complement of the verb *rohangál* 'run, hurry, scurry' can either function as an adjunct specifying the time-frame of the event, or it can also be construed as an argument of the verb in another diathesis. In this case, the sentence describes a hurried chase aimed at getting lunch somehow. Since this PP is headed by a postposition, the adjectivalizing suffix *-i* can be added to it. The result is ambiguous, since (145b) either has the adjunct reading of the PP or the argument reading. The *való*-construction, on the other hand, can only be interpreted as the complex event nominalization of the argument-PP construction. Thus, if both strategies of **attributivization** are available, the *való*-construction creates complex event nominals with the preferred argument reading of the PP complement, if such reading is available.

A further difference between event nominals and non-eventive nouns is that the former inherit the verb modifiers of the input verb, which can occupy a prehead position in the complex event noun phrase without any attributivizing device. Thus in (146a), the directional *Londonba* 'to London' occupies the immediate prehead position, in analogy with the verb modifier position that it would occupy in finite verbal structures.

(146) • Verb modifiers in event nominalizations

a. János London-ba érkez-és-e
János London-Ill arrive-Nmn-Poss
'János's arrival in London'

b. János meg-érkez-és-e London-ba
János Perf-arrive-Nmn-Poss London-Ill
'János's arrival in London'

The pre-head position is occupied by the verbal particle *meg* in (146b), which makes it possible for the illative PP to stay in the post-head zone – provided it is a title, or the whole DP is a nominative or accusative argument of the verb. Otherwise, as we have seen above, the PP is extraposed or it is expressed in the pre-head zone of the noun phrase with the help of *való*.

5.6. Summary

This chaper discussed the grammar of so-called participant PPs in Hungarian, and it has argued in particular that a systematic distinction can be drawn between core and non-core arguments of verbal and adjectival predicates. While the former are obligatory (or at least they are entailed by the predicate) and their adpositional head is selected by the predicate, the latter are optional and they have variable morphological realization. We surveyed the grammar of a representative array of participant PPs selected by verbal and adjectival heads in Hungarian. The issue of PP complementation in Noun Phrases has been discussed separately, and we focused on the distinguishing morphosyntatic behaviour of deverbal and deadjectival nominalizations. Since both verb modifiers in general, and verbal particles in particular play an important role in the construction of the Hungarian clause, the chapter commenced with an inventory of the various different types of particle verb constructions that the language has and with an overview of the variation between verbs that select one PP argument as a verb modifier and verbs that do not.

5.7. Bibliographical notes

Komlósy (1992, 1994), Alberti (1997) and Kiefer (2008) provide in depth discussions of argument structure phenomena in Hungarian, including many of the PP constructions we have discussed in this chapter. The following works focus on respective Hungarian PP types that are covered here: Nemesi (2003), Komlósy (2000), Horvath and Siloni (2011) and Bartos (2011) make comments on the behavior of comitative PPs in Hungarian causative constructions; Rákosi (2003, 2008) presents a detailed description of comitative PPs in reciprocal verb constructions; Bibok (2018) and Rákosi (2013) discuss instrumental PPs; Rákosi (2006, 2009a) investigates dative experiencers as well as other recipient or goal-type PPs; and Rákosi (2009b, 2012a) studies cause PPs in Hungarian. Komlósy (1992, 1994), as well as Gábor and Héja (2006) develop Hungarian specific tests to distinguish arguments from adjuncts. Rákosi (2006, 2009a,b) argues on the basis of mainly Hungarian data that core argument PPs are to be distinguished from optional thematic dependants of predicates, which he analyzes as thematic adjuncts. Kálmán (2006) argues against the assumption that the argument-adjunct distinction is a dichotomy, and proposes to treat relevant phenomena as an instance of gradient, rather than discrete categorization.

Kiefer and Ladányi (2000b), É. Kiss (2006a) and Surányi (2009c) are comprehensive surveys of the grammar of verbal particles in Hungarian. Particle verb constructions in which both a particle and a PP associate are present have received particular attention in the literature. Ackerman (1987), Ackerman and Webelhuth (1997), É. Kiss (1998), Laczkó and Rákosi (2011, 2013), as well as Rákosi and Laczkó (2011) treat these particle verb complexes essentially as lexical units, which may take complement PPs. É. Kiss (2002), Ürögdi (2003) and Surányi (2009a,b) propose that verbs and particles combine in the syntax. The PP complement inside the verb phrase is in an appositive relation to the particle for É. Kiss (2002), whereas Ürögdi (2003) and Surányi (2009a,b) argue that they form a chain in the case of particle types that show agreement morphology (i.e., case markers and inflecting postpositions used as particles).

Laczkó (1995, 2003) offers a detailed overview of how PP complements of noun phrases are licensed in Hungarian, and É. Kiss (2000) also includes pertinent discussion within a general survey of the grammar of the Hungarian noun phrase.

Chapter 6
PPs used as obligatory adjuncts

Katalin É. Kiss

6.1. Introduction

A large set of verbs require the presence of a PP adjunct if their internal argument is a definite or specific indefinite DP. Interestingly, these verbs impose no constraint on the thematic role of the adjunct that they need; they accept temporal, locative, instrumental, manner, cause, purpose, etc. adverbials alike. The obligatory adjunct occupies the preverbal focus position (the focus is marked by small capitals). For example:

(1) a. *Van a pénz.
is the money
'There is the money.'

b. HONNAN van a pénz?
where.from is the money
'Where is the money from?'

c. A pénz KÖLCSÖN-BŐL van.
the money loan-Ela is
'The money is from a loan.'

d. A pénz A FIÓK-BAN van.
the money the drawer-Ine is
'The money is in the drawer.'

e. A pénz A LAKODALOM-RA van.
the money the wedding-Sub is
'The money is for the wedding.'

f. A pénz NEK-ED van.
the money Dat-2Sg is
'The money is for you.'

(2) a. *A baba született.
the baby was_born
'The baby was born.'

b. A baba TEGNAP született.
the baby yesterday was_born
'The baby was born yesterday.'

c. A baba IDŐ-RE született.
the baby time-Sub was_born
'The baby was born on time.'

d. A baba a Szent István Kórház-ban született.
the baby the Saint Stephen Hospital-Ine was_born
'The baby was born in the Saint Stephen hospital.'

e. A baba FOGÓ-VAL született.
the baby forceps-Ins was_born
'The baby was born with forceps.'

f. A baba CSÁSZÁRMETSZÉS-SEL született.
the baby C-section-Ins was_born
'The baby was born by C-section.'

g. A baba GAZDAG CSALÁD-BA született.
the baby rich family-Ill was_born
'The baby was born into a rich family.'

h. A baba hormon-kezelés eredmény-e-képpen született.
the baby hormone-therapy result-Poss-FoE was-born
'The baby was born as a result of a hormone therapy.'

These adverbial adjuncts are free in the sense that they are thematically independent of the verb, and they are obligatory in the sense that their absence renders the sentence ungrammatical.

This section shows that the need for an obligatory adjunct arises in contexts displaying the so-called Definiteness Effect. Section 6.2 describes the types of verbs, whereas Section 6.3 describes the types of internal arguments that 'conspire' to require the presence of an obligatory adjunct. Section 6.4 discusses the correlation between the presence of an obligatory adjunct and the aspectual value of the clause. Section 6.5 demonstrates that a focus (other than the internal argument) neutralizes the Definiteness Effect, and an obligatory adjunct is needed in Definiteness Effect contexts to serve as a focus.

6.2. Definiteness Effect verbs

6.2.1. Verbs of coming-into-being and creation

A large set of verbs, those expressing the existence of their subject, such as *van* 'be' and *akad* 'occur', or its coming into being, such as *születik* 'be born', *keletkezik* 'arise', *támad* 'arise', *alakul* 'be formed', *létrejön* 'come into being', *készül* 'be prepared', and *épül* 'be built', or its appearance, such as *érkezik* 'arrive', do not allow a definite subject. These verbs can take either a subject with an indefinite determiner such as *egy* 'a, one', *két* 'two', *három* 'three',..., *néhány* 'some', *pár* 'a couple of', *sok* 'many, much', *rengeteg* 'a lot of', etc. (4), or a bare singular or bare plural subject (5):

(3) a. *Az énekkar alakult.
the choir formed
'The choir was formed.'

b. *Alakult az énekkar.
formed the choir
'The choir was formed.'

(4) a. Alakult egy/ két / három énekkar.
formed a / two / three choir
'A choir was formed.' / 'Two/three choirs were formed.'

b. Alakult néhány / pár / sok / rengeteg énekkar.
formed some / couple / many / lot choir
'Some / [a couple of] / many /[a lot of] choirs were formed.'

(5) a. Énekkar alakult.
choir formed
'A choir was formed.'

b. Énekkar-ok alakultak.
choir-s formed
'Choirs were formed.'

Remark 1. Verbs expressing coming into being or creation have the Definiteness Effect only in the perfective aspect. If they occur in the progressive aspect, the definiteness/specificity feature of their internal argument is not constrained – see (i) and the discussion in 6.4.

(i) Már alakult a hipotézis a fejében.
already formed the hypothesis the head.Poss.3Sg.Ine
'The hypothesis was already forming in his head.'

The definiteness constraint imposed by these verbs on their internal argument is a consequence of their meaning. They mean 'exist' like *van* 'be' and *akad* 'occur', or 'come to exist' like *születik* 'be born', *keletkezik* 'arise', or 'come to exist in the domain of discourse' like *érkezik* 'arrive', i.e., they all contain an EXIST meaning component. They assert the existence of the referent of their subject, whose existence therefore cannot be presupposed. Definite noun phrases carry an existential presupposition; they refer to an individual already present in the universe of discourse. Asserting the existence of an individual presupposed to exist would be a tautology, and is not tolerated by the language (Szabolcsi 1986).

The Definiteness Effect is displayed not only by unaccusative verbs meaning the existence or coming into being of the referent of their subject, but also by transitive verbs meaning the creation of the referent of their object. Creation verbs include achievement verbs like *talál* 'find', *kap* 'get', and accomplishment verbs like *épít* 'build', *varr* 'sew', *főz* 'cook', *készít* 'prepare', e.g.:

(6) a. *Találtuk a pénzt.
find.Past.DefObj.1Pl the money.Acc
'We found the money.'

b. Találtunk egy csomó pénzt.
find.Past.1Pl a lot money.Acc
'We found a lot of money.'

c. Pénzt találtunk.
money.Acc find.Past.1Pl
'We found some money.'

Remark 2. As will be explained in 6.5, the contrastive focusing of the verb in (6a) can save the sentence.

(7) a. *Kaptam Mari kinőtt ruháját.
receive.Past.DefObj.1Sg Mari outgrown dress.Poss.Acc
'I received Mari's outgrown dress.'

b. Kaptam egy új ruhát.
receive.Past.1Sg a new dress.Acc
'I received a new dress.'

c. Új ruhát kaptam.
new dress.Acc receive.Past.1Sg
'I received a new dress.'

The transitive verbs in (6)-(7) can be regarded as causative coming-into-being verbs. They, too, contain an EXIST meaning component; they mean that x causes y to come to exist in a particular way. What the meanings of e.g. *varr* 'sew' and *épít* 'build', or *kap* 'get' and *talál* 'find' differ in is the specific way in which the referent of their internal argument is caused to come to exist (in the domain of discourse). These verbs cannot cooccur with a definite object because asserting the coming-into-being of the referent of the object and presupposing its existence would be tautologous (cf. Piñón 2006a).

The set of creation verbs is practically open. Almost any verb denoting an activity as a result of which a particular individual appears in the domain of discourse can behave as a creation verb, requiring an indefinite internal argument (cf. Wacha 1976). For example, (8b) describes the creation of an ironed shirt, and (9b) describes the creation of some wine in the domain of discourse:

(8) a. ?*Vasaltam neked ezt az inget.
iron.Past.DefObj.1Sg Dat.2Sg this.Acc the shirt.Acc
'I have ironed this shirt for you.'

b. Vasaltam neked egy inget.
iron.Past.1Sg Dat.2Sg a shirt.Acc
'I have ironed a shirt for you.'

(9) a. ??Hoztuk a bort.
bring.Past.DefObj.1Pl the wine.Acc
'We have brought the wine.'

b. Hoztunk bort.
bring.Past.1Pl wine.Acc
'We have brought some wine.'

The elicitation of the intended 'creation' interpretation is often supported by naming the beneficiary of the creation event – see *neked* 'for you' in (8b).

6.2.2. Change-of-state counterparts of verbs of coming-into-being and creation

Many Definiteness Effect verbs can be supplied with a lexically selected telicizing verbal particle, e.g.: *születik* – *meg-születik* 'be born', *alakul* – *meg-alakul* 'be formed', *támad* – *fel-támad* 'arise', *van* – *meg-van* 'be'. The particle verb versions do not behave as Definiteness Effect verbs; what they mean is not existence or coming into being but a change of state. Their particle is a resultative element expressing that the change of state has been, or will be, completed. These particle verbs presuppose the existence of the referent of their subject, hence they require a definite (10b), (11b) or a specific indefinite (12b) subject:

(10) a. *Gyerekek meg-születtek.
children Perf-were_born
'Children were born.'

b. Mari gyereke meg-született.
Mari child.Poss Perf-was_born
'Mari's child was born.'

(11) a. *Szél fel-támadt.
wind up-rose
'A wind rose.'

b. A szél fel-támadt.
the wind up-rose
'The wind rose.'

(12) a. *Meg-van pénz.
Perf-is money
'There is money.'

b. Meg-van a pénz.
Perf-is the money
'[I/We] have the money/the money has been obtained.'

Remark 3. (9b) has a version which apparently contradicts the generalization that particle verbs do not show the Definiteness Effect :

(i) Hoztunk fel bort.
bring.Past.1Pl up wine.Acc
'We brought up some wine.'

However, this *fel* 'up', whose presence is optional in (i), does not behave as a telicizing secondary predicate. It does not occupy the preverbal position, the default position of predicative PPs, where they form a complex predicate with the verb. It behaves as a directional adjunct, i.e., it can be analyzed as an adverb independent of the verb – as discussed in connection with examples (75)-(77) in Chapter 4.

The verbal particle also turns a verb of creation into a change-of-state verb, which presupposes the existence of its object, and is consequently immune from the Definiteness Effect. Compare the interpretations of the creation verb in (13a) and the change-of-state verbs in (13b-c). (13a) expresses the finding of an unexpected, unknown item, whereas (13b-c) express the reemerging of a lost object, whose existence was known previously to the participants of the discourse.

(13) a. Találtam egy gyűrűt.
find.Past.1Sg a ring.Acc
'I found a ring.'

b. Meg-találtam a gyűrűt.
Perf-find.Past.DefObj.1Sg the ring.Acc
'I found the ring.'

c. Meg-találtam egy gyűrűt.
Perf-find.Past.1Sg a ring.Acc
'I found a ring [of the missing objects].'

The meaning difference between minimal pairs like (14a,b) and (15a,b) can be delicate (Kálmán 1995; Maleczki 1995; Bende-Farkas 2001):

(14) a. Péter *szervezett* egy konferenciát.
Péter organized a conference.Acc
'Péter organized a conference.'

b. Péter *meg-szervezett* egy konferenciát.
Péter Perf-organized a conference.Acc
'Péter organized a conference.'

(15) a. *Írtam* egy verset.
write.Past.1Sg a poem.Acc
'I wrote a poem.'

b. *Meg-írtam* egy verset.
Perf-write.Past.1Sg a poem.Acc
'I wrote a poem.'

In (14a) and (15a), the objects introduce completely new individuals. In the case of (14b) and (15b), on the contrary, the objects are assumed to have existed as a plan prior to the organizing and writing events. Thus (14a) or (15a) could well represent the initial sentence of a discourse, whereas (14b) and (15b) require some preceding context. In (16), for example, *egy konferenciát* 'a conference.Acc' is understood as one of the tasks mentioned in the preceding sentence:

(16) Minden feladatot én végeztem. Meg-szerveztem egy konferenciát.
every task.Acc I perform.Past.1Sg Perf-organize.Past.1Sg a conference.Acc
'It was me who performed every task. I organized a conference.'

6.3. Types of internal arguments blocked by the Definiteness Effect

The types of internal arguments that Definiteness Effect verbs do not allow include definite noun phrases (17a), proper names (17b), definite pronouns (17c), possessive constructions (17d), and universally quantified noun phrases (17e):

(17) a. *A vendég érkezett.
the guest arrived

b. *Mari született.
Mari was_born

c. *Én születtem.
I was_born

d. *Mari gyereke született.
Mari child.Poss was_born
'Mari's child was born.'

e. *Minden énekkar alakult.
every choir was_formed

The quantifier *valamennyi* 'x-many' is potentially ambiguous between the interpretations 'all' and 'some', as illustrated by (18). (The two interpretations have different intonation patterns; *valamennyi* 'all' is pronounced as a regular quantifier bearing a pitch accent with a falling tone, whereas *valamennyi* 'some' is destressed, and it requires the fall-rise intonation of contrastive topics.) If *valamennyi* determines the internal argument of a Definiteness Effect verb, the pitch accent and the universal interpretation of *valamennyi* are blocked, as shown by (19).

(18) (")Vala-mennyi énekkar "fel-lépett.
x-many choir up-performed
a. 'All the choirs performed.'
b. 'Some choirs performed.'

(19) Vala-mennyi énekkar "alakult.
x-many choir was_formed
'Some choirs were formed.'

In Hungarian, definiteness has a morphological test: definite objects elicit verbal agreement (in other words, they elicit the definite conjugation), as illustrated by the contrast in (20a,b). Noun phrases containing the universal quantifier *minden* do not elicit the definite conjugation – see (20c):

(20) a. Ismer-ek egy nyelvészt.
know-1Sg a linguist.Acc
'I know a linguist.'

b. Ismer-em azt a nyelvészt.
know-DefObj.1Sg that.Acc the linguist.Acc
'I know that linguist.'

c. Ismer-ek minden nyelvészt.
know-1Sg every linguist.Acc
'I know every linguist.'

Definiteness Effect verbs do not allow either a definite, or a universally quantified indefinite object, hence what they do not tolerate cannot be the definiteness of their internal argument. In fact, they do allow an internal argument modified by *mindenféle* 'all kinds':

(21) a. Érkezett minden-féle vendég.
arrived all-kind guest
'All kinds of guests arrived.'

b. Alakult minden-féle egyesület.
formed all-kind association
'All kinds of associations were formed.'

The prohibition that the internal arguments of Definiteness Effect verbs must observe is a prohibition against specificity/familiarity; the referent of the internal argument cannot exist prior to the coming-into-being or creation event described in the sentence. A definite internal argument is always specific, and so is a universally quantified internal argument (unless its quantifier is *mindenféle* 'all kinds'), hence they are ruled out by this constraint. An indefinite cannot occur as the internal argument of a Definiteness Effect verb if it refers to an element of a previously introduced set. Observe the second clause in (22a), containing a creation verb with an indefinite object. The object cannot be interpreted specifically, i.e. its referent cannot represent a subset of the referent of the subject of the previous clause. Hence the complex sentence is incoherent. This is not the case in (22b), where the particle verb of the second clause requires the specific, i.e., familiar interpretation of the object:

(22) a. #Kett-en el-tévedtek, de hamar találtunk egy lányt.
two-Adv away-get.lost.Past.3Pl but soon find.Past.1Pl a girl.Acc
'Two persons got lost but we soon found a girl.'

b. Kett-en el-tévedtek, de egy lányt hamar *meg-találtunk.*
two-Adv away-get.lost.Past.3Pl but a girl.Acc soon Perf-find.Past.1Pl
'Two persons got lost but we have soon found a girl [of them].'

Another piece of evidence testifying to the non-specificity of the indefinite internal argument of Definiteness Effect verbs is that it cannot take scope over negation; it must be in the scope of negation. An indefinite in the scope of negation is obligatorily accompanied by the minimizing particle *sem* in Hungarian.

(23) a. *János nem írt egy verset.
János not wrote a poem.Acc
'János did not write a poem.'

b. János nem írt egy verset *sem.*
János not wrote a poem.Acc Min
'János did not write any poem.'

At the same time, the internal arguments of coming-into-being and creation verbs can be referred to by a definite pronoun in the subsequent discourse (see (24)), therefore, they are said to be post-specific.

(24) János írt egy verset. *Azt* olvasták fel az ünnepély-en.
János wrote.3Sg a poem.Acc that.Acc read.Past.3Pl up the ceremony-Sup
'János wrote a poem. It was read out at the ceremony.'

6.4. Definiteness Effect and aspect

6.4.1. Verbs of creation and coming-into-being are accomplishment predicates

Verbs eliciting the Definiteness Effect include a couple of stative verbs expressing existence (e.g. *van* 'be'), and a large number of accomplishment and achievement verbs expressing coming into being (e.g. *készül* 'be prepared') or creation (e.g. *készít* 'prepare').

In Hungarian, situation aspect is marked by a verbal particle. Accomplishment and achievement predicates are verbal complexes consisting of a verb and a preverbal resultative secondary predicate (usually a verbal particle) in the default case (25b) – see Chapter 4 Section 4.3, whereas stative and activity predicates are bare verbs (25a). Compare:

(25) a. János [✓egész délután] / [*fél nap alatt] *festette* a kerítést.
János whole afternoon / half day during painted the fence.Acc
'János was painting the fence [the whole afternoon] / [*in half a day].'

b. János [*egész délután] / [✓fél nap alatt] *be-festette* a kerítést.
János whole afternoon/ / half day during in-painted the fence.Acc
'János painted the fence [*the whole afternoon] / [in half a day].'

The bare verb in (25a) can only be understood to denote an activity in progress, whereas the particle verb in (25b) can only be understood to represent a completed event. Accordingly, (25a) is only compatible with a durative time adverbial, whereas (25b) is only compatible with a delimiting time adverbial.

Verbs of coming into being and verbs of creation are exceptions to the above generalization; they describe accomplishments and achievements, i.e., completed events, without a verbal particle:

(26) a. János fél nap alatt festett egy képet.
János half day during painted a picture.Acc
'János painted a picture in half a day.'

b. [Fél órán belül] / Öt-kor kaptam egy emailt.
half hour within / five-Tmp receive.Past.1Sg an email.Acc
'I received an email [within half an hour] / [at five].'

If an achievement predicate, like *meg-kap* 'get', occurs without a verbal particle, it is an achievement which expresses coming into being or creation and evokes the Definiteness Effect. Being an achievement verb, it cannot occur with a durative time adverbial (27a), and being a creation predicate, it does not allow a definite object (27b).

(27) a. *Fél óra hosszat egy emailt kaptam.
half hour long an email.Acc receive.Past.1Sg
Intended meaning: 'I was receiving an email for half an hour.'

b. *Fél órán belül az emailt kaptam.
half hour within the email.Acc receive.Past.DefObj.1Sg
Intended meaning: 'I received the email in half an hour.'

Unlike achievement verbs, accomplishment verbs without a verbal particle can also be understood as activities denoting a change of state or change of location, in which case they can take a durative time adverbial (28a), and elicit no Definiteness Effect (28b) (cf. Peredy 2008):

(28) a. János (egész délután) festett egy képet.
János whole afternoon paint.Past.3Sg a picture.Acc
'János was painting a picture the whole afternoon.'

b. János (fél óra hosszat) festette a képet.
János half hour long paint.Past.DefObj.3Sg the picture.Acc
'János was painting the picture for half an hour.'

The activity described in (28), and activities in general affect an existing object, hence they are not predicates of coming into being or creation. Verbs predicating the coming into being or the appearance or the creation of a new individual are always accomplishments or achievements.

Remark 4. In the case of *eszik* 'eat', *iszik* 'drink', and *fogyaszt* 'consume', it is not quite clear why they behave syntactically as Definiteness Effect verbs. If these verbs take an indefinite object, they can be understood as accomplishments; if they take a definite object, they are understood as activities in progress (see (i)-(ii); cf. also (iii)).

(i) a. János evett egy pörköltet.
John ate.3Sg a stew.Acc
'János ate/has eaten a stew.'

b. János ette a pörköltet.
John ate.DefObj.3Sg the stew.Acc
'János was eating the stew.'

(ii) a. János ivott egy sört.
János drank.3Sg a beer.Acc
'János drank/has drunk a beer.'

b. János itta a sört.
János drank.DefObj.3Sg the beer.Acc
'János was drinking the beer.'

(iii) a. János meg-ivott egy sört.
János Perf-drank.3Sg a beer.Acc
'János drank a beer.'

b. János meg-itta a sört.
János Perf-drank.DefObj.3Sg the beer.Acc
'János drank the beer.'

It is perhaps the meaning component that they share with *szerez* 'obtain', meaning 'cause to come to exist in the domain of discourse', that licenses their creation-verb-like behavior.

6.4.2. Weak versus strong accomplishments

Accomplishment verbs predicating the coming into being or the creation of a new individual represent a special type of accomplishments, called weak accomplishments (Piñón 2006b). Strong accomplishments denoted by particle verbs describe complex events consisting of an activity and the resultant state of the internal argument affected by the activity. Weak accomplishments, on the contrary, cannot be divided into two subevents; the result of the activity is not a new state of the internal argument but the internal argument itself. This difference can be highlighted by two tests. A strong accomplishment modified by *almost* is ambiguous: it has a scalar and a counterfactual interpretation. In the case of a weak accomplishment, only the counterfactual interpretation is present. Compare:

(29) János majdnem be-festette a kerítést.
János almost in-paint.Past.DefObj.3Sg the fence.Acc
a. 'János almost painted the fence [but he did not start it]'.
b. 'János almost painted the fence [but he did not complete it]'.

(30) János majdnem festett egy képet.
János almost paint.Past.3Sg a picture.Acc
'János almost painted a picture [but he did not start it]'.

If we negate a strong accomplishment, negation can apply either to the resultant state of the internal argument or to the whole event. In the case of weak accomplishments, negation always applies to the whole event.

(31) János nem *festette* *be* a kerítést.
János not paint.Past.DefObj.3Sg in the fence.Acc
a. 'János did not paint the fence [he did not start it].'
b. 'János did not paint the fence [he did not complete it].'

(32) János nem *festett* egy képet sem.
János not paint.Past.3Sg a picture.Acc Min
'János did not paint any picture [he did not start any].'

In sum: when we talk about verbs of coming into being and verbs of creation, we mean particleless verbs with an accomplishment or achievement interpretation that elicit the Definiteness Effect. Verbs which are homophonous with verbs of coming into being and creation but are interpreted as activities in progress are not Definiteness Effect verbs.

6.5. Neutralizing the Definiteness Effect by a focused adjunct

The Definiteness Effect elicited by verbs of existence, coming into being, and creation is neutralized if the sentence contains a preverbal focus constituent other than the internal argument:

(33) A gyerek *MÁJUS-BAN* született.
the baby May-Ine was_born
'The baby was born in May.'

If the sentence in (33) contains no focus constituent, in which case the main stress falls on the verb (34a), or if the preverbal focus is the internal argument (34b), the sentence is unacceptable:

(34) a. *A gyerek "*született*.
the baby was_born
b. *A "*GYEREK* született.

The explanation of the disappearance of the Definiteness Effect in the presence of a focus is that in a focus construction, the non-focus section of the sentence is presupposed (É. Kiss 1995). (35), for example, does not assert the coming-into-being of a child anymore; it asserts that the familiar event of the child being born took place in May. Since the event of the child being born is known to have taken place, the indefiniteness, more precisely, the non-specificity requirement associated with the internal argument, is void:

(35) [Ez a gyerek]/ Jancsi/ [A család minden gyereke] *MÁJUS-BAN* született.
this the child / Jancsi / the family every child.Poss May-Ine was_born
'This child / Jancsi / [Every child of the family] was born in May.'

What we achieve by the introduction of a focus is that the internal argument becomes part of the presupposition. In sentences of existence and coming into being, the internal argument is the only argument, hence it can be (part of) the presupposition if either the verb or an adjunct is focused. Since a focused verb remains in situ, and it does not involve any stress shift (the default phrasal stress also falls on the verb), its focus function can only become apparent if it is set into an explicit contrast, which is not always possible. For example, the verb *talál* 'find' can easily be contrasted with *lop* 'steal', but it is unclear what alternative the verb *születik* 'be born' could be contrasted with; hence (36) is grammatical, whereas (34a) was uninterpretable:

(36) A pénzt "találtam, nem loptam.
the money.Acc found.DefObj.1Sg not stole.DefObj.1Sg
'I found the money; I didn't steal it.'

Adverbial adjuncts expressing the time, place, instrument, source, purpose, etc. of the action are focused by movement into preverbal position, i.e. they require no explicit contrast for the focus interpretation to arise. Furthermore, alternative times, places, instruments, etc., which facilitate the focus interpretation pragmatically, are easy to accommodate.

Thus an adverbial adjunct is obligatory if a verb of existence or coming-into-being, or a verb of creation cooccurs with a definite or specific indefinite internal argument. It is obligatory in the sense that if it is omitted, the sentence becomes either ungrammatical ((37b) and (38b)), or ungrammatical under a perfective interpretation (39b), though acceptable in the progressive:

(37) a. A *ZSEB-EM-BEN* van [a pénz] / [János pénze].
the pocket-Poss.1Sg-Ine is the money / János money.Poss
'[The money] / [János's money] is in my pocket.'

b.*"Van [a pénz] / [János pénze].
is the money / János money.Poss
'[The money] / [János's money] is.' / 'There is [the money] / [János's money].'

(38) a. A vonat *ÖT-KOR* / [*AZ ELSŐ VÁGÁNY-RA*] / *IDŐ-BEN* érkezett.
the train five-Tmp / the first platform-Sub / time-Ine arrived
'The train arrived [at five] / [on platform one] / [in time].'

b. *A vonat "érkezett.
the train arrived

(39) a. A ruha [*KÉT NAP ALATT*] / *SELYEM-BŐL* / *KÉZ-ZEL* készült.
the dress two day under / silk-Del / hand-Ins was_made
'The dress was made [in two days] / [from silk] / [by hand].'

b. #A ruha "készült.
the dress was_made
'The dress was made.'

In the case of transitive verbs of creation, the subject is also a potential focus, i.e., either a focused subject or a focused adverbial adjunct (or a focused verb) is needed to license the definite or specific indefinite subject:

(40) a. #A házat "építette János.
the house.Acc built.DefObj.3Sg János.Nom
'János built the house.'

b. A házat *JÁNOS* építette.
the house.Acc János.Nom built.DefObj.3Sg
'The house was built by JÁNOS.'

c. A házat TAVALY / KŐ-BŐL / VÍZPART-ON / [KÉT ÉV ALATT] / KÖLCSÖN-BŐL / SAJÁT-KEZ-Ű-LEG építette János.
the house.Acc last.year / stone-Del / waterfront-Sup / two year during / loan-Del / own-hand-Adj-Adv built.DefObj.3Sg János.Nom
'János built the house [last year] / [from stone] / [on the waterfront] / [in two years] / [from loan] / [on his own].'

In some cases, the Definiteness Effect appears to be neutralized by the focusing of the internal argument itself, which would be unexpected if the purpose of focusing is the relegation of the internal argument to the presupposed sentence part. In fact, such sentences are reactions to a preceding sentence where a constituent other than the internal argument is focused, i.e., where the internal argument has already become the part of the presupposition. For example:

(41) – A kislány "*TEGNAP* született.
the little.girl yesterday was_born
'It was yesterday that the little girl was born.'

– Nem. A "KISFIÚ született '*tegnap*.
no the little_boy was_born yesterday
'No. It is the little boy who was born yesterday.'

The second sentence in (41) involves the correction of the presupposition of the previous sentence.

An adverbial adjunct can save the definite internal argument of a verb of existence, coming-into-being, and creation if it is semantically compatible with the given predicate, i.e. if it denotes a circumstance (e.g. place, time, purpose, cause, instrument, etc.) of the coming-into-being or creation event. It must also be focusable; thus sentence adverbials, e.g. speech act adverbs such as *frankly*, or modal adverbs such as *probably*, which cannot be focused, cannot function as obligatory adjuncts:

(42) *"*Szerencsére* van a pénz.
luckily is the money
'Luckily, the money is.'/'Luckily, there is the money.'

The question arises why verbal particles neutralizing the Definiteness Effect, discussed above in Section 6.2.2 are not assimilated to preverbal foci – after all, they are also of the category PP, and they also occupy the immediately preverbal position. In other respects, however, particles and foci act differently both from a syntactic and a semantic point of view. It has been demonstrated (first by Brody 1990) that a preverbal focus and a preverbal verbal particle occupy different positions. The focus surfaces preverbally because it attracts the verb from behind the particle as discussed in connection with the examples in (88) in Chapter 4 Section 4.5.2. Their different syntactic positions are most apparent under negation: whereas a negated focus construction involves the order 'negative particle, focus, verb', a negated particle verb displays the order 'negative particle, verb, verbal particle':

(43) a. A gyerek *nem MÁJUS-BAN* született.
the child not May-Ine was_born.3Sg
'It wasn't in May that the child was born.'

b. A gyerek még *nem* született *meg*.
the child yet not was_born Perf
'The child has not been born yet.'

Particles and foci also differ semantically. In a focus construction, everything but the focus is presupposed, whereas a particle verb only requires its internal argument to be presuppositional. Its presuppositionality/specificity, however, is obligatory (44a). A focus construction, on the contrary, allows both a specific and a non-specific internal argument (44b).

(44) a. *Meg-született *gyerek*.
Perf-was_born child

b. A SZABÓ CSALÁD-BAN született *gyerek*.
the Szabó family-Ine was_born child
'It is the Szabó family where a child was born.'

6.6. Summary

Adverbial adjuncts – whether PPs or adverbs – can be obligatory constituents of the clause also when they are not selected arguments of the verb. This happens when the verb means existence, coming into being/appearance or creation, i.e., when the sentence asserts the existence, the coming into being/appearance, or the creation of the referent of its internal argument. In this clause type, the internal argument cannot be represented by a syntactic category associated with an existential presupposition, i.e. it cannot be a name, a definite pronoun, a definite or a specific indefinite noun phrase, or a possessive construction. (A verb of coming into being/appearance or creation can be homophonous with an activity verb denoting the change of state or change of location of an existing internal argument. However, the two verbs differ aspectually; whereas the activity verb is atelic, describing a change in progress, the verb of coming into being is a telic accomplishment or achievement, describing a completed event.) The prohibition against the definiteness of the internal argument of verbs of existence, coming into being/appearance and creation, the so-called Definiteness Effect, is neutralized by the presence of a focus. An adjunct is obligatory when it serves as the focus licensing the definite internal argument of a Definiteness Effect verb. In the case of an unaccusative Definiteness Effect verb, a definite or a specific indefinite internal argument can be licensed by the focusing of an adjunct, or, if pragmatics allows, by the focusing of the verb. The definite or specific indefinite internal argument of a transitive verb of creation can be saved by the focusing of either an adjunct or the subject (or, in special pragmatic conditions, by the focusing of the verb).

6.7. Bibliographical notes

The special syntactic and aspectual properties of verbs of creation was first noticed by Wacha (1976). It was Szabolcsi (1986) who discovered that this large set of verbs display the semantically motivated syntactic behavior known as the Definiteness Effect, observed in connection with the English *there is* construction. É. Kiss (1995) supplemented Szabolcsi's theory by deriving the role of obligatory adjuncts in the neutralization of the Definiteness Effect from the focus–presupposition structure that they create. Kálmán (1995) and Maleczki (1995) proposed alternative semantic explanations of Szabolcsi's observations. Bende-Farkas (2001) studied the Definiteness Effect in the framework of Discourse Representation Theory. Peredy (2008) investigated the aspectual role of obligatory adjuncts neutralizing the Definiteness Effect. Piñón (2006a,b) gave a formal semantic analysis of the properties of Definiteness Effect constructions.

Chapter 7
PPs as adjuncts

Barbara Egedi

7.1. Introduction

This chapter is concerned with non-argument adpositional phrases, i.e. adverbial adjuncts that are neither selected by a verb, nor used predicatively. Adjuncts are not exclusively PPs, they include adjectival phrases and relative clauses that are normally used to modify a nominal expression. (These modifiers are discussed in the volume on Adjectival Phrases.)

This chapter will only discuss adverbial adjuncts that modify non-nominal constituents, i.e. a predicate, or a more extended, clause-level category (simple and complex events, propositions and speech acts). PP adjuncts modifying other PP phrases, nouns and verbal particles have been dealt with in Chapter 2 (Sections 2.2.1.6, 2.2.2.2.6, 2.2.2.3.6, 2.2.1.5, and 2.2.3.4).

Note that most of the adverbial expressions discussed in this chapter may also function as arguments (1) or as secondary predicates (2). The first two cases are discussed in Chapter 5 and Chapter 4, respectively, while the present chapter concentrates on adverbial modification (3).

(1) Félix át-adta a meghívót *a vendégek-nek.* [PP as argument]
Félix over-gave the invitation.Acc the guests-Dat
'Félix handed the invitation to the guests.'

(2) Félix *vendég-nek* tekintette a felügyelőt. [PP as secondary predicate]
Félix guest-Dat considered the inspector.Acc
'Félix considered the inspector as a guest.'

(3) Félix volt a nap hőse *a vendégek-nek.* [PP as adjunct]
Félix was the day hero.Poss the guests-Dat
'Félix was the man of the day for the guests.'

It is not always obvious whether something is an optional argument or a free adjunct. This chapter aims only to deal with adverbial expressions that are clearly not arguments. The properties of non-core arguments are discussed in detail in Chapter 5, while Chapter 6 addresses the patterns involving the so-called obligatory adjuncts.

This chapter is structured as follows. Section 7.2 overviews the categorial types in which adverbial adjuncts can appear as well as the basic formal properties of these categories. Section 7.3 discusses the various adjunct classes from a semantic point of view, while Section 7.4 addresses the placement properties and prosodic features of these elements and their relative order within the sentence. Some peculiar cases will be discussed in separate sections, such as the obligatorily stressed high adverbials, or the case of obligatorily focused exclusive adverbials.

7.2. Categorial types and formal properties of adverbial adjuncts

This section introduces the grammatical categories in which adverbial adjuncts can appear as well as the basic formal properties of these categories. After a brief overview of the morphological structures of adjuncts, they will be categorized according to their semantic and syntactic properties. First of all, a distinction will be made between VP-adverbials and clausal adverbials through applying a series of tests (paraphrases, focusing, etc.), and separate sections will be dedicated to adverbials that seem to have a dual nature in this respect.

7.2.1. Categorial types in terms of morphology

Strictly speaking, not all types of adverbial adjuncts can be analyzed as adpositional phrases, but the majority have the morphological structure of a PP. The following inventory provides a representative listing of the possible types of Hungarian adverbial adjuncts as far as their morphological makeup is concerned. (For an exhaustive listing and detailed discussion of these formal properties, consult Chapter 2 in this volume.)

7.2.1.1. PPs

The majority of Hungarian adverbials are PPs, i.e. noun phrases furnished with a case suffix (4), a case-like postposition (5), or a case-assigning postposition (6):

(4) A kapitány *idő-ben* / *szerencsé-re* / *kapás-ból* / *szív-vel-lélek-kel*
the captain time-Ine / luck-Sub / catching-Ela / heart-Ins-soul-Ins
teljesítette a feladatot.
fulfilled the task
'The captain fulfilled the task [in time] / luckily / [off the cuff] / [with all his heart].'

(5) A kapitány [*idő előtt*] / [*három nap alatt*] teljesítette a feladatot.
the captain time before / three day under fulfilled the task
'The captain fulfilled the task [before time] / [in three days].'

(6) A kapitány [*határidő-n túl*] / [*átlag-on alul*] teljesítette a feladatot.
the captain deadline-Sup over / average-Sup below fulfilled the task.Acc
'The captain fulfilled the task [after the deadline] / [below average].'

7.2.1.2. Adverbials without a transparent PP structure

In what follows, an inventory of adverbial modifiers will be provided which can be categorized as adverbs, i.e., which are PPs with a non-canonical or non-transparent inner structure.

A class of adverbials have been formed from adjectives with a selection of productive derivational suffixes, namely *-n/-an/-en* (7), *-ul/-ül* (8), or *-lag/-leg* (9), which are equivalents of the English *-ly* suffix in the majority of the cases.

(7) A kapitány *lelkes-en* / *gyors-an* teljesítette a feladatot.
the captain enthusiastic-ly / quick-ly fulfilled the task.Acc
'The captain fulfilled the task enthusiastically / quickly.'

(8) A kapitány *türelmetlen-ül* / *rossz-ul* teljesítette a feladatot.
the captain impatient-ly / wrong-ly fulfilled the task.Acc
'The captain fulfilled the task impatiently / wrongly.'

(9) A kapitány *állító-lag* / *valószínű-leg* teljesítette a feladatot.
the captain alleged-ly / probable-ly fulfilled the task.Acc
'The captain allegedly / probably fulfilled the task.'

Note the variation in (10), where the clausal modifier 'in principle' might be formed by either of the above illustrated morphological strategies:

(10) A kapitány *elv-ben* / *elvi-leg* teljesítette a feladatot.
the captain principle-Ine / principled-ly fulfilled the task.Acc
'The captain in principle fulfilled the task.'

Though most of the apparently monomorphemic adverbs, too, were originally derived by once productive suffixes, their morphological make-up is either only partially transparent, or fully opaque.

(11) • Semi-transparent items
gyakran, mindig, hiába, ezennel
'often, always, in vain, hereby'

(12) • Opaque items
kint, ott, otthon, ma, mindjárt, ismét, valaha, most, majd,
'outside, there, at.home, today, instantly, again, ever, now, later,
talán, inkább, szinte
perhaps, rather, almost'

There are a few unanalyzable forms possibly derived by shortening, e.g. *gyalog* (< *gyalogosan* 'on foot'), *soká* (< *sokára* 'after a long time' / *sokáig* 'for a long time'):

(13) a. A kapitány *gyalog* (<gyalog-os-an) érkezett a kastély-ba.
the captain on_foot (< afoot-Adj-An) arrived the castle-Ill
'The captain arrived in the castle on foot.'

b. A kapitány *soká* (<soká-ra) érkezett a kastély-ba.
the captain long (< long-Sub) arrived the castle-Ill
'The captain arrived in the castle after a long time.'

c. A kapitány *soká* (<soká-ig) maradt a kastély-ban.
the captain long (< long-Ter) remained the castle-Ine
'The captain remained in the castle for a long time.'

Adverbs homophonous with bare noun phrases are mainly used in temporal expressions. Observe that most of the items either form a compound ending in *-nap* 'day', or have a possessive suffix on their heads (e.g. *hónap-ja* month-Poss):

(14) A kapitány *reggel* / *este* / *teg-nap* / *vasár-nap* teljesítette a feladatot.
the captain morning / evening / yester-day / Sun-day fulfilled the task.Acc
'The captain fulfilled the task in the morning / in the evening / yesterday / on Sunday.'

(15) A kapitány *két het-e* / *három hónap-ja* / *négy év-e* beteg.
the captain two week-Poss / three month-Poss / four year-Poss ill
'The captain has been ill for two weeks / for three months / for four years.'

Remark 1. When used as nominals, these expressions may be case-marked, or appear as the complement of a postposition (i).

(i) reggel-re, reggel-től, reggel előtt, otthon-ra, má-ra
morning-Sub morning-Ela morning before home-Sub today-Sub
'by morning, since morning, before morning, for home, for today'

Adverbial participles may also function as adverbials (and some of these uses seem to also have lexicalized as adverbs, e.g. *készakarva* 'ready_intend-Part' in (16)):

(16) A kapitány *bizakod-va* / *készakar-va* / *játsz-va* teljesítette a feladatot.
the captain hope-Part / ready_intend-Part / play-Part fulfilled the task.Acc
'The captain fulfilled the task confidently / purposely / with ease.'

Some adverbial modifiers even lexicalized from reduced clauses, as the variation in the following examples shows. In (17a), the modifier is still to be analyzed as a clause, which is clearly reflected by the intonational pattern: breaks must be inserted around the adjunct in postverbal position. As illustrated in (17b), the more lexicalized variants of the same expression may appear in the same position without a marked prosody.

(17) a. Nem veszett el *hála isten-nek* semmije.
not lost away thank God-Dat nothing.Poss.3Sg
'Thank God s/he didn't lose anything.'

b. Nem veszett el *hálisten-nek* / *hálisten* semmije.
not lost away thank_God-Dat / thank_God nothing.Poss.3Sg
'Thank God s/he didn't lose anything.'

7.2.2. VP-adverbials versus clausal adverbials

The main distinction between VP-adverbials and clausal adverbials was originally proposed by Jackendoff (1972). VP-adverbials (or predicate adverbials) modify the verb phrase, or the core predicative part of the sentence, while clausal adverbials (or sentence adverbials) modify larger constituents both in a semantic and in a syntactic sense: they take scope over whole sentences, more precisely over propositions, or even speech acts.

(18) • VP-adverbial
A felügyelő '*könny-en* döntés-re jutott.
the inspector easy-ly decision-Sub got
'The inspector easily arrived at a decision.'

(19) • Clausal or sentence adverbial:
A felügyelő *szerencsé-re* 'döntés-re jutott.
the inspector luck-Sub decision-Sub got
'The inspector luckily arrived at a decision.'

VP-adverbials and clausal adverbials are often referred to as low and high adverbials, respectively, which reflect their prototypical structural positions. In the examples above, this distinction remains hidden if one merely observes the data on the basis of the linear order of the elements. The least marked position for both adverbial types is the one after the topic constituent, preceding the predicate.

The prosodic properties of the sentence, however, make it clear that the VP-adverbial in (18) forms one intonational unit with the predicate, while the clausal adverbial in (19) precedes the verb modifier + verb complex bearing primary stress. (On the prosody of the clause, see the volume on Sentence Structure.) VP-adverbials or low adverbial adjuncts, in the unmarked case, directly precede the predicate and follow the topic constituent(s). This means that they typically appear before the complex predicate formed by a verb modifier and a verb, and a primary stress falls on the adverbial (18). Clausal adverbials, on the other hand, may precede or follow the topics and may also intervene between them. When located between the topic(s) and the predicate, they only bear a reduced stress (19). Structurally speaking, we assume that VP-adverbials such as the manner adverbial *könnyen* 'easily' are adjoined to the core predicate in Hungarian (PredP, rather than VP, but the labels 'VP-adverbial' or 'VP-adjunct' will be kept throughout the chapter for the sake of convenience). Clausal adverbials such as the evaluative adverbial *szerencsére* 'luckily' are adjoined higher in the hierarchical structure of the sentence, they are assumed to adjoin to the extended predicate phrase. (For the functional structure of the Hungarian simple sentence and the hierarchy of elements before the core predicate, see the volume on Sentence Structure.)

It follows from the positional distinction that when it comes to combine these two basic adverbial types in the same sentence, clausal adverbials precede VP-adverbials. To put it differently, their relative order is not arbitrary, and is strictly fixed in the preverbal field. Note that restrictions on word order only apply preverbally. The postverbal word order of these adjuncts appears to be completely free; the variation and their impact on scope interpretation will be discussed extensively in Section 7.4.

The relative order of preverbal clausal and predicative adverbial adjuncts is given in (20):

(20) • S-Adv > VP-Adv

a. A felügyelő *szerencsé-re 'könny-en* döntés-re jutott.
the inspector luck-Sub easy-ly decision-Sub got
'Luckily, the inspector easily arrived at a decision.'

b. *A felügyelő *'könny-en szerencsé-re* döntés-re jutott.
the inspector easy-ly luck-Sub decision-Sub got
Intended meaning: 'Luckily, the inspector easily arrived at a decision.'

In what follows, various tests will be presented to support the legitimacy of the clausal adjunct – VP-adjunct distinction, as well as to provide criteria for the classification of specific adjuncts.

There is a rather simple test to distinguish between VP-adverbials and clausal adverbials. The paraphrase type I in (21), can only apply to low adverbials (21a); it is inapplicable in the case of high adverbials (21b).

(21) • Paraphrase test I

a. A felügyelő döntés-re jutott, és azt *könny-en* tette.
the inspector decision-Sub got and that.Acc easy-ly did
'The inspector arrived at a decision and she did it easily.'

b. *A felügyelő döntés-re jutott, és azt *szerencsé-re* tette.
the inspector decision-Sub got and that.Acc luck-Sub did
Intended meaning: 'The inspector arrived at a decision and she did it luckily.'

Similarly, sentences with a clausal adverbial can be paraphrased as in (22a), while the same strategy does not work when paraphrasing the sentence with a VP-adverbial (22b):

(22) • Paraphrase test II
a. *Szerencsé-re* az a helyzet, hogy a felügyelő döntés-re jutott.
luck-Sub that the situation that the inspector decision-Sub got
'It is luckily the case that the inspector arrived at a decision.'

b. **Könny-en* az a helyzet, hogy a felügyelő döntés-re jutott.
easy-ly that the situation that the inspector decision-Sub got
Intended meaning: 'It is easily the case that the inspector arrived at a decision.'

VP-adverbials can normally be focused (23a) , while clausal adverbials cannot (23b) . Note that the presence of a focus constituent is also reflected by the fact that the finite verb must be adjacent to it and the verb modifier must be postverbal. (In neutral sentences without a focus, the verb modifier precedes the verb, see the volume on Sentence Structure.)

(23) • Focus test
a. A felügyelő KÖNNY-EN jutott döntés-re.
the inspector easy-ly got decision-Sub
'The inspector arrived at a decision EASILY.'

b. *A felügyelő SZERENCSÉ-RE jutott döntés-re.
the inspector luck-Sub got decision-Sub
Intended meaning: 'The inspector arrived at a decision LUCKILY.'

Clausal adverbials can precede the topic (24a), or even intervene between two topics (24b), while VP-adverbials cannot (25) – at least with an unmarked intonational pattern.

(24) • Relative order with respect to topic constituents: clausal adverbial
a. *Szerencsé-re* a felügyelő 'döntés-re jutott.
luck-Sub the inspector decision-Sub got
'Luckily, the inspector arrived at a decision.'

b. A nyomozó *szerencsé-re* a gyilkost 'el-kapta a falu-ban.
the detective luck-Sub the murderer.Acc away-caught the village-Ine
'Luckily, the detective caught the murderer in the village.'

(25) • Relative order with respect to topic constituents: VP-adverbial
a. **Könny-en* a felügyelő 'döntés-re jutott.
easy-ly the inspector decision-Sub got
Intended meaning: 'The inspector arrived at a decision easily.'

b. *A nyomozó *könny-en* a gyilkost 'el-kapta a falu-ban.
the detective easy-ly the murderer.Acc away-caught the village-Ine
Intended meaning: 'The detective caught the murderer easily in the village.'

It must be noted, however, that referential adverbials (e.g., participant PPs or locative modifiers, the nominal parts of which may refer to a specific person, object or place) can easily be topicalized in Hungarian, and, as a consequence, may land in a predicate-external position, namely, in the topic field. Once in topic position, such adverbial adjuncts can freely appear in any order with respect to other topic constituents: in (26), the locative modifier 'in the village' has been topicalized, while in (27), the participant modifier 'with the new witness' occupies one of the topic positions.

(26) (A falu-ban) a nyomozó (a falu-ban) '*könny-en* el-kapta
the village-Ine the detective the village-Ine easy-ly away-caught
a gyilkost.
the murderer.Acc
'The detective easily caught the murderer in the village.'

(27) (Az új tanú-val) a nyomozó (az új tanú-val) '*könny-en* el-kapta
the new witness-Ins the detective the new witness-Ins easy-ly away-caught
a gyilkost.
the murderer.Acc
'The detective easily caught the murderer with the new witness.'

It follows that the above test referring to the relative ordering of adjuncts with respect to topic constituents is only applicable to non-referential adjuncts.

VP-adverbials normally fall into the scope of sentential (interrogative (28a), conditional (28b), or negative (28c)) operators. Clausal adverbials are either infelicitous in sentences containing a sentential operator (29a-b), or they are interpreted outside the scope of the operator (29c).

(28) • In scope of operators: VP-adverbial

a. A felügyelő '*könny-en* döntésre jutott?
the inspector easy-ly decision-Sub got
'Did the inspector arrive easily at a decision?'

b. Ha a felügyelő '*könny-en* döntés-re jut-na...
if the inspector easy-ly decision-Sub get-Cond.3Sg
'If the inspector easily arrived at a decision...'

c. A felügyelő 'nem jutott *könny-en* döntés-re.
the inspector not got easy-ly decision-Sub
'The inspector did not arrive easily at a decision'

(29) • In scope of operators: clausal adverbial

a. ?*A felügyelő *szerencsé-re* 'döntés-re jutott?
the inspector luck-Sub decision-Sub got
Intended meaning: 'Did the inspector arrive luckily at a decision?'

b. ?Ha a felügyelő *szerencsé-re* 'döntés-re jut-na...
if the inspector luck-Sub decision-Sub get-Cond.3Sg
'If the inspector luckily arrived at a decision...'

c. A felügyelő 'nem jutott *szerencsé-re* döntés-re.
the inspector not got luck-Sub decision-Sub
'Luckily, the inspector did not arrive at a decision'

Some adverbial adjuncts are ambiguous in that they can be used either as a VP-adverbial or as a clausal adverbial. If the adverbial *szokatlanul* 'oddly' remains unstressed, it has a wide scope and a sentential reading (30a); it can even precede the topic (30b), and the clause can be paraphrased as in (30c). If, however, the same adverbial appears in focus position, it can only have a (VP-modifying) manner reading (31a), and can only be paraphrased as in (31b).

(30) a. A szomszéd *szokatlan-ul* 'ajtót nyitott.
the neighbor odd-ly door.Acc opened
'Unexpectedly, the neighbor opened the door.'

b. *Szokatlan-ul*, a szomszéd 'ajtót nyitott.
odd-ly the neighbor door.Acc opened
'Unexpectedly, the neighbor opened the door.'

c. *Szokatlan-ul* az történt, hogy a szomszéd ajtót nyitott.
odd-ly that happened that the neighbor door.Acc opened
'It was unexpected that the neighbor opened the door.'

(31) a. A szomszéd SZOKATLAN-UL nyitott ajtót.
the neighbor odd-ly door.Acc opened
'The neighbor opened the door ODDLY.'

b. A szomszéd ajtót nyitott, és azt SZOKATLAN-UL tette.
the neighbor door.Acc opened and that.Acc odd-ly did
'The neighbor opened the door and he did it oddly.'

There are a few adverbial modifiers that have two readings and can occur in the same position with either of the two interpretations. In such cases, stress assignment makes the only distinction between the two readings, as demonstrated in the minimal pair below:

(32) Olívia *'helyes-en* meg-oldotta a feladványt. [manner]
Olívia correct-ly Perf-solved the problem.Acc
'Olívia solved the problem correctly.'

(33) Olívia *helyes-en* 'meg-oldotta a feladványt. [evaluative]
Olívia correct-ly Perf-solved the problem.Acc
'Rightly, Olívia solved the problem.'

At the same time, one may observe that in the scope of a question (34), or a negation (35) only the manner reading is available:

(34) a. Olívia '*helyes-en* meg-oldotta a feladványt? [manner]
Olívia correct-ly Perf-solved the problem.Acc
'Did Olívia solve the problem correctly.'

b. ?*Olívia *helyes-en* 'meg-oldotta a feladványt? [evaluative]
Olívia correct-ly Perf-solved the problem.Acc
Intended meaning: 'Was it right of Olívia to solve the problem?'

(35) a. Olívia 'nem oldotta meg *helyes-en* a feladványt. [manner]
Olívia not solved Perf correct-ly the problem.Acc
'Olívia didn't solve the problem correctly.' (Not: 'It wasn't right of Olívia to solve the problem.')

b. Olívia *helyes-en* 'nem oldotta meg a feladványt. [evaluative]
Olívia correct-ly not solved Perf the problem.Acc
'Rightly, Olívia did not solve the problem.'

Spatial and temporal adverbial adjuncts form a special group inasmuch as they all behave ambiguously: they can modify the sentence as a whole by adding a general, temporal or spatial frame to the clause (hence they are often referred to as framing adverbials, or scene-setting adverbials), but they can also modify a smaller domain, namely the core predicate. Distinction between the two uses is not straightforward, as the tests listed above fail to work in this case. Spatiotemporal adjuncts can freely appear in any possible position, but they can also be topicalized or focalized themselves. They appear both outside and inside the scope of operators.

There is another group of adjuncts that are conventionally not referred to as framing adverbials but show quite similar properties to what have been claimed for spatiotemporals above. These adjuncts introduce an additional circumstance into the proposition, typically a cause, a purpose, or a result. This type will be referred to as contingency adverbial adjuncts and discussed along with spatiotemporals in Section 7.2.4, which is fully devoted to the overview of PP adjuncts that take their scope in a flexible way.

To conclude, the most important features that distinguish VP-adjuncts from clausal adjuncts are the following. VP-adverbials modify the (core) event and the minimal predicate of the sentence. Only Paraphrase I can apply to VP-adjuncts, they can be focused or be questioned by means of a *wh*-phrase. They bear a primary stress when occupying their canonical position at the left edge of the predicate phrase. They normally fall into the scope of sentential operators, and never precede topic constituents. Clausal adverbials typically appear in a sentence initial position, often even preceding the topic constituents(s). Only Paraphrase II can apply to the members of this class. They cannot be focused or questioned by means of a *wh*-phrase. They bear secondary stress or remain unstressed; they precede the locus of primary stress at the left edge of the predicate phrase. Semantically, they do not fall into the scope of other sentential operators, such as interrogation, negation or conditional.

7.2.3. Something in-between: degree and aspectual adverbial adjunct

There are two sets of adjuncts to which neither of the two paraphrase tests applies, and they also behave ambiguously with respect to the focus-test and the pre-topic test. Degree modifiers form a special group of adverbials in this respect, as their contribution to the meaning of a sentence cannot be paraphrased by either of the above used strategies. Consider the approximatives *majdnem* 'almost' and *szinte* 'nearly' in (36), the paraphrases of which are nearly uninterpretable (37)–(38).

(36) A felügyelő *majdnem* / *szinte* döntés-re jutott.
the inspector almost / nearly decision-Sub got
'The inspector almost arrived at a decision.'

(37) • Paraphrase-test I
*A felügyelő döntés-re jutott, és azt *majdnem* / *szinte* tette.
the inspector decision-Sub got and that.Acc almost / nearly did
'*The inspector arrived at a decision and she did it almost.'

(38) • Paraphrase-test II
?**Majdnem* / ?**szinte* az a helyzet, hogy a felügyelő döntés-re jutott.
almost / nearly that the situation that the inspector decision-Sub got
Intended meaning: 'It is almost the case that the inspector arrived at a decision.'

Nevertheless, a sort of interspeaker variation has been observed here: some speakers readily accepted (38) above, while other speakers found this type of sentences slightly better if the reference time of the main clause in Paraphrase II had been changed:

(39) • Paraphrase-test II - modified
?*Majdnem* / ?*szinte* az volt a helyzet, hogy a felügyelő döntés-re jutott.
almost / nearly that was the situation that the inspector decision-Sub got
'It was almost the case that the inspector arrived at a decision.'

As was claimed above, paraphrase test I can only apply to low adverbials, and is inapplicable in the case of high adverbials. At the same time, paraphrase test II can only apply to clausal adverbials, and fails with a VP-adverbial. On the basis of these data, the adjuncts under discussion cannot be classified either as VP-adverbials or as clausal adverbials.

It must also be noted that adjuncts of these types cannot be focused either and will never appear before topic constituents, as demonstrated by the following, ungrammatical examples:

(40) • Focus test
*A felügyelő MAJDNEM / SZINTE jutott döntés-re.
the inspector almost / nearly got decision-Sub
'The inspector ALMOST / NEARLY arrived at a decision'

(41) • Pre-topic test
**Majdnem / *szinte* a felügyelő döntés-re jutott
almost / nearly the inspector decision-Sub got
Intended meaning: 'The inspector almost/nearly arrived at a decision'

Summarizing the results, the category of approximative degree adverbials cannot be determined based on the tests we used to distinguish VP-adjuncts from clausal adjuncts.

There is another class of adjuncts that confuses the picture, as far as the dichotomy of VP-adverbials vs. clausal adverbials is concerned. These can be grouped together because they all contribute to the aspectual properties of the clause, and, at the same time, resemble quantifiers. Nevertheless, the paraphrases, the focus test and the pre-topic test do not characterize them as a homogeneous class. To illustrate these aspectual adjuncts, a habitual adverbial, *általában* 'usually' will be examined below.

(42) A felügyelő *általában* döntés-re jutott.
the inspector usually decision-Sub got
'The inspector usually arrived at a decision.'

The habitual *általában* 'usually' fails at both paraphrase tests:

(43) • Paraphrase-test I.
*A felügyelő döntés-re jutott, és azt *általában* tette.
the inspector decision-Sub got and that.Acc usually did
Intended meaning: 'The inspector arrived at a decision and she did it usually.'

(44) • Paraphrase-test II
**Általában* az a helyzet, hogy a felügyelő döntés-re jutott.
usually that the situation that the inspector decision-Sub got
Intended meaning: 'It is usually the case that the inspector arrived at a decision.'

Again, Paraphrase II can be repaired by changing the reference time of the main clause, as in (45):

(45) • Paraphrase-test II - modified
Általában az volt a helyzet, hogy a felügyelő döntés-re jutott.
usually that was the situation that the inspector decision-Sub got
'It was usually the case that the inspector arrived at a decision.'

The adverbial is normally not focused (46), but may precede a topic constituent (47):

(46) • Focus test
*A felügyelő ÁLTALÁBAN jutott döntés-re.
the inspector usually got decision-Sub
'*The inspector arrived at a decision USUALLY.'

(47) • Pre-topic test

Általában a felügyelő döntés-re jutott.
usually the inspector decision-Sub got
'The inspector usually arrived at a decision.'

The test results suggest that the habitual aspectual adjunct is a high adverbial but modifies a smaller domain within the sentence than a prototypical speaker-oriented adverbial such as *szerencsére* 'luckily' does. The latter adds a sort of attitude or evaluation on behalf of the speaker and scopes over the sentence as whole, including the speech-act of the proposition. Adverbials like *általában* 'usually' and other quantifier-like PP adjuncts might be assumed to modify the extended predicate of the clause, though having a smaller scope than prototypical clausal adjuncts, which makes it reasonable to treat them as a separate class.

To summarize these observations, degree adverbial adjuncts and aspectual adverbial adjuncts cannot clearly be classified either as VP-adjuncts or as clausal adjuncts but appear to be something in-between. The semantic properties of this middle class will be discussed in sections 7.3.9 and 7.3.10, while their possible syntactic positions and restrictions on their placement will be discussed in Section 7.4.1.2.

7.2.4. Flexible scope taking: Spatial, temporal and contingency adverbial adjuncts

Spatial and temporal adverbials seem to share properties both with VP-adjuncts and with clausal adverbials. This means that they can be used in both functions: they are either quasi-external, framing elements, or they are VP-adjuncts, anchoring the event at a certain location or time. This can be readily observed through paraphrases. A sentence such as (48) can be paraphrased both as in (49), and as in (50), i.e., by using the strategies that were suggested above to distinguish between VP-adverbials and clausal adverbials.

(48) *London-ban* a felügyelő döntés-re jutott.
London-Ine the inspector decision-Sub got
'In London, the inspector arrived at a decision.'

(49) • Paraphrase-test I

A felügyelő döntés-re jutott, és azt *London-ban* tette.
the inspector decision-Sub got and that.Acc London-Ine did
'The inspector arrived at a decision and she did it in London.'

(50) • Paraphrase-test II

London-ban az a helyzet, hogy a felügyelő döntés-re jutott.
London-Ine that the situation that the inspector decision-Sub got
'The situation in London is that the inspector arrived at a decision.'

Spatial and temporal adverbials can freely appear in practically any sentence position: they either precede or follow the topic constituent (51a-b), may intervene between topics and may appear postverbally (51c).

(51) a. *London-ban* / *hajnal-ban* a felügyelő döntés-re jutott.
London-Ine / dawn-Ine the inspector decision-Sub got
'[In London] / [At dawn], the inspector arrived at a decision.'

b. A felügyelő *London-ban* / *hajnal-ban* döntés-re jutott.
the inspector London-Ine / dawn-Ine decision-Sub got
'[In London] / [At dawn], the inspector arrived at a decision.'

c. A felügyelő döntés-re jutott *London-ban* / *hajnal-ban.*
the inspector decision-Sub got London-Ine / dawn-Ine
'[In London] / [At dawn], the inspector arrived at a decision.'

As a matter of fact, when they appear in the topic field, preceding/following a topic constituent, it is impossible to decide whether they are framing adverbials that have been adjoined in a relatively high position in the sentence, or they have been themselves topicalized into the left periphery and were originally adjoined to the predicate. Framing adjuncts and true (discourse) topics can only be distinguished in context, that is to say, taking into consideration the information structural status of the spatial or temporal expression we are dealing with in a given sentence.

Spatial and temporal adverbials can freely appear in the structural focus position.

(52) a. A felügyelő LONDON-BAN jutott döntés-re.
the inspector London-Ine got decision-Sub
'The inspector arrived at a decision IN LONDON.'

b. A felügyelő HAJNAL-BAN jutott döntés-re.
the inspector dawn-Ine got decision-Sub
'The inspector arrived at a decision AT DAWN.'

Spatial and temporal adverbials can also cooccur in the same clause, in either of the following orderings:

(53) a. *London-ban hajnal-ban* a felügyelő döntés-re jutott.
London-Ine dawn-Ine the inspector decision-Sub got
'In London, at dawn, the inspector arrived at a decision.'

b. *Hajnal-ban London-ban* a felügyelő döntés-re jutott.
dawn-Ine London-Ine the inspector decision-Sub got
'At dawn, in London, the inspector arrived at a decision.'

Spatial and temporal adverbials may be interpreted within as well as outside the scope of operators, e.g. negation (54a), or question (54b). When the adverbial gets focused, the readings are disambiguated and reflected by the word order: (55a) can only mean that the inspector did arrive at a decision but it did not take place in London, while (55b) exclusively or contrastively identifies the place where the inspector did not arrive at a decision with London.

(54) a. A felügyelő nem jutott döntés-re *London-ban.*
the inspector not got decision-Sub London-Ine
'The inspector did not arrive at a decision in London.'

b. A felügyelő döntés-re jutott *London-ban*?
the inspector decision-Sub got London-Ine
'Did the inspector arrive at a decision in London?'

(55) a. A felügyelő nem LONDON-BAN jutott döntés-re.
the inspector not London-Ine got decision-Sub
'The inspector did not arrive at a decision in LONDON.'

b. A felügyelő LONDON-BAN nem jutott döntés-re.
the inspector London-Ine not got decision-Sub
'The inspector did not arrive at a decision in LONDON.'

Spatial and temporal adverbials with a sentential scope, however, differ from other, non-spatial/non-temporal clausal adjuncts both in their semantics and in their syntactic properties. The difference can most easily be captured by the fact that framing adverbials do not pose any requirement with regard to the structure or the semantic representation of the clause they adjoin to, while the position of non-spatiotemporal adjuncts is more restricted within the sentence. This will be one of the topics discussed in Section 7.4.

Contingency adverbials establish a circumstance upon which the process or event denoted by the predicate is contingent. Most typically, this circumstance is a cause or a purpose, and contingency adverbials seem to behave like spatiotemporal adjuncts in that they can behave either as VP-adjuncts, or as framing adverbials taking a wide scope. Observe the two paraphrase tests applied to an adverbial adjunct of cause below:

(56) A felügyelő *az új bizonyítéknak köszönhető-en* döntés-re jutott.
the inspector the new proof.Dat owing-Adv decision-Sub got
'The inspector arrived at a decision owing to the new proof.'

(57) • Paraphrase-test I
A felügyelő döntés-re jutott, és azt *az új bizonyítéknak*
the inspector decision-Sub got and that.Acc the new proof.Dat
köszönhető-en tette.
owing-Adv did
'The inspector arrived at a decision and he did it owing to the new proof.'

(58) • Paraphrase-test II
Az új bizonyítéknak köszönhető-en az a helyzet, hogy a felügyelő
the new proof.Dat owing-Adv that the situation that the inspector.
döntés-re jutott
decision-Sub got
'Owing to the new proof, the situation is that the inspector arrived at a decision.'

Contingency adverbials can freely appear in focus position (59), and may precede the topic constituent (60).

(59) • Focus test

A felügyelő AZ ÚJ BIZONYÍTÉKNAK KÖSZÖNHETŐ-EN jutott döntés-re.
the inspector the new proof.Dat owing-Adv got decision-Sub
'The inspector arrived at a decision OWING TO THE NEW PROOF.'

(60) • Pre-topic test

Az új bizonyítéknak köszönhető-en a felügyelő döntés-re jutott.
the new proof.Dat owing-Adv the inspector decision-Sub got
'Owing to the new proof, the inspector arrived at a decision.'

As a matter of fact, such adverbials can easily be found in any sentence position in which adjuncts can appear.

(61) (Az új bizonyítéknak köszönhető-en) a felügyelő
the new proof.Dat owing-Adv the inspector
(az új bizonyítéknak köszönhető-en) döntés-re
the new proof.Dat owing-Adv decision-Sub
jutott (az új bizonyítéknak köszönhető-en).
got the new proof.Dat owing-Adv
'The inspector arrived at a decision owing to the new proof.'

Contingency adverbials are ambiguous in scope relations, in a similar fashion to what has been shown for spatial and temporal adjuncts above (62a). However, focusing the PP adjuncts leaves no uncertainty in the interpretation: (62b) can only mean that the inspector's decision-making did not happen because of the new proof, while (62c) explicitly says that the inspector did not arrive at a decision as a consequence of the new proof.

(62) a. A felügyelő nem jutott döntés-re *az új bizonyítéknak köszönhető-en.*
the inspector not got decision-Sub the new proof.Dat owing-Adv
'The inspector did not arrive at a decision owing to the new proof.'

b. A felügyelő nem AZ ÚJ BIZONYÍTÉKNAK KÖSZÖNHETŐ-EN
the inspector not the new proof.Dat owing-Adv
jutott döntés-re.
got decision-Sub
'The inspector did not arrive at a decision OWING TO THE NEW PROOF.'

c. A felügyelő AZ ÚJ BIZONYÍTÉKNAK KÖSZÖNHETŐ-EN nem jutott
the inspector the new proof.Dat owing-Adv not got
döntés-re.
decision-Sub
'The inspector did not arrive at a decision OWING TO THE NEW PROOF.'

To conclude, contingency adverbials can also be claimed to be flexible in scope taking as they can be used both as a VP-adjunct and as a clausal adjunct.

7.3. Semantic types of adverbial adjuncts

This section offers a semantic classification of adverbial adjuncts, with some necessary overlap with Section 2.3 in Chapter 2. In each case, after providing a basic description of the semantic class, typical forms of the type will be defined and illustrated. The classification is not intended to serve as an exhaustive listing; it rather aims to present the relevant groups of PP adjuncts in a comprehensible and representative way.

It is important to note that the referential properties of the internal nominal part of PP adjuncts have a crucial effect on their behavior. Several classes of adjuncts will be listed below, and many types, such as spatiotemporal PPs, or participant PPs, typically contain a noun phrase that can be referential. In this case the PP constituent can easily be topicalized, i.e. it can function as the logical subject of predication.

7.3.1. Spatial and temporal adverbial adjuncts

7.3.1.1. Spatial adverbial adjuncts

Spatial adpositional phrases may refer to a location (a point or a region in space), and to a change in location (path, or direction). However, adjuncts are more likely to be locative in the first sense. Directional adpositional phrases, which assume a goal, a path or a source, tend to function as arguments or thematic adjuncts in the sentence. As has already been discussed above, in Section 7.2.4, spatial adverbials share properties both with VP-adjuncts and with clausal adjuncts, in accordance with the fact that they can be used in both functions.

The typical forms of spatial adjuncts are noun phrases with either a locative (inessive, superessive, adessive) case suffix (63a-c) or a case-like (63d) or case-assigning postposition (63e).

(63) a. Félix leveleket gépelt *a nappali-ban.*
Félix letters.Acc typed the living-room-Ine
'Félix was typing letters in the living room.'

b. Félix leveleket gépelt *az erkély-en.*
Félix letters.Acc typed the balcony-Sup
'Félix was typing letters on the balcony.'

c. Félix leveleket gépelt *a kandalló-nál.*
Félix letters.Acc typed the fireplace-Ade
'Félix was typing letters at the fireplace.'

d. Félix leveleket gépelt *a kandalló mellett.*
Félix letters.Acc typed the fireplace next_to
'Félix was typing letters beside the fireplace.'

e. Félix leveleket gépelt *a kandalló-hoz közel.*
Félix letters.Acc typed the fireplace-All close_to
'Félix was typing letters close to the fireplace.'

In all the examples cited, the adjuncts contain a referential element, for this reason the PP phrase can be topicalized.

(64) (*A kandalló mellett*) Félix (*a kandalló mellett*) 'leveleket gépelt.
the fireplace next_to Félix the fireplace next_to letters.Acc typed
'Félix was typing letters beside the fireplace.'

It must be noted again, however, that the same adverbial adjuncts can also be analyzed as mere framing adverbials, instead of functioning as aboutness topics. A distinction can only be made relying on the discourse and taking into consideration the role these phrases play in the information structure of the given sentence.

When a spatial adverbial adjunct refers to a path, rather than to a specific location, its form and semantics is close to the duration reading of temporal adverbials.

(65) a. A kapitány *az erdő-ben* biciklizett. [location]
the captain the forest-Ine cycled
'The captain cycled in the forest.'

b. A kapitány *az erdő-ig* biciklizett. [path]
the captain the forest-Ter cycled
'The captain cycled as far as the forest.'

When two locative adverbials are combined, the more general frame normally precedes the more specific one:

(66) a. A nyomozó *a falu-ban a polgármester pincé-jé-ben* el-kapta a gyilkost.
the detective the village-Ine the mayor cellar-Poss-Ine away-caught the murderer.Acc
'The detective caught the murderer in the village, in the mayor's cellar.'

b. $^{?}$A nyomozó *a polgármester pincé-jé-ben, a falu-ban* el-kapta a gyilkost.
the detective the mayor cellar-Poss-Ine the village-Ine away-caught the murderer.Acc
'The detective caught the murderer in the mayor's cellar, in the village.'

7.3.1.2. Temporal adverbial adjuncts

Temporal adpositional phrases are either punctual or durative, i.e. they refer to a point or a duration in time. In a more fine-grained classification, the following five types may be distinguished (after Kiefer 2006, 2009): time span adverbials (e.g. *két órán át* 'for two hours', see (67e)), durative-delimitative adverbials (e.g. *két óra alatt* 'in two hours', see (67d)), time point adverbials (e.g. *két órakor* 'at two o'clock', see (67b)), adverbials denoting the length of a resulting state (e.g. *két órára* 'for two hours', see (67a)), adverbials denoting an endpoint of a process or activity (e.g. *két óráig* 'until two o'clock', see (67c)).

The morphological realization of temporal adjuncts shows considerable variation: they may either appear as PPs furnished with a case-suffix (e.g. locative suffixes (67a), the temporal suffix *-kor*, the iterative suffix *-(V)nta/-(V)nte* (67b), the terminative suffix *-ig* (67c)), or appear as postpositional phrases with either a case-like (67d) or a case-assigning postposition (67e). Many temporal adverbials are PPs without a transparent inner structure (67f).

(67) a. Félix le-gépelt *dél-ben* / *hétfő-n* / *két órá-ra* egy levelet.
Félix down-typed noon-Ine / Monday-Sup / two hour-Sub a letter.Acc
'Félix typed a letter [at noon] / [on Monday] / [for two o'clock].'

b. Félix *három-kor* / *het-ente* le-gépelt egy levelet.
Félix three-Tmp / week-Iter down-typed a letter.Acc
'Félix typed a letter [at three o'clock] / [every week].'

c. Félix *három-ig* leveleket gépelt.
Félix three-Ter letters.Acc typed
'Félix was typing letters until three o'clock.'

d. Félix *két óra alatt* le-gépelt egy levelet.
Félix two hour under down-typed a letter.Acc
'Félix typed a letter in two hours.'

e. Félix *két órá-n át* leveleket gépelt.
Félix two hour-Sup through letters.Acc typed
'Félix was typing letters for two hours.'

f. Félix *egész este* / *ma* leveleket gépelt.
Félix whole evening / today letters.Acc typed
'Félix was typing letters [the whole evening] / today.'

The compatibility of temporal adverbials with different event types has long been observed and examined across languages. The basic observation is that accomplishment and achievement predicates, presenting a completed event, are compatible with delimiting time adverbials (68), while stative and activity predicates are compatible with durative time adverbials (69).

(68) Félix le-gépelt egy levelet *két óra alatt* / **két órá-n át.*
Félix down-typed one letter.Acc two hour under / two hour-Sup through
'Félix typed a letter [in two hours] / [*for two hours].'

(69) Félix leveleket gépelt *két órá-n át* / **két óra alatt.*
Félix letters.Acc typed two hour-Sup through / two hour under
'Félix was typing letters [for two hours] / [*in two hours].'

Accusative-marked PPs can also serve as temporal adjuncts (as durative / time-span adverbials, see (70)), but their distribution is far more restricted than that of temporal adjuncts in general, including its quasi-synonymous pair, the durative postposition *át* 'through/for/via'. For instance, they are slightly degraded before another VP-adverbial (71), and rather degraded in combination with a true accusative argument (72).

(70) Félix *két órá-t* / *két órá-n át* dolgozott.
Félix two hour-Acc / two hour-Sup through worked
'Félix was working for two hours.'

(71) a. Félix *két órá-n át* keményen dolgozott.
Félix two hour-Sup through hard worked
'Félix was working hard for two hours.'

b. ?Félix *két órá-t* keményen dolgozott.
Félix two hour-Acc hard worked
'Félix was working hard for two hours.'

(72) a. Félix *két órá-n át* levelek-et gépelt.
Félix two hour-Sup through letters-Acc typed
'Félix was typing letters for two hours.'

b. ??Félix *két órá-t* levelek-et gépelt.
Félix two hour-Acc letters-Acc typed
'Félix was typing letters for two hours.'

When two temporal adverbials are combined, the more general frame normally precedes the more specific one:

(73) a. A nyomozó *kedd-en hajnal-ban* el-kapta a gyilkost.
the detective Tuesday-Sup dawn-Ine away-caught the murderer.Acc
'The detective caught the murderer on Tuesday, at dawn.'

b. ?A nyomozó *hajnal-ban, kedd-en* el-kapta a gyilkost.
the detective dawn-Ine Tuesday-Sup away-caught the murderer.Acc
'The detective caught the murderer at dawn, on Tuesday.'

7.3.2. Contingency adverbial adjuncts

Contingency adverbials establish a circumstance upon which the action/event denoted by the predicate is contingent. As has already been discussed above, in Section 7.2.4, contingency adverbials share properties both with VP-adjuncts and with clausal adjuncts, and accordingly, they can be used in both functions.

7.3.2.1. Contingency adverbials: cause

Contingency adverbials may express a cause. The cause can be established objectively or might appear as a subjectively considered reason.

Cause adverbials can be formed, for instance, by a causal-final case-marked PP (74a), by a sublative case-marked PP (74b), by a postpositional phrase (74c), but the same semantic role may be fulfilled by alternative forms as well, such as e.g. an inessive or an ablative PP expression (74d-e).

(74) a. Félix *valami-ért* kihagyta az ebédszünetet.
Félix something-Cau out-left the lunch.break.Acc
'Félix skipped the lunch break for some reason.'

b. Félix *a felügyelő kérésé-re* leveleket gépelt.
Félix the inspector request.Poss-Sub letters.Acc typed
'Félix typed some letters at the inspector's request.'

c. Félix *az esős idő miatt* leveleket gépelt.
Félix the rainy weather because_of letters.Acc typed
'Félix typed some letters because of the rainy weather.'

d. Félix *rossz kedvé-ben* leveleket gépelt.
Félix bad mood.Poss.3Sg-Ine letters.Acc typed
'Félix typed some letters due to his low spirits.'

e. Olívia *a fejfájás-tól* dühbe gurult.
Olívia the headache-Abl anger.Ill rolled
'Olívia got angry because of the headache.'

7.3.2.2. Contingency adverbials: purpose

Another circumstance might be some kind of purpose to which the action/event denoted by the predicate is related.

Purpose adverbials are typically expressed with the same PP-types as cause adverbials, e.g. by a causal-final case-marked PP (75a), by a postpositional phrase (75b), or they may appear in further alternative forms that express a similar semantic function (75c).

(75) a. Olívia *a nyomozás lezárásá-ért* fel-hívta a felügyelőt.
Olívia the investigation closing.Poss-Cau up-called the inspector.Acc
'Olívia called the inspector in order to close the investigation.'

b. Olívia *a nyomozás lezárása miatt / végett* fel-hívta a felügyelőt.
Olívia the investigation closing.Poss because_of / for_the_purpose_of up-called the inspector.Acc
'Olívia called the inspector in order to close the investigation.'

c. Olívia *a sikeres nyomozás érdeké-ben* fel-hívta a felügyelőt.
Olívia the successful investigation interest.Poss-Ine up-called the inspector.Acc
'Olívia called the inspector for the sake of successful investigation.'

7.3.2.3. Contingency adverbials: result

Result adverbials introduce a circumstance as the expected result of the action/event denoted by the predicate.

A result adverbial may appear, for instance, in the form of a sublative (76a) or a causal-final case-marked PP (76b):

(76) a. Félix *a felügyelő megelégedésé-re* le-gépelte a levelet.
Félix the inspector satisfaction.Poss-Sub down-typed the letter.Acc
'Félix typed the letter to the inspector's satisfaction.'

b. Félix *a rend kedvé-ért* le-gépelte a levelet.
Félix the order sake.Poss-Cau down-typed the letter.Acc
'Félix typed the letter for order's sake.'

Note that cause, purpose and result interpretations cannot always be clearly distinguished. The actual interpretation may depend on the discourse and on the point of view adopted by the speaker/addressee. Accordingly, (75b) is ambiguous between cause and purpose, while (76b) between purpose and result.

7.3.2.4. Contingency adverbials: concession

Concessive adverbials refer to a circumstance the effect of which fails to manifest, in spite of the expectation of the interlocutors.

The typical form of the concessive adverbial is a postpositional phrase headed by a possessive P *ellenére/dacára* 'despite'. (For this type of postpositions, see Section 2.4.2 in Chapter 2.)

(77) Félix *a fejfájása ellenére / dacára* legépelte a levelet.
Félix the headache.Poss.3Sg despite / despite down-typed the letter.Acc
'Félix typed the letter despite his headache.'

7.3.3. Manner adverbials

Manner adverbials specify the manner in which the action is performed. Manner adverbials are prototypical VP-adjuncts, they directly precede the core predicate in Hungarian and bear a primary stress. They can be focused and can be questioned by a *wh*-phrase. Their characteristic form is an adverb derived from an adjective (78).

(78) a. Félix *könny-en* le-gépelte a levelet.
Félix easy-ly down-typed the letter.Acc
'Félix easily typed the letter.'

b. Félix *hibátlan-ul* le-gépelte a levelet.
Félix flawless-ly down-typed the letter.Acc
'Félix flawlessly typed the letter.'

A group of negative adverbials of manner always must be focused. (The same holds for a group of negative adverbials of degree and frequency. This phenomenon will be discussed in detail in Section 7.4.3.)

(79) Félix ROSSZ-UL gépelte le a levelet.
Félix wrong-ly typed down the letter.Acc
'Félix typed the letter incorrectly.'

(80) Félix GONDATLAN-UL gépelte le a levelet.
Félix careless-ly typed down the letter.Acc
'Félix typed the letter carelessly.'

Lassan 'slowly' and *gyorsan* 'quickly' seem to be typical manner adverbs semantically, but they can also be used as adjuncts with a special, aspectual meaning. *Lassan* 'slowly' as a higher adverbial means 'soon, in a little while', whereas *gyorsan* 'quickly' means 'right now, without deferring', both modifying the time of the preparation preceding the event, rather than the process itself (cf. Eszes 2009). The higher adverbial version of these adverbs can freely co-occur with an apparently antonymous adjective without any contradiction arising:

(81) *Lass-an* összeütök egy gyors levest.
slow-ly slapdash.1Sg one quick soup.Acc
'In a little while, I throw together a quick soup.'

(82) *Gyors-an* táncoljunk még egy lassú csárdást!
quick-ly dance.Subj.1Pl still one slow chardash.Acc
'Right now, let us dance a slow chardash, too!'

7.3.4. Subject-oriented adverbials

Subject-oriented adverbials specify the relation of the acting/affected person to the action/event denoted by the predicate, informing about the volition, attitude or mental state of the subject. The class is also referred to as the class of agent-oriented or volitional adverbials. The prototypical subject-oriented adjunct is an adverb derived from an adjective (83), but it may also be expressed by a case-marked PP, or a lexicalized adverbial participle (84).

(83) a Félix *véletlen-ül* / *szándékos-an* fel-bontotta a levelet.
Félix accidental-ly / deliberate-ly up-opened the letter.Acc
'Félix opened the letter [by accident] / deliberately.'

b. Félix *kelletlen-ül* / *lelkes-en* fel-bontotta a levelet.
Félix unwilling-ly / zealous-ly up-opened the letter.Acc
'Félix opened the letter unwillingly / zealously.'

(84) Félix *öröm-mel* / *vonakod-va* fel-bontotta a levelet.
Félix pleasure-Ins / begrudge-Part up-opened the letter.Acc
'Félix opened the letter [with pleasure] / reluctantly.'

A subtype of subject-oriented adverbials reflects the speaker's evaluation of the subject of the clause in relation to the predicate, rather than the mental state or volition of the subject itself.

(85) Félix *okos-an* / *diszkrét-en* le-gépelte a levelet.
Félix clever-ly / tactful-ly down-typed the letter.Acc
'Félix cleverly / tactfully typed the letter.'

The VP-adjunct status of subject-oriented adverbials is not self-evident, since they may appear quite high in the clause, even preceding the quantifier field (cf. Section 7.4.1.3). Volitional adverbials can be focused, while those evaluating the subject's way of acting are often ambiguous between the evaluating and the pure manner reading, like in the case of *okosan* 'cleverly' where only the manner interpretation is available in focus position. Accordingly, *okosan* 'cleverly' is slightly degraded in (86), because it is difficult to accommodate the manner reading with the process of letter-typing expressed in the predicate part of the clause.

(86) Félix SZÁNDÉKOS-AN / DISZKRÉT-EN / $^{?}$OKOS-AN gépelte le a levelet.
Félix deliberate-ly / tactful-ly / clever-ly typed down the letter.Acc
'Félix typed the letter deliberately / tactfully / cleverly.'

7.3.5. Participant PPs

An event may have various participants that are not entailed by the predicate, and as such, are optional. Chapter 5 treats them as non-core arguments of the verb as opposed to subcategorized core arguments (see Section 5.3.1). In this chapter, however, these participant PPs are classified as VP-adjuncts. They can be questioned by means of a *wh*-phrase, they can be focused, and from a semantic point of view, they modify the core predicate in a similar way as other VP-adjuncts do. At the same time, participant PPs have a nominal part inside the adjunct phrase, which are often referential. Therefore, the unmarked position for a participant PP is not the one directly preceding the predicate; it rather appears postverbally, or else, sentence initially as a discourse topic (see some examples at the end of this section).

Under the cover term of participant PPs, instrumentals, comitatives and benefactives will be grouped together.

7.3.5.1. Instrumental adverbials

Instrumental adverbials specify the instrument (87a) or means (87b) used in performing the action. The prototypical instrumental adverbial is a PP with an instrumental case suffix (87), but the same semantic role may be fulfilled by alternative forms as well, e.g. by a superessive-marked PP (88).

(87) a. Félix le-gépelte a levelet *az új piros írógépé-vel.*
Félix down-typed the letter.Acc the new red typewriter.Poss.3Sg-Ins
'Félix typed the letter with his new red typewriter.'

b. Olívia el-menekült *egy taxi-val.*
Olívia away-escaped a taxi-Ins
'Olívia escaped by a cab.'

(88) Félix le-gépelte a levelet *az új piros írógépé-n.*
Félix down-typed the letter.Acc the new red typewriter.Poss.3Sg-Sup
'Félix typed the letter on his new red typewriter.'

7.3.5.2. Comitative adverbials

Comitative adverbials establish the co-agents of the action/event denoted by the predicate. The prototypical comitative adverbial is an instrumental-marked PP (89).

(89) Olívia keringőt táncolt *a kapitány-nyal.*
Olívia waltz.Acc danced the captain-Ins
'Olívia danced a waltz with the captain.'

A special case of comitative modifiers is expressed by a PP formed with the sociative suffix *-(V)stul/-(V)stül* (90). (For the forms and use of this special suffix, see Section 2.2.4.1.2 in Chapter 2.)

(90) A kapitány *felesége-stül* érkezett Argentíná-ból.
the captain wife-Soc arrived Argentina-Ela
'The captain arrived from Argentina with his wife.'

7.3.5.3. Benefactive adverbials

Benefactive adverbials establish discourse participants for the sake of whom the action/event denoted by the predicate is performed. Benefactive adverbials are typically realized as PPs involving a noun phrase supplied with a dative case suffix (91) or with a corresponding postposition (92).

(91) Olívia keringőt táncolt *az új ügyfelek-nek.*
Olívia waltz.Acc danced the new clients-Dat
'Olívia danced a waltz for the new clients.'

(92) Olívia keringőt táncolt *az új ügyfelek számára.*
Olívia waltz.Acc danced the new clients for
'Olívia danced a waltz for the new clients.'

As was mentioned above, instrumentals, comitatives and benefactives can also be grouped together on the basis that they often have a referential element in their nominal part. Therefore, they are easy to topicalize. In the examples below, the sentence initial PPs all serve as discourse topics, which means that the 'red typewriter' and the 'new clients' must have been introduced into the discourse previously.

(93) • instrumental
Az új piros írógépé-vel Félix le-gépelte a levelet.
the new red typewriter.Poss.3Sg-Ins Félix down-typed the letter.Acc
'Félix typed the letter with his new red typewriter.'

(94) • benefactive
Az új ügyfelek-nek Olívia keringőt táncolt.
the new clients-Dat Olívia waltz.Acc danced
'Olívia danced a waltz for the new clients.'

7.3.6. Domain adverbials

Domain adverbials restrict the action/event denoted by the predicate to a certain domain. Prototypical domain adverbials are adverbs derived from an adjective.

(95) a. A nyomozó *elvi-leg / gyakorlati-lag* a lakásán dolgozott.
the detective principled-ly / practical-ly the flat.Poss.3Sg.Sup worked
'The detective [in principle] / practically worked in his apartment.'

b. A kapitány *jogi-lag* el-vesztette az ügyet.
the captain legally away-lost the case.Acc
'The captain legally lost the case.'

Domain adverbials behave more like clausal adjuncts. Only paraphrase-test II applies to them, they can hardly be focused (98), but can freely precede topic constituents (100).

(96) • Paraphrase-test I

a. *A nyomozó a lakásán dolgozott, és azt
the detective the flat.Poss.3Sg.Sup worked and that.Acc
elvi-leg / *gyakorlati-lag* tette.
principled-ly / practical-ly did
'*The detective worked in his apartment and he did it [in principle] / practically.'

b. ??A kapitány el-vesztette az ügyet, és azt *jogi-lag* tette.
the captain away-lost the case.Acc and that.Acc legal-ly did
'The captain lost the case and he did it legally.'

Remark 2. It is to be noted that Paraphrase-test I is more difficult to apply if the verb in the predicate is not agentive, like in (97b) . In such cases, the schema used in the paraphrase-test could be changed, e.g.:

(i) ??A kapitány el-vesztette az ügyet, és az
the captain away-lost the case.Acc and that
jogi-lag történt vele.
legal-ly happened Ins.3Sg
'The captain lost the case and it happened to him legally.'

(97) • Paraphrase-test II

a. *Elvi-leg* / *gyakorlati-lag* az a helyzet, hogy a nyomozó
principled-ly / practical-ly that the situation that the detective
a lakásán dolgozott.
the flat.Poss.3Sg.Sup worked
'[In principle] / practically, it is the case that the detective worked in his apartment.'

b. *Jogi-lag* az a helyzet, hogy a kapitány el-vesztette az ügyet.
legally that the situation that the captain away-lost the case.Acc
'Legally it is the case that the captain lost the case.'

(98) • Focus test

a. ??A nyomozó ELVI-LEG / GYAKORLATI-LAG dolgozott a lakásán.
the detective principled-ly / practical-ly worked the flat.Poss.3Sg.Sup
Intended meaning: 'The detective worked in his apartment [IN PRINCIPLE] / PRACTICALLY.'

b. ?A kapitány JOGI-LAG vesztette el az ügyet.
the captain legal-ly lost away the case.Acc
'The captain lost the case LEGALLY.'

But note that focusing is available if more possible domains associated with the predicate can be contrasted. (99) can be used, if the captain did not lose the case from another, e.g. intellectual, perspective.

(99) A kapitány JOGI SZEMPONT-BÓL / JOGI ÉRTELEM-BEN vesztette
the captain legal viewpoint-Ela / legal sense-Ine lost
el az ügyet.
away the case.Acc
'The captain lost the case [from a legal perspective] / [in a legal sense].'

(100) • Pre-topic test

a. *Elvi-leg* / *gyakorlati-lag* a nyomozó a lakásán dolgozott.
principled-ly / practical-ly the detective the flat.Poss.3Sg.Sup worked
'The detective [in principle] / practically worked in his apartment.'

b. *Jogi-lag* a kapitány el-vesztette az ügyet.
legally the captain away-lost the case.Acc
'Legally, the captain lost the case.'

Even if placed after the negative particle and the verb, domain adverbials are normally interpreted outside the scope of negation (101), or other sentential operators. This observation supports the claim that these adverbials are clausal adjuncts.

(101) a. A nyomozó nem dolgozott *elvi-leg* / *gyakorlati-lag* a lakásán.
the detective not worked principled-ly / practical-ly the flat.Poss.3Sg.Sup
'[In principle] / practically, the detective did not work in his apartment.'

b. A kapitány nem vesztette el *jogi-lag* az ügyet.
the captain not lost away legal-ly the case.Acc
'Legally, the captain did not lose the case.'

7.3.7. Speaker-oriented adverbials

Speaker-oriented adverbials express the speaker's attitude or evaluation with respect to the situation described in the sentence. They are clausal adverbials, which typically appear in a sentence initial position, often even preceding the topic constituents(s). Only Paraphrase II can apply to the members of this class. They cannot be focused or questioned by means of a *wh*-phrase. They bear secondary stress or remain unstressed; they precede the locus of primary stress at the left edge of the predicate phrase. Semantically, they do not fall into the scope of other sentential operators, such as interrogation, negation or conditional.

They have the whole sentence in their scope, but their scope relative to one another is asymmetric in as much as speech-act adverbials (e.g. *őszintén szólva* 'honestly speaking') have scope over evaluative adverbials, e.g. *szerencsére* 'luckily', which have scope over epistemic adverbials, e.g. *valószínűleg* 'probably' (cf. Section 7.4.2 on this issue).

7.3.7.1. Epistemic/modal adverbials

Modal adverbial adjuncts express the speaker's epistemic judgments or comments on the proposition, i.e. on the likelihood of the actual event expressed in the proposition. The adjuncts themselves may express various levels of commitment of the speaker to the truth of the propositions based on his/her own belief or evidence.

Typical modal adverbials are adverbs derived from adjectives, their forms being similar to manner adverbs.

(102) Félix *valószínű-leg* / *feltehető-en* / *kétségtelen-ül* le-gépelte a levelet.
Félix probable-ly / supposed-ly / undoubted-ly down-typed the letter.Acc
'Félix probably / supposedly / undoubtedly typed the letter.'

Evidential adverbial adjuncts can also refer to the source of the information on the basis of which such judgments have been formed. The adjunct in (103) refers to direct evidence, perceived by the speaker himself, while the one in (104) shows that the source is not necessarily identifiable.

(103) Félix *látható-an* le-gépelte a levelet.
Félix visible-ly down-typed the letter.Acc
'Félix evidently typed the letter.'

(104) Félix *állító-lag* le-gépelte a levelet.
Félix alleged-ly down-typed the letter.Acc
'Félix allegedly typed the letter.'

Certain PP adjuncts serve to show that the truth of the assertion is compatible with the knowledge or the information state of the speaker (105a), or the other way round, the speaker shifts the responsibility to someone else (105b).

(105) a. *Szerintem* Félix le-gépelte a levelet.
according_to.1Sg Félix down-typed the letter.Acc
'In my opinion, Félix typed the letter.'

b. *A kapitány szerint* Félix le-gépelte a levelet.
the captain according_to Félix down-typed the letter.Acc
'According to the captain, Félix typed the letter.'

7.3.7.2. Evaluative adverbials

Evaluative adverbials provide a subjective evaluation of the proposition expressed by the clause, rather than commenting on its truth value. The speaker's evaluation might communicate a positive as well as a negative attitude towards the event (106), or might express, more objectively, how the proposition is related to what was previously expected in the discourse (107).

Typical evaluative adverbials are case-marked PPs, or adverbs derived from adjectives, their forms being similar to manner adverbs.

(106) Félix *szerencsé-re* / *sajnos* le-gépelte a levelet.
Félix luck-Sub / unfortunately down-typed the letter.Acc
'Félix luckily / unfortunately typed the letter.'

(107) Félix *váratlan-ul* / *természetes-en* le-gépelte a levelet.
Félix unexpected-ly / natural-ly down-typed the letter.Acc
'Unexpectedly / naturally, Félix typed the letter.'

7.3.7.3. Speech-act adverbials

So-called speech-act adverbials provide additional information about the speech-act associated with the sentence (they are also referred to as pragmatic adverbials).

The typical speech-act adjunct is an adverb derived from an adjective, the forms being similar to manner adverbials.

(108) *Rövid-en* / [*őszinté-n (szól-va)*], Félix le-gépelte a levelet.
brief-ly / honest-ly speak-Part Félix down-typed the letter.Acc
'Briefly / [honestly (speaking)], Félix typed the letter.'

7.3.8. Discourse-oriented adverbials

Discourse-oriented adverbials function similarly to conjunctions, relating the clause they modify to previous utterances, i.e. to the discourse. Discourse-oriented adverbials are clausal adjuncts with a maximal scope. This means that they take scope over evaluative adverbials (e.g. *szerencsére* 'luckily') and other speaker-oriented adjuncts as well.

The forms of discourse-oriented adverbials show considerable variation. A typical morphological structure, with the derivational formal suffix *-képpen* 'in the way/manner', can be observed in the example below:

(109) *Következés-képpen* / *hasonló-képpen*, Félix le-gépelte a levelet.
consequense-For / similar-For Félix down-typed the letter.Acc
'Consequently / similarly, Félix typed the letter.'

In some of the conjunction words, a transparent PP-structure can still be reconstructed, even though they are already used as indecomposable items. For instance, in the conjunction *mindazonáltal* 'nevertheless', the postposition *által* 'by/through' has the universal quantifier *mind* 'all' and the demonstrative *az-on* 'that-Sup' in its complement, but the phrase has already lexicalized into a plain conjunction:

(110) *Mindazonáltal*, Félix le-gépelte a levelet.
nevertheless Félix down-typed the letter.Acc
'Nevertheless, Félix typed the letter.'

7.3.9. Aspectual adverbial adjuncts

7.3.9.1. Habitual adverbials

Habitual adverbials express the idea that the situation described by the clause is characteristic of an extended period of time. Habituality is usually associated with adverbials expressing characteristically, but not necessarily frequent recurrence such as *általában* 'generally', and *rendszeresen* 'regularly', thus the existential *néha* 'sometimes', *olykor* 'occasionally', and *időnként* 'from time to time' also belong to this group, displaying the same properties.

The form of the habitual adverbial can be a PP including a case suffix, an adverb derived from an adjective (e.g. *rendszeres-en* 'regularly'), a lexicalized postpositional phrase (e.g. *rend-szerint* 'order' + 'according to' cf. (111)), or a synchronically non-transparent adverb (e.g. *néha* 'sometimes').

(111) A nyomozó *általában* / *rendszerint* /*néha* el-kapta a gyilkost.
the detective usually / ordinarily / sometimes away-caught the murderer.Acc
'The detective usually/ordinarily/ sometimes caught the murderer.'

Habituals, e.g., *általában* 'usually', fail at Paraphrase-test I (112), and they only satisfy Paraphrase-test II (113) if the reference time of the main clause is assimilated to that of the embedded clause, as in (114):

(112) • Paraphrase-test I

*A nyomozó el-kapta a gyilkost, és azt
the detective away-caught the murderer and that.Acc
általában / *rendszerint* / *néha* tette.
usually / ordinarily / sometimes did
'*The detective caught the murderer and he did that usually / ordinarily / sometimes.'

(113) • Paraphrase-test II

**Általában* / *rendszerint* / *néha* az a helyzet, hogy a nyomozó
usually / ordinarily / sometimes that the situation that the detective
el-kapta a gyilkost.
away-caught the murderer.Acc
'*It is usually / ordinarily / sometimes the case that the detective caught the murderer.'

(114) • Paraphrase-test II - modified

Általában / *rendszerint* / *néha* az volt a helyzet,
usually / ordinarily / sometimes that was the situation
hogy a nyomozó el-kapta a gyilkost.
that the detective away-caught the murderer.Acc
'It was usually / ordinarily / sometimes the case that the detective caught the murderer.'

The latter fact follows from the function of habitual adverbials: they express that the situation described is characteristic of an extended period of time, which is specified as past tense in the given example.

Habitual adjuncts cannot bear primary stress. They cannot normally be focused (115), but may precede a topic constituent (116):

(115) • Focus test

*A nyomozó ÁLTALÁBAN / RENDSZERINT / NÉHA kapta el
the detective usually / ordinarily / sometimes caught away
a gyilkost.
the murderer.Acc
'*The detective caught the murderer USUALLY / ORDINARILY / SOMETIMES.'

(116) • Pre-topic test

Általában / *rendszerint* / *néha* a nyomozó el-kapta a gyilkost.
usually / ordinarily / sometimes the detective away-caught the murderer.Acc
'Usually / ordinarily / sometimes, the detective caught the murderer.'

Habitual adverbials are usually interpreted outside the scope of negation (117a) but may be interpreted within the scope of an interrogative operator (117b).

(117) a. A nyomozó nem kapta el *általában* a gyilkost.
the detective not caught away usually the murderer.Acc
'The detective usually did not catch the murderer.'

b. A felügyelő 'döntés-re jutott *általában*?
the inspector decision-Sub got usually
'Did the inspector arrive at a decision usually?'

These tests indicate that habitual adverbials cannot be classified unambiguously. They take a larger scope than VP-adjuncts, which modify the core predicate, but can fall into the scope of sentential operators (117b), and they are always in the scope of speaker-oriented adverbials (118), which means that they are not as high as canonic clausal adjuncts are. Habitual adverbials, as well as other aspectual adjuncts listed in the subsequent sections, seem to have scope over the extended predicate phrase.

(118) *Szerencsé-re,* a nyomozó *általában* / *rendszerint* / *néha*
luck-Sub the detective usually / ordinarily / sometimes
el-kapta a gyilkost.
away-caught the murderer.Acc
'Luckily, the detective usually / ordinarily / sometimes caught the murderer.'

7.3.9.2. Repetitive adverbials

A large set of adverbial adjuncts express the repeated occurrence of the situation described in the sentence. Within this set, we apply the term repetitive to the adverbials that denote a single repetition. They are elements derived by a suffix, e.g., *ismételt-en* 'repeated-ly', *új-ból* new-Ela 'anew', or synchronically unanalyzable adverbs e.g. *ismét* 'again', *megint* 'again'.

(119) Félix *újra* / *megint* / *ismét* le-gépelte a levelet.
Félix again / again / again down-typed the letter.Acc
'Félix typed the letter again.'

According to the paraphrase tests (120)-(121) and the focus test (122), these adjuncts are clausal adverbials, but they are not felicitous sentence initially, before a topic constituent (123), as speaker-oriented and discourse-oriented high adverbials are. (Note that – depending on the aspectual properties of the clause – Paraphrase-test II might require the adjustment of the reference time of the paraphrase.)

(120) • Paraphrase-test I
*Félix le-gépelte a levelet, és azt *újra* / *megint* / *ismét* tette.
Félix down-typed the letter.Acc and that.Acc again / again / again did
'Félix typed the letter and he did it again.'

(121) • Paraphrase-test II
Újra / *megint* / *ismét* az (volt) a helyzet, hogy Félix
again / again / again that was the situation that Félix
le-gépelte a levelet.
down-typed the letter.Acc
'It is / was again the case that Félix typed the letter.'

(122) • Focus test

*Félix ÚJRA / MEGINT / ISMÉT gépelte le a levelet.
Félix again / again / again typed down the letter.Acc
Intended meaning: 'Félix typed the letter AGAIN.'

(123) • Pre-topic test

**Újra / megint / ismét* Félix 'le-gépelte a levelet.
again / again / again Félix down-typed the letter.Acc
Intended meaning: 'Félix typed the letter again.'

Repetitive adverbials normally fall into the scope of a logical operator, such as, for instance, negation (124).

(124) Félix nem gépelte le *újra / megint / ismét* a leveleket.
Félix not typed down again / again / again the letters.Acc
'Félix didn't type the letters again.'

Újra and *megint* also have a restitutive meaning, i.e., (125) is ambiguous between a repetitive reading, expressing the repetition of the opening of the door, and a restitutive reading, expressing the restitution of the former open state of the door:

(125) A szomszéd *újra* ki-nyitotta az ajtót.
the neighbor again out-opened the door.Acc
'The neighbor has opened the door again.'

The restitutive meaning is only accessible if *újra* 'again' immediately precedes the minimal predicate (verb modifier plus verb), as in (125) above. If a focus or a manner adverbial intervenes between them, only the repetitive reading is available:

(126) Az ajtót *újra* A SZOMSZÉD nyitotta ki.
the door.Acc again the neighbor opened out
'It is the neighbor who has opened the door again.'

(127) A szomszéd *újra* *óvatos-an* ki-nyitotta az ajtót.
the neighbor again careful-ly out-opened the door.Acc
'The neighbor has carefully opened the door again.'

7.3.9.3. Continuative adverbials

Continuatives are expressions like *még* 'still', *még mindig* (lit. still always) 'still', and complexes involving *még* 'still' and the distributive particle *is* 'also', which surround a temporal expression specifying a reference time or reference period when the situation still holds, such as *még nyolckor is* 'at eight even still', *még most is* 'even now still'.

(128) Félix *még mindig* veri az írógépet.
Félix still always clatters the typewriter.Acc
'Félix is still clattering away at the typewriter.'

(129) Félix *még nyolc-kor is* veri az írógépet.
Félix still eight-Tmp also clatters the typewriter.Acc
'Félix is clattering away at the typewriter at eight even still.'

Continuative adverbials satisfy both Paraphrase-test I and Paraphrase-test II (if the matrix verb shares the tense of the embedded predicate):

(130) • Paraphrase-test I
Félix veri az írógépet, és azt *még mindig* teszi.
Félix clatters the typewriter.Acc and that.Acc still always does
'Félix is clattering away at the typewriter and is still doing it.'

(131) • Paraphrase-test II
Még mindig az a helyzet, hogy Félix veri az írógépet.
still always that the situation that Félix clatters the typewriter.Acc
'It is still the case that Félix is clattering away at the typewriter.'

Continuative adverbials cannot precede the topic (132), and they cannot be focused (134) .

(132) • Pre-topic test
**Még mindig* Félix 'gépeli a leveleket.
still always Félix types the letters.Acc
Intended meaning: 'Félix is still typing the letters.'

(133) • Focus test
*Félix MÉG MINDIG bontja ki a leveleket.
Félix still always opens out the letters.Acc
Intended meaning: 'Félix is STILL opening the letters.'

Note that (133) is only ungrammatical with focus intonation (see the volume on Sentence Structure), when primary stress falls unto the focus constituent and the subsequent words get deaccentuated. The fact that in (134) the verbal particle *ki* 'out' follows the finite verb instead of preceding it (the latter word order is expected in a non-focused, neutral sentence), may be due to the progressive aspect of the clause, rather than to the presence of a focus. The progressive reading is, of course, not unexpected in combination with a continuative adverbial. In this case, however, the prosodic pattern of the clause crucially differs:

(134) Félix *még 'mindig* 'bontja (')ki a 'leveleket. [progressive reading]
Félix still always opens out the letters.Acc
'Félix is still opening the letters.'

Continuative adverbials can occur in the scope of an interrogative and a conditional operator:

(135) a. Félix *még mindig* gépeli a leveleket?
Félix still always types the letters.Acc
'Is Félix still typing the letters?'

b. Ha Félix *még mindig* gépel-né a leveleket, akkor...
if Félix still always type-Cond.3Sg the letters.Acc then
'If Félix were still typing the letters, then...'

Még (mindig) 'still' cannot occur in the scope of negation; its negative counterpart is used, i.e. the combination of *már* 'already' and *nem* 'not' (136). However, *még (mindig)* 'still' can scope over negation (137).

(136) Félix *már* *nem* gépel leveleket.
Félix already not types letters.Acc
'Félix doesn't type letters anymore.'

(137) Félix *még mindig* nem gépelte le a levelet.
Félix still always not typed down the letter.Acc
'Félix still hasn't typed the letter.'

7.3.9.4. Preparatory adverbials

Aspectual adverbials like *rögtön* 'immediately', *azonnal* 'instantly', and *hamarosan* 'soon' modify the preparatory time of the process expressed in the predicate. Note that some manner adverbials (e.g. *gyorsan* 'quickly') can also express this function when used as an aspectual adjunct (see Section 7.3.3 above).

The form of the preparatory adverbials can be a case-marked PP (*azon-nal* that-Ins 'instantly'), or a derived adverb (e.g. *hamar-os-an* soon-Adj-ly 'soon'), and sometimes their form is not any more analyzable (e.g. *rögtön* 'immediately').

(138) Félix *rögtön* / *azonnal* le-gépelte a levelet.
Félix immediately / instantly down-typed the letter.Acc
'Félix immediately / instantly typed the letter.'

Preparatory adverbials only satisfy the modified (temporally adjusted) Paraphrase-test II, cannot be focused (141), and do not precede the topic constituents (142).

(139) • Paraphrase-test I
*Félix le-gépelte a levelet, és azt *rögtön* / *azonnal* tette.
Félix down-typed the letter.Acc and that.Acc immediately / instantly did
'Félix typed the letter and he did it immediately / instantly.'

(140) • Paraphrase-test II - modified
Rögtön / *azonnal* az volt a helyzet, hogy Félix le-gépelte a levelet.
immediately / instantly that was the situation that Félix down-typed the letter.Acc
'It was immediately / instantly the case that Félix typed the letter.'

(141) • Focus test
*Félix RÖGTÖN / AZONNAL gépelte le a levelet.
Félix immediately / instantly typed down the letter.Acc
Intended meaning: 'Félix typed the letter IMMEDIATELY / INSTANTLY.'

(142) • Pre-topic test:
**Rögtön / *azonnal* Félix le-gépelte a levelet.
immediately / instantly Félix down-typed the letter.Acc
Intended meaning: 'Immediately / instantly Félix typed the letter.'

Preparatory adverbials normally occur in the scope of a logical operator, such as, for instance, negation (143).

(143) Félix nem gépelte le *azonnal* a leveleket.
Félix not typed down instantly the letters.Acc
'Félix didn't type the letters instantly.'

7.3.9.5. Frequentative adverbials

Frequentative adverbials express the repeated occurrence of the situation or the activity or state described in the sentence (144).

The form of the frequentative adverbial can be a case-marked PP (e.g. *számos alkalom-mal* several occasion-Ins 'on several occasions'), or an adverb derived from an adjectival or verbal root (e.g. *gyakr-an* 'frequent-ly', *folyt-on* 'continuous-ly'). A typical form for frequentatives is the multiplicative suffix (*-szor/szer/ször*) combined with a definite or indefinite numeral (e.g. *öt-ször* 'five times', *sok-szor* 'many times'. *Több-ször* 'several times' and multiplicatives derived from definite numerals can be combined with the distributive particle *is* 'also'.

(144) Félix *gyakran* / *többször* / [*többször is*] le-gépelte a levelet.
Félix often / several_times / several_times also down-typed the letter.Acc
'Félix typed the letter often / [several times].'

Paraphrase-test I does not provide unambiguous results here, since native speakers' judgements varied between complete acceptance and complete rejection (145). The individual judgements also changed with changing the time or aspect of the event. As for Paraphrase test II, frequentatives only satisfy it if the reference time has been adjusted in the matrix clause (146), as was observed with other aspectual adverbial adjuncts as well. Frequentatives are not felicitous sentence initially, before the topic (147).

(145) • Paraphrase-test I
%Félix le-gépelte a levelet, és azt *gyakran* / *többször* tette.
Félix down-typed the letter.Acc and that.Acc often / several_times did
'Félix typed the letter and she did that often / several times.'

(146) • Paraphrase-test II - modified
Gyakran /*többször* az volt a helyzet, hogy Félix le-gépelte a levelet.
often / several_times that was the situation that Félix down-typed the letter.Acc
'It was often / several times the case that Félix typed the letter.'

(147) • Pre-topic test
?**Gyakran* / ?*többször Félix le-gépelte a levelet.
often / several_times Félix down-typed the letter.Acc
Intended meaning: 'Félix typed the letter often / several times.'

It is important to observe, however, that unlike the other aspectual adjuncts, frequentatives can easily be focused, except for those combined with the distributive particle *is* 'also'.

(148) • Focus test

a. Félix GYAKRAN / TÖBBSZÖR / KÉTSZER gépelte le a levelet.
Félix often / several_times / twice typed down the letter.Acc
'Félix typed the letter often / several times / twice.

b. *Félix KÉTSZER IS gépelte le a levelet.
Félix twice also typed down the letter.Acc
Intended meaning: 'Félix typed the letter TWICE.'

For adverbials expressing negative frequency, focusing is obligatory (cf. Section 7.4.3 on this phenomenon):

(149) A nyomozó KEVÉS-SZER utasít el ügyfeleket.
the detective few-Mult turns away clients.Acc
'The detective turns down clients FEW TIMES.'

Frequentatives can fall into the scope of sentential operators (150a); but they can also take scope over them (150b).

(150) a. Félix nem gépelte le *többször* *is* a leveleket.
Félix not typed down several_times also the letters.Acc
'Félix did not type the letter more than once.'

b. Félix *többször* *is* nem gépelte le a leveleket.
Félix several_times also not typed down the letters.Acc
'On several occasions, Félix did not type the letters.'

Even though frequentatives behave slightly differently with respect to the other aspectual adverbials discussed above, they all share the property that they cannot clearly be categorized either as clausal or as VP-adjuncts. They rather appear in the middle field of the clause and seem to modify the extended predicate.

7.3.10. Degree adverbial adjuncts

7.3.10.1. Approximatives

Degree adverbials express the degree or intensity of an action or a property, hence they can modify not only verbal predicates, but adjectival expressions and adverbs, as well (see the volume on Adjectival Phrases). Approximatives express the nearness of the completion of the action or nearness of the completeness of the property denoted by the modified expression. The typical degree adverbial is a morphologically non-transparent adverb (151).

(151) A nyomozó *majdnem* / *szinte* el-kapta a gyilkost.
the detective almost / nearly away-caught the murderer.Acc
'The detective almost caught the murderer.'

Both paraphrase tests seem to fail with approximatives. Note, however, that some speakers find Paraphrase II slightly better, if the reference time of the main clause is changed:

(152) • Paraphrase-test I

*A nyomozó el-kapta a gyilkost, és azt *majdnem / szinte* tette.
the detective away-caught the murderer.Acc and that.Acc almost / nearly did
'*The detective caught the murderer and he did it almost.'

(153) • Paraphrase-test II

**Majdnem / szinte* az a helyzet, hogy a nyomozó el-kapta
almost / nearly that the situation that the detective away-caught
a gyilkost.
the murderer.Acc
'It is almost the case that the detective caught the murderer.'

(154) • Paraphrase-test II - modified

?*Majdnem / szinte* az volt a helyzet, hogy a nyomozó el-kapta
almost / nearly that was the situation that the detective away-caught
a gyilkost.
the murderer.Acc
'It was almost the case that the detective caught the murderer.'

Approximative adjuncts cannot be focused, and never appear before topic constituents:

(155) • Focus test

*A nyomozó MAJDNEM / SZINTE kapta el a gyilkost.
the detective almost / nearly caught away the murderer.Acc
Intended meaning: 'The detective ALMOST caught the murderer.'

(156) • Pre-topic test

**Majdnem / szinte* a nyomozó el-kapta a gyilkost.
almost / nearly the detective away-caught the murderer.Acc
Intended meaning: 'The detective almost caught the murderer.'

Approximative adverbials are usually interpreted outside the scope of negation (157a) but seem to fall into the scope of an interrogative operator (157b).

(157) a. A nyomozó nem kapta el *majdnem* a gyilkost.
the detective not caught away almost the murderer.Acc
'The detective nearly did not catch the murderer.'

b. A felügyelő '*majdnem* döntés-re jutott?
the inspector almost decision-Sub got
'Did the inspector almost arrive at a decision?'

As a consequence, approximative degree adverbials cannot be classified either as VP-adverbials or as clausal adverbials, as has also been shown in Section 7.2.3.

7.3.10.2. Intensifiers

Intensifying adverbials amplify the degree or intensity of the action or property expressed by a verbal predicate (or by an adjective or adverbial expression).

Intensifying adverbials can be adverbs derived from adjectives by an adverbial derivational suffix (158a), or even derived from an adjective by a case suffix (158b):

(158) a. Artúr *nagy-on* / *túlságos-an* meg-locsolta a virágokat.
Artúr great-ly / over-ly Perf-watered the flowers.Acc
'Artúr watered the flowers very much / too much.'

b. A felügyelő *elég-gé* el-fáradt.
the inspector quite-TrE off-tired
'The inspector got quite tired.'

Some of the intensifiers lexicalized from pejorative manner adverbs. Their original meanings have bleached in this use, and they simply function as intensifiers meaning 'very.'

(159) Olívia *szörny-en* / *borzasztó-an* / *durvá-n* le-késte a vonatot.
Olívia terrib-ly / dreadful-ly / brutal-ly down-missed the train.Acc
'Olívia terribly / dreadfully / brutally missed the train.'

Paraphrases practically do not apply. The second paraphrase test cannot be repaired by manipulating the reference time of the main clause, either. Intensifiers cannot be focused (162), and never appear before topic constituents (163):

(160) • Paraphrase-test I
??Artúr meg-locsolta a virágok-at, és azt *nagy-on* / *túlságos-an* tette.
Artúr Perf-watered the flowers-Acc and that.Acc great-ly / over-ly did
Intended meaning: 'Artúr watered the flowers and he did it [very much] / [too much].'

(161) • Paraphrase-test II
**Nagy-on* / *túlságos-an* az a helyzet, hogy Artúr meg-locsolta
great-ly / over-ly that the situation that Artúr Perf-watered
a virágokat.
the flowers.Acc
Intended meaning: 'It is [very much] / [too much] the case that Artúr watered the flowers.'

(162) • Focus test
*Artúr NAGY-ON / TÚLSÁGOS-AN locsolta meg a virágokat.
Artúr great-ly / over-ly watered Perf the flowers.Acc
Intended meaning: 'Artúr watered the flowers [VERY MUCH] / [TOO MUCH].'

(163) • Pre-topic test
**Nagy-on* / *túlságos-an* Artúr meg-locsolta a virágokat.
great-ly / over-ly Artúr Perf-watered the flowers.Acc
Intended meaning: 'Artúr watered the flowers [very much] / [too much].'

Intensifiers are normally interpreted within the scope of sentential operators, such as e.g. negation (164a), or conditional (164b).

(164) a. A felügyelő 'nem fáradt el *nagy-on.*
the inspector not tired off great-ly
'The inspector did not get tired very much.'

b. Ha Artúr *túlságos-an* meg-locsol-ná a virágokat...
if Artúr over-ly Perf-water.Cond.3Sg the flowers.Acc
'If Artúr watered the flowers too much...'

Intensifiers cannot be classified either as VP-adverbials or as clausal adverbials. It is to be noted, however, that there is a special subgroup of intensifiers, the so called downtoners, which provide slightly different results with respect to the usual tests. Downtoners rather diminish the degree or intensity of the action or property expressed by a verbal predicate (or an adjective or adverbial expression).

(165) Olívia *kicsit* meg-vizsgálta az iratot.
Olívia little.Acc Perf-examined the document.Acc
'Olívia examined the document a little.'

Downtoners can easily be focused (166), moreover, the downtoners that have a positive, intensifying counterpart are obligatorily focused (167):

(166) Olívia KICSIT vizsgálta meg az iratot.
Olívia little.Acc examined Perf the document.Acc
'Olívia examined the document ONLY A LITTLE.'

(167) a. Olívia ALIG vizsgálta meg az iratot.
Olívia hardly examined Perf the document.Acc
'Olívia HARDLY examined the document.'

b. *Olívia *alig* meg-vizsgálta az iratot.
Olívia hardly Perf-examined the document.Acc
Intended meaning: 'Olívia hardly examined the document.'

7.3.11. Measure adverbials

Measure adverbials appear to be akin to degree adverbials from a semantic point of view. They modify the predicate by adding information as to what extent a process has been carried out or completed. Whereas degree and certain manner adverbials evoke a scale (see Section 7.4.3), measure adverbials are neither scalar in this sense, nor gradable.

The form of measure adverbials can be a case-marked PP, or a suffixed element derived from an adjective (e.g. *teljes-en* 'complete-ly').

(168) Félix *fél-ig* / *rész-ben* / *teljes-en* le-gépelte a levelet.
Félix half-Ter / part-Ine / complete-ly down-typed the letter.Acc
'Félix typed the letter halfway / partially / completely.'

Paraphrase-test II clearly fails (170), while Paraphrase-test I is slightly or strongly degraded, depending on the choice of the lexical items (169). The latter can be due to the fact that the predicate expresses a telic event with an inherent endpoint, and paraphrases such as (169) below yield either a contradiction (in the cases of *halfway* and *partially*) or a tautology (in the case of *completely*).

(169) • Paraphrase-test I
??Félix le-gépelte a levelet és azt *fél-ig* / *rész-ben* / *teljes-en* tette.
Félix down-typed the letter.Acc and that.Acc half-Ter / part-Ine / complete-ly did
Intended meaning: 'Félix typed the letter and he did it halfway / partially / completely.'

(170) • Paraphrase-test II
**Fél-ig* / *rész-ben* / *teljes-en* az (volt) a helyzet, hogy Félix
half-Ter / part-Ine / complete-ly that was the situation that Félix
le-gépelte a levelet.
down-typed the letter.Acc
'*It is/was halfway / partially / completely the case that Félix typed the letter.'

Measure adjuncts can easily be focused (171), but cannot precede the topic constituents (172).

(171) • Focus test
Félix FÉL-IG / RÉSZ-BEN / TELJES-EN gépelte le a levelet.
Félix half-Ter / part-Ine / complete-ly typed down the letter.Acc
'Félix typed the letter halfway / partially / completely.'

(172) • Pre-topic test
**Fél-ig* / *rész-ben* / *teljes-en* Félix 'le-gépelte a levelet.
half-Ter / part-Ine / complete-ly Félix down-typed the letter.Acc
Intended meaning: 'Félix typed the letter halfway / partially / completely.'

Measure adverbials fall into the scope of logical operators, as the following negated example show:

(173) Félix nem gépelte le *fél-ig* / *rész-ben* / *teljes-en* a levelet.
Félix not typed down half-Ter / part-Ine / complete-ly the letter.Acc
'Félix did not type the letter halfway / partially / completely.'

7.4. Placement and prosody

7.4.1. Position of the major types of PP adjuncts within the sentence

Apparently, PP adjuncts do not have a designated syntactic position in Hungarian and can freely appear in several sentence positions, both preverbally and postverbally. On a closer look, however, one may observe that this is not completely true and there are certain restrictions on their placement, depending on the class to which a given adverbial adjunct belongs.

There is a crucial difference between preverbal and postverbal adjunction: restrictions on the relative ordering of various adverbial types only apply preverbally. The postverbal word order of these adjuncts appears to be completely free (cf. Section 7.4.5 on some postverbal phenomena). In the following sections, some generalizations will be established on the possible positions of PP adjuncts within the sentence as well as with respect to each other.

The schema in (174) shows how constituents are ordered in the preverbal field of the Hungarian simple sentence (see the volume on Sentence Structure). The left periphery is occupied by the topic constituent(s), followed by a field for operators: quantifiers, negation and the structural focus position. With negation ignored for the moment, the main constituents are the following:

(174) Topic(s) / Quantifier(s) / Focus / (neutral or core) Predication

There are PP adjuncts, principally the framing modifiers, i.e. the spatial and temporal PPs, as well as the contingency adverbials that can appear in any structural position with respect to these operators: preceding the topic constituent(s), between the topic(s) and the quantifier field, between the quantifiers and the Focus or predicate part, or they can be focused themselves. Of course, they can always appear inside the predication, following the finite verb.

7.4.1.1. PPs with a flexible position

Spatial, temporal and contingency PPs may freely appear in various sentence positions. They can have scope over other adverbials or, alternatively, fall into the scope of other adverbials (see below, in Section 7.4.2.1). In the following examples, a locative PP *Londonban* 'in London' and an adverbial of reason/purpose *a biztonság kedvéért* 'for safety's sake' will be used to illustrate the behavior of the members of these classes.

All the examples below are to be interpreted under a non-contrastive intonational pattern. Some of the orderings may sound more natural than others, but there is no completely ungrammatical permutation in the following set of data. Adjuncts between the quantifier and the verb modifier plus finite verb complex are degraded. They become, however, readily accepted if the quantifier expression they follow can be topicalized (see the volume on Sentence Structure).

(175) (London-ban) a nyomozó (London-ban) minden gyilkost
London-Ine the detective London-Ine every murderer.Acc
(??London-ban) 'elkapott (London-ban).
London-Ine away-caught London-Ine
'The detective caught every murderer in London.'

(176) (London-ban) a nyomozó (London-ban) minden gyilkost
London-Ine the detective London-Ine every murderer.Acc
(??London-ban) 'TITOKBAN kapott (London-ban) el (London-ban).
London-Ine in_secret caught London-Ine away London-Ine
'The detective caught every murderer in London SECRETLY.'

(177) A nyomozó minden gyilkost 'LONDON-BAN kapott el.
the detective every murderer.Acc London-Ine caught away
'The detective caught every murderer in LONDON.'

(178) (A biztonság kedvé-ért) Artúr (a biztonság kedvé-ért) három
the safety sake.Poss-Cau Artúr the safety sake.Poss-Cau three
erkélyen (a biztonság kedvé-ért) meg-locsolta
balcony.Sup the safety sake.Poss-Cau Perf-watered
(a biztonság kedvé-ért) a virágokat (a biztonság kedvé-ért).
the safety sake.Poss-Cau the flowers.Acc the safety sake.Poss-Cau
'For safety's sake, Artúr watered the flowers on three balconies.'

(179) Artúr A BIZTONSÁG KEDVÉ-ÉRT locsolta meg a virágokat.
Artúr the safety sake.Poss-Cau watered Perf the flowers.Acc
'Artúr watered the flowers FOR SAFETY'S SAKE.'

The only position from which PP adjuncts are strictly banned is between the verbal particle/modifier and the finite verb on the one hand (180a) and between the focus and the finite verb on the other (180b). This position is not available for other intervening constituents of any sort either (see the volume on Sentence Structure), which means that the ill-formedness of (180a) and (180b) follows from independent reasons (Surányi 2008: 168).

(180) a. *A nyomozó minden gyilkost 'el *London-ban* kapott.
the detective every murderer.Acc away London-Ine caught
Intended meaning: 'The detective caught every murderer in London.'

b. *A nyomozó minden gyilkost CSAK OLÍVIA SEGÍTSÉGÉVEL
the detective every murderer.Acc only Olívia help.Ins
London-ban kapott el.
London-Ine caught away
Intended meaning: 'The detective caught every murderer in London ONLY WITH THE HELP OF OLÍVIA.'

7.4.1.2. PPs with a fixed position – high, middle and low adjuncts

The placement of all other types of adjuncts is not completely free. Nevertheless, these adjuncts can also be classified into larger groups, according to the possible domain in which they can appear with respect to the preverbal operator fields of the sentence (see the volume on Sentence Structure). The choice of the adjunction zone in which these adverbials enter the clause is determined by the semantically motivated selectional requirements of the individual PP adjuncts (cf. Ernst 2002). Although the domains may overlap, adverbial adjuncts can normally be assigned to one of these main groups. Based on the positions they can occupy with respect to the sentence initial topic(s), the quantifier field, and the structural focus position, three such groups may be distinguished: high adverbial adjuncts, low adverbial adjuncts, and middle adverbial adjuncts. In what follows, the semantically classified adjunct types of the previous sections (sections 7.3.3–7.3.11) will be discussed again, but rearranged according to the domains, or adjunction zones in which they usually appear. Note that all the examples below are to be interpreted with an unmarked, non-contrastive intonational pattern, with no intonational breaks around the adjuncts.

7.4.1.2.1. High adverbial adjuncts

High adverbial adjuncts can precede topics and can also precede the quantifier field. If a quantifier is present in the clause, discourse-oriented and speaker-oriented adverbials are never located between the quantifier and the predicate phrase. However, habitual and domain adverbials may occupy all the possible preverbal positions, even the one between the quantifier and the predicate phrase. High adverbial adjuncts cannot be focused.

(181) • Discourse-oriented adverbials

a. (Következésképpen) a felügyelő (következésképpen) minden kérdés-ben
consequently the inspector consequently every question-Ine
(*következésképpen) döntés-re jutott.
consequently decision-Sub got
'Consequently, the inspector arrived at a decision on every issue.'

b. *A felügyelő KÖVETKEZÉSKÉPPEN jutott döntés-re.
the inspector consequently got decision-Sub
'*The inspector arrived at a decision CONSEQUENTLY.'

(182) • Speech-act adverbials

a. (Őszintén szólva) a felügyelő (őszintén szólva) minden kérdés-ben
honestly speak.Part the inspector honestly speak.Part every question-Ine
(*őszintén szólva) döntés-re jutott.
honestly speak.Part decision-Sub got
'Honestly speaking, the inspector arrived at a decision on every issue.'

b. *A felügyelő ŐSZINTÉN SZÓLVA jutott döntésre.
the inspector honestly speak.Part got decision-Sub
'*The inspector arrived at a decision HONESTLY SPEAKING.'

(183) • Evaluative adverbials

a. (Szerencsére) a felügyelő (szerencsére) minden kérdés-ben
luckily the inspector luckily every question-Ine
(?*szerencsére) döntés-re jutott.
luckily decision-Sub got
'Luckily, the inspector arrived at a decision on every issue.'

b. *A felügyelő SZERENCSÉRE jutott döntés-re.
the inspector luckily got decision-Sub
'*The inspector arrived at a decision LUCKILY.'

(184) • Epistemic / modal adverbials

a. (Valószínűleg) a felügyelő (valószínűleg) minden kérdés-ben
probably the inspector probably every question-Ine
(*valószínűleg) döntés-re jutott.
probably decision-Sub got
'The inspector probably arrived at a decision on every issue.'

b. *A felügyelő VALÓSZÍNŰLEG jutott döntés-re.
the inspector probably got decision-Sub
'*The inspector arrived at a decision PROBABLY.'

(185) • Habitual adverbials
a. (Általában) a felügyelő (általában) minden kérdés-ben (általában) döntés-re jutott.
usually the inspector usually every question-Ine usually decision-Sub got
'The inspector usually arrived at a decision on every issue.'

b. *A felügyelő ÁLTALÁBAN jutott döntés-re.
the inspector usually got decision-Sub
'*The inspector arrived at a decision USUALLY.'

(186) • Domain adverbials
a. (Elvileg) Olívia (elvileg) három iratot (elvileg) 'meg-vizsgált.
principled-ly Olívia principled-ly three document.Acc principled-ly Perf-examined
'In principle, Olívia examined three documents.'

b. *Olívia ELVILEG vizsgálta meg az iratokat.
Olívia principled-ly examined Perf the documents.Acc
Intended meaning: 'Olívia examined the documents IN PRINCIPLE.'

7.4.1.2.2. Middle adverbial adjuncts

Middle adverbial adjuncts cannot precede topics. However, they can precede the quantifier field and they can also appear between the quantifier and the predicate phrase. Whereas frequentatives and subject-oriented (volition) adverbials can be focused, the other adjunct types listed here cannot appear in a focus position.

(187) • Repetitive adverbials
a. (*Újra) a felügyelő (újra) minden kérdés-ben (újra) döntés-re jutott.
again the inspector again every question-Ine again decision-Sub got
'The inspector arrived at a decision on every issue again.'

b. *A felügyelő ÚJRA jutott döntés-re.
the inspector again got decision-Sub
Intended meaning: 'The inspector arrived at a decision AGAIN.'

(188) • Continuative adverbials
a. (*Még mindig) Olívia (még mindig) két kérdés-ben (még mindig) egyet-ért a szakáccsal.
still always Olívia still always two question-Ine still always one.Acc-mean.3Sg the cook.Ins
'Olívia still agrees with the cook on two issues.'

b. *Olívia MÉG MINDIG ért egyet a szakáccsal.
Olívia still always mean.3Sg one.Acc the cook.Ins
'*Olívia agrees with the cook STILL.'

(189) • Preparatory adverbials

a. (*Rögtön) a felügyelő (rögtön) minden kérdésben (rögtön)
instantly the inspector instantly every question-Ine instantly
döntés-re jutott.
decision-Sub got
'The inspector instantly arrived at a decision on every issue.'

b. *A felügyelő RÖGTÖN jutott döntés-re.
the inspector instantly got decision-Sub
Intended meaning: 'The inspector arrived at a decision INSTANTLY.'

(190) • Frequentative adverbials

a. (*Gyakran) a felügyelő (gyakran) minden kérdés-ben (gyakran)
often the inspector often every question-Ine often
döntés-re jutott.
decision-Sub got
'The inspector often arrived at a decision on every issue.'

b. A felügyelő GYAKRAN jutott döntés-re.
the inspector often got decision-Sub
'The inspector arrived at a decision OFTEN.'

(191) • Subject-oriented adverbials

a. (*Önként) a nyomozó (önként) két gyilkost (önként) el-engedett.
voluntarily the detective voluntarily two murderer.Acc voluntarily away-released
'The detective voluntarily released two murderers.'

b. A nyomozó ÖNKÉNT engedett el két gyilkost.
the detective voluntarily released away two murderer.Acc
'The detective released two murderers VOLUNTARILY.'

There is another important feature that can distinguish middle adjuncts from low adjuncts: middle adverbials can typically modify predicates with a constituent focus (192). Low adverbials can be focused themselves (except for degree adverbials), but normally only modify a neutral, non-focused predicate. Observe the ungrammaticality of (193) in which a manner modifier is combined with a focus.

(192) A felügyelő gyakran CSAK GYAKORLATI KÉRDÉSEK-BEN jutott döntés-re.
the inspector usually only practical questions-Ine got decision-Sub
'The inspector usually arrived at a decision ON PRACTICAL ISSUES ONLY.'

(193) *A felügyelő könnyen CSAK GYAKORLATI KÉRDÉSEK-BEN jutott döntés-re.
The inspector easily only practical questions-Ine got decision-Sub
Intended meaning: 'The inspector easily arrived at a decision ON PRACTICAL ISSUES ONLY.'

7.4.1.2.3. Low adverbial adjuncts

Low adverbial adjuncts can never precede topics or quantifiers. Normally, they can be focused, except for degree adverbials.

(194) • Manner adverbials

a. (*Könnyen) a felügyelő (*könnyen) minden kérdés-ben (könnyen)
easily the inspector easily every question-Ine easily
döntésre jutott.
decision-Sub got
'The inspector easily arrived at a decision on every issue.'

b. A felügyelő KÖNNYEN jutott döntés-re.
the inspector easily got decision-Sub
'The inspector arrived at a decision EASILY.'

(195) • Measure adverbials

a. (*Félig) Olívia (*félig) három iratot (félig) meg-vizsgált.
half.Ter Olívia half.Ter three document.Acc half.Ter Perf-examined
'Olívia examined three documents halfway.'

b. Olívia FÉLIG vizsgálta meg az iratokat
Olívia half.Ter examined Perf the documents.Acc
'Olívia examined the documents HALFWAY.'

(196) • Participant PP adjuncts (instrument/comitative/benefactive)

a. (*Esővíz-zel) Artúr ($^{?}$*esővíz-zel) három erkélyen (esővíz-zel)
rainwater-Ins Artúr rainwater-Ins three balcony.Sup rainwater-Ins
meg-locsolta a virágokat.
Perf-watered the flowers.Acc
'Artúr watered the flowers on three balconies with rainwater.'

b. Artúr ESŐVÍZ-ZEL locsolta meg a virágokat.
Artúr rainwater-Ins watered Perf the flowers.Acc
'Artúr watered the flowers WITH RAINWATER.'

Participant PPs frequently contain a referential nominal element, and accordingly can easily undergo topicalization. Note that in Hungarian, PPs can function as ordinary topics if their nominal part is referential/specific. (see M2.3.3.1) When topicalized, the adjunct may appear in both pre-topic and post-topic positions, hence in all the possible positions under discussion.

(197) • Participant PP adjuncts (instrument/comitative/benefactive) – referential

a. (A piros kanná-val) Artúr (a piros kanná-val) három erkélyen
the red can-Ins Artúr the red can-Ins three balcony.Sup
(a piros kanná-val) meg-locsolta a virágokat.
the red can-Ins Perf-watered the flowers.Acc
'Artúr watered the flowers on three balconies with the red can.'

b. Artúr A PIROS KANNÁVAL locsolta meg a virágokat.
Artúr the red can-Ins watered Perf the flowers.Acc
'Artúr watered the flowers WITH THE RED CAN.'

(198) • Degree, approximative adverbials

a. (*Majdnem) a felügyelő (#majdnem) három kérdés-ben (majdnem)
almost the inspector almost three question-Ine almost
döntés-re jutott.
decision-Sub got
'The inspector almost arrived at a decision in three questions.'

b. *A felügyelő MAJDNEM jutott döntés-re.
the inspector almost got decision-Sub
Intended meaning: 'The inspector ALMOST arrived at a decision.'

Note that *majdnem* 'almost' may appear before the quantifier expression, but can only be interpreted with a narrow scope, i.e., as 'It was almost three questions in which the inspector arrived at a decision'.

(199) • Degree, intensifier adverbials

a. (*Nagyon) Artúr (*nagyon) három erkélyen (nagyon)
greatly Artúr greatly three balcony.Sup greatly
meg-locsolta a virágokat.
Perf-watered the flowers.Acc
'Artúr watered the flowers on three balconies very much.'

b. *Artúr NAGYON/ TÚLSÁGOSAN locsolta meg a virágokat.
Artúr greatly / overly watered Perf the flowers.Acc
Intended meaning: 'Artúr watered the flowers VERY/TOO MUCH.'

7.4.1.3. The role of prosody

As has been shown above, the domains of the possible adjunction sites may overlap. This means that PPs of different types can appear in the same position with respect to the other constituents of the clause. For most of the adverbial adjunct types, the least marked position is the one after the topic constituent, preceding the predicate. Accordingly, both VP-adverbials and clausal adverbials often occupy this position.

In such cases, prosody has a crucial role in distinguishing the major classes. VP-adverbials or low adverbial adjuncts typically form a single intonational unit with the predicate, and, in the unmarked case, a primary stress obligatorily falls on the adverbial placed at the left edge of the predicate (200). Clausal adverbials only bear a reduced stress in the very same position (201).

This contrast reveals a structural difference, namely, that VP-adjuncts, such as the manner adverbial *könnyen* 'easily', are adjoined to the predicate phrase (PredP), while clausal adjuncts, such as the evaluative adverbial *szerencsére* 'luckily', are adjoined higher in the hierarchical structure of the sentence.

(200) • VP-adjunct – with primary stress

A felügyelő '*könny-en* döntés-re jutott.
the inspector easy-ly decision-Sub got
'The inspector easily arrived at a decision.'

(201) • Clausal adjunct – reduced stress

A felügyelő *szerencsé-re* 'döntésre jutott.
the inspector luck-Sub decision-Sub got
'The inspector luckily arrived at a decision.'

As was already pointed out in Section 7.2.2, a few adverbial modifiers have two readings and can occur in the same position with either of the two interpretations. In such cases, stress assignment (and optional comma intonation) makes the distinction between the two readings:

(202) a. Olívia '*helyes-en* meg-oldotta a feladványt. [manner]
Olívia correct-ly Perf-solved the problem.Acc
'Olívia solved the problem correctly.'

b. Olívia *helyes-en* 'meg-oldotta a feladványt. [evaluative]
Olívia correct-ly Perf-solved the problem.Acc
'Rightly, Olívia solved the problem.'

In the following table, the possible placement of the major PP adjunct types is summarized, according to the three main domains arranged hierarchically.

Table 1: Position of PP adjuncts

TYPE	EXAMPLE	PRE-TOP	PRE-QUANT	POST-QUANT & PRE-PRED	FOCUS
SPATIAL/TEMPORAL	*Londonban* 'in London'	✓	✓	✓	✓
CONTINGENCY	*a biztonság kedvéért* 'for safety's sake'	✓	✓	✓	✓
HIGH					
DISCOURSE-ORIENTED	*következésképpen* 'consequently'	✓	✓	–	–
SPEECH-ACT	*őszintén szólva* 'honestly speaking'	✓	✓	–	–
EVALUATIVE	*szerencsére* 'luckily'	✓	✓	–	–
EPISTEMIC	*valószínűleg* 'probably'	✓	✓	–	–
HABITUAL	*általában* 'usually'	✓	✓	✓	–
DOMAIN	*elvileg* 'in principle'	✓	✓	✓	–
MIDDLE					
REPETITIVE	*újra* 'again'	–	✓	✓	–
CONTINUATIVE	*még mindig* 'still'	–	✓	✓	–

PREPARATORY	*rögtön* 'instantly'	–	✓	✓	–
FREQUENTATIVE	*gyakran* 'often'	–	✓	✓	✓
SUBJECT-ORIENTED	*önként* 'voluntarily'	–	✓	✓	✓
LOW					
MANNER	*könnyen* 'easily'	–	–	✓	✓
MEASURE	*félig* 'halfway'	–	–	✓	✓
PARTICIPANT	*a kannával* 'with the can'	(✓)	(✓)	✓	✓
APPROXIMATIVE	*majdnem* 'almost'	–	–	✓	–
INTENSIFIER	*nagyon* 'very much'	–	–	✓	–

7.4.2. Relative ordering of PP adjunct types

In the previous section we have seen that adjuncts can be grouped according to the possible domains in which they appear in the preverbal operator field of the sentence. In this section, the order of adjuncts with respect to each other will be discussed. Under a neutral intonation, the linear ordering of scope-taking elements normally reflects the scope relations in the preverbal field: the adverbial that comes first has the wider scope (postverbal phenomena will be discussed later, in Section 7.4.5). Again, it seems to be important to make a distinction between PPs with a flexible position (spatial, temporal and contingency adverbials) on the one hand, and PPs with a fixed position on the other hand.

7.4.2.1. PPs with a flexible position

PPs with a flexible position and other types of adverbial adjuncts can reciprocally have scope over each other. This is illustrated below through the combination of a temporal adverb with a speaker-oriented modal adjunct.

(203) • temporal > modal

Tegnap valószínű-leg a nyomozó el-kapta a gyilkost.
yesterday probable-ly the detective away-caught the murderer.Acc
'Yesterday, the detective probably caught the murderer.'

(204) • modal > temporal

Valószínű-leg a nyomozó *tegnap* el-kapta a gyilkost.
probable-ly the detective yesterday away-caught the murderer.Acc
'The detective probably caught the murderer yesterday.'

7.4.2.2. PPs with a fixed position – high, middle and low adjuncts

According to whether a PP adjunct belongs to the group of high, low or middle adverbials, it takes different portions of the proposition in its scope. Semantically speaking, they can scope over a core event, a proposition or even over a speech act, and this is also reflected in their relative syntactic ordering. Accordingly, those which are higher in this hierarchy have scope over those that are lower. In what follows, the most important observations in this respect will be presented and illustrated.

VP-adverbial adjuncts are low adverbials and follow clausal or high adverbials as a rule.

(205) • clausal adverbial > VP-adverbial

a. A felügyelő *szerencsé-re 'könny-en* döntés-re jutott.
the inspector luck-Sub easy-ly decision-Sub got
'Luckily, the inspector easily arrived at a decision.'

b. *A felügyelő *'könny-en szerencsé-re* döntés-re jutott.
the inspector easy-ly luck-Sub decision-Sub got
Intended meaning: 'Luckily, the inspector easily arrived at a decision.'

Clausal adverbial adjuncts normally precede both middle and low adverbial adjuncts:

(206) a. A felügyelő *szerencsé-re gyakran* könny-en döntés-re jutott.
the inspector luck-Sub often easy-ly decision-Sub got
'Luckily, the inspector often arrived at a decision easily.'

b. ?*A felügyelő *gyakran szerencsé-re könny-en* döntés-re jutott.
the inspector often luck-Sub easy-ly decision-Sub got
Intended meaning: 'The inspector often luckily arrived at a decision easily.'

Aspectual adjuncts, which are typically middle adverbials, precede VP-adverbial adjuncts. The adverbial *újra* 'again' can also be attested with the reverse word order (208), but in this case, only its restitutive reading is available.

(207) • frequentative / repetitive > manner

a. A nyomozó *gyakran / újra könny-en* el-kapja a gyilkost.
the detective often / again easy-ly away-catches the murderer.Acc
'The detective often / again catches the murderer easily.' (i.e. murderers in general)

b. *A nyomozó *könny-en gyakran / újra* el-kapja a gyilkost.
the detective easy-ly often / again away-catches the murderer.Acc
'*The detective easily often / again catches the murderer.'

(208) • manner > *újra* 'again' (restitutive)

A nyomozó *könny-en újra* el-kapja a gyilkost.
the detective easy-ly again away-catches the murderer.Acc
'The detective easily catches the murderer again.' (i.e., the same murderer)

Habitual aspectual adjuncts precede other aspectual adjuncts, like the repetitive in (209).

(209) • habitual > repetitive

a. Olívia *általában újra* fel-hívja a kapitányt.
Olívia usually again up-calls the captain.Acc
'Olívia usually calls the captain again.'

b. *Olívia *újra általában* fel-hívja a kapitányt.
Olívia again usually up-calls the captain.Acc
'*Olívia again usually calls the captain.'

When degree adjuncts appear in combination with manner adverbials, degree adverbials are preferred to come first. At the same time, a characteristic comma intonation can be observed in this case (210a), otherwise degree adjuncts tend to be interpreted as the modifier of the manner adverb itself (i.e. with a narrow scope), rather than as the modifier of the predicate (210b).

(210) • degree > manner

a. Félix *majdnem* □ *hibátlan-ul* le-gépelte a levelet.
Félix almost flawless-ly down-typed the letter.Acc
'Félix almost typed the letter, flawlessly.'

b. Félix *majdnem hibátlan-ul* le-gépelte a levelet.
Félix almost flawless-ly down-typed the letter.Acc
'Félix typed the letter almost flawlessly.'

Within the domain of high adverbials, in an unmarked case, evaluative modifiers precede modals. Evaluatives are factives, which means that they imply that the proposition is true. Consequently, it is not surprising that an epistemic/modal adverbial cannot have wider scope than the evaluative does.

(211) • evaluative > modal

a. A nyomozó *szerencsé-re valószínű-leg* el-kapta a gyilkost.
the detective luck-Sub probab-ly away-caught the murderer.Acc
'Luckily, the detective probably caught the murderer.'

b. *A nyomozó *valószínű-leg szerencsé-re* el-kapta a gyilkost.
the detective probab-ly luck-Sub away-caught the murderer.Acc
'*Probably, luckily, the detective caught the murderer.'

At the same time, speech-act modifiers precede evaluatives, and discourse-oriented modifiers precede speech-act modifiers.

(212) • speech-act > evaluative

a. *Rövid-en,* a nyomozó *szerencsé-re* el-kapta a gyilkost.
brief-ly the detective luck-Sub away-caught the murderer-Acc
'In short, the detective luckily caught the murderer.'

b. *A nyomozó *szerencsé-re rövid-en* el-kapta a gyilkost.
the detective luck-Sub briefly away-caught the murderer.Acc
Intended meaning: 'The detective luckily, shortly speaking, caught the murderer.'

(213) • discourse-oriented > speech-act

a. *Következésképpen, őszintén szólva,* Artúr hibát vétett.
consequently honestly speak.Part Artúr mistake.Acc erred
'Consequently, honestly speaking, Artúr made a mistake.'

b. ??*Őszintén szólva, következésképpen,* Artúr hibát vétett.
honestly speak.Part consequently Artúr mistake.Acc erred
'Honestly speaking, consequently, Artúr made a mistake.'

Subject-oriented adverbials precede low adverbials like manner adverbs on the one hand (214), and follow (any types of) clausal adverbials on the other (215). In this way, they behave as other middle adverbials.

(214) • subject-oriented > manner

a. A nyomozó *önként könnyedén* el-kapta a gyilkost.
the detective voluntarily lightly away-caught the murderer.Acc
'The detective voluntarily caught the murderer without a hitch.'

b. ?*A nyomozó *könnyedén önként* el-kapta a gyilkost.
the detective lightly voluntarily away-caught the murderer-Acc
'*The detective effortlessly voluntarily caught the murderer.'

(215) • modal > subject-oriented

a. *Valószínűleg* a nyomozó *önként* el-kapta a gyilkost.
probably the detective voluntarily away-caught the murderer.Acc
'Probably, the detective voluntarily caught the murderer.'

b. *A nyomozó *önként valószínűleg* el-kapta a gyilkost.
the detective voluntarily probably away-caught the murderer-Acc
'*The detective voluntarily probably caught the murderer.'

7.4.3. Exclusive adverbials

Adverbials representing one and the same category are expected to appear in the same sentence position, hence it comes as a surprise that the placement of frequentative, degree, and manner adverbials depends on whether they express a positive or negative frequency, a positive or negative degree, or a positive or negative quality. (The whole section below is based on É. Kiss 2006d, 2009b.) Compare the following minimal pairs:

(216) • frequentative

a. A felügyelő *gyakran* el-fárad.
the inspector often off-tire.3Sg
'The inspector often gets tired.'

b. A kapitány RITKÁN fárad el.
the captain rarely tire.3Sg off
'The captain RARELY gets tired.'

(217) • degree

a. A felügyelő *nagy-on* el-fáradt. [intensifier]
the inspector great-ly off-tired
'The inspector got tired very much.'

b. A kapitány ALIG fáradt el. [downtoner]
the captain barely tired off
'The captain BARELY got tired.'

(218) • manner

a. Olívia *jól* meg-oldotta az ügyet.
Olívia well Perf-solved the case.Acc
'Olívia solved the case well.'

b. Artúr ROSSZ-UL oldotta meg az ügyet.
Artúr bad-ly solved Perf the case.Acc
'Artúr solved the case BADLY.'

Whereas the positive adverbs of the (a) examples occupy the pre-VP/PredP position, immediately preceding the verbal modifier, the negative adverbs of the (b) examples are in the focus position, immediately preceding the verb and the verbal modifier. The positive frequency and manner adverbs of (216a) and (218a) can also be focused; however, this is not true for the positive adverb of degree (220a) . For the negative adverbs of the (b) examples, the position immediately before the verb modifier plus verb complex is not available. Compare with (220b)-(220b), and (221b):

(219) a. A felügyelő GYAKRAN fárad el.
the inspector often tire.3Sg off
'The inspector OFTEN gets tired.'

b. *A kapitány *ritká-n* el-fárad.
the captain rare-ly off-tire.3Sg
Intended meaning: 'The captain rarely gets tired.'

(220) a. *A felügyelő NAGYON fáradt el.
the inspector greatly tired off
Intended meaning: 'The inspector got tired VERY MUCH.'

b. *A kapitány *alig* el-fáradt.
the captain barely off-tired
Intended meaning: 'The captain barely got tired.'

(221) a. Olívia JÓL oldotta meg az ügyet.
Olívia well solved Perf the case.Acc
'Olívia solved the case WELL.'

b. *Artúr *rossz-ul* meg-oldotta az ügyet.
Artúr bad-ly Perf-solved the case.Acc
Intended meaning: 'Artúr solved the case badly.'

The phenomenon illustrated in (222) concerns scalar expressions. The interpretation of scalar expressions, in principle, involves no upper boundary; i.e., if the scalar element is a number *n*, it means 'at least *n*', '*n* or more'. E.g.:

(222) a. Az új ügyfél-nek van 500 dollár-ja.
the new client-Dat is 500 dollar-Poss.3Sg
'The new client has (at least) 500 dollars.'

b. 500 dollár-ja mindegyik ügyfél-nek van.
500 dollar-Poss.3Sg each client-Dat is
'Each client has (at least) 500 dollars.'

Though the 'at least *n*' interpretation of numerals is always possible logically, in languages like English, it is only elicited by specific contexts; the default interpretation is the upper-bounded, 'exactly *n*' reading. This is different in Hungarian; here the upper bounded interpretation is associated with the focus position (223).

(223) Az új ügyfél-nek 500 DOLLÁR-JA van.
the new client-Dat 500 dollar-Poss.3Sg is
'The new client has (exactly) 500 dollars.'

If a scalar element appears in a position other than the immediately preverbal focus slot, speakers tend to infer that it is not in focus position because it is to be interpreted without an upper boundary. The same holds for scalar adverbials of frequency, degree, and manner; in a position other than focus, they elicit an unbounded reading. (216a) can also be true if the inspector is nearly always tired; (217a) could also be truly said if the inspector was totally exhausted; and (218a) is also appropriate if Olívia solved the case perfectly.

Focusing supplies scalar adverbials with an upper boundary. Put differently, to achieve an interpretation with an upper boundary, scalar adverbials of frequency, degree, and manner must be focused:

(224) Olívia JÓL oldotta meg az ügyet, de nem tökéletesen.
Olívia well solved Perf the case.Acc but not perfectly
'Olívia solved the case WELL, but not perfectly.'

In the case of bidirectional scales, the unbounded interpretation of scalar values from the negative domain of the scale would yield unwanted results. Whereas *well done* can describe something perfectly done, *frequently done* can describe something nearly always done, and *very much broken* can describe something totally damaged, the phrase *badly done* cannot be applied to something well done, *rarely done* cannot be applied to something frequently done, and *little damaged* cannot be applied to something very much damaged. The need of negative scalar adverbials to be upper bounded has been grammaticalized in Hungarian as a need to be focused. Positive, intensifying degree adverbials such as *nagyon* 'very much' represent the opposite case: they are barred from the focus position because they cannot be supplied with an upper boundary.

7.4.4. Obligatorily stressed high adverbials

There is a small number of epistemic adverbial adjuncts, such as *mindenképpen* 'by all means', *feltétlenül* 'uncondionally', *okvetlenül* 'definitely', which seem to bear a primary stress, contrary to all the so far established generalizations.

(225) Olívia *'feltétlen-ül* egyetért a szakáccsal.
Olívia uncondional-ly agrees the cook.Ins
'Olívia agrees with the cook unconditonally.'

Another small group of adverbial adjuncts show ambiguity in this respect. Undoubtedly, the most interesting case is provided by the adverbial *biztosan* 'surely, certainly' with its three different readings. In (226a), it has a manner reading, while in the other two sentences below the same adverbial *biztosan* 'surely, certainly' has a clausal reading, but with a slight difference in meaning: (226b) expresses strong probability, while (226c) actual certainty. In the third example, the adverbial *biztosan* gets stressed (with a simultaneous stress reduction in the subsequent domain of the clause). This characteristic prosody expresses the speaker's belief that the situation corresponds to what figures in the proposition.

(226) a. • manner
A kapitány *'biztos-an* 'eltalálta a 'céltábla 'közepét.
the captain sure-ly hit the target middle.Acc
'The captain hit the bull's eye confidently.'

b. • clausal 1: probability
A kapitány *biztos-an* 'eltalálta a céltábla közepét.
the captain sure-ly hit the target middle.Acc
'Very probably, the captain hit the bull's eye.'

c. • clausal 2: certainty
A kapitány *'biztos-an* eltalálta a céltábla közepét.
the captain sure-ly hit the target middle.Acc
'Certainly, the captain hit the bull's eye.'

Unlike canonical clausal PP adjuncts, stressed clausal adverbials fall into the scope of other sentential operators:

(227) a. A felügyelő *'biztos-an* döntés-re jutott?
the inspector sure-ly decision-Sub got
'Is it certain that the inspector arrived at a decision?'

b. A felügyelő 'nem jutott *biztosan* döntés-re.
the inspector not got surely decision-Sub
'It is not certain that the inspector arrived at a decision.'

Unlike canonical clausal PP adjuncts, stressed clausal adverbials cannot precede the topic and the quantifier fields:

(228) (**Feltétlen-ül*) Olívia (**feltétlen-ül*) két kérdésben ('*feltétlen-ül*)
unconditional-ly Olívia unconditional-ly two question.Ine unconditional-ly
egyetért a szakáccsal.
agrees the cook.Ins
'Olívia agrees with the cook in two questions unconditionally.'

All these facts point to the direction that such stressed clausal adverbials should be considered middle adverbials. They seem to be adjoined to the predicate directly, or to the predicate extended with a focused constituent.

Semantically speaking, the adverbials under discussion all express some kind of certainty with respect to the truth of the proposition on behalf of the speaker. It can be assumed that they modify propositions that involve a so called *verum*-focus (Egedi 2009a and 2009b). The associated intonation pattern also conveys stress reduction (or deaccentuation, cf. Varga 2002) after the primary stress, in the same way as it can be observed in constituent focus structures (cf. Vogel and Kenesei 1987).

Verum-focus emphasizes the truth of the proposition; or in other words, it reasserts or denies the hearer's presupposition. It is also called polarity focus since it contrasts the interpretation of the whole sentence to its negation. There is a set of modifiers, such as *valóban, tényleg, csakugyan, igazán* 'indeed, really', which are obligatorily stressed and modify identificational focus constructions (229), or *verum*-focus (230), but are conventionally classified as pragmatic/modal particles:

(229) Olívia '*tény-leg* A SZAKÁCCSAL ért egyet.
Olívia fact-ly the cook.Ins mean.3Sg one-Acc
'It is really THE COOK whom Olívia agrees with.'

(230) A felügyelő '*való-ban* döntés-re jutott.
the inspector truth-Ine decision-Sub got
'The inspector really arrived at a decision.'

7.4.5. Postverbal phenomena

As has been shown above, Hungarian adverbial adjuncts may appear both preverbally and postverbally, but only their preverbal order is strictly fixed. In the postverbal field the order of the elements is relatively free in spite of the fact that the adverbs maintain their scope, and usually their stress properties as well.

A postverbal sentence adverb may have scope over a preverbal one (231), and two postverbal adverbs may also show scope hierarchy independently of their position and their relative order in the sentence (232).

(231) A nyomozó *valószínűleg* 'el-kapta *szerencsére* a gyilkost.
the detective probably away-caught luckily the murderer.Acc
'Luckily, the detective probably has caught the murderer.'

(232) A nyomozó 'el-kapta *titokban valószínűleg* a gyilkost.
the detective away-caught secret.Ine probably the murderer.Acc
'The detective probably has caught the murderer in secret.'

The postverbal section of the Hungarian sentence is assumed to be linearized freely, and all the constituents, including PP adjuncts, can be ordered randomly. There are some adverbial expressions, however, that remain ambiguous between the manner and clausal reading in the postverbal field, when the prosodic properties are neutralized. Observe the case of *szokatlanul* 'oddly', which can have a manner reading as well as a clausal, evaluative reading, The two readings are disambiguated by prosody: primary stress falls on the manner adverb that is adjoined directly to the predicate (233a), while the same adjunct in a clausal adverbial function remains unstressed (or bears a reduced stress) (233b):

(233) a. • manner

A kertész *'szokatlanul* biciklizett az állomás-ig.
the gardener oddly cycled the station-Ter
'The gardener cycled to the station oddly.'

b. • evaluative

A kertész *szokatlanul* 'biciklizett az állomás-ig.
the gardener oddly cycled the station-Ter
'Unexpectedly, the gardener cycled to the station.'

When appearing postverbally, in the scope of certain operators (e.g. in the scope of negation), the original prosodic contrast is lost, and only the manner reading is available under normal intonation:

(234) • manner

A kertész 'nem biciklizett *szokatlanul* az állomás-ig.
the gardener not cycled oddly the station-Ter
'The gardener did not cycle to the station oddly.'

To get the clausal reading, the adverbial must be associated with an independent intonational phrase, involving a short interval before and after the adjunct, i.e. by the insertion of a pause. With this marked prosodic pattern, the adjunct has a clausal, evaluative reading and has scope over the negation.

(235) • evaluative

A kertész 'nem biciklizett □ *szokatlanul* □ az állomás-ig.
the gardener not cycled oddly the station-Ter
'Unexpectedly, the gardener did not cycle to the station.'

With the adverbial types discussed in Section 7.4.4, beyond the manner reading, one of the clausal readings is also accessible, but only in the verum-modifier sense:

(236) • manner; clausal 2: certainty

A kapitány 'nem találta el *biztosan* a céltábla közepét.
the captain not hit away surely the target middle.Acc
(i) 'The captain did not hit the bull's eye confidently.'
(ii) 'The captain did not certainly hit the bull's eye.' (i.e., It is not certainly true that he hit it.)

7.5. Summary

This chapter discussed adverbial adjuncts, i.e. PPs that are neither arguments nor predicates. These adjuncts modify different nonnominal portions of the clause, the core predicate being the smallest, while the proposition including the speech-act being the largest over which adjuncts may have a scope. The chapter has been divided into three major parts: the first section overviewed the morphological properties and the categorial types of adverbial adjuncts providing basic tests to distinguish the so-called VP-adjuncts from clausal adjuncts. The tests clearly showed that there are in-between categories of adjuncts that cannot be classified either as VP-adjuncts or clausal adjuncts: aspectual and degree adverbials must be discussed separately in this respect. Furthermore, there are adjuncts that take their scope in a flexible way, as was claimed for spatial, temporal and contingency adverbials.

Section 7.3 discussed the various adjuncts from a semantic point of view, classifying them into eleven major types: spatial and temporal adjuncts, contingency adverbial adjuncts, manner adverbials, subject-oriented adverbials, participant PPs, domain adverbial adjuncts, speaker-oriented adverbials, discourse-oriented adverbials, aspectual adverbial adjuncts, degree adverbial adjuncts and measure adverbial adjuncts.

Section 7.4 addressed the placement properties and prosodic features of high, middle and low adverbials as well as their relative order within the sentence. At the end of Section 7.4, three individual subsections have been devoted to some special features to be accounted for in Hungarian: the case of exclusive adverbials that must be focused obligatorily, the stressed clausal adverbials that appear to modify the so called verum-focus in the middle field, and finally some postverbal phenomena which are relevant in the case of adverbials with ambiguous readings.

7.6. Bibliographical notes

As for the categorial types and semantic groups of Hungarian adverbial adjuncts, the chapter has not adopted any of the known systems in the literature, but has been inspired by several works on the topic (Cinque 1999, Ernst 2002), and also aimed to follow, as closely as possible, the relevant chapter on adverbial modifiers of the verb phrases in Broekhuis, Corver & Vos (2015). Certain parts of this chapter heavily rely on the volume *Adverbs and adverbial adjuncts at the Interfaces* edited by Katalin É. Kiss (Berlin: Mouton de Gruyter, 2009).

The observation that speaker-oriented adverbs have a rather restricted distribution (e.g. they are degraded in questions, imperatives and antecedents of conditionals, and they do not occur in the scope of negation) was first made by Bellert (1977). On the semantically motivated selectional requirements of the individual PP adjuncts, consult first of all Ernst (2002). According to Ernst's (2002) event-based semantic theory, several layers of event types and proposition types can be built on a basic event until the representation of a sentence is completed. This model assumes that the relative order and scope relations of the adjuncts of different subclasses can be derived from their requirements for specific semantic event-arguments. For similar approaches, cf. Haider (2000), Frey (2003). For the cartographic approach of the syntax of adjuncts and for a proposal of a universal hierarchy behind their ordering, see Cinque (1999). Tenny (2000) further groups this hierarchical order of functional projections into six semantic zones. See also Ramat & Ricca (1998) for cross-linguistic observations on the ordering of sentence adverbs.

Descriptive literature on Hungarian adjuncts may be found in Keszler (2000). Kugler (2003) also discusses clausal adverbials, even though from a radically different perspective from ours. See also Prószéky (1989) on free adjuncts in Hungarian. Surányi (2008) deals with the distribution of Hungarian adverbial adjuncts in the preverbal field, distinguishing three main classes according to their syntactic position. The descriptive generalizations proposed in this chapter have similar results to what has been proposed in Surányi's paper.

For the classification of Hungarian temporal adverbial adjuncts, see Kiefer (2006, 2009). For some semantic properties of time adverbs, see Csirmaz (2006a), while for accusative marked temporal adjuncts, cf. Csirmaz (2006c). For the aspectual reading of *gyorsan* 'quickly', see Eszes (2009). On the repetitive vs. restitutive readings of *újra* 'again', see Csirmaz (2015, 2016); Hegedűs (2020).

On scalar adverbials of frequency, degree, and manner, and on the special case of exclusive adverbials see É. Kiss (2006d, 2009b). On the semantic and syntactic properties of 'verum focus', see first of all Höhle (1992), Han and Romero (2004). For Hungarian, cf. Kenesei (1998), Egedi (2009a,b). Egedi's papers also analyze adverbial adjuncts with ambiguous readings, as well as postverbal prosodic and disambiguating strategies. About pragmatic particles cf. Kugler (2003), as for modal particles, see Kiefer (1988). É. Kiss (2009a) derives the postverbal positions and the free order of Hungarian adverbs.

Subject index

A

D

S

T

U

V

References

Abondolo, Daniel. 1998. *Hungarian Inflectional Morphology*. Budapest: Akadémiai Kiadó.

Ackermann, Farrell. 1984. Verbal modifiers as argument taking predicates: Complex verbs as predicate complexes in Hungarian. *Groninger Arbeiten zur Germanistischen Linguistik* 25: 23–71.

Ackerman, Farrell. 1987. Pronominal incorporation: The case of prefixal adverbs. In *Approaches to Hungarian Volume 2*, ed. István Kenesei, 213–260. Szeged: JATE.

Ackerman, Farrell and Adele E. Goldberg. 2001. The pragmatics of obligatory adjuncts. *Language* 77: 798–814.

Ackerman, Farrell and Gert Webelhuth. 1997. The composition of (dis)continuous predicates: lexical or syntactic? *Acta Linguistica Hungarica* 44: 317–340.

Alberti, Gábor. 1997. *Argument Selection*. Frankfurt am Main: Peter Lang.

Antal, László. 1961. *A magyar esetrendszer* [The Hungarian case system]. Budapest: Akadémiai Kiadó.

Asbury, Anna. 2005. Adpositions as case realizations: Structures and consequences. *Leiden Papers in Linguistics* 2: 69–92.

Asbury, Anna. 2008. Marking of semantic roles in Hungarian morphosyntax. In *Approaches to Hungarian Volume 10. Papers from the Veszprém Conference*, eds. Christopher Piñón and Szilárd Szentgyörgyi, 9–30. Budapest: Akadémiai Kiadó.

Asbury, Anna, Berit Gehrke and Veronika Hegedűs. 2007. One size fits all: Prefixes, particles, adpositions and cases as members of the category P. In *UiL OTS Yearbook 2006*, ed. Cem Keskin, 1–17. Utrecht: Utrecht University.

Bartha, Csilla. 1997. Helységneveink ragozása határainkon innen és túl [Inflecting place names in and outside of Hungary]. In *Hungarológia 9. Tudományos, oktatásmódszertani és tájékoztató füzetek*, eds. Katalin Erdős, Rita Hegedűs and Zoltánné Kőrösi, 179–193. Budapest: Nemzetközi Hungarológiai Központ.

Bartos, Huba. 1999. *Morfoszintaxis és interpretáció. A magyar inflexiós jelenségek szintaktikai háttere* [Morphosyntax and interpretation. The syntactic background of Hungarian inflexional phenomena]. PhD dissertation. Budapest: Eötvös Loránd University.

Bartos, Huba. 2000. Az inflexiós jelenségek szintaktikai háttere [The syntactic background of inflectional phenomena]. In *Strukturális magyar nyelvtan 3. Morfológia*, ed. Ferenc Kiefer, 653–761. Budapest: Akadémiai Kiadó.

Bartos, Huba. 2011. Hungarian external causatives: Monoclausal but bi-eventive. In *Approaches to Hungarian Volume 12. Papers from the 2009 Debrecen Conference*, eds. Tibor Laczkó and Catherine O. Ringen, 1–38. Amsterdam: John Benjamins.

Behaghel, Otto. 1932. *Deutsche Syntax* IV. Heidelberg: Carl Winters.

Bellert, Irena. 1977. On semantic and distributional properties of sentential adverbs. *Linguistic Inquiry* 8: 337–351.

Bende-Farkas, Ágnes. 2001. *Verb-object dependencies in Hungarian and English: a DRT-based approach*. PhD dissertation. Stuttgart: University of Stuttgart.

Benkő, Loránd (ed.) 1967. *A magyar nyelv történeti-etimológiai szótára 1. A-Gy*. [A historical-etymological dictionary of Hungarian. Vol 1. A-Gy.] Budapest: Akadémiai Kiadó.

Benkő, Loránd (ed.) 1970. *A magyar nyelv történeti-etimológiai szótára 2. H-Ó*. [A historical-etymological dictionary of Hungarian. Vol 2. H-Ó.] Budapest: Akadémiai Kiadó

Benkő, Loránd (ed.) 1976. *A magyar nyelv történeti-etimológiai szótára 3. Ö-Zs*. [A historical-etymological dictionary of Hungarian. Vol 3. Ö-Zs.] Budapest: Akadémiai Kiadó.

Benkő, Loránd. 1980. *Az Árpád-kor magyar nyelvű szövegemlékei* [Hungarian texts from the time of the Árpád dynasty]. Budapest: Akadémiai Kiadó.

Benkő, Loránd (ed.) 1994. *Etymologisches Wörterbuch des Ungarischen. Vol II. Kor–Zs*. Budapest: Akadémiai Kiadó.

Bibok, Károly. 2018. Instrument-subject alternation: A further case study in lexical pragmatics. In *Boundaries Crossed, at the Interfaces of Morphosyntax, Phonology, Pragmatics and Semantics*, eds. Huba Bartos, Marcel den Dikken, Zoltán Bánréti and Tamás Váradi, 33–50. Cham: Springer International Publishing.

Brassai, Sámuel. 1863–5. A magyar mondat [The Hungarian sentence]. *Akadémiai Értesítő. A Nyelv- és Széptudományi Osztály Közlönye* 1: 279–399; 2: 3–128, 3: 173–409.

Brody, Michael. 1990. Some remarks on the focus field in Hungarian. In *UCL Working Papers in Linguistics II*, ed. J. Harris, 201–225. London: University College London.

Broekhuis, Hans, Norbert Corver and Riet Vos. 2015. *Syntax of Dutch: Verbs and Verb Phrases*. Amsterdam: Amsterdam University Press.

Chisarik, Erika and John Payne. 2001. Modelling possessor constructions in LFG: English and Hungarian. In *Proceedings of the LFG'01 Conference*, eds. Miriam Butt and Tracy Holloway King, 33–46. Stanford: CSLI Publications.

Cinque, Guglielmo. 1999. *Adverbs and Functional Heads. A Cross-Linguistic Perspective*. Oxford Studies in Comparative Syntax. New York/Oxford: Oxford University Press.

Citko, Barbara. 2014. On headed, headless and light-headed relatives. *Natural Language and Linguistic Theory* 22/1: 95–126.

Creissels, Denis. 2006. Suffixes casuels et postpositions en hongrois. *Bulletin de la Société de Linguistique de Paris* 101/1: 225–272.

Csirmaz, Anikó. 2006a. A typology of Hungarian time adverbs. *Acta Linguistica Hungarica* 53/3: 249–289.

Csirmaz, Anikó. 2006b. Particles and a two-component theory of aspect. In *Event Structure and the Left Periphery. Studies on Hungarian*, ed. Katalin É. Kiss, 107–128. Dordrecht: Springer.

Csirmaz, Anikó. 2006c. Accusative case and aspect. In *Event Structure and the Left Periphery. Studies on Hungarian*, ed. Katalin É. Kiss, 159–200. Dordrecht: Springer.

Csirmaz, Anikó. 2015. Re Hungarian *again*. *Acta Linguistica Hungarica* 62/3: 263–295.

Csirmaz, Anikó. 2016. Repetitive adverbs in English and Hungarian. *University of Pennsylvania Working Papers in Linguistics* 22/1: 91–99.

De Groot, Casper. 2017. The essives in Hungarian. In *Uralic Essive and the Expression of Impermanent State*, ed. Casper de Groot, 325–351. Amsterdam/Philadelphia: John Benjamins.

Dékány, Éva. 2011. *A Profile of the Hungarian DP. The Interaction of Lexicalization, Agreement and Linearization with the Functional Sequence.* PhD dissertation, Tromsø: University of Tromsø.

Dékány, Éva. 2014. Argument structure and functional projections in Old Hungarian verbal gerunds. *Acta Linguistica Hungarica* 61/3: 317–361.

Dékány, Éva. 2015. The syntax of anaphoric possessives in Hungarian. *Natural Language and Linguistic Theory* 33/4: 1121–1168.

Dékány, Éva. 2018. The position of case markers relative to possessive agreement: variation within Hungarian. *Natural Language and Linguistic Theory* 36/2: 365–400.

Dékány, Éva and Veronika Hegedűs. 2015. Word order variation in Hungarian PPs. In *Approaches to Hungarian Volume 14: Papers from the Piliscsaba Conference*, eds. Katalin É. Kiss, Balázs Surányi and Éva Dékány, 95–120. Amsterdam: John Benjamins.

Dér, Csilla. 2012. Mennyire (prototipikus) névutók a ragvonzó névutók a magyarban? [How prototypical postpositions are case-assigning postpositions in Hungarian?] In *Konstrukció és jelentés. Tanulmányok a magyar nyelv funkcionális kognitív leírására*, eds. Gábor Tolcsvai Nagy and Szilárd Tátrai, 11–29. Budapest: ELTE BTK.

Dér, Csilla. 2013. A kontextus szerepe a magyar ragvonzó névutók viselkedésében [The role of context in the distribution of Hungarian case-assigning postpositions]. In *Grammatika és kontextus – új szempontok az uráli nyelvek kutatásában III.* (Uralisztikai tanulmányok 20.), eds. Márta Csepregi, Kata Kubínyi and Jari Sivonen, 9–19. Budapest: ELTE Finnugor Tanszék.

Dikken, Marcel den. 2018. *Dependency and Directionality*. Cambridge: Cambridge University Press.

D. Mátai, Mária. 1989. Igekötőrendszerünk történetéből [On the diachrony of the system of verbal particles]. *Magyar Nyelv* 85: 9–28, 151–171.

D. Mátai, Mária. 1991. Az igekötők [Verbal particles]. In *A magyar nyelv történeti nyelvtana I. A korai ómagyar kor és előzményei*, eds. Loránd Benkő, Erzsébet E. Abaffy and Endre Rácz, 433–441. Budapest: Akadémiai Kiadó.

D. Mátai, Mária 1992. Az igekötők [Verbal particles]. In *A magyar nyelv történeti nyelvtana II/1. A kései ómagyar kor morfematikája*, ed. Loránd Benkő, 662–695. Budapest: Akadémiai Kiadó.

Egedi, Barbara. 2009a. Adverbial (dis)ambiguities. Syntactic and prosodic features of ambiguous predicational adverbs. In *Adverbs and Adverbial Adjuncts at the Interfaces,* ed. Katalin É. Kiss, 103–132. Berlin: Mouton de Gruyter.

Egedi, Barbara. 2009b. A magyar kétértelmű mondathatározók és hatókör-viszonyaik [Ambiguous sentence adverbs in Hungarian and their scope relations]. In *A mai magyar nyelv leírásának újabb módszerei VII. Modellek, elméletek és elvek érvényessége nyelvi adatok tükrében*, eds. Márta Maleczki and Enikő Németh T., 67–85. Szeged: SZTE Általános Nyelvészeti Tanszék.

É. Kiss, Katalin. 1977. Topic and Focus in Hungarian Syntax. *Montreal Working Papers in Linguistics* 8: 1–42.

É. Kiss, Katalin. 1995. The Definiteness Effect revisited. In *Approaches to Hungarian Volume 5*, ed. István Kenesei, 63–88. Szeged: JATE.

É. Kiss, Katalin. 1998. Verbal prefixes or postpositions? Postpositional aspectualizers in Hungarian. In *Approaches to Hungarian Volume 6*, eds. Caspar de Groot and István Kenesei, 123–148. Szeged: JATE.

É. Kiss, Katalin. 1999. Mi tartozik a névutók osztályába? [What belongs to the category of postpositions?]. *Magyar Nyelvjárások* 37: 167–172.

É. Kiss, Katalin. 2000. The Hungarian Noun Phrase is like the English Noun Phrase. In *Approaches to Hungarian Volume 7*, eds. Gábor Alberti and István Kenesei, 121–149. Szeged: JATE Press.

É. Kiss, Katalin. 2002. *The Syntax of Hungarian*. Cambridge: Cambridge University Press.

É. Kiss, Katalin. 2005. First steps towards a theory of the verbal particle. In *Approaches to Hungarian Volume 9*, eds. Christopher Piñón and Péter Siptár, 57–88. Budapest: Akadémiai Kiadó.

É. Kiss, Katalin. 2006a. The function and the syntax of the verbal particle. In *Event Structure and the Left Periphery. Studies on Hungarian*, ed. Katalin É. Kiss, 17–56. Dordrecht: Springer.

É. Kiss, Katalin. 2006b. From the grammaticalization of viewpoint aspect to the grammaticalization of situation aspect. In *Event Structure and the Left Periphery. Studies on Hungarian*, ed. Katalin É. Kiss, 129–158. Dordrecht: Springer.

É. Kiss, Katalin. 2006c. Apparent or real? On the complementary distribution of identificational focus and the verbal particle. In *Event Structure and the Left Periphery. Studies on Hungarian*, ed. Katalin É. Kiss, 201–224. Dordrecht: Springer.

É. Kiss, Katalin. 2006d. *Jól megoldottuk? Rosszul oldottuk meg?* Az összefoglaló és a kirekesztő kifejezést tartalmazó mondatok szórendjének magyarázata [*Jól megoldottuk? Rosszul oldottuk meg?* Explanation of the word order of sentences with inclusive and exclusive expressions]. *Magyar Nyelv* 102: 442-459.

É. Kiss, Katalin. 2009a. Syntactic, semantic and prosodic factors determining the position of adverbial adjuncts. In *Adverbs and Adverbial Adjuncts at the Interfaces,* ed. Katalin É. Kiss, 21–38. Berlin: Mouton de Gruyter.

É. Kiss, Katalin. 2009b. Scalar adverbs in and out of focus. In *Adverbs and Adverbial Adjuncts at the Interfaces,* ed. Katalin É. Kiss, 297–316. Berlin: Mouton de Gruyter.

É. Kiss, Katalin. 2009c. *Nekem el kell menni/el kell mennem/el kell, hogy menjek/el kell menjek/el kellek menni*. In *Nyelvelmélet és dialektológia*, ed. Katalin É. Kiss and Attila Hegedűs, 213–231. Piliscsaba: PPKE.

É. Kiss, Katalin (ed.) 2009d. *Adverbs and Adverbial Adjuncts at the Interfaces*. Berlin: Mouton de Gruyter.

É. Kiss, Katalin and Henk van Riemsdijk (eds.) 2004. *Verb Clusters. A Study of Hungarian, German and Dutch*. Amsterdam: John Benjamins.

Elekfi, László. 1980. *Azokat – őket* (Nyelvművelésünk tudományosságáért) [*Azokat – őket* (For a scientific approach to language cultivation)]. *Magyar Nyelv* 76: 176–187, 323–330.

Ernst, Thomas. 2002. *The Syntax of Adjuncts*. Cambridge: Cambridge University Press.

Eszes, Boldizsár. 2006. Verbal particles telicizing stative psych verbs. In *Event Structure and the Left Periphery. Studies on Hungarian*, ed. Katalin É. Kiss, 57–74. Dordrecht: Springer.

Eszes, Boldizsár. 2009. Aspect and adverb interpretation – the case of *quickly*. In *Adverbs and Adverbial Adjuncts at the Interfaces,* ed. Katalin É. Kiss, 269–294. Berlin: Mouton de Gruyter.

Farkas, Donka F. and Jerrold M. Sadock. 1989. Particle climbing in Hungarian. *Language* 65: 318–338.

Farkas, Imola-Ágnes. 2017. Miért nem tud Mari két óra alatt sétálni egyet? Az ige + *egyet* szerkezet és az *alatt* határpontos időmódosító összeférhetetlenségéről [Why can't Mary take a walk in two hours? On the incompatibility between the verb + *egyet* 'one.ACC' construction and the delimiting *alatt* 'in' time adverbial]. *Nyelv- és Irodalomtudományi Közlemények* 61/2: 119–138.

Farkas, Imola-Ágnes and Éva Kardos. 2018. Non-maximal event delimitation in Hungarian. *Argumentum* 14: 368–382.

Fejes, László. 2013. Mi az a *szerte*? [What is *szerte*?] *Nyelv és Tudomány* 2013. június 24.

Fekete, István. 2013. Hungarian *gyerekestül* vs. *gyerekkel* ('with [the] kid'). *Hungarian Cultural Studies. e-Journal of the American Hungarian Educators Association* 6: 96–119.

Forgács, Tamás. 2004. Grammaticalisation and preverbs. *Acta Linguistica Hungarica* 51/1-2: 45–84.

Frey, Werner. 2003. Syntactic conditions on adjunct classes. In *Modifying Adjuncts*, ed. Ewald Lang, Claudia Meienborn and Cathrine Fabricius-Hansen, 163–209. Berlin: Mouton de Gruyter.

Gábor, Kata and Enikő Héja. 2006. Predikátumok és szabad határozók [Predicates and adjuncts]. In *KB 120. A titkos kötet: Nyelvészeti tanulmányok Bánréti Zoltán és Komlósy András tiszteletére*, ed. László Kálmán, 135–163. Budapest: MTA NYTI & Tinta Kiadó.

Haider, Hubert. 2000. Adverb placement – convergence of structure and licensing. *Theoretical Linguistics* 26: 95–134.

Halm, Tamás. 2015. Free choice and aspect in Hungarian. In *Approaches to Hungarian Volume 14. Papers from the 2013 Piliscsaba Conference*, eds. Katalin É. Kiss, Balázs Surányi and Éva Dékány, 167–185. Amsterdam: John Benjamins.

Han, Chung-hye and Maribel Romero. 2004. Disjunction, Focus, and scope. *Linguistic Inquiry* 35: 179–217.

Hegedűs, Veronika. 2006. Hungarian spatial PPs. *Nordlyd: Tromsoe University Working Papers in Linguistics* 33: 220–233.

Hegedűs, Veronika. 2013. *Non-verbal Predicates and Predicate Movement in Hungarian*. PhD dissertation, Tilburg University. Published as Volume 337 of the LOT Dissertation Series, LOT: Utrecht.

Hegedűs, Veronika. 2014. The cyclical development of Ps in Hungarian. In *The Evolution of Functional Left Peripheries in Hungarian Syntax*, ed. Katalin É. Kiss, 122–147. Oxford: Oxford University Press.

Hegedűs, Veronika. 2015. The grammaticalization of postpositions in Old Hungarian. In *Syntax over Time*, ed. Theresa Biberauer and George Walkden, 72–85. Oxford: Oxford University Press.

Hegedűs, Veronika. 2020. Back to restitutives (again): A syntactic account of restitutive and counterdirectional verbal particles in Hungarian. *Acta Linguistica Academica* 67/3: 319–345.

Hegedűs, Veronika and Éva Dékány. 2017. Two positions for verbal modifiers: evidence from derived particle verbs. In *Approaches to Hungarian Volume 15. Papers from the 2015 Leiden Conference,* eds. Anikó Lipták and Harry van der Hulst, 65–94. Amsterdam: John Benjamins.

Horvath, Julia. 1978. Verbal prefixes: a non-category in Hungarian. *Glossa* 12/2: 137–162.

Horvath, Julia and Tal Siloni. 2011. Causatives across components. *Natural Language and Linguistic Theory* 29: 657–704.

Höhle, Tilman N. 1992. Über Verum–Fokus im Deutschen. In *Informationsstruktur und Grammatik.* Linguistische Berichte Sonderhefte 4, ed. Joachim Jacobs, 112–141. Opladen: Westdeutscher Verlag.

H. Varga, Márta. 2008. Redundáns jelenségek a magyar grammatikában [Redundancies in Hungarian grammar]. *Magyar Nyelvőr* 132/3: 354–366.

Jackendoff, Ray. 1972. *Semantic Interpretation in Generative Grammar*. Cambridge, MA: MIT Press.

J. Soltész, Katalin. 1959. *Az ősi magyar igekötők* [Ancient Hungarian verbal particles]. Budapest: Akadémiai Kiadó.

Kádár, Edit. 2009. Adverbial versus adjectival constructions with *be* and the category Adv. In *Adverbs and Adverbial Adjuncts at the Interfaces,* ed. Katalin É. Kiss, 171–195. Berlin: Mouton de Gruyter.

Kalivoda, Ágnes. 2018. Hungarian particle verbs in a corpus-driven approach. In *Computational Linguistics and Intelligent Text Processing: 18th International Conference, CICLing 2017, Budapest, Hungary, April 17–23, 2017. Revised Selected Papers, Part I,* ed. Alexander Gelbukh, 123–133. Cham: Springer.

Kalivoda, Ágnes. 2020. *Igekötős szerkezetek a magyarban* [Particle verb constructions in Hungarian]. PhD dissertation. Budapest: Pázmány Péter Catholic University.

Kálmán, László. 1995. Definiteness effect verbs in Hungarian. In *Approaches to Hungarian Volume 5*, ed. István Kenesei, 221–242. Szeged: JATE.

Kálmán, László. 2006. Miért nem vonzanak a régensek? [Why do predicates not attract?] In *KB 120. A titkos kötet: Nyelvészeti tanulmányok Bánréti Zoltán és Komlósy András tiszteletére*, ed. László Kálmán, 229–246. Budapest: MTA NYTI & Tinta Kiadó.

Kenesei, István. 1992. Az alárendelt mondatok szerkezete [The structure of embedded clauses]. In *Strukturális magyar nyelvtan 1. Mondattan*, ed. Ferenc Kiefer, 529–714. Budapest: Akadémiai Kiadó.

Kenesei, István. 1994. Subordinate clauses. In *The Syntactic Structure of Hungarian.* Syntax and Semantics 27, eds. Ferenc Kiefer and Katalin É. Kiss, 275–354. San Diego/New York: Academic Press.

Kenesei, István 1998. Adjuncts and arguments in VP-focus in Hungarian. *Acta Linguistica Hungarica* 45: 61–88.

Kenesei, István. 2000. Szavak, szófajok, toldalékok [Words, word classes, affixes]. In *Strukturális magyar nyelvtan 3. Morfológia*, ed. Ferenc Kiefer, 75–136. Budapest: Akadémiai Kiadó.

Kenesei, István. 2005. Nonfinite clauses in derived nominals. In *Approaches to Hungarian Volume 9,* eds. Christopher Piñón and Péter Siptár, 161–186. Budapest: Akadémiai Kiadó.

Kenesei, István. 2007. Semiwords and affixoids: The territory between word and affix. *Acta Linguistica Hungarica* 54/3: 263–293.

Kenesei, István. 2014. On a multifunctional derivational affix: Its use in relational adjectives or nominal modification, and phrasal affixation in Hungarian. *Word Structure* 7/2: 214–239.

Kenesei, István, Robert Vago and Anna Fenyvesi. 1998. *Hungarian.* London: Routledge.

Keszler, Borbála. 2000. A határozók [Adverbials]. In *Magyar grammatika*, ed. Borbála Keszler, 423–443. Budapest: Nemzeti Tankönyvkiadó.

Kiefer, Ferenc. 1988. Modal particles as discourse markers in questions. *Acta Linguistica Hungarica* 38: 107–125.

Kiefer, Ferenc. 1995/1996. Prefix reduplication in Hungarian. *Acta Linguistica Hungarica* 43: 175–194.

Kiefer, Ferenc. 2000a. A ragozás [Inflection]. In *Strukturális magyar nyelvtan 3. Morfológia*, ed. Ferenc Kiefer, 569–618. Budapest: Akadémiai Kiadó.

Kiefer, Ferenc. 2000b. *Jelentéselmélet* [*Semantics*]. Budapest: Corvina.

Kiefer, Ferenc (ed.) 2000c. *Strukturális magyar nyelvtan 3. Morfológia* [A structural grammar of Hungarian 3. Morphology]. Budapest: Akadémiai Kiadó.

Kiefer, Ferenc. 2003. Alaktan [Morphology]. In Katalin É. Kiss, Ferenc Kiefer and Péter Siptár, *Új magyar nyelvtan,* 189–285. Budapest: Osiris.

Kiefer, Ferenc. 2006. *Aspektus és akcióminőség különös tekintettel a magyar nyelvre.* Budapest: Akadémiai Kiadó.

Kiefer, Ferenc (ed.) 2008. *Strukturális magyar nyelvtan 4. A szótár szerkezete* [A structural grammar of Hungarian 4. The structure of the lexicon]. Budapest: Akadémiai Kiadó.

Kiefer, Ferenc. 2009. Types of temporal adverbials and the fine structure of events. In *Adverbs and Adverbial Adjuncts at the Interfaces,* ed. Katalin É. Kiss, 247–267. Berlin: Mouton de Gruyter.

Kiefer, Ferenc and Mária Ladányi. 2000a. Morfoszintaktikailag semleges képzések [Morphosyntactically netural derivations]. In *Strukturális magyar nyelvtan 3. Morfológia*, ed. Ferenc Kiefer, 165–214. Budapest: Akadémiai Kiadó.

Kiefer, Ferenc and Mária Ladányi. 2000b. Az igekötők [Verbal particles]. In *Strukturális magyar nyelvtan 3. Morfológia,* ed. Ferenc Kiefer, 453–518. Budapest: Akadémiai Kiadó.

Kiefer, Ferenc and Boglárka Németh. 2012. Amikor az igekötő nem telicizál [When the verbal particle does not telicize]. *Nyelvtudományi Közlemények* 108: 267-273.

Klemm, Antal. 1928. *Magyar történeti mondattan* [Hungarian diachronic grammar]. Budapest: Magyar Tudományos Akadémia.

Komlósy, András. 1992. Régensek és vonzatok [Predicates and arguments]. In *Strukturális magyar nyelvtan 1. Mondattan*, ed. Ferenc Kiefer, 299–528. Budapest: Akadémiai Kiadó.

Komlósy, András. 1994. Complements and adjuncts. In *The Syntactic Structure of Hungarian.* Syntax and Semantics 27, eds. Ferenc Kiefer and Katalin É. Kiss, 91–178. New York: Academic Press.

Komlósy, András. 2000. A műveltetés [Causation]. In *Strukturális magyar nyelvtan 3. Morfológia*, ed. Ferenc Kiefer, 215–292. Budapest: Akadémiai Kiadó.

Koopman, Hilda and Anna Szabolcsi. 2000. *Verbal Complexes*. Cambridge, MA: MIT Press.

Kornai, András. 1989. A főnévi csoport egyeztetése [Agreement with the noun phrase]. *Általános Nyelvészeti Tanulmányok* 17: 183–211.

Kugler, Nóra. 2003. *A módosítószók funkciói* [The functions of modifier words]. Nyelvtudományi Értekezések 152. Akadémiai Kiadó: Budapest.

Laczkó, Tibor. 1995. On the status of *való* in adjectivalized constituents in noun phrases. In *Approaches to Hungarian Volume 5*, ed. István Kenesei, 125–152. Szeged: JATE.

Laczkó, Tibor. 1995. *The Syntax of Hungarian. Noun Phrases. A Lexical-Functional Approach.* Frankfurt am Main: Peter Lang.

Laczkó, Tibor. 1997. Action nominalization and the possessor function within Hungarian and English noun phrases. *Acta Linguistica Hungarica* 44/3-4: 413–475.

Laczkó, Tibor. 2000. Az ige argumentumszerkezetét megőrző főnévképzés [Noun derivation retaining verbal argument structure]. In *Strukturális magyar nyelvtan 3. Morfológia*, ed. Ferenc Kiefer, 293–407. Budapest: Akadémiai Kiadó.

Laczkó, Tibor. 2003. On oblique arguments and adjuncts of Hungarian event nominals. In *Nominals: Inside and Out*, eds. Miriam Butt and Tracy Holloway King, 201–234. Stanford: CSLI Publications.

Laczkó, Tibor. 2009. On the -Ás Suffix: Word Formation in the Syntax? *Acta Linguistica Hungarica* 56/1: 23–114.

Laczkó, Tibor. 2010. A new account of possessors and event nominals in Hungarian. In *The Semantics of Nominalizations across Languages and Frameworks*. Interface Explorations 22, eds. Artemis Alexiadou and Monika Rathert, 81–106. Berlin: Mouton de Gruyter.

Laczkó, Tibor. 2015. Nominalization in Hungarian. In *Word-Formation: An International Handbook of the Languages of Europe*. Handbooks of Linguistics and Communication Science (HSK) 40/2, eds. Peter O. Müller, Ingeborg

Ohnheiser, Susan Olsen and Franz Rainer, 1241–1253. Berlin/New York: De Gruyter.

Laczkó, Tibor and György Rákosi. 2011. On particularly predicative particles in Hungarian. In *The proceedings of the LFG 11 Conference*, eds. Miriam Butt and Tracy H. King, 299-319. Stanford: CSLI Publications.

Laczkó, Tibor and György Rákosi. 2013. Remarks on a novel LFG approach to spatial particle verb constructions in Hungarian. In *Approaches to Hungarian Volume 13. Papers from the 2011 Lund Conference*, eds. Johan Brandtler, Valéria Molnár and Christer Platzack, 149–178. Amsterdam: John Benjamins.

Levin, Beth and Malka Rappaport Hovav. 1995. *Unaccusativity: At the Syntax–Lexical Semantics Interface*. Cambridge, MA: The MIT Press.

Lipták, Anikó. 2008. On the correlative nature of Hungarian left peripheral relatives. In *Dislocated Elements in Discourse. Syntactic, Semantic and Pragmatic Perspectives*, eds. Benjamin Shaer, Philippa Cook, Werner Frey and Claudia Maienborn, 398–430. New York: Routledge.

Lipták, Anikó. 2012. Correlative topicalization. *Acta Linguistica Hungarica* 59/3: 245–302.

Lipták, Anikó and Andres Saab. 2014. No N-raising out of NPs in Spanish: ellipsis as a diagnostic of head movement. *Natural Language and Linguistic Theory* 32/4: 1247–1271.

Maleczki, Márta. 1995. Definiteness effect in Hungarian. A semantic approach. In *Approaches to Hungarian Volume 5*, ed. István Kenesei, 261–285. Szeged: JATE.

Marácz, László. 1984. Postposition stranding in Hungarian. In *Groninger Arbeiten zur Germanistischen Linguistik 24*, eds. Werner Abraham and Sjaak de Mey, 127–161. Groningen: University of Groningen.

Marácz, László. 1986. Dressed or naked: The case of the PP in Hungarian. In *Topic, Focus and Configurationality*, eds. Werner Abraham and Sjaak de Meij, 227–252. Amsterdam/Philadelphia: John Benjamins.

Marácz, László. 1989. *Asymmetries in Hungarian*. PhD dissertation, Rijksuniversität Groningen.

Moravcsik, Edith. 2003. Inflectional morphology in the Hungarian noun: A typological assessment. In *Noun Phrase Structure in the Languages of Europe*, ed. Frans Plank, 113–252. Berlin/New York: Mouton de Gruyter.

Nádasdy, Ádám and Péter Siptár. 1994. A magánhangzók [Vowels]. In *Strukturális magyar nyelvtan 2. Fonológia*, ed. Ferenc Kiefer, 42–182. Budapest: Akadémiai Kiadó.

Nemesi, Attila László. 2003. A magyar műveltető szerkezet esetkiosztásának kérdéséhez. [On case-assignment in the Hungarian causative construction]. *In LingDok 2. Nyelvész-doktoranduszok dolgozatai*, ed. Zsuzsanna Gécseg, 71–94. Szeged: SZTE Nyelvtudományi Doktori Iskola.

Olsson, Magnus. 1992. *Hungarian Phonology and Morphology*. Lund: Lund University Press.

Oravecz, Csaba, Tamás Váradi and Bálint Sass. 2014. The Hungarian Gigaword Corpus. In *Proceedings of the Ninth International Conference on Language Resources and Evaluation (LREC'14)*, eds. Nicoletta Calzolari, Khalid

Choukri, Thierry Declerck, Hrafn Loftsson, Bente Maegaard, Joseph Mariani, Asuncion Moreno, Jan Odijk and Stelios Piperidis, 1719–1723. European Language Resources Association.

Payne, John and Erika Chisarik. 2000. Demonstrative constructions in Hungarian. In *Approaches to Hungarian Volume 7. Papers from the Pécs Conference*, eds. Gábor Alberti and István Kenesei, 181–198. Szeged: JATE.

Peredy, Márta. 2008. A kötelező határozók aspektuális szerepe [The aspectual role of obligatory adjuncts]. *Magyar Nyelv* 104: 39–50, 143–153.

Piñón, Christopher. 1991. Falling in paradise: verbs, preverbs, and reduplication in Hungarian. Handout of a talk at the syntax workshop 21 May, 1991, Stanford University.

Piñón, Christopher. 2001. Töprengtem egyet: azon, hogy mit jelent az *egyet*. [I wondered about the meaning of one.ACC]. In *Újabb tanulmányok a strukturális magyar nyelvtan és a nyelvtörténet köréből*, eds. Marianne Bakró-Nagy, Zoltán Bánréti and Katalin É. Kiss, 182–198. Budapest: Osiris.

Piñón, Christopher. 2006a. Definiteness effect verbs. In *Event Structure and the Left Periphery*, ed. Katalin É. Kiss, 75–90. Dordrecht: Springer.

Piñón, Christopher. 2006b. Weak and strong accomplishments. In *Event Structure and the Left Periphery*, ed. Katalin É. Kiss, 91–106. Dordrecht: Springer.

Prószéky, Gábor. 1989. Határozók, szabad határozók [Adverbials, free adverbials]. *Általános Nyelvészeti Tanulmányok* 17: 213–240.

Rácz, Endre. 1968, 1988 (7th edition). Mondattan [Syntax]. In *A mai magyar nyelv*, ed. Endre Rácz, 205–458. Budapest: Tankönyvkiadó.

Rácz, Endre. 1986. *Mondattani elemzések* [Syntactic analyses]. Budapest: Nemzeti Tankönyvkiadó.

Radics, Katalin. 1992. Fossilized gerunds with possessive endings in Hungarian. In *Approaches to Hungarian Volume 4*, eds. István Kenesei and Csaba Pléh, 283–300. Szeged: JATE.

Rákosi, György. 2003. Comitative arguments in Hungarian. In *Uil-OTS Yearbook 2003*, eds. Willemijn Heeren, Dimitra Papangeli and Evangelia Vlachou, 47–57. Utrecht: Utrecht Institute of Linguistics OTS.

Rákosi, György. 2006. *Dative Experiencer Predicates in Hungarian.* PhD dissertation, University of Utrecht. Published as Volume 146 of the LOT Dissertation Series, Utrecht: LOT.

Rákosi, György. 2008. The inherently reflexive and the inherently reciprocal predicate in Hungarian: each to their own argument structure. In *Reciprocals and Reflexives. Theoretical and Typological Explorations.* Trends in Linguistics Studies and Monographs 192, eds. Ekkehard König and Volker Gast, 411–450. Berlin/New York: Mouton de Gruyter.

Rákosi, György. 2009a. The diversity of dative experiencers. In *Merging Features: Computation, Interpretation and Acquisition*, eds. José M. Brucart, Anna Gavarró and Jaume Solà, 215–234. Oxford: Oxford University Press.

Rákosi, György. 2009b. Ablative causes in Hungarian. In *Approaches to Hungarian Volume 11. Papers from the 2007 New York Conference*, eds. Marcel den Dikken and Robert M. Vago, 167–196. Amsterdam/Philadelphia: John Benjamins.

Rákosi, György. 2010. On snakes and locative binding in Hungarian. In *Proceedings of the LFG10 Conference*, eds. Miriam Butt and Tracy Holloway King, 395–415. Stanford: CSLI Publications.

Rákosi, György. 2012a. In defense of the non-causative analysis of anticausatives. In *The Theta System: Argument Structure at the Interface*, eds. Martin Everaert, Marijana Marelj and Tal Siloni, 177–199. Oxford: Oxford University Press.

Rákosi, György. 2012b. A magyar birtokos szerkezetű viszonyjelölőkről, avagy kígyók szájfénnyel és esernyővel [On Hungarian locatives with a possessive structure, or snakes with lipbalms and umbrellas]. In *Nyelvelmélet és dialektológia* 2, eds. Katalin É. Kiss and Attila Hegedűs, 154–173. Pilliscsaba: PPKE BTK.

Rákosi, György. 2013. Down with obliques? In *From Quirky Case to Representing Space: Papers in Honor of Annie Zaenen*, eds. Tracy Holloway King and Valeria de Paiva, 127–138. Stanford: CSLI Publications.

Rákosi, György. 2014. A case of disagreement: on plural reduplicating particles in Hungarian. In *The Evidential Basis of Linguistic Argumentation*, eds. András Kertész and Csilla Rákosi, 179–189. Amsterdam/Philadelphia: John Benjamins.

Rákosi, György and Tibor Laczkó. 2011. Inflecting spatial particles and shadows of the past in Hungarian. In *The Proceedings of the LFG 11 Conference*, eds. Miriam Butt and Tracy Holloway King, 440–460. Stanford: CSLI Publications.

Ramat, Paolo and Davide Ricca. 1998. Sentence adverbs in the languages of Europe. In *Adverbial Constructions in the Languages of Europe*. Eurotyp 20-3., ed. Johan van der Auwera, 187–275. Berlin/New York: Mouton de Gruyter.

Rebrus, Péter. 2000. Morfofonológiai jelenségek [Morphophonological phenomena]. In *Strukturális magyar nyelvtan 3. Morfológia*, ed. Ferenc Kiefer, 763–949. Budapest: Akadémiai Kiadó.

Roberts, Ian G. and Anna Roussou. 2003. *Syntactic Change. A Minimalist Approach to Grammaticalization*. Cambridge: Cambridge University Press.

Sebestyén, Árpád. 1965. *A magyar nyelv névutórendszere* [The postpositional system of Hungarian]. Budapest: Akadémiai Kiadó.

S. Hámori, Antónia and József Tompa 1961, 1970 (2nd ed.). A ragozás [Inflection]. In *A mai magyar nyelv rendszere. Leíró nyelvtan I*, ed. József Tompa, 473–586. Budapest: Akadémiai Kiadó.

Simonyi, Zsigmond. 1888. *A magyar határozók* [Adverbials in Hungarian]. Vol. 1. Budapest: Magyar Tudományos Akadémia.

Simonyi, Zsigmond. 1892. *A magyar határozók* [Adverbials in Hungarian]. Vol. 2. Budapest: Magyar Tudományos Akadémia.

Simonyi, Zsigmond. 1895. *Tüzetes magyar nyelvtan történeti alapon* [Detailed Hungarian grammar on a diachronic basis]. Budapest: Magyar Tudományos Akadémia.

Siptár, Péter and Miklós Törkenczy. 2000. *The Phonology of Hungarian*. New York/ Oxford: Oxford University Press.

Spencer, Andrew J. 2008. Does Hungarian have a case system? In *Case and Grammatical Relations. Studies in Honor of Bernard Comrie*, eds. Greville C. Corbett and Michael Noonan, 35–56. Amsterdam: John Benjamins.

Spencer, Andrew J. and Gregory Stump. 2013. Hungarian pronominal case and the dichotomy of content and form in inflectional morphology. *Natural Language and Linguistic Theory* 31/4: 1207–1248.

Surányi, Balázs 2008. Határozóosztályok és mondattartományok [Adverbial classes and clausal domains]. *Nyelvtudományi Közlemények* 105: 164–192.

Surányi, Balázs. 2009a. Adpositional preverbs, chain reduction and phases. In *Approaches to Hungarian Volume 11. Papers from the 2007 New York Conference*, eds. Marcel den Dikken and Robert M. Vago, 217–250. Amsterdam: John Benjamins.

Surányi, Balázs. 2009b. "Incorporated" locative adverbials in Hungarian. In *Adverbs and Adverbial Adjuncts at the Interfaces,* ed. Katalin É. Kiss, 39–74. Berlin: Mouton de Gruyter.

Surányi, Balázs. 2009c. Verbal particles inside and outside *v*P. *Acta Linguistica Hungarica* 56/2–3: 201–249.

Szabó, Ildikó Emese. 2016. Low vowel "lengthening" in Hungarian. *Linguistica* 56/1: 273–279.

Szabolcsi, Anna. 1983. The possessor that ran away from home. *The Linguistic Review* 36/1: 89–102.

Szabolcsi, Anna. 1986. From the definiteness effect to lexical integrity. In *Topic, Focus, and Configurationality*, eds. Sjaak de Mei and Werner Abraham, 321–348. Amsterdam: John Benjamins.

Szabolcsi, Anna and Tibor Laczkó. 1992. A főnévi csoport szerkezete [The structure of the Noun Phrase]. In *Strukturális magyar nyelvtan 1. Mondattan*, ed. Ferenc Kiefer, 179–298. Budapest: Akadémiai Kiadó.

Szendrői, Kriszta. 2004. A stress-based approach to climbing. In *Verb Clusters. A Study of Hungarian, German and Dutch,* ed. Katalin É. Kiss and Henk van Riemsdijk, 205–224. Amsterdam: John Benjamins.

Talmy, Leonard. 1972. *Semantic Structures in English and Atsugewi*. PhD dissertation. Berkeley: University of California.

Tenny, Carol. 2000. Core event and adverbial modification. In *Events as Grammatical Objects*, eds. Carol Tenny and James Pustejovsky, 285–334. Stanford: CSLI Publications.

Tompa, József (ed.) 1961. *A mai magyar nyelv rendszere. Leíró nyelvtan* [*The grammatical system of contemporary Hungarian. A descriptive grammar*] *Vol. I.* Budapest: Akadémiai Kiadó.

Tompa, József. 1968. *Ungarische Grammatik*. Berlin: Mouton de Gruyter.

Tompa, József. 1980. Földrajzi nevek helyhatározóragjai [Spatial adverbial suffixes of geographical names]. In *Nyelvművelő kézikönyv A–K,* ***eds. László*** Grétsy and Miklós Kovalovszky, ***675–677.*** Budapest: Akadémiai Kiadó.

Tóth, Ildikó. 2002. Can the Hungarian infinitive be possessed? *Approaches to Hungarian Volume 8*, eds. István Kenesei and Péter Siptár, 134–160. Budapest: Akadémiai Kiadó.

Tóth, Ildikó. 2011. A *-t* képzős igeneves szerkezet használata az ómagyarban [The use of *-t* suffixed participial constructions in Old Hungarian]. In *Nyelvelmélet és diakrónia*, eds. Katalin É. Kiss and Attila Hegedűs, 121–132. Piliscsaba: PPKE BTK.

Trommer, Jochen. 2008. "Case suffixes", Postpositions and the Phonological Word in Hungarian. *Linguistics* 46/2: 403–437.

Ürögdi, Barbara. 2003. Feature doubling, aspectual structure, and expletives. In *Proceedings of the North East Linguistic Society 33*, eds. Makato Kadowaki and Shigeto Kawahara, 425–444. Amherst: University of Massachusetts.

Ürögdi, Barbara. 2006. Predicate fronting and dative case in Hungarian. *Acta Linguistica Hungarica* 53/3: 291–332.

Vago, Robert M. 1980. *The Sound Pattern of Hungarian*. Washington D.C.: Georgetown University Press.

Varga, Diána. 2013. *A magyar felszólító mondatok szerkezete* [The structure of Hungarian imperative clauses]. PhD dissertation. Piliscsaba: Pázmány Péter Catholic University.

Varga, László. 2002. *Intonation and Stress: Evidence from Hungarian*. Houndmills, Basingstoke: Palgrave Macmillan.

Vendler, Zeno. 1967. *Linguistics in Philosophy*. Ithaca, NY: Cornell University Press.

Vicente, Luis. 2007. *The syntax of heads and phrases: A study of verb (phrase) fronting*. PhD dissertation, Leiden University. Published as Volume 154 of the LOT Dissertation Series Utrecht: LOT.

Vogel, Irene and István Kenesei. 1987. The interface between phonology and other components of grammar: The case of Hungarian. *Phonology Yearbook* 4: 243–263.

Wacha, Balázs. 1976. Az igeaspektusról [On verbal aspect]. *Magyar Nyelv* 72: 59–69.

Zwarts, Joost. 2005. Prepositional Aspect and the Algebra of Paths. *Linguistics and Philosophy* 28/6: 739–779.

Zsilinszky, Éva. 1992. A névutók [Postpositions]. In *A magyar nyelv történeti nyelvtana II/1. A kései ómagyar kor. Morfematika*, eds. Loránd Benkő and Erzsébet E. Abaffy, 696–715. Budapest: Akadémiai Kiadó.

The *Syntax of Hungarian* will include the following volumes:

Nouns and Noun Phrases Volume 1 & Volume 2 [appeared in 2018]
eds. Gábor Alberti and Tibor Laczkó

Postpositions and Postpositional Phrases [this volume]
eds. Katalin É. Kiss and Veronika Hegedűs

Sentence Structure

Verb Phrases in General and Finite Verb Phrases

Adjectival Phrases

Non-finite and semi-finite verb phrases

Finite embedding

Coordination and Ellipsis